MARRIAGES AND FAMILIES

Coping with Change

MARRIAGES AND FAMILIES

Coping with Change

Second Edition

Leonard Cargan

Wright State University

Prentice Hall
Englewood Cliffs, New Jersey 07632

Library of Congress Cataloging-in-Publication Data

Marriages and families : coping with change / [edited by] Leonard
  Cargan.—2nd ed.
      p.   cm.
    Rev. ed. of: Marriage and family / Leonard Cargan. c1985.
    Includes bibliographical references.
    ISBN 0-13-558792-1
    1. Family life education. 2. Marriage. 3. Family. I. Cargan,
  Leonard. II. Cargan, Leonard. Marriage and family.
  HQ10.C27 1991
  306.8—dc20   90-43109
                                                                CIP

Editorial/production supervision and
   interior design: Fred Dahl
Cover design: Circa 86, Inc.
Manufacturing buyer: Debbie Kesar

© 1991 by Prentice-Hall, Inc.
A Division of Simon & Schuster
Englewood Cliffs, New Jersey 07632

Printed in the United States of America
10 9 8 7 6 5 4 3 2 1

ISBN 0-13-558792-1

Prentice-Hall International (UK) Limited, *London*
Prentice-Hall of Australia Pty. Limited, *Sydney*
Prentice-Hall Canada Inc., *Toronto*
Prentice-Hall Hispanoamericana, S.A., *Mexico*
Prentice-Hall of India Private Limited, *New Delhi*
Prentice-Hall of Japan, Inc., *Tokyo*
Simon & Schuster Asia Pte. Ltd., *Singapore*
Editora Prentice-Hall do Brasil, Ltda., *Rio de Janeiro*

Contents

Preface

An examination of textbooks in introductory sociology would reveal that society consists of various institutions designed to meet its basic needs. The major ones are economics, education, the family, politics, and religion. The most pervasive of these is considered to be the family because all persons are born into some form of family. Through its role as socializer of the young, the family transmits society's norms and values and thus becomes society's traditional culture-bearer. This outcome of a family function makes it difficult to accept and adjust to social changes that are, in turn, affecting family relations. Thus, controversies abound in regard to gender roles, sexual behavior, alternatives to traditional marriage, family roles, childbearing, living with children, and even the future of the family. A resulting problem for the family is the difficulty in obtaining the necessary information for dealing with these controversies. The primary objective of this anthology is to provide this link for dealing with the issues brought about by change.

The first step in providing this framework for the text was the identification of those issues considered to be the most important. As the cross-chapters list in the *Instructor's Manual* indicates, numerous marriage-and-family texts were examined. The result is that this text examines the important controversies marking the family of today. The second step was an exhaustive search of the literature for materials dealing with these controversies. The result is a balance of articles in each section that is both interesting and highly readable. Finally, the resulting extensive introductions to each section of the anthology discuss the major themes of that topic section, noting how each article relates to these themes. The study questions at the beginning of each reading help to highlight important items in the readings. It is suggested that these questions be answered as the material is read.

Because the anthology is so comprehensive it can be used in several ways to aid in the instructional process, to expand student comprehension of main topics, to illustrate lecture materials, and to provide a basis for class discussion. Articles that deal with controversial issues can be used for debate or as the basis of small-group activities.

For the convenience of the instructor, the *Instructor's Manual* cross-lists chapters in major marriage-and-family texts with corresponding sections in this anthology. This list facilitates the use of this text with almost all of the major marriage-and-family texts. The *Instructor's Manual* also contains an abstract of each article's major theme, findings, and conclusions; multiple-choice and essay questions for testing purposes; and a film list by subject matter.

I would like to thank the authors and publishers of the articles for their permission to use them in *Marriages and Families: Coping with Change*. Thanks is also offered to the departmental secretaries, Lynn Morgan and especially, Glena Buchholtz, to Mary Cargan for her excellent proofreading, and to the Department of Sociology and College of Liberal Arts for their support. To all I give a very large "thank you!"

Leonard Cargan

MARRIAGES AND FAMILIES

Coping with Change

1   *The Changing Picture*

A glance at American history since the turn of the century reveals that the institution of marriage and family is not a static one. As with other social institutions, the structure and meaning of these twins of personal intimacy have and are undergoing change.

The contemporary American family can trace its roots to the ancient Hebrews, Greeks, Romans, and Christians. These societies had strong patriarchal systems. Women had few rights but were usually treated with respect as long as they retained their virtue and did their duties. Throughout the early period of the United States, there was little change in this system despite a growing tendency toward free choice of a mate. The family form most familiar to us began to take shape with the beginning of the Industrial Revolution and its evolutionary concomitant—the growth of cities. Structurally, the families that emerged during this period were different from earlier families: the marriage was based on affection and mutual respect; the wife's primary role was the care of children and household maintenance; the parents' efforts and resources were increasingly centered on rearing their children; and the average size of the family decreased significantly (Degler 1980). For much of the first half of this century, then, tradition and family custom were an important part of family life. Family unity was usually a more important consideration than were personal needs and attitudes. The result was clearly defined and limited gender and age roles in which individual liberty was sacrificed for continuity and security (Duggan 1981).

Seemingly supportive of these values, the married portion of the population had increased throughout this period despite a temporary setback during the depression. The popularity of the traditional marriage

1

and family arrangement was reinforced with its dramatic rise in the post-World War II period of the 1950s and the early 1960s. The number of married people increased from 60 percent to 67 percent of the adult population (U. S. Bureau of the Census 1989). With two-thirds of its adult population married and a baby boom underway, the United States had become, much more than ever before, a marriage- and family-oriented society. It became known as the golden age of the family.

The mass circulation magazines emphasized this seeming priority of marriage with articles criticizing the lifestyles of what were then known as bachelors and spinsters. Some representative titles were: "When Being Single Stops Being Fun"; "The Necessary Melancholy of Bachelors"; "There Is No Place in Heaven for Old Maids." They also promoted marriage directly with such titles as, "How Come a Nice Girl Like You Isn't Married?"; "129 Ways to Get a Husband"; "How to Be Marriageable" (Cargan and Melko 1982, pp. 229–230). Social scientists also added to this emphasis on being married by focusing their research on dating behavior and on ways to achieve marital success and satisfaction. For example, in a survey of various studies of marital adjustment, it was indicated that being older and having more education are important predictors of a successful marriage. Other important factors are that the partners know each other for some time before marriage, that the quality of the premarital relationship was good, that the partners are religious and of the same faith, that neither of the partners is previously divorced, that the woman is not pregnant before the marriage, and that the parents were happily married.

The social unrest of the mid-1960s—protests for social and civil rights and against the Vietnam conflict revealed that the mood of solace and content in marriage was for many an illusionary one. A surface indicator of this discontent was the rising divorce rate. Within ten years of the high point in marriage euphoria, the divorce rate almost doubled (from 2.1 percent to 4.4 percent per 1,000 females) to a figure even higher than that which followed the end of World War II and the termination of many quickie marriages (U.S. Bureau of the Census 1989). Other signs of this disaffection with the institution of marriage were seen in a declining marriage rate; in movements to such alternative lifestyles as remaining single, living in communes and cohabitation; in changes in what was referred to as proper sexual conduct; and in a movement for the rights of women. Even beliefs about the family were under suspicion with increasing knowledge and concern over marital and child abuse, parental sexual molestation of their children, and the rising statistics on premarital pregnancy and abortion. A demystification of family life was underway.

In fact, some scientists speculated that the "death" of the family was underway since the family had lost many of its functions to other institutions, and the divorce rate was reaching new highs. Granted, structural, demographic, and value changes had led to changes in the basis for marriage, greater emphasis on personal satisfaction and gratification, and a new freedom to leave unsatisfactory marriages, but then change can also be considered an important indicator of life. Thus, as other institutions took over the economic, educational, and protective work of the family, the family, it was believed, could perform its retained functions better (Mitterauer & Siedler 1982). That is, it could better provide its social and personal functions when relieved of functions which could be carried out more efficiently by institutions specifically designed for them. Thus, the family was still seen as providing continuity, stability, support, love, and an intimacy that cannot be easily achieved elsewhere. This belief continues today, as evidenced by the fact that marriage is still the norm of society. Thus, about 90 percent of young adults will eventually marry, although somewhat later than their counterparts in the 1950s and 1960s. The brisk rate of remarriage reaffirms the belief that Americans are not losing interest in marriage. Divorce, then, may simply be replacing death as a way to end marriage, as society places an ever higher value on personal fulfillment. However it is difficult to comprehend the strength of the family since changes in the family are emphasized by the increase in the "negative" indicators of family disruption and dissolution. Rather than emphasizing the increase in one-parent families, "it could be said that 89% of the population were living in families" and that "81% of the families with children under 18 had both parents present" (Kitagawa 1981, pp. 13–14). In sum, the majority of Americans marry, remain married, and have children. Thus, the family is functioning better than critics would have us believe since it is still the prime source of intimacy and nurturing albeit now in more accepted variations.

The end of the conflict in Vietnam seemingly marked another change in attitudes toward marriage and the family. Just as the golden age of the family in the 1950s could be referred to as a "we" decade and the idealistic social commitment of the 1960s as an "us" decade, the calculating approach of the 1970s could be called a "me first" decade. The emphasis had shifted from a joining of partners in what appeared to be an ideal state to a getting together with others to protest what appeared to be inequalities in that state, to a preoccupation with one's own fulfillment. From such therapists as Abraham Maslow, Rollo May, Fritz Perls, and Carl Rogers came the idea of self-fulfillment through a liberated self via self-actualization and self-expression (Chilman 1983). This emphasis encouraged a "me first" attitude that was suspected in the breakdown of the traditional family unit. For example, single-parent families increased more quickly than the traditional two-parent families.

So far, the 1980s would seem to be both a continuation of the trend begun in the mid-1960s and a concern with the effects of those trends. However, the pace of change has slowed as we enter the 1980s and society adjusts to the new patterns that have formed in recent years. Nonetheless, controversies abound: Marriage is a sacred and social obligation versus it is a means of personal fulfillment; traditional gender role behavior is more fulfilling for the child versus it should be a gender role of androgyny; the questioning of the role of sex as either traditional versus expressive and as a factor in versus out of marriage; prospective marital roles should be traditional versus involve equitable task sharing. It would appear that the belief noted above of a slowing pace of change would appear to be much needed.

These changes in our concepts concerning marriage and family are shown in the articles of the initial chapter. In the first article, David Mace discusses the issues involved in marriage and companionship, sex, parenthood, and stability and concludes that marriage will continue due to these relationships. Daniel Yankelovich, in the second article, also examines the changes that have occurred by comparing past and current family attitudes. In comparing several national polls, he finds that Americans are increasingly accepting of women working, of smaller families, of women staying single, of abortion up to the first three months, and of dual-parent care for children. On the other hand, the use of drugs and having extramarital affairs still command majority condemnation. Yankelovich concludes that a desire by the majority to return to the perceived image of family life of the 1950s may be in contradiction to the currently accepted rules of domestic life.

This seeming contradiction would seem to be in line with the fact that social change has always been accepted with ambivalence. Few would wish to return to the family its lost functions by closing schools, day care centers, frozen and fast food operations, homes for the elderly, educational and job opportunities for women, or for that matter, by restricting the acceptability of sexual activity outside of marriage. Yet, it is these very changes in functions that have led to the debate referred to as the "death of the family." This is due to the difference in the perception of change. In most technical areas, change is standard and is seen as progress. However, change in such social institutions as the family involves our own personal experiences and so limits our ability to be objective. As Arlene Skolnick notes in the third article, the rosy hue of the family of the past does not coordinate with its reality. Familiarity also leads to two other difficulties in understanding marriage and family behavior: the ethnocentric belief that our family cultural patterns are natural and thus superior, and a romanticizing of the past—a past that never was. For example, the extended family was no more prevalent in colonial society than it is today, more families have two parents alive today than in those days, today's working mothers probably devote as much time to their children as did yesterday's mothers since the latter had to do housework without labor-saving devices, and although divorce is more prevalent and is replacing death as the family disrupter it has the advantage that most divorced people remarry.

REFERENCES

1. Cargan, L., & M. Melko. 1982. *Singles: Myths and Realities.* Beverly Hills, CA: Sage.

2. Chilman, C. S. 1983. "Prologue: The 1970's and the American Families (A Comitragedy)." In *Contemporary Families and Alternative Lifestyles*, E. Macklin & R. H. Rubin (eds.). Beverly Hills, CA: Sage.

3. Degler, C. N. 1980. *At Odds: Women and the Family in America from the Revolution to the Present.* New York: Oxford University.

4. Duggan, M. 1981. "Violence in the Family." In *Understanding the Family*, C. Getty & W. Humphreys (eds.). New York: Appleton-Century-Crofts.

5. Kitagawa, E. M. 1981. "New Life-Styles: Marriage Patterns, Living Arrangements and Fertility Outside of Marriage." *Annals* (January).

6. Mitterauer, M., & R. Siedler. 1982. *Has the Family Lost Its Functions? The European Family.* Chicago: University of Chicago.

7. U. S. Bureau of the Census. 1989. *Statistical Abstracts of the United States.* Washington, DC: United States Department of Commerce.

1 *Contemporary Issues in Marriage*

David R. Mace

STUDY QUESTIONS

1. Why has marriage existed throughout human history?
2. Do you agree that men and women will seek to enter marriage more eagerly than in the past? Why?

MARRIAGE IN THE PAST

The archaeologists now tell us that we have had at least a million years of man. They are not able to report with equal confidence that we have had a million years of marriage; but I strongly suspect that we have. We can be certain that, during those million years, the continuity of the race was provided for by the fact that women had babies. We know that they couldn't have had babies without first having had sexual intercourse with men. We know that the experience of motherhood makes a woman vulnerable, and in the grim struggle for existence we can assume that the woman whose man stayed with her and supported her through the experience of motherhood would have a better chance of survival than the woman left to fend for herself. The search for food and shelter and safety was probably most successfully carried out by small groups of people cooperating with one another; and the most natural nuclear grouping, in terms of mutual needs and mutual service, is a man, a woman, and their children. So it is a reasonable supposition that marriage of some sort has existed throughout the entire period of human history.

This was the view of Edward Westermarck, who wrote the classical three-volume *History of Human Marriage* nearly eighty years ago. One of his major conclusions was that marriage is a universal human institution and has been part of the social structure of all settled societies; but that it is also a very

Source: David R. Mace, "Contemporary Issues in Marriage." Southwest Council of Family Relations, 1968 Annual Meeting. Used by permission.

flexible institution, and has existed in many forms. He defined marriage as "a relation of one or more men to one or more women which is recognized by custom or law and involves certain rights and duties both in the case of the parties entering the union and in the case of the children born of it."

Another of the major findings of Westermarck was summarized in his famous dictum that "marriage is rooted in the family, and not the family in marriage." What he meant was that human survival depends upon providing the best possible conditions for the birth and upbringing of children, that experience has shown these conditions to be best provided in family life, and that therefore marriage must be controlled and safeguarded by the community in order to ensure the continuity of the family.

This concept of marriage as subsidiary to the family, and therefore subservient to it, has dominated human history and has never been seriously challenged until our own time. But we are living today through an era of tremendous cultural change, in which all our institutions are being severely shaken; and marriage is no exception. In fact, marriage is changing so much that it is literally being turned inside out. If you think this sounds like dramatic exaggeration, let me assure you that I mean it quite literally; and let me explain what I mean.

In the entire sweep of human history, there have been only two major changes in our way of life—changes so vast that I prefer to call them "social mutations." The first was when man stopped being a wandering hunter and food-gatherer, a puny pigmy fighting against the enormous forces of a hostile nature, and learned to cooperate with nature by growing his food and taming wild animals and enlisting them in his service. This was the change from the nomadic to the agricultural way of life. It led to a long period of relative prosperity, with people living on the land in comparative security. The family was the basic unit of society, and it was generally a large or "extended" family of one kind or another, in which the kinship groups were united in cooperating with one another for the common good. The family was a very rigid institution, resisting all change and dedicated to maintaining the *status quo* from generation to generation.

Then came what we call the Industrial Revolution, which led to the second major social mutation in human history. We are in the midst of this now, and there has never been anything like it before. It began in England with the building of the first factories, and the flocking of the people from the land to the cities. We know all about this change, because we are part of it. The enormous advances of science and technology have now given man power over nature, so that its great forces are more and more coming under his direct control. This is changing radically the entire pattern of human living. Because it is happening gradually, we are not aware how profound the change is. It is almost as if the human race were being transferred from one planet to another, and having to adapt to almost entirely new conditions.

What is important for us is that our new environment is breaking up all our traditional institutions and forcing us to create new ones of quite a different kind. Professor J. K. Whitehead, the English social philosopher, expressed this very well when he said that before the Industrial Revolution, an institution could survive only if it had rigidity and stability; whereas since the Industrial Revolution, the qualities needed for survival are the opposite, namely flexibility and adaptability. These were in fact qualities that the traditional type of marriage could not tolerate. Consequently, marriage and the family as we have known them in the past, throughout most of human history, are breaking down, and must break down. There is absolutely no possibility that they will survive in the new urban-industrial culture that is taking shape everywhere in the world today.

Many people take alarm at this, because they assume that marriage and the family are themselves breaking down. It is very important to stress the fact that this is not so. The disintegration of the old rigid patterns is not something unhealthy, but something healthy. It is the inevitable prelude to the establishment of new patterns that will be much more appropriate to our new way of life. The family is changing, not breaking down. And, as Clark Vincent pointed out in a speech at an N.C.F.R. Conference, the family is showing its fundamental health by proving, after long centuries of rigidity, that it is actually capable of considerable adaptation to our new environment.

In the process of this adaptation, marriage is being turned inside out. In the old days, the central goal in marriage was that it must fulfill certain social and familial obligations—the continuation of the family line, the family inheritance, the family tradition—while somewhere out on the periphery there was a pious hope that the couple might get along harmoniously together. But so long as the familial obligations were met, nobody cared very much whether the couple were happy or unhappy in their interpersonal life. That was quite secondary.

Today, however, the central goal in marriage is personal fulfillment in a creative relationship, and the traditional familial and social obligations have moved out to the periphery. The mood of today is that if your marriage doesn't turn out to be happy, you quit, because finding happiness in marriage is the fulfillment of its fundamental objective.

Some people consider this change of goal as a manifestation of selfishness and irresponsibility. But the change of goal actually corresponds with the change of environment. In the old rural-agricultural society, the major business of life was economic survival and physical safety, and marriage had to conform to these requirements. But in an affluent society, economic survival is taken for granted; and the police, though they have troubles, do their best to assure us of physical safety. In our urban-industrial society, many of the traditional functions of marriage and the family—education, economic production, recreation, and many others—have been taken over by the state. And now our deepest need is for *emotional* security, for the survival of our sense of personal worth and individual significance in a vast world of people in which the individual often doesn't seem to count for anything. By shifting its focus, marriage has now become the primary means by which this individual need for comfort and support and love and understanding can be met. Gibson Winter calls this the "quest for intimacy." In our study of the Soviet family, my wife and I found that in the days of Stalinist terror, marriage was sometimes the only means by which people could keep sane. Surrounded by insecurity, they found their security in the openness and the cathartic communication they could enjoy as husband and wife, when they were alone together. There is a sense in which this kind of need, though not in the same extreme sense, is pervading the whole of modern life. And if marriage can meet that need, it will simply be manifesting one of its dormant potentialities which was almost totally neglected in the past, but is highly relevant today.

MARRIAGE IN THE PRESENT

This brings us to the point at which we can look at contemporary issues in marriage. There are so many of these that it is hard to choose; but for this discussion I have selected four:

1. Marriage as Companionship. You will remember that Ernest Burgess, who might be called the father of family sociology, summarized the fundamental change that is taking place today in the title *Marriage: From Institution To Companionship*. So our focus today is upon marriage as a relationship. This is what we are concerned about, this is what more and more of what we are writing about marriage focuses upon, this is what marriage counselors are working with and trying to facilitate. So I would say that the primary issue in modern marriage is how we can make it a really creative relationship for husband and wife.

When we think of marriage in these terms, however, we begin to realize that husband and wife enter not into one relationship, but into two relationships, which coexist and interact, and yet can be clearly distinguished from each other. There is the relationship between two persons living together as partners, sharing life on an equal basis; and there is the relationship between a man and a woman, which is not equal at all, but reciprocal and complementary. In simple language, married couples have to contrive to be both good partners and good lovers. Failure in one of these areas will not compensate for success in the other. There must be a reasonable measure of satisfaction in both.

The concept of husband and wife as equal partners, sharing life in openness and intimacy, represents a radical break with tradition. Of course there have always been marriages in which good partnership was achieved; but there has never before been a time in which this was a primary criterion of success applied to *all* marriages. Indeed, traditional societies devised two means by which the concept of equal partnership, and of the two-vote marriage, was carefully avoided. First, a hierarchical distinction was made between husband and wife, the husband being acknowledged as having almost all the power, and the wife being compliant and obedient. Second, the spheres of influence of husband and wife were rigidly segregated, so that there was the minimum chance that they might compete or clash with one another. These devices were highly developed, and there is no doubt that they were based on the discovery that attempts to make marriage a relationship of close sharing led to explosive consequences that must be avoided in the interest of family stability.

But in our modern world we have deliberately given a central place to this concept of the shared life; and the explosive possibilities are very much with us! It would not be too much to say that interpersonal conflict, far from being an extraneous element in modern marriage, actually represents the raw material out of which an effective marital partnership has to be shaped. Unless we clearly recognize this, and deliberately teach young people to expect conflict in marriage, and to cope with it adequately, we simply doom large numbers of them to inevitable disillusionment and even disaster. Conflict in marriage is simply the emotional manifestation of disagreement, which is an inevitable consequence of difference. And difference cannot be avoided between two people who live in continuing intimacy, because it is unreasonable to imagine that two different people would always want to do the same thing in the same way at the same time. By insisting on homogamy as a primary condition for successful marriage, we have contrived to minimize interpersonal conflict. But I am not at all sure that the marriages of people with a minimum of difference are necessarily the best marriages. There are enormous potentials for creativity and growth in two people who begin with a good deal of difference, but have the maturity to resolve it and grow together.

When we consider the other relationship in marriage, that of husband and wife as lovers, we encounter at once the fascinating but baffling question of masculine-feminine interaction. For long centuries this has been rather naively interpreted in terms of dominance and submission, or even as superiority and inferiority. One of the somewhat bizarre side-effects of the emergence today of the idea of marriage as companionship is the open revolt of youth against the extreme stereotypes of masculinity as hairy-chested male aggressiveness on the one hand, and docile female compliance on the other. Modern youth has dramatized this protest in the long-haired boy who is not ashamed to identify himself with femininity by looking like a girl, and the modern girl who does not feel any loss of womanhood when she engages in activities that hitherto were reserved exclusively for men.

2. Marriage and Sex. There is an argument going on at the present time as to whether there is a sexual revolution or not. I am in no doubt whatever about this question. There is, emphatically, a sexual revolution. But the confusion is caused by the fact that people are arguing not about the revolution, but about the consequences of it. In my judgment, a revolution is by definition a complete change, a reversal of what previously was believed. But a revolution also, in my view, always takes place in the realm of ideas, and then is gradually translated into changed patterns of living. In these terms, we can say emphatically that the sexual revolution is not only here; it is now almost complete. It began about three-quarters of a century ago, and has resulted in a total change in the way we think about sex. Beginning with an attitude that considered sex essentially negatively, as unwholesome and regrettable though perhaps an unavoidable necessity, we have moved to an attitude which sees sex positively, as something essentially good and creative, though of course capable like everything else of misuse. If a change of this magnitude is not a revolution, I can think of no other radical change in human thinking that is worthy of the name.

DAVID R. MACE

However, this revolution has led to many consequences, and one of them concerns the relationship between sex and marriage. In the older cultures, where sex was officially recognized only as a means of procreation for married people, and unofficially as a clandestine pastime in which men exploited women with little regard for the interpersonal implications, a state of uneasy equilibrium could with a little difficulty be maintained. But our new attitude to sex has broken this up completely, and forced us to reevaluate the total situation.

What has precipitated the crisis is the change in our concepts of mate selection. So long as the parents or village elders chose your husband or wife for you, there was no need for boys and girls to be exposed to the risks of meeting socially and forming friendships. Indeed, Confucius insisted that after the age of seven a boy and girl must never even sit together in public! But once the principle was established that young people could choose each other, they naturally wanted to do so on a basis of personal compatibility, and personal compatibility has to be tested out in a period of friendship. Once this has been conceded in any culture, the flood gates are open to the free association of unmarried men and women. This means that it is henceforth impossible to confine sex to marriage by the appeal to force or fear, and sexual morality becomes a question of conscious and deliberate choice based on an acceptance of certain values, which all men and women will not necessarily accept.

Once a principle is established that a man and woman who are unmarried may respond to each other emotionally, and carry that response as far as they personally choose, it becomes impossible to exclude married people from the same privileges. Once premarital chastity has become a matter of conscious choice, marital fidelity follows suit. The consequences of infidelity for the married are of course generally more serious, and this introduces restraints, but we should not be realistic if we did not recognize that one of the major issues in marriage today, in an era where increasingly effective contraceptives are available, is the question of how far married couples generally will accept the principle of sexual exclusiveness, and what is likely to happen to marriage if they don't.

3. Marriage and Parenthood. We all recognize that there has been a radical change in our pattern of marriage, but we are not so ready to see that there has been a corresponding change in parenthood. The societies of the past were rigidly structured, and had little use for individualists who refused to accept the roles allocated to them. The son was expected to follow in his father's footsteps, or to go in whatever direction the family decided was appropriate for him. The task of families was therefore to bring up children to be obedient conformists, who would do what they were told without expressing individual preferences or asking awkward questions. Parenthood was therefore essentially a task of molding human beings to accept their lot without resistance or complaint.

Today, in our open society, obedient conformists become social misfits. In a world where the individual must stand on his own feet and shape his own destiny, qualities that are desirable are the opposite of those needed in the past—namely, autonomy and self-reliance, and the capacity to handle a degree of personal freedom seldom experienced in the past. To prepare children for living in this new world, parents have to accept completely new roles. Their task now is not to mold the child into conformity, but to cooperate with him flexibly in learning to use freedom with wisdom and restraint. This is a much more difficult task, and puts a heavy strain on modern families.

One aspect of this strain is the need for a child to see in his parents the effective exercise of freedom in good relationships and cooperation. We used to accept, without critical examination, the principle that one of the child's primary needs was to be brought up in a home where his father and mother were both present. But the question is now being asked, whether the mere presence of father and mother is enough, if their relationship is vitiated by destructive conflict. We would all agree with the principle that a warm, loving relationship between husband and wife creates the perfect emotional climate for the healthy development of the child. But we have been less willing to examine what the atmosphere created by a bad marriage does negatively to the emotional life of the child. In the close and confining atmosphere of the nuclear family, a continued state of unresolved marital conflict might well be a breeding-ground of psychopathology. In the old extended family, this was unlikely to happen, because there were always other family members in whom the child could find emotional compensation when his immediate parents caused him anxiety and distress.

4. Marriage and Stability. We have seen that in the past the continuity of the family was absolutely essential, and everything else had to be sacrificed to it. Today, our values are different. In the old days, the married couple were shut up in a box together and had to get on with the familial tasks that were committed to them, whether they were happy together or not. I once asked a group of Indians what an Indian wife could do if she found herself in an intolerable marital situation. Quite seriously, I was told that the correct solution for this problem was suicide! This was true throughout the Orient, and there are plenty of illustrations that it was resorted to on occasions. The stability of marriage was the primary value, and nothing else mattered in comparison.

Today the emphasis has shifted, and I believe the shift is permanent. We must face realistically the fact that in the future it will be impossible to hold marriages together by coercion from outside. They will only be held together by cohesion from within. What this means is that the principle that an unhappy marriage must be tolerated for the sake of the stability of the institution, which is an article of Catholic dogma, will be less and less readily accepted in the future. People who consider their marriages unhappy will get out of them, either to remarry or to abandon marriage as a way of life. I think we are moving to the point at which the primary value in marriage will no longer be stability, but creativity. We may not like this, or approve of it. But we can hardly suggest that the difference between stability and creativity in marriage can be equated to the difference between good and evil.

What seems to be clear from our discussion is that the case for a good marriage is overwhelming. A good marriage results in the kind of companionship that marriage is ideally fitted to provide in our modern world. A good marriage finds its own satisfactory solution of the sexual needs of the partners, and provides the atmosphere for happy and successful parenthood. But a bad marriage, or a poor marriage, or a mediocre marriage, poses problems for the persons involved, and for the society to which they belong, which can no longer be avoided or neglected.

What is clear is that marriage in contemporary culture raises all kinds of problems and questions which simply did not bother our ancestors. Those of us who are workers and specialists in this field have been facing these problems and questions. As I perceive the situation, there are three basic tasks that confront us. The first is study and research, so that we may identify the true nature and dimensions of the problems. The second is a massive program of education to enlighten people concerning what is happening to marriage today, and to give them some intelligent understanding of the task they assume when they get married. The third is to develop counseling services to tide married people through the crises that are inevitable in the close and intimate kind of relationship they are asking marriage to provide. The programs we have developed have been on the right lines, and we have made considerable headway with them. What we now need is the widespread support of the community, and the money to provide the services that are needed. This will come only when the community and the nation recognize that good marriages are their most precious asset, and that bad marriages lead to costly and destructive consequences.

MARRIAGE IN THE FUTURE

I have tried to indicate that the changes that are taking place in marriage are a healthy adaptation to the new functions marriage must serve in the altogether different environment in which our children and our children's children will have to live. In the vast, impersonal world of the future, technology will achieve miracles in ministering to human need. But what technology cannot do is to provide for that deep need in all of us that can only be met through intimate relationships in which we know ourselves to be loved and cherished, supported and sustained. There are many ways in which this need can be met, but none that can compare with the experience of a really happy marriage. None of us can predict what life will be like on this planet for distant future generations. But in the foreseeable future, I believe men and women will seek to enter marriage not less eagerly, but more eagerly, than in the past. And as our knowledge increases, and as we learn to make it available and assimilable through sound education and effective counseling, I think the chances are that people will become more mature and more creative, so that they are able to enter into the relationships in depth that make marriages truly happy and successful. In short, as I look into the future of marriage I feel rather optimistic. I do not share the gloomy forebodings that I often hear expressed by those around me. As I look ahead, my feeling is that the potentialities of marriage have not been exhausted. On the contrary, they have not yet begun to be fully developed. I think there is a good chance that what the children of today will see, in their lifetime, is not marriage sinking ignominiously into obsolescence, but blossoming and flourishing as it has never done before in human history.

2   *The New Norms of Domestic Life*

Daniel Yankelovich

STUDY QUESTIONS

1. With which of the normative changes would you agree? Why?

2. With which of the normative changes would you disagree? Why?

Many observers have concluded from the news coverage of the past year—the Reagan sweep, the disarray of political liberalism, the tighter constraints of our economy, the emergence of fundamentalist groups opposed to the ERA, abortion, and sex education—that the United States is swinging back to the disciplined, self-sacrificing habits that ruled American life before the heyday of affluence. But that inference is incorrect.

When I asked young women in the 1950s why they cherished marriage, family, and children as their inevitable destiny, many were rendered tongue-tied. My question struck them as unanswerable, meaningless. Asked why she wanted to get married and have children, one woman replied, sarcastically, "Why do you put on your pants in the morning? Why do you walk with two feet instead of one?"

We all know that very little can be taken for granted any longer when it comes to Americans' attitudes toward sexual relations, marriage, family, and childbearing. Some of the changes that have taken place are so profound that we may not realize that they may yet be evolving into newer forms, forms that can now be only dimly discerned. However, to get a perspective on what may be happening, we need to appreciate the shifts of the past few decades.

A variety of surveys point to at least 20 major normative changes in American life in recent years. These 20 are not necessarily the most important

Source: Excerpted from Daniel Yankelovich, *New Rules: Searching for Self-Fulfillment in a World Turned Upside Down.* New York: Random House, 1981. Reprinted by permission.

changes; they simply are the ones that have been measured in surveys. (See the chart on page 16.) But at least half of them have to do with domestic norms and portray the virtual abandonment of some of our most deeply entrenched beliefs about marriage and the family. (In some instances we have trend data going back to the 1930s; in others the comparisons go back only 10 or 20 years or even less; and, in a few instances, there are no previous measures, so we must infer from other evidence that a change has taken place.)

The study I conducted in the late 1950s among single and married women in their teens and early 20s demonstrated the strength of marriage norms. All the single women I interviewed assumed they would marry and have children. The married women who did not yet have children all stated that they planned to have them; most wanted three or four children or more. The mothers in the study were all married, and each pronounced herself thoroughly satisfied with being a mother. Although several of the young mothers admitted that they had become pregnant without intending to, none of them felt comfortable saying outright that she did not want to have a child.

These attitudes toward marriage and children were confirmed by a study conducted by the University of Michigan at about the same time. The study asked a national cross section of Americans what they thought of anyone, man or woman, who rejected the idea of marriage. An overwhelming majority—a full 80 percent—severely criticized those who preferred the single state, stigmatizing them as "sick" or "neurotic" or "immoral." The remaining 20 percent were neutral, neither condemnatory nor approving. Fewer than one percent had anything good to say about the unmarried state.

By the late 1970s the country's interpretation of the kind of person who would deliberately choose to remain unmarried had shifted strikingly. In another Michigan study, condemnatory attitudes shrunk from 80 percent to a mere 25 percent—from virtual consensus to minority standing. A three-fifths majority (61 percent) swung into the neutral column, and a significant number (14 percent) praised the choice of the unmarried state as a valid and positive way of life. In other words, in the late 1950s, 80 percent of all Americans held that being unmarried was an unnatural state for a man or woman: to be normal was to be married. By the late 1970s, a mere generation later, virtually the same proportion (75 percent) had changed their normative premise.

According to Elizabeth Douvan, a Michigan researcher associated with the study, "Norms about marriage and parenthood have changed dramatically over the past 20 years. Today marriage and parenthood are rarely viewed as necessary, and people who do not choose these roles are no longer considered social deviants."

Furthermore, and also in sharp contrast with the past, it has become normal to think of marriage as not being permanent. When an NBC/Associated Press poll asked Americans in 1978 whether they thought "most couples getting married today expect to remain married for the rest of their lives," a 60 percent majority said no. As Sheila M. Rothman writes in *Woman's Proper Place*: "In the 1950s as in the 1920s, diamonds were 'forever.' In the 1970s diamonds were for 'now'."

These shifts are not just a matter of our changing attitudes and values.

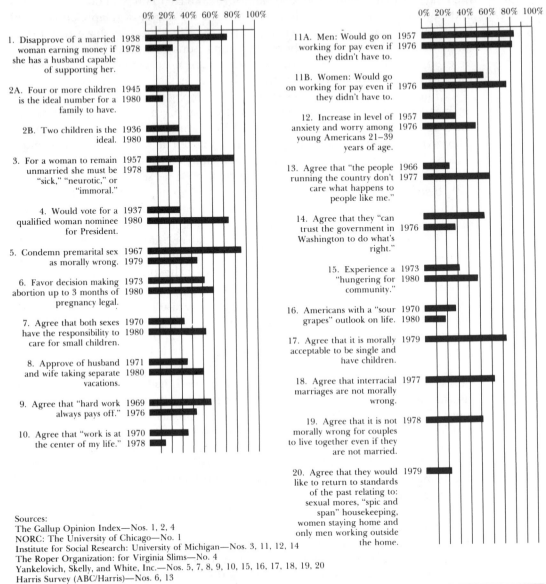

1. Disapprove of a married 1938 / woman earning money if 1978 / she has a husband capable / of supporting her.

2A. Four or more children 1945 / is the ideal number for a 1980 / family to have.

2B. Two children is the 1936 / ideal. 1980

3. For a woman to remain 1957 / unmarried she must be 1978 / "sick," "neurotic," or / "immoral."

4. Would vote for a 1937 / qualified woman nominee 1980 / for President.

5. Condemn premarital sex 1967 / as morally wrong. 1979

6. Favor decision making 1973 / abortion up to 3 months of 1980 / pregnancy legal.

7. Agree that both sexes 1970 / have the responsibility to 1980 / care for small children.

8. Approve of husband 1971 / and wife taking separate 1980 / vacations.

9. Agree that "hard work 1969 / always pays off." 1976

10. Agree that "work is at 1970 / the center of my life." 1978

11A. Men: Would go on 1957 / working for pay even if 1976 / they didn't have to.

11B. Women: Would go on working for pay even if 1976 / they didn't have to.

12. Increase in level of 1957 / anxiety and worry among 1976 / young Americans 21–39 / years of age.

13. Agree that "the people 1966 / running the country don't 1977 / care what happens to / people like me."

14. Agree that they "can / trust the government in 1976 / Washington to do what's / right."

15. Experience a 1973 / "hungering for 1980 / community."

16. Americans with a "sour 1970 / grapes" outlook on life. 1980

17. Agree that it is morally 1979 / acceptable to be single and / have children.

18. Agree that interracial 1977 / marriages are not morally / wrong.

19. Agree that it is not 1978 / morally wrong for couples / to live together even if they / are not married.

20. Agree that they would 1979 / like to return to standards / of the past relating to: / sexual mores, "spic and / span" housekeeping, / women staying home and / only men working outside / the home.

Sources:
The Gallup Opinion Index—Nos. 1, 2, 4
NORC: The University of Chicago—No. 1
Institute for Social Research: University of Michigan—Nos. 3, 11, 12, 14
The Roper Organization: for Virginia Slims—No. 4
Yankelovich, Skelly, and White, Inc.—Nos. 5, 7, 8, 9, 10, 15, 16, 17, 18, 19, 20
Harris Survey (ABC/Harris)—Nos. 6, 13

Norms influence behavior. Single households (defined by the U.S. Census Bureau as men or women living alone or with an unrelated person) have had an explosive growth rate, increasing 66 percent from 1960 to 1980. During this same period, single-parent families (mainly women, but now including more than one and a half million men) also grew rapidly—from 9 percent of all households in 1960 to 14 percent now. Together, these two categories constitute nearly four out of 10 households. Marriage and traditional family life are growing less universal all the time.

DANIEL YANKELOVICH

Between 1960 and 1977 it is estimated that the number of unmarried couples living together more than doubled—from 439,000 to 957,000. *Time* magazine quotes one woman, a 27-year-old graduate student living in Kansas, describing her parents' reaction to the news that she was living with a man: "When I first told my parents I had a new roommate, they immediately knew what was going on. My mother's first words were, 'Don't do all the cooking and cleaning'." When Yankelovich, Skelly, and White asked in surveys for *Time* whether people thought it was "morally wrong for couples who are not married to live together," more than half (52 percent) answered no.

There has been a dramatic change in attitudes toward childbearing as well. From the once universally held norm that a childless woman was, by definition, barren and not a complete woman, we have moved to a widespread acceptance of childlessness without stigma. A study by my firm shows that virtually all Americans (83 percent) now believe it is acceptable to be married and not have children. A majority (59 percent) reject even the weaker version of that concept, that "people who do not have children are selfish." In the same tolerant spirit, three out of four Americans say it is now morally acceptable to be single and have children—an astonishing turnabout in mores when one recalls the scandal and disgrace formerly associated with having a child out of wedlock.

Here, too, changes in behavior parallel the shift in norms. In recent years the fertility of American women has followed a steady downward trend—from 118.3 births per 1,000 women of childbearing age in 1955, to 66.7 in 1975. In the period from 1955 to 1959, a woman in her childbearing years could expect to have 3.7 births; in 1965 to 1969, 2.6 births; in 1977, 1.8. In the 1950s married young women who did not want babies were reluctant to admit it. Now I often encounter the reverse situation in interviews: many young women deny any interest in having babies; they admit to harboring a "curiosity" about the experience of childbirth and mothering only if pressed.

So much has been written in recent years about changing sexual norms that we need not dwell on them at length. A few survey findings sum up the story. As recently as 1967, a Yankelovich, Skelly, and White survey for CBS News found that most parents of college-age youths (85 percent) condemned all premarital sex as morally wrong. Now, a majority (63 percent) condone it: "If two people love each other, there's nothing morally wrong with having sexual relations." Nearly the same majority (57 percent) reject the norm that a woman should be a virgin when she gets married. And most Americans now reject the old double standard: "If a husband plays around a little, that's excusable, but a wife never should."

In another form, the double standard lives on. Its existence can be documented in the mere 45 percent plurality of Americans who find male nudes in women's magazines acceptable, as compared with the nearly 60 percent who accept female nudes in men's periodicals. The divergence is merged again, however, in the nearly doubled acceptance of total nudity in films and plays in the last 10 years.

Another change: for the first time in American society, only minorities of adults report discomfort at "having friends who are homosexuals," and while slim majorities still feel that homosexual relations may be morally wrong, there is declining willingness to restrict the sexual preferences of consenting adults by law; barely one-quarter of the population (21 percent) express a desire for a return to traditional standards in sexual relations.

Not surprisingly, normative changes relating to sexuality, childbearing, and marriage also affect sex roles: the male/female division of effort in the family. Changing norms of what a woman is "supposed to do" as wife and mother and what a man is "supposed to do" as husband and father are transforming the institutions of the workplace and the family. Probably no set of shifting norms carries greater significance for the culture.

Norms affecting whether a wife should work outside the home have reversed themselves within a single generation. It should be kept in mind that some women in America have always worked outside the home. In recent years the number of working women has increased, but the phenomenon is not novel. What is new is not the fact of women working, but its cultural meaning. In the 18th century, and particularly in the 19th, it was not unusual for the whole family—the husband, his wife, and his children—to work for pay outside the home. In the late 19th and early 20th century, as the nation industrialized and its wealth grew, it became a source of pride for a man to be so successful as a provider that his children and even his wife no longer had to work outside the home. In the early post-World War II years, the majority of women with children who worked were blue collar, not bluestocking. When middle-class women worked outside the home, couples spun elaborate rationalizations to ensure that the husband's position as chief bread-winner not be undermined, either in his own eyes or in the eyes of others. The social meaning of his wife's working was that the husband was incapable of providing for his family—he was less than a man.

This shared meaning, which equated manliness with earning power, persisted with great force until the late 1960s. One of my favorite survey questions asks people to define what they mean when they use the phrase "real man." Until the late 1960s, an 85 to 90 percent majority defined a real man as someone who is a good provider for his family. Other meanings—sexual potency, physical strength, being a responsible and caring human being, being handy around the house—always fell far behind this root cultural meaning. In recent years, however, the definition of a real man as a good provider declined from the No. 1 spot to the No. 3 position and slipped from 86 percent in 1968 to 67 percent a decade later. The cultural definition persists, but in attenuated form.

Even more strikingly, the change in the female work population reflects a marked shift in social meanings. Whereas in the past it was mainly blue-collar women who worked for pay, now it is the better educated, upper-middle-class women who increasingly work outside the home, seeking the satisfactions of paid employment that include the financial but are not limited to it.

The cultural meaning of a woman working outside the home has shifted subtly from an act that diminishes the manliness of the "head of household" to one that enhances the status of the woman without adversely affecting the man. As recently as 1970 only a minority of Americans (42 percent) wanted unstintingly to strengthen women's status in our society. By the end of that decade, a two-thirds majority in a Harris survey (64 percent) approved this goal, and work outside the home has become the key to achieving it.

Our research indicates that husbands and wives have different perceptions of the stresses caused by women working. A substantial 25 percent of working wives say their husbands are bothered by having them away from home so much; only one percent of the husbands admit to being so bothered. One out of five working wives claims her husband is disturbed that the home is not as neat and clean as it was before she went out to work, but virtually none of the husbands say that bothers them. Husbands, on the other hand, do admit to disliking pressure to help around the house and say their wives underestimate the discomfort to the whole family caused by the fact that they worked outside the home.

The dual-earner family is rapidly becoming the norm, now accounting for a majority of upper-income households. Economic need pushes many women to take paying jobs outside the home rather than do housekeeping or voluntary work, but it is not always easy to define economic need. In many families, both spouses work in order to maintain a standard of living that they have come to enjoy and expect, though they hardly "need" it, in a literal sense. Indeed, an impressive 67 percent of women who work say that they do so for reasons of self-fulfillment as well as for economic reasons. The majority of women today, including those who work for pay *and* those who stay at home, state that their ideal of the woman who is truly fulfilling herself is someone who can manage a career as well as a home.

As in the case with so many norms, the path of change proceeds along the lines of age and education. Most of the women over 55 feel comfortable with a sharp cleavage of responsibilities between men and women, while only a minority of those under 35 like rigid divisions. Similarly, the old roles are endorsed by a minority of those with some college education (37 percent) and by a majority (57 percent) of those with a high school education or less.

One of the most far-reaching changes in social norms relates to what parents believe they owe their children and what their children owe them. Nowhere are changes in the unwritten social contract more significant or agonizing.

The overall pattern is clear: today's parents expect to make fewer sacrifices for their children than parents did in the past, but they also demand less from their offspring in the form of future obligations than their parents demanded from them. Measures of these attitudes in previous eras do not exist, largely because no one thought of the parent-child bond as anything but permanent. But the data now available are unmistakable.

In a series of studies on the American family carried out by Yankelovich, Skelly, and White in the 1970s for General Mills, the following key findings came to light:

Nearly two-thirds of all American parents (63 percent) reject the idea that parents should stay together for the children's sake even if the parents are unhappy with each other.

A similar majority (66 percent) feel that "parents should be free to live

Traditional Norms That Still Command Majority Assent

90%
Would still have children if they "had it to do over again"
1

87%
Feel use of hard drugs is "morally wrong"
2

84%
Feel it's up to parents to educate teenagers about birth control
3

81%
Feel "mate swapping is "morally wrong"
4

79%
Disapprove of married women having affairs
5

76%
Disapprove of married men having affairs
6

77%
Agree that a woman should put her husband and children ahead of her career
7

74%
Want their children to be better off and more successful than they are
8

57%
Agree that it's best to "demand a lot" from children: they have to "do their best to get ahead"
9

55%
Feel "it's more important for a wife to help her husband's career than to have one herself"
10

51%
Believe that "strict, old-fashioned upbringing and discipline" are still the best ways to raise children
11

Sources
1976–77 General Mills American Family Report: Raising Children in a Changing Society—Nos. 1, 8, 9
1978–79 General Mills American Family Report: Family Health in an Era of Stress—Nos. 3, 11
TIME Magazine/Yankelovich Survey; July, 1977, and March, 1978—Nos. 2, 4, 5, 6, 7
NORC General Social Survey, 1977—No. 10

their own lives even if it means spending less time with their children." And an almost equal number of parents (63 percent) endorse the view that they have the right to live well now and spend what they have earned "even if it means leaving less to the children."

On the other hand, most parents recognize that in the name of fairness, if they reduce their level of sacrifice for the children, then the children should not be burdened with future obligations to them. Sixty-seven percent believe that "children do not have an obligation to their parents regardless of what their parents have done for them."

I've saved for the end of this discussion of the new domestic norms one survey finding that encapsulates the ambivalence Americans feel about these changes. The sweeping normative changes in marriage, family life, and the relationship to children I have described fill many people with sadness and nostalgia. The changes create a sense of loss, almost of grief, and give rise to many inconsistencies and contradictions. The large two-thirds majority that express a reduced commitment of parents to children and children to parents also wish to see "a return to more traditional standards of family life and parental responsibility." (See the chart above [on p. 20] for some of the traditional norms that retain widespread support.)

Why the contradiction? A related survey finding provides the key: majorities may claim, in the abstract, that they want to return to the family life of the past, but when it comes to specifics, only one out of five (21 percent) has any hankering to go back to traditional standards of sexual relations, to the spic-and-span housekeeping norms of the past, or to the male monopoly on working outside the home. Americans long for the warmth and closeness they associate with family life in earlier decades, but not if it means going back to the old rules.

How to preserve warmth and closeness while at the same time holding on to the new freedom to choose? That is the preeminent question about our domestic lives that is now confronting our culture.

3 *The Paradox of Perfection*

Arlene Skolnick

STUDY QUESTIONS

1. Why does Skolnick believe that the family can be both a cherished value and a troubled institution at the same time?

2. What does Skolnick mean when she claims that even "normal" families are less than ideal?

The American Family, as even readers of *Popular Mechanics* must know by now, is in what Sean O'Casey would have called "a terrible state of chassis." Yet, there are certain ironies about the much-publicized crisis that give one pause.

True, the statistics seem alarming. The U.S. divorce rate, though it has reached something of a plateau in recent years, remains the highest in American history. The number of births out-of-wedlock among all races and ethnic groups continues to climb. The plight of many elderly Americans subsisting on low fixed incomes is well known.

What puzzles me is an ambiguity, not in the facts, but in what we are asked to make of them. A series of opinion polls conducted in 1978 by Yankelovich, Skelley, and White, for example, found that 38 percent of those surveyed had recently witnessed one or more "destructive activities" (e.g., a divorce, a separation, a custody battle) within their own families or those of their parents or siblings. At the same time, 92 percent of the respondents said the family was highly important to them as a "personal value."

Can the family be at once a cherished "value" and a troubled institution? I am inclined to think, in fact, that they go hand in hand. A recent "Talk of the Town" report in *The New Yorker* illustrates what I mean:

Source: Arlene Skolnick, "The Paradox of Perfection." From the *Wilson Quarterly*, Summer 1980. Copyright 1980 by The Woodrow Wilson International Center for Scholars. Reprinted by permission.

A few months ago word was heard from Billy Gray, who used to play brother Bud in "Father Knows Best," the 1950s television show about the nice Anderson family who lived in the white frame house on a side street in some mythical Springfield—the house at which the father arrived each night swinging open the front door and singing out "Margaret, I'm home!" Gray said he felt "ashamed" that he had ever had anything to do with the show. It was all "totally false," he said, and had caused many Americans to feel inadequate, because they thought that was the way life was supposed to be and that their own lives failed to measure up.

As Susan Sontag has noted in *On Photography*, mass-produced images have "extraordinary powers to determine our demands upon reality." The family is especially vulnerable to confusion between truth and illusion. What, after all, is "normal"? All of us have a backstairs view of our own families, but we know The Family, in the aggregate, only vicariously.

Like politics or athletics, the family has become a media event. Television offers nightly portrayals of lump-in-throat family "normalcy" ("The Waltons," "Little House on the Prairie") and even humorous "deviance" ("One Day at a Time," "The Odd Couple"). Family advisers sally forth in syndicated newspaper columns to uphold standards, mend relationships, suggest counseling, and otherwise lead their readers back to the True Path. For commercial purposes, advertisers spend millions of dollars to create stirring vignettes of glamorous-but-ordinary families, the kind of family most 11-year-olds wish they had.

All Americans do not, of course, live in such a family, but most share an intuitive sense of what the "ideal" family should be—reflected in the precepts of religion, the conventions of etiquette, and the assumptions of law. And, characteristically, Americans tend to project the ideal back into the past, the time when virtues of all sorts are thought to have flourished.

We do not come off well by comparison with that golden age, nor could we, for it is as elusive and mythical as Brigadoon. If Billy Gray shames too easily, he has a valid point: While Americans view the family as the proper context for their own lives—9 out of 10 people live in one—they have no realistic context in which to view the family. Family history, until recently, was as neglected in academe as it still is in the press. [The summer 1980] White House Conference on Families is "policy-oriented," which means present-minded. The familiar, depressing charts of "leading family indicators"—marriage, divorce, illegitimacy—in newspapers and newsmagazines rarely survey the trends before World War II. The discussion, in short, lacks ballast.

Let us go back to before the American Revolution.

Perhaps what distinguishes the modern family most from its colonial counterpart is its newfound privacy. Throughout the 17th and 18th centuries, well over 90 percent of the American population lived in small rural communities. Unusual behavior rarely went unnoticed, and neighbors often intervened directly in a family's affairs, to help or to chastise.

The most dramatic example was the rural "charivari," prevalent in both Europe and the United States until the early 19th century. The purpose of these noisy gatherings was to censure community members for familial transgressions—unusual sexual behavior, marriages between persons of grossly discrepant ages, or "household disorder," to name but a few. As historian Edward Shorter describes it in *The Making of the Modern Family*:

> Sometimes the demonstration would consist of masked individuals circling somebody's house at night, screaming, beating on pans, and blowing cow horns. . . . [O]n other occasions, the offender would be seized and marched through the streets, seated perhaps backwards on a donkey or forced to wear a placard describing his sins.

The state itself had no qualms about intruding into a family's affairs by statute, if necessary. Consider 17th-century New England's "stubborn child" laws that, though never actually enforced, sanctioned the death penalty for chronic disobedience to one's parents.

If the boundaries between home and society seem blurred during the colonial era, it is because they were. People were neither very emotional nor very self-conscious about family life, and, as historian John Demos points out, family and community were "joined in a relation of profound reciprocity." In his *Of Domestical Duties*, William Gouge, a 17th-century Puritan preacher, called the family "a little community." The home, like the larger community, was as much an economic as a social unit; all members of the family worked, be it on the farm, or in a shop, or in the home.

There was not much to idealize. Love was not considered the basis for marriage but one possible result of it. According to historian Carl Degler, it was easier to obtain a divorce in colonial New England than anywhere else in the Western world, and the divorce rate climbed steadily throughout the 18th century, though it remained low by contemporary standards. Romantic images to the contrary, it was rare for more than two generations (parents and children) to share a household for the simple reason that very few people lived beyond the age of 60. It is ironic that our nostalgia for the extended family—including grandparents and grandchildren—comes at a time when, thanks to improvements in health care, its existence is less threatened than ever before.

Infant mortality was high in colonial days, though not as high as we are accustomed to believe, since food was plentiful and epidemics, owing to generally low population density, were few. In the mid-1700s, the average age of marriage was about 24 for men, 21 for women—not much different from what it is now. Households, on average, were larger, but not startlingly so: A typical household in 1790 included about 5.6 members, versus about 3.5 today. Illegitimacy was widespread. Premarital pregnancies reached a high in 18th-century America (10 percent of all first births) that was not equaled until the 1950s.

FORM FOLLOWS FUNCTION

In simple demographic terms, then, the differences between the American family in colonial times and today are not all that stark; the similarities are sometimes striking.

ARLENE SKOLNICK

The chief contrast is psychological. While Western societies have always idealized the family to some degree, the *most vivid* literary portrayals of family life before the 19th century were negative or, at best, ambivalent. In what might be called the "high tragic" tradition—including Sophocles, Shakespeare, and the Bible, as well as fairy tales and novels—the family was portrayed as a high-voltage emotional setting, laden with dark passion, sibling rivalries, and violence. There was also the "low comic" tradition—the world of henpecked husbands and tyrannical mothers-in-law.

It is unlikely that our 18th-century ancestors ever left the Book of Genesis or *Tom Jones* with the feeling that their own family lives were seriously flawed.

By the time of the Civil War, however, American attitudes toward the family had changed profoundly. The early decades of the 19th century marked the beginnings of America's gradual transformation into an urban, industrial society. In 1820, less than 8 percent of the U.S. population lived in cities; by 1860, the urban concentration approached 20 percent, and by 1900 that proportion had doubled.

Structurally, the American family did not immediately undergo a comparable transformation. Despite the large families of many immigrants and farmers, the size of the *average* family declined—slowly but steadily—as it had been doing since the 17th century. Infant mortality remained about the same and may even have increased somewhat, owing to poor sanitation in crowded cities. Legal divorces were easier to obtain than they had been in colonial times. Indeed, the rise in the divorce rate was a matter of some concern during the 19th century, though death, not divorce, was the prime cause of one-parent families, as it was up to 1965.

Functionally, however, America's industrial revolution had a lasting effect on the family. No longer was the household typically a group of interdependent workers. Now, men went to offices and factories and became breadwinners; wives stayed home to mind the hearth; children went off to the new public schools. The home was set apart from the dog-eat-dog arena of economic life; it came to be viewed as a utopian retreat or, in historian Christopher Lasch's phrase, a "haven in a heartless world." Marriage was now valued primarily for its emotional attractions. Above all, the family became something to worry about.

The earliest and most saccharine "sentimental model" of the family appeared in the new mass media that proliferated during the second quarter of the 19th century. Novels, tracts, newspaper articles, and ladies' magazines—there were variations for each class of society—elaborated a "Cult of True Womanhood" in which piety, submissiveness, and domesticity dominated the pantheon of desirable feminine qualities. This quotation from *The Ladies Book* (1830) is typical:

> See, she sits, she walks, she speaks, she looks—unutterable things! Inspiration springs up in her very paths—it follows her footsteps. A halo of glory encircles her, and illuminates her whole orbit. With her, man not only feels safe, but actually renovated.

In the late 1800s, science came into the picture. The "professionalization" of the housewife took two different forms. One involved motherhood and childrearing, according to the latest scientific understanding of children's special physical and emotional needs. (It is no accident that the publishing of children's books became a major industry during this period.) The other was the domestic science movement—"home economics," basically—which focused on woman as full-time homemaker, applying "scientific" and "industrial" rationality to shopping, making meals, and housework.

The new ideal of the family prompted a cultural split that has endured, one that Tocqueville had glimpsed (and rather liked) in 1835. Society was divided more sharply into man's sphere and woman's sphere. Toughness, competition, and practicality were the masculine values that ruled the outside world. The softer values—affection, tranquility, piety—were worshipped in the home and the church. In contrast to the colonial view, the ideology of the "modern" family implied a critique of everything beyond the front door.

What is striking as one looks at the writings of the 19th-century "experts"—the physicians, clergymen, phrenologists, and "scribbling ladies"—is how little their essential message differs from that of the sociologists, psychiatrists, pediatricians, and women's magazine writers of the 20th century, particularly since World War II.

Instead of men's and women's spheres, of course, sociologists speak of "instrumental" and "expressive" roles. The notion of the family as a retreat from the harsh realities of the outside world crops up as "functional differentiation." And, like the 19th-century utopians who believed society could be regenerated through the perfection of family life, 20th-century social scientists have looked at the failed family as the source of most American social problems.

None of these who promoted the sentimental model of the family—neither the popular writers nor the academics—considered the paradox of perfectionism: the ironic possibility that it would lead to trouble. Yet it has. The image of the perfect, happy family makes ordinary families seem like failures. Small problems loom as big problems if the "normal" family is thought to be one where there are no real problems at all.

One sees this phenomenon at work on the generation of Americans born and reared during the late 19th century, the first generation reared on the mother's milk of sentimental imagery. Between 1900 and 1920, the U.S. divorce rate doubled, from four to eight divorces annually per 1,000 married couples. The jump—comparable to the 100 percent increase in the divorce rate between 1960 and 1980—is not attributable to changes in divorce laws, which were not greatly liberalized. Rather, it would appear that, as historian Thomas O'Neill believes, Americans were simply more willing to dissolve marriages that did not conform to their idea of domestic bliss—and perhaps try again.

A "FUN" MORALITY

If anything, family standards became even more demanding as the 20th century progressed. The new fields of psychology and sociology opened up whole new definitions of familial perfection. "Feelings"—fun, love, warmth, good orgasm—

ARLENE SKOLNICK

acquired heightened popular significance as the invisible glue of successful families.

Psychologist Martha Wolfenstein, in an analysis of several decades of government-sponsored infant care manuals, has documented the emergence of a "fun morality." In former days, being a good parent meant carrying out certain tasks with punctilio; if your child was clean and reasonably obedient, you had no cause to probe his psyche. Now, we are told, parents must commune with their own feelings and those of their children—an edict which has seeped into the ethos of education as well. The distinction is rather like that between religions of deed and religions of faith. It is one thing to make your child brush his teeth; it is quite another to transform the whole process into a joyous "learning experience."

The task of 20th-century parents has been further complicated by the advice offered them. The experts disagree with each other and often contradict themselves. The kindly Dr. Benjamin Spock, for example, is full of contradictions. In a detailed analysis of *Baby and Child Care*, historian Michael Zuckerman observes that Spock tells mothers to relax ("trust yourself") yet warns them that they have an "ominous power" to destroy their children's innocence and make them discontented "for years" or even "forever."

As we enter the 1980s, both family images and family realities are in a state of transition. After a century and a half, the web of attitudes and nostrums comprising the "sentimental model" is beginning to unravel. Since the mid-1960s, there has been a youth rebellion of sorts, a new "sexual revolution," a revival of feminism, and the emergence of the two-worker family. The huge postwar Baby-Boom generation is pairing off, accounting in part for the upsurge in the divorce rate (half of all divorces occur within seven years of a first marriage). Media images of the family have become more "realistic," reflecting new patterns of family life that are emerging (and old patterns that are re-emerging).

Among social scientists, "realism" is becoming something of an ideal in itself. For some of them, realism translates as pluralism: All forms of the family, by virtue of the fact that they happen to exist, are equally acceptable—from communes and cohabitation to one-parent households, homosexual marriages, and, come to think of it, the nuclear family. What was once labeled "deviant" is now merely "variant." In some college texts, "the family" has been replaced by "family systems." Yet, this new approach does not seem to have squelched perfectionist standards. Indeed, a palpable strain of perfectionism runs through the pop literature on "alternative" family lifestyles.

For the majority of scholars, realism means a more down-to-earth view of the American household. Rather than seeing the family as a haven of peace and tranquility, they have begun to recognize that even "normal" families are less than ideal, that intimate relations of any sort inevitably involve antagonism as well as love. Conflict and change are inherent in social life. If the family is now in a state of flux, such is the nature of resilient institutions; if it is beset by problems, so is life. The family will survive.

2 *Role Changes*

At first glance it would appear that the subject matters listed under this heading are related but mutually exclusive. Appearances notwithstanding, a major factor affecting both sexual and dating behavior is that of gender, and in the current milieu, sexual expression may be what intimate relationships, such as dating, are all about.

A belief held in society is that the child's gender at birth will determine the child's future gender behavior. Because men and women have differing sex characteristics—chromosomes, hormones, and physiology—society has ingrained expectations of stereotypical attitudes and behaviors—gender differences—characteristic of men and women. That is, such instrumental traits as assertiveness, competitiveness, and independence have been expected of men because they are usually bigger and stronger, while such expressive traits as possessiveness, nurturance, and dependency have been ascribed to women because of their childbearing capacity. Changing roles for women are now raising the question of whether gender traits are biologically determined (nature) or learned after birth (nurture).

Advocates of a nature perspective attempt to account for reported sex differences by referring to the findings on sex-related chromosome combinations, recessive traits, hemispheric specialization, and prenatal hormone exposure (Adams 1987). Though chromosomal and hormonal differences do influence susceptibility to disease, physical development, and aggression, it is not clear that other typically masculine or feminine behaviors are biologically determined. A study of various societies by Margaret Mead (1935) reveals that there was no one biologically "natural" male or female behavior. She found societies in which men and women do not behave in ways considered appropriate for their sex in Western society.

Advocates of the nurture perspective say that sex differences result from socialization. They refer to findings related to family socialization, role identification, peer and school influences, and other training and formal instruction efforts (Adams 1987).

Michael Lewis and Marsha Weinraub, in the first article of Chapter 2, summarize this debate by examining the relationship between the biological, the environmental, and the cognitive factors of role development. Their findings lead to the conclusion that gender-specific behavior continues because of a gender-typed environment with its gender-typed structure and messages. That is, children are guided in their gender identity by the socializing agents of parents and social institutions. An example of this gender socialization by parents is seen in the second article of this chapter by Carol Adair Finn. She reveals how the beliefs of the parents are turned into realities via different treatment. It is these expectations and actions that bring about the very behavior they expected.

Social institutions also constantly reinforce stereotypical gender behavior through children's books, comic strips, cartoons, and television programs. Women are underrepresented; appear as housewives, sex objects, and victims; achieve only indirectly; and are trivialized in the media. Schools, too, encourage traditional gender behaviors by giving more attention to boys and channeling children into traditional roles.

There is a growing questioning of this "proper" gender behavior. Socialization into stereotypical behavior for either sex has been found to be related to anxiety and poor self-esteem and may keep people from realizing their full human potential by forcing them into restrictive molds. Thus negative attitudes toward feminine behavior led women to have less self-confidence and a lower idea of their capabilities than men have. Also, the learning of the male gender role may result not in an inability to be expressive but in the male's thinking that he is not supposed to be expressive (Balswick & Peek 1977). Traditional gender behaviors also cause marital problems: inequitable family relations, communication problems, hostility toward women, and emotional inexpressiveness.

These results of traditional gender socialization have led to the idea that children should be socialized with both expressive and instrumental traits as a means of promoting mental health, the ability to deal with stress, and to derive the personal satisfaction that results from access to the full range of human behavior. Psychological androgyny "allows men and women to be both independent and tender, both assertive and yielding, both masculine and feminine." In other words, psychological androgyny expands the range of behavior to everyone (Bem 1977). The last two articles in this chapter echo these beliefs. Phyllis LaFarge, in the third article, describes the impact of the feminist movement on women. Basically, it includes an expanded sense of identity and the belief that the humble work of maintenance and nurturance is valuable and should be shared with men. In the final article, Betty Friedan concludes that American men are at the cutting edge of a tidal wave of change, of new adventure, in the struggle for wholeness, for openness to feeling, for living and sharing on equal terms with women—a change in their very identity as men.

However, raising children androgynously is complicated by:

a. psychological resistance to change in traditional gender roles,

b. fear of increased homosexuality,

c. possible disadvantages to men of instrumental traits in women,

d. a nonsupportive occupational system, and

e. the parents' own lack of experience with androgynous upbringing.

What this chapter on gender reveals, then, is that the content of each gender's "proper" behavioral script reflects the patriarchal social tradition on which the American family is based. Since many beliefs and powerful subgroups support the perpetuation of these expectations, they will be hard to change.

REFERENCES

1. Adams, G. 1987. "Sex Differences: A Brief Commentary from a Developmental Science Perspective." *Journal of Early Adolescence* (Vol. 7, No. 1, pp. 129–132).

2. Balswick, J. D., & C. W. Peek. 1977. "The Inexpressive Male: A Tragedy of American Society." *The Family Coordinator* (October).

3. Bem, S. L. 1977. "Beyond Androgyny: Some Presumptuous Prescriptions for a Liberated Sexual Identity." In *Family in Transition*, 2nd ed., A. Skolnick & J. Skolnick (eds.). Boston: Little, Brown.

4. Mead, M. 1935. *Sex and Temperament in Three Primitive Societies*. New York: Morrow.

4 Origins of Early Sex-Role Development

Michael Lewis / Marsha Weinraub

STUDY QUESTIONS

1. According to the authors, what are the three influences on gender formation and in what manner do they operate?

2. Which of the three influences on gender behavior is, in your opinion, the most important and why?

The conceptualization of sex-role development traditionally has centered on the influences of three rather separate and distinct factors: biological, environmental, and cognitive. Although all theorists and researchers recognize the interactive influence of these three factors, differences exist in emphasis. Those who focus on the role of biological factors argue that sex-role development is biologically tied to gender; individuals' sex roles, in large part, are determined by their gender. Thus, boys behave like boys because they are males. These theorists argue that human sexual dimorphism exists and accounts for the observed differences in sex-role development.

Those who focus on the role of environmental factors argue that sex roles are learned primarily as a consequence of differentially rewarded behavior of the child by adults and other children. Such a view holds that the individual's sex-role behavior is to a large degree learned as a result of cultural reinforcement patterns. Even though there is a paucity of supporting data demonstrating a direct relationship between differential reinforcement and child's sex-role behavior, this view has a considerable number of adherents. However, given that the rejection of this view often implies the acceptance of the biological view, it is no wonder that the importance of environmental factors is accepted even without sufficient evidence.

Source: Michael Lewis and Marsha Weinraub, "Origins of Early Sex-Role Development." *Sex Roles* 512(1979): 135–153. Reprinted by permission.

There is, of course, an alternative to both the biological and social reinforcement views of sex-role development—what we will call the cognitive approach. In both the biological and social learning views, the role of the infant and child is rather passive; in the first, passive vis-à-vis the child's biological gender, and in the second, passive vis-à-vis the differential reinforcement patterns of others in the child's social environment. In both of these views, the child is acted upon by external forces and the child's behavior is passively altered. In contrast to these two passive views, the cognitive approach to sex-role development assumes an active organism, one which participates in, is influenced by, and influences the forces which help to determine its development. Such a model of the developing child in regard to sex-role behavior emphasizes the influence of the child's cognitions and the child's abilities to plan, to ask questions about behavior of self and of others, and to test self-generated hypotheses.

While the contribution of each of these three factors—biological, environmental, and cognitive—will be reviewed in the following pages, it is the last factor—the child's active construction of sex role through cognition—that we consider most important for the development of early sex-role behavior. As we shall demonstrate, development in general, and sex-role behavior in particular, is influenced by both biological and environmental factors. However, the coalescence of these factors around the child's growing cognitive abilities, specifically the child's social cognition—knowledge of self, other, and the relationship of self to other—is the critical factor in the development of sex roles.

In order to arrive at such a conclusion, we must examine the contribution of biological and social reinforcement processes before we turn our attention to the influences of cognition on the development of sex-role behavior.

BIOLOGICAL INFLUENCES

The individual's genetic structure at birth—XX or XY—determines the differentiation of the fetal gonads into testes or ovaries. From then on, biological sexual differentiation appears to be under hormonal control. Hormones not only influence the differentiation of internal reproductive structures and external genitalia but also seem to affect perinatal brain organization and subsequent brain development. These neurological effects may have lasting and important behavioral consequences. . . .

Money and Ehrhardt offer human analogies to the nonhuman studies of the effects of hormones on behavior. In their studies of individuals whose assigned sex was different from their genetic sex or from their hormonal histories, Money and Ehrhardt (1972) and Ehrhardt and Baker (1974) have illuminated the role of hormonal factors in contributing to temperamental, attitudinal, and behavioral sex differences. Two of the abnormal syndromes they have studied include progestin-induced hermaphroditism and fetal androgenization in females. Either as a result of genetic defect or maternal drug experience, these genetic females had been exposed perinatally to androgens (male hormones). Surgical intervention was used to correct masculinized external genitalia; in the case of the latter syndrome, cortisone therapy was administered to ensure subsequent feminine hormonal levels. All of these individuals were reared as females. They saw themselves and were seen by others as normal females. Nevertheless, in comparison to a matched sample of girls, these early-androgenized girls tended to be more masculine in attitudes, preferences, and behavior. They were more likely to be perceived as tomboys; they showed increased energy levels in play; they preferred cars, trucks, and building materials to dolls; they showed little interest in clothing, hairdos, and jewelry; and they were more likely to think about careers in their futures (Ehrhardt & Baker, 1974). These observations suggest that hormonal factors around birth may contribute to the development of temperamental and attitudinal differences even in humans. Ehrhardt and Baker suggest that hormones may affect a wide variety of behaviors by affecting preferred levels of energy expenditure both across and possibly within the sexes.

Sex differences observed early in life, particularly those which continue into later life, are often cited (Hutt, 1972) to demonstrate the role of biological influences in human sex-role development. Physiologically, a number of sex differences are apparent from birth and continue into adulthood. First, there are clear size and strength differences. Like adult males, male babies have larger muscle to fat ratios, are taller in stature and heavier in weight, and have higher metabolic rates than do females of the same age (Tanner, 1970). In addition, at all points over the life span, males are more vulnerable to injury, disease, and developmental problems (for reviews, see Maccoby & Jacklin, 1974; Sherman, 1971). Finally, males have slower rates of physiological maturation. They have a longer gestational period, longer term to permanent dentition, and longer terms to skeletal and phallic maturity (Tanner, 1970).

Research on cerebral dominance suggests that sex differences in maturational rates may also be related to the earlier and stronger development of cerebral lateralization in girls (Buffrey & Gray, 1972). Left hemispheric functioning in girls may begin to predominate over right hemispheric functioning as early as 3 or 4 years of age; in boys, such lateralization does not appear until about a year later. This earlier maturation in girls may facilitate verbal development, while inhibiting development of spatial skills. There still is a great deal of controversy and contradictory information on this topic (Maccoby & Jacklin, 1974). Nevertheless, it is clear that sex differences in cerebral dominance are probably *not* responsible for the appearance of sex differences before the fourth year of life.

Behavioral sex differences in the first year or two of life are not consistently observed. . . . In general, the inconsistency and slight differences between the sexes in perceptual-cognitive development suggest that these early differences are not robust and may occur only under limited conditions.

Sex differences in infant temperament have been infrequently observed except in a few specific areas. After rigorous investigation, researchers have generally concluded that boy and girl infants do not differ in activity level (Birns, 1976; Maccoby & Jacklin, 1974). Likewise, despite a number of investigations, few sex differences in the Brazelton Scale of Neonatal Behavior have been reported. However, replicated findings demonstrate higher levels of irritability and lesser amounts of sleep in boys than girls under 3 months of age (Moss, 1967; Sander, 1973). Along the same line is evidence that male infants are more affected by stress than female infants. A large number of studies show that infant boys are more distressed following maternal separation than girls (Brooks & Lewis, 1974; Corter, Rheingold, & Eckerman, 1972; Feldman & Ingham, 1975; Shirley & Poyntz, 1941; Young & Lewis, in press; Weinraub & Frankel, 1977; Weinraub & Lewis, 1977). Since greater male distress upon maternal absence is contrary to stereotype, these differences may fit into the more general biological pattern of male vulnerability to stress.

That sex-role behavior may be influenced by biological factors is supported by such studies demonstrating the existence of early sex differences. However, just because differences between males and females are observed early in life does not mean that these differences are necessarily biological in origin. Indeed, as early as sex-differential infant behavior has been observed, so has differential parental behavior been observed. For example, Watson (1969) has reported that infant girls as young as 12 weeks of age show greater attention to auditory stimuli than do same-aged boys. However, parent-infant interaction data on 12-week-old infants show that girls are talked to more than boys by their mothers and that when a girl infant vocalizes, her mother is more apt to respond with a vocalization than when a boy vocalizes (Lewis & Freedle, 1973). This being the case, are girls more attentive to auditory signals because of some biological differences—for example, better lateralization? If so, the biological differences in infant attentiveness could have influenced the mother's behavior; mothers are more likely to talk to someone who is "interested" than one who is not. On the other hand, the differential maternal behavior may be responsible for sex differences observed in infants' behavior; mothers who talk more to their infants may have infants who become more interested in auditory stimuli. Caution must be used in attributing early differences in behavior to biological factors.

Thus, the direct role of biological factors in influencing sensory, attentional, and temperamental sex differences in infants and young children is open to question. The picture that emerges of sex difference in the first two years of life is a limited one. Physiological sex differences are clearly observed; sensory, attentional, and temperamental differences are less consistently observed.

Often ignored, however, is the *indirect* role of biological sex differences on the development of sex roles. It is possible that biological differences in structure and function—not just in infancy but over the entire life span—may affect cultural expectations for males and females. As a result of differential expectations, adult behavior toward infants and young children may differ in order to prepare children for their adult roles. For example, if adults expect that certain children will eventually be larger and have greater energy levels than other children, then their early behavior toward these children and the types of experiences they provide these children may be different than if they expected the children to be smaller and less strong. Multigenerations of such learning within cultures may have led, quite adaptively, to differential behaviors towards boys and girls, feeding into the development of sex roles and exaggerating minimal biological differences. In the next section, the effects of environmental influences—specifically, differences in social reinforcement—will be considered.

ENVIRONMENTAL INFLUENCES

Even before children appear, there are differences in parents' preferences for and attitudes toward sons and daughters. A recent nationwide study by Hoffman (cited in Hoffman, 1977) showed that although parents want to have children of both sexes, boys are still preferred more frequently than girls, especially by fathers. Preference for male children is also demonstrated by the fact that couples who have only daughters are more likely to continue having children. In addition, reasons women give for wanting boys and girls are different. According to Hoffman, women want boys to please their husbands, to carry on the family name, and to serve as a companion for the husband; women want daughters for companionship and as play toys. Women also feel that daughters will be more obedient and easier to raise, can help with family chores, and will be cuter and sweeter and less mean than sons (Hoffman, 1977).

College-aged adults, soon-to-be parents, hold clear stereotypical expectations about boys and girls. When college students were asked to categorize 2-year-old play activities as appropriate for either boys or girls or appropriate for both boys and girls (Fagot, 1973); adults saw roughhouse play, vehicular play, and aggressive behavior as more appropriate for boys than girls, and doll play, dress-up games, and mirror looking as more appropriate for girls than boys. Likewise, parents of 6-year-olds describe the behavior of "typical boys" and "typical girls" very differently. Boys are seen as rough at play, noisy, willing to defend themselves, defiant of punishment, physically active, competitive, risk-taking, and enjoying mechanical things; girls are seen as neat and clean and quiet and reserved, easily frightened, helpful around the house, sensitive to others' feelings, well-mannered, and easily upset (Lambert, Yackley, & Hein, 1971).

Immediately after their baby is born, parents—especially fathers—describe and interpret their infants' behaviors along sex-stereotyped lines. Daughters are seen as softer, finer featured, smaller and more attentive, while sons are seen as fussier, larger featured, better coordinated, more alert, stronger, and hardier. Newborn daughters are likely to be described as beautiful, pretty, or cute much more often than newborn sons (Rubin, Provenzano, & Luria, 1974).

In light of differential attitudes toward and expectations regarding sons and daughters, it is not surprising to find sex differences in early parent-infant interaction. Up to 3 months of age, boys are touched more frequently and handled more roughly (Lewis, 1972a; Moss, 1967; Parke & O'Leary, 1975; Yarrow, Rubenstein, Pedersen, & Jankowski, 1972). Touching behavior towards girls remains stable over the first few months, but it declines dramatically in boys, so that by 6 months of age and probably thereafter, girls are touched more (Lewis, 1972b). Girls may be verbally stimulated more frequently than boys (Lewis, 1972a; Lewis & Cherry, 1977; Lewis & Goldberg, 1969; Moss 1967; Thoman, Leiderman, & Olson, 1972; Weinraub & Lewis, 1978) particularly in the first six months of life. By preschool age, teachers respond to boys very differently than they respond to girls (Cherry, 1977; Serbin, O'Leary Kent, & Tonick, 1973).

Although it is not always clear in these studies whether differences in infant behavior elicit differences in maternal behavior or vice versa, the greater incidence of sex differences in adult behavior relative to sex differences in infant behavior suggests that sex-differentiated parental behavior may be more a cause than a result of sex differences in infant behavior. Recent studies designed to tease out the effects of infant sex and adult expectations regarding infant sex suggest that sex differences in certain adult behaviors, particularly touching may depend more on adult expectation than real infant sex difference (Frankel & Weinraub, 1977; Seavey, Katz, & Zalk, 1975).

Through a variety of behaviors—from choice of name, clothes, and toys to room decor and assignment of household chores—parents make the child's gender very clear to the child as well as to all individuals within the child's social network. Children are given clearly sex-differentiated names. They are dressed in conformity to their sex role—blue for boys, pink for girls, with dresses and frills reserved for girls (Brooks & Lewis, 1974). Room decor is clearly differentiated on the basis of child sex, and as early as the first few months, the child is surrounded with toys in keeping with the proper sex role (Rheingold & Cook, 1975). Boys and girls are still assigned household chores in keeping with sex-role division of adult household tasks (Duncan, Schuman, & Duncan, 1973). Even into this last decade, parents, especially fathers, actively encourage their children to choose appropriate-sexed play activities, and they become upset when their children, especially their sons, express interest in opposite-sex activities (Fling & Manosevitz, 1972; Goodenough, 1957; Lansky, 1967). Thus, there is no doubt that parents play an important role in helping the child and others to differentially categorize little boys and little girls and that parents selectively encourage appropriate-sexed toys and activity preferences.

What role do parents play in nurturing the development of psychological differences between boys and girls—differences in aggression, verbal and spatial abilities, career and achievement striving, anxieties, self-esteem, dominance, competitiveness, and adult compliance behaviors? It is clear that parents think of and often behave differently to their boy and girl children. For example, parents are more concerned over the physical well-being of daughters than sons (Minton, Kagan, & Levine, 1971; Pedersen & Robson, 1969), and parents exert more pressure to control the expression of affect on sons than on daughters. The effect of this differential behavior can be seen as part of a general socialization in which the current values of the society are passed along by the parents to their children from the moment of birth onward. But to what extent do parents differentially reinforce boys and girls for appropriate-sexed behavior? The data in this area are controversial (Block, 1977; Maccoby & Jacklin, 1974). According to Maccoby and Jacklin, "the reinforcement contingencies for the two sexes are not as different as might be expected, if parents were socializing children for stereotyped adult roles" (p. 342). There appears to be no consensus that parents differentially reinforce boys and girls for aggressive behavior, for autonomous behavior, for dependent behavior, or for competitive behavior. Although there is some evidence that punishment for inappropriate sex-typed behavior is more widespread than reinforcement for appropriate sex-typed behavior (Maccoby & Jacklin, 1974), so far the relative effectiveness of punishment and even of intermittent reinforcement on the development of sex-typed behaviors have not been investigated.

Whether or not parents do differentially reinforce appropriate-sexed behaviors, relationships between parental reinforcement patterns and children's performance of sex-typed behaviors have not been clearly demonstrated. While Goldberg and Lewis (1969) showed that sex difference in maternal touching at 6 months was related to boys and girls touching their mothers at 1 year, relatively little data of this kind are available. In addition, there has been consistent failure in correlating parental attitudes toward sex-typing and parental attempt to encourage sex-typed behavior with children's conformity to sex roles (Fling & Manosevitz, 1972; Mussen & Rutherford, 1971; Sears, Rau, & Alpert, 1965).

Whether or not parental reinforcement contributes to the development of sex-typed behavior in preschool children, differential parental behavior may make its most critical contribution to the development of sex roles by clarifying and even emphasizing the differences between the sexes. In addition, parental reinforcement behaviors in the area of clearly sex-typed toy and activity preferences may set a precedent for the child, which demonstrates that rewards can be obtained by conforming to sex-appropriate standards.

Parents may be helpful to the child by serving as prototypes for two important models—male and female—and by providing information about the child's own gender. The child's task may be to develop sex-role knowledge and to choose appropriate-sexed behaviors. It is to this active, organismic approach that we now turn.

COGNITIVE INFLUENCES

Cognitive influences in the development of sex-role-appropriate behavior receive far less attention than they deserve, since the theoretical argument usually revolves around the issue of environment versus biology. Our premise is that both the biological and environmental factors provide the information the child needs to produce socially acceptable behavior. Thus, while not discounting the role of environment and biology, the emphasis of any cognitive theory is that these forces, while important in their own right, have most importance vis-à-vis the information they supply to the young organism.

Working from a cognitive explanation, Kohlberg (1966) argues that the child's social cognitions—the child's gender identity and awareness of sex-role stereotypes—play a critical role in the development of sex-typed behaviors. According to the cognitive-developmental position, children first become aware of their own gender label, become aware of differential behaviors, attitudes

MICHAEL LEWIS / MARSHA WEINRAUB

and preferences common to that sex, and then find the opportunity to do like-sexed behaviors rewarding. Kohlberg's cognitive-developmental explanation is often contrasted with Mischel's social learning explanation (1966). According to Mischel, the child wants rewards, finds he or she is rewarded for like-sexed activities, and therefore assumes he or she is a boy or a girl. Although there are some major differences between the two approaches, common to both positions is the child's awareness of the culture's division of people, behavior, and attitudes into two different categories based on gender. In addition, according to both approaches, the child is aware that the behaviors in one of these categories are more likely to be rewarded than behaviors in the opposite category. Thus, in both explanations, the child's social cognitions play a critical role in the acquisition of sex-typed behaviors. The child develops a category of male and female behavior, attitudes, and preferences; the child places himself or herself into one of these categories; and then the child actively strives to adopt behavior, preferences, and attitudes in keeping with his or her like-sexed group.

These social cognitions are the products of the child's "active structuring of his own experiences, they are not the passive products of social training" (Kohlberg, 1966, p. 85). Although the child's parents may influence the child's sex-role stereotypes, it is unlikely that children's stereotypes are the results only of direct parental tuition. For example, young children show more rigorous, clear-cut sex-role stereotypes than do adults or older children (Kohlberg, 1966; Masters & Wilkinson, 1976). . . .

In regard to social cognition concerning gender, sex role, and sex-typed behavior, we hold that knowledge of the self and other is vital and, along with a desire to act consistently with others similar to the self, determines the young child's behavior. In order to facilitate our exposition, let us first state the general principles and then explore the conditions that are necessary:

I. The infant acquires knowledge about itself and at the same time the infant acquires knowledge about others.

II. Gender and sex-role knowledge is acquired early.

III. The infant acts in a manner consistent with "like" objects.

Lewis and Brooks (1975, Lewis & Brooks-Gunn, in press) in a series of studies have shown that the infant's knowledge of self, as measured through self-recognition, begins within the first year of life and that by 2 years the infant demonstrates a clear self-knowledge. The use of personal referents and personal pronouns such as "That's mine" appears before 2 years of age. That the child demonstrates knowledge of himself comes as no surprise, given the large social and cognitive competencies the child shows in other areas. Moreover, the child's knowledge of others is considerable (Lewis & Feiring, 1979, in press; Weinraub, Brooks, & Lewis, 1977), and it is difficult to imagine the child's knowledge of the complex social space does not include knowledge of self.

These results have been supported by the works of others (for example, Amsterdam, 1972; Bernathal & Fisher, 1978; Dixon, 1957).

While it is not difficult to demonstrate the child's acquisition of self-knowledge through self-recognition, the child's knowledge about his or her own gender is a bit more difficult to demonstrate. Lewis and Brooks (1975) have already reported on the perceptual data that show infants tend to look more at same-sex pictures than at opposite-sex pictures of other infants, and these data have been partially replicated (Lewis & Brooks-Gunn, in press).

The child's knowledge of others follows both logically and empirically. From an interactional position, it has been argued that knowledge of the other—most often an object—is acquired through interaction with the other. Let us consider object permanence. How could an organism learn of the existence of objects independent of one's perception of them without at the very same time learning about oneself and one's own existence? The study of social cognition requires that we consider the self, since to know of another is at the same time to know of yourself. Our work on social perception and social relationships (Lewis & Brooks, 1975; Lewis & Weinraub, 1976) indicates that infants have knowledge of others, and one aspect of infants' knowledge of others is knowledge of their gender (Lewis & Feiring, 1979). Perhaps the most convincing data is on verbal labeling and comprehension. In a series of tasks, infants were asked to label or point to an assortment of social objects (Lewis & Brooks-Gunn, in press; Brooks-Gunn & Lewis, in press). By 18 months of age, when most infants had some labeling ability, infants labeled adults correctly on the basis of gender 90% of the time. Of the infants who had labels for boy and girl, approximately 80% applied these labels correctly. Whether we hold to the dual process of social cognition or some other explanation, it does appear that infants acquire information about themselves and others quite early and that this knowledge emerges at about the same time as sex-differentiated behavior. Remember, we make no claim about the form of this knowledge (without verbal ability, this is hard to explore), nor do we believe the knowledge is fixed; certainly, these concepts are just emerging. Nevertheless, some form of knowledge both of self and of others is present by 18 months of age.

Proposition III addresses the motivational aspects of sex-role behavior. Our motivational system rests on the assumption that if I am an "A" and I can differentiate other "A" and "not A" ($\overline{A}$), I will, under most conditions, act like the other "A." An example of this principle from the point of view of friendship highlights this process. Edwards and Lewis (1979) have shown that by 3 years of age, children have some knowledge of age and prefer different social objects for different functions. Thus, other children are preferred for play and adults are preferred when the child needs help or is hurt. In one study, 3-year-olds were asked to choose who they would like to play with. The choice was between a picture of a 3-, 7-, or 20-year-old. These same children at a later time were asked which picture they were most like. Interestingly, children who preferred to play with the 7-year-old also picked the 7-year-old as most like. In terms of gender, the data are less clear. First, Lewis and Brooks (1975; Lewis & Brooks-Gunn, in press) have shown that infants within the first 2 years, but especially in the 15-to-18-month period, prefer to attend to pictures of infants with the same sex. Thus, from a perceptual point of view, infants prefer to look at like-sex objects. Moreover, there is some evidence that children under 3 years of age prefer to play with the same-sex children (Jacklin & Maccoby, 1978). More impressive is the data on parent-child preferences as a function of likeness of sex. Weinraub and Lewis (1973) found that during free play, children were more likely to look up at the same-sex than opposite-sex parent. Similar same-sex relationships between parent and child were found by Lamb (1975). Although Maccoby and Jacklin's review (1974) notes that children do not consistently imitate same-sex adult models, the data do suggest imitation of same-sex parents between the ages of 3 and 5 years. Of the four studies of children under 5 years of age imitating parental behavior that Maccoby and Jacklin review, three show that children are more likely to imitate the behavior of same-sex parents (DuHamel & Biller, 1969; Hartup, 1962; Hetherington, 1965; Hetherington & Frankie, 1967).

We believe that the infant is evolving knowledge about self and other within the first years of life; this knowledge involves gender, sex roles, and sex-typed behavior. Moreover, as an active organism—one that acts on its environment and constructs the schema that govern its actions—the infant chooses to be like those who have similar characteristics and labels. This choice and active cognitive process, based on the level of development at any specific time, provide the material for the next phase of construction. In this way, additional information continually leads to increased conformity. Thus, the earliest forms of knowledge may be based on the smallest differences, for example, hair length or the color and nature of clothes. These provide the first information necessary for differentiation of self and other. On the basis of this differentiation and on the principle of attraction, the infant moves towards conformity with sex-role stereotypes.

THE ROLE OF BIOLOGY, REINFORCEMENT, AND COGNITION

In order to incorporate the various theoretical positions which center on the child's acquisition of sex-role and sex-typed behavior, we must make clear our notion of the human infant and young child as a complex, competent, and active organism. We hold to an active, constructivist position (Lewis & Brooks, 1975) where the infant actively interprets the environment and has plans and intentions (certainly by the secondary circular reaction stage of means and ends development—Lewis, 1977). The infant can act on the environment, can influence it as well as be influenced by it (Lewis & Rosenblum, 1974). In terms of sex roles, we acknowledge the sexual dimorphism of the species and the existence of early sex differences. What we caution against is the interpretation of early observed differences in terms of sex-role stereotypes or the use of these early differences to explain the development of later sex-role behaviors. Thus, while it is true that infant girls open their eyes wider than boys when approached by a stranger (Haviland & Lewis, 1976), this observation cannot be interpreted to mean that girls at this age are more frightened than boys, nor does this early sex difference account for later sex differences in fearfulness. Similarly, the fact that males have more muscle mass as early as birth cannot be interpreted to mean that infant males are braver, nor does it explain later sex differences in risk-taking behaviors. From a constructivist position, this early sexual dimorphism serves only to impart information to the organism regarding the existence of two sexes and their differences. The organism uses this information to form schema used to differentiate others, to construct categories in which to place others, and to locate the self vis-à-vis others. Given the universality of this differentiating feature—in all times and places males and females are at least in some physical way different—one basis for differentiation and location of the self must be gender. It is important to remember, however, that this sexual dimorphism only demonstrates the existence of differences and not their meaning or value. The meanings and value of these differences are often exaggerated societal interpretations which serve, not infrequently, as self-fulfilling expectations.

The content of the difference is located in the cultural values and goals which lay claim to the particular meaning system. For example, sexual dimorphism might dictate the style of dress (even this could be argued), but it certainly could not dictate the color of the clothes or the meaning of the colors. The emphasis on and interpretation of sex-role and sex-typed behavior by the society is all-pervasive. It presents the child with the means to differentiate others and self, and at the same time provides the content and meaning of the differentiation. The child uses this information in differentiating its social world and in striving to be similar to other like-labeled individuals. In this way, the environmental influences are additive to the biological in the differentiation of classes of people and, in addition, supply specific meaning systems. From toys, colors, attitudes, and language, the child can easily learn to differentiate others—first on simple dimensions, then on more complex. At the same time, the child begins to classify himself or herself as a member of one of the two classes. The process is gradual and continuing. With the child's increasingly complex experiences and developments in cognitive ability comes a more sophisticated knowledge of sex roles and gender. That the child can be fooled by simple transformations of hair lengths or clothing (Emmerich et al., 1977) is no reason to suppose that the child's cognitive concept of gender is absent, only that these concepts are still open to further experience and learning.

We find the interrelationship of these forces compelling. We do not wish to reject the contribution of biological and environmental factors, nor do we wish to accept the tyranny of genes or reinforcement. The existence of biologically based sexual dimorphisms means that we will be different. The meaning of these differences is determined by the culture. The child processes and makes use of this information (regarding sexual dimorphism and cultural differences) to construct a notion of self and others. Having done so, the child chooses to be like those like the self. In this way, the self actively and creatively develops culturally designated sex-role behavior.

REFERENCES

Amsterdam, B. K. Mirror self-image reactions before age two. *Developmental Psychology*, 1972, *5*, 297–305.

Bernathal, B. I., & Fisher, K. E. Development of self-recognition in the infant. *Developmental Psychology*, 1978, *14*, 44–50.

Birns, B. The emergence and socialization of sex differences in the earliest years. *Merrill-Palmer Quarterly*, 1976, *22*, 229–254.

Block, J. H. Assessing sex differences: Issues, problems and pitfalls. *Merrill-Palmer Quarterly*, 1977, 140–147.

Brooks, J., & Lewis, M. Attachment behavior in thirteen-month-old, opposite sex twins. *Child Development*, 1974, *45*, 243–247.

Brooks-Gunn, J., & Lewis M. "Why Mama and Papa?" The development of social labels. *Child Development*, in press.

Buffrey, A. W. H., & Gray, J. A. Sex differences in the development of spatial and linguistic skills. In C. Ounsted & D. C. Taylor (Eds.), *Gender differences: Their ontogeny and significance*. Baltimore: Williams & Wilkins, 1972.

Cherry, L. The preschool teacher-child dyad: Sex differences in verbal interaction. *Child Development*, 1977, *46*, 532–536.

Corter, C. M., Rheingold, H. L., & Eckerman, C. O. Toys delay the infant's following of his mother. *Developmental Psychology*, 1972, *6*, 138–145.

Dixon, J. C. Development of self recognition. *Journal of Genetic Psychology*, 1957, *91*, 251–256.

DuHamel, T. R., & Biller, H. B. Parental imitation and nonimitation in young children. *Developmental Psychology*, 1969, *1*, 772.

Duncan, D., Schuman, H., & Duncan, B. *Social change in a metropolitan community*. New York: Russel Sage, 1973.

Edwards, C. P., & Lewis, M. Young children's concepts of social relations: Social functions and social objects. (Paper presented at the Conference on the Origins of Behavior: The Social Network of the Developing Infant, Princeton, December 1977.) In M. Lewis & L. Rosenblum (Eds.), *The child and its family: The genesis of behavior* (Vol. 2). New York: Plenum, 1979.

Ehrhardt, A. A., & Baker, S. S. Fetal androgens' human central nervous system differentiation and behavior sex differences. In R. Friedman and R. Vandeville (Eds.), *Sex differences in behavior*. New York: Wiley, 1974. Pp. 33–51.

Emmerich, W., Goldman, K. S., Kirsh, B., & Sharabany, R. Evidence for a transitional phase in the development of gender constancy. *Child Development*, 1977, *48*, 930–936.

Fagot, B. I. Sex-related stereotyping of toddlers' behaviors. *Developmental Psychology*, 1973, *9*, 429.

Feldman, S., & Ingham, M. Attachment behavior: A validation study in two age groups. *Child Development*, 1975, *46*, 319–330.

Fling, S., & Manosevitz, M. Sex typing in nursery school children's play interests. *Development Psychology*, 1972, *7*, 146–152.

Frankel, J., & Weinraub, M. *Adult-infant interaction: Effects of infant real sex, infant labeled sex, and adult sex.* Paper presented at the Southeastern Psychological Association meetings, Miami, May, 1977.

Goldberg, S., & Lewis, M. Play behavior in the year old infant: Early sex differences. *Child Development*, 1969, *40*, 21–31.

Goodenough, E. W. Interest in persons as an aspect of sex differences in the early years. *Genetic Psychology Monographs*, 1957, *55*, 287–323.

Hartup, W. W. Some correlates of parental imitation in young children. *Child Development*, 1962, *33*, 85–96.

Haviland, J., & Lewis, M. Infants' greeting to strangers. (Paper presented at the Human Ethology session of the Animal Behavior Society meeting, Wilmington, N.C., May 1975.) *Research Bulletin 76–2*, Princeton: Educational Testing Service, 1976.

Hetherington, E. M. A developmental study of the effects of sex of the dominant parent on sex-role preference, identification, and imitation in children. *Journal of Personality and Social Psychology*, 1965, *2*, 188–194.

Hetherington, E. M., & Frankie, G. Effects of parental dominance, warmth, and conflict on imitation on children. *Journal of Personality and Social Psychology*, 1967, *6*, 119–125.

Hoffman, L. W. Changes in family roles, socialization, and sex differences. *American Psychologist*, 1977, *32*, 644–657.

Hutt, C. *Males and females.* London: C. Nichols & Co., 1972.

Jacklin, C. N., & Maccoby, E. E. Social behavior at 33 months in same-sex and mixed-sex dyads. *Children Development*, 1978, *49*(3), 557–569.

Kohlberg, L. A. Cognitive-developmental analysis of children's sex-role concepts and attitudes. In E. E. Maccoby (Ed.), *The development of sex differences*. Stanford: Stanford University Press, 1966. Pp. 82–173.

Lamb, M. E. Fathers: Forgotten contributors to child development. *Human Development*, 1975, *18*, 245–266.

Lambert, W. E., Yackley, A., & Hein, R. N. Child training values of English Canadian and French Canadian parents. *Canadian Journal of Behavioral Science*, 1971, *3*, 217–236.

Lansky, L. M. The family structure also affects the model: Sex-role attitudes in parents of preschool children. *Merrill-Palmer Quarterly*, 1967, *13*, 139–150.

Lewis, M. Parents and children: Sex-role development. *School Review*, 1972, *80*(2), 229–

Lewis, M. State as an infant-environment interaction: An analysis of mother-infant interaction as a function of sex. *Merrill-Palmer Quarterly*, 1972, *18*, 95–121. (b)

Lewis, M. *The infant and its caregiver: The role of contingency.* Paper presented at the Conference on Infant Intervention Program at the University of Wisconsin, Milwaukee, June 1977.

Lewis, M., & Brooks, J. Infants' social perception: A constructivist view. In L. Cohen & P. Salapatek (Eds.), *Infant perception: From sensation to cognition* (Vol. 2). New York: Academic Press, 1975. Pp. 101–143.

Lewis, M., & Brooks-Gunn, J. *Social cognition and the acquisition of self.* New York: Plenum, in press.

Lewis, M., & Cherry, L. Social behavior and language acquisition. In M. Lewis & L. Rosenblum (Eds.), *Interaction, conversation, and the development of language: The origins of behavior* (Vol. 2). New York: Wiley, 1977.

Lewis, M., & Feiring, C. The child's social world. In R. M. Lerner & G. D. Spanier (Eds.), *Child influences on marital and family interaction: A life-span perspective.* New York: Academic Press, 1978.

Lewis, M., & Feiring, C. The child's social network: Social object, social functions and their relationship. (Paper presented at the Conference on the Origins of Behavior: The Social Network of the Developing Infant, Princeton, N.J., December 1977.) In M. Lewis & L. Rosenblum (Eds.), *The child and its family: The genesis of behavior* (Vol. 2). New York: Plenum, 1979.

Lewis, M., & Freedle, R. Mother-infant dyad: The cradle of meaning. In P. Pliner, L. Krames, & T. Alloway (Eds.), *Communication and affect: Language and thought.* New York: Academic Press, 1973. Pp. 127–155.

Lewis, M., & Goldberg, S. Perceptual-cognitive development in infancy: A generalized expectancy model as a function of the mother-infant interaction. *Merrill-Palmer Quarterly,* 1969, *15*(1), 81–100.

Lewis, M., & Rosenblum, L. (Eds.), *The effect of the infant on its caregiver: The origins of behavior* (Vol. 1). New York: Wiley, 1974.

Lewis, M., & Weinraub, M. The father's role in the child's social network. In M. E. Lamb (Ed.), *Role of the father in child development.* New York: Wiley, 1976.

Maccoby, E. E., & Jacklin, C. N. *The psychology of sex differences.* Stanford: Stanford University Press, 1974.

Minton, C., Kagan, J., & Levine, J. A. Maternal control and obedience in the two-year-old. *Child Development,* 1971, *42,* 1873–1894.

Money, J., & Ehrhardt, A. *Man and woman, boy and girl.* Baltimore: Johns Hopkins University Press, 1972.

Moss, H. A. Sex, age and state as determinants of mother-infant interaction. *Merrill Palmer Quarterly,* 1967, *13,* 19–36.

Mussen, P. H., & Rutherford, E. Parent-child relations and parental personality in relation to young children's sex-role preferences. *Child Development,* 1971, *42,* 1873–1894.

Parke, R. D., & O'Leary, S. Father-mother-infant interaction in the newborn period: Some findings, some observations, and unresolved issues. In K. Riegel & J. Meachan (Eds.), *The developing individual in a changing world, Vol. II, Social and environmental issues.* The Hague: Mouton, 1975.

Pedersen, F. A., & Robson, K. S. Father participation in infancy. *American Journal of Orthopsychiatry,* 1969, *39,* 466–472.

Rheingold, H. L. & Cook, K. V. The content of boys' and girls' rooms as an index of parents' behavior. *Child Development*, 1975, *46*, 459–563.

Rubin, J. Z. Provenzano, F. J., & Luria, Z. The eye of the beholder: Parents' views on sex of newborns. *American Journal of Orthopsychiatry*, 1974, *44*, 512–519.

Sander, L. *Twenty-four distributions of sleeping and waking over the first month of life in different infant caretaking systems.* Paper presented at the meeting of the Society for Research in Child Development, Philadelphia, 1973.

Sears, R. R., Rau, L., & Alpert, R. *Identification and child rearing.* Stanford: Stanford University Press, 1965.

Seavey, C. A., Katz, P. A., & Zalk, S. R. Baby X. The effect of gender label on adult responses to infants. *Sex Roles*, 1975, *2*, 103–109.

Serbin, L. A., O'Leary, K. D., Kent, R. N., & Tonick, I. J. A comparison of teacher response to the pre-academic and problem behavior of boys and girls. *Child Development*, 1973, *44*, 796–804.

Sherman, J. A. *On the psychology of women.* Springfield, Ill.: Charles C Thomas, 1971.

Shirley, M., & Poyntz, L. The influence of separation from the mother on the child's emotional responses. *Journal of Psychology*, 1941, *12*, 251–282.

Tanner, J. M. Physical growth. In P. H. Mussen (Ed.), *Carmichael's manual of child psychology.* New York: Wiley, 1970.

Thoman, E. B., Leiderman, P. H., & Olson, J. P. Neonate-mother interaction during breast feeding. *Developmental Psychology*, 1972, *6*, 110–118.

Watson, J. S. Operant conditioning of visual fixation in infants under visual and auditory reinforcement. *Developmental Psychology*, 1969, *1*, 408–416.

Weinraub, M., & Frankel, J. Sex differences in parent-infant interactions during free play, departure and separation. *Child Development*, 1977, *48*, 1240–1249.

Weinraub, M., & Lewis, M. *Infant attachment and play behavior: Sex of child and sex of parent differences.* Unpublished manuscript, 1973.

Weinraub, M., & Lewis, M. The determinants of children's responses to separation. *Monographs of the Society for Research in Child Development*, 1977, *42* (4, Serial No. 172).

Weinraub, M., Brooks, J., & Lewis, M. The social network: A reconsideration of the concept of attachment. *Human Development*, 1977, *20*, 31–47.

Yarrow, L. J., Rubenstein, J. L., P edersen, F. A., & Jankowski, J. J. Dimensions in early stimulation and their differential effects on infant development. *Merrill-Palmer Quarterly*, 1972, *18*, 205–218.

Young, G., & Lewis, M. Effects of familiarity on social interaction between infants. *Merrill-Palmer Quarterly*, in press.

5   *Congratulations! It's a Baby!*

Carol Adair Finn

STUDY QUESTIONS

1. Finn claims that although seemingly harmless, sex-role stereotypes can limit life opportunities. Why?
2. According to Finn, the best thing is to think of toys for children rather than for a specific gender. Why and what should such toys accomplish?

"Too bad," the man said, good naturedly, "but keep trying. Maybe next time you'll have a son!" The first time it had happened, Barry, proud father of a baby girl, had laughed it off—this time he had trouble containing his anger because his daughter was old enough to hear the insult. Since the time of her birth, perfect strangers had come up to him to express sympathy that he had not had a son. "I can't believe the ignorance of some people," Barry says. "Not only are they dead wrong, but they have to say these things in front of my daughter!"

Sex role stereotypes often are held unconsciously and transmitted to our children. What seems harmless in the beginning—pink and blue booties at birth—is potentially destructive when it undermines a child's self-concept or limits opportunities in life.

In most countries boys and girls are instructed differently, given different play materials and opportunities, and—most importantly—given different role models to emulate. Many of these differences in expectations and treatment are defended on the basis of the idea that "normal" or "appropriate" sexual behavior has been adequately defined by the traditions of a given society. For example, in the United States men traditionally are breadwinners and women

Source: Carol Adair Finn, "Congratulations! It's a Baby!" *The Single Parent*, November/December 1987, pp. 14–16. Reprinted by permission.

the primary child-rearers, and their respective upbringing prepares them for these roles.

But the consequences of such differential treatment cannot be overlooked. For example, it is well-documented that in the United States twice as many women as men experience serious depression sometime in their lives.

Psychologists agree that the passive and indirect psychological attitudes that women have been encouraged to develop are not those considered desirable for mental health. These attitudes often result in low self-esteem, role conflict, and fear of success. It is the men who have been encouraged to make direct attempts to use all available psychological resources toward establishing a grounded, self-determined sense of self.

Although our society is changing, many women feel their upbringing has been a handicap that they've had to overcome in order to compete with men in commercial and professional endeavors. Similarly, men who are now expected to take a greater role in child-rearing than their fathers and grandfathers did have had to "unlearn" a lot of traditional masculine behavior.

How can the restrictions of sex role stereotyping be avoided? Many people believe that sexism can only be avoided if consistent efforts are made when children are still young. "Female and male infants will only grow as equals in an environment where equality between the sexes is daily modeled by all who care for them," says Selma Greenberg, author of *Right from the Start*.

Yet, "some parents go too far in trying to avoid sexual stereotypes," charges Lawrence Brain, M.D., a child psychiatrist in Bethesda, Md., "and their children have a hard time knowing what's expected of them. Not all stereotypes are bad."

How does one avoid going overboard? Concerned parents ask how they can create an egalitarian environment for their children without endangering their children's sexual identity. When they are single, these parents are especially concerned that the absence of an equal partner—and role model—of the opposite sex will make it more difficult for their children to avoid a sexually biased upbringing.

"I wish Robert had a male around more often," says Kitty Dale, a single parent of two small children, Robert, 4, and Elizabeth, 6, "—just to do man things every once in a while—throw a ball around in the back yard, or go fishing. And I think there's a special relationship between a girl and her father." Kitty has managed to establish a community of friends to give her children a variety of role models, yet she is conscious of the one-sided nature of her children's family life.

Kitty is not alone. There are realistic difficulties for single parents: A single parent cannot provide everything and shouldn't feel obligated to do so. The fact is that one parent often attempts to provide most of the parenting, even within an intact marriage. "He was rarely here anyway," recalls Kitty of her husband, "so I tried to be both mother and father. It was when he left that I stopped trying to do it all because I realized that it was impossible!"

Nevertheless, "the single mother can have an important influence on her son," psychiatrist Brain says, "by being very supportive, by admiring and encouraging aspects of his masculinity—but not overly. The single mother

CAROL ADAIR FINN

needs to be careful not to put her son into the role of man of the house because that is not a child's role. Not to expect him to be macho or not to cry—not to expect things from him that one might expect from a spouse. She should support and acknowledge the masculine [characteristics] but also encourage her son to express his feelings."

Similarly, a father can have an important influence on his daughter. A girl is valued for her femininity by her father in a different way than she is by her mother, according to Brain. "The father's role does have an effect on the daughter's future relationships with the opposite sex," he says.

In short, instead of ignoring a child's gender or attempting to ignore the issue of sexual identity, parents should be discriminating about which aspects of masculinity and femininity to encourage and which to avoid. For example, a stereotype such as "women should be passive and submissive, and men should be dominant" is undesirable for the individual and for today's society. Parents can help their children avoid the cultural transmission of this stereotype by showing respect for one another and by encouraging one another toward self-actualization.

On the other hand, attempts to avoid the issue of sexual identity altogether can backfire. "The idea of encouraging boys to play with dolls to help them develop a more equal view of the world can be confusing," Brain says. "When you make everything unisex, you detract from the child's capacity to differentiate for themselves."

Still, girl-toys and boy-toys teach different things. Toys and play activities for girls are usually inside-based, use small muscle coordination, and encourage learning through imitation and re-enactment. Toys for boy are outside-based, encourage exploration of the dimensions of physical space, and use a step-by-step instructional style that gives them a good basis for learning science and mathematics. Perhaps the best thing for parents to do is to think in terms of toys for *children* instead of toys specifically designed for boys or girls.

A wide variety of toys and play activities enables children to develop a full range of skills and interests. Ideally, all children should have adequate opportunities for:

- Small and large muscle development;
- Active and quiet behavior;
- Outdoor and indoor activities;
- Predominantly verbal and nonverbal play; and
- Imitation, creativity, exploration and discovery.

There are important stages in the development of a child's sexual identity. Ages 3 to 7 and the teenage years are probably the most turbulent. Parents who are aware of difficulties can educate themselves to provide their children with valuable support, especially during these times.

Some experts feel that boys and girls are somewhat "genderless" until age 3—they play with the same toys, for example, and identify chiefly with their mother, who is usually the primary care-giver. At age 3, however, boys and girls supposedly begin to act differently as they discover anatomical differences. If parents are comfortable with their own sexuality, they can provide an open and friendly environment toward sex that enables their children to explore and begin to understand. The following guidelines are taken from a variety of child-rearing manuals:

- Accept the gender of your child. If the parent is happy with the gender of his or her child, then chances are the child will be happy with it.

- Provide adequate models for your child to learn from. Both parents have important roles to play and should be careful to spend enough time with their children to be a good influence.

- Don't be too rigid or stereotypic about encouraging a child's gender identity. Provide dress-up clothes for dramatic play for both boys and girls, for example. "We need to allow our preschoolers to play out roles and feelings appropriate to the opposite sex as well as their own," asserts Dr. Fitzhugh Dodson in *How to Parent*.

Adolescence provides a different set of problems, some of which are particularly difficult for single parents. For example, the single mother of an adolescent boy must find a way to help her son through the confusion of sexual attraction to his mother without the neutralizing influence a father usually provides. A single father often establishes a buddy-buddy relationship with his teenage son and consequently finds it hard to protect his son from overexposure to the father's sex life.

When there is a boyfriend or girlfriend, the single parent can demonstrate—without being overtly sexual or provocative—that this is my child and this is my adult friend and I have a separate life with the other adult," Brain says. "The parent needs to show that there are adult things and children's things to do and not break down the generational barriers."

Regardless of their marital status, many parents are worried that their efforts to provide nonsexist child-rearing for their children are nullified by the influences their children encounter in school. They have good reason to be concerned. "Sexism is the only form of prejudice still socially acceptable," says Aileen Pace Nilsen, in her article, "Alternatives to Sexist Practices in the Classroom" (*Young Children*, July, 1977).

Sexism in schools has been traced from preschool to college, and appears prevalent today. On Nov. 11, 1986, the *Washington Post* reported two recent studies by American University professors Myra and David Sadker, showing that boys get far more attention of all kinds from their teachers in school. "When girls come into school, they are ahead of boys in reading and math and writing. When they leave school at the end of the 12th grade . . . boys are outscoring them.

"Girls are the only group that leave school performing worse," states David Sadker. Furthermore, the Sadkers conclude that "sex bias is far worse in college than it is in grammar school."

In the schools studied, it was not only that instructional practices were biased but also that teaching materials promoted boys at the expense of girls. These findings were supported by a study of Caldecott Award-winning books for kids showing that male protagonists outnumbered female counterparts 10 to one.

Parents should never forget that they can influence the course of public education if they believe that it is in the best interests of children to do so. Classroom practices that contribute to sex bias and discrimination usually exist because no one has recognized their detrimental effects. For example:

- The arrangement of preschool and early elementary school classrooms often suggests and perpetuates the segregation of traditional male and female activities. A more realistic arrangement would be one that combines activities—such as a kitchen and shop class in which pliers and hammers are found with cooking utensils.
- The curriculum should include references to both males and females in every subject area, so that Madame Curie is not the exception to the myth that girls don't like science!
- "Good conduct" in school often reflects attitudes that categorize feminine and masculine behavior. For example, boys are often expected to fight things out while girls are expected to resolve disputes through talk. Children should learn to consider both love and aggression to be natural emotions and develop a variety of problem-solving strategies.
- Schools often channel girls and boys into traditionally female and male occupations. Efforts can be made to provide children with a broader range of experiences and greater encouragement in nontraditional areas.

No matter how good a parent's intentions are, avoiding potentially deterimental sex-role stereotyping is a difficult task. The fact is that there is no clear or reliable definition of appropriate sex-role behavior to fit every situation—no one knows where the line is drawn between nature and nurture on this issue. "I used to think that as a parent I could teach my children how to act. But they come out with their own personalities!" says Dale, a single parent. "Elizabeth was a little delicate feminine girl from the beginning—even the way she reached for things with her little fingers, while Robert has always grabbed with his whole hand."

But most parents want their children to be the best that they can be and that is the goal of nonsexist child-rearing. Why limit a child to the sex-role stereotypes that perpetuate inequality and confine men and women in their choices and chances for success in life? Barry, now a full-time father of two daughters, expresses it this way: "I just want my daughters to be unafraid of the world and to know that they can be anything they want to be."

6   *The New Woman*

Phyllis LaFarge

STUDY QUESTIONS

1. What does LaFarge mean when she says that the feminist movement has expanded the identity of women?
2. How does the feminist movement view household duties and nurturing?

"I'm not alone any more," Freda Branch said when I asked her why she thought the women's movement had made her life better. Freda is 24 years old and a resident of University City, Missouri. Until pregnancy interrupted her studies, she had been preparing for a career as a dental technician while working at a tennis club, where she books court time. I asked her in what way she had felt alone. "Well," she replied, "when I was a kid people always said, 'Oh, you're not going to do that. That's something men do.' I always wanted to be a doctor, but at that time people thought that was something just for men."

Being a doctor was not Freda's only ambition when she was growing up: she wanted to be the statistician for her high school baseball team. "Boys had always done it," she recalled, "but I asked the coach and he said, 'Can you do it?' I said, 'You don't think I can, but I can,' and he gave me a chance. It was great. I got to travel with the team."

When Freda says she is no longer alone, she is acknowledging that she is part of a revolution that has swept over America—the revolution of the women's movement. Despite the clear changes this revolution has brought—the enormously increased numbers of women entering the professions, for instance—the women's movement is in many ways an intangible revolution. Although in recent years women have begun to feel differently about themselves and their place in the world, we are often not sure of just how they feel different and whether the difference is for better or worse.

To measure the impact of the women's movement, *Parents* sponsored a

Source: Phyllis LaFarge, "The New Woman." *Parents*, October 1983. Reprinted by permission.

telephone poll of a national sample of women 21 to 35. The results confirmed that Freda is far from alone—and that her sisters are far from being the braless ideologues or briefcased executives often portrayed as feminist stereotypes.

WHAT IS THE WOMEN'S MOVEMENT TELLING US?

Before we look at the impact of the movement, however, let's look at its core messages. They concern identity. The women's movement supports an expanded identity for women. Giving a contemporary formulation to an age-old attitude, psychoanalyst Erik Erikson once postulated that woman's domain was the world of "inner space"—of childbearing, child rearing, and the intimate life of family. According to this formulation, men's domain was the less intimate, more public "outer" world beyond the home, often thought of as the world of work for pay or the "world of action." The women's movement has questioned the sex-linked nature of these distinctions and in doing so legitimized women who, like Freda, sensed that in order to be fully themselves, they must be free to find a place and play a role or roles in the "outer" world.

This expanded sense of identity is the aspect of the women's movement most reinforced by the media. But the movement carries another message as well, usually missed by the media but central to many feminists. This message concerns the special and enduring value of women's traditional role as maintainers of the fabric of daily life, including the fabric of intimate, daily relationships. According to this line of feminist thinking, women should not have to do this job alone—it should be shared with men—but whoever is doing it, the humble work of maintenance and nurturance should be valued as it historically never has been.

With the media tending to associate the women's movement with the expansion of women's identity, it's hard for many women to be alert to this alternative message, but some are. Cindy Keeling, for instance, of Rogers, Arkansas, is 27 years old and the mother of four children—Cliff, 8, Mandy, 4, and Carrie and Lindsey, 1-year-old twins. When I spoke with her, she had a job assembling B.B. guns at the Daisy Manufacturing Company, where her husband, Luther, also is employed, but she was working only because her family needed her paycheck. When asked what matters most to her, being a wife and mother or having a career outside the home, she answered, "I'm working, but it's more fulfilling being at home with my children." (Subsequently Cindy has been able to quit her job because her husband has taken over his father's part-time saw-sharpening business in order to supplement the family income.)

It would be easy to conclude from these statements that Cindy's life has been untouched by the women's movement, but this is not how she herself sees it. "The women's movement," she commented, "has made me a better wife and mother. It has made me aware of things I wasn't aware of before." What kind of things? It was hard for Cindy to answer, but when she did, she said, "I feel that I'm more valuable than, say, a woman in the fifties would have felt. Being a wife and mother was what women then were expected to do. Today being a wife and mother is more like a career choice." It is the value the women's movement places on nurturance that helps Cindy feel the way she does.

But her words reflect another aspect of feminist thinking as well. Cindy feels she has a choice in life. The women's movement has helped women feel that they have the right to shape their own lives as well as a true possibility of doing so. This belief in a right to self-realization is a common thread in much contemporary psychological and political thinking and is not an exclusive attribute of the women's movement. But it is an especially potent message when applied to women.

Traditionally, women's destiny was molded not only by the same political and economic forces that shape men's lives but by the hazards and inevitability of childbearing and by a social "place" in society that reflected both the necessities of child rearing and the power of men. Technology has greatly changed all this—and very rapidly. Reliable birth control, better gynecological care, and easier home maintenance have liberated women so that nurturance and maintenance can be part of life rather than the whole. At the same time, technology has changed the nature of work and patterns of consumption, virtually necessitating the two-pay-check marriage. In the light of these changes, an expanded identity for women is an inevitability, and it's no coincidence that the women's movement has been a force for the last fifteen years: the movement provides ideological and emotional support for women seeking to find their way in a historically new situation.

THE ACCEPTANCE OF THE WOMEN'S MOVEMENT

With these changes in mind—and not forgetting Freda's attitudes or Cindy's—let's look at how widely accepted the movement is. At least among women under 35, it has gained wide acceptance: two-thirds of our poll respondents (67 percent) agree with its overall goals, and 42 percent believe that it has made their lives better. This conviction is not restricted to the upper middle class or to professional women: 46 percent of women with incomes under $15,000 a year, 40 percent of nonwhite women, and 38 percent of blue-collar women think they are leading better lives.

Women's thinking on a number of issues on which feminists have taken a stand is at least as revealing as their avowed allegiance to the movement itself: two-thirds feel that the Equal Rights Amendment should have been passed; 61 percent believe that advertising stressing women's sexual attractiveness is insulting to women; 56 percent think that homosexuals should be allowed to teach in the public schools; 82 percent think that stricter measures should be taken to reduce the amount of pornography available; 80 percent believe that job quotas to ensure equal opportunity are a good thing. Perhaps most astounding of all, 57 percent believe that abortions should be available to any woman who wants one.

HOW WOMEN SEE THE MOVEMENT

We'll return to these very liberal attitudes, but first let's consider how women see the movement. For the most part they see it in terms of support for an expanded identity: When asked to identity the goals of the women's movement, 76 percent mentioned the opening up of job opportunities for women and 73 percent an end to discrimination. This is corroborated by the fact that women are even more likely to agree with the goals of the movement and to believe they have benefited by it if they are well educated and in a managerial position—characteristics of individuals who are likely to want and enjoy expanded opportunities in their lives.

But to see women's acceptance of the women's movement only in terms of their desire for expanded opportunity in the outer world does not take into account the complexity of women's opinions and feelings. When asked what they regard as necessary for a fulfilling life, 76 percent say that love is necessary and 76 percent mention a good family life. Only 30 percent mention career as essential, although another 47 percent see it as important but not essential. How do these attitudes toward fulfillment dovetail with those they have toward the women's movement?

The answer is that although women today need and want opportunities in the "outer world" they have in no way let go of the values traditionally associated with the private "inner" world of family life. They are the adventurous, ambitious Freda, but they are the more traditional Cindy, too. A look at women's attitudes toward their own accomplishments and toward their work outside the home underlines the degree to which this is true. Sixty percent of our respondents regard their family life as their greatest accomplishment, and 66 percent believe that even when they are old they will still look on their family in this way. When asked which is most important to them, being a wife and mother or their work outside the home, 60 percent chose wife and mother, and only 18 percent chose work. (Eighteen percent refused to choose between the two options and said both were equally important, and this figure might have been higher if the question had not been worded to force a choice between a "career" and a "wife-mother" answer.) But at the same time, two-thirds work outside the home and most of those who are not employed at present expect to work in the future. Moreover, more report that they work because they enjoy it (32 percent) rather than because they need the money—26 percent— although among nonwhite respondents the figure is 36 percent. Forty-two percent say they are motivated equally by enjoyment and need. Three-quarters of those working say they would continue working even if they could maintain their standard of living without doing so. Interestingly, the presence of young children scarcely affects this point of view: 71 percent of those with children under five would continue working even if they could maintain their standard of living without doing so.

Many women, however, even when they seek through work personal satisfaction and a measure of independence from their husband and family, are reluctant to give their ambitions or their work the same value as their husband's. Often they see their work in nurturant terms as "helping out" their husband and family. Thus Kathy Ramin, who works in Williamsport, Pennsylvania, assembling radar tubes, says, "I'd be bored if I didn't work, and I think when you don't work you feel your husband is doing you a favor giving you spending money. And the chores you do are insignificant." But in the next breath she commented, "When you work, you're helping your husband, helping him bring home the bread while you're taking care of your own needs for independence."

When you listen to a woman like Kathy, or a woman like Cindy, you realize the extent to which the ideas of the women's movement have penetrated the society: it's more than likely that fifteen years ago neither of them would have thought in the terms they do today.

It's equally clear, however, that the movement would never have achieved the measure of acceptance it has if it were its narrowest stereotype; that is, a relentless pursuit of economic equality with an implied contempt for traditional feminine roles and an implied belief that paid work is the only real and valuable work of the society. And to the degree that the women's movement is perceived as its stereotype, it may be even less accepted than it might be. This is suggested by the fact that women who are opposed to the movement tend to see it as pushing women in the direction of career at the expense of family, while those who identify strongly with its goals tend to see it as encouraging women to combine family life and work outside the home. In the light of what we know about women's enduring commitment to the values of the intimate world it is not surprising that they would reject any set of beliefs they perceived as asking them to turn their backs on their central course of fulfillment.

How can we characterize the women who have taken the goals of the women's movement to heart—but without surrendering traditional values? Mary Jo Bane, associate professor at Harvard's Kennedy School of Government, sees them as "a very special generation": "These are all baby-boom women. The oldest ones were born in 1947. That means their mothers produced the baby boom and subscribed to the ideology of children, family, and staying home. The older ones were in their twenties; and the younger, coming of age when feminist ideas came along. These women tend to be better educated than their mothers and more of them have worked before they married. Coming of age, they were the first generation in history for whom good birth control was available and acceptable. They realized, as their mothers were beginning to realize, that children and family are part of life but not the whole. Their attitudes are very liberal indeed, and what's so interesting is that these younger women have these very liberal attitudes at the same time they are so devoted to children and family. The stereotype is that liberal social attitudes are associated with a lack of caring about home and family.

"It's not a trivial finding, either," Professor Bane continued, "that 26 percent of these women characterize themselves as 'very religious' and another 55 percent as 'somewhat religious.' That means that you don't have a bunch of crazies here but very mainstream people subscribing to very liberal attitudes."

WOMEN AND THEIR WORK

How is widespread acceptance of the goals of the women's movement changing women's lives? A solid majority (61 percent) of women see increased job opportunity as the principal effect of the movement and 83 percent feel they can expect equal pay for equal work—a somewhat surprising finding in the face of the fact that women still earn only 60 cents for every dollar earned by men.

Women in all lines of work believe that opportunity has increased. Carol Doran, an attorney with the Internal Revenue Service in Washington, D.C., commented, "Only in the last decade has my division hired women attorneys, but I think they've tried very hard to hire a lot of women."

Pat Stephens, who works in a central Oregon lumber mill, felt discrimination "is not near as bad" and that opportunity has increased. "Back in the sixties," she recalled, "three of us were working on a finger joint machine. We were all women and we'd been at the mill two years. We were making $2.65 an hour and they hired a boy just out of high school and paid him $3 to start. That wouldn't happen today."

But although discrimination "is not near as bad," it has not disappeared. "One thing I've noticed," Pat said, "is that lately they've been hiring all men. They are trying to phase out women, and they do seem to prefer the cutesy ones."

DISCRIMINATION: STILL WITH US

Only a minority of women (20 percent) feel that the women's movement has eliminated discrimination (whereas 73 percent believe that its elimination is a central message of the movement), and many have been touched by it in painful ways. Jacqueline Haloszka of Wheeling, West Virginia, for instance, is a single mother. After her divorce she looked for work as a bookkeeper with an accounting firm. Describing her feelings while job hunting, she said, "I was worried, because I'm a mother, too. So I told them right off what my situation was; I couldn't work nights and weekends during the tax season." Although she was promised that it wouldn't make any difference, she was the first to go when her firm merged with another.

Perhaps the most striking change with respect to the world of work that the women's movement has brought about is a kind of ferment of activity in women themselves: whatever obstacles women still encounter in the job market, they are continuing their education, starting their own businesses, and seeking advancement on the job. The bid system at the lumber mill allows Pat to try for a better job, and right now she is being trained for a position that will earn her nearly a dollar an hour more than she is making at present. Jacqueline Haloszka, who now works as comptroller for a construction company, is going to school to complete her training as an accountant—and is thinking of starting a business of her own. This ferment is not only a response to actual opportunity—which in some communities is not all that great—it's a response to the permission and encouragement to seek an expanded identity that is at the core of the women's movement. It is also evidence of women's greatly increased self-confidence—which women themselves tend to see as virtually as important a consequence of the women's movement as increased opportunity on the job. As Freda Branch puts it, "More women are venturing out and saying to heck with staying in their place. They're working, going to school, and having a good social life."

However, the advantage that numerous women are taking of new opportunities and new confidence, combined with the media's narrow definition of the women's movement—often emphasizing a "briefcase," "corporate success" image—can be undermining to women who are staying home to raise their children, even when they have made the choice to do so freely and are happy with the choice. "It makes you feel funny even if you are happy," commented Deanna Kimble of Wheeling, West Virginia. "If you have kids and you feel happy, you still feel odd." When a woman like this no longer feels "funny" or "odd"—and, be it said, when another sort of woman doesn't need to phrase a personal ad in the following manner: "Cute little neuroscientist looking for smart single men to knit socks for" (*New York Review of Books*, April 14, 1983)— the fullest, deepest messages of the movement will have been accepted by the society.

WOMEN AND MEN

It's much harder to tell how women feel the women's movement has changed their relationship with men than it is to tell what they feel it has done to their work opportunities. Only 20 percent feel that it has made it harder to hold marriages together. Although more than 60 percent of the women had married by the time they were 22, only 26 percent thought a husband was necessary to a fulfilling life—as compared with the 76 percent who thought love and a good family life necessary. And 19 percent thought a husband was not at all related to fulfillment. The figure of 26 percent may be as low as it is, according to Mary Jo Bane, because respondents were asked if they considered a husband *absolutely* necessary, but even so it is striking and surprising and would undoubtedly have been higher for their mothers at a comparable age.

It is hard to be entirely clear how much these figures reflect changes brought about by the women's movement and how much they reflect a very broad change in the society of which the women's movement constitutes only a part.

Referring to this broader change, Dr. Peggy McIntosh, a program director at the Wellesley College Center for Research on Women, commented, "Today I think people are aware that there are many forms of love you can experience in the course of your life. The definition of love has diffused in a healthy way. You can get love from friends, children, lovers, as well as husbands. Human warmth is necessary—women are sure of that—but the romantic twosome does not have an exclusive grip on women's imagination as it did for so many in the forties and fifties."

It may be, too, that the low figure of 26 percent represents a realistic attitude given the number of marriages that fail and the number of years a woman can expect to spend alone over the course of her life. (Ten percent of the women interviewed were divorced or separated and only 43 percent of these hope to remarry, although 22 percent characterize themselves as "unsure" with respect to remarriage.) The low figure of 43 percent reinforces the message of independence suggested by the attitudes toward marriage described above. It may also hint at pessimism about the possibilities of being one's own person within "a romantic twosome."

Many women are aware that, without actually leading to the breakup of a marriage, the expanded identity encouraged by the women's movement can cause difficulties in their relations with men. Margaret Wilkerson, director of the Center for the Study, Education and Advancement of Women at the University of California at Berkeley, commented, "I think one reason women are staying single is that they want more of a relationship than they can find."

For some very able women in the professions the situation can appear quite bleak. Attorney Carol Doran, who is not married, commented, "It's difficult, if not impossible, to combine marriage and a profession because of the difficulty of finding a sympathetic man. The attitudes of the men haven't caught up with women. Most men want someone who will stay home with kids and who will look up to them because they make a lot of money. If you're a professional, you're not what they're looking for."

Carol's position is a minority one, however; a substantial majority of women (70 percent) report that their husbands approve of their working. Nevertheless, this is a more positive response than women give when asked more impersonally if a wife and mother can expect her husband to feel threatened if she works. In reply to this more general question 26 percent think it very likely; and 56 percent, somewhat likely. Only 17 percent felt their husbands would not be threatened. It may be that women are much more ready to consider the possibility of being threatening in the abstract than they are in relation to their actual husbands. Perhaps this is all the more true because most women strongly believe that combining career and motherhood leads to greater self-esteem (72 percent feel that it is "very likely" that a woman will feel better about herself if she does so): it is hard to admit that what enhances your self-esteem may in fact be threatening to someone you love.

THE HOUSEWORK DILEMMA

Housework—or rather the sharing of housework—is another area in which the ideas of the women's movement have the potential to affect the relationship of husband and wife. In fewer than one in five marriages do couples share housework equally. Interestingly, the figures are not radically different among women who identify strongly with the women's movement. Only 24 percent of such women share housework equally with their husbands.

Why do men resist sharing housework—beyond the fact that anyone would avoid it if he or she could? The reason may lie in the fact that if a man shares housework or more than cursory child care, he assumes a new role—expands his identity. This may be far more threatening than perhaps continuing in an established role but experiencing it as somewhat diminished, as is the case when his wife works and he is no longer the sole provider. Sensing this, women may hold back from pushing their husbands to share housework and child care. The closer a change comes to intimate life and, particularly, to challenging the self-image of a loved one, the harder it may be for women to push for.

It would be wrong, however, to suggest that women do not think that men have been affected by the revolution in attitudes of which the women's movement is a part. Thirty percent of our respondents felt that a central message of the movement was the encouragement of men to be more expressive in ways usually associated with women—in other words to allow themselves to express feelings such as tenderness or vulnerability. And 20 percent thought the fact that men realized they could do so was a major consequence of the women's movement. These figures are not large, but they are of great interest given the fact that there is as yet little support among men themselves for change in this direction, and there is a lot for them to be threatened by in the women's movement.

Even women who are quite conservative may perceive that the women's movement has had an effect on their husbands. Deanna Kimble, for instance, is basically opposed to the women's movement. She feels that it has created unrealistic expectations among women, made the position of women more difficult, and made it harder to hold marriages together. Most of all, she believes that because the women's movement pressures women to work outside the home, children suffer. "When you come home at 5 you're tired and you don't get time to do anything special with the kids."

But a discussion of her husband's situation qualified her point of view. At the time Deanna was interviewed, her husband, Brian, had been laid off from his job in the shipping department of a tool company and Deanna had taken a part-time job in a fast-food restaurant to supplement the family income. She and Brian share the care of their four-year-old daughter. Deanna felt that the messages of the women's movement concerning men's roles made Brian's unemployed situation a little more tolerable for him. "It's easier with the women's movement for men to help out with housework and help with kids. I tease Brian about women's lib all the time in front of his friends, but they're doing the same thing. I think it's acceptable to him." Although Deanna states that the movement has made her life neither easier nor more difficult, it may in fact have made it easier by providing some societal support of the role temporarily forced on her husband.

FEMINIST CHILD REARING

The women's movement has profoundly influenced women's attitudes toward rearing children. Whereas the mothers and grandmothers of today's women would not have thought at all about the issue of innate biological differences between the sexes versus socialization—and, if pressed, would have favored biology—the ideas the women's movement has popularized about nurture versus nature have led 76 percent of our respondents to believe that social and behavioral differences between the sexes are the result of the way children are taught to behave. Only 9 percent think these differences are the result of biology, and only 12 percent think nature and nurture have an equal effect. By implication this belief in the power of socialization leads parents to believe they have a role and choice in their children's development that earlier generations would not have perceived in the same way.

How do women see themselves exercising this influence? Fifty-one percent would like to diminish the differences between boys and girls but not eliminate them altogether, and 30 percent would like to try for as few differences as possible. Thirty-nine percent of nonwhite respondents would like to try for as few differences as possible—a figure that Margaret Wilkerson finds "not surprising." "My hunch," she says, "is that it reflects a kind of historical egalitarianism that undergirds the black community. [Going back to slavery] both men and women worked in the fields and in the kitchen. More recently, both men and women have to work to support a family." Only 13 percent of our poll respondents would like to see the current range of differences continue in the next generation. This may be the most remarkable finding of the study. It suggests an extraordinary acceptance of a set of ideas that had hardly touched public consciousness twenty years ago as well as a very rationalist attitude toward human potential. And it's worth pointing out that these attitudes are shared even by those who see themselves as very religious or as political conservatives: only 14 percent of the very religious and only 17 percent of the politically conservative would like to see the socialization of children continue as now.

At the same time that the women's movement has changed attitudes toward the rearing of children, it has changed women's outlook on the place of children in their lives. Important as family life and children continue to be for them, the goal of an expanded identity has made it acceptable to women to consider postponing children while they build a base for themselves through work or study in the "outer world." When asked if a woman planning a career should start her career first and postpone children or vice versa, 60 percent of our respondents favored postponing children, and 29 percent were in favor of postponing career (11 percent were not sure). In fact, there are indications that these women are practicing what they preach, since of those who have children, less than 16 percent are 25 or under.

The same goal of an expanded identity leads women to believe that it is realistic to combine a career with motherhood: 77 percent of our respondents believe that it is possible to do so successfully—a point of view their mothers and grandmothers would not have shared to the same degree at all. However, when questioned on the more specific and sensitive issue of whether pre-school children will thrive without the fulltime care of their mothers, only 59 percent thought they did not need their mothers' fulltime care, whereas 38 percent believed that preschoolers *do* require it. "You're still getting a lot of people who think it's a good thing to stay home when kids are young," Mary Jo Bane commented, "but these days 'young' gets defined as six or three, not eighteen."

A closer look at our sample reveals the way in which opportunity for an expanded identity influences these attitudes: 75 percent of those in management or professional positions feel that preschoolers can thrive without their mothers' fulltime care, whereas far fewer women feel this way if they have less opportunity in their lives: only 54 percent of women who had no more than a high school education felt this way. Moreover, the ideological character of these attitudes is suggested by the fact that 72 percent of those who identify strongly with the women's movement think that young children flourish without their mothers' fulltime care, but among women who identified themselves as political conservatives only a slim majority—53 percent—felt this way.

HIDDEN CONFLICTS

Although women want a role in the "outer world" while raising their children, pursuing it inevitably involves some degree of conflict—conflict that, given their commitment to balancing many roles, they may not always be entirely ready to admit to—at least in a telephone interview. When asked if they personally spent less time on family life than they liked because of work, only 13 percent said they did so frequently, although 38 percent said they did occasionally. Only 4 percent said they frequently left their children with child care they were less than entirely happy with while they went to work, and only 17 percent did so occasionally. However, when asked in much less direct and personal terms if a woman who combines career and motherhood will doubt that she is a good enough wife and mother, 25 percent of respondents said that it was very likely that she would do so; and 56 percent, somewhat likely. Moreover, 48 percent thought it somewhat likely that her children would get in trouble, and 26 percent thought it somewhat likely that the children would have emotional difficulties.

Traditionally women have tended to handle inner conflict over their sense of responsibility to their family by choosing work that is not too pressured or is in one way or another a good fit with family life. Implicitly if not explicitly, the "brief-case," "corporate success" stereotype of the message of women's movement discourages this approach in its attempt to help women better adapt to the world of work, particularly highly competitive work in the contemporary corporate setting. A profound aspect of women's nature and socialization is thus downplayed. "We women are trained to work for the decent survival of all," Peggy McIntosh comments. "That's the heritage we were raised with by virtue of our socialization, even if we're not aware of it."

Combining motherhood with most work situations is no threat to the "decent survival of all" as long as good child care is available, but a woman may feel it is an issue if she enters a highly competitive field and wishes to be outstanding. Our respondents' awareness of this problem was reflected in their answers to a hypothetical question concerning "Sara," a lawyer who would have to work 60 hours a week, as the men did in her firm, if she wished to become a partner. Fifty-eight percent of the sample thought she should give up the hope of being outstanding and settle for a lesser role in the firm so that she could spend time with her child; 26 percent thought she should devote herself to her career; and 15 percent were not sure what she should do. A commitment to the "decent survival of all" still has the majority voice, but the "briefcase," "corporate success" message of the women's movement has won at least theoretical concurrence from a quarter of the women.

Percentages, however, cannot suggest what it feels like for real women as opposed to the hypothetical Sara when they try to resolve conflicts between doing well by their family and fully pursuing their talents and ambitions. For many the solution—or the nearest thing to a solution—may be starting a family late and keeping it small. Carol Reagan, for instance, of Skokie, Illinois, is married and 30 years old. She works as a field representative for a county agency on aging and is meanwhile studying for a master's degree in public administration. So far she has not had a child. "I like my freedom and I don't think I should go into child rearing feeling that way," she said. "If I had one child," she continued, "it would be easier. I think perhaps I could manage one child with day care. If I had more than one child, I'd have to have a housekeeper." When asked if she thought her employer would be somewhat flexible to help her balance her job with mothering, she said, "My agency is flexible to a certain extent, but not my husband's company. And he certainly wouldn't get any paternity leave. And given the current economic situation I don't see that organizations are going to become more flexible. I think they're going to become more inflexible."

By implication Carol's remarks raise an important issue. As more women work outside the home the kind of family nurturance and maintenance provided preponderantly by women will have to be shared if families are not to live with a high degree of stress—particularly for children. Where is this support going to come from? From husbands? But they are not going to provide it unless they experience a wider, deeper change of consciousness than they now have— one profound enough to make them join women in insisting on modifications in the structure of the workplace. Or will it come from public-policy changes— but policy changes do no come unless people press for them—men as well as women—and it goes against the American grain to press for public solutions to what we tend to see as individual problems. Our American cult of the individual makes us think that families should solve their own problems—and to see help as intrusion or proof of weakness. The difficulty is that our very belief in opportunity for the individual, now that it has been extended to women, has created an unprecedented situation. We have created a "nurturance gap" in the society that cannot be filled without changes and solutions that go beyond what individual families can do. It is this nurturance gap that Carol Reagan, like many other women, struggles with when she thinks of having a child. Or, put more concretely, in the words of Margaret Wilkerson, "The findings of the *Parents* poll have strong implications for national childcare supports."

VOTING FOR CHANGE

It seems likely that awareness of the "nurturance gap" is an important part of the much publicized "gender gap"—the discrepancy between male and female voting patterns. Women want for themselves not only job opportunities and an end to discrimination but support for the values of nurturance and family life—and, in terms of the wider society beyond the family, help in assuring the "decent survival of all." This is what the political attitudes of the women in our sample suggest, particularly if one considers their views in the context of their values—their enduring commitment to family life, which a wish for an expanded identity has not changed. "Women in this age category," Margaret Wilkerson comments, "do not want to reject traditional roles but want to bring traditional values into the public arena."

Although the total sample characterized themselves as 23 percent conservative, 45 percent moderate, and 21 percent liberal, clear majorities endorsed federally guaranteed job opportunities (68 percent), job quotas to ensure equal opportunity for women (80 percent), and quotas for blacks and other minorities (73 percent). More striking, 73 percent thought that President Reagan's handling of issues especially important to women was fair or poor. Seventy-one percent thought that his handling of the economy was fair or poor—and this figure can be compared with 70 percent of women and 57 percent of men questioned in a national poll by NBC/Associated Press a month after *Parents'* poll was conducted in September, 1982 (but the NBC/AP poll sample included men and women of all ages, not just 21 to 35).

So far we have examined the ways in which the women's movement has changed women themselves and modified their attitudes toward work and their relationships within their families. But the question for the next decade may well be the impact of the women's movement on the society as a whole. As a remarkably liberal generation of women now in their twenties and thirties enter their prime and gain greater power, pressure is going to build for policies that guarantee "the decent survival of all."

7   *Their Turn: How Men Are Changing*

Betty Friedan

STUDY QUESTIONS

1. Friedan notes ways that the feminist movement is affecting men. Think of other ways that men are changing and note whether these are also a result of the feminist movement.

Source: Betty Friedan, "Their Turn: How Men Are Changing." *Redbook*, May 1980. Reprinted by permission.

I believe that American men are at the edge of a tidal wave of change—a change in their very identity as men. It is a change not yet clearly visible, not really identified or understood by the experts and not even, or seldom, spoken about by men themselves. Yet this change will be as basic as the change created for women by the Women's Movement, even though it is nothing like the Women's Movement. Nobody is marching or making statements. There is no explosion of anger, no enemy to rage against, no list of grievances or demands for benefits and opportunities clearly valuable and previously denied, as with women.

This is a quiet movement, a shifting in direction, the saying of no to old patterns, a searching for new values, a struggling with basic questions that each man seems to be going through alone. At the same time, he continues the outward motions that always have defined men's lives, making it (or struggling to make it) at the office, the plant, the ball park . . . making it with women . . . getting married . . . having children . . . yet he senses that something is happening with men, something large and historic, and he wants to be part of it. He carries the baby in his backpack, shops at the supermarket on Saturdays, with a certain showing-off quality.

It started for many men almost unwillingly, in response to the Women's Movement. The outward stance of hostility and bristling defensiveness that the rhetoric of the first stage of the Women's Movement almost demanded of men obscured the reality of the first changes among them, the real reasons those changes were threatening to some men and the surprising relief, support—even envy—many men felt about the Women's Movement.

At first glance, all it looked like was endless arguments about his doing a fair share of the housework, the cooking and the cleaning; and his responsibility for helping with the children, getting them to bed, into snowsuits, to the park, to the pediatrician. Because now it wasn't *automatic* that her job was to take care of the house and all the other details of life while his job was to support everyone. Now she was working to support them too.

But then, even if she didn't have a job outside the home, she suddenly had to be treated as a person too, as he was. She had a right to her own life and interests; at night, on weekends, he could help with the children and the house.

He felt wronged, injured. He had been working his can off to support her and the children and now he was her "oppressor," a "male chauvinist pig," if he didn't scrub all the pots and pans to boot. "You make dinner," she said. "I'm going to my design class."

He felt scared when she walked out like that. If she didn't need him for her identity, her status, her sense of importance, if she was going to get all that for herself and have a life independent of him, wouldn't she stop loving him? Wouldn't she just leave? He was supposed to be the big male oppressor, yeah? How could he admit the big secret—that maybe he needed her more than she needed him? That he felt like a baby when he became afraid she would leave. That suddenly he didn't know what he felt, what he was *supposed* to feel—as a man.

I believe much of the hostility of men comes from their very dependence on our love, from those feelings of need that men aren't supposed to have—just as the excess of our attacks on our male "oppressors" stemmed from our dependence on men. That old, excessive dependence (which was supposed to be natural in women) made us feel we had to be *more* independent than any man in order to be able to move at all. Our explosion of rage and our attacks on men masked our own timidity and fear at risking ourselves, in a complex and competitive world, in ways we never had had to before.

And the more a man was pretending to a dominant, cool, masculine superiority he didn't really feel—the more he was forced to carry the burden alone of supporting everyone against the rough odds of that grim, outside economic world—the more threatened and the more hostile he felt.

Sam, a foreman for an aerospace company in Seattle, Washington, believes that the period when his wife "tried to be just a housewife" was the worst time in his marriage. "If you decide you're going to stay home and be taken care of," he says, "and you have to depend for everything on this guy, you get afraid. *Can he do it?* It all depended on me, and I was in a constant panic, the way our business is now, but I'd say, 'Don't worry.'

"Susie was tired of her job anyhow," explains Sam. "It wasn't such a great job—neither is mine, if you want to know—but she had an excuse. She said she wanted to be home with the children. The pressure was on me. But it was crazy. Here I was, not knowing where the next paycheck was coming from after our Government contract ran out, suddenly supporting a wife and children all by myself.

"It's better now that she's working and bringing some money in," Sam insists. "And I don't just *help* with the kids. She has to be at work before I do, so I give them breakfast and get them off to school. The nights she works late, I make dinner, help with the homework and get everyone to bed. But I don't feel so panicky now—and she isn't attacking me anymore."

Phil Kessler, a young doctor who started out to be a surgeon, but who now has a small-town family practice in New Jersey talks to me as he makes pickles and his children run around underfoot in the country kitchen that is next to his office.

"I was going to be a surgeon, super cool in my gleaming white uniform," he says "—the man I was supposed to be but knew I wasn't. So I married a nurse and she stayed home to raise our children, and she was supposed to fulfill herself through my career. It didn't work for either of us.

"I went through torture before every operation," Phil explains. "Then Ellen started turning against me. I always said the children needed her at home full time. Maybe because I was so scared inside. Maybe she didn't have the nerve to do her own thing professionally. All she seemed to want was revenge against me, as if she were locked into some kind of sexual battle against me, playing around, looking elsewhere for true love.

"When Ellen finally got up the nerve to do her own thing—she's a nurse-midwife now—it was a relief," says Phil. "The other stuff stopped. She could come back to being my wife. And I'm *redefining myself*, no longer in terms of success or failure as a doctor, though I still am a doctor, and not as superior or inferior to her. It was a blow to my ego, but what a relief to take off my surgical mask! I'm discovering my own value to the family.

"Now that I'm not so hurt and angry and afraid that she'll leave me, I can see that it's a hell of a fight for a woman to be seen as a person. I think she was afraid of trying to accomplish something on her own, so she made me the villain. But it's as hard for me to feel like a person as it is for her. We couldn't—either of us—get that from each other."

The new questions are harder for men because men have a harder time talking about their feelings than women do. That's part of the masculine mystique. And after all, since men have the power and the top-dog position in society that women are making all the fuss about, why should men want to change—unless women make them?

"Maybe men feel more need to pretend," says a sales engineer in Detroit, Michigan, who is struggling to take "equal responsibility" for the children and the house, now that his wife has gone to work in a department store. "I don't think men thought much about what it was to be a man," he explains, "until women suddenly were talking about what it was to be a woman—and men were left out of the equation.

"Now men are thinking about what it means to be a man. The Women's Movement forced us to start rethinking the way we relate to women and to our families. Now men are going to have to rethink the way they relate to their work. Our sense of who we are was always profoundly based on work, but men are going to begin to define themselves in ways other than work.

"In the '80s," this man says, "we're going to see more men dropping away from traditional male roles, partly because of the economy, partly because men are beginning to find other goodies at the table, like their children—areas where men were excluded before. Being a daddy has become very important to me. When I used to see a man on the street with his children on a weekday, I assumed that he was unemployed, a loser. Now it's so common—daddies with their children, at ease."

The truth is that many of the old bases for men's identity have become shaky. If being a man is defined, for example, as being *dominant, superior*—as *not-being-a-woman*—the definition gets shaky when most of the important work of society no longer requires brute muscular force. The Vietnam war probably was the beginning of the end of the old caveman-hunter, gun-toting, he-man mystique. The men I have been interviewing around the country these past months are the men who fought in Vietnam or who went to graduate school to stay out of the war.

Vietnam was somehow a watershed. If men stop defining themselves by going to war or getting power from jobs women can't have, what is left? What does it mean to be a man, except *not-being-a-woman*—that is, physically superior and able to beat up everyone else? The fact is, when a man admits to those "messy feelings" that men as well as women have, he can't *play* the same kind of man any more.

Tony Kowalski, of the Outer Banks of North Carolina, was a pilot in Vietnam when it started for him. "I was a captain, coming up for major," he says. "I had all the medals, and I would have gone on for twenty years in the Air Force. Sitting up there over Nam, the commander, under heavy fire, the guys screaming into the mikes, the bombers and fighters moving in, me giving the orders, I was caught up in it, crazy-wild, excited. And then I woke up one day, coming out of Special Forces camp, and found myself clicking my empty gun at civilians. I knew I had to get out."

Tony can fly any piece of machinery. He took a job with an airline. "All I wanted was security," he says. "After one year I was furloughed because the company was having financial difficulties. There was no security. So I came back to this town where I grew up and took a job as a schoolteacher, working with seventh and eighth graders who were reading at the second-grade level. It was the 'reading lab,' the pits, the bottom—and traditionally a 'woman's job.' It's the hardest job I've ever done and it gets the least respect. Flying a three-hundred-and-twenty-three-thousand-pound Lockheed Starlifter can't compare." As a pilot Tony made $34,000 a year; as a teacher he makes $12,000.

"But maybe now," he says, "with the ladies moving in and picking up some of the financial slack—my wife works for a florist and as a waitress nights—a guy can say, 'I'm not going to get much of anywhere with the money anyhow. Why don't I do something really worthwhile from a human point of view?"

Another man, a West Point graduate of the class of '68, whose father and grandfather were Army men, insists that: "Men can't be the same again after Vietnam. It always defined men, as against women, that we went to war. We learned it in the locker room, young. The worst insult was to be called all the four- and five-letter words for women's sex. Now that women are in the locker rooms at West Point, how can that work?

"Women have a powerful advantage," this man adds, "because they aren't brought up to believe that if someone knocks you down, *he* has the courage, so you have to knock *him* down. Women aren't stuck with the notion that that kind of courage is necessary. It seems to me, ever since the Vietnam war, more and more men are reaching a turning point, so that if they don't get beyond these games, they start to die. Women will make a mistake if they reach that turning point and start to imitate men. Men can't be role models for women, not even in the Army. We badly need some new role models ourselves."

At first it seems as if men and women are moving in exactly opposite directions. Women are moving out of the home and into the men's world of work and men are shifting toward a new definition of themselves *in* the home. As we move into the '80s social psychologist and public-opinion analyst Daniel Yankelovich is finding that a majority of adult men in the United States no longer are seeking or are satisfied by conventional job success. Only one in every five men now says that work means more to him than leisure.

"Men have come to feel that success on the job is not enough to satisfy their yearnings for self-fulfillment," says Yankelovich. "They are reaching out for something more and for something different."

Certain large signs of this movement are reported in the newspapers almost daily. Corporation heads complain that young executives refuse to accept transfers because of "the family." Economists and government officials bewail increased absenteeism and declining productivity among workers. In the past ten years, more than half of West Point's graduates have resigned as Army career officers. College and graduate-school enrollments are dropping among men (as they continue to increase among women), and not just because it isn't necessary for men to evade the draft any more.

In the book *Breaktime*, a controversial study of men "living without work in a nine-to-five world," Bernard Lefkowitz reports a 71-per-cent increase in the number of working-aged men who have left the labor force since 1968 and who are not looking for work. According to Lefkowitz, the "stop-and-go pattern of work" is becoming the predominant pattern, rather than the lifetime jobs and careers men used to pursue both for economic security and for their masculine identity.

"In the depression of the '30s," says Lefkowitz, "men were anxious because they were not working. In the '70s men became anxious because their work was not paying off in the over-all economic security they had expected."

Bob O'Malley, 33, quit his rising career in a big New York City bank to sell real estate on the tip of Long Island.

"I asked myself one day, if my career continued going well and I really made it up the corporate ladder, did I want to be there, fifteen years from now, with the headaches of the senior executives I saw being pushed off to smaller offices, their staffs, secretaries, status, taken away, or having heart attacks, strokes? Men who had been loyal to the company twenty-five years— it governed their whole lives—and to what end? I didn't want to live my life like that. I wanted to be more independent—maybe not making so much money but living more for myself."

The trouble is that once men disengage themselves from the old patterns of masculinity and success, they are just as lost for role models as women are. Moreover, if a man tries to get out of his own bind by *reversing roles* with his wife—if he yearns for a superwoman to support him as she used to yearn for a strong man who would take care of her—it makes his wife uneasy.

"My husband wants me to have another child, and he says he'll quit his job and stay home to take care of the children," a woman in Vermont tells me. "But why should that work for him when it didn't work for me? And maybe I don't want him to take over the family that much. Maybe I'd resent it—just working to support him."

It's a situation that didn't work when Dr. Phil Kessler, in the first flush of relief after dropping his surgical mask, tried reversing roles with his wife. In the first place, his wife couldn't make as much money as a nurse-midwife as he could make as a doctor. And somehow when she came home from work the house was never "clean enough," the meat loaf wasn't seasoned "right" and he'd also forgotten to put the potatoes on. So she would rush around, tired as she was, doing everything over, making him feel just as guilty as she had in the old days.

"Then I began to feel like a martyr," he says. "Nobody appreciated how hard I worked, taking care of the house and the children. Now that I'm doing my own work again—and bringing money in—I don't have to feel guilty if the house isn't all that clean. And now that they're treating her like a professional at the hospital, she doesn't notice the dust on the windowsills so much, either."

It takes trial and error, of course, to work out the practicalities, the real trade-offs, of the new equality between the sexes when both try to share home and work responsibilities. And it may be harder for men because the benefits of the trade-offs for them aren't that obvious at first. Women, after all, are fighting for an equal share in the activities and the power games that are rewarded in this society. What are men's rewards for giving up some of that power?

Jimmy Fox, a blue-collar worker in Brooklyn, New York, won't admit that there are any rewards for him in the trade-offs he's been "forced" to work out with his wife. "In our community," says Jimmy, "men don't freely accept women's equality. It's got to be slowly pushed down their throats. Men are the ones who go to the bar on the corner, drink, come home when the heck they want and expect supper to be on the table, waiting for them. When that starts changing, it scares them to death. It scared me.

"I didn't know what was going on," he says. "First thing I knew, my wife is going out to a women's organization, the National Congress of Neighborhood Women, and she wants to go do this, do that. She's learning, letting me know that things are wrong with our marriage. What am I supposed to do? It took five years before we got to the point where she went out to work and found her own role."

Today Jimmy makes $9,000 a year and his wife makes $9,000. "And when she's out working," says Jimmy, "I'm taking care of the baby. It's no picnic. Any man who wants to change places with his wife when his wife stays home and takes care of the house and children has got to be a maniac. Her job in the house was twice as hard as mine at the plant. I work ten, twelve hours. She works from when she gets up in the morning until she goes to bed."

When Linda Fox first started working, she says, "there were many, many battles between Jimmy and me. I wanted equality, which I thought meant that if he put three hours and twenty-two minutes into housework, then I would put in three hours and twenty-two minutes. I wanted a blow-by-blow division and I was fanatical about it. Jimmy was so happy to be relieved of some of the burden of being the only one with the paycheck that he was willing to do that, although I know he was teased by the guys at the bar."

The first payoff for men then, obviously, is economic survival. Unfortunately, few of the other big trade-offs of equality can be measured as mechanically as men's and women's making exactly the same amount of money (women on the average still earn only 59 cents to a man's $1) or their spending exactly the same amount of time on housework.

"What I've gained," says Avery Corman, who wrote the novel *Kramer versus Kramer*, on which the movie was based, from his own experience of taking over the children when his wife started a business, "is the joy—and it is a joy—of having my children really rely on me. I've gained this real participation in their upbringing because I've been active in it on a daily basis."

Unlike the Kramers, the Cormans remain happily married, and, he says, "what I've given up is being waited on myself. There are times when I'd really like to be the prince of patriarchs and sit around with my pipe and slippers with my wife and children tiptoeing around, but it sure isn't like that now and it never will be again. A secret part of me would sometimes like a less-equal marriage, would like to be catered to the way guys used to be.

"But the real payoff," he says, "is that men can begin to think about who they are *as men*. I can ask myself what I really want in life. With my wife out there earning, I don't have to be just a breadwinner."

Another big trade-off for men while women become more independent is more independence—more "space"—for them. An Atlanta cotton broker, now married at 30 to a woman with her own career, recalls his first marriage, to a woman who depended on him for everything.

"She made me feel suffocated," he says. "Living with a completely dependent woman is debilitating. You don't know why, but you just feel awful. She's breathing your air. She's passing her anxiety on to you. She's got no confidence in herself and she's looking to you for everything; but what she does is always put you down, make you feel you won't make it."

"She may be very sweet," he explains further. "She may be lovely, but all you know is that you don't have room to breathe. I never heard of any ruling class resigning, but as men realize that it's better to live with a nondependent woman the change will come about because the payoff is real—economic and emotional."

Paradoxically, part of the trade-off is that when women share the economic burden—and declare themselves equal persons in other ways—men are able to put a new value on personal qualities once considered the exclusive domain of women. It's the new American frontier for men, this exploration of their inner space, of the "messy feelings" we all have but that for too long were considered awesome and mysterious and forbidden territory for men.

When women share the work burden and relieve men of the need to pretend to false strengths, men can open up to feelings that give them a real sense of strength, especially when they share the daily chores of life that wives used to shield them from. "It grounds me—I have to admit it," says a man named Bernie, who for the first time, after 30 years of his mother's and wife's doing it for him, is cooking, shopping and washing clothes. "I like the relief from always thinking about my job, feeling like a disembodied head chained to a typewriter."

Or as a man named Lars Hendrix, of Oakland, California, expresses it: "It makes me feel alive. I don't have to pretend to be so strong because I feel good. I feel grounded. The silence that most men live with isolates them not only from women but also from other men. My wife's assault on my silence was at first extremely painful. She made me share my feelings with her. It brought an incredible sense of liberation, and maybe for the first time in my adult life a sense of reality, that I can *feel* my feelings and share them with her.

"But there'll still be a loneliness, for me and for other men," says Lars, "until we can share our feelings with each other. That's what I envy most about the Women's Movement—the way women share their feelings and the support they get from each other. Do you know how isolated and lonely and weak a man feels in that silence, never really making contact with another man?"

There is another, major problem. As men seek for themselves the liberation that began with the Women's Movement, both men and women have to confront the conflict between their human needs—for love, for family, for purpose in life—and the demands of the workplace.

A family therapist in Philadelphia, Pennsylvania, the father of a three-year-old son, talks about the conflict in terms of his own profession and personal needs. "I was working at one of the top family-training centers in the country," he says. "There was a constant theoretical discussion about getting the father back into the family, but the way the jobs were set up there, you had to work fifty, sixty hours a week. To really get anywhere you had to put in seventy hours and work nights, weekends. You didn't have time for your own family. I won't do that. My family is number one—my job is only to be a good therapist."

Recent managerial studies have shown that the long working hours and the corporate transfers that keep many men from strong daily involvements with their families or with other interests are not always necessary for the work of the company. But the long hours and the transfers do serve to keep a man *dependent* for his very identity, as well as his livelihood, on the corporation—dependent as a "company man."

Recently, at the National Assembly on the Future of the Family sponsored by the NOW Legal Defense and Education Fund, corporation heads and union leaders joined feminists and family experts in confronting the need for "practical and innovative" solutions to balancing the demands of the workplace and the family. The agenda for the '80s must include restructuring the institutions of work and home to make equality livable and workable—for women and men.

Women can't solve the problem alone by taking everything on themselves, by trying to be "superwomen." And women don't have the power to change the structure of the workplace by themselves. But while more and more men decide that they want some self-fulfillment beyond their jobs and some of the life-grounding that women always have had in the family—as much as women now need and want some voice and active power in the world—there will be a new, combined force for carrying out the second stage of liberation for us all.

It seems strange to suggest that there is a new American frontier, a new adventure for men, in the struggle for *wholeness*, for openness to feeling, for living and sharing life on equal terms with women. But it is a new frontier where both men's and women's needs converge. Men need new role models now as much as women do.

Men also need to share their new questions and feelings about work and family and self-fulfillment with other men. And Redbook invites them to do that, to share their questions and thoughts, in the pages of the magazine in coming months. To help each other. To begin to break out of their isolation and become role models for each other, as women are doing in the second stage of the struggle for liberation.

The dialogue has gone on too long in terms of women alone. Let men join women in the center of the second stage.

BETTY FRIEDAN

3 *Sexual Expression*

Unlike the changes in gender behavior, the changes in sexual behavior have been both rapid and widespread. Historical fluctuation in society's norms of sexual permissiveness led in the Victorian period to an extreme sexual restrictiveness which prevailed with little change until the 1960s and 1970s. At that time ideological changes toward gender equality and technological changes, such as improved contraception, combined with a greater accessibility of erotic materials, a higher divorce rate, and a larger singles' population to bring about the idea that sexual activity is acceptable and necessary for pleasure; for both sexes, in or outside of marriage. The result of these changes is, as Reiss notes in the first article of Chapter 3, the delineation of areas of sexual controversy concerning genetic differences of the sexes, sexual normality, exploitation and pornography, abortion, and the change to a new mood that sees sex as a form of play rather than of sin. He concludes that these controversies are the result of conflicting sexual scripts, a traditional-romantic ideology that sees sexuality redeemed from its guilt by love versus a modern naturalistic alternative that sees the goals of sexuality as physical pleasure and psychological intimacy.

This growth in permissive sex is one primarily affecting the female due to the presumptions of a double standard in which coitus was seen as a need for men but not for women. A survey of sex manuals reveals this change in the role of women over the past thirty years, a change from the role of being different-and-unequal to one of humanistic sexuality to one of sexual autonomy. Reflecting changing ideas of sexuality, the different-and-unequal model suggested that women can and should enjoy sex. However, sex for women was different than for men—it was more dormant and emotional and so needed the animalistic sexuality of the male to be awakened. The humanistic version deinstitutionalized female sexuality by portraying it as a human quality present between two loving partners. Spurred by the feminist movement, a new model emerged in which women were portrayed as independent agents in charge of their own sexuality (Weinberg et al. 1983). These changed sexual ethics received mixed reviews as to the effects for women's liberation. The permissive sex ethic was seen as essentially a premarital sex ethic that gives females the same sexual rights and privileges that men enjoy whereas some believed that the new sexual permissiveness for women has made "a new reservoir of available females . . . for traditional sexual exploitation, disarming women of even the little protection they had so painfully acquired" (Firestone 1970).

Regardless of which of the above views is correct, understanding the gender differences in sexual scripts will improve the understanding of sexuality and provide an understanding of its relationship to sex roles. As a means toward this end, Shirley Radlove in the second article of this chapter examines the relationship between the biophysical, the psychosocial, and the social values involved in sexual activity. She concludes that gender differences arise from learned psychosocial and social values since research reveals that men and women have similar biophysical responses.

Another outgrowth of the acceptance of permissive sex has been a seemingly explosive growth in teenage pregnancy. The great number of 15- to 24-year-old females during the 1960s and 1970s and their increased willingness to keep their babies has led to the perception of an epidemic of teenage pregnancies when in fact pregnancy rates have been declining since about 1980; however, there are still over one million teenage pregnancies a year (Adams et al. 1989).

Perhaps a reasonable question to ask at this point is why there is so much growth in teenage pregnancy in a period of increasing feasibility of conception control. The reasons for this include:

a. parents' discomfort with sexual communication and the resultant lack of sex education for their children,

b. inaccurate sex information from their peers,

c. anxiety and guilt about consciously engaging in "immoral" activity,

d. ignorance about the proper use of contraceptives, and

e. the desire to become pregnant or to impregnate.

The result may mean, as Anne Kates in the third article of Chapter 3 notes, becoming a mother with the attendant hardships of being a single parent.

The high costs to society of teenage childbearing—less healthy, poorly raised children, and the employment and financial problems of their mother—is one of the issues in the abortion debate since over 400,000 teenagers end their pregnancy in this manner (Kantrowitz 1987). Yet less than half of Americans approve of abortion for educational or employment reasons or because the mother is single, whereas more than 80 percent approve in cases of endangerment of the mother's life, chance of serious birth defect, or rape. The reason given by some for this ban or restriction is the supposed psychiatric after-effects of abortion, but research has shown these effects to be very limited. It would appear, then, that the abortion issue is an ideological one. Kristin Luker, in the fourth article of this chapter, examines this ideology.

Another outcome of the growth of permissive sex is seen in the spread of sexually transmitted diseases (STDs). Some 10 to 15 million Americans each year contract such diseases as gonorrhea, syphilis, genital herpes, and AIDS (Centers for Disease Control 1987). Ignorance, use of the pill rather than condoms, feelings of invulnerability, and difficulties in detection mean that about 75 percent of reported venereal disease cases occur among 15-to-30-year-olds, with the rate among 16-to-20-year-olds triple that of the rest of the population. Since few heterosexual Americans appear sufficiently informed or concerned about AIDS to change their sexual behavior, the above figures on STDs among teenagers indicate that adolescents are likely to be next high-risk group for this disease. Geeta Dardick, in the fifth article of Chapter 3, gives the facts for dealing with this deadliest of the STDs.

Sexual behavior, however, is not only premarital and the marrieds also have problems to consider. Problems specific to married couples include spillover from other aspects of their marriages, lack of planning for intimacy, and personal and societal conditions leading to an increase in extramarital sex. Also, the problem of marital rape must be taken seriously since it is more common than generally realized. There are, however, advantages of marital over premarital and extramarital sex. Carol Botwin, in the final article of this chapter, provides a guide for retaining this sexual advantage.

REFERENCES

1. Adams, G., S. Adams-Taylor, & K. P. Pittman. 1989. "Adolescent Pregnancy and Parenthood: A Review of the Problem, Solutions, and Resources." *Family Relations* (April), pp. 223–230.

2. Centers for Disease Control. 1987. *Sexually Transmitted Disease Statistics*. Atlanta: Centers for Disease Control.

3. Firestone, S. 1970. *The Dialectic of Sex.* New York: Morrow.

4. Kantrowitz, B. 1987. "Kids and Contraceptives." *Newsweek* (February 16), pp. 54–65.

5. Weinberg, M. S., R. G. Swenson, & S. K. Hammersmith. 1983. "Sexual Autonomy and the Status of Women: Models of Female Sexuality in U.S. Sex Manuals from 1950 to 1980." *Social Problems* (February).

8 Some Observations on Ideology and Sexuality in America

Ira L. Reiss

STUDY QUESTIONS

1. What are the controversies surrounding the issues of genetic differences of the sexes and that of sexual normality?

2. Compare the sexual scripts of traditional-romantic ideology and modern-naturalistic alternatives.

There is nothing new about the assertion that our ideologies severely limit our vision of the social world in which we live. Karl Marx popularized this notion by asserting that ideologies were the tools which capitalists utilized to rationalize their own economic interests. Marx's classic assertion was:

> The mode of production of material life conditions the social, political and intellectual life process in general. It is not the consciousness of men that determines their being, but on the contrary, their social being that determines their consciousness (Marx and Engels, 1962:363).

One may disagree with Marx's view of the singular power of economic interests but still believe in the power of ideologies to blind us to the realities of our social system. Surely most sociologists would accept such a general proposition and yet it has never been systematically applied to the area of human sexuality. My basic purpose in this paper will be to exhume some of the fundamental ideological beliefs in America concerning human sexuality and to show the value of a sociological approach to this area. Recent evidence indicates a new

Source: Ira L. Reiss, "Some Observations on Ideology and Sexuality in America." *Journal of Marriage and the Family,* May 1981, pp. 271–283. Copyrighted 1981 by the National Council on Family Relations, 3989 Central Ave., N.E., Suite #550, Minneapolis, MN 55421. Reprinted by permission.

growth of ideological fervor in the area of sexuality during the last several years and thus this analysis is quite relevant to understanding our current milieu.

Ideologies are firmly held doctrines of particular philosophical groups. The doctrine of economic determinism held by Marxist philosophers and the doctrine of original sin held by fundamentalist Christian groups are such ideological beliefs. I will attempt to indicate some of the ideological underpinnings of our American sexual beliefs and practices and thereby show how they like all ideologies, blind us to various realities of our sexual lives. Of necessity, this investigation will have to rely on illustrative examples, current day events, and some speculation, as well as on more strongly established empirical data. But I will attempt to explicate the reasoning and evidence for each assertion. This article is an attempt to establish the value of this approach to sexuality and encourage further scientific investigation.

I will seek to derive and analyze our American sexual ideologies by means of an examination of five controversial substantive areas relevant to sexuality: (1) abortion, (2) genetic differences of the sexes, (3) exploitation and pornography, (4) sexual normality, and (5) sexual history. Surely, these areas do not completely cover human sexuality but they are central and will be used to show the value of this type of analysis.

ABORTION

In August of 1980, the CBS-*New York Times* poll gathered some rather interesting data on attitudes of American adults toward abortion. Two of their questions and the resulting marginals appear below:

> Do you think there should be an amendment to the Constitution prohibiting abortions, or shouldn't there be such an amendment?
>> 29% yes, 62% opposed, and 9% uncertain
> Do you believe there should be an amendment to the Constitution protecting the life of the unborn child, or shouldn't there be such an amendment?
>> 50% yes, 39% opposed, and 11% uncertain.

Clearly, if one were pro-choice, the question that would be more favorable to that position would be the first one; and if one were pro-life, the question most favorable to that perspective would be the second one. The public declarations of opposed groups on abortion indicate just such selective use of questions like those in the CBS poll.

To further show the complexity of our ideology regarding abortion, let us examine the results of the 1980 National Opinion Research Center poll (NORC) of 1,500 adults. The findings show that over half their sample *opposed* abortion *if* the question stated that abortion should be granted "for any reason the woman wants" or if "the woman doesn't want more children" or if "the woman is single." But less than 20 percent *opposed* abortion *if* the stipulation

IRA L. REISS

was that the pregnancy was due to rape or if child defects were suspected or if the mother's health was at risk (NORC, 1980: 142, 144, 164). A 1980 Gallup Poll shows that 25 percent of their respondents felt that abortion should be legal under all circumstances; 53 percent accepted abortion only under some conditions, and 18 percent said abortion should be illegal under all circumstances (*Minneapolis Tribune*, 1980). Thus, by choosing the precise question it is easy to show that the majority of people favor or oppose a particular position on abortion.

It is precisely in situations such as this that those with a strong ideological commitment on one side or the other of the abortion issue will tend to utilize the research findings to their own advantage. This is one example of how sexual ideologies can and do bias our utilization of data. Even more relevant is the conclusion that there is a need for sociological analysis of such data so that somewhere there is available a reasonably objective account of just what are American attitudes toward areas like abortion. Of course, this is not always easy to accomplish. Sociologists also have their ideological training in our culture and have strong peer-group feelings which pressure against publishing any results that could be used by an opposing ideology. Nevertheless, sociology can offer a refuge from politicized approaches to social reality if it becomes conscious of the need to do so. Of course, science has its own ideology concerning methods of discovering and organizing knowledge but that ideology is not necessarily attached to any private moral position concerning controversial issues like abortion. The scrutiny of published research by other scientists helps insure the avoidance of private moral biases in one's scientific work. In addition, research indicates that views on abortion are not isolated from our other values. Recent studies show that those who oppose abortion are more likely to be in favor of traditional male dominance and of traditional sexual views in other areas (Granberg and Granberg, 1980; Walfish and Myerson, 1980). Thus, the sociological study of abortion can increase our awareness of some broad ideological positions as well as increase our scientific knowledge of the abortion controversy.

GENETIC DIFFERENCES OF THE SEXES

Ideology often enters in to bias our approach to genetic differences. Those who favor equalitarian gender roles strive to minimize all known genetic differences between the sexes and those who wish to have segregated gender roles strive to enlarge the area of known genetic sex differences. From a sociological perspective, both groups labor in vain. Surely there are some hormonal differences like those attested to by writers such as Maccoby and Jacklin (1974). For example, males have several times the androgen levels of females. In numerous studies, and in primate research, such hormonal difference is predictive of aggressive differences. Maccoby and Jacklin conclude that this is true of humans and that males are inherently more aggressive than females. Androgen is also related to sexual motivation in that androgen is the common treatment for females who lack sexual interest. Are we to conclude from this that males are therefore inevitably more sexually motivated and more aggressive than females? Not at all.

What this means is that, on the average, males may have the potential to differ from females in the above fashion; but this is only a tendency, and many males and females overlap even in terms of tendency. Further, androgen levels are not predictive of sexual activity or interest in any straightline fashion (Brown *et al.*, 1978; Schwartz *et al.*, 1980). More importantly, groups who wish to produce males and females who are equal on aggression or sexuality can do so by training. Clearly, human aggression and sexual interest vary tremendously *within* each sex and between the sexes in various cultures (Beach, 1977). In sum, then, genetic differences are just averages and tendencies and they can and are altered by training. They do not set immutable boundaries.

Relatedly, we know that females have more of the hormone called oxytocin and that this hormone can produce erect nipples and lactation at the sound of a crying infant, and yet most American mothers do not feel compelled to nurse their infants. Thus, training does and can alter our hormonal tendencies. Finally, even if we wanted to produce gender differences where there were no hormonal differences, we could do that, too. The debate about genetic differences then really has very little to do with unalterable gender-role differences or sexual-drive differences. Learning is so powerful a force in the human situation that such average tendencies do not necessarily predetermine very much at all. Our ideologies will determine our gender roles and our sexuality far more than our hormonal differences. It takes a sociologist and other social scientists to deliver this message to those who come prepared to do battle for their ideological position about genetic differences. The battle may still occur but at least we will have played out our role as scientists and made it possible for others to eventually grasp the situation in which they are involved.

EXPLOITATION AND PORNOGRAPHY

In today's public discussions of sexuality, one often hears the charges of sexual "exploitation." To what precisely does the term exploitation refer? Does a pornographic film exploit females in the film? Is pornography generally exploitive of females? There is no way to answer such questions unless we have a relatively clear definition of the term exploitation. However, the term is seldom defined in public dialogue because those who oppose pornographic films are convinced they are "bad" and, therefore, another "bad" term like exploitation is certainly appropriate. Relatedly, those who approve of pornographic films and literature are convinced that they are alright and, thus, they do not deserve the negative label of exploitation. One thing is clear, the term exploitation is used to apply to something thought to be negative but exactly what sort of negative thing is not clear.

The dictionary basically states that exploitation is to make use of someone for one's own advantage or to take more than one is giving. One way to define this is subjectively. We can ask persons if they think that they are using others for their own advantage and we can ask the potentially exploited person if they feel that they are being taken advantage of. If the answer is no, then even if we totally disapprove, we would have to agree that there is no exploitation occurring. But to my knowledge, few people have ever asked porno stars if they feel that in making a porno film they are getting as much as they are giving. They have not asked because most people are rushing to their own moral judgment and not asking how the persons involved feel. This judgment is made even though in other professions we use people's bodies for our pleasure and do not consider it exploitation, *e.g.*, professional football, nursing, and physical labor. It is an ideological and not a scientific conclusion that asserts that women in porno films *must* be exploited. This conclusion is based upon the premise that such use of our bodies is bad. I would suggest that it is our negative evaluation of body-centered sexuality that causes some Americans to label such sexuality in films as exploitive. The use of the body in these other professions is not sexual and thus is judged acceptable.

A second way that one can define exploitation is to state that it is an act against a particular moral code. In this case, the judgment could be made that if one's moral code says sexuality without affection (body-centered) is "bad," then such an act would, by definition, be exploitative, even if the actress involved protested that she did not feel exploited. This is compatible with Marx's notion of "false consciousness" wherein workers fail to see that they are "really" being exploited by the bourgeoise. Such an imposed definition of exploitation asserts that this act must "degrade" the actor and is therefore subject to such negative labels as exploitation. This is the more common usage and, clearly, it is quite vague and subject to meaning whatever the definer of the act thinks is "degrading."

I would contend that the strong ideological underpinnings that make one label pornography as exploitative are based upon the belief that sexuality which centers on the body and is without affection is wrong and, thus, there must be many negative consequences of such a wrong act. For example, consequences of pornography are at times asserted to be rape and violence against women. Here, too, the sociologist has an important role in trying to ascertain whether such consequences actually follow from pornography and, if so, in what way and for whom. One relevant research study in this area is that of Edward Donnerstein's (1980). Donnerstein has examined whether those subjects who viewed sexually violent films (rape) were more willing to administer shocks to other people than people who saw an erotic nonviolent film or a neutral film. The results indicate that those who saw violent-erotic films were more willing to administer electric shocks to women subjects in the study. But what can be objectively concluded from this? A great many pornographic films and magazines do not portray violent sexuality, that is, they do not show physical violence against females (Malamuth and Spinner, 1980). Further, the Donnerstein findings do not contradict the report of the Commission on Obscenity and Pornography (1970); rather, they extend and qualify those findings. The Commission has reported that pornographic materials do not promote sex offenses and that, in fact, sex offenders have been exposed to a *below* average amount of pornography. Donnerstein's work notes that it was predominantly from *violent* pornography that one gets results indicating an increase in violence towards females. Actually, mild forms of pornography (*Playboy* photos) have been found to *reduce* aggression towards females (Donnerstein *et al.*, 1975). There is also the question of sensitivity to violent pornography. Certain types of males may be more ready than others to respond to such stimuli; therefore, the effects of increased violence may be quite selective. Donnerstein and others are interested in pursuing just this type of specification of their results in terms of facilitating and inhibiting factors and, thus, draw no overall conclusions at this time.

Often the public reaction to pornography is not based upon an understanding of the research evidence but upon the way that evidence appears once it has been filtered through their ideological positions. Some people have taken the Donnerstein findings as a basis for wanting to ban all pornography. Donnerstein himself does not accept such an interpretation of his study; for, as noted above, he does report that nonviolent pornography did not have the same effects as did violent pornography. Most pornography is not violent. Furthermore, the audience in a porno film often consists of 50-year-old males while rapists are usually young men (Chappell *et al.*, 1977; Groth, 1979). Thus, any general unqualified causal connection between pornography and rape and violence is not called for by the evidence we possess today. As with the term exploitation, many would use the concept of "violence" broadly, *i.e.*, to be more than just physical abuse but to include "moral abuse." Such usage, of course, makes the term violence mean many different things and makes scientific conclusions difficult, since one would be free to label anything one didn't like as "violence."

American attitudes toward pornography are quite complex and contradictory. In the 1980 National Opinion Research Center national survey, it was found that most Americans view pornography as possibly leading to rape, but an even greater majority feel that sexual materials provided an outlet for bottled-up impulses. Further, most Americans do not want laws against such materials for adults (NORC, 1980). Clearly, social science analysis of this area could be helpful in furthering our understanding of causal connections and in the development of a typology of pornography and its users and an examination of its consequences.

Related to this issue of the consequences of pornography is the issue of body-centered sexuality in general. As noted above, those who oppose pornography generally oppose body-centered coitus or coitus that lacks affection or a personal quality and instead focuses on the bodily pleasures of sexuality. It may well be that opposition to pornography is, in good part, based upon opposition to body-centered coitus. So it is worthwhile to briefly look at this possible connection.

Every recorded civilization has had body-centered sexuality whether it be in the form of prostitution, orgiastic celebrations, or generally sanctioned body-centered sexuality. The physical body is a basic aspect of sexual attraction and it seems rather unlikely that any society could structure things to avoid this reality. Therefore, in any society, whatever body types are culturally decreed to be attractive will, at times, be sought not for love or romantic reasons but for themselves. What distinguishes cultures around the world, with very few exceptions, is not the absence or presence of body-centered sexuality but the evaluation of such sexuality. Some cultures, such as those in Polynesia, rate body-centered sexuality as good and desirable although not preferable to person-centered sexuality (Marshall and Suggs, 1971; Beach, 1977). Other cultures create a larger chasm between body and person-centered sexuality, although both are accepted. Western society is in the minority in its condemnation of body-centered sexuality as being below the acceptable level. I should note that there is a gender difference since most all societies accept body-centered sexuality for males, and it is predominately the strongly double-standard cultures which condemn such sexuality for females.

In part, the rejection of body-centered sexuality is rooted in an objection to the traditional view of women as exclusively sexual objects. Thus, some groups, in order to overcome this sexual-object view of females, wish to eliminate body-centered sexuality as evidenced in pornography and elsewhere. Whether this is right or wrong is beside the point—the point is that such a move is not likely to succeed. If changing the cultural image of females is desired, then *adding* other "favorable" female traits such as intelligence, sensitivity, and friendship to the common view of females will be much more effective in breaking down the existing stereotypes. It is notable that males do not often object to female admiration of the male body. This is most likely because males know that there are other things for which they are also valued. Thus, it would seem that the pathway to being treated as an equal is not by denying the undeniable physically attractive body, but rather by stressing the full range of human traits that is possessed by that group in addition to physical beauty. The dominant negative view of body-centered sexuality blinds many Americans to these other alternatives. Of course, there are groups who praise body-centered sexuality, but they are not as often heard from.

Another interesting aspect of our negative view of body-centered sexuality and pornography is that this criterion is almost never used in references to males. Who asks if male porno stars are exploited? Who asks if 16 and 17-year-old males are into prostitution? There is much less furor about such male activities because the concern for female body-centered sexuality is largely a part of the double standard. Therefore, in true double-standard fashion, we primarily talk about how female sexuality can be destructive while ignoring male sexuality. When we have strong ideological commitments, we often are unaware of just what we are overlooking. Many of those who oppose body-centered coitus also oppose the double standard. However, they fail to see how their views are congruent with male-domination viewpoints concerning the greater rights of males to practice body-centered sexuality.

Finally, the strong opposition in America to body-centered coitus is evidenced in our laws on pornography and obscenity. The legal definition is that any book or film which appeals predominantly to prurient interests is thereby pornographic and obscene. That means that if such a book or film is aimed at just giving us sexual excitation, it is illegal. This clearly shows our orientation to sexuality. Sexual pleasure is viewed as something to be condemned unless it is "purified" by love and affection in a person-centered relationship. Some of those who support this ideology against body-centered coitus do not realize the implication of such support for their overall view of sexuality.

SEXUAL NORMALITY

Probably the most obvious place to look for evidence of ideological blinders is in a culture's conception of what is "normal" and "abnormal" sexuality. Let me illustrate this by using the example of premature ejaculation. American males go to therapists for treatment of the "problem" of premature ejaculation. Now what does it mean to be a premature ejaculator? Premature for what? Since an orgasm does occur it is not a case of inability to achieve orgasm but rather achieving it too quickly in terms of some culturally imposed standard. The standard is the orgasm of the female partner—if orgasm occurs so quickly that the female has no opportunity to achieve orgasm in coitus, then the male orgasm is labelled premature. That this view is a specific cultural perspective should be apparent. In cultures that are more male dominant (*e.g.,* South American societies), a man who achieves an orgasm in 20 seconds after insertion might well be admired as virile and strong and no problem would be assumed. It is with the advent of equalitarian sexual ideas that premature ejaculation comes to be viewed as a problem. Thus, the "illness" is not a medical one in the strict sense; rather, it is one created by a particular cultural approach to human sexuality. The problem aspect in premature ejaculation is more analogous to the desire for cosmetic surgery than it is to the desire to treat kidney failure or a slipped disc. In this sense, what is defined as a sexual problem informs us about our cultural values concerning sexuality.

It is even more revealing to examine how premature ejaculation is treated by therapists in America. One very common technique is called the "squeeze technique." The objective is to have the female squeeze the penis to prevent orgasm and to thereby gradually teach the male how to control his orgasmic response. Given our focus on sexual intercourse as the major normal outlet for sexuality, such a technique is not surprising. However, if we think logically of what possibilities are available to deal with the desire not to leave the woman unsatisfied, we realize just how selective our therapy is. For example, one simple way to handle premature ejaculation is to instruct the male to bring the female to orgasm orally or manually. Why is this "solution" not typically utilized by therapists? I would suggest the reason is that our sexual ideology is coitally focused. We believe that coitus is the predominant way to express sexuality and that equal or preferable emphasis on other ways of achieving orgasm is not desirable. Some Freudian analysts still assert that to remove the emphasis from coitus is to encourage what they would label as "abnormal" or "disturbed" psychosexual development (Gadpaille, 1972). In part, this focus on coitus may be historically due to our traditional desire to produce more offspring who can serve as workers or warriors. In part, though, it also reflects a male-derived emphasis on a sexual act which is pleasurable.

Now let us go one step further and examine the nature of what we call sexual intercourse. Clearly, it is an act that is aimed at promoting male orgasm more than female orgasm. By definition sexual intercourse must entail contact with the penis and thereby make male orgasm very likely. Some dictionaries stress the "deposit of sperm" and thereby also point to male orgasm as central. There is no necessary contact in coitus with the female clitoris which would increase the likelihood of female orgasm. Given the types of physical contact involved in sexual intercourse, it is no wonder that females have had more orgasmic problems than males. In addition, sexual intercourse has been "stage directed" by the male. It is the male who is supposed to be the initiator, and at least on first coitus, it is he who decides what positions will be utilized and what sequence of sexual events will occur. Once again, then, the act is set up when the male is ready and to his specifications. Consequently, it is no wonder that more wives than husbands have "headaches." As this situation changes and females become more assertive sexually, I would predict that more husbands may well develop headaches!

But the important conclusion to draw from the above discussion of sexual intercourse is that the act which in Western cultures has become the ultimate sexual act is a male-controlled and male orgasm-oriented act and thus fits with the male dominance which is prevalent in the culture. Therefore, it is no surprise that our therapy is aimed at integrating male orgasm with female orgasm, especially in coitus, for that is the preferred sexual act. Once again, our cultural sexual ideology is writ large in the way we define problems and also in the way we seek to resolve them.

On this same topic of normality let us examine our attitudes toward homosexuality. In a 1980 poll (NORC, 1980), approximately 70 percent of adult Americans stated that homosexuality was "always wrong." Again, we can assert that our focus on heterosexual coitus is also involved in this judgment. A homosexual act clearly does not involve heterosexual coitus and in addition it involves two people of the same gender—a second violation of our sexual ideology. One can also discern here the American view of sexuality as being a very powerful force and one to be feared. This comes through in our view which seems to assert that homosexuality is virtually "infectious." If we have too much contact with a homosexual or allow a homosexual to talk to our children, then we may spread the homosexual's "ailment." This viewpoint not only displays our view of sexuality as overpowering but it also exhibits our lack of confidence in our commitment to heterosexuality. We are frightened that our heterosexuality can be changed if homosexuals are given any degree of public acceptance. The repeal of some equal treatment laws for homosexuals which has occurred in Florida and Minnesota is testimony to precisely this sort of viewpoint.

Again, our view of normality seems based upon a view of heterosexual coitus as the prime "normal" state for adults. This is a view that Freud expressed in his emphasis upon the genital stage of development (Money and Musaph, 1977). Freud may well have been strongly influenced by Western culture just as we are today. However, when we examine our primate cousins, we find homosexuality to be quite common, although virtually never a preferred form of sexuality. The learned aspect of homosexuality in other primates can be seen in the recent findings that monkeys raised with siblings of only one sex display more homosexual behavior than monkeys raised with siblings of both sexes (IASR, 1980). Looking at other cultures, we find homosexuality frequently accepted. Thus, it is difficult for us to scientifically label such behavior as necessarily "disturbed" or "abnormal" (Beach, 1977). It would seem that such behavior is in our genetic line (other primates) and that it can be easily learned and accepted in other cultural settings. This should cause us to question the medical basis for calling it abnormal. However, there is an ideological basis for labelling homosexuality as abnormal. This basis involves our allegiance to heterosexual coitus as the standard for all to abide by, but this is hardly a medical basis. The moral position that homosexuality is abnormal is often passed off as being founded on sexual "health" notions, but as I have briefly noted above, there is no convincing scientific base for such a viewpoint (Bell and Weinberg, 1978; Reiss, 1980a). I should add here that there are many psychiatrists who would not view homosexuality as an abnormality but there are also many who do, and the public view, though somewhat more tolerant today, is still quite critical. The removal of homosexuality from the American Psychiatric Association's list of pathologies in 1973 should not be taken as proof that most all psychiatrists view homosexuality as a normal variation.

Our concepts of normality, health, and abnormality seem heavily influenced by our sexual ideology. Further sociological analysis can detail this state of affairs and afford us some additional perspective on ourselves that otherwise would be lacking. We should remember that in the 19th century many medical doctors were performing clitoridectomies on women who were "too" sexually responsive. This was done in the interests of "sexual health," as they then defined it (Comfort, 1967). We do not perform these operations today but there are scores of American wives who have recently undergone surgery, performed by a doctor in Dayton, Ohio, to redesign the coital area so that the clitoris is more easily contacted by the penis in the traditional male-above position (IASR, 1977). Here, again, we have dramatic evidence of the influence of our culture, not only on our mental concepts, but on our bodies also. The ideological dictates of a culture can pressure our bodies, as well as our acts and thoughts, toward conformity.

SEXUAL HISTORY

If our sexual ideology affects our conceptions of normality and reality in so many ways, then surely it must affect our conception of our sexual past. There is still in America a widespread belief that at sometime in our past we lived in a society in which most young people remained virginal until they married and then learned about sexuality in the marital bed and remained faithful to each other until death did part them. The Puritan period is often mentioned as one such time. But Arthur Calhoun's (1945) classic work indicates that nonvirginity was rather common during the end of the Puritan period in the 18th century. For example, in one church in Groton, Massachusetts, he reports that one third of the brides married confessed fornication to their minister. The nonvirginity rate was likely higher than this for it was predominantly pregnant brides who confessed fornication so that their babies might be accepted for baptism. Those nonvirgins who were not pregnant would not be under such pressure to confess. This sort of situation is not unusual historically. I have read the anthropological literature extensively in search for a culture in which males reach physical maturity (say, age 21) with the majority of them virginal. I have yet to find such a culture anywhere in the world at any time in history. Now, there may be a few such cultures that I have missed but surely they are quite rare.

The reasons for male nonvirginity are not difficult to discern. Males are normatively dominant in almost every society that has ever existed. This means that virtually all of our sexual codes are established by males. The reasons for this history of male dominance can only be speculated upon but it may be due to the fact that during our two million years on this planet we have been hunters and gatherers for all but the last 12,000 years. Male physical strength must have given males an advantage in such a setting and the tie to newborn infants via nursing must have weakened the competition from females. Such male dominance seems to have been strengthened in agricultural societies (Gough, 1971) but has been weakening in the industrial societies which began to appear approximately 200 years ago.

When a group in power sets up a code, it is set to their felt advantage. Accordingly, males set up a sexual code which allowed themselves to enjoy sexuality under a wide variety of conditions: premaritally, maritally, and extramaritally. But they also set up a provision that restricted their wives and daughters from much of the sexual enjoyment they decreed for themselves. This basic contradiction between male freedom and female restrictions is at the heart of the explanation of why human sexuality has been secretive and guilt ridden. If wives and daughters cannot engage in premarital or extramarital sexuality, then the majority of possible partners for males are eliminated. One source of female partners would be to violate some weaker group of males and take their wives and daughters or set up a class of prostitutes composed of females whose kinship ties have in some way been broken. But such patchwork solutions do not resolve the basic contradiction inherent in allowing males more sexual rights than females and there still are many males violating the restrictions on sexuality with in-group wives and daughters. This occurrence forces secrecy on sexuality and creates guilt feelings concerning the violation of the double-standard restrictions on wives and daughters. It is no wonder, then, that sexuality, particularly in the West, has come down to the 20th century with strong guilt, secrecy, and psychological qualms woven into its basic fabric.

Over the centuries, Western culture has worked out a modification of the traditional double standard by building up the cult of romantic love. Sexuality has indeed been viewed as negative behavior, but if it is done for the sake of a great love feeling, then perhaps the negative aspect in it can be exorcised by the goodness in love. Thus, love has become the great justifier and purifier of sexuality (Reiss, 1960; 1967). Of course, males have had cultural support for their sexuality so the love justification has been predominantly a female belief. For centuries sexuality which involves love has been viewed as more acceptable, even if not fully acceptable, for premarital couples. In fact, the Groton, Massachusetts data discussed above is testimony to the fact that 200 years ago couples were commonly engaging in sexual intercourse before marriage. What acceptance there was then of premarital coitus was in good measure a result of the fact that it occurred after a declaration of love and intention to marry.

We are still a double-standard culture (Reiss, 1980a). One illustration of this occurred in a sociologist's (Pepper Schwartz) class at the University of Washington. She asked her class a question about how many premarital sexual partners it was proper to have. Those who approved of premarital intercourse still allowed males to have many more sexual partners than they allowed for females. This is a modification of the traditional double standard, but there still are two codes: one to judge females and one to judge males, and that is the essence of any double standard.

Basically, then, our historical background, as far as actual behavior and operational norms go, is one of the double standard and not one of abstinence. Henry Kissinger was correct about the relation of power to sexuality. Power does have a way of legitimizing sexual rights and males have had greater power in virtually all societies. We can observe the relation of power to sexuality by noting that public opinion is much harsher when a black male rapes a white female than when a white male rapes a black female (LaFree, 1980). Equality in sexual rights for males and females will help achieve greater gender equality in other areas of life. Conversely, equality in overall gender roles is also very helpful in creating equality in sexual relations. We do not remove our social positions when we take off our clothes even though there are moments in sexual relations when our social positions are much less in focus than our physical position.

IDEOLOGIES: OLD AND NEW

The five areas I have briefly explored in this search for our basic sexual ideologies surely do not exhaust those that can be explored nor is the evidence fully in on even these five areas. The purpose of this paper is merely to open up such an exploration, not to complete it. I will now derive some basic ideological tenets from the above examination of ideologies and connect them with what I believe are the two major sexual ideologies of our day. I will first derive tenets that are part of what I shall call our Traditional-Romantic Ideology.

First and most fundamental to the Traditional-Romantic Ideology is the belief in the primacy and rightfulness of the double standard. Most explicitly, this expresses itself in the belief that gender roles should be segregated and distinct with the male role clearly being the dominant one. I would state this ideological tenet as:

1. Gender roles should be distinct and interdependent, with the male gender role as dominant.

This tenet underlies many of the traditional positions taken on the five controversial areas we have examined, but it is most central to our discussion of genetic sex differences.

A second tenet of the Traditional-Romantic Ideology is that body-centered sexuality is of lowest worth, particularly for females. This can be simply stated as:

IRA L. REISS

2. Body-centered sexuality is to be avoided by females.

This tenet appeared most clearly in our earlier examination of sexual exploitation and pornography.

Sexuality as a very powerful emotion and one to be feared was a theme we mentioned in the discussion of sexual normality. Here, too, there is a double standard aspect since the belief usually asserts that males are more driven by such sexual forces and that females best be careful to avoid males when they are in such states of possession. The third tenet of the Traditional-Romantic Ideology then would be:

3. Sexuality is a very powerful emotion and one that should be particularly feared by females.

Also in our discussion of sexual normality we pointed out how coitally centered and male dominated our sexual ideology was. So our fourth tenet would be:

4. The major goal of sexuality is heterosexual coitus and that is where the man's focus should be placed.

Here, too, there is double-standard input because according to the Traditional-Romantic perspective such a goal is considered proper for males to feel and for females to accept.

The fifth and last tenet of the Traditional-Romantic Ideology concerns the relation of love and guilt to sexuality. Sexuality, because it violates the sexual prohibition for wives and daughters, entails guilt feelings. Females in particular have devised, as a partial justification for sexual behavior, the great power and value of romantic love. While men are viewed as driven by the power of lust, women are viewed as driven by the power of love. Love, at least in part, redeems and explains the female interest in sexuality. So the fifth tenet is:

5. Love redeems sexuality from its guilt, particularly for females.

We discussed the evidence for this tenet in our comments on historical views of sexuality.

The major theme running through all five of these ideological tenets of the Traditional-Romantic view of sexuality is the double standard. Male dominance is explicitly present in each tenet. These five tenets could be applied with reasonable accuracy to most cultures in the Western world although some modifications would need to be made for differences in the Mediterranean and Scandinavian subgroupings (Bourguignon, 1980; Reiss, 1980b). Many people in the Western world lack awareness of what adherence to these beliefs force them to include and exclude from their life styles. One purpose of this paper is to increase such awareness.

The 20th century has witnessed a challenge to these ideological beliefs. One of the reasons why it is now easier to become aware of the Traditional-

Romantic Ideology in sexuality is that there is a new ideology that has set up opposing tenets. The new ideology is one I shall call the Modern-Naturalistic Ideology and it directly challenges each of the five tenets listed above.

In order to display the key differences, I will list below the five alternative tenets that the Modern-Naturalistic view would assert as part of its ideology:

1. Gender roles should be similar for males and females and should promote equalitarian participation in the society.
2. Body-centered sexuality is of less worth than person-centered sexuality, but it still has a positive value for both genders.
3. One's sexual emotions are strong but are manageable, by both males and females, in the same way as are other basic emotions.
4. The major goals of sexuality are physical pleasure and psychological intimacy in a variety of sexual acts and this is so of both genders.
5. A wide range of sexuality should be accepted without guilt by both genders providing it does not involve force or fraud.

The basic underlying principle in this newer ideology is the equalitarian relationship of males and females. There is relatedly a naturalistic view of sexuality and of its acceptability. The expression of sexuality is considered a good and proper part of much of human social life. Knowing what we know about equalitarian gender trends throughout this century, we as sociologists could have predicted that the Traditional-Romantic Ideology would be challenged by the Modern-Naturalistic Ideology. Let it be explicit that the newer ideology is based upon a fundamental way of thinking—most obviously, it eliminates the older ideological ways. Also, the newer ideology is based upon a fundamental moral view of the genders which assumes equality. One can easily deduce the different ways that an adherent of the Modern-Naturalistic Ideology and an adherent of the Traditional-Romantic Ideology would evaluate the issues of abortion, genetic differences, exploitation and pornography, sexual normality, and our sexual past. What we are witnessing in the 1980s in America in reference to sexual issues can be interpreted as fundamentally a clash of these two basic ideologies regarding human sexuality.

It should be clear that many people today are in transition and so they will adhere to elements of both the old and the new sexual ideologies. Furthermore, there are others who will display tenets which have not been explored in this paper. But many of the essentials of the two dominant ideologies have been outlined and this should be helpful in understanding our sexual customs.

Let us briefly look at the Bendix Corporation case involving the promotion of Mary Cunningham as one illustration of our sexual ideologies. Such a single case can only be illustrative, but I do believe it is instructive regarding our current ideology. I will not try to deal with the morality of the case or with the controversy about it. Rather, I will examine how the mass media handled this case and what that tells us about our sexual ideology. This story appeared in our mass media during October of 1980 and involved the suggested promotion

IRA L. REISS

in September, 1980 of Mary Cunningham to Vice President for Strategic Planning at Bendix. The promotion was put forth by her boss, Chief Executive William Agee. Rumors spread that Agee and Cunningham were sexually involved and that her promotion should therefore be denied. In October, 1980, she resigned from Bendix. From the ideological point of view several things are interesting in this case. First, almost all the news media coverage centered around the one question of whether Cunningham and Agee were sleeping together. The assumption appeared to be that if they were sexually involved then it was a foregone conclusion that her promotion should be denied. This popular view involves several tenets of the Traditional-Romantic sexual ideology. It stresses the all-powerful nature of the sexual emotion assuming that sexual relations will likely occur when a man and woman are together in business and, furthermore, such an emotion will dominate the evaluation of the woman for promotion. Also involved in many of the statements was the amazement that Cunningham could really be ready for such a promotion in just one year. Agee himself had been a "boy wonder" of Bendix and moved up in rank at a very fast pace without any questions being raised. Thus, the tenets concerning the separate treatment of each gender and the dominance of males also enter into the media coverage. Frequently a promotion in business is put forth by a man who is a close friend of the man up for promotion. Seldom is that situation judged as improper. Here, again, the powerful view of sexuality is much more distorting than friendship and the accepted dominance of males is visible in this interpretation of reality.

From a broader perspective one could have asked if Cunningham was qualified for promotion. The available evidence cited in the press indicated that she was thought to be qualified by those who examined her record. The conflict over her promotion could have been handled by having an outside impartial committee evaluate her qualifications for promotion. Such a routine procedure could avoid a favoritism charge in such cases. Yet no article that I read mentioned such a suggestion for future use in business or for this case. This was so, I believe, because in the popular press the focus was on the sexual aspects of the case. The key issue clearly seemed to be the sexual relations of Cunningham and Agee.

The Modern-Naturalistic Ideology asserts that sexual emotions are manageable, gender roles should be equal, and sexuality is generally acceptable, and it would have led to a different public treatment of the issue in the media. Of course, both ideologies express value judgments and neither is scientifically "better," but the point I am making here is that the predominance of the Traditional-Romantic Ideology in the public handling of the Cunningham case indicates that the newer ideology, although an increasingly popular one, is not the dominant position. The treatment of this case also shows how our ideology determines what we see as the "crucial issues" in any social situation involving sexuality. Of course, this is but one case, but the similarity in the mass media treatment was impressive. It would be valuable to do more careful analysis of a variety of such instances to develop a more considered judgment as to the relative use of our two major ideologies in the mass media.

CONCLUSIONS

The ways in which our sexual ideologies blind us to the totality of choices and interpretations has been the central topic of this paper. I have conceptualized the specific tenets of the two major ideologies as an aid to future conceptualization in this area. But the most important conclusion to be drawn from this analysis is that social science research can help us immensely in understanding the basic assumptions and values upon which we base our sexual life styles. Knowledge of such basic ideological elements will give us an excellent predictive base and will also provide clinicians and individuals with information that can help them in their work and in their personal lives.

In just the last several years, the evidence has mounted that the conservative forces in this country have organized to become an effective force, particularly in the religious and political spheres. Some have taken this as a sign that the society is moving to the "right." However, polls have consistently indicated very little change in the proportion of people who favor various positions on abortion, premarital sexuality, pornography, etc. (Reiss, 1980a). What has happened is that the conservative forces have organized more effectively and thereby increased their power if not their numbers. The signs are clear that the "left wing" forces are organizing more effectively now and that the 1980s will reverberate with the sounds of conservative-liberal battles over many sexual issues. It is precisely because of this recent organization that ideologies have become more prominent and the ability to obtain a nonideological view of human sexuality has accordingly decreased. This is precisely the time when a scientific perspective can add clarity and help define the issues.

Adherents to both major ideologies make claims to scientific support for specific aspects of the various positions they take. It is time that social scientists get off the sidelines and speak to the scientific issues involved in terms of what research has been done and in terms of our theoretical understanding of the situation. If we remain silent, then we will have given up our rightful claim to explain human social behavior even in areas as emotionally charged as sexuality. Of course, science cannot settle which ideology is "best" but it can deal with scientific questions such as genetic differences between the sexes, consequences of aborting or not aborting, meanings and uses of terms like normality and exploitation, and knowledge of our past sexual customs. Sociology and other social sciences offer a comprehensive perspective on the competing ideologies and an overview of the social scene that is not available elsewhere.

I have tried to show some ways in which sociology can address the issues raised in our ideologies. My attempt has been to encourage future work, for, admittedly, I have not fully explored all the issues raised nor has there always been full evidence available and, thus, some of my observations surely require additional examination. Finally, it should be clear that we will never have a society without ideologies, but we can have our ideologies tempered and examined by our social sciences.

Of course, as members of our society, we are also strongly emotionally committed to ideological positions of our own and this may make us hesitate to do anything that might weaken the successful outcomes of our private

IRA L. REISS

ideologies. Also, some may fear being attacked by those whose ideological beliefs are brought under scrutiny. But if the value of scientific inquiry is to prevail, then we need to pursue a scientific understanding of these private ideologies that we all possess. In this paper, I stress the value of following the *ideology* of science. Surely science, too, is based on ideological tenets regarding the nature of the world and the value of knowing it scientifically. Science, too, must be chosen on faith as one source for understanding the nature of the world. Nevertheless, in a time of ideological conflict, the ideology of science can serve as a predominant means of gaining understanding of our sexual ideologies and their place in our lives today. Social science can offer a perspective that is missing in the two dominant ideologies that are now grappling with each other on our national stage.

REFERENCES

Beach, F. A. (ed.) 1977 *Human sexuality in four perspectives*. Baltimore: Johns Hopkins University Press.

Bell, A. P., and M. S. Weinberg 1978 *Homosexualities*. New York: Simon and Schuster.

Bourguignon, E. (ed.) 1980 *A world of women*. New York: Praeger.

Brown, W. B., P. M. Monti, and D. P. Corrineau 1978 Serum testosterone and sexual activity and interest in men. *Archives of Sexual Behavior* 7 (March):97–103.

Calhoun, A. W. 1945 *A social history of the American family* (3 vols.). New York: Barnes and Noble Books.

CBS-New York Times 1980 August 1980 News Poll. Cited in Minneapolis Tribune. August 24, 1980, p. 9A.

Chappell, D., R. Geis, and G. Geis (eds.) 1977 *Forcible rape*. New York: Columbia University Press.

Commission on Obscenity and Pornography 1970 *The Report of the Commission on Obscenity and Pornography*. Washington, D.C.: Government Printing Office.

Donnerstein, E., M. Donnerstein, and R. Evans 1975 Erotic stimuli and aggression: Facilitation or Inhibition? *Journal of Personality and Social Psychology* 32:237–44.

Donnerstein, E. 1980 Aggressive erotica and violence against women. *Journal of Personality and Social Psychology* 39 (August):269–77.

Gadpaille, W. J. 1972 Research into the physiology of maleness and femaleness. *Archives of General Psychiatry* 26 (March):193–206.

Gough, K. E. 1971 The origins of the family. *Journal of Marriage and the Family* 33 (November):760–70.

Granberg, D., and B. W. Granberg 1980 Abortion attitudes: 1965–1980: Trends and determinants. *Family Planning Perspectives* 12 (September/October):250–61.

Groth, A. N. 1979 *Men who rape: The psychology of the offender*. New York: Plenum.

IASR, International Academy of Sex Researchers 1977 Paper presented by J. C. Burt at the Annual Meeting in Bloomington, Indiana.

    1980   Paper presented by D. Goldfoot of the University of Wisconsin (Madison) at the Annual Meeting in Tucson, Arizona.

LaFree, G. D. 1980 The effect of sexual statification by race on official reactions to rape. *American Sociological Review* 45 (October):842–54.

Maccoby, E. E., and C. Jacklin 1974 *The psychology of sex differences*. Stanford: Stanford University Press.

Malamuth, N. M., and B. Spinner 1980 A longitudinal content analysis of sexual violence in the best-selling erotic magazines. *Journal of Sex Research* 16 (August):226–37.

Marshal, D. S., and R. C. Suggs 1971 *Human sexual behavior*. New York: Basic Books.

Marx, K., and F. Engels 1962 *Marx and Engels: Selected Works* (Vol. 1). Moscow: Foreign Languages Publishing House.

Minneapolis Tribune 1980 August 24, 1980, p. 9A.

Money, J., and A. Ehrhardt 1972 *Man and woman, boy and girl*. Baltimore: Johns Hopkins University Press.

Money, J., and H. Musaph (eds.) 1977 *Handbook of sexology*. New York: Elsevier Press.

National Opinion Research Center (NORC) 1980 *General social survey*. Chicago: University of Chicago Press.

Reiss, I. L. 1960 *Premarital sexual standards in America*. New York: Macmillan.

    1967   *The social context of premarital sexual permissiveness*. New York: Holt, Rinehart and Winston.

    1980a   *Family systems in America*, 3d ed. New York: Holt, Rinehart and Winston.

    1980b   Sexual customs in Sweden and America: An analysis and interpretation." In *Research on the interweave of social roles: women and men*, ed. by H. Lopata. Greenwich, Conn.: JAI Press.

Schwartz, M. F., R. C. Kolodny, and W. H. Masters 1980 Plasma testosterone levels of sexually functional and dysfunctional men. *Archives of Sexual Behavior* 9 (October):355–66.

Walfish, S., and M. Myerson 1980 Sex role identity and attitudes toward sexuality. *Archives of Sexual Behavior* 9 (June):199–205.

9 *Sexual Response and Gender Roles*

Shirley Radlove

STUDY QUESTIONS

1. What are the three sexual response systems and their impacts?

2. Why does Radlove suggest androgyny as an alternative?

In the movie *Sleeper*, Miles Monroe (Woody Allen), part-owner of the Happy Carrot Health Food Restaurant in Greenwich Village, has a major problem. In 1973 he went to the hospital for a minor ulcer operation, but something went wrong. So he was wrapped in aluminum foil and frozen (as hard as a South African lobster tail), only to wake up 200 years later, defrosted, in a new world.

Miles is the first to admit to the inhabitants of this advanced new world that he is an uncurable coward. As he himself points out, "I was once beaten up by Quakers." The world in which Miles finds himself is thus rather alarming to him—a "worst dream come true," you might say. He comes across chickens that are 12 feet tall and bananas as big and as long as canoes. There are robot servants and robot dogs, and at the end of a dinner party, a hostess comments, "I think we should have had group sex but there weren't enough people." Miles is shocked to learn that group sex consists of nothing more than passing around a small crystal ball from guest to guest.

It seems apparent that in this new society all the men are impotent and all the women are frigid. What has evolved is a very simple and efficient "orgasm machine" (a tall contraption called an Orgasmitron) used for automatic (and solo) sexual release. The Orgasmitrons look like white metal shower stalls big enough for one person to enter, climax, and exit—all in the space of about 30 seconds. There is an Orgasmitron available in the home of almost every well-to-do person in this new world. When Luna (Diane Keaton), a beautiful

Source: Shirley Radlove, "Sexual Response and Gender Roles." In *Changing Boundaries*, E. R. Algeier & N. B. McCormick (eds.). Palo Alto: Mayfield Publishing, 1983, pp. 87–105. Reprinted by permission.

but slightly flaky right-wing poet, tells Miles that she earned her Ph.D. in oral sex, it is clear to the film audience that she studied something as potentially unnecessary and as dead as ancient Greek.*

In Woody Allen's futuristic fantasy of a society where sexual release is fully automated and conveniently relegated to a mechanical contrivance called an "Orgasmitron," and group sex is literally a ball but orgasm is always achieved solo, something seems definitely awry. In this new world rather helpless females are still the standard model of womanliness, and sexual behavior between consenting adults has apparently become obsolete.

Why might the inhabitants of such a new world opt to reject traditional concepts of sexual behavior? Perhaps they felt there were simply too many complex and puzzling problems associated with traditional sex.

For example, why do men in our society, of whom the traditional gender role requires continuous demonstrations of strength, power, and control, often find themselves totally unable to fend off an oncoming orgasm? Why are women, who are supposed to have the biological potential to be multiorgasmic, often not orgasmic at all? Why do men and women seem to have so many problems, concerns, and difficulties in the area of sexual behavior?

Sexual response is supposed to be a healthy, pleasurable, natural phenomenon. Quite often, however, something intervenes, creating barriers and obstacles to this natural act. In this chapter, I focus on some of these intervening variables, including gender-role norms, stereotypes, attitudes, and self-concepts. The emphasis will be on how these gender-role issues can interfere with sexual behavior and cause problems in sexual response.

First, I describe the physiological components of sexual response and use this material to show that men and women are quite similar in their physiological response to sexual stimulation. This provides a foundation for understanding the differences in male and female sexual response in terms of gender-related issues and attitudes.

Second, I consider three overlapping systems involved in effective and healthy sexual functioning. Disruptive influences in any or all of these systems can result in a wide array of sexual difficulties. I define some of these difficulties in relation to sexual attitudes and gender-role norms covered in the third section of the chapter.

Third, in the last section I offer alternatives and suggestions for change. I look at some behaviors related to androgyny, describe some ways to effect personal change, and consider how to approach the resolution of sexual problems.

Of course, all this material will immediately become obsolete with the invention of an Orgasmitron. Should this come to pass, I suggest that you remember to check your circuits periodically, replace worn fuses, thank Woody Allen, and make sure your voltage is always properly regulated.

---

*Adapted from Vincent Canby's review of Woody Allen's film *Sleeper, New York Times*, December 18, 1973.

THE PHYSIOLOGICAL COMPONENTS OF SEXUAL RESPONSE: MASTERS AND JOHNSON'S FINDINGS

Prior to the publication of *Human Sexual Response* by Masters and Johnson (1966), our knowledge of the physiological components of human sexual response and potential was sketchy, at best. Many small studies and a few major studies (for example, Kinsey et al., 1948, 1953; Terman, 1951), had been conducted. However, these were mainly survey studies of sexual attitudes and reported behaviors. That is, they described what people said they did, not what they were observed to do. Research in the area was not only costly but was typically hampered by narrow attitudes, embarrassment, and heated controversy. Sexual behavior was not considered a respectable topic for study, and those who did try to study it met with strong resistance.

As a result, few scientists had the definitive information badly needed and repeatedly sought by direct-service health professionals (physicians, psychologists, and social workers) who were typically called on for advice and treatment of sexual concerns.

According to gynecologist William H. Masters (Tom Snyder television interview, 1975), physicians were being asked the same unanswerable questions over and over again by their female patients:

"Am I *supposed* to have orgasms?"

"I've never had an orgasm; is there something wrong with me?"

"Will I be more sexually satisfied after my child is born?"

"How can my husband control himself longer when we're having sex?"

Responsible physicians could not answer. Science had not supplied the answers. Physicians fielded these and many other questions as best they could, but their bottom-line responses had to be "I just don't know. No one knows—the research is just not in yet."

In 1954, Dr. Masters began an intensive 10-year investigation of the anatomy and physiology of human sexual response. His results were published in 1966, a definitive and rather astonishing contribution to our knowledge of human sexual response. From a physiological standpoint, the research was apparently in.

The Sexual Response Cycle

In their report of the results, Masters and his co-researcher Virginia Johnson (1966) described four phases of human physiological response to effective sexual stimuli. These phases were (1) excitement, (2) plateau, (3) orgasm, and (4) resolution.

Excitement Phase. In the male, the first physiological responses to sexual stimulation are the swelling and erection of the penis and partial elevation of the testes. Female excitement results in the production of vaginal lubrication, accompanied by clitoral swelling. The clitoris gets longer, and the vagina increases in width and length.

Plateau Phase. With continued sexual stimulation, the circumference of the head (coronal ridge) of the penis increases. The testes become 50 percent larger than they are in their unstimulated state. In the female, the clitoris begins to withdraw into its hood, and there is a further increase in the width and depth of the vagina. Extreme swelling can be seen in the lips of the vulva.

Orgasmic Phase. In the male, this phase is characterized by three or four contractions of the entire length of the urethra, at 0.8-second intervals. This is followed by several seconds of minor contractions, which are lower in frequency and expulsive force. The female experiences three to six intense contractions of the outer third of the vagina, at 0.8-second intervals, followed by several seconds of minor contractions, also reduced in frequency and intensity.

Resolution Phase. After orgasm, the male's penis begins a rapid loss of swelling and erection. This is followed by a slower shrinking of the penis until it returns to its normal state. In the female, the clitoris returns to its normal position, followed by a slower reduction in size and level of swelling.

Similarities in the Sexual Responses of Men and Women

Throughout their lengthy report of the results just reviewed, Masters and Johnson emphasized the similarities rather than the differences in male and female sexual response. They did report one striking difference between men and women: women seemed to have a unique biological capability for multiple orgasm.

After her initial orgasm, a woman can immediately experience additional orgasms as long as effective stimulation continues and until the woman chooses to stop or becomes exhausted. Men, on the other hand, were said to experience a refractory period: an interval of time (approximately 30 minutes), after ejaculation, during which a man could not return to orgasmic levels of response. Thus, researchers thought men were not multiorgasmic.

More recent research, however, has shown that males too, may have a biological capability for multiple orgasms. Robbins and Jensen (1978) found that men who had taught themselves to be orgasmic without ejaculating could return to repeated orgasms with the same speed and facility observed in women. It was only after these men chose to have an orgasm accompanied by ejaculation that they experienced the refractory period noted by Masters and Johnson (1966).

Apparently, even where the issue of multiple orgasm is concerned, men and women are similar in their sexual response. If there is any remaining difference between the sexes, is it perhaps that only men can ejaculate and women cannot? There is new evidence indicating that such an assumption is unwarranted.

In a series of studies concerning ejaculation in women, researchers noted that women have a biological capability for ejaculation (Addiego et al., 1981;

Belzer, 1981; Perry & Whipple, 1981). In women, orgasm may be accompanied by an expulsion of liquid from the urethra. Chemical analysis indicates that it is not urine. Interestingly, Belzer (1981) hypothesized that orgasm accompanied by ejaculation in women may also be followed by a temporary inability to be multiorgasmic—a refractory period, as in men.

Multiple orgasm in males and ejaculation in females are behaviors that are not currently found with great frequency in the population (Robbins & Jensen, 1978; Perry & Whipple, 1981). They do exist, however, as sexual behaviors that can be developed through learning. Although Masters and Johnson (1966) did not observe male multiple orgasm and female ejaculation in their research subjects, it is doubtful these behaviors would have been researched without their initial impetus. In short, the concept of similarity between the sexes had valuable impact on the scientific community.

The Impact of Masters and Johnson's Research

Human Sexual Response was written for physicians and scientists, in terms that few laypeople would ordinarily find captivating. It was not long, however, before journalists began translating the material into popular language, and it began to appear in a number of popular magazines and newspaper articles, and as a topic on television interviews. For instance, Tom Snyder interviewed Masters and Johnson and featured their findings on one of his television programs in 1975.

In a questionnaire designed for a couples sexual communication workshop (Radlove, 1979), men and women were asked if they had read the results of Masters and Johnson's research or other articles describing their work, and if so, whether it had any impact on their attitudes, behavior, or significant relationships. Many of the individuals who shared their insights and experiences indicated that the Masters and Johnson data did indeed have an impact on them.

Women, it seemed, were accorded a new physiological status (sexually speaking). Those who had never been orgasmic, or had never given much thought to their sexual selves, now sought sexual fulfillment from their partners. Others, who worried whether or not their technique for achieving orgasm was legitimate, took comfort in Masters and Johnson's conclusion that orgasms were the same, no matter how achieved. Specifically, there was a serious challenge to the Freudian assumption that women had two kinds of orgasms (see Deutsch, 1944, 1945). The new research seemed to refute the existence of two separate types of female orgasms, a vaginal orgasm reached without clitoral stimulation by sexual intercourse alone and a clitoral orgasm reached when a partner or the woman herself stimulated the clitoris directly. Women's feelings about their sexual functioning improved when they were no longer told that needing clitoral stimulation for orgasmic release was somehow less mature and feminine than achieving orgasm through sexual intercourse (Hite, 1976; Kaplan, 1974).

The new doctrines about sexuality liberated many women, but it was not all "roses." Many men, feeling threatened by the new message, found their own sexual problems exacerbated. Some who had earlier functioned effectively now seemed to falter under the pressure to provide their partner with multiple orgasms. Old "shoulds" were replaced by new ones; people continued to be anxious about their sexual adequacy.

The major question raised by Masters and Johnson was "Why do so many more women than men suffer from sexual dysfunction? If there is no longer a physiological and/or anatomical rationale for this, what is the problem?"

In 1970, Masters and Johnson published another book describing their work with sexually dysfunctional men and women. Their book was not written for the layperson, and, although it did seem to create some stir among the general population, it offered no easy solutions. It did, however, provide repeated and compelling indications that sexual problems in both men and women could best be understood in terms of disruptive influences on one or more of three overlapping systems involved in sexual response.

THREE SEXUAL RESPONSE SYSTEMS

Each person has three sexual response systems. The *biophysical system*, based on our biological capacity to respond to sexual stimulation, determines the physiological limits of sexual response. The *psychosocial system*, based on the culture's sexual scripts for appropriate male and female sexual behavior, and the *sexual value system*, an individual's unique set of beliefs about sexuality, are equally important. People are not naturally sexual. They must learn scripts that tell them how to have sex, who to have it with, and even the extent to which they are allowed to take advantage of their biophysical capacity for responsiveness (Gagnon & Simon, 1973; Gagnon, 1977).

The Biophysical System

The biophysical system involves the body's natural capacity to respond to sexual stimulation. It includes the genitals, the internal sex organs, the nervous system, the circulatory system, and every physiological structure and process involved in sexual response. This system tends to be dominant. That is, it is not easily disrupted or wiped out by negative influences such as anger or resentment toward one's partner or the attitude that sexual response or excitement is bad or dirty. However, negative attitudes and beliefs can partially diminish the body's natural tendency to respond to sexual stimulation. For example, a woman may experience high levels of physiological tension and excitement during masturbation or intercourse. But she may not be orgasmic if she is frightened or ashamed by the intensity of her sexual response.

The Psychosocial System

The psychosocial system involves the learned and internalized messages and myths transmitted to men and women by the culture. For example, men receive permission to value and explore their sexual feelings by our society, while women are taught to conceal their sexual feelings and remain naive. Men are directed to increase their sexual knowledge and sexual performance skills via masturbation and/or multiple-partner experience, while women are advised to avoid sexual self-exploration and multiple-partner experience lest they be labeled oversexed or promiscuous. In addition, although the culture dimly approves when men's sexual tensions find outlet in casual sex, the resolution of women's sexual tensions are permitted only in the context of love, affection, commitment, and/or movieland romanticism.

The psychosocial system—all the culturally imposed limitations to free-flowing biophysical response—does not automatically create sexual problems for men and women. Problems occur, however, when the realities of individual experience fall short of cultural ideals. For example, if a man has not fully developed his sexual skill and sexual technique, it is unlikely that he will be able to satisfy appropriately and effectively a naive and inexperienced woman who is completely dependent on him for sexual direction. Similarly, if a woman ignores the cultural directive to remain sexually unsophisticated until romantically committed and/or married, she may find that her partner responds to her sexual expertise with erectile difficulties grounded in his perception of her as loose or immoral.

The Sexual Value System

The sexual value system involves the individual's sexual attitudes and beliefs. It consists of family attitudes and personal learning beyond that which is generally transmitted by the culture at large. For example, although the culture may approve and promote sexual skill building via exploration of the male's sexuality, an individual man's religious beliefs may be such that he prefers to remain sexually inexperienced prior to marriage.

North American culture imposes many restrictions as to what sexual behaviors are more appropriate for women or for men. It does not, however, advance the notion that sex is dirty, sinful, or painful for either gender. These negative perceptions are learned in a more personal context. A woman who is raped, for example, may come to devalue sex as a painful and frightening experience. Similarly, men and women whose religion has taught them that masturbation and any other nonreproductive sexual activity is dirty or sinful may bury their natural potential for sexual response and may associate sex with guilt and shame. Such individuals would be said to have a negative sexual value system.

In sum, although men and women are quite similar in their biophysical potential for sexual response, they tend to be dissimilar with regard to their cultural learning of sexual behavior norms. They may also differ greatly (from each other as well as the culture at large) in their sexual value system—the degree to which they value or devalue sexuality. For women, the available research seems to show that cultural learning of feminine role behaviors may be implicated in female sexual problems. In men, sexual problems seem to be more often related to negative sexual values than to a stereotypic masculine role.

GENDER-ROLE AND SEXUAL PROBLEMS IN WOMEN

Statistics compiled by Kinsey and his colleagues (1953) and by Fisher (1973) suggested that approximately 60 percent of North American women have orgasms very rarely or not at all, during sexual intercourse. The currently held belief (for example, see Masters & Johnson, 1970; Kaplan, 1974) is that women seldom get or seek the sexual stimulation they need in order to reach orgasm. Orgasmic dysfunction in females is seldom associated with emotional disturbance, negative sexual attitudes, physiological problems, and/or anatomical abnormalities (Cooper, 1969; Fisher, 1973; Masters & Johnson, 1966; Pomeroy, 1965; Raboch & Bartak, 1968; Radlove, 1977; Winokur, Guze, & Pfeiffer, 1959).

However, many research clues suggest that identification with the traditional feminine role may be related to women's reluctance to ask for or go after the sexual stimulation they need. For example, Masters & Johnson (1970) and Kaplan (1974) report that, in part, the achievement of orgasm requires some behavioral independence or sexual autonomy in a person—the ability and desire to take active responsibility for one's own pleasure. They indicate that a woman (or a man) must be capable of behaving in what they called a "sexually selfish" manner. That is, the individual must be able to focus at times only on his or her own sexual sensations and pleasure. Such focus may be particularly difficult for women, for several reasons.

First, the culture has not traditionally given women the same tacit permission to be fully sexual, with honor and/or praise, that it has given men. That is, during her formative years, a woman learns to repress her sexual needs and feelings in order to abide by cultural norms calling for her to remain a "good girl" (see Chapters 1 and 2). If women are taught to avoid sexual exploration and sexual experience in order to remain "good girls," how are they supposed to learn and understand what their sexual needs are, much less focus on them?

Second, if indeed orgasm requires independence, autonomy, and active responsibility for the self, it is no wonder that so many women are nonorgasmic. How can a woman take active and independent responsibility for her sexual self, when the culture does not promote or support these behaviors in her nonsexual self?

Early research suggesting a link between gender-role norms and orgasmic dysfunction was done by Terman (1951). He noted that nonorgasmic women were less likely to "rebel inwardly at orders" and were also less persistent and more emotionally sensitive than were orgasmic women. No attempt was made by Terman to interpret these findings in terms of traditional or socially approved expressions of femininity. Nevertheless, they do seem to describe traditionally feminine role characteristics, including passivity, dependency, altruism, sensitivity, and harmony. Similarly, Fisher (1973) found a relationship between consistent achievement of orgasm and a typically masculine characteristic (endurance) often associated with traits such as persistence, task orientation, and other instrumental approaches to life.

More recent research indicates that women who take an active, autonomous, and responsible role in their own sexuality not only tend to be orgasmic and/or multiorgasmic but also have a greater likelihood of experiencing ejaculation than women who do not. For example, Kegel (1949, 1952) reported that sexual feeling in the vagina is closely related to muscle tone and that women can increase the probability of coital orgasm by engaging in voluntary contractions of the pubococcygeus muscle ("Kegel exercises"). Perry and Whipple (1981) noted that women who revealed an active and independent effort to condition their sexual muscle tone, doing Kegel exercises for many months, often had orgasms accompanied by ejaculation.

It seems clear that gender-role norms directing women to be passive and dependent, rather than active and autonomous, can prevent many women from becoming orgasmic. How is it, then, that some women are able to overcome such normative influences and/or behave actively and independently in spite of these influences? Quite simply, the behavior of individuals is not entirely or exclusively controlled by gender-role norms. Many individuals achieve a sense of self or unique identity that can supersede psychological allegiance to a set of stereotyped role behaviors.

By actively interacting with the environment and testing our limits, we eventually establish ourselves as adult human beings with unique traits, talents, and abilities. When this is accomplished, we can begin to define ourselves in terms of our special traits as a person rather than in terms of a collection of gender-role traits. That is, we may know that in addition to having traits typically associated with being male or female, we also have traits that are neither masculine nor feminine (for example, we may be skillful, musically talented, successful). Unfortunately, the early learning and acceptance of gender roles may delimit the development of a personalized self-definition or unique identity in many women.

Wynne (1958), for example, conceived of the achievement of unique identity as requiring an environment in which the individual is motivated to test a large variety of behaviors during the course of development. When the environment does not encourage active self-testing, the probability of achieving an identity outside of one's gender role is substantially diminished. In such a case, the culturally prescribed role may become a substitute for a unique self. Wynne further noted that the individual may then invest a great deal of psychological energy in maintaining the stereotypical role, because underneath this pseudo-identity there is no other person: there is a void.

Bardwick and Douvan (1971) noted that establishing a unique identity may be particularly difficult for the majority of presumably healthy women, given socialization practices that reward conformity, dependence, and passivity in women, rather than independence, self-sufficiency, and objective achievement. In other words, many women may be highly dependent on gender-role norms for self-definition. This situation seems additionally serious in that women may have to step out of their stereotypic feminine role in order to function well sexually.

Masters and Johnson (1970) and Kaplan (1974) noted that the likelihood of orgasm is increased when a woman takes the woman-above position during intercourse. This position creates an increase in clitoral pressure and sexual stimulation. Similarly, it is believed to be helpful for a woman to engage periodically in active coital thrusting. But many women reportedly perceive such behaviors as "masculine," and thus inappropriate for them. Perhaps this is why women gave more negative evaluations of a couple depicted in photographic slides of intercourse in the woman-above position in Allgeier and Fogel's (1978) research (see Chapter 3). Consistent with this, Kaplan (1974) reported that the woman-above position seems to give rise to anxieties in nonorgasmic women. These women fear that they will be sexually unattractive in the woman-above position. Moreover, Kaplan noted, these fears may have some basis, for husbands may in fact become resentful or rejecting if they feel their role is being preempted.

The possibility that women may monitor themselves in line with what they believe to be role-appropriate behavior is also implied in clinical reports of progress in sex therapy. Masters and Johnson (1970) and Kaplan (1974) have noted that the nonorgasmic woman seems to have difficulty abandoning herself to the sexual situation, behaving more like a passive spectator than an active participant in sexual intercourse.

Although researchers have long sensed there might be a relationship between gender-role identity and sexual dysfunction, the relationship could not be strongly substantiated (Terman, 1951; Fisher, 1973). This was probably because early tests of gender-role identification could only reveal whether a woman was masculine *or* feminine; these tests could not tell the *extent* to which a woman was masculine or feminine. With the advent of Bem's (1974) measure of gender role identification described in Chapter 2, however, it became possible to ask whether a feminine woman might be more likely to have sexual problems than a woman who is more androgynous (both masculine and feminine) in her gender-role identification.

In a study designed to explore the relationship between female orgasm and gender-role identification, I found that androgynous women tended to achieve orgasm more often than feminine women (Radlove, 1977). Androgynous women were also more likely than feminine women to take active responsibility for their own clitoral stimulation. Compared to feminine women, androgynous women were more likely to perceive active sexual behaviors such as coital thrusting or being on top of one's partner as equally appropriate for men and women. Thus, it appears that feminine role norms can be a disruptive influence in women's sexual behavior. Women who do not define themselves solely in terms of the female stereotype are more apt to be orgasmic than women whose gender-role identification is strictly feminine.

GENDER-ROLE AND SEXUAL PROBLEMS IN MEN

Although men are not free of sexual difficulties, far fewer men than women have sexual problems that seem directly related to gender-role stereotypes. Men, for example, do get the stimulation they need in order to reach orgasm. The behaviors that lead to the stimulation necessary for orgasm in both the male and female are apparently already a part of the masculine gender-role repetoire. That is, the masculine role involves behaving in an active, instrumental manner. When men are sexually dysfunctional, the source of the problem is more often traced to sexual values and attitudes than to adherence to gender-role norms.

For example, in discussing the inability to achieve erection under any circumstances, Masters and Johnson (1970) reported that long-term negative sexual attitudes seem to be at the core of the problem. In the majority of cases they treated, sexual histories revealed restrictive sexual attitudes—a perception of sex as "dirty" or only for purposes of procreation—originating with intense religious training. For these men, the overwhelming psychological barrier against sexual pleasure tended to wipe out completely the body's natural ability to respond to physical stimulation.

Similarly, in the majority of males treated for the inability to have orgasm during coitus,* Masters and Johnson noted that the problem appeared to stem from severe religious training, dislike or open disgust for the marital partner, and/or sexual trauma, more often than to gender-role norms. In some cases, a man's earlier excessively intimate relationship with his mother resulted in overwhelming sexual guilt and a maze of unconscious defenses against "letting go" with any woman. Other men revealed that the problem began after they had been ridiculed by impatient prostitutes for "not coming fast enough."

In the case of premature ejaculation—the inability to exert control over speed of ejaculation—it appears that attitudes are again a major factor. In this case, however, it is less often a result of negative sexual attitudes per se, and more often a result of naivetè and/or lack of concern for the sexual needs of women. For example, Masters and Johnson (1970) reported that grade school or early high school dropouts rarely request treatment for premature ejaculation. When treatment is sought, it is usually the wife, not the husband, who seeks it. The husbands of these women seem to be quite unaware and/or unconcerned that their speedy ejaculation is leaving their partners sexually frustrated. Masters and Johnson further noted that men's level of concern for controlling ejaculation and sexually satisfying their partners seems to increase in direct parallel to their level of formal education.

Interestingly, it might be hypothesized that males who are sexually aware and well educated, and who tend to be more profeminist in their attitudes, might also have problems. Overly invested with a sense of responsibility for satisfying the potentially multiorgasmic female, these men may exercise high levels of control—possibly diminishing their own sexual pleasure.

The foregoing overview of the association of various attitudes to the development of a number of male sexual dysfunctions is not meant to imply that identification with the stereotypic masculine role is never a factor in male sexual dysfunction. In the case of the inability to maintain an erection, Masters and Johnson (1970) clearly seem to suggest that identification with the stereotypic masculine role can be a major factor in the onset of the problem. Such men usually have a history of success in having erections. For a variety of reasons, including exhaustion, alcohol excess, and marital tension, they may

*Penis-in-vagina intercourse.

have an initial experience with erectile dysfunction. Such a man may look on this as a sign that his manhood is in danger. To overcome the difficulty, he may become quite tense, hoping erection can be achieved if he works at it. It is as if he is convinced that by the sheer force of his masculine strength and will, he can forcibly produce an erection. However, forcing, exerting, and demanding are masculine gender-role characteristics that tend to work against the man with erection problems. Healthy responses generally come only when he allows himself the luxury of not trying at all. In other words, he should give in to the moment, become somewhat more passive sexually, so as to let the erection occur naturally, of its own accord. Like the woman, he may be better off sexually if he is less psychologically bound to traditional gender-role behaviors and is able to behave in either an active or passive manner depending on the situation.

It is surprising that the incidence of sexual dysfunction among men tends to be less than among women. The sexual myths that men learn in North American culture seem to be enough to give any man an overdose of performance anxiety. Zilbergeld (1978) devoted two chapters in his book on male sexuality to a discussion of these myths. Although Zilbergeld, tongue-in-cheek, refers to these myths as the "Fantasy Model of Sex," he clearly believes the effects of the fantasy model to be psychologically and behaviorally disturbing to most men . . . Zilbergeld closes his discussion of the cultural myths with the saddest myth of all: "In this enlightened age, the preceding myths no longer have any influence on us" (p. 53).

ALTERNATIVES AND SUGGESTIONS FOR CHANGE

We have seen that from a physiological perspective, males and females are quite similar in their sexual response. We have seen too, that from a psychosocial perspective, gender-role behaviors can diminish sexual pleasure and create problems for otherwise healthy men and women. The remaining issue is what to do about it. And here, unfortunately, the scientific literature does not provide much help.

Are there alternatives to the traditional masculine and feminine gender roles that tend to reduce our options and cause difficulties in the sphere of sexual behavior? Can we give up a one-dimensional set of role behaviors and still maintain our unique sense of pride and value as male and female partners in sexual activity?

Androgyny as an Alternative

One possible answer may be found in S. L. Bem's (1972, 1974, 1975) concept of the androgynous person. A number of studies seem to indicate a positive relationship between an androgynous role orientation and effective functioning in general, as well as effective sexual functioning. Allgeier (1975), for example, reported that androgynous individuals felt less guilt over masturbation and tended to begin their contraceptive education at a younger age than nonandrogynous individuals. Spence, Helmreich, and Stapp (1975) examined the relationship between androgyny and self-esteem in men and women, and found that androgynous subjects tended to be higher in self-esteem than were traditionally gender-typed individuals.

However, recent evidence (Jones, Chernovetz, & Hansson, 1978) indicates that self-esteem, flexibility, and overall emotional adjustment tend to be associated with masculinity more often than with androgyny for both males and females. Furthermore, research by Allgeier (1981) shows that where heterosexual interaction is concerned, the strength of the androgyny variable seems to diminish. Apparently, engaging in behaviors defined by the culture as "role inappropriate" can be very difficult in a heterosexual context even for androgynous individuals. Perhaps, in a heterosexual context, the possibility of rejection by a person of the other gender can make the translation of androgynous attitudes into androgynous behavior much more risky.

At the present time, very little in the literature on androgyny indicates clearly how one can become more androgynous. It appears that a great deal more work must be accomplished in this area before androgyny can be seen as a truly viable alternative to the restrictive gender roles implicated in sexual dysfunction.

Personal Change

Regardless of whether or not it is possible simply to choose to become more androgynous, a number of options are open to an individual who wants to effect personal behavior change in the context of a sexual relationship. One such option may be to engage in the desired behaviors despite the psychological discomforts that may initially be associated with these behaviors.

D.J. Bem (1972) has shown that the observation of oneself actually engaging in a particular behavior tends to shape our perceptions of our internal attitudes and emotions. In other words, actually doing so-called role-inappropriate sexual behaviors can positively change our own perception of "appropriateness."

Because any sexual partnership obviously involves more than one person, however, the suggestion that one person might independently engage in new behavior without the understanding and cooperation of the other seems, at best, to greatly undermine the probability of a successful result.

Although it is often suggested that partners in sexual interaction need to communicate more, it seems more important to suggest that they need to communicate more effectively. Appropriate ways to communicate feelings, needs, desires, hurts, and/or fears, in a nonthreatening and nondemanding way, may be found in classes, workshops, and reading material on effective couple communication or training in assertiveness (Bloom, Coburn, & Pearlman, 1975; Alberti & Emmons, 1978; Bower & Bower, 1976).

Another way to effect personal change may be found in books specifically designed for self-help. Barbach's (1975) book on female sexuality and Zilbergeld's (1978) book on male sexuality give exercises for improving sexual response.

Where sexual problems already exist or are suspected to exist, however, professional help may be useful. Some of the issues an individual may want to consider are (1) the need for gynecological and/or urological examination (to rule out physical or anatomical pathology), (2) the need to choose wisely from available sex therapists by asking questions regarding the therapist's professional background and training in the treatment of sexual concerns, and (3) the desirability of placing sexual concerns in the context of a relationship. Masters and Johnson (1970, p. 2) note, "There is no such thing as an uninvolved partner in any marriage (or relationship) in which there is some form of sexual dysfunction. *Sexual response represents . . . interaction between people*" (or emphasis). Where there is a breakdown in the nonsexual aspects of a relationship—a long-term buildup of resentment, a loss of trust, or a lessening of mutual concern and respect—it is typically reflected in the sexual aspect of the relationship. Thus, the initial focus in sex therapy is often the relationship itself (Kaplan, 1974; Masters & Johnson, 1970).

Whatever an individual chooses to do to resolve or prevent sexual difficulties, the effort can be greatly enhanced by a more open and accepting view of one's own behavior and that of others. With such a view, the restrictive roles we fill as men and women may eventually give way to a healthier, more spontaneous, and more productive reality for all.

10 *Early Motherhood*

Anne Kates

STUDY QUESTIONS

1. Why does Kates claim that the overwhelming majority of unwed mothers are unprepared for growing up and raising a child at the same time?

2. Kates claims that you can cut down on the damage from teenage pregnancy. How?

Source: Anne Kates, "Early Motherhood." *The Single Parent.* July/August 1985, pp. 18–21, 30. Reprinted by permission.

ANNE KATES

Portrait of a teenage mother: She's not likely to have clear-cut educational or career goals; she's likely to be economically underprivileged or emotionally deprived; she's often a low achiever with little self esteem—and there's a good chance she was born before her own mother was 20. We expect her to be a Superwoman, to balance school books with diaper bags and to balance a budget with meager resources.

According to statistics compiled by the Alan Guttmacher Institute, based on the most recent data from the National Center for Health statistics, 523,530 girls under the age of 20 gave birth in 1982—accounting for about 15 percent of all births in the United States. Of those giving birth, 269,300 were unmarried. Ninety-six percent of the unmarried teen mothers chose to keep their babies. According to the National Association of Social Workers, based on the same 1982 data, four out of 10 14-year-old girls will become pregnant before they reach the age of 20; two out of 10 will give birth.

Teenage parenthood is not a phenomenon limited to any single socioeconomic or racial group. "Today we're recognizing that teen parenthood is cutting across all social class boundaries," says Dr. Joyce Ladner, a professor of Social Work at Howard University and chairwoman of Washington D.C. Mayor Marion Barry's Blue Ribbon Panel on teenage pregnancy. One reason is that there are not as many sanctions imposed by society on the teenager who choses to have a child out of wedlock, explains Ladner.

Changing societal attitudes have had a significant effect on the birth rate for white teenagers. The National Center for Health Statistics reports that the difference in birth rates between black and white teenagers has narrowed considerably, principally because the birth rate for unmarried white teenagers increased by 40–65 percent during the 70s, while rates for unmarried black teenagers declined by 14 percent.

Middle-income girls are also expressing some of the reasons for wanting to keep and raise their babies that poor girls have always expressed, says Ladner. That is: wanting someone to love and to call their own. "That's a sentiment that seems to cut across all racial, geographical and social class boundaries."

When their babies are first born, a lot of teen mothers spend an inordinate amount of time dressing the babies up, combing their hair, taking them out, showing them off. "It's almost as though they were dolls," Ladner notes. "But a sober awakening comes fairly soon. Reality sets in when she suddenly realizes she can't just get up and go, her routine has been interrupted by this child. That's one of the most sobering experiences that she has."

At a time when society is telling women that they can have it all, girls don't see that having a child will keep them from returning to school, for instance. "They register to return to school in an almost ceremonial way," says Ladner. "But unless they have child care and other support services they do not remain in school."

Not surprisingly, high on the list of what adolescent mothers miss most after having a baby is the active social life they enjoyed before becoming pregnant. Before I got pregnant my friends used to call me, invite me places," says 15-year-old Earline, whose daughter Nicole is 20 months old. "Now nobody calls."

Girls are often surprised when their expectations of support from family, friends and professional service providers aren't matched by reality. When the pregnancy is announced, the girls are the focal point of lots of attention. They're pleased at being treated as an adult for the first time. But after giving birth they soon find out that friends who offered to babysit are never available. Grandmothers—who may only be in their late 20s, early 30s themselves—are usually working and often unwilling to become a surrogate mother for the child. And federal, state and community services, when they exist, can sometimes be so inconvenient as to be virtually inaccessible. "Hardly anybody was honest with me," says Kim, the 17-year-old mother of 2-year-old Freddie.

Every aspect of a girl's life is affected when she becomes a parent. She needs assistance from what one social worker describes as a palette of medical, educational, social and income support services. According to Dr. Martha Burt, Director of Social Services Research at the Urban Institute, Washington, D.C., the first priorities for a teen mother are: not having another baby (Guttmacher statistics show that 17 percent of teen mothers become pregnant again within a year of giving birth to their first child); staying in school; being a good parent.

The most immediate priority is obtaining prenatal medical care. The risk of delivering a low-birth-weight baby increases the younger the mother is. Vital statistics show that in 1981, 14 percent of babies born to mothers under 15 years old weighed under 2,500 grams (about 6 pounds) at birth, compared with 11 percent for mothers aged 15–17 and nine percent for mothers in the 18–19 year age group. Low-weight babies are subject to higher rates of infant mortality, mental retardation and birth defects.

Most of the risks associated with low-birth weight can be reduced by adequate prenatal care. Unfortunately, teen mothers are more likely to delay seeking prenatal care, or receive no care at all. "Adequate prenatal care is clearly the major predictor in determining a healthy pregnancy," says Dr. Richard Jones, a practicing pediatrician who treats adolescent mothers and their babies and assistant professor of pediatrics at Georgetown University Medical School.

Prenatal care is usually delayed because of late confirmation of pregnancy, ignorance of the importance of prenatal care, or denial that the pregnancy exists. "Denial is the primary defense mechanism," says Jones. He remembers one 15-year-old girl who came into his office eight months pregnant and denied ever having sex. The girl's mother did not realize her daughter's condition.

Teenage mothers are also at risk for other medical problems, says Jones, including a higher incidence of toxemia and a greater likelihood of complications in delivery. And the children of adolescents are more likely to be maltreated than children of older mothers. Although studies show that the children of teen mothers most often suffer from inadequate nutrition and other symptoms of physical neglect, Jones notes that the spectrum of maltreatment ranges from a failure of the infant to grow strong and thrive to actual physical abuse at the hands of the mother.

Most experts agree that the risk of abuse or neglect can be offset if a teen mother lives with her parent(s) or with some other responsible adult. When the mother's relationship with her family makes living with them impossible, experts advocate visits to the girl's home by health-care professionals.

ANNE KATES

"There needs to be an adult in the home to monitor how well the girl takes care of the baby, to help teach her to care for the child," Howard University's Ladner says. She once knew a girl who would hang her baby upside down out the window when the baby was colicky. "It always seemed to quiet the baby," the girl explained.

"It's the ignorance that comes from youth, the inexperience. Most teens don't know how to parent, and there's no reason to expect that they should know. They still need so much socialization, so much training, so much teaching," Ladner says. "The problem with teenage pregnancy is that they're teenagers, they're just kids."

Teen mothers need to be taught, but they also need vocational training and most of all—a basic high-school education. Many experts argue that the best place to put special services for teen mothers is in the public schools. In an effort to decrease the teenage-dropout rate, many schools have established programs to keep pregnant teens in school and to make it easier for teenage mothers to return.

It's an uphill battle. Vital statistics show that in 1982, the median years of school completed by mothers in the 15–19 year age group was 11.4 years. "I didn't want to come back to school," says Michelle, 17. "My father pressured me. I knew all the responsibilities I was going to have after having a child, (added to the pressures of) going to school too." Michelle, whose son Terrell is 3 months old, decided to return to school. She holds a parttime job as well.

Some school districts offer homebound instruction, where students can continue classes, during the late stages of pregnancy and for several weeks after delivery. But the toughest assignment is keeping a teen mother in school after she has the added responsibility of an infant to care for, and tailoring a curriculum to meet her special needs.

Some school districts offer evening classes; some place programs for teen parents in separate, satellite school buildings. Other programs are housed in the regular school building, where pregnant and parenting teens are mainstreamed with other students in academic classes but also enrolled in special parenting, child-development, consumer-education or vocational-training classes. A few schools provide daycare on the premises.

Groveton High School, in Fairfax County, Va., is one of the few which does. More than 500 teenagers became mothers in Fairfax County last year. Groveton, the only school in its district offering daycare for the children of students, is licensed to care for 15 babies. The girls are required to take an adolescent parenting class and to spend half that class time interacting with their babies in the school's infant center, under the supervision of a public-health nurse and other professional care givers.

The program is designed to foster a stimulative learning environment for the students and their babies, as well as a sense of parental responsibility in the adolescent mothers. It seems to work. During one adolescent parenting class at Groveton, the girls discussed their criteria for choosing a babysitter for their children. Although most of the girls lamented their inability to lead active social lives because of their childcare responsibilities, when it came to choosing a babysitter, not even family members were exempt from scrutiny worthy of top-secret government clearance. "I don't trust babysitters," says Michelle, 16, whose son is 1.

Groveton's objectives aren't limited to providing parenting skills. Most adolescent mothers exhibit a lack of self-esteem, low academic achievement and spotty attendance before becoming pregnant, explains the Groveton program's co-founder Pam Robertson. Those problems still need to be addressed. "We can't be naive; adolescent pregnancy goes beyond the moral or sexual issue," says Robertson. Groveton staff monitor school attendance and call home when absences mount. Once a week, a therapist comes in to conduct group workshops and individual counseling.

But programs like Groveton's find little support in some school districts. Administrators argue that day care is a social service beyond the realm of the school system's educational mandate and that it should not be funded through the school system's budget. Others argue that providing such services only encourages teenage parenthood. Some schools, unwittingly or not, even discourage pregnant or parenting teens from remaining in school.

Margaret Dunkle, co-director of the Equality Center in Washington, D.C., studied the way schools treat pregnant and parenting teens from the perspective of Title IX—the law that prohibits sex discrimination in schools. Title IX makes it illegal to discriminate against pregnant or parenting students. But Dunkle found that "schools can't force a student out, but they often nudge her out." School systems can effectively force a girl to change schools after she becomes pregnant if, for instance, only certain schools in the district offer special programs for pregnant or parenting teens. The school to which she transfers is often academically inferior, says Dunkle. Transportation to the new school may not be provided, forcing teenagers who don't drive to lug books, baby, carseat, diaper bag, etc. across town on public transportation, or to depend on others for rides. Naturally teens are reluctant to leave familiar surroundings and old friends. They're apprehensive about how they'll be accepted by students at the new school. Some teens would rather drop out. "Everyone around here is hostile," says a 16-year-old mother who's been at her new school six months.

Schools that don't allow for the conditions of pregnancy can force a girl out, says Dunkle. Schools can make allowances for pregnant students by establishing a more lenient absence policy. Tardiness on account of morning sickness should not be registered as a demerit. Girls should be allowed to make up classwork or exams missed because of clinic appointments. Girls in the late stages of pregnancy with mobility problems should be let out of class five minutes early so they can get to their next class on time without getting crushed in crowded hallways. And pregnant girls experiencing pressure on their bladders should be able to go to the bathroom without having to fight for a hall pass.

Teenagers often choose to drop out of school because they're anxious to work. But completing a high-school education is critical to a teenager's chances of entering and remaining in the labor force. According to 1984 statistics from the Department of Labor, the unemployment rate for high school dropouts in the 16–24 year age group was 27.8 percent for whites, and a staggering 52.9 percent for blacks.

Staying in school also provides adolescent mothers with another, less-obvious advantage: It reduces the chances of repeat pregnancies. Dunkle compares the high school dropout's situation with that of the woman who is on a leave of absence from work—to write a Ph.D. dissertation, for example. "While I'm home, it's a good time to have a baby," they both reason. But the stakes are higher for the high-school dropout. "With each additional child it becomes exponentially more difficult to become economically self-sufficient," says Dunkle.

Teenagers have to be made aware of options in life other than child-bearing—and those options must be viewed as attractive. Social workers have found that those girls most likely to become teen mothers are the ones with no educational or career goals. "They're like ships out at sea," says Ladner, "sometimes they get blown off course. Maybe the girls who don't get pregnant have an internal compass, a more focused sense of direction."

"The girl who becomes a teen parent has the most stereotypical picture of herself as a woman," says Ann Aukamp, clinical social-work administrator with the Maryland Department of Human Resources. Girls who become pregnant often visualize themselves as being taken care of in a marriage, never becoming a part of the paid labor force—a fantasy that rarely comes true.

Getting married increases the chances that a teen mother will quickly become pregnant again, but unfortunately for the teenager who's had two or more babies, it also increases the likelihood of eventually becoming divorced. Census data for 1980 show that 21.8 percent of the girls 19 and under who married for the first time during the '70s were divorced by 1980, compared with 13.2 percent of the women in the 20–24 age group. "We have to give these kids some real hope and real aspirations other than becoming a traditional parent in an ivy-covered cottage," says Aukamp.

Motivation to achieve personal goals must be present before any of the social programs aimed at teen mothers can succeed. For example, while many experts consider the lack of daycare to be a primary impediment to a teenager's returning to school or joining the labor force, according to the Urban Institute's Burt, the availability of daycare in and of itself is not an effective inducement to accomplishing these goals. She cites research that shows only 10 percent of those teen mothers who said they would accomplish a certain task if only they had daycare actually accomplished the task when daycare was made available.

By the same token, the availability of welfare benefits and services is no inducement to teenagers to have babies. A study of international trends in teenage childbearing by the Guttmacher Institute found that pregnancy rates in Sweden, France, the Netherlands, England and Canada were far lower than those in the United States, even though welfare benefits were more generous in the foreign countries.

According to the U.S. Congress, the median assistance from Aid to Families with Dependent Children received by a two-person family was $272 a month in January 1985. As of 1983, families in which the mother was 18 or under accounted for 3.3 percent of the total AFDC enrollment, or 120,483 families.

Most experts agree that some income support is a necessary ingredient for a successful transition from adolescent mother to adult provider. Few teenagers can finish school, acquire a marketable job skill, raise a child—and make a living at the same time. "It's unrealistic to put expectations on teens that 30-year-olds can't handle," says Burt.

Recent changes in eligibility rules require that a girl's parents and other minor siblings be counted as part of the AFDC assistance unit when the girl lives with her family. A portion of the family's income is assumed available to the adolescent mother and her baby. Advocacy groups have argued that the changes financially penalize a girl who lives with her family. But proposed changes would require that a minor parent receiving AFDC benefits live with her own parents, unless the minor has been on her own for a year or more, or the minor's health or safety would be jeopardized by living at home.

Some girls who are eligible for assistance don't apply for it. They may be unaware that they're eligible for benefits, they may not understand the application procedures, or they may fear the stigma attached to getting welfare by their families or community. "It's a tremendously complicated, tremendously negative experience for anyone to apply for welfare," says Aukamp.

Applying for welfare is a complicated undertaking, but just part of the bureaucratic maze through which teens must wend their way. Scheduling conflicts and transportation difficulties often force a teenager to choose between keeping a clinic appointment or going to school, picking up her child on time from the daycare center or leaving work early.

Schools and community-service providers need to communicate with each other and coordinate their services, says the Equality Center's Dunkle. "Teen pregnancy is not a single problem, there's no single solution. We're dealing with the same child in pieces; we have to know where the gaps are." Dunkle adds, "Professionals should navigate the system rather than the 14-year-old mother."

Making sure that teens get the comprehensive care that they need— educational, medical, social and counseling services—can be done in one of two ways: The services can be coordinated through a system of referrals together with the establishment of complimentary schedules, or the services can be delivered at a single site.

Cities and Schools, a national organization with 42 programs in 17 cities, chose the latter approach when it established its Adolescent Health Center in Washington, D.C. four years ago. The success of its comprehensive, holistic approach has put similar projects on the drawing board in other cities, says Outreach Director Donald Robinson.

The center is funded by public/private partnerships. Community agencies often donate services and many of its professional staff members are volunteers. Health care runs the gamut from pregnancy testing to postnatal care; educational services include GED preparation, vocational training, home economics and parenting; social services include daycare placement, career workshops and interpersonal communications workshops. Individual and family counseling is available. The center goes one step further by organizing physical and recreational activities such as group sports and drama productions.

Although organizations like Cities and Schools can go far in providing a model for communities to follow, no single program or combination of services is going to solve all the problems of teenage pregnancy. Says Dunkle, "You can't totally eliminate teenage pregnancy, but you can cut down on the damage."

ANNE KATES

For more information on teenage pregnancy and parenting programs, check with your local school district, county health department or planned parenthood organization.

TEEN FATHERS

Everyone knows that it takes two to create a pregnancy. In the past, teen fathers were expected "to do the right thing" by marrying their pregnant girlfriends. That societal pressure no longer carries the same force it once did. Nor should it, experts say.

Although the teen mother's life is inarguably the one most affected by an unplanned pregnancy, the birth of a baby also can have lasting ramifications on the father's life. If paternity is established, he will be held financially accountable for the child. Increasingly tougher child-support enforcement laws are designed to make sure that responsibility is fulfilled.

But parenting goes far beyond financial support. Service providers are beginning to realize that teen fathers, too, need to be taught how to parent. And what's more, teen fathers today are becoming avid students.

Preliminary research from the Teen Father Collaboration, a national research and demonstration project, shows that 78 percent of the teen fathers involved in the project see their child every day whether or not they live with the child's mother; 55 percent make financial contributions toward raising the child; 62 percent contribute goods, such as toys, diapers, baby furniture; 87 percent consider the child's mother and themselves as parts of an intact couple.

Funded by the Ford Foundation, the Teen Father Collaboration has established eight programs throughout the country. The programs are monitored by the Bank Street College of Education. Among the services they found most effective in helping teen fathers become successful parents are:

- Prenatal and Parenting Classes—focusing on fetal development, the birth process, nutrition and child care.
- Family Planning Workshops—focusing on effective contraception.
- Educational Programs—assisting teen fathers in finishing high school or obtaining an equivalency degree.
- Vocational Training—developing marketable job skills.
- Job Placement Services—teaching teen fathers to find jobs, write resumes, interview successfully.
- Individual and Group Counseling—addressing day-to-day problems and promoting a sense of self-worth.
- Couples Counseling—helping teen fathers and mothers develop a nurturing family environment for their child.

For more information, contact the Bank Street College of Education, 610 West 112 Street, New York, NY 10025 (212) 663-7200.

11 Motherhood and Morality in America

Kristin Luker

STUDY QUESTIONS

1. What are the values involved in the abortion issue?
2. Compare the social background of the activities on both sides of the abortion issue.

According to interested observers at the time, abortion in America was as frequent in the last century as it is in our own. And the last century, as we have seen, had its own "right-to-life" movement, composed primarily of physicians who pursued the issue in the service of their own professional goals. When abortion reemerged as an issue in the late 1950s, it still remained in large part restricted debate among interested professionals. But abortion as we know it has little in common with these earlier rounds of the debate. Instead of the civility and colleagueship that characterized the earlier phases of the debate, the present round of the abortion debate is marked by rancor and intransigence. Instead of the elite male professionals who commanded the issue until recently, ordinary people—and more to the point, ordinary women—have come to predominate in the ranks of those concerned. From a quiet, restricted technical debate among concerned professionals, abortion has become a debate that seems at times capable of tearing the fabric of American life apart. How did this happen? What accounts for the remarkable transformation of the abortion debate?

The history of the debate, as examined in previous chapters in this book, provides some preliminary answers. Technological advances in obstetrics led to a decline in those abortions undertaken strictly to preserve the life of the woman, using the narrowly biological sense of the word *life*. These technological

Source: "Motherhood and Morality in America." In *Abortion and the Politics of Motherhood* by Kristin Luker. Berkeley: University of California Press, 1984, pp. 192–215. Copyright © 1984 by the University of California. Reprinted by permission.

advances, in turn, permitted (and indeed forced) physicians over time to make more and more nuanced decisions about abortion and eventually brought to the fore the underlying philosophical issue that had been obscured by a century of medical control over abortion: is the embryo a person or only a potential person? . . .

But this is only part of the story. This chapter will argue that all the previous rounds of the abortion debate in America were merely echoes of the issue as the nineteenth century defined it: a debate about the medical profession's right to make life-and-death decisions. In contrast, the most recent round of the debate is about something new. By bringing the issue of the moral status of the embryo to the fore, the new round focuses on the relative rights of women and embryos. Consequently, the abortion debate has become a debate about women's contrasting obligations to themselves and others. New technologies and the changing nature of work have opened up possibilities for women outside of the home undreamed of in the nineteenth century; together, these changes give women—for the first time in history—the option of deciding exactly how and when their family roles will fit into the larger context of their lives. In essence, therefore, this round of the abortion debate is so passionate and hard-fought *because it is a referendum on the place and meaning of motherhood.*

Motherhood is at issue because two opposing visions of motherhood are at war. Championed by "feminists" and "housewives," these two different views of motherhood represent in turn two very different kinds of social worlds. The abortion debate has become a debate among women, women with different values in the social world, different experiences of it, and different resources with which to cope with it. How the issue is framed, how people think about it, and most importantly, where the passions come from are all related to the fact that the battlelines are increasingly drawn (and defended) by women. While on the surface it is the embryo's fate that seems to be at stake, the abortion debate is actually about the meanings of *women's* lives. . . .

WHO ARE THE ACTIVISTS?

On almost every social background variable we examined, pro-life and pro-choice women differed dramatically. For example, in terms of income, almost half of all pro-life women (44 percent) in this study reported an income of less than $20,000 a year, but only one-fourth of the pro-choice women reported an income that low, and a considerable portion of those were young women just starting their careers. On the upper end of the income scale, one-third of the pro-choice women reported an income of $50,000 a year or more compared with only one pro-life woman in every seven.

These simple figures on income, however, conceal a very complex social reality, and that social reality is in turn tied to feelings about abortion. The higher incomes of pro-choice women, for example, result from a number of interesting factors. Almost without exception pro-choice women work in the paid labor force, they earn good salaries when they work, and if they are married, they are likely to be married to men who also have good incomes. An astounding 94 percent of all pro-choice women work, and over half of them have incomes in the top 10 percent of all working women in this country. Moreover, one pro-choice woman in ten has an annual *personal* income (as opposed to a family income) of $30,000 or more, thus putting her in the ratified ranks of the top 2 percent of all employed women in America. Pro-life women, by contrast, are far less likely to work: 63 percent of them do not work in the paid labor force, and almost all of those who do are unmarried. Among pro-life married women, for example, only 14 percent report any personal income at all, and for most of them, this is earned not in a formal job but through activities such as selling cosmetics to groups of friends. Not surprisingly, the personal income of pro-life women who work outside the home, whether in a formal job or in one of these less-structured activities, is low. Half of all pro-life women who do work earn less than $5,000 a year, and half earn between $5,000 and $10,000. Only two pro-life women we contacted reported a personal income of more than $20,000. Thus pro-life women are less likely to work in the first place, they earn less money when they do work, and they are more likely to be married to a skilled worker or small businessman who earns only a moderate income.

These differences in income are in turn related to the different educational and occupational choices these women have made along the way. Among pro-choice women, almost four out of ten (37 percent) had undertaken some graduate work beyond the B.A. degree, and 18 percent had an M.D., a law degree, a Ph.D., or a similar postgraduate degree. Pro-life women, by comparison, had far less education: 10 percent of them had only a high school education or less; and another 30 percent never finished college (in contrast with only 8 percent of the pro-choice women). Only 6 percent of all pro-life women had a law degree, a Ph.D., or a medical degree.

These educational differences were in turn related to occupational differences among the women in this study. Because of their higher levels of education, pro-choice women tended to be employed in the major professions, as administrators, owners of small businesses, or executives in large businesses. The pro-life women tended to be housewives or, of the few who worked, to be in the traditional female jobs of teaching, social work, and nursing. (The choice of home life over public life held true for even the 6 percent of pro-life women with an advanced degree; of the married women who had such degrees, at the time of our interviews only one of them had not retired from her profession after marriage.)

These economic and social differences were also tied to choices that women on each side had made about marriage and family life. For example, 23 percent of pro-choice women had never married, compared with only 16 percent of pro-life women; 14 percent of pro-choice women had been divorced, compared with 5 percent of pro-life women. The size of the families these women had was also different. The average pro-choice family had between one and two children and was more likely to have one; pro-life families averaged between two and three children and were more likely to have three. (Among the pro-life women, 23 percent had five or more children; 16 percent had seven or more children.) Pro-life women also tended to marry at a slightly younger age and to have had their first child earlier.

KRISTIN LUKER

Finally, the women on each side differed dramatically in their religious affiliation and in the role that religion played in their lives. Almost 80 percent of the women active in the pro-life movement at the present time are Catholics. The remainder are Protestants (9 percent), persons who claim no religion (5 percent), and Jews (1 percent). In sharp contrast, 63 percent of pro-choice women say that they have no religion, 22 percent think of themselves as vaguely Protestant, 3 percent are Jewish, and 9 percent have what they call a "personal" religion. We found no one in our sample of pro-choice activists who claimed to be a Catholic at the time of the interviews.

When we asked activists what religion they were raised in as a child, however, a different picture emerged. For example, 20 percent of the pro-choice activists were raised as Catholics, 42 percent were raised as Protestants, and 15 percent were raised in the Jewish faith. In this group that describes itself predominantly without religious affiliation, therefore, only 14 percent say they were not brought up in any formal religious faith. By the same token, although almost 80 percent of present pro-life activists are Catholic, only 58 percent were raised in that religion (15 percent were raised as Protestants and 3 percent as Jews). Thus, almost 20 percent of the pro-life activists in this study are converts to Catholicism, people who have actively chosen to follow a given religious faith, in striking contrast to pro-choice people, who have actively chosen not to follow any.

Perhaps the single most dramatic differences between the two groups, however, is in the role that religion plays in their lives. Almost three-quarters of the pro-choice people interviewed said that formal religion was either unimportant or completely irrelevant to them, and their attitudes are correlated with behavior: only 25 percent of the pro-choice women said they *ever* attend church, and most of these said they do so only occasionally. Among pro-life people, by contrast, 69 percent said religion was important in their lives, and an additional 22 percent said that it was very important. For pro-life women, too, these attitudes are correlated with behavior: half of those pro-life women interviewed said they attend church regularly once a week, and another 13 percent said they do so even more often. Whereas 80 percent of pro-choice people never attend church, only 2 percent of pro-life advocates never do so.

Keeping in mind that the statistical use of averages has inherent difficulties, we ask, who are the "average" pro-choice and pro-life advocates? When the social background data are looked at carefully, two profiles emerge. The average pro-choice activist is a forty-four-year-old married women who grew up in a large metropolitan area and whose father was a college graduate. She was married at age twenty-two, has one or two children, and has had some graduate or professional training beyond the B.A. degree. She is married to a professional man, is herself employed in a regular job, and her family income is more than $50,000 a year. She is not religiously active, feels that religion is not important to her, and attends church very rarely if at all.

The average pro-life woman is also a forty-four-year-old married woman who grew up in a large metropolitan area. She married at age seventeen and has three children or more. Her father was a high school graduate, and she has some college education or may have a B.A. degree. She is not employed in the paid labor force and is married to a small businessman or a lower-level white-collar worker; her family income is $30,000 a year. She is Catholic (and may have converted), and her religion is one of the most important aspects of her life: she attends church at least once a week and occasionally more often.

INTERESTS AND PASSIONS

To the social scientist (and perhaps to most of us) these social background characteristics connote lifestyles as well. We intuitively clothe these bare statistics with assumptions about beliefs and values. When we do so, the pro-choice women emerge as educated, affluent, liberal professionals, whose lack of religious affiliation suggests a secular, "modern," or (as pro-life people would have it) "utilitarian" outlook on life. Similarly, the income, education, marital patterns, and religious devotion of pro-life women suggest that they are traditional, hard-working people ("polyester types" to their opponents), who hold conservative views of life. We may be entitled to assume that individuals' social backgrounds act to shape and mold their social attitudes, but it is important to realize that the relationship between social worlds and social values is a very complex one.

Perhaps one example will serve to illustrate the point. A number of pro-life women in this study emphatically rejected an expression that pro-choice women tend to use almost unthinkingly—the expression *unwanted pregnancy*. Pro-life women argued forcefully that a better term would be a *surprise* pregnancy, asserting that although a pregnancy may be momentarily unwanted, the child that results from the pregnancy almost never is. Even such a simple thing—what to call an unanticipated pregnancy—calls into play an individual's values and resources. Keeping in mind our profile of the average pro-life person, it is obvious that a woman who does not work in the paid labor force, who does not have a college degree, whose religion is important to her, and who has already committed herself wholeheartedly to marriage and a large family is well equipped to believe than an unanticipated pregnancy usually becomes a beloved child. Her life is arranged so that for her, this belief is true. This view is consistent not only with her values, which she has held from earliest childhood, but with her social resources as well. It should not be surprising, therefore, that her world view leads her to believe that everyone else can "make room for one more" as easily as she can and that therefore it supports her in her conviction that abortion is cruel, wicked, and self-indulgent.

It is almost certainly the case that an unplanned pregnancy is never an easy thing for anyone. Keeping in mind the profile of the average pro-choice woman, however, it is evident that a woman who is employed full time, who has an affluent lifestyle that depends in part of her contribution to the family income, and who expects to give a child as good a life as she herself has had with respect to educational, social, and economic advantages will draw on a different reality when she finds herself being skeptical about the ability of the average person to transform unwanted pregnancies into well-loved (and well-cared-for) children.

KRISTIN LUKER

The relationship between passions and interests is thus more dynamic than it might appear at first. It is true that at one level, pro-choice and pro-life attitudes on abortion are self-serving: activists on each side have different views of the morality of abortion because their chosen lifestyles leave them with different needs for abortion; and both sides have values that provide a moral basis for their abortion needs in particular and their lifestyles in general. But this is only half the story. The values that lead pro-life and pro-choice women into different attitudes toward abortion are the same values that led them at an earlier time to adopt different lifestyles that supported a given view of abortion.

For example, pro-life women have *always* valued family roles very highly and have arranged their lives accordingly. They did not acquire high-level educational and occupational skills, for example, because they married, and they married because their values suggested that this would be the most satisfying life open to them. Similarly, pro-choice women postponed (or avoided) marriage and family roles because they chose to acquire the skills they needed to be successful in the larger world, having concluded that the role of wife and mother was too limited for them. Thus, activists on both sides of the issue are women who have a given set of values about what are the most satisfying and appropriate roles for women, and they have made *life commitments that now limit their ability to change their minds.* Women who have many children and little education, for example, are seriously handicapped in attempting to become doctors or lawyers; women who have reached their late forties with few children or none are limited in their ability to build (or rebuild) a family. For most of these activists, therefore, their position on abortion is the "tip of the iceberg," a shorthand way of supporting and proclaiming not only a complex set of values but a given set of social resources as well. . . .

In consequence, anything that supports a traditional division of labor into male and female worlds is, broadly speaking, in the interests of pro-life women because that is where their resources lie. Conversely, such a traditional division of labor, when strictly enforced, is against the interest of pro-choice women because it limits their abilities to use the valuable "male" resources that they have in relative abundance. It is therefore apparent that attitudes toward abortion, even though rooted in childhood experiences, are also intimately related to present-day interests. Women who oppose abortion and seek to make it officially unavailable are declaring, both practically and symbolically, that women's reproductive roles should be given social primacy. Once an embryo is defined as a child and an abortion as the death of a person, almost everything else in a woman's life must "go on hold" during the course of her pregnancy: any attempt to gain "male" resources such as a job, an education, or other skills must be subordinated to her uniquely female responsibility of serving the needs of this newly conceived person. Thus, when personhood is bestowed on the embryo, women's non-reproductive roles are made secondary to their repro-ductive roles. The act of conception therefore creates a pregnant woman rather than a woman who is pregnant; it creates a woman whose life, in cases where roles or values clash, is defined by the fact that she is—or may become—pregnant.

It is obvious that this view is supportive of women who have already decided that their familial and reproductive roles are the major ones in their lives. By the same token, the costs of defining women's reproductive roles as primary do not seem high to them because they have already chosen to make those roles primary anyway. For example, employers might choose to discriminate against women because they might require maternity leave and thus be unavailable at critical times, but women who have chosen not to work in the paid labor force in the first place can see such discrimination as irrelevant to them.

It is equally obvious that supporting abortion (and believing that the embryo is not a person) is in the vested interests of pro-choice women. Being so well equipped to compete in the male sphere, they perceive any situation that both practically and symbolically affirms the primacy of women's reproductive roles as a real loss to them. Practically, it devalues their social resources. If women are only secondarily in the labor market and must subordinate working to pregnancy, should it occur, then their education, occupation, income and work become potentially temporary and hence discounted. Working becomes, as it traditionally was perceived to be, a pastime or hobby pursued for "pin money" rather than a central part of their lives. Similarly, if the embryo is defined as a person and the ability to become pregnant is the central one for women, a woman must be prepared to sacrifice some of her own interests to the interests of this newly conceived person.

In short, in a world where men and women have traditionally had different roles to play and where male roles have traditionally been the more socially prestigious and financially rewarded, abortion has become a symbolic marker between those who wish to maintain this division of labor and those who wish to challenge it. Thus, on an intimate level, the pro-life movement is women's version of what was true of peasants in the Vendeé, the part of France that remained Royalist during the French Revolution. Charles Tilly has argued that in the Vendeé, traditional relationships between nobles and peasants were still mutually satisfying so that the "brave new world" of the French Revolution represented more loss than gain, and the peasants therefore resisted the changes the Revolution heralded. By the same logic, traditional relationships between men and women are still satisfying, rewarding, and meaningful for pro-life women, and they therefore resist the lure of "liberation." For pro-choice women, however, with their access to male resources, a division of labor into the public world of work and the private world of home and hearth seems to promise only restriction to "second-class" citizenship.

Thus, the sides are fundamentally opposed to each other not only on the issue of abortion but also on what abortion *means*. Women who have many "human capital" resources of the traditionally male variety want to see motherhood recognized as a private, discretionary choice. Women who have few of these resources and limited opportunities in the job market want to see motherhood recognized as the most important thing a woman can do. In order for pro-choice women to achieve their goals, therefore, they *must* argue that motherhood is not a primary, inevitable, or "natural" role for all women; for pro-life women to achieve their goals, they *must* argue that it is. In short, the

KRISTIN LUKER

debate rests on the question of whether women's fertility is to be socially recognized as a resource or as a handicap. . . .

Because of their commitment to their own view of motherhood as a primary social role, pro-life women believe that other women are "casual" about abortions and have them "for convenience." There are no reliable data to confirm whether or not women are "casual" about abortions, but many pro-life people believe this to be the case and relate their activism to their perception of other people's casualness. For example:

> Every time I saw some article [on abortion] I read about it, and I had another friend who had her second abortion in 1977 . . . and both of her abortions were a matter of convenience, it was inconvenient for her to be pregnant at that time. When I talked to her I said, "O.K., you're married now, your husband has a good job, you want to have children eventually, but if you became pregnant now, you'd have an abortion. Why?" "Because it's inconvenient, this is not when I want to have my child." And that bothered me a lot because she is also very intelligent, graduated magna cum laude, and knew nothing about fetal development.

The assertion that women are "casual" about abortion, one could argue, expresses in a short-hand way a set of beliefs about women and their roles. First, the more people value the personhood of the embryo, the more important must be the reasons for taking its life. Some pro-life people, for example, would accept an abortion when continuation of the pregnancy would cause the death of the mother; they believe that when two lives are in direct conflict, the embryo's life can be considered the more expendable. But not all pro-life people agree, and many say they would not accept abortion even to save the mother's life. (Still others say they accept the idea in principle but would not make that choice in their own lives if faced with it.) For people who accept the personhood of the embryo, any reason besides trading a "life for a life" (and sometimes even that) seems trivial, merely a matter of "convenience."

Second, people who accept the personhood of the embryo see the reasons that pro-abortion people give for ending pregnancy as simultaneously downgrading the value of the embryo and upgrading everything else but pregnancy. The argument that women need abortion to "control" their fertility means that they intend to subordinate pregnancy, with its inherent unpredictability, to something else. As the pro-choice activists . . . have told us, that something else is participation in the paid labor force. Abortion permits women to engage in paid work on an equal basis with men. With abortion, they may schedule pregnancy in order to take advantage of the kinds of benefits that come with a paid position in the labor force: a paycheck, a title, a social identity. The pro-life women in this study were often careful to point out that they did not object to "career women." But what they meant by "career women" were women whose *only* responsibilities were in the labor force. Once a woman became a wife and a mother, in their view her primary responsibility was to her home and family.

Third, the pro-life activists we interviewed, the overwhelming majority of whom are full-time homemakers, also felt that women who worked *and* had families could often do so only because women like themselves picked up the slack. Given their place in the social structure, it is not surprising that many of the pro-life women thought that married women who worked outside the home were "selfish"—that they got all the benefits while the homemakers carried the load for them in Boy and Girl Scouts, PTA, and after school, for which their reward was to be treated by the workers as less competent and less interesting persons.*

Abortion therefore strips the veil of sanctity from motherhood. When pregnancy is discretionary—when people are allowed to put anything else they value in front of it—then motherhood has been demoted from a sacred calling to a job.** In effect, the legalization of abortion serves to make men and women more "unisex" by deemphasizing what makes them different—the ability of women to visibly and directly carry the next generation. Thus, pro-choice women are emphatic about their right to compete equally with men without the burden of an unplanned pregnancy, and pro-life women are equally emphatic about their belief that men and women have different roles in life and that pregnancy is a gift instead of a burden.

The pro-life activists we interviewed do not want equality with men in the sense of having exactly the same rights and responsibilities as men do, although they do want equality of status. In fact, to the extent that *all* women have been touched by the women's movement and have become aware of the fact that society often treats women as a class as less capable than men, quite a few said they appreciated the Equal Rights Amendment (ERA), except for its implied stand on abortion. The ERA, in their view, reminded them that women are as valuable *in their own sphere* as men are in theirs. However, to the extent that the ERA was seen as downplaying the differences between men and women, to devalue the female sphere of the home in the face of the male sphere of paid work, others saw it as both demeaning and oppressive to women like themselves. As one of the few married employed pro-life women argued:

> I oppose it [the ERA]. Because I've gotten where I am without it. I don't think I need it. I think a woman should be hired on her merits, not on her sex or race. I don't think we should be hiring on sex or on race. I think we should be taking the competent people that are capable of doing the job. . . . I don't think women should be taking jobs from the bread-winner, you know. I still think that our society should be male . . . the male should be the primary breadwinner. For example, my own husband cannot hope for promotion because he is white and Anglo, you know, I mean white male. He's not going to get a promotion. If he could get the

---

* In fact, pro-life women, especially those recruited after 1972, were *less* likely to be engaged in formal activities such as Scouts, church activities, and PTA than their pro-choice peers. Quite possibly they have in mind more informal kinds of activities, premised on the fact that since they do not work, they are home most of the time.

** The same might be said of all sacred callings—stripped of its layer of the sacred, for example, the job of the clergy is demanding, low status, and underpaid.

KRISTIN LUKER

promotion that others of different minorities have gotten over him, I probably wouldn't have to work at all. So from my own point of view, purely selfishly, I think we've got to consider it. On the other hand, if I'm doing the same job [as a man], I expect to get the same pay. But I've always gotten it. So I really don't think that's an issue. I see the ERA as causing us more problems than it's going to [solve]. . . . As I see it, we were on a pedestal, why should we go down to being equal? That's my feeling on the subject. . . .

The genetic basis for the embryo's claim to personhood has another, more subtle implication for those on the pro-life side. If genetic humanness equals personhood, then biological facts of life must take precedence over social facts of life. One's destiny is therefore inborn and hence immutable. To give any ground on the embryo's biologically determined babyness, therefore, would by extension call into question the "innate," "natural," and biological basis of women's traditional roles as well.

Pro-choice people, of course, hold a very different view of the matter. For them, social considerations outweigh biological ones: the embryo becomes a baby when it is "viable," that is, capable of achieving a certain degree of social integration with others. This is a world view premised on achievement, but not in the way pro-life people experience the world. Pro-choice people, believing as they do in choice, planning, and human efficacy, believe that biology is simply a minor given to be transcended by human experience. Sex, like race and age, is not an appropriate criterion for sorting people into different rights and responsibilities. Pro-choice people downplay these "natural" ascriptive characteristics, believing that true equality means achievement based on talent, not being restricted to a "women's world," a "black world," or an "old people's world." Such a view, as the profile of pro-choice people has made clear, is entirely consistent with their own lives and achievements.

These differences in social circumstances that separate pro-life from pro-choice women on the core issue of abortion also lead them to have different values on topics that surround abortion, such as sexuality and the use of contraception. With respect to sexuality, for example, the two sides have diametrically opposed values; these values arise from a fundamentally different premise, which is, in turn, tied to the different realities of their social worlds. If pro-choice women have a vested interest in subordinating their reproductive capacities, and pro-life women have a vested interest in highlighting them, we should not be surprised to find that pro-life women believe that the purpose of sex is reproduction whereas pro-choice women believe that its purpose is to promote intimacy and mutual pleasure.

These two views about sex express the same value differences that lead the two sides to have such different views on abortion. If women plan to find their primary role in marriage and the family, then they face a need to create a "moral cartel" when it comes to sex. If sex is freely available outside of marriage, then why should men, as the old saw puts it, buy the cow when the milk is free? If many women are willing to sleep with men outside of marriage, then the regular sexual activity that comes with marriage is much less valuable an incentive to marry. And because pro-life women are traditional women, their primary resource for marriage is the promise of a stable home, with everything it implies: children, regular sex, a "haven in a heartless world."

But pro-life women, like all women, are facing a devaluation of these resources. As American society increasingly becomes a service economy, men can buy the services that a wife traditionally offers. Cooking, cleaning, decorating, and the like can easily be purchased on the open market in a cash transaction. And as sex becomes more open, more casual, and more "amative," it removes one more resource that could previously be obtained only through marriage.

Pro-life women, as we have seen, have both value orientations and social characteristics that make marriage very important. Their alternatives in the public world of work are, on the whole, less attractive. Furthermore, women who stay home full-time and keep house are becoming a financial luxury. Only very wealthy families *or families whose values allow them to place the nontangible benefits of a full-time wife over the tangible benefits of a working wife* can afford to keep one of its earners off the labor market. To pro-life people, the nontangible benefit of having children—and therefore the value of procreative sex—is very important. Thus, a social ethic that promotes more freely available sex undercuts pro-life women two ways: it limits their abilities to get into a marriage in the first place, and it undermines the social value placed on their presence once within a marriage.

For pro-choice women, the situation is reversed. Because they have access to "male" resources such as education and income, they have far less reason to believe that the basic reason for sexuality is to produce children. They plan to have small families anyway, and they and their husbands come from and have married into a social class in which small families are the norm. For a number of overlapping reasons, therefore, pro-choice women value the ability of sex to promote human intimacy more (or at least more frequently) than they value the ability of sex to produce babies. But they hold this view because they can afford to. When they bargain for marriage, they use the same resources that they use in the labor market: upper-class status, an education very similar to a man's, side-by-side participation in the man's world, and, not least, a salary that substantially increases a family's standard of living.

It is true, therefore, that pro-life people are "anti-sex." They value sex, of course, but they value it for its traditional benefits (babies) rather than for the benefits that pro-choice people associate with it (intimacy). Pro-life people really do want to see "less" sexuality—or at least less open and socially unregulated sexuality—because they think it is morally wrong, they think it distorts the meaning of sex, and they feel that it *threatens the basis on which their own marital bargains are built. . . .*

Pro-choice women, therefore, value (and can afford) an approach to sexuality that, by sidelining reproduction, diminishes the differences between men and women; they can do this *because they have other resources on which to build a marriage.* Since their value is intimacy and since the daily lives of men and women on the pro-choice side are substantially similar, intimacy in the bedroom is merely an extension of the intimacy of their larger world.

　　　　　　　　　　　　　　　　　　　　　　　　　　　　KRISTIN LUKER

Pro-life women and men, by contrast, tend to live in "separate spheres." Because their lives are based on a social and emotional division of labor where each sex has its appropriate work, to accept contraception or abortion would devalue the one secure resource left to these women; the private world of home and hearth. This would be disastrous not only in terms of status but also in terms of meaning; if values about fertility and family are not essential to a marriage, what support does a traditional marriage have in times of stress? To accept highly effective contraception, which actually and symbolically subordinates the role of children in the family to other needs and goals, would be to cut the ground of meaning out from under at least one (and perhaps both) partners' lives. Therefore, contraception, which sidelines the reproductive capacities of men and women, is both useless and threatening to pro-life people.

THE CORE OF THE DEBATE

In summary, women come to be pro-life and pro-choice activists as the end result of lives that center around different definitions of motherhood. They grow up with a belief about the nature of the embryo, so events in their lives lead them to believe that the embryo is a unique person, or a fetus; that people are intimately tied to their biological roles, or that these roles are but a minor part of life; that motherhood is the most important and satisfying role open to a woman, or that motherhood is only one of several roles, a burden when defined as the only role. These beliefs and values are rooted in the concrete circumstances of women's lives—their educations, incomes, occupations, and the different marital and family choices they have made along the way—and they work simultaneously to shape those circumstances in turn. Values about the relative place of reason and faith, about the role of actively planning for life versus learning to accept gracefully life's unknowns, of the relative satisfactions inherent in work and family—all of these factors place activists in a specific relationship to the larger world and give them a specific set of resources with which to confront that world.

The simultaneous and on-going modification of both their lives and their values by each other finds these activists located in a specific place in the social world. They are financially successful, or they are not. They become highly educated, or they do not. They become married and have a large family, or they have a small one. And at each step of the way, both their values and their lives have undergone either ratification or revision.

Pro-choice and pro-life activists live in different worlds, and the scope of their lives, as both adults and children, fortifies them in their belief that their own views on abortion are the more correct, more moral, and more reasonable. When added to this is the fact that should "the other side" win, one group of women will see the very real devaluation of their lives and life resources, it is not surprising that the abortion debate has generated so much heat and so little light.

12 *The Facts About AIDS*

Geeta Dardick

STUDY QUESTIONS

1. What are safe and unsafe sexual behaviors?

2. What does Dardick claim children should know about sexual behavior?

WHAT IS AIDS?

Public information about AIDS reveals the following data. AIDS is a contagious disease that is caused by a virus. The initials A-I-D-S stand for Acquired Immune Deficiency Syndrome. The virus or germ which causes AIDS is typically called the HIV virus.

The HIV virus destroys the immune system by attacking the white blood cells within a person's bloodstream. Without a functional immune system, a person loses the normal ability to fight off disease. At that point, he/she is diagnosed with AIDS.

There is currently no cure for AIDS. The disease has killed men and women, homosexuals and heterosexuals, and persons of every age, and every race. People who have AIDS are dying from a range of health problems including cancer, pneumonia, and meningitis. They are highly susceptible to opportunistic infections because their immune system is rendered useless. As one health officer put it: "When you have a full blown case of AIDS, your body's immune response can drop to zero. It's like phoning 911 and receiving no answer."

When the HIV virus enters an individual's bloodstream, the body tries to fight off the virulent germs by producing antibodies. Unfortunately these antibodies are not strong enough to subdue the HIV virus. However, the antibodies can be used to give an indication of whether or not a person has

Source: Geeta Dardick, "The Facts About AIDS." *The Single Parent,* July/August 1985, pp. 17–20, 46. Reprinted by permission.

been infected with the virus. Most infected persons will show antibodies (in a blood sample) within a three-month period.

After becoming infected with the HIV virus, people can pass it on to others, even though they may show no symptoms of having AIDS. At the current time, about one and one-half million people have the HIV virus, and it is not known how many of these persons will develop full-blown cases of AIDS. But whether or not infected persons come down with AIDS, they can still pass the virus on to others. Unfortunately, close to a million people who now carry the virus probably don't even realize they are infected.

HOW AIDS IS PASSED FROM ONE PERSON TO ANOTHER

AIDS is a preventable disease. AIDS is NOT spread like a cold or flu through everyday, casual contact. Instead, AIDS is spread through the exchange of bodily fluids, or blood to blood (white-cell to white-cell) contact.

The HIV virus can be spread in several, very distinct ways. People who use intravenous drugs can spread the virus by sharing hypodermic needles that are contaminated by infected blood. Pregnant women who have AIDS can pass the virus on to their unborn children. Transfusions of infected blood have passed the virus to recipients, such as persons with hemophilia. Sexual contact (penis-vagina, penis-rectum, mouth-rectum, mouth-vagina, and mouth-penis) with infected persons can move the virus from one person to another.

The HIV virus can be transferred through various sexual acts because sperm and vaginal fluids contain white blood cells. If these fluids are infected with the virus, then the disease can be transmitted into the other person's bloodstream through microscopic rips in the walls of the vagina, rectum, penis or gums. (Saliva and tears can also contain the virus, but in an amount that has not been determined dangerous. Nevertheless, deep, french kissing with persons who could be infected is not advisable).

SAFE AND UNSAFE BEHAVIORS

Health officials state that shaking hands, hugging, dry kissing, coughing and sneezing will NOT transmit the HIV virus. AIDS is NOT contacted from sharing eating utensils or bed linens. You can NOT get AIDS from toilet seats, telephones or swimming pools. Contact with dogs and cats will NOT give you AIDS. A mosquito bite will NOT give you AIDS. Body massages and masturbation will NOT give you AIDS. Going to school with a child who has AIDS, or working in an office with someone who has AIDS, will not give you AIDS. In summary, most behaviors are NOT considered dangerous.

Two behavior patterns definitely increase the risk of getting AIDS. These are: sexual contacts with infected persons and the sharing of syringes and needles with infected intravenous drug users.

The safest solution is to avoid having sexual contacts with infected persons, or with persons who have had multiple partners. The more sex partners you have, the greater your risk of developing AIDS. . . .

As for sharing needles during intravenous drug use, the obvious solution is not to shoot any drugs. If you do use drugs you should not share your syringes or "works" with anyone.

TALKING TO YOUR CHILDREN

When you talk about AIDS with your children, you will need to vary the content of your conversation according to their ages. You can teach young children about the concept of infections, and how to protect themselves from the germs that surround us. With children in the primary grades, you will want to begin teaching about their bodies and how they function. Basically you want to give your children a thorough health education, explaining how they can co-exist safely in an environment which contains various viruses and germs. Teaching them to cover their mouths when they cough, or to wash and bandage cuts on their knees, will get across the concept of wise, precautionary health care.

Scaring young children unnecessarily will serve no purpose. However, they do need to know that becoming "blood brothers" or "blood sisters" with their friends (as so many adults used to do as children) is completely out of the question. Times change, and what was fine for Huck Finn is no longer fun or safe.

Child development experts say children should know all about the reproductive and sexual acts—the penis, vagina, uterus, intercourse, the sperm and egg, the mouth, the rectum everything, by the fifth or sixth grade. . . .

By seventh and eighth grade, you will definitely want to make sure your children understand the dynamics of relationships, that it is normal to develop sexual feelings for others. Teach them that some people respond to their own sex and become homosexuals or lesbians, whereas others (most people) respond sexually to persons of the opposite sex.

Some parents fear that talking about sex with children will promote sexuality but statistics don't back this up. In fact, the statistics (10 to 15 percent of parents talk about sex, whereas 30 to 50 percent of children are already engaging in sex) would suggest that NOT discussing sex may lead to increased sexual activity.

Your children need to understand their own bodies and appreciate their sexuality before ideas like safe sex will make much sense. You definitely need to teach them to say "no" assertively, but it also may be practical to teach them how to say "yes" and be well-prepared. Says Dr. John Holland, "Besides teaching children how to avoid sexual contacts, parents may want to assume that their children will become active sexually, and teach them how to fully protect themselves."

Your talks with your children should reflect your own style, and your own moral convictions. The most important thing you can do is keep channels of communication open, and talk together about the connections between sexuality and AIDS, and drug abuse and AIDS. Silence could be your most dangerous option. . . .

Don't worry about talking about AIDS too much. Children may pretend they are bored or not listening, but they still will be hearing everything you tell them. For some youngsters, family round-table talks may offer their first lessons about AIDS. Your kids may have already heard about the epidemic on television and in school classes and playground discussions. Your children may be experiencing a great deal of alarm and fear about AIDS, or they may act unconcerned and disinterested. Some young people tell their parents that they find the topic depressing, and don't want to hear anything more about AIDS. Others spout myths that are definitely incorrect. You need to be prepared to handle all types of responses from your children. Your main goal will be to convey the facts on AIDS in a clear, comprehensive and unbiased manner.

A parent who practices warm, loving and caring communications with his/her children on *all* topics will have the easiest time talking about AIDS. If you can create a relaxed atmosphere where you listen to your children, they, in turn, will be more inclined to listen to you.

The Surgeon General of the United States, Dr. C. Everett Koop, says: "Education about AIDS should start in early elementary school and at home so that children can grow up knowing the behavior to avoid to protect themselves from exposure to the AIDS virus. The threat of AIDS can provide an opportunity for parents to instill in their children their own moral and ethical standards.

"Those of us who are parents, educators and community leaders, indeed all adults, cannot disregard this responsibility to educate our young. The need is critical and the price of neglect is high. The lives of our young people depend on our fulfilling our responsibility."

AIDS RESOURCES

You and your children can expand your understanding of AIDS through reading available pamphlets and telephoning questions to AIDS hotlines. Besides gathering relevant information for your family, you might consider creating an AIDS library for your church or school. Today, many concerned parents and teens are acting as volunteers to teach others the facts about the disease. Some are giving classes, and others are developing local hotline services. You may want to help form an AIDS task force in your area, or join an already existing association. Your involvement could save lives.

All of the following organizations can give you information about AIDS.

Public Health Service AIDS Hotline
1-800-342-AIDS

National Sexually Transmitted Disease Hotline
1-800-227-8922

National Gay Task Force AIDS Information Hotline
1-800-221-7044
(212) 807-6016 (in NY state)

Maryland Teen-AIDS Hotline
(301) 340-AIDS

American Red Cross Aids Education Office
1730 D Street, NW
Washington, D.C. 20006
(202) 737-8300

U.S. Public Health Service
Public Affairs Office
Hubert H. Humphrey Building, Room 725-H
200 Independence Ave., SW
Washington, D.C. 20201
(202) 245-6867

American Association of Physicians for Human Rights
P.O. Box 14366
San Francisco, CA 94114
(415) 558-9353

AIDS Action Council
729 Eighth Street, SE
Suite 200
Washington, D.C. 20003
(202) 547-3101

Gay Men's Health Crisis
P.O. Box 274
132 West 24th Street
New York, NY 10011
(212) 807-6655

Hispanic AIDS Forum
c/o APRED
853 Broadway, Suite 2007
New York, NY 10003
(212) 870-1902

Los Angeles AIDS PROJECT
7362 Santa Monica Boulevard
Los Angeles, CA 90046
(213) 876-AIDS

Minority Task Force on AIDS
c/o NY City Council of Churches
475 Riverside Drive, Rm. 456
New York, NY 10115
(212) 749-1214

Mothers of AIDS Patients (MAP)
c/o Barbara Peabody
3403 E Street
San Diego, CA 92102
(619) 234-3432

National AIDS Network
729 Eighth Street, SE
Suite 300
Washington, D. C. 20003
(202) 546-2424

National Association of People with AIDS
P.O. Box 65472
Washington, D.C. 20035
(202) 483-7979

National Coalition of Gay Sexually Transmitted Disease Services
c/o Mark Behar
P.O. Box 239
Milwaukee, WI 53201
(414) 277-7671

National Council of Churches/AIDS Task Force
475 Riverside Drive, Rm. 572
New York, NY 10115
(212) 870-2421

San Francisco AIDS Foundation
333 Valencia Street, 4th Floor
San Francisco, CA 94103
(415) 863-2437

The Women's Health Research Foundation
700 Arizona
Santa Monica, CA 90401
(213) 459-6567

13 *The Back-to-Basics Sex Guide*

Carol Botwin

STUDY QUESTIONS

1. What are three areas of communication that affect sex?
2. What factors regarding your own responsibility are important in sexual behavior?

Too many couples, once they're married, assume that sex will take care of itself. Actually, to keep your sex life exciting and satisfying even after years together, you have to make it a top priority—particularly after the honeymoon stage is over. That's when you may begin to take each other for granted, if you're not careful. Of course, there's no way to recapture the wonder and thrill of first love. But a different kind of passion can take over once you know each other well, and it can be more powerful, more of a binding force, than you ever dreamed possible. In fact, married sex can be the best sex of all—if you remember the basics that brought you together in the first place. They are the very same things that can help you keep your love life alive and thriving. Here, from the experts, 23 ways to rekindle the loving feelings, renew your initial attraction and make sex better than ever.

1. EVALUATE YOUR LOVE LIFE

There is nothing wrong with a husband and wife periodically conducting a sexual "check-up." Ask yourself and your partner questions like: Is there anything wrong? What is good about what we are doing—and could we be doing that more often? Are we really enjoying ourselves? Don't analyze yourself

Source: Carol Botwin, "The Back-to-Basics Sex Guide." *Redbook*, March 1985, pp. 102–103, 197. In *Is There Sex After Marriage?* New York: Little, Brown. Copyright © by Carol Botwin. Reprinted by permission of Little, Brown and Company.

or your partner during the actual sexual experience; at a nonsexual time, make an overall review of the state of your sexual life.

2. MAKE TIME FOR SEX

Don't let sex become something that you squeeze in, if you can, *after* chores, the children, work, sports, gardening. Set aside prime time—when you aren't exhausted—for erotic enjoyment. And allot sufficient time so that lovemaking isn't hurried. Sex is just as important as watching TV, cooking a fancy dinner, fixing a leaky faucet, or taking the kids to a movie—maybe more so: It renews your relationship as a couple.

3. CONTINUE TO COURT EACH OTHER

"After marriage, couples tend not to woo or seduce one another," says Dr. Harvey Caplan, a San Francisco psychiatrist and sex therapist. He suggests that one of the best things you can do for your sex life is to continue the courtship once you've "landed" your mate—even after many years together. Take time to keep the vital signs alive in your marriage by letting your partner know that you still think he is valuable and special. You can do this by making an effort to look nice; by telling him what you like about him; by saying "I love you" unexpectedly; by giving him hugs and kisses apart from sexual situations; by concocting little surprises—anything that says, "I'm thinking of you."

Sex therapist Dr. Helen Singer Kaplan, a *Redbook* contributing editor who is studying happy long-term relationships, has noted that the eyes of her subjects seem to light up every time their partner enters the room: "She knows she is giving him a present by being there. He knows he is giving her a present by being there." When was the last time your eyes lit up for your spouse?

4. DON'T BE AFRAID TO TALK ABOUT SEX

Good communication includes telling your partner specifically and explicitly what you want or need. "Touch me down there" isn't good enough. Tell him exactly where you want to be touched. Show him by leading his hand to the right place and demonstrating the exact pressure, rhythm and amount of stimulation that you enjoy, and that ultimately brings you to orgasm.

Telling your partner what you don't like is just as important, but try to offer a positive alternative. For example, if you don't like your breasts touched a certain way, let your partner know what you do like.

Beware of trying to communicate by doing to your partner what you want done to you. It may not work. One woman wanted to be touched more gently, and she thought that she was showing her husband this by touching him very lightly. He, however, liked to be touched very firmly, so he responded by touching her more heavily. Only when this couple finally started talking to each other were they able to understand each other.

If you hate doing something that your partner has suggested, you must talk that over, too. One wife had a good sex life with her husband for 15 years until he announced one day that he would like to try oral sex. The wife agreed but found it totally repugnant. Instead of telling her husband this, though, she started to avoid sex with him. She was afraid that he would want more oral sex. Sex, which had been frequent until this point, started to dwindle—all because of this couple's lack of communication and inability to discuss what they really wanted in bed.

Sometimes partners can negotiate and find acceptable alternatives when sexual tastes are different—they bring their likes and dislikes into the open. For example, the woman just described might have suggested to her husband that she bring him to climax manually instead of orally, or, since he seemed to be in search of variety, that they try out several different sexual positions, different surroundings, or even new props or sex toys.

One subject that couples rarely discuss is frequency of sex. Various studies have shown that dissatisfaction with sexual frequency is often a silent problem in marriage: one partner may want more sex, the other less, but neither is willing to talk about it. Experts find that mutually acceptable compromises can often be worked out—three times a week instead of five, or twice a week instead of once, for example, but only if the matter is discussed.

5. GIVE POSITIVE FEEDBACK

Let your mate know when you are enjoying yourself. You can say, for example, "I like that," or "Keep that up; it really turns me on." Or you can express your delight by making satisfied sounds. That way, partners learn about each other's preferences and know when they are doing the right thing. And let your mate know that you feel turned on when he looks or acts a certain way, in or out of bed. Positive feedback and affection in the rest of the relationship also contributes to nurturing good sex.

6. NEVER FAKE ORGASMS

Faking orgasms is primarily a female problem, although some men also pretend. Most people who moan and groan in phony ecstasy are afraid of being considered inferior sex partners, or are trying to cover up sexual dysfunctions, and think that they might be rejected if the truth comes out. Many women who feign orgasms feel that they are protecting their partner's ego. But covering up—keeping a sexual secret—is destructive. Your partner never learns about your needs or preferences and is misled into thinking that you both are doing just fine. You cheat yourself out of genuine sexual pleasure that might come about if you're honest with him, if you told him what you really want and if you then explored and experimented in different ways together.

7. USE POSITIVE REINFORCEMENT

If you are consistently turned off by something your partner does—for example, your husband usually forgets to shave or shows up in a T-shirt when you've planned a nice dinner—try a positive approach to effect change. When he's clean-shaven, act sexy and affectionate and attempt to seduce him. If you do this often enough, he may begin to realize that a certain behavior or appearance leads to a reward: you respond sexually.

8. TUNE IN TO YOUR OWN SEXUALITY

Unless you understand how you tick sexually, you can never be a really good sex partner. You have to know what you need or want before you can tell someone else. Although this news may seem shocking, most sex therapists believe that masturbation is an excellent way to get acquainted with yourself as a sexual being—even when you're married. Without a partner, whose presence might inhibit or distract you, you can think about yourself and learn what excites you, what you don't respond to, and what fantasies give you an erotic charge. This sexual self-exploration can enrich your marital sex life. When you are slow to respond to your partner, you can summon up the fantasy that excited you during masturbation. You can ask your partner to touch you in that way.

Another way to understand yourself better sexually is to pay more attention to the sensual part of your personality. Take note of the erotic or sexual responses you have as you go through your day-to-day life. What kind of music makes you feel romantic or sexual? What kind of setting? Does a silk blouse or a leather jacket rubbing against your skin put you in a sensual mood? Leading sex therapist Dr. Harold Lief often recommends keeping a daily journal of sexual thoughts, feelings and fantasies. If you start to tune in to erotic responses that you may have shut out before, you will be cultivating the sexual side of yourself as well as learning things about yourself that you could put into play with your partner. For example, music that makes you feel romantic can be used as background to lovemaking. Or you can drape yourself in the silky cloth that you discovered feels so sensual against your skin, and let your partner slowly peel it away.

9. REMEMBER THAT OUR SEXUAL SELVES ARE PART OF OUR ENTIRE SELVES

Psychological problems, such as fear of getting really close to someone, or inability to tolerate much pleasure, or an unconscious desire to see a spouse as a parent, can get in the way of full erotic enjoyment. Negative or angry feelings toward a partner have to be brought into the open and resolved before sex can be expected to improve.

CAROL BOTWIN

10. DON'T BE AFRAID TO SAY NO

In all marriages situations will arise when one or both partners will not want to have sex. Partners may get angry at one another; there may be trouble with jobs or children; a person can be unusually fatigued, or may not feel well, or, for one reason or another, simply might not be in the mood. Experts advise couples to be straight with each other—to say, "I don't feel like it tonight," followed by a simple, honest explanation of why so that the partner does not feel personally rejected. Unfortunately, most people use devious tactics to avoid sex—such as staying up later than their mate, working on a home-repair project, or even starting an argument. Instead of saying, "I'm not in the mood," they make up an excuse such as, "I'm too tired," or "I have a stomachache." Behind all such lies and evasions is the feeling that somehow it isn't ever right to refuse sex in marriage and that your mate will get angry at you if you do.

Respect each other's right to occasionally not feel like making love, and make a pact ahead of time that you will not be afraid to tell each other the truth. Discuss in advance the possibility of sexual refusals, and how each of you will handle them. Agree to try to avoid evasions or excuses, which often create hurt feelings or misunderstanding ("I'm getting older; he doesn't think I'm attractive anymore," or "I must have done something to irritate him," or "She must be mad at me for some reason."

11. RECOGNIZE THE DANGERS IN SEXUAL SIGNALS

Many couples use all sorts of private signals—spoken or unspoken—to indicate whether they're ready for sex. For example, a phrase like "I'm going to bed early" can be an invitation, whereas "I feel like staying up late" can be a way of saying "No sex tonight." There are some intrinsic problems in such signals. According to sex researcher John Gagnon, they can become a form of negotiation between husband and wife—one reason why sexual frequency declines with age. "As we get older, such negotiation gets more tiring," he explains. "We say to ourselves, Well, maybe tomorrow (even though we have fewer tomorrows)." Still another danger of sexual signals is that they may not be clearly understood by both partners because they have never been discussed. If you use sexual signals, agree on them so that they're clear to both of you.

12. RESPECT EACH OTHER'S TASTES

If your partner doesn't like the smell of your face cream, or can't stand bitten fingernails, or wants the lid put back on the peanut butter jar, respect his preferences. To some people, looks or surroundings don't matter; to others, appearances are important to sexual interest. Similarly, bodily smells excite some people but turn others off. Don't ignore or put down his tastes; cater to them as much as possible. And expect the same consideration.

13. CREATE PRIVACY

The Study Group of New York recently published a book entitled *Children and Sex*, the results of a survey of 225 parents. They discovered that the parents' bedroom was often used by the children as the TV room, a reading room and a gym, with the bed used as a trampoline; it was also where group discussions and cuddling sessions took place. No wonder surveys show that couples' sex lives deteriorate markedly with children around!

In order for their sex life to flourish, a couple has to create an atmosphere in which they will not be afraid of being interrupted—one where they can concentrate on enjoying each other and put everything else out of their minds for the moment. Installing a lock on the bedroom door and teaching the kids that they must knock before entering is one answer. So is putting the TV in another room and encouraging the children to get in the habit of playing elsewhere.

14. GUARD AGAINST RIGID ROUTINES

A typical rut is only-on-Wednesday-and-Saturday-night, or only on Sunday morning, or only at night before going to sleep, or only in the same one or two ways every time. Although some couples thrive on complete predictability, most find fixed schedules and repertories boring or uninspiring, especially as time goes on. Variety and spontaneity keep sex interesting and prevent it from dwindling. Experiment—even if you feel silly or embarrassed at first. Try different positions, times of day, lighting, places to have sex. Take weekend or one-day vacations: sexual desire and frequency increase during holidays. Dullness in the rest of your relationship is often reflected in the bedroom, so try regularly to plan anything that will be exciting and fun for both of you.

15. REMEMBER THAT SEX IS A WAY OF EXPRESSING LOVE

Too many people think of sex as just a way of relieving tension. In marriage, sex should have a dual role: physical release, as well as the expression of affection, tenderness and caring. If you really believe that sex is a loving experience, you won't be tempted to use it to reward or punish your partner. You can emphasize affection by occasionally caressing and fondling each other without going on to intercourse. And remember that a little affection at nonsexual times can mean more satisfying sex later.

16. USE YOUR FANTASIES

The majority of experts encourage the use of fantasies in a couple's sex life. New excitement can be injected into tired sex lives if couples learn to reveal their sexual fantasies and sometimes act them out together. You can use

CAROL BOTWIN

fantasies solo, as well—by thinking private exciting thoughts or even by dressing in something that turns you on while you are making love to your spouse.

Many people feel that it is wrong to think of someone besides their partner during a sexual fantasy, to think of something they regard as perverted or to play out kinky stuff from their fantasies. The consensus among sex authorities, however, is that to do all of these things is normal, common and often beneficial. The well-known marriage counselor Dr. Clifford Sager has written that "playing out romantic or in-danger-of-being-caught situations, mild sadomasochistic play, master-slave fantasies, call-girl fantasies, Don Juan, gay or troilism [group-sex] fantasies are included in the repertoire of many married couples."

In addition to fantasy, many experts feel that sexual interest can be maintained, or a flagging libido revived, by the occasional use of titillating literature, erotic movies, sexy clothing, body oils or vibrators—if these aids don't go against a couple's values and they find them sexually stimulating.

17. TAKE RESPONSIBILITY FOR YOUR OWN PLEASURE

You may think that it's up to your partner to make you enjoy sex; it's actually up to you. This means, first of all, giving yourself and your partner permission to enjoy sex. A surprisingly large number of men and women have internal censors that tell them not to take pleasure in sex.

Taking responsibility for your own pleasure means letting your partner know about your sexual needs instead of hoping that he'll read your mind or stumble onto what you want. Be active—initiate sex instead of always waiting for him, try different positions, make suggestions. Educate yourself.

18. DON'T TURN YOURSELF OFF

Husbands and wives who have lost sexual interest generally blame their partner ("She doesn't turn me on anymore," or "He turns me off"), but Dr. Helen Singer Kaplan maintains, "People who say, 'I am turned off,' are usually turning themselves off without realizing it. When something about the other person evokes a wish not to have sex, it is involuntary and unconscious, but you can learn to control it."

Here's what happens: You are angry at your partner or inhibited about receiving sexual pleasure. When your partner approaches you, you automatically summon up negative thoughts without realizing what you're doing. You think about something your partner does that riles you, or concentrate on your mate's most unattractive feature.

If you feel turned off, start to examine your thoughts just before sex. When negative notions float through your head, send them packing. Think about your mate's attractive qualities instead of his drawbacks, or concentrate on pleasure itself.

19. DON'T EXPECT SEX TO BE GREAT ALL THE TIME

If you think your sex life should always be fantastic, you're setting yourself up for keen disappointment. Highs and lows are normal: our sexual appetite and hormone levels fluctuate; our physical or mental well-being changes. Sometimes sex will be good, sometimes so-so, sometimes downright disappointing. You and your partner aren't machines; don't expect too much of each other.

20. AVOID TURNING SEX INTO WORK

If you try too hard, sex backfires. Sex experts say that performance anxiety—constant worry over whether you are a good or perfect partner—is rampant; people turn each sexual experience into a test. Do take your partner's needs into consideration, but also remember that to be really good at sex, you have to learn to concentrate on your own sexual pleasure.

21. REMEMBER THAT THE FOUNDATION OF GOOD SEX IS RESPECT AND TRUST

Dr. Fred Gottlieb, director of the Family Therapy Institute of Southern California, maintains that the single most significant factor in staying turned on to a mate is respect—the ability to take a long view of your partner and to continue to feel proud and pleased to be a part of his environment. Respect, he says, implies "that you are both equals. Neither of you feels superior or is caught in a scramble based on feeling inferior and wanting to catch up."

As for trust, New Jersey psychiatrist Edward L. Parsons says that it means "Not only feeling secure that your partner will protect and support you but also that he is interested in your personal growth, so that there is room for both of you to change over the years." Trust means knowing that your mate has your best interests at heart and can consider them as well as his own.

If for some reason a husband and wife do not respect each other or if the trust is broken, their sexual relationship often suffers.

22. DON'T NEGLECT A SEXUAL PROBLEM

If you suffered from a physical ailment that lingered, you would see a doctor. Adopt the same attitude toward sexual functioning. Don't ignore a sexual problem, including lack of desire, because you are embarrassed or fearful to discuss it with your spouse. Sometimes you can solve a minor difficulty just by talking. However, if the problem seems major, see a reputable sex therapist.

In the case of sexual dysfunction, like lack of desire, Dr. Helen Singer Kaplan says that "The faster you recognize it, the better the chance of curing it." But don't give up hope if you have had sexual problems for many years. You can be helped at any age, or at any stage of a relationship, provided that both partners are mutually determined to do so and are firmly committed to each other.

23. PAY SPECIAL ATTENTION TO SEX AS YOU GROW OLDER

Too many couples, starting in their forties and fifties, begin to let their sex lives evaporate. It is important for men and women to understand that sexual responses may slow down because of the aging process—but they don't disappear altogether. As they age, couples should talk to each other about their changing sexual needs, and should be willing to experiment together to find out how they can accommodate new needs as they arise. More direct stimulation of the genital area, the use of additional lubrication, gratifying each other sexually through means other than actual intercourse, a change to positions that might make sex more comfortable and the attitude that successful sex can be stroking and holding without copulation are all possible adjustments. With flexibility and the feeling that sex does not end with old age, couples can go on giving each other pleasure for the rest of their lives.

Dr. Helen Singer Kaplan tells of a happy couple in their eighties married 60 years. Dr. Kaplan broached the subject of sex when she was alone with the woman. "Well," said the octogenarian, "since Jake had his pacemaker put in, we keep it down to once a week."

Is there sex after marriage? You bet!

4 *Developing Intimacy*

Another aspect of intimacy—dating—is dealt with in this chapter. Taken for granted, the custom of dating is a relatively recent social phenomenon. Before World War I, most people lived and died in the same small community, a situation that meant everyone knew everyone else and so such formal introductions were unnecessary.

Dating as we know it came with the changes brought about by rapid industrialization and urbanization. With the exodus from small towns and the use of the telephone and automobile, control by parents was lessened and dating became more an aspect of recreation and adult role socialization than an aspect of mate selection, although it still functions as a significant element in this regard.

Until recently, the cultural scripts reflected in dating were those of the male's dominant role and the differing male/female goals of sexual pursuit versus seeking a commitment. Now a more spontaneous, informal pattern prevails. However, elements of the old male-domination script seem to be combining with the new sexually permissive script to produce a high incidence of sexual assaults on dates. Levine and Kanin in the first article of Chapter 4 discuss these effects of the changing sexual mores on dating norms.

Goals for dating vary with age and include recreation in that dating is fun; it is also a means of evaluating one's own personality and sexuality, of raising one's status, and selecting a mate. Difficulties concerning dating basically revolve around meeting potential dates. Means to this end are blind dates, ads, dating services, and self-introduction, often using bait and flirting behavior. Janet Jacobsen in the second article of this chapter discusses these means for obtaining an introduction.

With the large jump in the divorce rate has come the problem of reentry dating. Added to their difficulty in meeting people, and their reluctance to risk commitment is the role of the newly separateds' children. Dating for the newly separated is quite different from their former dating relationship. It includes a number of growth stages. In the first stage there is the fear of social contact due to the long absence from the dating game; the "candy factory" stage is an attempt to build one's ego by multiple dating or a number of short-term relationships; the "latching on" stage is an entering into an immediate relationship in order to avoid the inevitable feelings of loss; when exploring the singles' world becomes lonely and empty due to its lack of closeness, there comes a search for commitment, for intimacy; the final stage is risking again with a close and loving relationship (O'Phelan 1983).

A seeming new extension of dating is seen in the extremely rapid growth of cohabitation in the past twenty years. Cultural, personal, and technological reasons based in part on dating's inability to help one build and maintain meaningful relationships has been the basis for the growing popularity of cohabitation. This popularity, however, does not mean that cohabitation is problem-free. Problems of cohabitation may include feelings of guilt, limiting of social contacts, conflicting goals, and an extra-legal status. It is this latter item that Patricia O'Toole discusses in the third article of Chapter 4—how to add protection to your premarital cohabitation.

An outcome of dating may be the development of a strong relationship involving physical attraction, friendship, intimacy, mutuality, and a feeling of transcendence—love. However, indiscriminate use of the term "love," mythical ideas of romantic love, and mistaken techniques for maintaining it lead to confusions about what love is. Robert Trotter, in the final article of this chapter, discusses Sternberg's three faces of love and the need to have all three—commitment, intimacy, and passion—in order to have love.

REFERENCE

1. O'Phelan, M L. 1980. "Once Upon a Time . . . Again." *The Single Parent* (May).

14 Sexual Violence Among Dates and Acquaintances

Edward M. Levine / Eugene J. Kanin

STUDY QUESTIONS

1. What are some factors that predispose males to avoid using sexual preliminaries in order to gain sexual gratification?

2. What do Levine and Kanin claim will be an outcome of sexual violence on future family formation?

INTRODUCTION

In recent years the crime of rape has received unprecedented attention and, as with other serious offenses, keen interest has developed regarding this trend. However, the rise in incidence that has been reported in the *Uniform Crime Reports* and in select cities in recent years has been largely discredited as real, largely because the increase in the rates of reported rape reflect a greater willingness of victims to report their having been victimized. And this has been variously attributed to the influence of the women's movement, the modification of rape statutes, and to the increase in the general level of education regarding the rights of rape victims (Sheley, 1985).

While it would be difficult to make a definitive case for a real increase in the rate of official forcible rape, rape among intimates—date and acquaintance rape—is another matter. Evidence can now be gathered to show that serious sexual violence (termed date rape) has increased dramatically during the last 30 years. Although the questionnaire studies of the late 1950s dealing with sexual aggression did not focus on rape, per se, case material collected at the

Source: Edward M. Levine and Eugene J. Kanin, "Sexual Violence Among Dates and Acquaintances: Trends and Their Implications for Marriage and Family." *Journal of Family Violence* 2:1(1987): 55–65. Reprinted by permission.

time from the sample populations show rape to have been an exceptional occurrence.

For example, from one study in which 82 cases were collected, only three cases of rape were identified, all of them date rapes (Kirkpatrick and Kanin, 1957). Another study of the experiences of high school seniors examined 91 case studies among whom only four date rape victims were found (Kanin, 1957). From 1957 to 1961, Kanin requested his female undergraduate students anonymously to report on their victimization experiences, and of the 372 reports of female victimization, 13 cases of forcible rape were found (3.5%), 11 of which were readily identified as date rape, the remaining 2 being acquantance rape victims. Thus, investigations revealed a date rape incidence of only 3.8%.

In contrast, recent studies of female college students revealed strikingly higher figures. Koss and Oros (1982) found that 8.2% of their sample of female college students reported having had forced sex; Wilson and Durrenberger (1982) reported 15% in their study; Parcell (1973) found 14.6%; and Rapaport (1984) reported 14%. And more recent data from a study of 727 college females found that slightly more than 15% of them had been victims of date rape (Kanin, 1985). In addition, Korman and Leslie's (1982) research found that there was a higher rate of sex aggression at the genital level experienced by college females, a trend that had been detected somewhat earlier by Kanin and Parcell (1977), who found that the incidence of sex aggression experienced by college females was shifting dramatically from stranger to date and acquaintance rape.

Other evidence pertinent to our case that serious sexual aggression has become more commonplace for university women in their dating-courtship relations can be culled from the sex aggression studies from the mid-1950s to the late 1970s. This has increased from 13% in the early 1970s—and to 20% in the late 1970s (Kirkpatrick and Kanin, 1957; Kanin and Parcell, 1977; Korman and Leslie, 1982). Korman and Leslie (1982) also noted that "sexually exploitative attempts are becoming more coitally direct and that more women are experiencing these attempts." . . .

Although this survey of evidence should be viewed with a degree of caution, since the studies from which they are drawn represent certain problems in sampling and contrasting populations from different institutions, there is nevertheless a preponderance of and a consistency in the evidence from the past 30 years indicating that the college female is increasingly finding herself a target of sexual victimization and violence. This is now also true for female high school seniors (and perhaps even younger teenagers). In addition, males much more frequently resort to sexual aggression with no preliminary erotic intimacies than they did 3 decades ago.

Because such fear-inducing experiences may engender profoundly troubling emotional problems among sexually victimized females with regard to their attitudes toward marriage and family, the purpose of this study is to describe certain of the sociocultural changes that have occurred during the past generation and that appear to be largely responsible for the emergence of these trends in aggressive sexual behavior among younger males.

TRADITIONAL SEX STANDARDS

The human desire for sexual gratification is not governed by an instinct, an autonomous force that compels men and women to seek sexual gratification irrespective of their wishes. Instead, human sexual feelings and behavior are stimulated by the sex drive or impulse which becomes most intense and powerful during adolescence and young adulthood, after which its influence over human behavior gradually diminishes. Furthermore, its expression is greatly limited by the constraining influence of the moral values of tradition and religion, norms, and individual preferences that are inculcated in children by their parents, as well as emphasized by society through social institutions such as the schools. Historically, these standards have generally served to protect females against the predatory sexual propensities of males.

These values were part of the same tradition that upheld a double standard of sexual rights and responsibilities for postpubertal males and females. That is, adolescent and young adult males were generally free to enjoy such sexual pleasures as they found or that were offered them by sexually congenial women. Once married, they were expected to observe marital fidelity, although their extramarital affairs were not exceptional.

By contrast, females were expected to remain chaste until marriage and be completely faithful to their husbands thereafter. Economically dependent on their husbands, who regarded them as the weaker sex, women were also envisaged as the guardians of sexual and other moral standards that were considered as being centrally important for the stability of the family and for human well-being. Thus, modesty was a cardinal virtue of unmarried females, while the sexual posturing and dalliances of bachelors were taken for granted and commonly overlooked.

After that point in history when parents arranged their children's marriages, single, young (and even older) women who worked were obliged to live at home until they married, while their male counterparts were free to come and go as they pleased. Teenage girls were expected to introduce their dates to their parents at home so the latter could learn something about their character and their families. Parents also knew where their daughters were going, and when their dates would bring them home. The most difficult choice then confronting most adolescent girls was whether or not to give a boy a goodnight kiss on the first date, for to do so might lead him to consider her forward and improperly interested in his amorous advances which might undermine her defenses against them. While these standards still hold for some adolescent females, they have weakened considerably during the past generation, and have been rejected or abandoned by numbers of them.

WOMEN'S INDEPENDENCE AND THE NEW SEXUAL FREEDOM

The use of the contraceptive pill and the concomitant erosion of traditional values related to marriage and family and sexual behavior by the cultural revolution of the late 1960s (Levine, 1981, 1985) were major factors leading to

EDWARD M. LEVINE / EUGENE J. KANIN

the fundamental changes in intersexual relationships that are so prevalent today. These changes gained considerable momentum from the successes of the Women's Movement in breaking down the barriers to women's social and economic inequality, with the result that the double sexual standard collapsed for ever-growing numbers of females. Many assertive young women contend that it relegated them to a subordinate status in their relationships with men and was, therefore, a completely out-moded standard that had lost its relevance.

Armed with college and professional degrees and enjoying the satisfaction of having jobs and careers and the financial independence this provided them, increasing numbers of young women went on to claim much the same social rights and options that men have traditionally enjoyed. For example, it is no longer unconventional for working women to pay for their luncheons and dinners when dating, to invite men to be their guests for an evening date, and to engage in premarital sex almost as freely and unperturbedly as do men. In brief, women's occupational and social independence has been translated into a sexual freedom that begins to approximate that which men have had throughout the ages.

These transforming changes in women's occupational and social roles, as well as in their values and attitudes concerning their social and sexual relationships with men, have led to corresponding changes in the lives of adolescent females. That is, once women attained equality with men, the next logical step was for them (and their husbands) to raise their daughters to become fully independent, with the schools and the mass media affirming and exemplifying female equality in all important spheres of life. Consequently, steadily growing numbers of young women have been attending college for a generation and more, but especially since the early 1970s. And adolescent girls, more than ever before, anticipate working several years before they marry, are much freer in deciding when and whom to date, and are generally much less limited by their parents' regulations. Furthermore, numbers of adolescent girls are unhesitant about calling boys for dates or merely to talk with them, and are also sexually active—alarmingly so for those who become pregnant in their early teens, which is no longer uncommon among white, middle class high school girls.

Today, adolescents are well aware that even if their parents understandingly and helpfully counsel them to remain sexually abstinent, they are also resigned, however ruefully, to their children being sexually active during their teen years. Adolescent boys guiltlessly ignore parental pieties about their behaving responsibly toward girls, and easily find girls as willing as they are to engage in sexual intercourse. The confluence of the equalized social relationships between the sexes, the sexual freedom so widely enjoyed today by adolescents and young adults, and females' greater willingness to engage in coitus make them more vulnerable to being raped.

The changing context within which the sexual victimization of females occurs is illustrated by earlier studies that provide substantial data indicating that aggressive sexual behavior followed after consensual sexual activity, such as kissing, petting, and more intensely erotic behavior (Kirkpatrick and Kanin, 1957; Kanin, 1957). However, female college students today report a surprisingly large percentage of both sexual aggression and rape that were spontaneously initiated by their male companions without any antecedent consensual, erotic activity. Approximately 44% of these sexual aggressions were not preceded by any form of consensual sex play (Kanin & Parcell, 1977). More explicitly, this phenomenon involved the males attempting to engage in sexual intercourse at once, rather than their engaging in a sequential seductive order involving kissing, fondling, and the like in order sexually to arouse the female.

The apparently growing tendency of males to dispense with such sexual preliminaries prior to seeking coercively to gain sexual gratification from their female companions may be partly due to the influence of the entertainment media. That is, these media often portray sexual settings in which males and females are intimately involved, but with the amorous or courtship sequences that might properly lead to this, being seldom, if ever, depicted. Thus, the trend in contemporary sexual behavior of date and acquaintance rapists suggests an equivalence of male and female sexuality in the sense that such males are heedless of females' rights when the former are highly sexually aroused, behavior that is partly legitimized by the entertainment media.

It may also be the case that adolescent and college males now have far higher expectations of gaining sexual gratification from casual dates because of the changes in the roles and attitudes of their female counterparts, and are, therefore, much less willing to allow them to frustrate their sexual desires. To the extent that young women are viewed as being uninhibited by traditional standards governing female sexual behavior, and are regarded as being equally knowledgeable about and interested in sex as are their dates, then males holding these views may expect females to treat coitus as casually as they do in thought and behavior. Consequently, the unwillingness of females to comply with their dates' demands for sexual intercourse may lead to sexual aggression or rape— which males may increasingly consider acceptable because they no long find clear-cut, generally respected standards ruling out such reactions. What they deem to be wholly unjustifiable is the refusal of their dates to accede to their demand for sexual gratification, since this is seen as a completely arbitrary response. In their eyes, sexual freedom for females does not countenance sexually frustrating their dates. Sex on demand on 1-night stands has become normative among many young males for whom a kiss good night or even mild petting are hopelessly juvenile responses.

A study that tends to affirm this interpretation found that numbers of adolescents of both sexes now believe that extenuating circumstances limit females' right to preserve their sexual integrity. In a sample of 432 adolescents, 54% of the males and 42% of the females agreed that forced sexual intercourse *is* permissible if the girls led the boy on, sexually excited him, or agreed to have sex with him and then changed her mind (Ehrhart and Sandler, 1985). Attesting to how greatly dating norms and environments have changed are data from another study reporting that 75% of the female college students in its sample said that they had experienced sexual aggression, that these incidents most often occurred during their senior year of high school or their first year of college—and that they had taken place on the *first* date in either their rooms or the room of their dates (Burkhardt, 1983). Other research mentioned in the *Chronicle of Higher Education* (1983) involving United States and Canadian male college students stated that 35% of the sample said that they might commit rape if they could be certain that they would not be apprehended. Although this probably reflects their fantasy life more than their inclination, it is nonetheless symptomatic of negative changes in young men's attitude toward young women, and a worrisome sign of the times.

THE CULTURE OF SEX AND THE EQUALIZATION OF WOMEN

The attenuation of the traditions and norms that protected adolescent and adult females against male sexual aggression and violence has been paralleled by the popularity of magazines that feature nude females in sexually explicit poses. Paradoxically, while these magazines have prospered by exploiting young women who are deliberately portrayed as sex objects, numbers of college women regard them as unobjectionable, partly because sex has become a common subject for social and public discussion, as well as because exposing oneself to the public, if not condoned, is considered by them to be a matter of individual choice, and its legitimacy a matter of personal opinion.

Insofar as opinions are based on personal choice and right, then they tend to be equalized, for all have rights to their opinions, however dubious or slanted others may judge them to be (Levine and Ross, 1977). This relativistic standard, in tandem with the growing educational, familial, and occupational equalization of females, has modified younger men's image of women. That is, inasmuch as adolescent and older females generally want to be regarded and dealt with primarily as individuals who are on an equal footing with males, and since the media flood the public with both suggestive and explicit sexual themes, images, and fantasies that demean and degrade female sexuality, males increasingly seem to view females primarily as asexual competitors, and secondarily in terms of their gender. Consequently, males may increasingly believe that bargaining, pressuring, and threatening are acceptable, if not truly legitimate, means to employ in attempting to induce women to be sexually compliant. Thus, male aggressiveness in intersexual relationships appears to become more prevalent the more closely the females' way of life and degree of sexual freedom approximate those of males. Indeed, while Janet Chafetz (1985) found that equality in marriages had a positive effect on spouses' intimacy, her insightful comment that intersexual equality also generated more marital disputes and conflict and increased the difficulty of resolving them is also pertinent here. . . .

CONCLUSION

An accumulating body of evidence indicates that the last 30 years have witnessed a disturbingly high increase in the sexual victimization of teenage and college females by dates and acquaintances. This trend seems to be partly the result of young females having much the same degree of freedom in their social and sexual relationships that their male counterparts enjoy. It is also attributable to the largely unrestrained ways in which human sexuality is featured in the mass media and popular culture, and which have diminished young people's inhibitions about seeking and gaining sexual gratification increasingly during their adolescent years. This is very likely facilitated by their widespread and growing use of alcoholic beverages.

Given this set of conditions and the declining influence of the standards that once protected unmarried females against male sexual predations, there is a strong likelihood that younger females, and perhaps older ones as well, will increasingly constitute an at-risk population with regard to being raped by dates and acquaintances, a trend that is all the more disconcerting in view of its ramifications for the well-being of marriage and family.

REFERENCES

Burkhart, B. (1983, December.) Presentation at Acquaintance Rape and Rape Prevention on Campus Workshop, Louisville, Ky.

Chafetz, J. (1985). Marital intimacy and conflict: Irony of spousal equality. *Free Inq. Creative Sociol.* 2: 191–199.

Chronicle of Higher Education (1983, August 31). p. 9.

Kanin, E. (1957). Male aggression in dating-courtship relations. *Am. J. Sociol.* 63: 197–204.

Kanin, E. (1985). *Rape among Intimates*, Paper presented at the Annual Meeting of the American Society of Criminology.

Kanin, E., and Parcell, S. (1977). Sexual aggression: A second look at the offended females. *Arch. Sexual Behav.* 6: 67–76.

Kirkpatrick, C., and Kanin, E. (1957). Male sex aggression on a university campus. *Am. Sociological Rev.* 22: 52–58.

Kornman, S., and Leslie, G. (1982). The relationship of feminist ideology and date expense sharing to perceptions of sexual aggression in dating. *J. Sex Res.* 18: 114–129.

Koss, M., and Oros, C. (1982). Sexual experiences survey: A research instrument investigating sexual aggression and victimization. *J. Consult. Clin. Psychol.* 50: 455–457.

Levine, E. (1981). Middle class family decline. *Society* 1: 72–78.

Levine, E. (1985). The plight of the middle class family. *J. Fam. Cult.* 1: 29–41.

Levine, E., and Kanin, E. (1986). Adolescent drug use: Its prospects for the future. *J. Fam. Cult.* 1: 4.

Levine, E., and Ross, N. (1977). Sexual dysfunctions and psychoanalysis. *Ame. J. Psychiatr.* 234: 646–651.

Rapaport, K. (1984). Quoted in: A disturbing look at rape. *National on-Campus Report.*

Wilson, W., and Durrenberger, R. (1982). Comparison of rape and attempted rape victims. *Psychological Rep.* 50: 198.

15 *Making Your Move*

Janet Jacobsen

STUDY QUESTIONS

1. What does Jacobsen mean by the term, "bait"?

2. Indicate several examples of "bait" and how they are used.

Unless we opt to give up the opposite sex completely, sooner or later every single comes to grips consciously or unconsciously with the issue of developing a primary relationship, possibly even marriage. The American way of creating relationships is by dating. Unfortunately, especially for those who are newly single, our training in "how to date" is generally limited to experience as teenagers. Dating for adults is a highly neglected subject.

After several years of teaching singles classes and workshops and earning a B.A. in interpersonal communication, I've found that there are some basic skills involved in what we could call "Beginning Dating." While trial and error is probably the most common way to learn, learning from the experience of others can be just as useful, and a lot less painful.

In order to develop a dating life, the first—and for some people most difficult—skill is in meeting people. There are three basic ways to meet people. One is to be introduced by others, a social convention sadly on the decline. Social life for all singles would be much brighter if we would just remember to introduce people to one another—and encourage others to do the same for us.

Waiting for the revival of introductions, however may take longer than we have, which leads us to the second method of meeting—introducing ourselves. Often we think that in order to speak to a stranger we need a brilliant "opening line." After asking hundreds of singles what opening line "works" best on them, I've found that you can actually say *anything*, provided it's honest and sincere. Obviously there was something that attracted you to the person.

Source: Janet Jacobsen, "Making Your Move." *The Single Parent,* April 1984, pp. 16, 23. Reprinted by permission.

Tell them what it is! "I'm about to die of terminal boredom waiting in this grocery line. Wanna talk?" Or "You look like such a cheerful person; I wanted to meet you. My name is . . ." Actually, you can stumble around, hem and haw, and wind up with something witty like "Hi," and still make a great impression, if you're sincere about it. We avoid this second method, however, because of fear of rejection, which we'll discuss shortly.

This leaves us with the third method of meeting—getting them to introduce *themselves.* This amounts to making it easy for other people to approach you. At group events or social functions, stand among the biggest crowd of people. Smile. Be willing to make eye contact with people, which doesn't mean staring anyone down. One of our reasons for not approaching others is not knowing what to talk about, so you can make it easy for others by having "bait." Bait consists of things like wearing a T-shirt or a button with a slogan, thus enabling others to say, "Oh, did you go to Florida State?" Unusual jewelry or clothing can spur conversation. People seem to like to comment on clothes that are embroidered, for instance. Carry a book with an interesting title. Carry a frisbee when you walk through the park. And who can resist coming over when you have a puppy or a kitten . . . or a Saint Bernard, for that matter. People who might be shy about coming up and talking to *you* seem to have no trouble coming over to meet your cocker spaniel. Being aware of bait also helps when you are going to take the risk of speaking first; look for bait. It gives you something to talk about.

Why *not* just talk to everyone? Single people constantly deal with that major social block—fear of rejection. We're afraid they might not *like* us. But let's be realistic. Rejection is essential. You *can't* accept everyone. If I said you must now be best friends with all the people in your neighborhood, you wouldn't be able to do it. Relationships take time, a limited resource for each of us. Maybe we would really like to be close friends with everyone, but we have to put priorities in our interactions, and so does everyone else. And we can't expect to make it to the top of everyone's list.

Think of the reasons we might be rejected. Perhaps we remind them of someone they'd rather not remember. Perhaps they're interested in or involved with someone else at the moment. Perhaps they're having a bad day and don't want to meet *anyone.* Maybe they just don't have the time for any more people in their lives right now. Or we may fit some negative stereotype they hold (such as avoiding smokers). Some people will reject us to keep us from rejecting them. And sometimes we're just not their type. It's as though we each have a little check list of qualities and characteristics that we find most attractive. Just because someone doesn't happen to match our list doesn't mean there's anything *wrong* with them, and there's nothing necessarily wrong with us just because we don't match someone else's list. Fortunately, there are many, many people in the world. All we have to do is meet them.

Often people find it difficult to "reject" others; we want to spare their feelings, so we spend all evening in a conversation with someone we don't really want to date, but we don't know how to tell them. Maybe not being able to tell them even goes so far as a few dates before we can find a way—either by finally talking it out or by being suddenly "busy"—to let them know we're not really interested.

But look what you've done. You've tied up an incredible amount of their time, energy, and possibly even money, and you've kept them from investing those resources in finding someone who would be interested. Sure it hurts a bit at the moment to be told, "Gee, I'm sorry, but I just don't think we're compatible," but it hurts a lot more when we prolong it.

Granted, sometimes we don't know how we feel about a person until we've spent some time getting to know him or her, but in any case, continuing to see someone just to "be kind" is not kind at all. And by the same token, anyone who rejects you has also done you a favor, by letting you get on to meeting the person who *is* right for you.

We seem to be trained to take rejection like a stab in the stomach, and it's not easy to learn to look at the experience in a positive way. Simply remember that the more people you meet, the more likely you are to find the people—and perhaps *the* person—who are right for you. Regard the ebb and flow as part of a normal process. Keep the big picture in mind, and the hardest part of dating will become much easier.

So what do you do when you meet someone who *is* interested? Asking for a date—traditionally the male role—is now an acceptable role for either sex. In fact, many women hesitate to take the initiative for fear of what the man will think, while time and again in surveys, I've found that the majority of men want and appreciate women taking more of the responsibility in dating. If you already know the person somewhat, and know some things you have in common, a good first date to ask for is something that reflects a mutual interest—such as tennis, or perhaps a concert.

If, however, the first date is being offered as a way of *getting* acquainted, then one of the best dates for either a man or woman to suggest is the "coffee" date. The coffee date has several safety features that make it more likely to be accepted. Generally you meet at a place, saving the ritual of meeting at someone's home. It implies a relatively short period of time, it encourages conversation, it's a public setting with other people around, and it's inexpensive. Often men still believe that it's important to spend a lot of money on a first date, while women often feel obligated or pressured because he's spending a lot of money, so for first dates with someone you don't already know well, both parties will generally be more comfortable with an inexpensive get-together. Meeting for lunch is also good, and many people find going to "brunch" on Sunday is a comfortable time for getting acquainted.

An important component in modern dating is the telephone. Some men I know see the first phone call as the first "date"—an opportunity to get better acquainted, look for common interests, possibly plan an activity. It's not necessary to assume that you have to ask for a date when you call. In fact, it might make the first call less stressful to think of it as merely checking in—"validating the number" as one man calls it. He also suggests that you call to "validate" within three or four days of getting the number.

One area of phone use too much neglected is for women to get the man's number. Do you *really* want him to have your number, if you're not also willing to ask for his? Certainly any time you've made a date, you should be sure to get the man's number. Too often, something goes wrong—you're detained at work, there's a family emergency—and if you don't have his number, there's no way to let him know. So getting his number can prevent problems, and also serves as a way of "screening" out married men, who are generally hesitant to give a home number.

Often, at the end of a relationship, people will wonder if there wasn't some way to know it would turn out the way it did, if there weren't some early warning signs they missed. Because each person's wants and needs are different in each relationship, there are no absolute rules to predicting success or happiness. However, there are some things to note that can give you valuable insights.

1. How do you feel when you part? Do you come away with good feelings about yourself? If not, what is happening that makes you feel bad?

2. Do you compete with each other? Some competition may be fun or stimulating, but be careful if you feel that your partner is always trying to win, be one-up, or overpower you.

3. How does your partner talk about other people? Is he or she critical behind someone's back? It's hard not to secretly fear that they will talk about you too.

4. How does your partner view the world? Doom and gloom, or rosy no matter what? How does that match your view?

5. Does your partner tend to hog conversations, doing all the talking or keeping the topic to things that only he/she is interested in?

6. Do they make jokes at the expense of other people's feelings?

7. Do they show appreciation to others, or take kindnesses for granted?

8. Does your partner tend to criticize, complain, or condemn often?

9. How did your partner's past relationships end? Are they still friends with past partners, or do they blame and criticize people in their past? If they do, perhaps you should expect the same some day.

10. Do they keep their commitments to you—are they on time, do what they say they will? If they treat you shabbily now, is it reasonable to expect things to get better?

Often, in the glow of a burgeoning relationship, we are all on our best behavior and treat the object of our affections with great respect and consideration. Many of the clues listed here deal with how your partner treats others outside the warmth of your romance. How important each one is depends on your own values and priorities.

There are no absolute rules, no absolute answers, and never any absolute guarantees in early dating or in the development of the relationship. But do consider these 10 questions. Love isn't really blind—usually it just forgets to look.

16 *It Pays to Get Your Affair in Order*

Patricia O'Toole

STUDY QUESTIONS

1. Explain four of the problems POSSLQs might encounter.

2. How would a living-together document aid POSSLQs?

Mention that you know a couple living together without benefit of clergy and you're likely to raise more yawns than eyebrows. This year [1983] 1.9 million couples fit the Census Bureau description of POSSLQ (persons of the opposite sex sharing living quarters)—more than triple the 1970 figure. Add to that a sizable but unknown contingent of same-sex couples and the total could surpass 2.5 million.

Although sheer numbers have helped render unconventional relationships more socially acceptable, unmarried couples still live in a cloudy and unpredictable legal climate. State courts are recognizing their rights, but, says New York attorney Doris Jonas Freed, an authority on family law, "The country still is riddled with old-fashioned judges."

Until the law catches up with the facts of unmarried life, couples who by choice or necessity leave the knot untied will operate at a distinct disadvantage compared with married partners. Among the major problems:

Inheritance. When a husband or wife dies without a will, state laws typically assure that the bulk of the person's property will pass to the surviving spouse. But when an unmarried person leaves no will, all of his or her earthly goods can be claimed by the next of kin. Even a loathsome great-aunt thousands of miles away stands ahead of a POSSLQ in the inheritance line.

Source: Patricia O'Toole, "It Pays to Get Your Affair in Order." *Money*, October 1983. Reprinted by permission.

Health insurance. Plans that cover a spouse almost never extend to an unmarried mate.

Children's rights. To protect their child's future claim to financial support and inheritance, both unmarried parents have to take the extra step of acknowledging in writing the paternity of the child.

Separation. In a divorce, state laws offer guidance for dividing property, but unmarried couples who split up are left to slug it out on their own.

Spread over these difficulties is a crazy quilt of state laws ranging from outright bans on cohabitation to various shades of permissiveness. In Georgia, unwed cohabitants risk a $1,000 fine and a year in jail. Although such laws rarely are enforced, they can tilt the way judges settle other legal problems. In a court dispute with a landlord, for instance, an unmarried couple with an entirely justified gripe may find themselves out on the sidewalk because their living arrangement is against the law.

Archaic statues can stymie other seemingly just claims. In Illinois a few years ago, the state supreme court denied a woman's pleas for an equal share of the assets accumulated by the man with whom she had lived for 15 years— even though she had borne him three children while he was establishing a dental practice. The court ruled that their relationship amounted to a common-law marriage, which the state outlawed back in 1905.

It's usually possible for couples to plug the holes in a legal system that predates POSSLQs and gay lib, but the remedies they have to take will mock their deliberately casual way of life. These involve drawing up contracts or agreements—precisely the kind of thing that the resounding majority of such couples find odious. "Contracts just don't go with moonlight and roses," sighs San Francisco lawyer Melvin Belli. Observes Elliot L. Evans, a lawyer in New York: "People who live together often do so because they don't want to define their relationship. They think that if they don't write things down, they won't lock themselves in."

Alas, by not writing things down, unmarried couples may inadvertently lock themselves out. Without written contracts, they often forfeit the legal protections of married couples. If disputes arise over an inheritance, ownership of property or financial obligations, POSSLQs may end up in court, where the outcome could have scant relation to what either wants done. And the absence of written agreements leaves the door wide open for the spurned lover to go to court to argue the existence of an unwritten contract. Michelle Triola Marvin established that precedent in California (but failed in her own claim) when she sued her ex-lover, actor Lee Marvin, for "palimony."

Mere utterance of the word *contract* calls up visions of inflexibility (ironclad, written in stone) and complexity (party of the first part and party of the second part). But contracts don't have to be complicated or, for that matter, permanent. In one common type of agreement, couples simply waive all financial claims on each other: what's his is his and what's hers is hers, period.

Contracts also can provide for regular revision. Dick Merritt and Mary Gannaway of Raleigh, North Carolina review their agreement every year. The

PATRICIA O'TOOLE

latest changes deal with Gannaway's return to college, which Merritt is under-writing with a long-term 7 per cent loan. She has guaranteed to repay him whether or not the two continue living together.

Nor is there any need for contracts to cover every aspect of couples' lives. Advises Doris Freed: "Focus on money and property. Don't get into who empties the garbage and who walks the dog." Instead of drawing up a single, compre-hensive contract, many couples write several agreements, each one focused on a specific bit of business. That is how Ralph Warner and Toni Ihara, two lawyers who live together in Berkeley, California handle ownership of their house and their interests in Nolo Press, which publishes *The Living Together Kit* ($12.95 at bookstores or from the publisher, 950 Parker St., Berkeley, California 94710) and other self-help legal material. Says Warner: "She and I have a written agreement covering the house. And every time we do a book together, we write that down. We don't have an agreement about things in the house because if we put them all out on the lawn, they probably wouldn't be worth more than $2,000."

As for how to draw up contracts, many lawyers say that couples with little money and no major assets usually can get by with the fill-in-blanks legal forms found in books on living together. If a couple's financial picture is more intricate, they should see an attorney—but first they should compose a rough draft as a way of clarifying their financial expectations of each other. When serious questions arise over individual interests, each partner should consult a different lawyer.

Whether prepackaged or tailor-made, contracts between unmarried cou-ples generally are recognized by courts as long as they violate no laws and as long as both parties enter into them freely. Leave out of the contract the nature of your relationship, especially in states where cohabitation and homosexuality are illegal. Never put in writing any words that could be construed as an agreement to exchange money for sex, lest you run afoul of prostitution laws. Living-together documents should be signed, witnessed and notarized in triplicate: one copy for each of you and the third entrusted to a relative or lawyer.

With or without contracts, unmarried couples make dozens of decisions that can have legal reverberations. The major considerations:

DAY-TO-DAY FINANCES

Wedded or not, as soon as couples set up housekeeping, they begin accumulating possessions—from stereo rigs to Cuisinarts. If a married couple call it quits, their divorce decree will spell out who gets what. For unmarried couples who split, the best protection against a needlessly bitter end is separate ownership. He buys the car, she buys the computer. "They should acquire as little as possible together and keep receipts or other records of what each of them buys," says New York matrimonial lawyer Raoul Lionel Felder. Unmarried couples should not have joint bank accounts or credit cards. Each person is 100 per cent responsible for debts incurred by the other in joint charge accounts, and creditors can seize bank assets that are deposited in both names.

The tidiest way to split household expenses is down the middle, which many POSSLQs do quite simply by initialing receipts, tossing them into a drawer and squaring accounts once a month. But if one person quits work, the situation may call for a written agreement.

Cindy Ornstein, a public relations account executive in Manhattan, says she and her ex-POSSLQ divided expenses evenly until he left his job to attend law school. Then, she says, "we wrote a contract that was basically a loan agreement. I was to pay considerably more of our living expenses while he was in school, and the contract set the terms for paying me back." Their romance eventually came apart, but because of their clear-cut agreement, his debt of about $6,000 was one thing they didn't argue about. He has agreed to start paying her back in January.

"Couples also need to plan what financial support they will provide each other in case one of them loses a job or gets sick," says Merle Horwitz, a Los Angeles lawyer and author of *Love is Love but Business Is Business: The Essential Guide to Living Together* (William Morrow, $4.95). "These plans should be part of their written contract. It's fine to make promises, but feelings change when there's stress on a relationship."

In prince-and-pauper partnerships, a proportional sharing of expenses may feel more comfortable than a fifty-fifty split, but the American Bar Association cautions that the law generally respects cash more than services. So if the prince contributed mostly money and the pauper mostly elbow grease, a judge might well view the toil as a gift—and deny the toiler's claim to any possessions paid for by the prince. In a written contract, however, the pair could spell out their intentions for sharing the fruits of their individual contributions.

HOUSING

The legal hazards facing POSSLQs here range from shared leases to disagreements over jointly acquired real estate. Roberta Springer and Michael Spitalnik leased an apartment together a few years ago, hoping to make a profitable investment if the building was converted to a co-op or condo. The building eventually was converted, but by then the couple had broken up and Springer had moved out. Since her name was still on the lease, though, the landlord insisted that the two of them would have to buy the apartment jointly to get the favorable price available to existing tenants. When he and she each pressed for the individual right to buy at the insider price, Spitalnik asked a New York State court to rule that he alone, as the occupant, should be allowed to buy the apartment. Their legal tiff, which is still going on, might have been avoided had they spelled out each person's share of any profit in case the place was bought and later sold.

"Business partners make these buy-sell agreements all the time," says Judith Zabalaoui, head of Resource Management, a financial-planning firm in

Metairie, LA. "The idea is that you negotiate the exit as you're making the entrance. That's when everybody has a nice, rosy glow and a concern for each other's interests."

TAXES

Here's one positive inducement for living together unwed. Even with recently enacted deductions for two-career couples, the tax code still requires many married people to pay more than their unmarried counterparts. The more nearly equal the unmarried partners' earnings, the bigger the benefit. A couple with two $30,000-a-year incomes and average deductions can keep the IRS smiling with about 15 per cent less tax if they're single.

But the rules turn against unwed couples if only one partner works. You can claim your POSSLQ as a dependent only by passing a stiff IRS test. Among the conditions for the $1,000 exemption: the state doesn't ban cohabitation, the taxpaying partner furnishes more than half of the other's support, and the dependent earns under $1,000 a year. State income tax laws might not look on unmarried couples even that tolerantly.

CHILDREN

The rights of children, especially to inheritances and financial support, are the same whether their parents marry or not. And child custody disputes usually are not decided on the basis of marital status. But parents should write a statement acknowledging the father's parenthood to assure that neither a parent nor a child will have to go to extravagant lengths to prove paternity.

A divorced mother who moves in with another man should know that her cohabitant's contributions to the household may cost her the loss of child support from her ex-husband. "If the unmarried couple have a written contract stating that the man does not contribute to the children's support, that would be a helpful piece of evidence if the issue went to court," says lawyer Merle Horwitz.

INSURANCE AND WILLS

Unmarried couples' problems with most types of insurance are minimal as long as they tell the truth on application forms. Homeowners' and renters' policies should carry both names so the possessions of both are clearly covered. One temptation to resist: registering his car in her name to escape the high premiums paid by unmarried men under 25. Says Bill Malcolm, president of the Professional Insurance Agents Association of Connecticut: "If there's an accident, she'll be liable even if he's driving. Judgments these days can be enormous, and any such award would stay on her insurance record." Settlement of a negligence claim would sharply raise her premium or perhaps cause the insurance company to cancel her policy.

Because employer-provided family health insurance does not extend to POSSLQs, unmarried couples have to buy their own protection against catastrophic medical costs if either of them isn't covered by a group plan. One advantage of unmarried couples over marrieds: they are not liable for each other's medical bills. One disadvantage: if an unmarried person is hospitalized with a serious illness, the hospital may grant visiting privileges only to kin. To get around such rules, draft a medical power of attorney that permits an unrelated person not only to visit but also to make medical decisions for a totally incapacitated patient.

Don't neglect to name your POSSLQ the beneficiary of your life insurance policies. Also arrange for your partner to receive the death benefits if you die before you collect your pension or profit-sharing proceeds. You should hit no obstacles with pension and profit-sharing plans, but life insurers have balked at making one unmarried person the beneficiary of another. An easy, perfectly legal way out is suggested by Bill Malcolm, the insurance agent: "Name a family member when you take out the policy, and change the beneficiary later." The owner of the policy can make such a change anytime—and many an ex-lover has done so.

Pension plans frequently offer a joint-and-survivor annuity, which allows the widow or widower of a pensioner to continue collecting at least part of the retirement benefit. But POSSLQs don't qualify for the joint-and-survivor option. An unmarried pair's only safe passage through the pension maze is to explore with the company's employee-benefits counselor other annuity options that provide a survivor benefit.

While money from life insurance and pensions goes directly to the beneficiaries, most other assets acquired over a lifetime are destined for the owner's estate. That's the domain ruled over by his or her last will and testament. To make sure their wishes are carried out in probate—and that no kinfolk, especially that loathsome great-aunt, inherit undeserved assets—an unmarried couple had better write their wills. A few years ago, when a New York writer died intestate, the apartment that he owned went to his co-op association instead of to his male live-in lover of 10 years.

SOCIAL SECURITY

The federal old-age system no longer pays higher retirement income to unmarried couples than to husbands and wives. People wed or unwed can draw their benefits from the individual accounts they built up during their working years. Although individual benefits earned while you're working are the same for unmarrieds as for marrieds, the Social Security system generally favors those who wed.

When a husband or wife is the only one getting retirement benefits and then dies, the spouse gets survivor's income; a POSSLQ has no such right. If one spouse worked only a short time and accrued only a small individual benefit, the law allows that person the option of drawing half the other spouse's benefit instead. So a wife entitled to $200 a month married to a man receiving $700 could raise her benefit to $350.

Unmarried couples cannot take advantage of this option. Nor do they qualify for the $255 lump sum paid at a spouse's death, except in states permitting common-law marriage. But children under 18, whether their parents marry or not, are entitled to monthly income if a parent dies or is totally disabled.

Proper documents, from wills to statements of who owns what, can yield peace of mind as well as legal and financial benefits, says Baila Zeitz, a New York City psychologist with a special interest in money problems. "Contracts form a basis for constructive discussion when things go wrong—as they invariably do. Even more important, they give people a way of knowing what's going to happen, which feels much better than not knowing." Until the law gives the same shelter to unmarried partners that it does to spouses, putting your intentions in writing is the best way to protect a joint venture of the heart.

17   *The Three Faces of Love*

Robert J. Trotter

STUDY QUESTIONS

1. Explain the three active ingredients in Sternberg's theory of love?

2. What is missing in such types of love as empty love, romantic love, and fatuous love?

Brains and sex are the only things in life that matter. Robert J. Sternberg picked up that bit of wisdom from a cynical high school classmate and appears to have taken it to heart. "I spent the first part of my career studying brains, and now along comes sex," he says, claiming to be only partly facetious.

Sternberg, IBM Professor of Psychology and Education at Yale University, has, in fact, made a name for himself as one of the foremost theoreticians and researchers in the field of human intelligence (see "Three Heads are Better than One," *Psychology Today*, August 1986), but in recent years he has turned a good deal of his attention to the study of love. Why? Because it's an understudied

Source: Robert J. Trotter, "The Three Faces of Love." *Psychology Today*, September 1986, pp. 46–50, 54. Reprinted with permission from *Psychology Today* magazine. Copyright © 1986 (PT Partners, L. P.).

topic that is extremely important to people's lives. "It's important to my own life," he says. "I want to understand what's happening."

Sternberg began his attempt to understand love with a study for which he and graduate student Susan Grajek recruited 35 men and 50 women between 18 and 70 years old who had been in at least one love relationship. Participants rated their most recent significant love affair using the well-tested scales of loving and liking developed by psychologist Zick Rubin and the interpersonal involvement scale developed by psychologist George Levinger. The participants also rated their love for their mothers, fathers, siblings closest in age and best friends of the same sex.

Sternberg and Grajek found that men generally love and like their lover the most and their sibling the least. Women tend to love their lover and best friend about the same, but they like the best friend more than they like the lover. Sternberg thinks he knows why. "Women are better at achieving intimacy and value it more than do men, so if women don't get the intimacy they crave in a relationship with a man, they try to find it with other women. They establish close friendships. They can say things to another woman they can't say to a man."

Sternberg and Grajek concluded that, while the exact emotions, motivations and cognitions involved in various kinds of loving relationships differ, "the various loves one experiences are not, strictly speaking, different." In other words, they thought they had proved that love, as different as it feels from situation to situation, is actually a common entity. They thought they had discovered the basis of love in interpersonal communication, sharing and support.

This research generated a lot of publicity in 1984, especially around St. Valentine's Day, and earned Sternberg the appellation "love professor." It also generated a lot of phone calls from reporters saying things like, "You mean to tell me the way you love your lover is the same as the way you love your 5-year-old kid? What about sex?" Sternberg had to rethink his position.

He analyzed various relationships to figure out what differentiates romantic love from companionate love, from liking, from infatuation and from various other types of love. He finally concluded that his original theory accounted for the emotional component of love but left out two other important aspects. According to Sternberg's new triangular theory, love has motivational and cognitive components as well. And different aspects of love can be explained in terms of these components (see "How Do I Love Thee?").

Sternberg calls the emotional aspect of his love triangle intimacy. It includes such things as closeness, sharing, communication and support. Intimacy increases rather steadily at first, then at a slower rate until it eventually levels off and goes beneath the surface. Sternberg explains this course of development in terms of psychologist Ellen Berscheid's theory of emotions in close relationships.

According to Berscheid, people in close relationships feel increased emotion when there is some kind of disruption. This is common early in a relationship primarily because of uncertainty. Since you don't know what the other person is going to do, you are constantly learning and experiencing new

ROBERT J. TROTTER

things. This uncertainty keeps you guessing but also generates new levels of emotion and intimacy. As the other person becomes more predictable, there are fewer disruptions and less expressed, or manifest, intimacy.

An apparent lack of intimacy could mean that the relationship and the intimacy are dying out. Or, says Sternberg, the intimacy may still be there in latent form. The relationship may even be thriving, with the couple growing together so smoothly that they are hardly aware of their interdependence. It may take some kind of disruption—time apart, a death in the family, even a divorce—for them to find out just how they feel about each other. "Is it any wonder," Sternberg asks, "that some couples realize only after a divorce that they were very close to and dependent on each other?"

The motivational side of the triangle is passion, which leads to physiological arousal and an intense desire to be united with the loved one. Unlike intimacy, passion develops quickly. "Initially you have this rapidly growing, hot, heavy passion," Sternberg says, "but after a while it no longer does for you what you want it to—you get used to it, you habituate."

Passion is like an addiction, Sternberg says. He explains it according to psychologist Richard Solomon's opponent process theory of motivation, which says that desire for a person or substance involves two opposing forces. The first is a positive motivational force that attracts you to the person. It is quick to develop and quick to level off. The negative motivational force, the one that works against the attraction, is slow to develop and slow to fade. The result is an initial rapid growth in passion, followed by habituation when the more slowly developing negative force kicks in. "It's like with coffee, cigarettes or alcohol," Sternberg says. "Addiction can be rapid, but once habituation sets in, even an increased amount of exposure to the person or substance no longer stimulates the motivational arousal that was once possible.

"And then when the person dumps you, it's even worse. You don't go back to the way you were before you met the person," Sternberg explains. "You end up much worse off. You get depressed, irritable, you lose your appetite. You get these withdrawal symptoms, just as if you had quit drinking coffee or smoking, and it takes a while to get over it." The slow-starting, slow-fading negative force is still there after the person or the substance is gone.

The cognitive side of Sternberg's love triangle is commitment, both a short-term decision to love another person and a long-term commitment to maintain that love. Its developmental course is more straightforward and easier to explain than that of intimacy or passion. Essentially, commitment starts at zero when you first meet the other person and grows as you get to know each other. If the relationship is destined to be long-term, Sternberg says, the level of commitment will usually increase gradually at first and then speed up. As the relationship continues, the amount of commitment will generally level off. If the relationship begins to flag, the level of commitment will decline, and if the relationship fails, the level of commitment falls back to zero. According to Sternberg, the love of a parent for a child is often distinguished by a high and unconditional level of commitment.

Levels of intimacy, passion and commitment change over time, and so do relationships. You can visualize this, says Sternberg, by considering how the love triangle changes in size and shape as the three components of love increase and decrease. The triangle's area represents the amount of love and its shape the style. Large amounts of intimacy, passion and commitment, for example, yield a large triangle. And in general, Sternberg says, the larger the triangle, the more love.

Changing the length of the individual sides yields four differently shaped triangles, or styles of love. A triangle with three equal sides represents what Sternberg calls a "balanced" love in which all three components are equally matched. A scalene triangle (three unequal sides) in which the longest leg is passion represents a relationship in which physical attraction plays a larger role than either emotional intimacy or cognitive commitment. A scalene triangle with commitment as its longest leg depicts a relationship in which the intimacy and passion have waned or were never there in the first place. An isosceles triangle (two equal sides) with intimacy as its longest leg shows a relationship in which emotional involvement is more important than either passion or commitment. It's more like a highgrade friendship than a romance.

Sternberg admits that this triangle is a simplification of a complex and subtle phenomenon. There can be a variety of emotions, motivations and types of commitment in a loving relationship, and each would have to be examined to completely diagnose a relationship. Beyond that, he says, every relationship involves several triangles: In addition to their own triangles, both people have an ideal triangle (the way you would like to feel about the person you love) and a perceived triangle (the way you think the other person feels about you).

Sternberg and graduate student Michael Barnes studied the effects these triangles have on a relationship by administering the liking and loving scales to 24 couples. Participants were asked to rate their relationship in terms of how they feel about the other person, how they think the other person feels about them, how they would feel about an ideal person and how they would want an ideal person to feel about them. They found that satisfaction is closely related to the similarity between these real, ideal and perceived triangles. In general, the closer they are in shape and size, the more satisfying the relationship.

The best single predictor of happiness in a relationship is not how you feel about the other person but the difference between how you would ideally like the other person to feel about you and how you think he or she actually feels about you. "In other words," Sternberg says, "relationships tend to go bad when there is a mismatch between what you want from the other person and what you think you are getting.

"Were you ever the overinvolved person in a relationship? That can be very dissatisfying. What usually happens is that the more involved person tries to think up schemes to get the other person up to his or her level of involvement. But the other person usually sees what's going on and backs off. That just makes the overinvolved person try harder and the other person back off more until it tears the relationship apart. The good advice in such a situation is for the overinvolved person to scale down, but that advice is hard to follow."

An underlying question in Sternberg's love research is: Why do so many relationships fail? Almost half the marriages in the United States end in divorce, and many couples who don't get divorced aren't all that happy. "Are people

ROBERT J. TROTTER

really so dumb that they pick wrong most of the time? Probably not," he suggests. "What they're doing is picking on the basis of what matters to them in the short run. But what matters in the long run may be different. The factors that count change, people change, relationships change."

Sternberg can't predict how people or situations will change, but he and his assistant Sandra Wright recently completed a study that suggests what will and won't be important in the long run. They put this question, what's important in a relationship, to 80 men and women from 17 to 69 years old, and divided them into three groups according to the length of their most recent relationship. The short-term group had been involved for up to two years, the mid-term group between two and five years, the others for more than five years.

Among the things that increase in importance as a relationship grows are willingness to change in response to each other and willingness to tolerate each other's imperfections. "These are things you can't judge at the beginning of a relationship," Sternberg says. "In the beginning," he explains, "some of the other person's flaws might not seem important. They may even seem kind of cute, but over the long term they may begin to grate on you. You both have to be willing to make some changes to make the relationship work and you both have to be willing to tolerate some flaws."

Another thing that becomes increasingly important is the sharing of values, especially religious values. "When you first meet," says Sternberg, "you have this love-overcomes-all-obstacles attitude, but when the kids come along you have to make some hard decisions about the religion issue. All of a sudden something that wasn't so important is important."

Among the things that tend to decrease in importance is how interesting you find your partner. "In the beginning," Sternberg says, "it's almost as if the other person has to keep you interested or the relationship will go nowhere. Later on, it's not quite as critical because there are other things in your life that matter."

In addition to asking what is important at different times, Sternberg and Wright asked how much of these various things people had at different times in their relationships. The answers were not encouraging. The ability to make love, for example, often goes just at the time when it is becoming more important. In fact, Sternberg says, almost everything except matching religious beliefs decreased over time. The ability to communicate, physical attractiveness, having good times, sharing interests, the ability to listen, respect for each other, romantic love—they all went down. "That may be depressing," says Sternberg, "but it's important to know at the beginning of a relationship what to expect over time, to have realistic expectations for what you can get and what is going to be important in a relationship."

And Sternberg feels that his triangular theory of love can help people in other ways. "Just analyzing your relationship in terms of the three components can be useful," he says. "Are you more romantic and your partner more companionate? It's helpful to know where you and your partner are well-matched and where you are not and then start thinking about what you can do to make yourselves more alike in what you want out of the relationship."

If you decide to take steps to improve a relationship, Sternberg offers a final triangle, the action triangle. "Often there's quite a gap between thought or feeling and action," he explains. "Your actions don't always reflect the way you feel, so it could help to know just what actions are associated with each component of love."

Intimacy, he suggests, might be expressed by communicating inner feelings; sharing one's possessions, time and self; and offering emotional support. Passion, obviously, is expressed by kissing, hugging, touching and making love. Commitment can be expressed by fidelity, by staying with the relationship through the hard times that occur in any relationship or by getting engaged or married. Which actions are most important and helpful will vary from person to person and from relationship to relationship. But Sternberg feels it is important to consider the triangle of love as it is expressed through action because action has so many effects on a relationship.

Citing psychologist Daryl Bem's theory of self-perception, Sternberg describes how actions can affect emotions, motivations and cognitions. "The way we act shapes the way we feel and think, possibly as much as the way we think and feel shapes the way we act." Also, he says, certain actions can lead to other actions; expressions of love, for example, encourage further expressions of love. Furthermore, your actions affect the way the other person thinks and feels about you and behaves toward you, leading to a mutually reinforcing series of actions.

"The point," Sternberg concludes, "is that it is necessary to take into account the ways in which people express their love. Without expression, even the greatest of loves can die."

HOW DO I LOVE THEE?

Intimacy, passion and commitment are the warm, hot and cold vertices of Sternberg's love triangle. Alone and in combination they give rise to eight possible kinds of love relationships. The first is nonlove—the absence of all three components. This describes the large majority of our personal relationships, which are simply casual interactions.

The second kind of love is liking. "If you just have intimacy," Sternberg explains, "that's liking. You can talk to the person, tell about your life. And if that's all there is to it, that's what we mean by liking." It is more than nonlove. It refers to the feelings experienced in true friendships. Liking includes such things as closeness and warmth but not the intense feelings of passion or commitment.

If you just have passion, it's called infatuated love—the "love at first sight" that can arise almost instantaneously and dissi-

pate just as quickly. It involves a high degree of physiological arousal but no intimacy or commitment. It's the 10th-grader who falls madly in love with the beautiful girl in his biology class but never gets up the courage to talk to her or get to know her, Sternberg says, describing his past.

Empty love is commitment without intimacy or passion, the kind of love sometimes seen in a 30-year-old marriage that has become stagnant. The couple used to be intimate, but they don't talk to each other any more. They used to be passionate, but that's died out. All that remains is the commitment to stay with the other person. In societies in which marriages are arranged, Sternberg points out, empty love may precede the other kinds of love.

Romantic love, the Romeo and Juliet type of love, is a combination of intimacy and passion. More than infatuation, it's lik-

ROBERT J. TROTTER

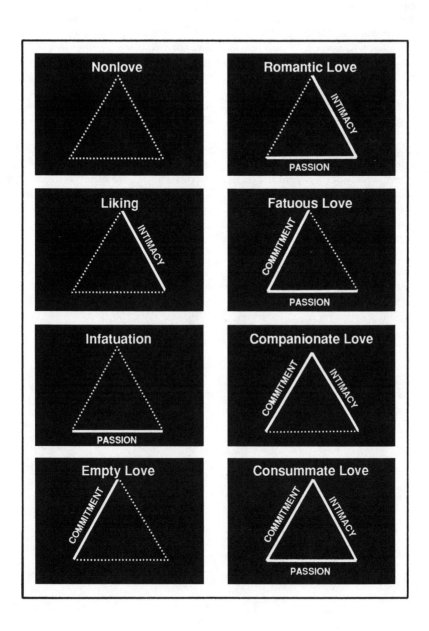

ing with the added excitement of physical attraction and arousal but without commitment. A summer affair can be very romantic, Sternberg explains, but you know it will end when she goes back to Hawaii and you go back to Florida, or wherever.

Passion plus commitment is what Sternberg calls fatuous love. It's Hollywood love: Boy meets girl, a week later they're engaged, a month later they're married. They are committed on the basis of their passion, but because intimacy takes time to develop, they don't have the emotional core necessary to sustain the commitment. This kind of love, Sternberg warns, usually doesn't work out.

Companionate love is intimacy with commitment but no passion. It's a long-term friendship, the kind of committed love and intimacy frequently seen in marriages in which the physical attraction has died down.

When all three elements of Sternberg's love triangle come together in a relationship, you get what he calls consummate love, or complete love. It's the kind of love toward which many people strive, especially in romantic relationships. Achieving consummate love, says Sternberg, is like trying to lose weight, difficult but not impossible. The really hard thing is keeping the weight off after you have lost it, or keeping the consummate love alive after you have achieved it. Consummate love is possible only in very special relationships.

5   *Making It*

The stages of marriage include the newlywed, parental, post-parental, and retirement periods, each of which has its particular characteristics and qualities. Each of these stages also has tasks which must be accomplished to aid its development. For example, the development tasks of the newly married couple center on establishing a home and financial support, allocating household responsibilities, building a satisfying emotional and sexual relationship, and planning for children. Monica McGoldrick and Elizabeth Carter in the first article in Chapter 5 describe these stages and developmental tasks from the unattached young adult through the post-parental period.

Being married is initially affected by the fact that the marriage contract is both a legal contract authorized by the state and a personal contract made by two unique people.

The state is an interested party in marriage because it desires to accomplish various functions via the marriage contract: to safeguard normal behavior by legitimizing sexual union; to protect the property rights of each individual as well as the couple; to protect the individuals involved from spouse and child abuse and from exploitation factors such as bigamy; to determine legitimacy of the children in regard to name and inheritance as well as in regard to social and financial responsibility; to safeguard against marriages within prohibited degrees of relationship such as incestual relations; to guarantee the legality of the contract by providing licensing and eligibility standards of the marriage and grounds for its dissolution (Albrecht & Boch 1975).

As a means of ensuring these interests, the state also makes four role-based assumptions about the marriage relationship and, in so doing, ignores the second part of the contract, that it is being made by two unique individuals. The four assumptions are: the husband is the head of the family and is responsible for support; the wife is responsible for domestic services and child care (Weitzman 1981). The first assumption is shown by the loss of an independent identity by the woman via the loss of her name, in having no right in determining residence, and in her treatment by various consumer groups. The second assumption is most forcefully seen at the time of separation or divorce in regard to support. The wife is usually obligated to support the children if the husband is unable to do so whereas the opposite is true for the husband in regard to support for the children. The third and fourth assumptions are also best demonstrated at the time of dissolution of the marriage since courts usually fail to provide reimbursement for the wife's services as a homemaker and usually assign any children to the mother since that is seen as her "natural and proper" role.

It would appear that the state, in making these assumptions, overlooked the individuality of the component parts—the husband and the wife. Despite recent court rulings, which have lessened the severity of some of these assumptions, the experience and desires of the couple are ignored. It is for this reason that many couples are beginning to write their own nuptial contract—a contract which reflects their own personal goals and expectations in regard to each other, to children, to sexual relations with others, to rights and obligations regarding financial matters, to household arrangements, and even in regard to termination of the contract. Although not legally binding, a premarital contract does bring to light subjects that will affect the continued happiness of the couple. It helps to clarify aims, expectations, and intentions by forcing discussion of important topics. Thus, it eases the transition to marriage by providing accurate information, aids the development of mutually realistic expectations, and clarifies transition procedures. In effect, the move to a personal contract reflects a change in the expectations of marriage. In the past, marriage was seen as a practical matter requiring certain responsibilities for each spouse whereas current expectations for marriage involve such personal factors as mutual affection, companionship, and individual growth.

Writing a prenuptial agreement recognizing these individual nuances of the marriage contract would appear to be calculating and a denial of the romantic love the partners hold for each other rather than a recognition that the qualities that usually arouse feelings of romance have little direct connection to the qualities that provide fulfillment in marriage. That is, the myths and unrealistic expectations that individuals bring to marriage may be a reason why the marital relationship does not live up to the expectations of its partners. Many of these myths revolve around the connection between love and marriage, such as "people marry because they are in love" and that "all problems can be solved if you're really in love."

Other myths dealing with how people operate can also sabotage your relationship. Chuck Hillig in the second article of this chapter describes these myths and their devastating effects. They are: Others can make you feel some emotion; you should always have good reasons for why you feel the way you do; and your partner should automatically know what you want.

Finally, the writing of a prenuptial agreement may overcome the state's lack of interest in preparing people for marriage by forcing people to balance the magic and marvelous attractiveness of courtship with the realities of marriage. Such contracts, however, do not solve all problems since many prospective mates are deficient in the skills that make a marriage work. One of the most important of these revolves around conflict resolution. Myths of romantic love make people too idealistic and fearful of conflict—which may arise because the couple have unshared meanings and value dissensions. However, fights can be bonding as well as alienating. Alienating behaviors involve such conflict avoidance techniques as refusing to fight by taking that proverbial walk, putting grievances into an imaginary gunnysack that will eventually burst rather than dealing with issues at the time (Bach & Wyden 1970), and using anger substitutes such as overeating. On the other hand, bonding fights require the clear stating of feelings—being specific as to what you want changed and how, in ways that do not attack the partner, using "you" messages; taking responsibility for one's own behavior and feelings—using "I" messages, providing feedback, clarifying the material; and negotiating the issues—being open to compromise.

Another difficulty revolves around what Marcia Lasswell and Norman Lobsenz refer to, in the third article of Chapter 5, as the intimacy that goes beyond sex. They conclude that there are barriers to the attainment of the different levels of intimacy and that various skills are needed to overcome these barriers.

In the fourth article of this chapter, Jeanette and Robert Lauer take a different tack for dealing with the difficulties of marriage by turning to the men and women who are involved in long-term marriages and noting their reasons for an enduring and happy marriage.

Other factors related to marital success have also been shown in various other studies. These factors include:

a. similarity in such cultural background items as age, class, education, ethnic/racial group, and religion,

b. good parental models,

c. good reasons for marriage,

d. maturity, and

e. good communication skills.

The idea of conflict in marriage also raises the specter of the possibility of spouse abuse—a major part of family violence, although underreported. As Robert Whitehurst notes in the final article of Chapter 5, the men as well as their victims have excuses for the battering of the spouse, but most of these appear to have little relationship to those factors consistently found in studies. These indicate that abuse arises from (Finkelhor 1981):

a. behavior learned from abusive parents,

b. cultural beliefs regarding the privacy of the home and the propriety of the family,

c. various psychological characteristics of both the abuser and the abused,

d. stressfull events, and

e. alcohol and drug problems.

Spouse abuse can be dealt with through jailing, mandatory counseling, and/or family therapy.

REFERENCES

1. Albrecht, R. E., & E. W. Bock. 1975. *Encounter: Love, Marriage, and Family.* Boston: Holbrook.

2. Bach, G. R., & P. Wyden. 1970. *The Intimate Enemy: How to Fight in Love and Marriage.* New York: Avon.

3. Finkelhor, D. 1981. "Common Features of Family Abuse." In *The Dark Side of Families,* D. Finkelhor (ed.). Beverly Hills CA: Sage.

4. Weitzman, L. 1981. *The Marriage Contract: Spouses, Lovers, and the Law.* New York: The Free Press.

18 *The Stages of the Family Life Cycle*

Monica McGoldrick / Elizabeth A. Carter

STUDY QUESTIONS

1. Briefly describe the six stages of the family life cycle.

2. Indicate at least one task required in each of the stages.

We now provide a very brief outline of the statistically predictable developmental stages of American middle-class families in the last quarter of the 20th century. Our classification of family life cycle stages highlights our view that the central underlying process to be negotiated is the expansion, contraction, and realignment of the relationship system to support the entry, exit, and development of family members in a functional way. . . .

THE UNATTACHED YOUNG ADULT

In outlining the stages of the family life cycle, we have departed from the traditional sociological depiction of the family life cycle as commencing at courtship or marriage and ending with the death of one spouse. Rather, considering the family to be the operative emotional unit from the cradle to the grave, we see a new family life cycle beginning at the stage of the "unattached young adult," whose completion of the primary task of coming to terms with his or her family of origin will most profoundly influence whom, when and how he or she marries and carries out all succeeding stages of the family life cycle. Adequate completion of his task requires that the young adult separate from the family of origin without cutting off or fleeing reactively to a substitute emotional refuge. Seen in this way, the "unattached young adult" phase is a

Source: "The Changing Family Circle." In *The Changing Family Life Cycle*, 2nd ed., edited by Monica McGoldrick & Elizabeth A. Carter. Boston: Allyn & Bacon, 1989. Copyright © 1989 Allyn & Bacon. Reprinted with permission.

cornerstone. It is a time to formulate personal life goals and to become a "self" before joining with another to form a new family subsystem. . . . This is the chance for them to sort out emotionally what they will take along from the family of origin and what they will change for themselves. Of great significance is the fact that until the present generation this crucial phase was never considered necessary for women, who were traditionally handed directly from their fathers to their husbands. Obviously, this tradition has had profound impact on the functioning of women in families, as the current attempt to change the tradition is now having. . . .

In the "unattached young adult" phase, problems usually center on either young adults' or their parents' not recognizing the need for a shift to a less interdependent form of relating, based on their now all being adults complementing each other. Problems in shifting status may take the form of parent's encouraging the dependence of their young adult children, or of young adults' either remaining dependent or breaking away in a pseudoindependent cutoff of their parents and families. It is our view, following Bowen (1978), that cutoffs never resolve emotional relationships and that young adults who cutoff their parents do so reactively and are in fact still emotionally bound to rather than independent of the family "program." The shift toward adult-to-adult status requires a mutually respectful and personal form of relating, in which young adults can appreciate parents as they are, needing neither to make them into what they are not, nor to blame them for what they could not be. . . .

THE JOINING OF FAMILIES THROUGH MARRIAGE:
THE NEWLY MARRIED COUPLE

Becoming a couple is one of the most complex and difficult transitions of the family life cycle. However, along with the transition to parenthood, which it has long symbolized, it is seen as the easiest and the most joyous. The positive and romanticized view of this transition may add to its difficulty, since everyone wants to see only the happiness of the shift. The problems entailed may thus be pushed underground, only to intensify and surface later on.

Weddings, more than any other rite of passage, are viewed as the solution to a problem, such as loneliness or extended family difficulties. The event is seen as terminating a process instead of beginning one. The myth "And they lived happily ever after" (with no further effort) causes couples and families considerable difficulty. Weddings, far from resolving a "status problem" of young unmarried adults, come in the middle of a complex process of changing family status.

Marriage requires that a couple renegotiate a myriad of personal issues that they have previously defined for themselves or that were defined by their parents, from when to eat, sleep, have sex, or fight, to how to celebrate holidays or where and how to live, work, and spend vacations. The couple must renegotiate their relationships with their parents, siblings, friends, and other relatives in view of the new marriage, and this will to some degree affect all personal relationships. It places no small stress on the family to open itself to

TABLE 5.1. The Stages of the Family Life Cycle

Family Life Cycle Stage	Emotional Process of Transition: Key Principles	Changes in Family Status Required to Proceed Developmentally
1. Between families: The unattached young adult	Accepting parent-offspring separation	a. Differentiation of self in relation to family of origin b. Development of intimate peer relationships c. Establishment of self in work
2. The joining of families through marriage: The newly married couple	Commitment to new system	a. Formation of marital system b. Realignment of relationships with extended families and friends to include spouse
3. The family with young children	Accepting new generation of members into the system	a. Adjusting marital system to make space for child(ren) b. Taking on parenting roles c. Realignment of relationships with extended family to include parenting and grandparenting roles
4. The family with adolescents	Increasing flexibility of family boundaries to include children's independence	a. Shifting of parent-child relationships to permit adolescents to move in and out of system b. Refocus on midlife marital and career issues c. Beginning shift toward concerns for older generation
5. Launching children and moving on	Accepting a multitude of exits from and entries into the family system	a. Renegotiation of marital system as a dyad b. Development of adult to adult relationships between grown children and their parents c. Realignment of relationships to include in-laws and grandchildren d. Dealing with disabilities and death of parents (grandparents)
6. The family in later life	Accepting the shifting of generational roles	a. Maintaining own and/or couple functioning and interests in face of physiological decline; exploration of new familial and social role options b. Support for a more central role for middle generation c. Making room in the system for the wisdom and experience of the elderly; supporting the older generation without overfunctioning for them d. Dealing with loss of spouse, siblings, and other peers, and preparation for own death. Life review and integration

an outsider who is now an official member of its inner circle. Frequently no new member has been added for many years. In addition, marriage involves a shifting of family boundaries for the members on both sides to some degree or other. Not only is the new spouse now a factor for each family, but priorities of both systems must now be negotiated in a complex set of arrangements of each system. As mentioned earlier, relationships with the third generation are of utmost importance in understanding the family life cycle, not only because of their historical importance to the system, but because of their direct, ongoing impact on the life of the next generations' family experiences.

In the animal kingdom, mating involves only the two partners. For mankind, it is the joining of two enormously complex systems. In fact, Haley has commented that the fact of having in-laws is the major distinguishing characteristic between man and all other forms of life. In any case, it is surely a complex transition and one that our rituals hardly prepare us for. And, although couples are marrying later and delaying having children more than ever before, the average age of marriage for women in 1975 was 21.3 and men 23.8; the birth of the first child came, on the average, 1½ years later. This means that there is still a relatively short time in which the couple and both families must adjust to this phase of their life cycle, with its accompanying stresses, before moving on. It may also be worth nothing that there seems to be an optimum timing for this phase, with those who fall outside it often having more difficulty. Women who marry before the age of 20 (38% of women) are twice as likely to divorce as those who marry in their 20s. Those who marry after 30 (6%) are half again as likely to divorce as those who marry in their 20s (Glick & Norton, 1977). Thus it appears that in our culture there is a time for coupling; while it may be better to marry later than sooner, those who fall too far out of the normative range on either end are more likely to have trouble making the transition. A number of other factors appear to make the adjustment to this life cycle transition more difficult:

1. The couple meets or marries shortly after a significant loss.
2. One or both partners wish to distance from family of origin.
3. The family backgrounds of each spouse are significantly different (religion, education, social class, ethnicity, age, etc.).
4. The couple have incompatible sibling constellations (Toman, 1976).
5. The couple reside either extremely close to or at a great distance from either family of origin.
6. The couple are dependent on either extended family financially, physically, or emotionally.
7. The couple marries before age 20 or after age 30.
8. The couple marries after an acquaintanceship of less than 6 months or after more than 3 years of engagement.
9. The wedding occurs without family or friends present.
10. The wife becomes pregnant before or within the first year of marriage (Christensen, 1963; Bacon, 1974).

MONICA MCGOLDRICK / ELIZABETH A. CARTER

11. Either spouse has a poor relationship with his or her siblings or parents.

12. Either spouse considers his or her childhood or adolescence as an unhappy time.

13. Marital patterns in either extended family were unstable. . . .

A number of other factors also add to the difficulty of adjusting to marriage in our time. Changing family patterns as a result of the changing role of women, the frequent marriage of partners from widely different cultural backgrounds, and the increasing physical distances between family members are placing a much greater burden on couples to define their relationship for themselves than was true in traditional and precedent-bound family structures. While any two family systems are always different and have conflicting patterns and expectations, in our present culture couples are less bound by family traditions and freer than ever before to develop male-female relationships unlike those they experienced in their families of origin. This is particularly so because of the changing role of women in families. It appears that the rise in women's status is positively correlated with marital instability (Pearson & Hendrix, 1979) and with the marital dissatisfaction of their husbands (Burke & Weir, 1976). When women used to fall automatically into the adaptive role in marriage, the likelihood of divorce was much lower. In fact, it appears very difficult for two spouses to be equally successful and achieving. There is evidence that either spouse's accomplishments may correlate negatively with the same degree of achievement in the other (Ferber & Huber, 1979). Thus, achieving a successful transition to couplehood in our time, when we are moving toward the equality of the sexes (educationally and occupationally), may be extraordinarily difficult. . . .

THE FAMILY WITH YOUNG CHILDREN

The shift to this stage of the family life cycle requires that adults now move up a generation and become caretakers to the younger generation. Typical problems that occur when parents cannot make this shift are struggles with each other about taking responsibility, or refusal or inability to behave as parents to their children. Often parents find themselves unable to set limits and exert the required authority, or they lack the patience to allow their children to express themselves as they develop. Typically, parents with children who present clinically [appear for counseling] at this phase are somehow not accepting the generation boundary between themselves and their children. They may complain that their 4-year-old is "impossible to control." Given their relative size, the difficulty here relates to the parents' difficulty exerting authority. From this perspective, whether parents placate and spoil their children, or whether they are endlessly critical, they are reflecting a failure to appreciate the new change in family status required in this stage of the family life cycle. . . .

THE FAMILY WITH ADOLESCENTS

While many have broken down the stages of families with young children into different phases, in our view the shifts are incremental until adolescence, which ushers in a new era because it marks a new definition of the children within the family and of the parents' roles in relation to their children. Families with adolescents must establish qualitatively different boundaries than families with younger children. The boundaries must now be permeable. Parents can no longer maintain complete authority. Adolescents can and do open the family to a whole array of new values as they bring friends and new ideas into the family arena. Families that become derailed at this stage are frequently stuck in an earlier view of their children. They may try to control every aspect of their lives at a time when, developmentally, this is impossible to do successfully. Either the adolescent withdraws from the appropriate involvements for this developmental stage, or the parents become increasingly frustrated with what they perceive as their own impotence. For this phase the old Alcoholics Anonymous adage is particularly apt for parents: "May I have the ability to accept the things I cannot change, the strength to change the things I can, and the wisdom to know the difference." Flexible boundaries that allow adolescents to move in and be dependent at times when they cannot handle things alone, and to move out and experiment with increasing degrees of independence when they are ready, put special strains on all family members in their new status with one another. This is also a time when adolescents begin to establish their own independent relationships with the extended family, and it requires special adjustments between parents and grandparents to allow and foster these new patterns.

Parents of adolescents often get stuck in attempting to get their children to do what the parents want at a time when this no longer be done successfully, or they let the children do whatever they want and fail to exert the needed authority. Children may become overly independent and adultlike, or they remain immature and fail to develop sufficient independent functioning to move on developmentally. . . .

LAUNCHING CHILDREN AND MOVING ON

This phase of the family life cycle is the newest and the longest, and for these reasons, it is in many ways the most problematic of all phases. Until about a generation ago, most families were occupied with raising their children for their entire active adult lives until old age. Now, because of the low birth rate and the long life span of most adults, parents launch their children almost 20 years before retirement and must then find other life activities. The difficulties of this transition can lead families to hold on to their children or can lead to parental feelings of emptiness and depression, particularly for women who have focused their main energies on their children and who now feel useless and unprepared to face a new career in the job world. The most significant aspect of this phase is that it is marked by the greatest number of exits and entries of family members. It begins with the launching of grown children and proceeds with the entry of their spouses and children. Meanwhile, it is a time when older parents are often becoming ill or dying; this, in conjunction with the difficulties of finding meaningful life activities during this phase itself, may make it a particularly difficult period. Parents must not only deal with the change in their own status as they make room for the next generation and move up to grandparental positions, but they must deal also with a different type of relationship with their own parents, who may become dependent, giving them considerable caretaking responsibilities.

This can also be a liberating time, in that finances may be easier than during the primary years of family responsibilities and there is the potential for moving into new and unexplored areas—travel, hobbies, new careers. For some families this stage is seen as a time of fruition and completion and as a second opportunity to consolidate or expand by exploring new avenues and new roles. For others it leads to disruption, a sense of emptiness and over-whelming loss, depression, and general disintegration. The phase necessitates a restructuring of the marital relationship now that parenting responsibilities are no longer required. As Solomon (1973) has noted, if the solidification of the marriage has not taken place and reinvestment is not possible, the family often mobilizes itself to hold onto the last child. Where this does not happen the couple may move toward divorce.

The family that fails to appreciate the need for a shift in relationship status at this stage may keep trying to fill their time with the old tasks, or the spouses may begin to blame each other for the emptiness they feel. If they can recognize the new efforts required in this period, they are much more likely to be able to mobilize the energy to deal with them than if they go along on the assumptions of the previous phase. . . .

THE FAMILY IN LATER LIFE

As Walsh (1980) has pointed out, few of the visions we are offered in our culture for old age provide us with positive perspectives for healthy later-life adjustment within a family or social context. Pessimistic views of later life prevail. The current myths are that most elderly people have no families; that those who do have families have little relationship with them and are usually set aside in institutions; or that all family interactions with older family members are minimal. On the contrary, the vast majority of adults over 65 do not live alone but with other family members. Over 80% live within an hour of at least one child (Walsh, 1980).

Another myth about the elderly is that they are sick, senile, and feeble and can be best handled in nursing homes or hospitals. Only 4% of the elderly live in institutions (Streib, 1972), and the average age at admission is 80. There are indications that if others did not foster their dependence or ignore them as functional family members, even this degree of dependence would be less.

Among the tasks of families in later life are adjustments to retirement, which may not only create the obvious vacuum for the retiring person but may put a special strain on a marriage that until then has been balanced in different spheres. Financial insecurity or dependence are also special difficulties, especially for family members who value managing for themselves. And while loss of friends and relatives is a particular difficulty at this phase, the loss of a spouse is the most difficult adjustment, with its problems of reorganizing one's entire life alone after many years as a couple and of having fewer relationships to help replace the loss. Grandparenthood can, however, offer a new lease on life, and opportunities for special close relationships without the responsibilities of parenthood.

Difficulty in making the status changes required for this phase of life are reflected in older family members' refusal to relinquish some of their power, as when a grandfather refuses to turn over the company or make plans for his succession. The inability to shift status is reflected also when older adults give up and become totally dependent on the next generation, or when the next generation does not accept their lessening powers or treats them as totally incompetent or irrelevant.

Even when members of the older generation are quite enfeebled, there is not really a reversal of roles between one generation and the next, because parents always have a great many years of extra experience and remain models to the next generations for the phases of life ahead. Nevertheless, because valuing older age is totally unsupported in our culture, family members of the next generation often do not know how to make the appropriate shift in relational status with their parents. . . .

CONCLUSION

In concluding this chapter, we direct the reader's thoughts toward the powerful (and preventive) implications of family life cycle celebration: those rituals, religious or secular, that have been designed by families in every culture to ease the passage of its members from one status to the next. As Friedman (1980) points out, all family relationships in the system seem to unlock during the time just before and after such events, and it is often possible to shift things with less effort during these intensive periods than could ordinarily be expended in years of struggle.

REFERENCES

Bacon L. Early motherhood, accelerated role transition and social pathologies. *Social Forces*, 1974, 52, 333–341.

Bowen, M. *Family therapy in clinical practice.* New York: Aronson, 1978.

Burke, R. J. & Weir, T. The relationships of wives' employment status to husband, wife, and pair satisfaction. *Journal of Marriage and the Family*, 1976, 2, 279–287.

Christensen, H. T. The timing of first pregnancy as a factor in divorce: A cross-cultural analysis. *Eugenics Quarterly*, 1963, 10, 119–130.

Ferber, M., & Huber, J. Husbands, wives and careers. *Journal of Marriage and the Family*, 1979, 41, 315–325.

Friedman, E. Systems and ceremonies: A family view of rites of passage. In E. A. Carter & M. McGoldrick (Eds.), *The family life cycle: A framework for family therapy.* New York: Gardner Press, 1980.

Glick, P., & Norton, A. J. Marrying, divorcing and living together in the U.S. today. In *Population Bulletin*, 32, No. 5. Washington, D.C.: Population Reference Bureau, 1977.

Hetherington, E. M., Cox, M., & Cox, R. The aftermath of divorce. In J. J. Stevens, Jr., & M. Matthews (Eds.), *Mother-child, father-child relations.* Washington, D.C.: National Association for the Education of Young Children, 1977.

Pearson, W., & Hendrix, L. Divorce and the status of women. *Journal of Marriage and the Family*, 1979, 41, 375–386.

Ransom, W., Schlesinger, S., & Derdeyn, A. P. A stepfamily in formation. *American Journal of Orthopsychiatry*, 1979, 49, 36–43.

Solomon, M. A developmental conceptual premise for family therapy. *Family process*, 1973, 12, 179–188.

Streib, G. Older families and their troubles: Familial and social responses. *The Family Coordinator*, 1972, 21, 5–19.

Toman, W. *Family constellation* (3rd ed.). New York: Springr, 1976.

Walsh, F. The family in later life. In E. A. Carter & M. McGoldrick (Eds.), *The family life cycle: A framework for family therapy.* New York: Gardner Press, 1980.

19 Your Beliefs Can Sabotage Your Relationships

Chuck Hillig

STUDY QUESTIONS

1. Explain how the three myths can affect your relationships.

2. Why do people accept these myths?

As a licensed marriage, family, and child counselor, I deal professionally with

Source: Chuck Hillig, M.A., MFCC, "Your Beliefs Can Sabotage Your Relationships." *The Single Parent*, October 1980. Reprinted by permission.

people who are having problems in their relationships. During my years in private practice, I have noticed that many couples entering therapy sincerely believe the same common myths about how people operate.

Myth #1 holds that other people, objects, or situations can, literally, *make* you feel some emotion. This single untruth probably helps to create more suffering, anger, and bitterness than the other myths combined.

For example, do you believe that other family members or friends are often responsible for your painful feelings? Before you answer that, think back to the times when you've accused others of having hurt you or of having made you angry. Sound familiar? I hear this from my clients every day.

Let's look at this closely. When you really believe that the cause of your emotional upset is somewhere *outside* of you, then you're implying that someone or something else is in charge of your painful experience. For example, if you believe that your spouse is, somehow, *forcing* you to react painfully, then you're admitting that you really have no other choice except to feel hurt and upset. When you believe that others are *making* you feel an emotion, then you are giving away your ability to *choose* your own responses.

This whole idea of choice is important because it is only through your choices that you are able to truly experience your own personal power. If you believe that you don't have any *choice* as to how you react, then you really have no *control* over the situation.

If you don't have any control, then it follows that you're not the one who is *responsible* for your painful experience. And if you're not responsible, then guess who ends up getting the blame?

Acting on the belief that "they" are "doing this terrible thing to me," it is easy then to *justify* your own behavior in response to them. "Since *they* have hurt me," you reason, "then *they* are also responsible for my negative reactions to them." For example, if I can point at my wife and say, "She made me get drunk because she made me angry," then I'm off the responsibility hook for my own actions.

It's all downhill from there. Once you've made that original decision that you're not responsible for your own discomfort, then you can give yourself permission to "get even" with those people who are "causing" you the emotional pain. But while you are justifying your own negative behavior, your mate is probably doing the very same thing to you. I have seen many couples who have believed this myth all of their lives and have created for themselves a relationship filled with resentment, bitterness, and isolation.

Many couples resist giving up this belief because they just don't want to accept the responsibility for creating their own pain in the relationship. If they openly admitted to themselves that they alone were the source of their own discomfort, then they might feel pressured into doing something different. But since changes can be scary, many people simply choose to continue living with their pain but to hold their mates responsible for it. They each can take the pressure off themselves to change their behavior by directing their energies into making the other person not-OK and deserving of punishment.

Myth #1 is so widespread because its philosophy is continually reinforced on TV, in movies, in books, and in our popular songs. For example, millions

CHUCK HILLIG

of us firmly accept without question that rainy days can *make* us sad or that wearing old clothes can *make* us embarrassed. The truth is that situations and inanimate objects cannot *make* us feel anything any more than other people can *make* us feel anything. We all create our own feelings. Period.

How did we ever get to accept this myth in the first place? Probably 99 percent of us were indirectly conditioned as pre-schoolers to begin believing that we could control other people's feelings. For example, when our parents would say, "Don't tell Aunt Sue that you don't like her present because *you'll hurt her feelings*," it implied that we had the power to *force* Aunt Sue into feeling bad. Indirectly, though, it also implied that Aunt Sue and others could force *us* into feeling bad, too.

The simple truth is that we humans just do not have that much power to literally *force* each other into feeling some emotion. Significant others, of course, can make it much *easier* for us to *choose* one feeling over another, but the final choice of what and how we are going to feel is entirely ours. To give up our responsibility as the creator and the source of our own feelings is to experience only half of our power.

Myth #2 holds that you should always have *good reasons* why you are feeling anxious or upset about something and yet were just not able to figure out why. It seems that many of us have gotten programmed into believing that we should *always* be able to understand and explain our feelings to ourselves and to others. We can probably all remember times when our parents would ask us *why* we were feeling some way. Most of the time we knew, but there were always situations when we simply were not aware of the causes behind our feelings.

If I believe that I must always have *good reasons* for feeling the way I do, then what happens when I'm not able to come up with an explanation? What we all too often do with feelings that we can't understand or justify is to try to deny them and keep them inside of us. But this, in turn, only works to limit our experience of ourselves by keeping us defensive and out of touch with our own momentary reality.

The truth is that, sooner or later, we will likely create for ourselves all of the potential feelings that we as humans are capable of experiencing.

Although we might have a desire to commit murder, suicide, incest, etc., we are never required to *act* on those feelings. If we all did exactly what we momentarily felt like doing, our social structure would collapse around us. Since we have a free will which can determine our choices, we can learn to simply acknowledge and own these feelings as they arise from our unconscious.

We can best do this by giving ourselves complete permission to have these feelings, no matter how outrageous, as our truth for that moment. I often tell my clients to remember the acronym J-U-D-E in order to help remind them that they don't have to *J*ustify, *U*nderstand, *D*efend or *E*xplain their feelings to either themselves or to others.

For example, a man begins to feel jealous of his mate's financial success. Although he has an excellent job himself, he feels threatened at some deep level. If he believes that he needs to first have a "good reason" to be threatened and is unable to come up with one, he will likely repress the jealousy that is arising in him. But since he needs to do *something* with that "jealous energy," he may transform it into anger, resistance, and withdrawal.

Because he will not give himself permission to have such an "unreasonable" feeling as jealousy as his truth for that moment, he denies what he's feeling. When he does not create a space in his own personal "myth" about himself that can include the possibility that he, too, has the potential of creating an experience of "unreasonable jealousy," then he's stuck with the negative energy. This in turn only creates distance between him and his mate because the *actual* feeling—the "unreasonable jealousy"—has neither been acknowledged nor shared.

It is far healthier for the relationship to learn how to stop judging your own feelings and those of your partner. A feeling is a feeling. The feeling doesn't hassle us nearly as much as the relationship that we set up in our own heads between the feeling itself and what we believe that we *should* be experiencing instead.

Learning to accept our feelings as they arise is really learning to say "yes" to our own experience of ourselves from moment to moment.

Myth #3 holds that my partner should automatically know what I want without me having to share this information with him or her. At some level, many people still want to believe in magic. Their reasoning is often, "Since my family loves me, they *should* know by now what I want and expect from them." However, this is a dangerous position because then it seems to follow that, if my partner doesn't automatically give me what I want, then he or she must *not* love me. Once these rejection mechanisms get triggered inside us, they create a fertile space for grudges, resentments, and hostility to grow.

The desire to have our wishes "divined" by our loved ones, probably has its origins in our unconscious memory as infants. Most of us had parents who fed us, changed our diapers, and generally attended to our needs. At a deep level, we probably became addicted to having our basic wishes satisfied consistently by some benevolent protector. Most importantly, this "all-powerful" guardian was miraculously able to predict what we wanted and to have it there for us. Although our needs were primitive and obvious at that age, many people still expect this kind of "magic" from their partners.

When we relieve ourselves of the responsibility of clearly communicating our needs to those around us, we unfairly place upon them the impossible burden of reading our minds. When they fail to pick up our signals or if they misinterpret our wants, it becomes easy for us to justify feeling hurt and angry.

Demanding that your mate automatically understand and fulfill your needs in the same way as your parents did when you were an infant is an unreasonable expectation. Clinging to such a belief is only setting yourself up to feel disappointed and betrayed.

The problem is, of course, that we don't easily see that we are holding these myths as infallible truths. They are *not truths*; they are only *belief systems*. Although these beliefs are often unconscious, we can become aware of them by observing our own behavior and by asking ourselves these questions: (1) Do I believe that someone or something else is responsible for my own painful feelings, or do I accept that I am always creating my own emotional experience?

(2) Do I believe that I need to justify, understand, defend, or explain my feelings, or do I just allow myself to feel them? (3) Do I believe that the people who love me should magically know what I want and expect of them, or do I clearly inform them of my needs and desires?

By honestly answering these questions, we can begin to become more conscious of how our own belief systems are likely to work in our relationships.

20 *The Intimacy That Goes Beyond Sex*

Marica Lasswell / Norman M. Lobsenz

STUDY QUESTIONS

1. What is and what isn't intimacy?

2. Explain the three barriers to intimacy.

A man and woman may be close to each other in every physical way, yet remain emotional strangers. To lock away one's thoughts and feelings inside the strongbox of the mind is to deprive a partner of the most significant gift one can offer—the intimacy that goes beyond all others. Even the dictionary recognizes this. "Sexual intercourse" is the secondary definition of the word "intimacy." Its primary meaning is the "close personal relationship" that springs from the "inmost self." Thus, intimacy between husband and wife cuts across the totality of a marriage not just its sexual aspect. It is, perhaps, what we really mean (but do not realize we mean) by "love."

This intimacy that goes beyond sex presents difficulties for many couples. We all need it, we all want it. But not all of us know how to find it, nor are able to give it. Intimacy can be one of the knottiest areas to deal with, since differences in our ability to give and receive intimacy often stem from deep psychological causes. A marriage empty of intimacy, for whatever reason, is likely to intensify doubt about our own worth and adequacy—a doubt that gets translated into a further retreat from intimacy and sets up a cycle of isolation.

But couples can make a beginning, at least, at improving their ability truly to share an intimate relationship by better understanding the levels of intimacy; by learning to recognize some of the barriers to it; and by developing the skill to overcome these barriers.

Source: Excerpt from "Sex and Other Intimacies" from *No-Fault Marriage* by Marcia Lasswell and Norman Lobsenz. Copyright © 1976 by Marcia Lasswell and Norman Lobsenz. Reprinted by permission of Doubleday & Company, Inc.

WHAT INTIMACY IS, AND ISN'T

There's been a good deal of foolishness put forth about intimacy. Some would have you believe that while it is a bonus in marriage its absence is not fatal, that a couple can find sufficient satisfaction in a "colleague" relationship where both persons function independently but get on well together. Others hold intimacy to be the only essential element of a good marriage. In the reality of wedlock, the truth would seem to fall somewhere between these extremes.

We don't expect any couple would score 100 percent on an "intimacy rating," if there were such a scale. Nor should they. Each individual rightly reserves close-held emotional space for private thoughts and feelings. Couples who assume that there is always *complete* intimacy in a good marriage thus naturally feel, from time to time, that something is wrong in their relationship. They have set a standard for themselves (or had it set by outsiders) that is impossible to achieve. Moreover, intimacy manifests itself in many forms: a smile across a room, a shared joke, a family ritual, a kiss, a touch, sex, even in a certain inflection of the voice. How intimate a couple are, and what forms their intimacy takes, depends on how they "negotiate" the difference between their individual desires for it. Intimacy cannot be a one-way proposition. Obviously, a marriage between an emotionally giving (or needy) person married to a very private person will have a hard time achieving a degree of intimacy acceptable to both; for them all the emotional flow will be going in one direction.

As a practical matter, the level of intimacy between husband and wife is constantly changing. Moments of intense closeness intersperse with periods of varying emotional distance. Try this experiment. Draw two circles on a sheet of paper. One represents you, the other your spouse. Where they intersect and overlap represents your area of intimacy. For example, during a particularly good sexual experience the circles may overlap almost completely, like this:

But there also may be times when intercourse, though still satisfying, is not quite such an intense merging experience. One of you may be worried, or tired, or just not as interested as the other. The circles in that case might look this way:

Yet the next evening, at a large noisy party—or just across a quiet living room—you may each look up from what you are doing and meet each other's eyes in a spontaneous exchange of silent affection. At that instant the circles will again be virtually superimposed—

MARCIA LASSWELL / NORMAN M. LOBSENZ

and you are just as intimately linked as you were in that earlier act of sex.

During much of the twenty-four hours, as a couple go about the routines of living, their circles may barely touch:

After a bitter argument, they may be widely separated:

And the silent sharing of a mood can bring them close again. Some years ago a writer friend described what he called "one of the most intimate moments of my married life." He and his wife were reading the papers on a lazy Sunday morning over second cups of coffee while the FM radio played in the background. "Suddenly," he said, "the music of Mozart flooded the room. Without exchanging a word or even a glance my wife and I simultaneously got up from our chairs, moved to the middle of the room, bowed to each other, and began to improvise the steps of a minuet. It all happened as if we had been one person. I shall never forget how close we felt."

In short, the circles constantly shift as each person gives and receives, withholds and blocks out.

BARRIERS TO INTIMACY

It may seem strange that anyone should want to avoid intimacy in marriage. Yet many people not only seek to avoid it but secretly fear it. Therapists believe the main reason is that intimacy, like trust, inevitably implies *vulnerability*. They are two sides of the same coin. Emotional sharing requires self-disclosure, and for many of us the idea of opening up our inmost centers is a scary prospect. Suppose we get hurt? Suppose we are rejected? Suppose we open up to find and to reveal to our partner that there is little or nothing inside?

Schopenhauer's parable about the porcupines which drew together for warmth but separated when their quills pricked each other illustrates the pull-and-push interplay of intimacy and vulnerability. Pained, the animals move apart; then, feeling the chill of the air they move close again, only to be hurt once more in the act of sharing warmth. We are often told that hate is the opposite of love, remoteness the reverse of intimacy. But it appears the real antagonist of both is the fear of being vulnerable to hurt, rejection or disillusionment.

One protection against vulnerability—and thus a secondary barrier to intimacy—is to avoid the risk of self-disclosure by masking your true self. That's why some people can be comfortable emotionally so long as they can play the "role" of husband and wife. Doing the conventional and saying the expected things, we are saved from having to deal with the real feelings of real people. Sadly, it's all too easy to get on life's treadmill and keep running so steadily or so fast that we can find no time for intimacy. For men and women who have a poor opinion of themselves to begin with, the marital "role" is a convenient cloak to hide insecurities and weak self-images.

The retreat into role-playing is often an outgrowth of the artifices some couples adopt in their dating days. Ideally, courtship should be the time when men and women reveal themselves to each other with increasing intimacy. But even today—when so many courting conventions have gone by the boards and young couples dissemble less and level more—even now they still tend to conceal realities that might threaten their relationship. And when the *part* one plays succeeds in attracting and holding the person one wants, it gets progressively harder to step out of that character. But by dodging true intimacy in courtship we make it harder to achieve in marriage.

Even sexual intercourse defies intimacy when two people become actors in bed. A wife who for years faked orgasm so her husband would not feel a failure as a lover said, "Now I am trapped. I would like to be honest with him because that would be a start at solving our difficulty. But it would mean admitting I deceived him all this time." Like all other kinds of intimacy, sexual intimacy depends on maximum *mutual* openness.

INTIMACY AND SEX

A pathetic paradox of these sexually "free" times is that Americans are making love more but enjoying it less.

William Masters and Virginia Johnson estimate that half the married couples in the United States have sexual problems. Much sexual unhappiness grows directly out of the fear of intimacy. In fact, some couples develop sexual problems as a result of the stress one or both partners feel about being emotionally committed to an intimate relationship. For these people, sex may be good before and early in marriage. But when the realization hits that a good marriage demands ever-higher degrees of intimacy, there may be a retreat from sex.

While sexual distancing is almost always a sign of intimacy problems, sexual contact is not always a sign of emotional closeness. That is another paradox couples need to bear in mind. For example, there are marriages in which sex is the only good thing the couple share, and is sufficiently rewarding to hold together a relationship that lacks most other assets. Even men and women who are separated or divorced may still be drawn together sexually. For other couples, intercourse may represent the search for an antidote to loneliness, the "skin hunger" that desperately needs assuaging by human touch. It may offer reassurance that one is still vigorous and desirable. Or it may be a frantic effort to prove one still actually *exists*. Widows and widowers are often shocked to find that quite soon after a spouse's death they want—or form—a new sexual liaison. Similarly, there's an upsurge of sexual activity after major disasters. In both instances people are denying death, expressing the life force, saying with their bodies: "*I* am still here."

Withholding sex—being "too tired" or having a "headache"—is a standard method for turning an intimate act into a power struggle. Spoiling sex—being passive or brusque, repressing a climax or ejaculating too quickly—are somewhat crueler refinements of the technique. One woman drove her husband to fury by making casual remarks about the day's events during intercourse.

Sometimes couples quarrel in order to feel sexy. Making up in bed after a fight is a common marital pattern. It is reassuring when the bond of intimacy survives an argument. But if it is often done deliberately one needs to ask *why* quarreling is a turn-on. Marital therapist Laura Singer has observed that "it may be a way for a couple to distance themselves from each other to avoid true merging. . . . Or the act may be an extension of the fight. People may perceive a fight as firing their libido, but what it really fires is their hostility."

All these "uses" or "mis-uses" of sex distort its function as the most intimate link in marriage. Even more startling, however, is the use of sex as an outright *substitute* for intimacy. A person who is so alienated as to fear any close relationship may turn to sex as the only nonthreatening way to be with another person. When there routinely is physical contact with no emotional attachments, the act of love becomes the *denial* of intimacy.

EXPRESSING INTIMACY

Some husbands and wives are genuinely puzzled by the suggestion that they try to raise the intimacy level of their marriage. They agree with the theory but they do not know how to put it into practice. They seem to assume that a talent for sharing feelings is an inborn skill which can't be learned. Or that it takes "too much time" to cultivate. Or that their responsibilities keep them too much on the go, or too far apart, to be able to create a basis for true intimacy.

But there are any number of ways every couple can find to enhance and to express their mutual intimacy:

1. Confiding in your spouse is an aspect of intimacy. Think back and ask yourself whether you often tell a friend or neighbor something you feel you cannot or do not want to tell your wife or husband. If you do, perhaps you should ask whether you are being emotionally fair to your partner—and why you are shutting him or her out, or shutting yourself away.

2. Sharing "trivialities" is a way of increasing intimacy. Some people feel it's "boring" to tell a spouse all the little things that occur during the day. But marriage is essentially made up of these small details; they are the "nuts and

bolts" of living together. True, they are usually routine. But if you wait for some major event to happen you may wait quite a while.

3. Intimate behavior does not have to involve only grand passion or high drama. Intimacy is built as well (if not more soundly) on lighter, slighter actions: reading aloud; putting a loving note in a lunch box; giving a small but unexpected present; doing a chore the other person hates (without being asked); telling the other person when you have had a warm thought about him or her.

4. Verbal communication is an important part of intimacy because unless we can put feelings into words our partners may never know we have them. Even an argument can contribute to marital intimacy. If a couple can have an honest fight without letting it deteriorate into aggression or anger, it often leaves them feeling closer when it's over. As one couple said after a furious battle: "You can get mad and know it's *because you care* about each other." Conversely, poor communication can handicap a couple's efforts to be close.

5. While sex is the peak physical expression of intimacy, it's essential to remember that there can be many kinds of marital sex. There can be an intense spiritual or emotional merging. There can be sex that makes you feel like the most desirable man or woman in the world. There is casual love-making, playful "seduction," intercourse for the release of tension, reluctant sex, or sex on the purely physical "let's do it" level. One brings a different expectation of intimacy to each kind of sexual experience, and it is important for both partners to know what kind of expectation the other has for each particular experience.

   The emphasis on sexual technique in recent years has cut many couples off from true intimacy. They get so caught up in mechanics and methods that they lose sight of the need for feelings and concerns. Good physical sex is obviously important—but no two persons' cycle of desire coincides exactly all the time. Not even the perfect orgasm is any guarantee of interpersonal intimacy. Orgasmic sex can make a good marriage better; but a good marriage, with a high level of emotional intimacy, can also make for more or better orgasms.

6. Many men and women find pleasure in varying degrees of physical intimacy short of sexual intercourse. That's why touching is such a key factor in conveying intimate feelings. Americans avoid touching. They tend to think of body contact not in terms of comfort and affection, but in terms of sex or combat—both of which are prickly with cultural and psychological taboos. Thus a wife may come to resent a husband's touch if she thinks all it means is that he wants sex. Likewise, she hesitates to touch him for fear *he* will think *she* wants sex.

   Yet touching is the most natural act in the world. A touch can calm anxiety, ease pain, soothe fear, provide emotional security.

If you have hesitated to express or receive intimacy through touching but would like to experiment with it, try these steps:

1. Discuss the idea first with your partner. Nothing is more disconcerting than when one person suddenly and without explanation becomes a "toucher."

2. Begin with simple physical contacts that are customary in many families: a good-morning and good-night kiss, a hug in greeting or farewell.

3. Become more aware of your spouse's physical presence. Many couples become so familiar with each other's bodies that, paradoxically, they forget how those bodies *really* look and feel.

4. Touch yourself more often to develop a sense of body awareness. We do it automatically while drying after a bath, shaving, putting on makeup. But we should learn to do it consciously on occasion.

Touching should never be an implied demand to be touched in return, or a camouflage for clinging to another person.

Learn to be sensitive to when the other person wants—or does not want—to be touched. The important thing is to respect each other's feelings about it.

Is it better to experience intimacy at the risk of some hurt, or to avoid it in order to feel safe?

That is what economists call a "cost-reward equation." As with all such questions, the answer lies in the balance between how much it costs to get the reward we desire. To a vulnerable person it always *seems* safer to keep feelings at arm's length. But retreating from intimacy is no guarantee that you will not be hurt by someone, somehow, anyway. In the long run, reaching out and opening up is not only more rewarding but also less risky.

21 *Marriages Made to Last*

Jeanette Lauer / Robert Lauer

STUDY QUESTIONS

1. On what factors do men and women agree for keeping a marriage going?

2. What are the major differences between men and women on the list of what keeps a marriage going?

Americans are keenly aware of the high rate of marital breakup in this country.

Source: Jeanette Lauer and Robert Lauer, "Marriages Made to Last." *Psychology Today*, June 1985, pp. 22–26. Reprinted with permission from *Psychology Today* magazine. Copyright © 1985 (PT Partners, L.P.).

More than a million couples a year now end their expectations of bliss in divorce; the average duration of a marriage in the United States is 9.4 years. The traditional nuclear family of husband, wife and children is less and less common. Indeed, it seems at times that no one out there is happily married. But in the midst of such facts and figures, another group tends to be overlooked: those couples who somehow manage to stay together, who allow nothing less than death itself to break them up.

Social scientists have long been concerned about the causes of marital disruption. There are numerous works that tell us why people break up. But as J. H. Wallis wrote in his 1970 book, *Marriage Observed*, "we have still not quite come to grips with what it is that makes marriages last, and enables them to survive." His conclusion remains valid. The books that tell couples how to construct a lasting and meaningful marriage tend to be based either upon the clinical experiences of those who have counseled troubled and dissolving marriages, or upon the speculations of those who believe that they have found the formula for success.

We recently completed a survey of couples with enduring marriages to explore how marriages survive and satisfy in this turbulent world. Through colleagues and students we located and questioned 351 couples married for 15 years or more.

Of the 351 couples, 300 said they were happily married, 19 said they were unhappily married (but were staying together for a variety of reasons, including "the sake of the children"); and among the remaining 32 couples only one partner said he or she was unhappy in the marriage.

Each husband and wife responded individually to our questionnaire, which included 39 statements and questions about marriage—ranging from agreement about sex, money and goals in life to attitudes toward spouses and marriage in general. We asked couples to select from their answers the ones that best explained why their marriages had lasted. Men and women showed remarkable agreement on the keys to an enduring relationship (see box).

The most frequently named reason for an enduring and happy marriage was having a generally positive attitude toward one's spouse: viewing one's partner as one's best friend and liking him or her "as a person."

As one wife summed it up, "I feel that liking a person in marriage is as important as loving that person. Friends enjoy each other's company. We spend an unusually large amount of time together. We work at the same institution, offices just a few feet apart. But we still have things to do and to say to each other on a positive note after being together through the day."

It may seem almost trite to say that "my spouse is my best friend," but the couples in our survey underscored the importance of feeling that way. Moreover, they told us some specific things that they liked about their mates—why, as one woman said, "I would want to have him as a friend even if I weren't married to him." For one thing, many happily married people said that their mates become more interesting to them in time. A man married for 30 years said that it was almost like being married to a series of different women: "I have watched her grow and have shared with her both the pain and the exhilaration of her journey. I find her more fascinating now than when we were first married."

JEANETTE LAUER / ROBERT LAUER

A common theme among couples in our study was that the things they really liked in each other were qualities of caring, giving, integrity and a sense of humor. In essence, they said, "I am married to someone who cares about me, who is concerned for my well-being, who gives as much or more than he or she gets, who is open and trustworthy and who is not mired down in a somber, bleak outlook on life." The redemption of difficult people through selfless devotion may make good fiction, but the happily married people in our sample expressed no such sense of mission. Rather, they said, they are grateful to have married someone who is basically appealing and likable.

Are lovers blind to each other's faults? No, according to our findings. They are aware of the flaws in their mates and acknowledge the rough times, but they believe that the likable qualities are more important than the deficiencies and the difficulties. "She isn't perfect," said a husband of 24 years. "But I don't worry about her weak points, which are very few. Her strong points overcome them too much."

A second key to a lasting marriage was a belief in marriage as a long-term commitment and a sacred institution. Many of our respondents thought that the present generation takes the vow "till death us do part" too lightly and is unwilling to work through difficult times. Successful couples viewed marriage as a task that sometimes demands that you grit your teeth and plunge ahead in spite of the difficulties. "I'll tell you why we've stayed together," said a Texas woman married for 18 years. "I'm just too damned stubborn to give up."

Some of the people in the survey indicated that they would stay together no matter what. Divorce was simply not an option. Others viewed commitment somewhat differently. They saw it not as a chain that inexorably binds people together despite intense misery but rather as a determination to work through difficult times. "You can't run home to mother when the first sign of trouble appears," said a woman married for 35 years.

"Commitment means a willingness to be unhappy for a while," said a man married for more than 20 years. "I wouldn't go on for years and years being wretched in my marriage. But you can't avoid troubled times. You're not going to be happy with each other all the time. That's when commitment is really important."

In addition to sharing attitudes toward the spouse and toward marriage, our respondents indicated that agreement about aims and goals in life, the desire to make the marriage succeed and laughing together were all important. One surprising result was that agreement about sex was far down the list of reasons for a happy marriage. Fewer than 10 percent of the spouses thought that good sexual relations kept their marriage together. Is sex relatively unimportant to a happy marriage? Yes and no.

Although not many happily married respondents listed it as a major reason for their happiness, most were still generally satisfied with their sex lives. Seventy percent said that they always or almost always agreed about sex. And indeed for many, "satisfied" seems too mild a term. A woman married for 19 years said: "Our sexual desire is strong, and we are very much in love." One man said that sex with his wife was like "a revival of youth." Another noted that for various reasons he and his wife did not have sex as frequently as they would like, but when they do "it is a beautiful act of giving and sharing as deeply emotional as it is physical."

While some reported a diminishing sex life, others described a relatively stable pattern and a number indicated improvement over time. "Thank God, the passion hasn't died," a wife said. "In fact, it has gotten more intense. The only thing that has died is the element of doubt or uncertainty that one experiences while dating or in the beginning of a marriage."

On the other hand, some couples said they were satisfied despite a less-than-ideal sex life. A number of people told us that they were happy with their marriage even though they did not have sex as frequently as they would like. Generally, men complained of this more than women, although a number of wives desired sex more than did their husbands. There were various reasons for having less sex than desired, generally involving one partner's exhaustion from work or family circumstances ("We are very busy and very involved," reported a husband, "and have a teenager who stays up late. So we don't make love as often as we would like to.").

Does this dissatisfaction with sex life lead to affairs? We did not ask about fidelity directly, but the high value that most of our subjects placed on friendship and commitment strikes us as incongruous with infidelity. And in fact only two of those we questioned volunteered that they had had brief affairs. One husband's view might explain the faithfulness of the group: "I get tempted when we don't have sex. But I don't think I could ever have an affair. I would feel like a traitor."

Such treason, in fact, may be the one taboo in enduring relationships. A wife of 27 years said that although she could work out almost any problem with her husband given enough time, infidelity "would probably not be something I could forget and forgive." The couples in our sample appear to take their commitment to each other seriously.

Those with a less-than-ideal sex life talked about adjusting to it rather than seeking relief in an affair. A woman married 25 years rated her marriage as extremely happy even though she and her husband had had no sexual relations for the past 10 years. "I was married once before and the marriage was almost totally sex and little else," she said. "So I suppose a kind of trade-off exists here—I like absolutely everything else about my current marriage."

Many others agreed that they would rather be married to their spouse and have a less-than-ideal sex life than be married to someone else and have a better sex life. As one wife put it, "I feel marriages can survive and flourish without today's emphasis on sex. I had a much stronger sex drive than my husband and it was a point of weakness in our marriage. However, it was not as important as friendship, understanding and respect. That we had lots of, and still do."

We found a few beliefs and practices among our couples that contradict what some therapists believe is important to a marriage. One involves conflict. Some marriage counselors stress the importance of expressing feelings with abandon—spouses should freely vent their anger with each other, letting out all the stops short of physical violence. According to them, aggression is a catharsis that gets rid of hostility and restores harmony in the marital relationship. But some social scientists argue that intense expressions of anger, resentment and dislike tend to corrode the relationship and increase the likelihood of future aggression.

Happily married couples in our survey came down squarely on the side of those who emphasize the damaging effects of intensely expressed anger. A salesman with a 36-year marriage advised, "Discuss your problems in a normal voice. If a voice is raised, stop. Return after a short period of time. Start again. After a period of time both parties will be able to deal with their problems and not say things that they will be sorry about later."

Only one couple said that they typically yelled at each other. The rest emphasized the importance of restraint. They felt that a certain calmness is necessary in dealing constructively with conflict.

Another commonly held belief that contradicts conventional wisdom concerns equality in marriage. Most social scientists note the value of an egalitarian relationship. But according to the couples in our sample, the attitude that marriage is a 50-50 proposition can be damaging. One husband said that a successful marriage demands that you "give 60 percent of the time. You have to be willing to put in more than you take out." A wife happily married for 44 years said she would advise all young couples "to be willing to give 70 percent and expect 30 percent."

In the long run, the giving and taking should balance out. If either partner enters a marriage determined that all transactions must be equal, the marriage will suffer. As one husband put it, "Sometimes I give far more than I receive, and sometimes I receive far more than I give. But my wife does the same. If we weren't willing to do that, we would have broken up long ago."

Finally, some marriage experts have strongly advocated that spouses maintain separate as well as shared interests. It is important, they argue, to avoid the merging of identities. But those in our survey with enduring, happy marriages disagree. They try to spend as much time together and share as many activities as possible. "Jen is just the best friend I have," said a husband who rated his marriage as extremely happy. "I would rather spend time with her, talk with her, be with her than with anyone else."

"We try to share everything," said another. "We even work together now. In spite of that, we often feel that we have too little time together."

We did not detect any loss of individuality in these people. In fact, they disagreed to some extent on many of the questions. Their intense intimacy—their preference for shared rather than separate activities—seems to reflect a richness and fulfillment in the relationship rather than a loss of identity. "On occasion she has something else to do, and I enjoy the time alone. But it strikes me that I can enjoy it because I know that soon she will be home, and we will be together again."

Our results seem to underscore Leo Tolstoy's observation that "Happy families are all alike." Those who have long-term, happy marriages share a number of attitudes and behavioral patterns that combine to create an enduring relationship. For them, "till death us do part" is not a binding clause but a gratifying reality.

Here are the top reasons respondents gave, listed in order of frequency.

Men	Women
My spouse is my best friend.	My spouse is my best friend.
I like my spouse as a person.	I like my spouse as a person.
Marriage is a long-term commitment.	Marriage is a long-term commitment.
Marriage is sacred.	Marriage is sacred.
We agree on aims and goals.	We agree on aims and goals.
My spouse has grown more interesting.	My spouse has grown more interesting.
I want the relationship to succeed.	I want the relationship to succeed.
An enduring marriage is important to social stability.	We laugh together.
We laugh together.	We agree on a philosophy of life.
I am proud of my spouse's achievements.	We agree on how and how often to show affection.
We agree on a philosophy of life.	An enduring marriage is important to social stability.
We agree about our sex life.	We have a stimulating exchange of ideas.
We agree on how and how often to show affection.	We discuss things calmly.
I confide in my spouse.	We agree about our sex life.
We share outside hobbies and interests.	I am proud of my spouse's achievements.

22 *The Social Construction of Male-Violence Rationales*

Robert N. Whitehurst

STUDY QUESTIONS

1. What are the rationales abusive males use for defending their violence?

2. Indicate the variables that create domestic violence potential.

Source: Robert N. Whitehurst, "The Social Construction of Male-Violence Rationales." American Sociological Association, 1979 Annual Meeting. Used by permission.

INTRODUCTION

Domestic violence has traditionally been handled in sociology either by presuming that it was perpetrated only by lower-class people or that it belonged as a part of a waste-basket category with other violent crimes. The many changes of consciousness over the past decade or so have included an increasing awareness of the narrowness of our previous definitions of the realities of domestic violence. We no longer believe it is only committed in poor or ethnic families or that it is only lower-class *men* who become violent. Although there have been advances in research and theory, much remains to be done, especially in terms of understanding male responses, attitudes and supports for violence under certain conditions and not other. . . .

In a previous paper, Whitehurst and Karcz (1978) described six orientations women bring to bear on their acceptance of violence as rule-governed behavior (Fig. 1). These run the gamut from a "no-violence" rule to accepting of violence as normal in a relationship. An earlier male-relationship typology suggested by Balswick and Peek (1971) was extended by Whitehurst and Booth (1980) to include six types of male orientations to relating. The aim of the development of the male-violence rationales typology is to be able to test for the amount of variance that can be accounted for by linking the types of responses in all three of the typologies.

Observation and the data available suggest the typology of male rationales, including these five types: She made me do it, I lost control, I wasn't myself, she needed it, and I needed it. The first three of these seem more or less clear to involve explanations that involve external locus of control notions. We know from other research that these people tend to have lower self-images, greater discrepancy between their ideal and real selves and do not feel as adequately in control of their lives as do those with internal locus of control perceptions of themselves (Chandler, 1976). The basic male dichotomy here is called Fatalists, who believe that they were not in control for some reason when they were violent, and Functionals, those who appear to take some responsibility for the violence, but excuse themselves on some ground (the violence has some functional value). In est terms, the fatalists (or externally controlled) are "at effect" of their environment or the people in it, and the functionals are more or less "at cause" (recognizing their own implication, culpability and responsibility for their actions). Female rules five and six, when combined with cowboy or playboy responses of males will most often eventuate in either the first or second male-violence kinds of rationales (she made me do it, or I lost control rationales). For our purposes now, I will discuss the dynamics of accounts in each of the five types of violence rationales.

The first response in the male rationales for violence (she made me do it) can be seen as both an excuse and a justification in Scott and Lyman's terms. Among the types of excuses that might apply to this type would be: accident, or an appeal of the offender to be understood in terms of his human incapacity to control his responses, and thus should be excused. This kind of response also crosses over into number three response (I wasn't myself) in that both the

FIGURE 1. Some Variables That Create Domestic Violence Potential

Unshared symbols,
meanings, negative
communications,
discounts, put-downs

       tensions in
       relationship,
       unresolved issues

              Poor
              accommodation
              potential

                     value and goal
                     dissensus

                            legitimacy of
                            the use of
                            violence,
                            violence
                            expectations

Female Rules, Male-Relationships and Violence Rationales

Female rules regarding violence (ORIENTATIONS)

1. No violence   (Non-acceptance)
2. "No violence"-but (you will be forgiven)
3. "I hope it will not happen-but it might"
4. "Resigned-accepters" (that's the way men are-not much can be done about it)
5. "The understanders" (I understand him-he had such a terrible childhood, has such a bad boss, etc.)- forgiveness
6. "Normal accepters"-(see violence as a normal part of   (Acceptance) life-not to be thought of too much if possible)

Modes of Male-Relating to Females (ORIENTATIONS TO RELATING)

1. Cowboy   (note potential for establishment of
2. Playboy   interpersonal credibility trust,
3. Fearful-ambivalent   acceptance, etc.)
4. Normal coper
5. Pragmatist
6. Happy-coper

Male violence-rationales

1. She made me do it (nagged me, etc.)
2. I lost control (due to problems)
3. I wasn't myself (alcohol, drugs, temporary insanity)
4. She needed it—(to once again set the relationship straight)
5. I needed it—(to straighten out my own life—and to regain a sense of loss of self-respect in my life)

                    ROBERT N. WHITEHURST

excuse and the rationale rely on a kind of at least temporary "not-me-ness." Men also tend to use other excuses, such as: defeasibility, in which a man claims that the act was not entirely within his will, biological drive, in which he asks to be understood as a part of a fatalistic reaction to "the way men are." Most obvious of all is the excuse category Scott and Lyman call scapegoating, which sees the violent responses as a function of attitudes of others.

In regard to justification, most men seem to engage in either denial of injury, even though the wife may protest that her injuries were more severe than the husband claims, and denial of the victim, in which the injured party is seen as deserving of the injury. Also involved at times is the condemnation of the condemners, in which a husband may see his violence as irrelevant compared with the worse offense of the wife (nagging, adultery, real or supposed—and neglect of duties).

The second rationale (I lost control) implies some awareness of culpability, but suggests a recourse to the excuse of accident (incapacity to control response) and defeasibility (my will was not free). Justifications are less likely to be called into play in these instances, and indeed some men simply say things like, "I know I shouldn't have hit her, but I just lost control and I know there is no excuse." This implicitly suggests that they know there can be few justifications that suffice so at times they do not attempt to make them.

In the third instance (I wasn't myself), the excuses of accident, defeasibility and biological drive provide rationales. At times, even scapegoating can be called upon, insofar as someone might blame others for getting him high on drugs or too drunk to keep control. There is no necessary linkage between any of the justifications and this type of rationale, thus justifications may or may not be a part of this response. Incapacity and loss of one's will are most clearly seen in this kind of case when a male sees himself as losing self-control and becoming someone other than himself—at least temporarily. The pre-dominating type of female response when women continue to tacitly approve of male violence against themselves is in female type five, the understanders, who can forgive men repeatedly who are perceived as very different when not drinking. Some therapies that deal with alcoholics and other kinds of more or less compulsive behavior do not accept the hypothesis that there is such a thing as "not-me-ness" when drunk. The presumption is that the inner dialogue continues in drunken states, albeit at a different level than while sober. The point is that we do not really lose control, even though there are obviously altered states of feeling, loss of inhibition and so forth.

In the case of the fourth adaptation (she needed it), scapegoating is the only potential excuse offered by males who use this rationale. Any of the justifications might be called upon but denial of the victim (she deserved what she got) and condemnation of the condemners is the most usual in the cases interviewed thus far. The presumption seems to be that were she to cease doing whatever it was that irritated him, he would desist from the violent reactions. There is, of course, little evidence to suggest that this is in fact very often a reality for couples. This analysis seems to suggest that men's violence may reside more within personality structures than in social situational factors. Previous research (Whitehurst, Booth, Hanif, 1979) suggests that violent males tend to go from one woman to another, continuing with violent modes of interaction when one woman escapes. This does not minimize situational factors, since there are obviously many women who are willing to play roles allowing violence; it only obscures the dynamics in an already unclear field of effort. In any case, many men get peer support for their definitions that a wife "needs" to be hit to keep the power relationship aligned; this adaptation may be nearly as common as losing control due to problems or excuses due to alcohol or drugs.

The last adaptation (I needed it) most clearly calls forth the scapegoating response kind of excuse. None of the justifications seems clearly appropriate from the data we have gathered to date. If a man says in effect, 'I needed that'—it seems that there is some kind of justification built into it on the face of the statement. This kind of statement seems to imply responsibility of a sort that does not displace the awareness of the conscious act of assigning cause to the aggressive act. In one sense, however, the justification of "appeal to loyalties" can be applied since a man may see other men as his chief referent for legitimacy of his violent actions toward his wife. He may view his status in the male group as becoming lowered if he does not keep his sense of self-respect when his wife may become "too" uppity or too dogmatic or bossy. His appeal to loyalties tends to be associated with his membership in a particular kind of male group that perceives women as a comparative group—useful to keep one's own self-respect intact by battering on occasion. . . .

SOME TENTATIVE CONCLUSIONS

Two conclusions seem justified—and of some importance—from all of this: one, men tell different stories and give different accounts of their violence in different settings. Why men do this is probably less important than recognizing the consequences of the second problem: that men by and large have found audiences to which they can provide more or less convincing stories they construct about their violence. It is this problem, the acceptance of rationales, that seems to me to be at least a part of the crux of continuing violence. On the one hand, we have a culture that promotes violence in a number of ways through socially structured means. On the other, we have made it possible for men to use rationales and have them more or less accepted; it is this acceptance, at whatever level it occurs that makes for the continuation of a high violence potential.

In some therapy circles, it is no longer fashionable to allow justifications for some kinds of behavior which were formerly called "compulsive" or of that order. What now seems to be more plausible than believing in some inner force or compulsion that causes people to act irrationally, including violently, is to believe that the inner dialogue is very much speeded up, not dispensed with or held in abeyance during episodes of violence. It is suggested here that the more or less witting acceptance of most violence rationales on the part of men (or women) tends to create an increased possibility that such behaviors will be continued, since "everyone" knows that it is possible to claim immunity on one

ROBERT N. WHITEHURST

or more grounds of either loss of control or by claiming that there is a justification for violence. In the case of women, it seems clear that they are deeply involved (albeit in an unwitting and typically female-socialized way) in their own victimization, most clearly in those cases of repeated assault. Our primary cause of dis-service is done to females by creating a belief system in women that they have few choices, that it is somehow proper to be at the mercy of a man, that it is more or less to be expected that a man might on occasion act violently. For men, our dis-service is located in the kinds of socialization that follows the "war model" (Whitehurst and Booth, 1980) that provides a number of rewards for toughness and aggressiveness, if not violence. More than that, to continue this system by more or less systematically accepting at some levels the excuses and rationalizations men give for their violence seems clearly to feed-back into more violence, since it is not really a clearly disapproved activity, since it is so obvious that many men not only get away with it, they have their stories believed and repeat their violence with impunity. Depriving women of their audiences which support their helplessness against men and depriving men of their audiences which give credibility to their violence seems necessary if progress in domestic violence is to be made. Obviously these kinds of change occur slowly, and in both cases some directions can be seen as emergent: women are more clearly now in a position to less often accept older definitions of themselves as helpless; the trend toward lesser acceptance of male violence and the accompanying rationales is much less clear. . . .

Our contemporary ways of dealing with men who behave in such a way seems to take one of three approaches: We may ignore or pass off such violence as unimportant, we may reject the person as a proper kind of human being and treat him with scorn, pejoratives, or otherwise surround him with negative definitions and thoughts. We may also treat him as a sick man in need of treatment. . . .

Recognizing the ways in which our normal roles and social structures feed the violence potential can lead to further actions which may increase consciousness of what we are doing and the effects of our beliefs and attributions on others. Above all, there is a need for a normative set of values which encourages persons to take responsibility for their own actions and to respect the dignity of others, not only in terms of their bodily space rights, but in terms of their rights to be heard and not discounted, put down, or otherwise treated as natural inferiors. Obviously there is much that needs to be done. The basic impetus will no doubt come from women with the help of some men who see equality as an idea whose time has come.

REFERENCES

Balswick, J. O. and Peek, C. W., "The Inexpressive Male: A Tragedy of American Society," *The Family Coordinator*, Vol. 20, No. 4, pp. 363–368, 1971.

Chandler, Theodore A., "Notes on the Relationship of Internality-Externality, Self-Acceptance and Self-Ideal Discrepancies," *Journal of Psychology*, 94, 1976, 145–146.

Scott, M. B. and Lyman, S. M., "Accounts," *American Sociological Review*, Vol. 33, No. 6, pp. 46–62, Dec. 1968.

Whitehurst, R., Booth, G. and Hanif, M., "Factors in Separation and Divorce," in *Sociological Footsteps*, ed. by Len Cargan and Joanne Ballentine, Houghton-Mifflin Co., New York: 1979.

Whitehurst, Robert N. and Booth, G. V., *Sexual Pluralism: Understanding Changing Identities*, Gage Publishing, Ltd., Agincourt, Ont.: 1980.

6 *Making It Equal*

Another aspect of marital interaction deals with the question of equality in the marital relationship. On the surface, this would appear to be a moot question since our ideology stresses the equality of all citizens, and this would appear to be especially so in a freely arranged marriage contract. However, as the discussion on the marital contract indicated, appearances can be deceiving. Besides the state's gender-role assumptions of the marriage contract, another element of inequality develops out of the marital custom of men marrying women who are slightly their inferiors. This marriage gradient reveals that older, more educated, higher-salaried, higher-status husbands are regularly matched with younger, less educated, lower-salaried, and lower-status wives. A legitimate question at this point would ask about the consequences of a pairing based on such an unequal relationship. A logical conclusion is that for a wife to deal with this inequality, that is, to gain some power, she must participate in the labor force. Actually, the concept of the child-centered housewife as a full-time occupation is a relatively recent one, which arose only after industrialization had separated male and female work locations and roles and which, in turn, led to the ideology of motherhood as woman's special calling. It should be recognized, however, that wives have always worked and contributed to the home via labor done in the home, such as taking in laundry, boarders, or the selling of canned goods. The change then, is a recognition that a substantial proportion of wives now earn their income away from the home in the paid labor force. The beginning of a movement that would lead a majority of women into the labor force was World War II. However, this participation was expected to be temporary. The surprise is that it has grown steadily every since, causing profound changes in marital roles, division of labor, and self-perception for both sexes. In the first article in Chapter 6, Jean Grambs sums up the hopes of the past and present situation with a glance at what she calls "the American dream."

Another logical question at this point would be, did the move to outside work accomplish its goal? Or, to put it another way, what are the benefits and penalties of this move? Barbara Chesser, in the second article of this chapter, notes thirteen such benefits as well as some recommendations that would ease the task. The penalties include stress, both internal and external, on the household. The internal stressors involve the discontinuity between early gender-role socialization and the present lifestyle, the conflicting demands of family and work, and role overload since the total volume of activities has been considerably increased. The external stressors include cultural strain due to lack of normative support, occupational inflexibility and demands for geographical mobility, and lack of time for social interaction with friends and relatives (Skinner 1980).

Since the social support structures have changed little in response to the increasing number of employed couples, how will dual-earner/dual-career homes cope with the stressors of their dual commitments? Linda Haas, in the third article of Chapter 6, believes the answer will be role-sharing symmetry in the family roles of breadwinner, decision making, and domestic chores. Such sharing, she concludes, provides both individual and family benefits, but it requires "wholehearted and enthusiastic willingness of both spouses to participate"—a condition which may not be in the fore since most husbands still help very little with household tasks. For the wife involved as well in her own career, there may be role strain since most professional jobs assume the traditional male worker's circumstances and having a career is not yet part of a woman's basic identity.

For the other members of the dual-career/employed family there are also benefits and penalties. Husbands in such households benefit from a second source of income and from their wives' broader experience and enthusiasm but may feel deprived of their wives' care and attention and even distressed at sharing the breadwinning role.

As Barbara Berg notes in the final article of Chapter 6, there is good news for mothers who work. The prevailing beliefs about the effects of working mothers on children are mostly myths. Children of two working parents do not seem to suffer at any age from good outside day care and may benefit from a greater range of role models, financial security, and the chance to develop independence. Lack of time and communication with parents are the most frequently cited drawbacks.

However, latch-key children are at greater risk for accidents and sex crimes.

Societal needs of dual-employed couples include:

a. access to appropriate and affordable day care,
b. flex-time or in-home employment,
c. changes in federal tax and aid programs, and
d. schools adopting child-care responsibilities.

REFERENCE

1. Skinner, D. A. 1980. "Dual-career Family Stress and Coping: A Literature Review." *Family Relations* (October).

23 Mom, Apple Pie, and the American Dream

Jean Dresden Grambs

STUDY QUESTIONS

1. What were the dreams or hopes of the past?

2. How has the dream been refined?

It was never true for most Americans, but still the story persisted that when far away, in strange countries with unfamiliar languages, the homesick American cherished a precious vision: Mom, her grey hair in a bun, with a white apron tied around her plump waist, lifting a steaming apple pie from the oven. Children, with faces Norman Rockwell would have loved, beam upon her with hunger and adoration, while the pipe-smoking man of the house stands in the kitchen door observing the homey scene with a misty paternal eye. Why would one ever go to the war or risk life and limb in horrible circumstances except to keep this vision alive? Or, nearer home, why would one spend arduous hours in boring, unpleasant, or uninteresting work at a desk or a factory, in a mine or a field, except to keep that vision pure? As a nation, it was said, Americans had an enduring love affair with Mom and her apple pie. Today, when Mom is more apt to be at the office than in the kitchen, and the apple pie is a defrosted supermarket product, this vision of the American Dream is less convincing than ever. Still, its presence obscures the reality.

For many years, Mom and apple pie symbolized the expected and rewarded role for women: to bear the children, nurture them, care for the man of the house, and consider the approval, affection, and success of these household members a lifelong justification. If, at the heavenly gates, a woman could say, "I have been a good wife and mother," then she could claim that her life had been worthwhile. How nice, how rosy, but how limiting a picture!

For millions of women of an earlier generation, this would have been a

Source: Joan Dresden Grambs, "Mom, Apple Pie, and the American Dream." Reprinted by permission from *Social Education* (Vol. 46, No. 6, October 1982, pp. 404–409).

true achievement, and would have been the fulfillment of their American Dream. These were the women who labored in sweatshop and factory for wages far lower than men's, as stoop labor on truck farms and unpaid labor on their husband's lands, who would have felt that their life goals would have been achieved had they been able to stay home and do domestic things comparable to the baking of apple pie. Most of these women never achieved that goal, but toiled unremittingly, bore many children, and died young.

For women fortunate enough to be able to stay home with their children and their baking, there was the knowledge that they were safe and secure—that is, as long as their husbands toiled. If they were prudent and unsentimental in their choice of a spouse, looking for a steady, ambitious, conservative partner, they could anticipate a lifelong sinecure. Even if the women turned dowdy and irritable, their mates could not deny them support; the law and social pressure saw to that. If the man strayed, his income at least stayed home. The woman was safe, her children protected, and she could devote herself to apple pie and other good works. Or she could be lazy, self-indulgent, and a terrible mother. What she could *not* be was ambitious in the way that men were, or do the kinds of jobs outside the home that men did.

Embedded also in this piece of the American Dream was a view of the special nature of women. They were viewed as weak and needing protection, as well as more pure in thought and deed and more moral and more virtuous than men. This conception of the sensitive and virtuous nature of women was part of the argument used to deny the first woman lawyer her license to practice, and to keep women out of the medical field for generations. It was also, however, the argument that women used when they asked to be part of the democratic process so that they could clean up the notorious election campaigns waged by men (Jacklin, 1981). To the consternation of men, women made Prohibition an issue, and, for an uncomfortable time, they were triumphant. Since then, men have not been quite so ardent in proclaiming the superior virtue of women, although some feminists today would argue that the greater affiliative needs of women and their greater concerns for others could be potent forces for world peace—if only more women were in charge.

It is important to understand that the Mom-and-apple-pie facet of the American Dream is not just a diabolical invention of the male of the species as a way of keeping women in thrall. Women have assiduously kept that vision viable. It has been essential in giving women a share of the American Dream. The other available options were so much worse. Women had a stake, therefore, in keeping their share—unequal, limited, but a share nonetheless—and to this extent the American white woman was at least ahead of her black sisters. As long as the good, white, Protestant, English-speaking American wife kept her husband attentively tuned to the siren song of the American dream—the achievement of material comfort and personal success based on merit for any man who worked hard enough—then the wife had every possibility of sharing in the resultant goodies, and so would her children. A car in every garage gave her some mobility, too; a chicken in every pot meant she could eat well and so could the rest of the family. The harder her man worked, the more she had to gain. She could—and did—promote the social perception that a man demonstrated his prestige and status by the way in which his wife dressed and embellished his home—a place where she spent many more hours than he. Any man worth his salt saw to it, as the times changed, that his wife had a color television, wall-to-wall carpeting, a dishwasher, and a diamond to last forever. The home and its furnishings, and the dress and appearance of those in it, were almost universally defined as something the husband got for his wife, and incidentally, the children. This woman's piece of the American Dream not only has served millions of women very well, but millions are totally dedicated to it as a rational and valued—if not God-given—way of life. But a significant and increasing number of both women and men are beginning to wonder.

There is ample documentation that Western civilization has evolved in a way which compartmentalizes sex roles, assigning to women activities which are private and personal. Public roles and social decision-making have been defined as the prerogatives of men. It was believed that accidents of history produced some extraordinary women, such as Elizabeth I of England and Catherine the Great of Russia. The demonstration of their talents did not result in any shift in the view that men were really the ones born to rule, although history was littered with the disasters perpetrated by men. Women's role was identified with the producing and rearing of children, and, in addition, with performing many economically significant activities related to food production and preparation. The biological necessity of providing for the continuation of the species makes such division of responsibility seem practical and sensible. Every species with sexual dimorphism establishes differential roles for male and female in caring for the young. With humans, while the female role has been almost indissolubly tied with reproduction, the male role has moved further and further away. The world of men—and, by extension, their monopoly of politics, religion, and the arts—has only the most tenuous connection with the primary world of women and children. It is very hard to see the connection between a foreman on the line at General Motors and the family at home. The link between man's work and home is now almost universally via the pay check. It does not really matter what the man of the family does as long as he brings home enough money to keep the family fed, housed, and schooled.

SHIFTING VIEWS OF THE AMERICAN DREAM

Up to this point, the American Dream has served women well, and far better than their counterparts almost anywhere else. Foreign visitors have noted for generations that the typical middle-class American woman has been more protected and provided with more benefits while doing increasingly less housework with fewer children than women in most other countries, while American men have been caricatured as henpecked nonentities in their own homes, even though they might command great power and influence elsewhere. Increased material affluence has made the American home a marvel of laborsaving devices which a provident and caring husband will make available to his wife. Until recently, then, these were the fruits of the American Dream that women enjoyed. They could enjoy these bounties—that is, if they married the right man and saw to it that he worked long and productively, and if they did not have too many children, and if they were not black or impoverished. The women who did not benefit from the American Dream nevertheless provided this vision of women's rightful rewards for their daughters. Maybe I have to work in a field or a factory or someone else's home, they told their daughters, but if you are smart and marry the right man, you won't have to.

This version of women's rightful place in the American Dream no longer seems to be working. The dream which kept Mom in the kitchen baking apple pie also kept Mom imprisoned and severely limited the exercise of her talents. She could not participate in business deals even though she might have a good sense of figures and futures; she could not be elected to office even if she were a good judge of character and potential; she could not preach in the pulpit even if she were the soul of piety and charity and had a voice that could carry three blocks. The Dream saw her only in the kitchen, with children. Outside that realm she was unwanted, derided, exploited, debauched, and denounced.

But some women were not all that lucky, even if they did stay home as they were supposed to. They married the wrong men—men who couldn't keep a job, beat them and/or the children, were criminals or alcoholics, or left them widows or divorcees. Moreover, there were terribly poor women who saw the American Dream as beyond the reach of even their granddaughters—if the dream depended on the bounty, good will, and good behavior of men.

A growing tide of dissatisfaction flooded forth in the 1960s, to the astonishment of a large portion of the populace. This dissatisfaction was not all that new, and not unprecedented. The newly found women's history has located dozens of women from the Middle Ages to the present who have been critical and unhappy over the restricted social role of women and the negative views of their intellectual and emotional capacity. These earlier voices found no popular response and few women knew about their works, since most women were illiterate. In more recent times, the leaders of the women's suffrage movement, once their goal was attained, subsided into a marginal political role. An ERA type of proposal has been before Congress for at least 50 years, but only in the last five has it been taken at all seriously.

There is no denying that there is a new face on women's activities in this decade. So impressive have been the changes in women's roles that social scientists now talk with academic certainty about the women's movement. The women's movement didn't just happen, however; like any other major social movement, it is the result of the convergence of many social forces and events. The Depression certainly helped to change women's perception of family security, which was deeply threatened by the loss of earning power of millions of men. Women found that they could not count on men as sole providers; they also had to count on their own skill and ingenuity. Then there was the massive dislocation of World War II; millions of women had to fend for themselves, and they were also actively recruited for nontraditional work in shipyards and industry. Women found that power drills and welding tools were not intimidating. Postwar affluence eased the life of mothers, and allowed daughters to opt for college at almost the same rate as their brothers.

The social convulsion of the Black civil rights movement which shocked much of White America was a lesson which women finally took to heart for themselves. If Blacks can ask for and expect to get equality, why can't women? This question was implicit in the biting analysis of women's self-deluding beliefs written by Betty Friedan (Friedan, 1963). Friedan was the first modern popular writer to point out to women the trap of the American Dream. The timing could not have been better; at the same time, scientists finally developed a birth-control device, the Pill, which could provide women with something they had not had before—effective, easily accessible, cheap, convenient, and private control over their own bodies (Dixon, 1976). Within a few years, the landmark Supreme Court decisions outlawing restrictions on the sale of birth control devices, and finally removing legal obstacles to abortion, resulted in the massive reexamination of women's roles and women's work which we have come to term "the women's movement." The women's movement challenged the old basis for the American Dream.

REDEFINING THE AMERICAN DREAM

How can we redefine that dream so that women, men, children, and families are comfortable with each other, and are able to develop a mutual dependence which also allows for mutual independence?

Earlier ways of feeling, believing, and perceiving are not easily modified. The feminist yearning for an equal role in all of the social arenas in which humans act and interact has given rise to slogans and rhetoric, but also seems to be at war with history and biology.

It is highly probable that women will accomplish some of the key goals of the women's movement; maybe not this year, or this decade, but within a few generations. These goals include the removal of the sexist tracking of women and men into different jobs with different, and lower, levels of achievement for women. The largest industries and corporations (as well as the smaller ones) will have able women, as well as men, in positions of great power, visibility, and prestige. Political leadership will be in the hands of women and men, very possibly in equal amounts. Intellectual and artistic achievements will include women's names as frequently as those of men. Spiritual leadership will be shared by women who are, in fact, the mainstay of organized religion. The work world will be desegregated, with men and women in approximately equal numbers in almost all job classifications, and earning the same pay for the same work.

These developments will take place because of the inevitable logic of the American democratic system (Lasch, 1978), tied to the massive equalizing messages of the mass media. Hard as this is for today's conservatives to understand, once the concept of equity has been acknowledged as referring to all human beings, and laws have been written which implement this concept, the movement of women into public life and the marketplace cannot be stopped.

Though we can predict this movement and its inevitability, the social order must still come to terms with the imperatives of childbearing, childrearing, and family maintenance. There is still Mom, whether she bakes apple pie or

JEAN DRESDEN GRAMBS

not. How much can and will male and female emotions engendered by creating and producing an infant change because women's lives have changed?

The historical association of women primarily with childbearing and childrearing, and the traditional view of pregnancy as a time of vulnerability requiring medical monitoring as though it were a disease, cannot be shrugged off. The political hysteria over the abortion issue is ample proof that the average American is extremely ambivalent about the "true" nature of women and their "rights" when it comes to reproduction (Leifer, 1980). Current statistics indicate that, although women are having fewer children, most women still intend to have at least two children, even if they postpone them into their late twenties and thirties (Census Bureau, 1981).

The baby boom generation is now in its childbearing years. It is this generation, which has seen women marching in impressive numbers into new vocations, deserting traditional careers in education, nursing, and social work, that is now launching into family life. These women, who have postponed childbearing as they concentrated on careers and further education, are acutely aware of the biological clock ticking away. These women will have different expectations of the world around them: more help from husbands is just a starter. They will be asking for more private and public investment in day care, more flexible working hours, and job protections (Samuelson, 1982). As Ross points out, when women are no longer completely dependent on men, divorce is not far behind. Furthermore, lacking other kinds of intimacy, "Marriage has been saddled with unprecedented ideological burdens" (Ross, 1980). She goes on to discuss the advice books on love with or without marriage, pointing out the extraordinary success of Marabel Morgan's *The Total Woman*, which was the best seller of all genres in 1975, and which "cheerily repudiated all the changes in marriage and women's situation since 1959."

Marriage, which is a social convention to provide security for the helpless newborn human infant, turns couples into parents. Although men do not bear children, psychologists are discovering that parenting and child-parent bonding, essential for good mental health, is not something which only women can provide (Gilligan, 1982). Men, too, can develop close attachment with infants—if they are around long enough and systematically enough to do so. After all, if the process of imprinting can make newborn ducks follow an adult male biologist, surely a newborn baby can become as much attached to its father as its mother. Such imprinting is part of the biological survival mechanism for many species. Whether women will, in fact, be able to share childrearing fully with fathers is a question for future generations. Little in the current rearing of boys or girls suggests this new model; yet, the revised American Dream, which takes Mom out of the kitchen, will elude women in the future as in the past, if they cannot face these consequences. Although increasing numbers of women want equity in the marketplace, most women have not been able to deal with the biological imperatives and social conditioning which make them feel and act as the major responsible parent. If both parents work, in 99% of the cases it is the mother who is called in case of a school emergency, and it is the mother who stays home with a sick child, who goes shopping for clothes, who arranges the child care and monitors the consequences. Those women are caught between the intellectual recognition of their right to equal market access and their acceptance of the full demands of careers, and their emotional acquiescence to the traditional motherhood expectations. The stress of trying to have it both ways is mounting (Rossi, 1980).

So we return again to the American Dream, that dream which has been the goal and despair of generations of Americans. The new culture which emerged in the new America in the seventeenth and eighteenth centuries was viewed with alarm, amusement, and envy by those in the Old World. The incredible keystone of this new culture—unlimited opportunity—was a siren song for millions of immigrants. Belatedly, after the perilous crossing was made, millions also found that this unlimited opportunity was to be selectively available. The Mayflower Compact, the pride of patriots as a demonstration of the democratic spirit that drove the earliest settlers to the bleak New England coast, was not signed by all aboard the little vessel: only gentlemen of property were allowed to sign. Women and "others" were not participants in this first "American" democratic pact.

The continuing story of the realization of the American Dream has been the struggle of the excluded groups to share the dream, although for many millions the dream has been a reality. For the ambitious, clever, hard-working, adventurous, white, English-speaking, Protestant male, the American Dream has been, indeed, worth dreaming. And this same group, which has benefited so extensively by achieving the promise of the dream, has been vigilant and tireless in protecting the monopoly of its benefits (Fishman, 1982).

WHAT IS IT THAT WOMEN WANT?

So it is, nearing the end of the twentieth century, that women are asking for their part of the American Dream. In the process, they must reconcile the traditional view of how that Dream is to be achieved, and their even more fundamental role of procreator. What is it, then, that women want? There are almost as many answers as there are writers on the subject. Here is one possible list:

Family-oriented social policies which will directly attack those social situations which have resulted in the feminization of poverty (Moynihan, 1982)

Sex-neutral work and educational policies

Affirmative action in education and in work to remedy past bias and to ensure future equal access (United States Commission on Civil Rights, 1978)

Recognition of the contributions of women on the basis of merit

Scholarly study to remedy the sex bias in social, medical, and historical research (Stewart and Platt, 1982)

Needed legal remedies to remove sex bias in the judicial system

Resolution of the moral right of women to choose how and under what circumstances they will bear children and to a full share in whatever medical decisions are made about them

The social studies educator has a responsibility to support women as they strive to realize these goals. Specifically, the social studies teacher can:

Make strenuous efforts to reeducate herself/himself about women's role in history, and transmit to students the ever-growing body of scholarly knowledge about how women lived and worked in previous eras, and the status of women in other countries and other cultures.

When reviewing public policy debates, include extensive discussion of issues related to women's equity, and, in particular, to those "women's issues" which are in the forefront of current concern: reproductive rights, Title IX and its implementation, affirmative action in education and work, and the unfinished business of achieving a non-sexist legal system (Pennsylvania Commission for Women, 1980).

Systematically expose girls and boys to opportunities in the political system as a right and a responsibility which they should aspire to as women and men. Demonstrate that women as well as men can be wise, courageous, and worthy leaders in local, state, national, and international affairs.

Provide ample opportunity for children and youth to identify role models who successfully and effectively have transcended the limitations of sex-stereotyped and archaic family and work roles. Provide opportunity for boys to take nurturing and supportive roles and for girls to experience significant intellectual competence and leadership.

REFERENCES

Census Bureau. 1981. *Fertility of American Women: June, 1980 (Advance Report)* P-20 No. 364. Washington, D.C.: U.S. Government Printing Office.

Dixon, Ruth. 1976. Measuring equality. *Journal of Social Issues*, Vol. 32, No. 3, pp. 19–32.

Fishman, Waldo K. 1982. *The New Right: Unraveling the Opposition to Women's Equality.* New York: Praeger.

Friedan, Betty. 1963. *The Feminine Mystique.* New York: W. W. Norton.

Gilligan, Carol. 1982. Why should a woman be more like a man? *Psychology Today* 16:68–77.

Jacklin, Pamela. 1981. The concept of sex equity in jurisprudence. In *Educational Policy and Management: Sex Differentials*, edited by Patricia A. Schmuck et al., pp. 55–72.

Lasch, Christopher. 1978. *The Culture of Narcissism: American Life in an Age of Diminishing Expectations.* New York: W. W. Norton.

Leifer, Myra. 1980. Pregnancy. *Signs* 5: 754–65.

Moynihan, Daniel Patrick. 1982. One-third of a nation: How will America care for its children? *New Republic*, June 9, pp. 18–21.

Pennsylvania Commission for Women. 1980. *Impact of the Pennsylvania State Equal Rights Amendment* (rev. ed.). Harrisburg, Pa: The Commission.

Ross, Ellen. 1980. 'The love crisis': Couples advice books of the late 1970's. *Signs* 6: 109–122.

Rossi, Alice. 1980. Life span theories and women's lives. *Signs* 6: 4–32.

Samuelson, Robert J. 1981. It's the boom, baby, that'll shape America. *The Washington Post*, Nov. 3, p. D1.

Stewart, Abigail J. and Marjorie B. Platt. 1982. Studying women in a changing world. *Journal of Social Issues*, Vol. 38, No. 1, pp. 1–124.

United States Commission on Civil Rights. 1978. *Social Indicators of Equality for Minorities and Women*. Washington, D.C.: The Commission.

24 *Building Family Strengths in Dual-Career Marriages*

Barbara Chesser

STUDY QUESTIONS

1. Indicate five of the issues involved in dual-career marriages.

2. Indicate five of the advantages of dual-career marriages.

INTRODUCTION

"Is a woman's place in the home?" Over 40 million women who work outside the home have said "No" to this question. Many of these women are the sole breadwinners for their families. They have no choice but to work outside the home. However, in all the families with a husband and wife present, 42% of the husbands and wives both work outside the home as compared to 29% in 1960. If projections are accurate, there will be an even greater increase of dual-career families in the future.

Because of the increasing number of dual-career families, all family life education efforts should deal with issues arising in dual-career families. Whether the efforts are preventive, enrichment, or interventional in nature, the marriages of the participants will be strengthened as they become more aware of the issues that arise in dual-career marriages. An increased awareness of these issues and possible ways to handle them constructively will increase the couple's coping skills and problem-solving abilities, thereby building family strengths.

Dual-career family as used in this paper means both husband and wife are pursuing careers and maintaining a family together. The word "career" usually refers to a job which requires a high degree of commitment and a fairly continuous developmental life. A career is different from a job or work, for work may involve any kind of gainful employment. Work may be full-time, part-time, and periodic over the years so that it can be easily changed to accommodate marital and childrearing responsibilities. Obviously the line of demarcation between a career and a job is not always clear. A career might be placed at one end of a continuum with higher levels of commitment, responsibilities, educational and emotional investment, whereas a job is at the other end of the continuum with lower levels of all these characteristics. The closer one comes to the career end of the continuum, the more likely the issues discussed in this paper will indeed be problematic within the marriage because of the higher level of commitment characteristic of a career as opposed to a job. The closer one approaches the job end of the continuum, the easier, relatively speaking, the issues will be to resolve because of less commitment and investment.

As family life educators share information about these issues, they should also assist their students in translating this information into new insights and problem-solving skills. By providing information and skills, a couple's array of alternatives for problem-solving is greater. Knowledge can add strength to a dual-career family.

In addition, advantages of dual-career families will be briefly examined. Recommendations for building strengths in dual-career families will be offered.

ISSUES

To work or not to work outside the home may be an issue arising before the couple is married. Many variables will feed into this decision, but for the decision for the wife to work outside the home to be successfully carried out, the wife must really want or need to work. *Want* and *need* may be difficult to differentiate for some persons. For the two million women who head families, there is no choice: they *need* to work. Because of inflation, some wives with working husbands may also feel that they have to work to help pay the rent, buy groceries, and to rear their children. For other women, working may be a way to raise the family's standard of living. Others may work mostly to be with other people. In a society that often measures human worth by how much money you can make or what you do, many women want to feel better about themselves.

A couple's knowing why the wife works may be important to her being able to work outside the home and manage a marriage. Traditionally, man's work was his commitment. Woman's work was for extras: extra money, extra fulfillment, and extra interests. Being able to sort out why each works may seem too trivial or too philosophical to be practical. But many of the practical decisions in a two-career marriage often rest on why each partner works. Why a farmer's wife works during a drought year may be quite different from why a wife who is a college professor works year after year. Issues and problems may develop on the homefront for each of these couples. And each may require different solutions to keep the marriage on an even keel.

But most couples describe common problems regardless of why they say the wife works. Extra demands on time and energy seem to plague every two-career marriage. The wife may try to do all the housework as well as meet the rigorous demands of a job or career. The husband traditionally views housework as female's work and may have trouble helping with it. He may feel clumsy, or housework may make him feel unmanly, or he may be exhausted from his career. His wife may not want him to help her. She may doubt her own value if he can do "her" work.

Another issue many dual-career couples grapple with is whether or not to have children. An increasing percentage are opting for a childfree marriage, but many career couples merely are postponing the birth of their first child. And most career families have fewer children than couples which include a non-working wife.

Determination of the "best" time for having a child rests on considerations such as educational plans and establishment of a career and the effects of time-off on these two considerations. Also the availability of maternity leaves may determine the "best" time.

For dual-career couples who have a child, childcare becomes a concern. Adequate childcare facilities are still not widely available. Finding a reliable babysitter to stay in the home may be a challenge. The financial cost of childcare is usually another concern. When the child is older and in school most of the day, childcare may not be such a problem. Problems may come when a child does not follow the usual schedule, for example, when he or she is sick. Who stays home? Who takes the child to the doctor? To the dentist? Who leaves work to go to the parent-teacher conference? To the Christmas play? To weekly music lessons? In a traditional marriage, the decision is easy: the mother's job always gives in to the demands of the children. As women increasingly express commitment to their careers, couples are compelled to establish new criteria for decisions regarding childcare.

Obviously these criteria are increasingly complicated if a child requires extra care and supervision because of a health problem or a handicap of some kind. Working out satisfactory childcare and supervision may also be compli-cated if the careers of one or both of the partners in a dual-career marriage require travel.

How to handle career relocation if one spouse is offered a promotion which requires moving is another issue confronting some couples at one time or another in their careers. Decision-making in this situation may be extra

BARBARA CHESSER

perplexing if it is the wife being offered the promotion. Our culture supports relocations made on the basis of the husband's promotion, not the wife's.

The issue of how to spend the combined earnings of a dual-career marriage confronts most couples. Should the discretionary income be spent on luxuries or travel, or should it be saved or invested? Dual-career families come face to face with this question. Other couples may find that there is no discretionary income. Taxes may take an extraordinary portion of their combined earnings. Transportation expenses for two careers eat up an unreasonable mount of money. Wardrobe demands may gnaw insidiously at the combined earnings. Childcare may take its unfair portion. Eating meals out or the purchase of convenience foods may require an undue portion of the paychecks. This is when the couple must scrutinize the value of two careers in one marriage, or they may be challenged to search for desirable ways to economize.

Survival of a two-career family may depend upon the ability of husband and wife to make decisions satisfying to both. Some marriages thrive on the husband making all the major decisions and others depend upon the wife to make them. But partners in most dual-career marriages have to work at learning how to make decisions together. Traditionally, the man made the money, therefore he had the authority to make the decisions. If both husband and wife work to make the money, both have the right to make decisions. Deciding *who* is going to decide and *how* the decisions are made is often more critical than the decisions. Couples able to decide mutually with occasional compromise seem to survive two-career marriages.

Some male egos may be too fragile to survive a two-career marriage. A working wife may signal his failure to make enough money to be considered "successful." Or a wife who makes more money than the husband may threaten a weak male ego. Husband and wife in similar careers may compete too keenly. A wife may occasionally put her husband in a double bind. She may pressure him to succeed in his job while pressuring him to be a terrific husband and father.

Some women may be uncomfortable out of a traditional homemaker role. Society still judges a man by his job and a woman by her homemaking, as a companion, mother, and hostess. Some women may be frustrated if they do better in the work world than their husbands. All husbands and wives it seems are pressured to do more and to do it better. Tensions may really mount in dual-career families if these issues are not dealt with realistically and constructively.

If two-career marriages survive these first few hurdles, they still have not completed the obstacle course. Careers make rugged demands on a husband's and wife's time and energy. So do the children's schedules. Little time and energy remain for friends or recreation. Most couples cannot maintain friendships with all they would like to. So they must make choices—a few friends from his acquaintances, a few from hers, or maybe a few from church, or from parents of their children's friends. Couples need skills in learning to say no to some activities so they can say yes to those they want to do.

Individual partners need to know what they expect of themselves as well as from their mates. They need to examine what they expect of the marriage itself. Couples must communicate these expectations to each other. One husband whose first two-career marriage ended in divorce but who was managing well in a second one shared: "You gotta have lots of heart-to-heart talks of what you want out of marriage and what you are willing to do to accomplish what you want." He explained that not only husband and wife but the kids must have a good understanding of what everyone wants out of the family and the responsibilities each is willing to assume. "Otherwise," he went on, "the family becomes like an explosion in a mattress factory: they never get it all together."

Marriage may be unsafe at any speed, but having unrealistic and unreasonable expectations may be the speed that kills. If this were true for the traditional marriage in which the husband is the breadwinner and the wife is the hearth-warmer, then it certainly is truer for the two-career marriage. Other survival tactics may help, but realistic expectations of self and partner are essential, as one college professor with three young children pointed out:

> You have to be realistic in what you expect of yourself and your marriage partner. It's impossible for one person to be terrific on the job, a terrific husband, a terrific father, and to keep the grass mowed all the time.

An enormous obstacle to two-career couples is the paucity of models of successful two-career marriages. And each two-career couple works through these issues in fairly unique ways that seem best for them. Their solution for a particular problem may not work for another couple.

Another complication is that many couples think other couples have solved most of these problems. Flashes of a superwoman haunt most women. This superwoman who knits marriage, career, and motherhood into a satisfying life without dropping a stitch is overwhelming and gives others miserable feelings of failure.

The foregoing discussion of some of the issues confronting most dual-career marriages may create a foreboding, ominous aura about the dual-career marriage. The marriages of those who do not work successfully through these issues, in fact, may be threatened. However, those who do at least to some extent successfully resolve some of the issues may enjoy some tangible benefits or advantages. Professionals should clearly outline these just as they teach about the issues that usually arise in a dual-career family.

ADVANTAGES

Some of the advantages which dual-career families may enjoy are briefly outlined as follows:

1. Dual-career families may enjoy some financial advantages. They may enjoy a higher standard of living. They may be able to accumulate savings. They may be able to provide financial security against possible disasters.
2. The wife may enjoy greater levels of creativity, self-expression, achievement,

and recognition. She may enjoy being herself, not an appendage to her husband. This may help her be a better mother and wife.

3. Dual-career marriages provide a greater range of role models for children of both sexes.

4. The husband may be relieved of some of the pressures to succeed and to make money. Thus, he will be able to function more effectively as a husband and/or father.

5. The husband may enjoy his wife more since she will have outside activities and interests to share.

6. Sexual interest in the marriage may heighten in an unstereotyped, dual-career marriage.

7. Parent responsibilities can be shared. Husbands can enjoy their children more, and children can profit from having an available father.

8. Children may learn to be more responsible and more resourceful when their mothers work outside the home. This may reinforce their feelings of achievement, pride, and self-esteem.

9. Children may learn to respect their parents more, especially their mothers, as individuals.

10. The empty-nest syndrome which affects some in later years may be avoided somewhat if the wife is engaged in a meaningful career outside the home.

11. Coping with widowhood may be somewhat easier for the woman who has had a meaningful career in addition to her marriage career.

12. Increased empathy with the demands of the roles of each other may foster mutual respect and facilitate communication.

13. The increased sharing of roles may create feelings of equality, thus strengthening the family.

RECOMMENDATIONS

. . . [There] are other general recommendations that all could work on which would strengthen the American family. Some of these are as follows:

1. There should be increased knowledge throughout the educational career about role flexibility and/or change. In other words, rigid or stereotyped sex roles should be avoided in textbooks and other learning materials.

2. Mass media should avoid perpetuating stereotypes.

3. Stereotypic assumptions about sex roles should be avoided (for example, "women are absent more from work").

4. Better parent education should be available for all people.

5. There should be more high-quality childcare for working parents. Perhaps more neighborhood childcare provisions as well as industrial childcare should be explored.

6. Business and government could provide more flexible working conditions, including more flexible working hours, sharing of positions, and more part-time positions without discrimination of benefits, promotions, etc. Increased flexibility would reduce conflict between the demands of parents' employment and the needs of their families. Flexible working hours would also help in battling the war against the traditional 8 to 5 schedule that is based on the assumption that the wife is at home and free to take care of business matters within this time frame.

7. More equitable provisions should be provided for taking time off for childbearing and childcare.

8. An integrated network of family services should be developed more fully. All families need easily available preventive services.

9. Marriage and family counseling should continually be developed into a more effective resource for helping members of two-career marriages cope with their stresses and strains.

10. More research is needed on the effects of two-career families. For example, the effects of long-distance marriages on the partners and the children might be explored.

Two-career families are probably a testing ground of things to come as sex roles become more flexible and interchangeable, as inflation continues, and as more careers are open to women. Professionals who are directly involved in activities to help build strengths in families must energetically carry out all of the foregoing suggested recommendations, and they must continue to be supportive and empathic in whatever ways will help strengthen two-career families. And we as professionals need to cherish our own family relationships to provide a model of ways to build strengths in the two-career family.

REFERENCES

Austin, H. S. 1969. *The woman doctorate in America: Origins, career, and family.* New York: Russell Sage Foundation.

Bailyn, L. 1970. Career and family orientation of husbands and wives in relation to marital happiness. *Human Relations* 23:97–113.

Bebbington, A. C. 1973. The function of stress in the establishment of the dual-career family. *Journal of Marriage and the Family* 35 (August):530–37.

Bem, S. L., and D. J. Bem. 1972. Training the woman to know her place. In L. K. Home (ed.), *The future of the family.* New York: Simon and Schuster.

Bernard, J. 1966. *Academic women.* New York: World.

Callahan, S. C. 1971. *The working mother.* New York: Macmillan.

Gannon, M. J., and D. H. Henrickson. 1973. Career orientations and job satisfaction among working wives. *Journal of Applied Psychology* 57:339–40.

Hall, D. T., and F. E. Gordon. 1973. Career choices of married women: Effects on conflict, role, behavior, and satisfaction. *Journal of Applied Psychology* 58:42–48.

Heckman, J. J. 1974. Effects of child care programs on women's work effort. *Journal of Political Economy* 82:S136–S163.

Holmstrom, L. L. 1973. *The two-career family.* Cambridge, Mass.: Schenkman.

Keniston, K., and The Carnegie Council on Children. 1972. *All our children: The American family under pressure.* New York: Harcourt Brace.

Slater, P. E. 1970. *The pursuit of loneliness: American culture at the breaking point.* Boston: Beacon Press.

Willett, R. S. 1971. Working in "a man's world": The woman executive. In V. Gornick and B. K. Moran (eds.), *Woman in sexist society.* New York: Basic Books.

Yarrow, M., et al. 1973. Child-rearing in families of working and non-working mothers. In M. E. Lasswell and T. E. Lasswell (eds.), *Love, marriage, family, a developmental approach.* Glenview, Ill.: Scott, Foresman.

25 *Role-Sharing Couples: A Study of Egalitarian Marriages*

Linda Haas

STUDY QUESTIONS

1. What are the individual benefits of role sharing?

2. What are the family benefits of role sharing?

Many observers of changes in family roles have discussed the completely egalitarian or role-sharing arrangement as a theoretical possibility (Bailyn, 1978; Bernard, 1973; Bott, 1971; Garland, 1972; Nye, 1976; Scanzoni, 1972; Young & Willmont, 1973). The purpose of this paper is to report some results of a detailed empirical study of couples who have attempted role-sharing and generally succeeded in putting it into practice. The goals of the study were to discover the reasons couples adopted this alternative family lifestyle, the problems they had adjusting to it, and the solutions they developed to combat the problems encountered.

Source: Linda Haas, "Role Sharing Couples: A Study of Egalitarian Marriages." *Family Relations* 29(1980):289–294. Copyrighted 1980 by the National Council on Family Relations, 3989 Central Ave., N.E., Suite 550, Minneapolis, MN 55421. Reprinted by permission.

A marriage style based on the equal sharing of traditionally sex-segregated roles is very rarely found in practice and subsequently has been generally unstudied by social scientists. There have been several studies of dual-career families, but these families generally do not practice role-sharing. While the wife is committed to a career, her basic family responsibilities typically remain intact and her husband's career has precedence over hers (Bryson, Bryson & Johnson, 1978; Holmstrom, 1973; Poloma & Garland, 1971; Rapoport & Rapoport, 1977). Studies have also been done on American parents who shared the childcare role (DeFrain, 1975; 1979) and Norwegian couples where both spouses chose part-time work (Grønseth, 1976; 1978). Yet even in these studies, the role-sharing arrangement was only partly in evidence: DeFrain's androgynous parents did not share housework or breadwinning equally and Grønseth's work-sharing couples did not share housework or childcare evenly. Sociologists have also paid some attention to discovering the actual division of labor and its determinants in the general population (e.g., Nye, 1976), but their samples have not been large enough to incorporate many role-sharing families, and thus have given us little insight into the role-sharing lifestyle.

As distinct from the partial steps toward sex-role equality discussed above, fully developed role-sharing can be defined as the sharing by husband and wife of each of the traditionally segregated family roles, including:

The breadwinner role. The husband and wife are equally responsible for earning family income; the wife's employment is not considered more optional or less desirable than the husband's. Consequently, the spouses' occupations are equally important and receive equal status, or at least the occupation which has more status is not determined by notions of the intrinsic supremacy of one sex over the other.

The domestic role. The husband and wife are equally responsible for performing housekeeping chores such as cooking, cleaning, and laundry.

The handyman role. The husband and wife are equally responsible for performing traditionally masculine tasks such as yardwork and repairs.

The kinship role. The husband and wife are equally responsible for meeting kinship obligations, like buying gifts and writing letters, which have traditionally been the wife's responsibility.

The childcare role. The husband and wife are equally responsible for doing routine childcare tasks and for rearing and disciplining of children.

The major/minor decision-maker roles. The spouses have generally equal influence on the making of major decisions which males have traditionally dominated and the minor decisions traditionally delegated to the female.

Specialization within any of these roles (e.g., husband cooks, wife launders) would be compatible with role-sharing, as long as specific tasks are not assigned to a spouse on the basis of sex (i.e., because they are deemed more appropriate for someone of his/her gender) and as long as the overall responsibility for the duties of each role is evenly shared.

LINDA HAAS

STUDY DESIGN

Since past studies of the family imply that role-sharing couples make up a very tiny proportion of the general population, a random sampling design could not be employed in this study without a great amount of expense and time. Therefore, a type of purposive or strategic sampling technique was employed (cf. Glaser & Strauss, 1967). In the liberal university community of Madison, Wisconsin, 154 couples were identified who had been referred by others or by themselves as sharing fairly evenly the responsibilities of breadwinning, housekeeping, childcare, and decision-making. Their names were obtained through contacts in various local institutions and associations (e.g., a daycare center, a chapter of the National Organization for Women, a liberal religious group, university organizations) and through announcements published in local newsletters and newspapers.

Each of these couples was contacted by telephone during January, 1976. Whoever answered the phone was asked several questions designed to ascertain in a rough fashion whether or not his or her relationship was characterized by role-sharing, as reputed. To be included for further study, both spouses had to be engaged in, looking for, or preparing for work and spending roughly the same number of hours per week on work or school-related pursuits. The wife's employment could not be seen as something less permanent than the husband's, and an unequivocally affirmative answer had to be given to the question, "Would you say that each of you has roughly the same amount of influence over family decisions?" When asked, "What percent of all the housework that's done in your household do you think you do?", the answer had to be in the 40–60% range, as did the answer to a similar question about childcare.

In the group of couples who were initially contacted by phone and willing to be interviewed, nearly half turned out not really to practice role-sharing in their marriages, according to the rough preliminary measures. Among the remaining couples who were tentatively labeled as role-sharers, some types were not included in the study. One type consisted of couples who hired outside help for housecleaning. Since being able to afford cleaning help is not available to all economic classes and I was primarily interested in studying the factors which promise to increase role-sharing among couples on a widespread basis, a decision was made to exclude those having housecleaning help. Another group of role-sharing couples not picked for further study were those not legally married since they might have unique arrangements that I was not prepared to study in detail. Several other couples were eliminated for miscellaneous reasons, such as living too far out of town for convenient interviewing.

After eliminating couples on such grounds, there were 31 remaining who qualified on the various criteria and were willing to participate in the study. The sample was fairly homogeneous, despite efforts to recruit a variety of types for the study. For the most part, the people in the sample were training themselves for or engaged in jobs in professional fields, usually in social service or the humanities. The sample couples tended to be young, with a majority of them being 26 to 30 years old. The mean number of years they had been married was six. Nearly half of them had children, most of which were not yet old enough to go to school.

Both the husband and wife in each of the 31 couples were interviewed three times from January through June of 1976. Averaging 1 1/2 hours each, these interviews usually took place in the couples' homes and were tape-recorded. The spouses were interviewed separately during most of the questioning. After the interviews, written forms were left with the individuals to be filled out and returned by mail. These included a time-budget and an attitudinal questionnaire.

The great majority of the 31 couples were later found to be generally as egalitarian as the preliminary phone measures suggested, when the extent and ways in which couples shared breadwinning, housekeeping, childcare, kinship obligations, and handyman chores were investigated. The family power structure was also studied by obtaining information on the process and outcome of several recent and hypothetical decision-making activities. Any departures from equality, were spread out, with no couples falling short on more than a small proportion of the numerous and fairly stringent standards for meeting an ideal of total role-sharing. Even those who failed to meet every last one of these standards showed themselves to be aspiring towards an ideal of marital equality not strived for by the general population or even by most dual-career couples. (See Haas, 1977, for a full description of all the indicators for role-sharing and specifics on how these couples measured up.)

RESULTS AND DISCUSSION

Motivations for Role-Sharing Behavior

In replies to open-ended questions about why they shared the responsibilities of breadwinning, decision-making, and domestic chores, each couple gave several motives for role-sharing. In the results which follow, couples are listed as giving a certain reason if either spouse reported it, but spouses usually answered the same way. Almost all of the couples in the sample revealed that they adopted role-sharing not as a result of an ideological commitment to sexual equality, but rather as a practical way of obtaining certain benefits which they perceived could not be realized in a traditional marriage with segregated husband-wife roles. The vast majority of couples said they became pessimistic about traditional marriage roles after trying a traditional pattern in their marriage in its early years. Over one-third of the individuals said they were also predisposed to attempt a non-traditional role pattern because they felt their parents had been constrained by the traditional familial division of labor. Finally, a handful of the respondents had been married previously and complained that conflict over sex-role expectations had been a major factor in their divorces.

The benefits attainable through role-sharing usually occurred to the wife first and more often aided her than the husband. However, a considerable part of the motivation to try a non-traditional pattern also involved a desire to liberate the husband from the confines of his traditional family role.

Benefits for the individual. One anticipated benefit for both spouses was a greater opportunity to develop their abilities and pursue personal interests without being limited by traditional role expectations. Over four-fifths of the sample adopted role-sharing so the wife could satisfy her desire to work outside the home for personal fulfillment. One-fifth of the couples reported picking the role-sharing lifestyle so that each spouse would have the freedom to quit outside employment for a time and pursue other interests.

Another motive for role-sharing was relief from the stress and overwork that results from having primary responsibility for a broad area of family life. Almost three-fourths of the couples wanted to eliminate the overload dilemmas faced by working women who remain primarily responsible for housework and childcare. This benefit of role-sharing did seem to have been realized, according to time-budget data collected in individual diaries for a week between the first and second interviews. Wives in the sample averaged 16.0 hours per week at housework, while men averaged 16.2.

Mothers in the study averaged 12.2 hours per week at specific childcare tasks, while fathers spent 10.4. The general equality of the workload was also evident in the finding that the women spent 26.8 hours per week at hobbies, watching television, socializing, organizational meetings, etc., compared to the men's average of 26.2 hours of leisure activities. In contrast, time-budget studies of the general population show employed husbands averaging almost $6\frac{1}{2}$ more hours of free-time activities a week than employed wives (Szalai, 1972).

Over half of the couples mentioned that the role-sharing lifestyle was adopted so that the husband would not be burdened more than the wife with the provider responsibility and its concomitant anxiety and stress. While this benefit was fully achieved by the majority of couples in the study, at least one partner in one-third (10) of the couples (usually the male) reported a little difficulty in completely letting go of the traditional idea that the man is more responsible for earning income than the wife, or that the wife was less obligated to work to provide family income. In most of these cases, it was the wife's newer or lesser interest in a career that was used as an explanation for the partial retention of this traditional sex-role expectation for men. These 10 couples said, however, that this was an idea they no longer wanted to believe in and certainly would not act on.

Another major motive for role-sharing cited by these couples was greater independence of the husband and wife. While the role-sharers in the study neither desired nor actually led completely independent lives within marriage, over one-fourth of them initiated role-sharing to avoid the economic dependence wives traditionally have had on husbands, while one-sixth wanted to avoid the dependence most husbands experience when it comes to getting domestic chores done—e.g., cooking, laundry, mending.

Benefits for the family. Several people who were happier because of new opportunities for self-fulfillment and relief from one-sided burdens reported themselves to be better marriage partners as a side benefit, however there were other ways in which couples tried to improve their family life directly through role-sharing. For instance, almost two-thirds of the couples cited a desire to cut down on the resentment and conflict that they saw resulting from husbands having more power in marriage. Generally, a shared decision-making pattern was the first aspect of role-sharing to be tried, and the one aspect that was relatively easy to establish. Several individuals commented that a positive but unanticipated consequence of a shared decision-making pattern was that it called for a considerable amount of discussion and this communicating in turn brought greater intimacy between husband and wife.

Another way couples thought role-sharing would improve husband-wife relations, reported by one-fifth of the couples, was in giving them more in common—with both spouses working and both having domestic responsibilities. Several individuals reported that having so much in common caused them to appreciate and sympathize with each other more. Each could appreciate problems the other had at work or school because they came up against the same things, and they were less likely to nag at each other if a task went undone because they personally knew how hard it was to get around to doing an undesirable chore. Several people also said the role-sharing gave them the opportunity to do more things together, increasing interaction and thus enhancing husband-wife closeness. A few couples were in the same occupational field, so they could profitably discuss their work and occasionally work on projects together. The spouses also had occasion to be together while domestic chores were being performed. Since the work hours of husbands and wives were approximately even and their work schedules were often similar, the couples had occasion to spend a lot of their free time together.

Besides an improvement in husband-wife relations, another major benefit of role-sharing cited for the family was improvement in parent-child relations. This was not a factor in the initial decision to adopt role-sharing, but it became a reason for continuing the arrangement. Five of the twelve women with children at home felt they had become better mothers because they worked outside the home and shared childcare with their husbands. They felt they were less bored, less hassled with managing two roles, and not resentful about shouldering the entire burden of childcare. Three of the 24 parents mentioned that sharing childcare meant that the children got to know their father better than they would in a traditional family, and three parents thought children benefited by being exposed to more than just the mother's outlook on things.

The final major benefit for the family that couples wanted to achieve with role-sharing was greater financial security. One-fourth of the couples said they chose a dual-earner arrangement to provide the family with more income on a permanent basis. Incidentally, the vast majority of couples pooled their incomes, and in all of the couples the wife's income was not saved for extras but was used for family expenses as much as was the husband's.

Problems with Role-Sharing

While these couples' efforts to implement role-sharing brought the benefits they anticipated, several difficulties with this arrangement were reported in responses to questions about problems with role-sharing. Some of these problems appeared to result from certain personal obstacles related to vestiges of traditional sex roles in the family. Others seemed to come from trying to transcend sex roles within family units in the context of a larger more traditional society. Still other problems seemed to be inherent in the role-sharing lifestyle itself.

Problems sharing the domestic role. Of all the areas of role-sharing, couples reported problems most often in the establishment of an egalitarian division of domestic chores. These problems can be grouped into four types, listed here in order of their frequency: disinclination to do non-traditional tasks, discrepancies in housekeeping standards, wife's reluctance to delegate domestic responsibility, and lack of non-traditional domestic skills.

The most common type of problem in sharing domestic chores, reported by over half of the couples, was that one or both spouses lacked the inclination to do some non-traditional tasks for which they had skills or for which no special skill was required. About one-third of the couples with this problem mentioned that it was hard to break with the traditional pattern they had observed in their parents' households. Over one-third claimed that it often seemed more efficient to let the traditional spouse perform the chore in the face of the other partner's inexperience, busy schedule, or laziness.

Couples had different solutions for this problem. Most often, the spouse who felt over-worked (usually the wife) complained and threatened to stop doing the chore or some other task until the lazy spouse resolved to do better. Sometimes a temporary system of rotation was agreed upon to get the recalcitrant spouse into the right habit. Occasionally the lazy spouse would develop more of a liking or tolerance for the chore or become so experienced at it that the problem would be solved. Some couples ended up agreeing to some specialization in order to avoid further conflict, especially if each spouse wanted to avoid certain non-traditional chores that the other spouse did not mind doing.

Another frequent problem in overcoming the traditional chore pattern involved the standards spouses had for housekeeping. Over half of the couples reported that at an earlier time in their marriage the wives had generally advocated a much higher standard of orderliness and cleanliness in the household than their husbands. This did not produce any conflict as long as the woman was in charge of getting the chores done, but when the decision to share responsibility for chores was reached, wives pushed for chores to be done as often as they wanted to see them done and in the manner they preferred. They fretted about the condition of the house all the time and experienced embarrassment if someone dropped in unexpectedly. Husbands, on the other hand, wanted to do the chores according to their own ideas on how often they needed to be done and in the manner (often unconventional) that appealed most to them. Husbands consistently felt wives were too finicky and wives regarded husbands as too sloppy.

Most of the couples coped with this discrepancy in standards by simultaneously having wives lower their expectations and husbands raise theirs. This change was usually precipitated by wives being busy with their jobs or schoolwork and it was accompanied by many heated discussions and practical experiments. Both spouses generally professed to be happier with the new standard, but the wives still tended to believe in a somewhat higher standard than their husbands. When asked, "Do you think that housework is done as often and as well as you want it to be?" almost one-half of the wives (but less than one-third of the husbands) expressed discontent with the level or orderliness and cleanliness of their homes. Wives were also more likely to mention spontaneously that they would like to hire outside help, while most of their husbands opposed hiring an outsider to do domestic chores.

Since both the husband and wife were busy with jobs or schoolwork, it is not surprising that many individuals felt anxious about their housekeeping standard. On the other hand, there was little evidence that their homes were in fact being neglected, for their homes generally seemed neat and clean to the interviewers. The actual number of hours spent at traditional housekeeping tasks (around 20 hours a week per couple) was still rather high, though not in the 30–40 hour range for working couples or the 50–70 range for housewives found in other studies (Robinson & Converse, cited in Babcock, 1975; Walker, 1970). Either the role-sharing couples were correct in their belief that they had a low housekeeping standard, in ways not apparent to a casual visitor, or they skipped a lot of unnecessary housework and kept house more efficiently than traditional couples.

A third problem, mentioned by half the couples, was the wife's reluctance to give up her traditional authority over many domestic chores. For all but one of these couples, this problem had been overcome by the time of the study. One-third of the women in the study reported that they expected to do all the traditionally female domestic chores when they got married because of socialization—their mothers had done them and they had learned it was the woman's duty to do those chores. Some of the women in the sample mentioned that they had actually enjoyed the challenge of trying to be simultaneously a great housewife and a successful professional.

The change to a more even sharing of domestic chores was not easy. Not only did the wives have to contend with the husband's disinclination to do chores, they also had to cope with guilt feelings about abandoning their traditional role and with the mixed feelings they had seeing their husbands do nontraditional tasks. As their strong interest in a profession consumed more and more of their mental and physical energy over the years, however, housework seemed increasingly tedious rather than challenging. In addition, the women's movement led them to believe that doing double work is unfair and made them feel better about sharing domestic chores with their husbands.

The last type of problem couples had in sharing domestic chores was a lack of skills on the part of one or the other of the spouses. Over one-third of the couples cited this as an impediment to the realization of equality. For half of these couples it was the husband's lack of expertise in areas such as cooking or sewing which had caused problems, and in the other half of the cases it was the wife's inability to do things like make repairs or handle the car which had inhibited an equal sharing of responsibility.

Couples sought to cope with this type of problem by having the more knowledgeable spouse teach the other one the new skill, or by having the incapable spouse develop the necessary ability on his or her own. This solution often failed to work out, for the spouse without a certain skill often lacked a desire to persist through the frustration and disappointment accompanying the learning experience. Other individuals claimed they were too busy with their careers or hesitated giving up valuable leisure time to learn a new skill and it seemed more efficient to let the expert spouse do the task. Many tasks also came up only in a crisis (stopped-up drain, faulty car brakes, popped-off button) and many individuals felt that this was not a good time to learn. Normalcy would be restored quicker if the expert fixed things up. Finally, in cases such as wives trying to learn car maintenance and home repairs, they had to interact with skeptical and hostile outsiders in the pursuit of these skills (e.g., hardware store personnel, garage mechanics). As a result, wives tended to shrink away from this type of contact and avoid learning the task.

Wives were generally less successful at acquiring the skills required for the husband's traditional chores than vice versa. Husbands on the average spent the same amount of hours doing traditionally feminine domestic chores as wives but wives spent less time on the average than husbands on "male" chores such as interior home repairs and yardwork (1.3 hours per week vs. 2.9, according to time-budget data). The figures are small, but they do suggest that the wives, who typically were the instigators of role-sharing, hadn't put much effort into sharing all of the husband's traditional family responsibilities. Interestingly, most of the couples did not perceive this difference to be a problem, perhaps because masculine domestic chores take up so little time compared to other types of domestic chores.

A few couples had succeeded in getting one spouse to pick up a skill once possessed only by the other. Husbands learning how to mend was the situation most often cited. In these cases it seemed that learning was aided by the wife restraining herself from nagging the husband to learn, and by her giving him positive verbal reinforcement of noncondescending type.

Conflicts involving jobs. Besides problems in sharing domestic responsibilities, couples also described several difficulties associated with having two jobs in the sample family. One serious problem was conflict between the spouses' jobs or studies. All but three of the couples felt that conflicts between jobs could be a problem in the future, when asked about a hypothetical situation where one spouse would be offered a job in a city different from that in which his or her spouse already worked. Most couples had already settled on strategies for dealing with this situation. A strategy most of them planned to employ was to give the spouse who had the *less* marketable skills or the poorer job opportunities their choice when a conflict arose. (Husbands' jobs were not any more likely to be given priority in the total sample than were wives'.) The next most common plan was establishing a long-distance marriage—that is, both spouses accepting their job offers, living in different cities, and visiting each other regularly. This possibility was mentioned by over half of the couples, most of whom did not yet have children. For the most part, couples did not like the idea of separating but were willing to consider it as a way to maintain a dual-career marriage. Another solution mentioned by some couples was for husband and wife to take turns holding the job of their choice. Finally, a few couples mentioned that one spouse's job offer in another city might be regarded as an opportunity for the other to do free-lance work, engage in independent research, or start a business. Several couples hoped to avoid making a decision about job priority by only looking for jobs at the same time in the same geographic area. This solution was only available to couples in which the husband and wife were at comparable stages in their careers, which was not common, since husbands tended to be older than wives.

Another common problem was conflict between jobs and family responsibilities. This was reported by over half of the total sample, by husbands a little more often than wives (in contrast to typical dual-career couples, where the wife usually reports job-family conflicts). Most of those individuals reporting job-family conflicts mentioned that their jobs interfered with family responsibilities in various ways: housework didn't get done, they lacked energy and patience to interact well with their children, or they did not have enough leisure time to spend with their families. About one-third of those reporting conflicts mentioned that family duties interfered with their job performance: they had to cut down on over-time work, had trouble doing job-related work at home, had to rearrange their schedules when children became ill, or had little time to attend job-related meetings in the evenings and on weekends.

The couples' strategies for dealing with job-family conflicts usually involved adjusting housework. The most common strategy, employed by over one-third of the couples, was to cut down on housework or at least to give it a very low priority—after meeting job or school responsibilities and after spending free time with family members. Next most common was for couples to maintain a regular schedule of housekeeping so it never got out of hand. Several couples mentioned that almost daily they engaged in negotiation and discussion regarding who would assume responsibility for the various family chores that would come up that day. By careful planning they were able to save considerable time while also assuring that chores got done. The two couples with the oldest children had encouraged their offspring to take care of themselves to a great extent (e.g., wash their own clothes) and to assume regular responsibility for some household chores.

Several couples mentioned that they tried to cut down on their jobs' interference with family life by segregating the two as much as possible. Both husbands and wives tried not bring work home and tried to reserve weekends and evenings for family activities. It was not clear whether role-sharing put these individuals at a real career disadvantage, although some observers have suggested that it would (Hunt & Hunt, 1977). Many of the role-sharers in the study were noticeably productive in their fields, so perhaps a role-sharing lifestyle contains some compensations that allow an individual to do well at a career (e.g., interaction with spouse on professional matters, more efficient time-use).

CONCLUSION

The problems and pitfalls experienced by the role-sharers in this study suggest that role-sharing is a lifestyle demanding the wholehearted and enthusiastic willingness of both spouses to participate. Both partners have to take into account each other's job and leisure activities when planning things that impinge on each other. For these couples, this kind of commitment to role-sharing seemed to derive from the expectation that the arrangement would produce benefits for both spouses which would outweigh the costs of implementing a new style of marriage.

REFERENCES

Babcock, B., A. Freedman, E. Norton, and S. Ross. 1975. *Sex discrimination and the law—causes and remedies.* Boston: Little, Brown.

Bailyn, L. 1978. Accommodation of work to family. In R. Rapoport and R. Rapoport (eds.), *Working couples.* New York: Harper and Row.

Bernard, J. 1973. *The future of marriage.* New York: Bantam.

Bott, E. 1971. *Family and social network.* New York: Free Press.

Bryson, R., J. Bryson, and M. Johnson. 1978. Family size, satisfaction, and productivity in dual-career couples. *Psychology of Women Quarterly* 3:66–77.

DeFrain, J. 1975. *The nature and meaning of parenthood.* Unpublished doctoral dissertation, University of Wisconsin-Madison.

———. 1979. Androgynous parents tell who they are and what they need. *The Family Coordinator* 28:237–43.

Garland, T. N. 1972. The better half? The male in the dual profession family. In C. Safillos-Rothschild (ed.), *Toward a sociology of women.* Lexington, Mass.: Xerox.

Glaser, B. G., and A. L. Strauss. 1967. *The discovery of grounded theory: Strategies for qualitative research.* Chicago: Aldine.

Grønseth, E. 1976. Work-sharing families. In A. G. Kharchev and M. B. Sussman (eds.), *Liberation of women, changing sex roles, family structure and dynamics.* New York.

———. 1978. Work sharing: A Norwegian example. In R. Rapoport and R. Rapoport (eds.), *Working couples.* New York: Harper & Row.

Haas, L. 1977. *Sexual equality in the family: A study of role-sharing couples.* Unpublished doctoral dissertation, University of Wisconsin-Madison.

Holstrom, L. 1973. *The two-career family.* Cambridge, Mass.: Schenkman.

Hunt, J., and L. Hunt. 1977. Dilemmas and contradictions of status: The case of the dual-career family. *Social Problems* 24, 404–16.

Nye, F. 1976. *Role structure and analysis of the family.* Beverly Hills: Sage.

Poloma, M., and T. N. Garland. 1971. The myth of the egalitarian family: Familiar roles and the professionally employed wife. In A. Theodore (ed.), *The professional woman*. Cambridge, Mass.: Schenkman.

Rapoport, R., and R. Rapoport. 1977. *Dual career families reexamined*. New York: Harper & Row.

Scanzonl, J. 1972. *Sexual bargaining*. Englewood Cliffs, N.J.: Prentice-Hall.

Szalal, A. 1972. *The use of time*. Paris: Mouton.

Walker, K. 1970. Time-use patterns for household work related to homemakers' employment. U.S. Department of Agriculture, Agricultural Research Service.

Young, M., and P. Willmont. 1973. *The symmetrical family*. New York: Pantheon.

26 *Good News for Mothers Who Work*

Barbara J. Berg

STUDY QUESTIONS

1. What is the good news for mothers who work?

2. What is the effect of day care on children?

At the Docs' home on any weeknight, candles illuminate a tablecloth, napkins, and such tempting food as veal marsala, salad, homebaked biscuits, and cake made from scratch. But Barbara Docs is not home all day preparing this lovely meal. Instead her four children divide the cooking among themselves while Barbara is at work. "We all make an effort to be home for dinner," explained Barbara, an administrative assistant with C.M. Offray, a New Jersey-based ribbon manufacturer. "Family closeness is very important to us. I love the chance to sit and talk with the children in a quiet, relaxed way, to hear about their day and tell them about mine."

Although other households with working mothers* may not want or be able to make candlelit dinners a priority, they do share the Docs' emphasis on family intimacy. In a nationwide survey of nearly 1,000 women of varying social and economic backgrounds that I conducted for my recent book, *The Crisis of the Working Mother: Resolving the Conflict Between Family and Work* (Summit Books),

Source: Barbara J. Berg, "Good News for Mothers Who Work." *Parents*, October 1982, pp. 103–108. Reprinted by permission.

*Editor's Note: "Working mother" is not an entirely satisfactory description of women who work outside the home since mothers who are at home work too, although differently. We use the term here for lack of a better one, but we welcome readers' suggestions.

my respondents' concern for the welfare of their children was paramount. In their attitudes, beliefs, and actions, working mothers were remarkable in their devotion to their children's needs. They consistently gave up any time for themselves in favor of spending it with their children. In fact, a recent study by United Media Enterprises found that "dual career parents are more likely to read and draw with their young children on a regular basis than traditional parents." Moreover, they are "more likely to supervise their children's school-work, take them to special events and talk to them about their school and friends."

ATTACKS ON THE WORKING MOTHER

However, women employed outside the home are increasingly attacked for neglecting the well-being of their families so that they can selfishly pursue their professional goals. In part this criticism is inspired by a Leave-It-to-Beaver image of the family with Dad as the breadwinner and Mom in the kitchen baking brownies. The cult of motherhood that is implicit in this image has a firm grip on the national psyche although it reflected the reality of American experience only briefly during the 1950's. With the exception of that decade when the majority of middle-class women did not hold jobs, mothers have worked throughout our nation's history. In fact, when female labor was required to keep the economy going, as it was in the Colonial period and during the major wars, women—the majority of them mothers—were publicly encouraged to work.

During World War II, for example, the United States Department of Labor reported ". . . it can hardly be said that any occupation is absolutely unsuitable for the employment of women." Rosie was not only a riveter but a truck driver, a tractor operator, and a stevedore. When the war started, 95 percent of the women with jobs said that they planned to quit when the men came home, but by 1945 more than 80 percent preferred to continue working. These wartime workers wanted employment for the same reasons as women today: financial necessity, a better life for their children, and personal fulfill-ment, but their hopes were eventually dashed by the conservative climate of the postwar years.

In a similar fashion, the current national drift to the right is responsible for some of the criticism of today's working mothers. President Reagan's opposition to the idea of comparable worth and to most of the enforcement provisions of the Equal Employment Opportunity Commission regulations threatens to erode much of the progress that women have made in the workplace over the past fifteen years. So does the growing influence of the fundamentalist movement, which stresses that a woman's role in life is child rearing and her place, the home. A strong proponent of these views is Beverly LaHaye, the wife of the Reverend Tim LaHaye, who directs the American Coalition for Traditional Values. Beverly LaHaye is president of Concerned Women for America, the largest counter-feminist organization in the country. With its reported 500,000 members. Concerned Women has a larger following than the

National Organization for Women, the National Women's Political Caucus, and the National League of Women Voters combined.

The media reflect this conservative climate and add to it. Whereas not so long ago magazines and television exalted the energy and capabilities of women who combined multiple roles, today they often feature women who have left the boardroom for the nursery.

DISPROVING THE MYTH OF THE "BAD" WORKING MOTHER

These influences—the national swing to the right, the pressure from fundamentalist groups, and the role of the press—reinforce myths about the "bad" working mother. In essence, these myths portray a mother who sacrifices her children's well-being to her own ambition, who neglects them and jeopardizes their development. There is no foundation for these myths. In an ongoing seven-year-old study, California psychologists Adele and Allen Gottfried have found no difference in the home environment or in the development of children whose mothers are employed and those who are not. How a child develops, they have concluded, has nothing to do with maternal employment.

In fact, when differences between children of working and nonworking mothers do emerge, they seem to favor the children of working mothers. Canadian psychologists Dolores Gold and David Andres have found that children of working mothers have broader conceptions of sex roles than children of nonemployed mothers. Moreover, women who work often provide very positive role models for their children, as the memories of women whose mothers were employed attest. "I always thought of my mother, who was a high school history teacher, as a lot more active and interesting than those women who stayed home," says Barbara J. Harris, Ph.D., a professor of history at Pace University: "Not only did I identify with her professionally, but personally also. She was very courageous, and when I find myself in a difficult situation, I often think back on how she would have handled it."

"My mother gave me a strong motivation to achieve, to strive for what I wanted," said another woman, Linda M. Martin, a senior vice-president with California Savings and Loan, whose mother worked in a factory.

Mollie Smilie, a comptroller from La Porte, Colorado, said. "My mother began as a secretary, but through her perseverance she worked herself up to personnel director for an engineering firm. Because of her example, I grew up believing that women can do whatever they set their minds to."

These working women remember growing up in families that thrived through everyone's efforts, families held together not by traditional patterns of domination and subordination but by the mutual respect and trust of all their members. When they became mothers themselves, they instilled the same values in their children. "We were very poor while I was growing up, but we had a strong sense of family. I always felt very loved and close to my mother, the way my son does to me," said Linda Martin. And Mollie Smilie says she has raised her fifteen-year-old son the way she was raised, "to be independent, self-reliant and to form his own opinions."

THE STRESS MYTH

Another aspect of the myth of the working mother has been the expectation that with so many different roles to fill she would be the victim of stress, dying at an earlier age than her more traditional counterpart, of coronary heart disease. This myth encouraged all kinds of gloomy predictions, but there is no evidence of increases in physical or mental stress-related illnesses or an increased mortality rate for women in the work force. In fact, recent studies show that work may well act as a buffer against stress in other areas of a woman's life. As Grace Baruch and Rosalind Barnett of the Center for Research on Women at Wellesley College document in a forthcoming study, the contemporary working woman's many spheres of activity can lead to enhanced self-esteem, control, and well-being.

This doesn't mean, of course, that working mothers don't become frustrated or tired or overwhelmed at times. Of course they do, just as homemakers do. But the sense of autonomy, security, self-worth, and independence they derive from their work more than compensates for occasional stress.

WOMEN WORKERS: HERE TO STAY

There are many reasons why it is important to correct the myths about the working mother. First of all, women are in the labor force to stay. Forty-five percent of the country's workers are women—all 43,951,000 of them.

Moreover, it is projected that by 1995, 59 million women will be working. The recent change in the participation of women with young children in the labor force is even more remarkable. Mothers of children under the age of three are the fastest-growing segment of women in the work force, and during the last ten years the participation of women with children under a year old has increased by more than 50 percent. In 1975, 30.8 percent of women with children under a year old worked outside the home; in 1985 that figure was 49.4 percent.

The vast majority of these women work for economic reasons. Edward Zigler, Ph.D., director of the Yale University Bush Center Advisory Committee on Infant Care Leave, pointed to recent studies showing that "only one job in four permits a man to make enough money to support four people. To make a decent level of income you need two people working, and *that's not going to change*," emphasized Dr. Zigler.

Second, the many misconceptions about working mothers' motives, values, and sense of responsibility create insecurity and guilt that have a negative impact on their personal and professional lives. All too common are examples of women engaging in such self-defeating behavior as overindulging their children or sabotaging their efforts at work out of an unnecessary sense of apology.

WILL MY CHILD STILL LOVE ME?

Third, the myth of the "bad" working mother makes women vulnerable to another set of myths, those portraying the dangers of any form of child care that is not provided by the mother herself.

All working mothers have to find child care, but this task—hard enough— is complicated further by dire predictions concerning some of its most common forms. The woman seeking a fulltime babysitter is cautioned that her child will become more attached to the care-giver than to herself. Woman after woman confided this fear to me, and yet it is unfounded. Jay Belsky, Ph.D., professor of human development at The Pennsylvania State University, has evaluated many studies of infants with some kind of day-care experience—babysitters, family day care and center-based care. He notes that the studies show the children to be emotionally attached to their mothers and to have a stronger preference for their mothers than for their care-givers. "While babies can develop affectional and emotional ties to the care-giver and, in fact, to a variety of people," Belsky says, "day-care givers do not replace and displace the mother as the primary source of the baby's affectional or emotional ties."

To compare the quality of the interaction between children and mothers who worked and those who did not and its effect on cognitive development, Helen Lerner, Ed.D., assistant professor of nursing at Lehman College, and her associates made two hundred home visits to two groups of families, one with employed mothers and the other with mothers who were not employed outside the home. In addition to direct observation they conducted in-depth interviews with the mothers and did developmental assessments of the babies who ranged from 12 to 30 months. They compared the manner in which the two groups of mothers interacted with their children—what they liked to do together, types of play, teaching activities, toys provided, and other aspects of the environment. They concluded that the interaction of working mothers with their children was not significantly different from mothers who did not work, nor was the environment they provided. And they found that the cognitive development of the two groups was equal.

Women considering putting their child in family day care or centerbased care are undermined by another myth that claims group care is inevitably damaging to a baby. This myth has been reinforced in the past several years by the discovery of instances of sexual abuse in day-care centers. Public demand for careful screening of care-givers has been immediate and appropriate, but unfortunately, a few incidents have led to blanket condemnations of group care rather than much needed public policy aimed not only at preventing these and other atrocities but at insuring optimum day care for all children.

There is a great range in the quality of group day care in this country. Some of it is first rate and some, just plain awful. But when parents have sufficient time and money to select a safe, stimulating environment with nurturing, capable care-givers and a low child-to-staff ratio (federal guidelines suggest 3–4:1 for infants or toddlers), the benefits to all can be great.

THE ADVANTAGES OF DAY CARE

The positive effects of day care have been documented by many studies. Psychologist Alison Clarke-Stewart's research, for example, suggests that children with day-care experience are more advanced socially and intellectually when they start school than children raised at home. While controversy exists among experts about the impact of group care on infants, most agree with Edward Zigler, who says that "in general children do well in good day care and poorly in bad day care."

Mothers confirm these findings. Mary Claire Ryan, a divorced mother from Illinois, has tried several kinds of care for her daughter Caroline; a day-care center is by far her favorite. "Caroline has thrived in an atmosphere where she can interact with other children, her social skills are excellent, and verbally she is well beyond her five years," said Mary Claire, who is the personnel manager of a Chicago law firm.

Another mother had similar impressions. "Our older daughter entered day care at seven weeks and from the beginning I felt that she was very stimulated by the environment," recalled Sandra Schiffman, a financial-planning manager at Xerox in Rochester, New York. "Her eyes opened wider, she seemed more alert and aware." Now with two children at the day-care center, Sandra marvels at the quality of their social interactions and their language development. "Even if my husband or I weren't working, the last expense on our budget that we would get rid of would be day care."

SAFE CHILDREN, HEALTHY CHILDREN

Myths about day care portray it as hazardous not only to the emotional well-being of children but to their physical safety and health as well. However, "there is absolutely no evidence that children in group care, either family or center-based, are less safe than children in the world at large," says Susan Aronson, M.D., who is consultant to the American Academy of Pediatrics on day care. "What's more, problems that are related to safety are fairly correctable," she adds. For example, the most frequent accidents in a day-care setting involve climbing. A proper impact-absorbing surface under climbing equipment—Dr. Aronson recommends a loose fill material like shredded tires, which costs about $150 a ton—prevents a lot of injuries at both day-care centers and other playgrounds. Proper staff supervision and well organized activities will also cut down on the number of mishaps.

The most recent evidence on the health effects of attending day care indicates that although day-care children are more apt to have diarrhea, hepatitis A, meningitis, and otitis media than children not in day care, and are possibly at somewhat greater risk for respiratory illness, these risks should not be exaggerated and should not be taken as a sign for alarm or as a reason to condemn day care. They do, however, underline the importance of maintaining high hygiene standards in day-care settings and the importance of low child-staff ratios.

Hepatitis and gastrointestinal illnesses occur most frequently in those states that permit a high child-to-staff ratio. Such as Arizona, Louisiana, or South Carolina, where one adult may supervise ten or twelve children. Proper hygiene procedures—hand washing and washing down and sanitizing the tops of changing tables—reduce the risk of these infections, according to Dr. Aronson.

There does appear to be one bacteria, *Haemophilis influenzae* type b, that is more common among children in group care. But there is a very safe vaccine against it that is effective for children over two and another is being perfected for children under two. All children, whether or not they are in group care, should be immunized against this disease, Dr. Aronson urged.

"Of course the few outbreaks of hepatitis or meningitis among children in day care get wide coverage and that scares everyone to death. But we have to think about the millions of children in day care who don't have these problems. That never gets reported," said Dr. Aronson.

Equally missing from the media is any recognition of the opportunity group-care settings offer for health education, including basic hygienic routines such as hand washing and toothbrushing, and for preventive medicine. Statistics show that children in day care are better immunized than children in the general population, but perhaps the best proof of the health advantages of day care is the fact that children enrolled in Head Start programs are, in general, healthier than those from the same background who are not enrolled. They have a lower incidence of pediatric problems, fewer cavities, and better nutrition.

AFTER-SCHOOL SELF-CARE

Self-care has attracted criticism just as group care has. Youngsters in self-care—latchkey children—have long been the subject of concern and pity. The general assumption has been that unattended by adults after school, they are prey to all kinds of physical and psychological dangers and are easily enticed into mischief.

As yet there is little conclusive research on the effects of self-care. Some studies have found that many self-care children are lonely and fearful and that their opportunities for play and friendship with their peers are restricted. However, the type of environment—urban, suburban, or rural—is an important factor in determining children's reactions, with urban children generally more prone to fear and more restricted.

Other studies, however, have been more positive in their findings. Hyman Rodman, Ph.D., director of the Family Research Center at the University of North Carolina at Greensboro, and his colleagues, David J. Pratto, Ph.D., and Rosemary Smith Nelson, Ph.D., compared a matched group of self-care and adult-care children. They measured the children's self-esteem, their sense of

BARBARA J. BERG

control over their own lives and environment, and their teachers' ratings of their social and interpersonal adjustments. They found no statistical difference between the two groups. It is reassuring to know that the self-care children had very uneventful afternoons. For the most part they did homework or chores or watched television, reported Rosemary Smith Nelson, who conducted interviews for the study. While these children were not formally supervised, there were very few who did not have almost immediate access to some adult. Nelson, who is a psychologist with a private practice in Winston-Salem, North Carolina, explained that we would be mistaken to think of these children as feeling isolated or lonely. "They are just normal kids," she said.

A similar study conducted by Deborah Vandell, a psychologist at the University of Texas at Dallas, reached the same general conclusion: self-care children are as well adjusted as those who go home to a parent or a babysitter after school.

There is no rule as to the age a child is ready for self-care, although as adolescence approaches most children want to take care of themselves. Parents must evaluate whether their child is ready to take care of himself or herself on an individual basis. Does he or she understand and follow family and school rules? Does the child usually demonstrate good judgment with friends and with adults? How well do parents believe their child would cope with the unexpected? How safe is their neighborhood? How accessible are other adults? If they can answer these questions positively, they can begin to experiment with short periods of self-care, which can gradually be extended.

SUPPORT FOR WORKING MOTHERS AND THEIR CHILDREN

A final reason it is important to correct myths about the working mother is that these myths deflect energy and attention from the search for solutions to some of the real difficulties that women face in combining roles. The many advantages that working mothers and their children enjoy are not uniformly shared. Mothers who are divorced or single are much more likely to be poor than women who are married, and women in general are still making only about 60 cents for every dollar earned by men. Moreover, recent studies show that the majority of employed women will continue to work in low-paying jobs dominated by women for some time to come. But when poverty, single parenthood and dead-end jobs cause problems for women and their families, the critics are quick to blame working mothers rather than to address the kinds of changes needed to enhance all of our lives.

For poor women, and for their better-off counterparts as well, finding good day care is often a problem. Until we have standards regulated by law to govern the staff-child ratio, there will continue to be great variation among states. And, in spite of a few celebrated examples like Stride Rite, only 120 corporations—a fraction of the country's 6 million total employers—provide on- or near-site child care.

Another problem working mothers face is insufficient or nonexistent maternity leave. While some employers grant sufficient maternity leave for a woman to get adjusted to motherhood and to investigate child-care facilities, many do not. The United States is the only industrialized nation in the world with no guaranteed parental leave.

More attempts to make flextime and job-sharing viable alternatives for men and for women, company-organized babysitter pools, visiting nurse services to care for the sick children of employees, all would help provide much needed family support. So would creating a corporate environment that enabled women to feel free to take off an afternoon to watch their sons play soccer or to take a sick child to the doctor. In short, a corporate atmosphere is needed that recognizes women as the complete, mature human beings they are.

As Dr. T. Berry Brazelton told me, "It's no longer a question of whether or not mothers should work. A woman's identity these days is really tied up with a career and with nurturing. The task ahead of us is to give her the most support possible to do both, for only then will we be helping parents and children to reach their fullest potential."

7 ***Parental Questions***

It would have been unnecessary to define the term "family" thirty years ago. The idealized image of a permanently married couple with at least two children, the husband as wage earner and the wife as homemaker, prevailed. Other alternatives such as cohabitation, childless marriages, single parenthood, working mothers, and communal living were all seen as deviant or pathological. Today, we have become relatively used to these alternative lifestyles. Thus, the topic of the family involves a number of related items covering the entire family cycle of before, during, and after children, as well as variations on this theme. It is this idea of a changing family with its variations in stages and roles that is the subject of the first article in Chapter 7 by Maris Vinovskis.

In the second article of this chapter, Maryann Brinley asks a question that a relatively few years ago was irrelevant—should you have a baby? This relatively new idea was made possible by advances in contraception technology and changing values. These advances in contraception are seen in the third item of this chapter—a chart indicating the advantages, disadvantages, effectiveness, and possible health effects of each method of birth control. Although technological developments now make child-bearing a matter of choice, most people will have children. It is seen as a natural component of the life cycle. Perhaps this is so or it may be due to a lack of awareness of the cultural pressures which induce people to satisfy society's basic need to reproduce itself. A strong procreation ethic is embodied in folklore beliefs, the mass media, and institutional policies. For example, both folklore beliefs and the mass media promote the joys of parenthood through such ideas or scenes as: "rearing children is fun," "children are sweet and cute," "children improve a marriage," and "child rearing is easier today because of modern medicine, modern appliances, child psychology, and so on" (LeMasters & DeFrain 1983). The various social institutions such as the government add to this pronatalist theme through tax exemptions and various support programs. There are, of course, personal reasons for wanting children such as the psychological needs for power, proof of personal competence, provision for economic security and personal immortality, and the experience and pleasure of raising a child (Berelson 1972) but the above pronatalist influences may mean that you are having a baby for the wrong reasons. Brinley's article summarizes these bad and good reasons for having children.

The list by Brinley indicates that the greatest perceived advantages of parenthood are the sense of family and source of love and affection children provide. The primary disadvantages would appear to be restrictions on lifestyle, economic strain, women's increasing economic independence, and liberalized views toward working and childless women. It is these latter factors that appear to be responsible for a growing trend toward smaller and even child-free families despite the continuing untrue beliefs that having a single child is detrimental to him/her (McCoy 1986) and that deliberately child-free women are maladjusted, immature, unfulfilled, and unhappily married (Veevers 1979). Actually, studies reveal that personal development, financial well-being, opportunities for career success, and marital happiness are all enhanced in child-free marriages. Lisa Rogers and Jeffry Larson, in the fourth article of Chapter 7, summarize these factors for going against tradition. A reflection of the changing values which enable couples to choose not to have children is seen in the growing use of the term "child-free" rather than "childless" to note this family situation. However, the biases and pronatalist pressures are so strong that most child-free women do not consciously reject parenthood; they simply postpone it to the point at which a de facto decision has been made.

REFERENCES

1. Berelson, B. 1972. *The Value of Children: A Taxonomical Essay.* The Population Council Annual Report.
2. LeMasters, E. E., & J. DeFrain. 1983. *Parents in Contemporary America: A Sympathetic View* 4th ed. Chicago: Dorsey.
3. McCoy, E. 1986. "Your One and Only." *Parents* (October).
4. Veevers, J. E. 1979. "Voluntary Childlessness: A Review of Issues and Evidence." *Marriage and Family Review* (Summer).

27 *The Changing Family*

Maris Vinovskis

STUDY QUESTIONS

1. The author claims that change has always been characteristic of the family. Explain.
2. As an example of the changing family, indicate how our treatment of children has changed.

There is widespread fear among policymakers and the American public today that the family is disintegrating. Much of that anxiety stems from a basic misunderstanding of the nature of the family in the past and a lack of appreciation for its resiliency in response to broad social and economic changes. The general view of the family is that it has been a stable and relatively unchanging institution through history and is only now undergoing changes; in fact, change has always been characteristic of it.

THE FAMILY AND HOUSEHOLD IN THE PAST

In the last twenty years, historians have been re-examining the nature of the family and have concluded that we must revise our notions of the family as an institution, as well as our assumptions about how children were perceived and treated in past centuries. A survey of diverse studies of the family in the West, particularly in seventeenth- eighteenth- and nineteenth-century England and America shows something of the changing role of the family in society and the evolution of our ideas of parenting and child development. (Although many definitions of *family* are available, in this article I will use it to refer to kin living under one roof.)

Source: Maris Vinovskis, "The Changing Family." *LSA*, Spring 1987, pp. 17–20. Reprinted by permission.

Although we have tended to believe that in the past children grew up in "extended households" including grandparents, parents, and children, recent historical research has cast considerable doubt on the idea that as countries became increasingly urban and industrial, the Western family evolved from extended to nuclear. Historians have found evidence that households in pre-industrial Western Europe were already nuclear and could not have been greatly transformed by economic changes. Rather than finding definite declines in household size, we find surprisingly small variations, which turn out to be a result of the presence or absence of servants, boarders, and lodgers, rather than relatives. In revising our nostalgic picture of children growing up in large families, Peter Laslett, one of the foremost analysts of the pre-industrial family, contends that most households in the past were actually quite small (mean household size was about 4.75). Of course, patterns may have varied somewhat from one area to another, but it seems unlikely that in the past few centuries many families in England or America had grandparents living with them.

However, as Philip Aries has argued in his well-known *Centuries of Childhood*, the medieval family was nevertheless quite different from its modern counterpart, largely because the boundary between the household and the larger society was less rigidly drawn, and the roles of parents, servants, or neighbors in the socialization of children were more blurred. Relationships within the nuclear family were not much closer, it seems, than those with neighbors, relatives, or other friends.

Another difference, according to Lawrence Stone, was that within property-owning classes, as in sixteenth-century England, for example, marriage was a collective decision, involving not only the immediate family, but also other kin. Protection of long-term interests of lineage and consideration for the needs of the larger kinship group were more important than individual desires for happiness or romantic love. In addition, because the strong sense of individual or family privacy had not yet developed, access to the household by local neighbors was relatively easy. But this type of family gave way in the late sixteenth century to a "restricted patriarchal nuclear family," which predominated from 1580 to 1640, when concern for lineage and loyalty to the local community declined, and allegiances to the State and Church and to kin within the household increased. The authority of the father, as head of the household, was enhanced and bolstered by State and Church support. This drive toward parental dominance over children was particularly characteristic of the Puritans and was not limited to the child's early years; upper-class parents, especially, sought to extend their control to their children's choices of both career and spouse.

By the mid-seventeenth century, the family was increasingly organized around the principle of personal autonomy and was bound together by strong ties of love and affection. The separation, both physical and emotional, between members of a nuclear family and their servants or boarders widened, as did the distance between the household and the rest of society. Physical privacy became more important, and it became more acceptable for individual family members to pursue their own happiness.

Throughout most of the pre-industrial period, the household was the central productive unit of society. Children either were trained for their future occupations in their own homes or were employed in someone else's household. As the economic functions of the household moved to the shop or factory in the late-eighteenth and nineteenth centuries, the household, no longer an economic focal point or an undifferentiated part of neighborhood activities, increasingly became a haven or escape from the outside world. Children growing up in fifteenth-century England were expected and encouraged to interact closely with many adults besides their parents, but by the eighteenth and nineteenth centuries, they had come to rely more and more upon each other and their parents for their emotional needs.

The families that migrated to the New World, especially the Puritans, brought with them the ideal of a close and loving family, and although the economic functions of the American household were altered in the nineteenth century, the overall change was less dramatic than it had been in Western Europe. Thus, although the relationship between parents and children has not remained constant in America during the past three hundred years, the extent of the changes is probably less than it was in Western Europe.

CHANGING PERCEPTIONS AND TREATMENT OF CHILDREN

We usually assume that an innate characteristic of human beings is the close and immediate attachment between the newborn child and its parents, especially its mother. Because abandonment or abuse of children seems to defy such beliefs, we are baffled by reports of widespread parental abuse of children. A look at the past may provide a different perspective on the present.

According to some scholars, maternal indifference to infants may have been typical of the Middle Ages. Aries says there is evidence that in the sixteenth and seventeenth centuries parents showed little affection for their children, and Edward Shorter argues that this indifference was probably typical among the ordinary people of Western Europe, even in the eighteenth and nineteenth centuries. The death of young children seems to have been accepted casually, and although overt infanticide was frowned upon, allowing children to die was sometimes encouraged, or at least tolerated. For example, in Western Europe it was common for mothers to leave infants at foundling hospitals or with rural wet nurses, both of which resulted in very high mortality rates. Whether these practices were typically the result of economic desperation, the difficulty of raising an out-of-wedlock child, or lack of attachment to an infant is not clear, but the fact that many well-to-do married women casually chose to give their infants to wet nurses, despite the higher mortality risks, suggests that the reasons were not always economic difficulty or fear of social stigma.

While the practice of overt infanticide and child abandonment may have been relatively widespread in parts of Western Europe, it does not seem to have been prevalent in either England or America. Indeed, authorities in both those countries in the sixteenth and seventeenth centuries prosecuted infanticide cases more vigorously than other forms of murder, and the practice of leaving infants with wet nurses went out of fashion in England by the end of the eighteenth century.

By the eighteenth century in Western Europe, parents were expressing more interest in their children and more affection for them, and by the nineteenth century, observers were beginning to criticize parents for being too child-centered. Nevertheless, parents were still not prevented from abusing their own children, as long as it did not result in death. Because the parent-child relationship was regarded as sacred and beyond State intervention, it was not until the late nineteenth century that reformers in England were able to persuade lawmakers to pass legislation to protect children from abusive parents. Ironically, efforts to prevent cruelty to animals preceded those to accomplish the same ends for children by nearly a half century.

Some of the earliest studies of colonial America suggested, that at that time childhood was not viewed as a distinct stage: children, these historians said, were expected to think and behave pretty much as adults from an early age. Although a few recent scholars of the colonial American family have supported this view, others have questioned it, pointing out that New England Puritans were well aware that children had different abilities and temperaments and believed that childrearing should be molded to those individual differences.

While young children in colonial America probably were not seen as miniature adults, they *were* thought to be more capable intellectually at a young age than their counterparts generally are today. The Puritans believed that because it was essential for salvation, children should be taught to read the Bible as soon as possible. Indeed, the notion that children could and should learn to read as soon as they could talk was so commonly accepted by educators that they did not think it necessary to justify it in their writings. The infant school movement of the late 1820s reinforced this assumption until it was challenged by Amariah Brigham, a prominent physician who claimed that early intellectual training seriously and permanently weakened growing minds and could lead to insanity later in life.

When the kindergarten movement became popular in the United States, in the 1860s and 70s, intellectual activities such as reading were deliberately avoided. Such examples are a clear indication of how the socialization of children is dependent on our perceptions of children, and one might even speculate that as we become increasingly willing to incorporate the latest scientific and medical findings into our care of the young, shifts in childrearing practices will increase in frequency.

YOUTH

Not only young children were perceived and treated differently in the past. Although there is little agreement among scholars either about when "adolescence" came to be viewed as a distinct stage or about the importance of education in the lives of nineteenth-century youths, many family historians have offered their perspectives on these topics. Surprisingly little, however, has been done to explore changes in teenage sexuality, pregnancy, and childbearing. Given

MARIS VINOVSKIS

the recent concern about the "epidemic" of adolescent pregnancies, we might expect more attention to be given to the attitudes of our forebears towards teenage parents.

Because of the stringent seventeenth-century prohibitions against pre-marital sexual relations and the low percentage of early teenage marriages, teenage pregnancy seems not to have been a problem in colonial New England. Early Americans were more concerned about pre-marital sexual relations, in general, than about whether teenage or adult women were involved. Not until the late nineteenth and early twentieth centuries did society clearly differentiate between teenage and adult sexual behavior, with a more negative attitude towards the former.

Only in the post-World War II period has the issue of teenage pregnancy and childbearing become a major public concern. But although the rates of teenage pregnancy and childbearing peaked in the late 1950s, the greatest attention to this phenomenon has come during the late 1970s and early 80s. The controversy over abortion, the great increase in out-of-wedlock births to adolescents, and the growing concern about the long-term disadvantages of early childbearing to the young mother and her child have made this issue more important today than thirty years ago.

PARENT-CHILD RELATIONS

Historically, the primary responsibility for the rearing of young children belonged almost exclusively to the parents, especially the father. It was not until the late nineteenth and early twentieth centuries that the State was willing to remove a young child from direct supervision of negligent or abusive parents. Even so, in order to reduce welfare costs to the rest of the community, a destitute family in early America, incapable of supporting its own members, was sometimes broken up and the children placed in other households.

During the eighteenth and nineteenth centuries the mother's role in the upbringing of children was enhanced: women became the primary providers of care and affection; and as men's church membership declined, women also became responsible for the catechizing and educating of young children, even though they often were less literate than men. While childrearing manuals continued to acknowledge the importance of the father, they also recognized that the mother had become the major figure in the care of the young.

Throughout much of Western history, as long as children remained in the home, parents exercised considerable control over them, even to the extent of arranging their marriages and influencing their career choices. Children were expected to be obedient and to contribute to the well-being of the family. And, perhaps more in Western Europe than in America, children were often expected to turn over almost all of their earnings directly to the parents— sometimes even after they had left home.

By the late eighteenth or early nineteenth century some of this control had eroded, and the rights of children as individuals were increasingly recognized and acknowledged. Interestingly, the development of children's rights has proceeded so rapidly and so far that we may now be in the midst of a backlash, as efforts are being made to re-establish parental responsibility in areas such as the reproductive behavior of minor children.

Clearly there have been major changes in the way our society treats children; but it would be very difficult for many of us to agree on the costs and benefits of these trends—whether from the viewpoint of the child, the parents, or society. While many applaud the increasing individualism and freedom of children within the family, others lament the loss of family responsibility and discipline. A historical analysis of parents and children cannot settle such disputes, but it can provide us with a better appreciation of the flexibility and resilience of the family as an institution for raising the young.

28 *Should You Have a Baby?*

Maryann Bucknum Brinley

STUDY QUESTIONS

1. What are several right reasons for undertaking parenthood? Why are they right?

2. What are several wrong reasons for undertaking parenthood? Why are they wrong?

My friend Lydia, a 34-year-old architect who lives and works in Washington, D.C., called me the other day with an urgent request.

"Quick. You're a mother. Tell me. Should I have a baby or shouldn't I? I've decided that I must decide now."

Lydia is a successful career woman—although her current position isn't perfect, she insistently reminds me—and she has a loving husband, a nifty house and is where she dreamed she'd be when we were roommates in college. The one feather that isn't currently in her cap is motherhood. She has, in fact, postponed having a child for so long, conscientiously warding off the threat of an unplanned pregnancy, that the prospect of having a baby leaves her petrified. For Lydia, it seems like an impossible and nearly unnatural step to have to take, and the decision has become an enormous burden. (Her husband assures her he'll be *there* for her, but she must make up her own mind.)

Where are the lists of practical and emotional do's and don'ts, rights and

Source: Maryann Bunknum Brinley, "Should You Have a Baby?" *McCall's*, January 1984, pp. 119–120. Reprinted by permission.

wrongs, for women caught in this bind? When we exchange birthday cards at age 45, Lydia wants to know, will she envy me my teenagers? (My children are five and two now.) She wonders if she'll become depressed or crazed or lonely as a result of never having exercised her baby option.

She also wonders whether her reasons for wanting a child are all wrong. And if so, can you have a baby for less than ideal reasons, in imperfect circumstances—and still live happily ever after? Moreover, are there any absolutely right, truly unselfish reasons for having a baby? (How, after all, can you be unself-centered in your love for a child during pregnancy, before he or she actually exists—except as an extension of your ego and physical self?)

According to New York psychotherapist Nancy Good, the decision to have a baby always includes some negative and positive aspects, some wrong and some right reasons, some silly and some sophisticated rationales. Moreover, she says, "any pregnancy begun for what might look like a 'wrong' reason can certainly turn out all right." (My youngest brother, my mother admits, was probably born for a "wrong reason." Nine years after she put the crib, which had been used and abused by five of us, into storage, she began to think wistfully about using it again. Work in the outside world looked pale when she compared it to the jobsite our home had been for so long. So Richard had been her way out . . . as well as her joy.)

Dr. Richard Formica, a New Jersey psychologist with ten years of experience running workshops for thousands of troubled parents, says that should's and shouldn'ts abound in this world, "and that's very sad. In fact, I hesitate to add more criteria to this very personal, very important decision. But there are considerations anyone can use to examine her readiness for parenthood."

None of the wrong reasons listed here is *absolutely* wrong. They are simply guidelines. Having a baby isn't, ultimately, a checklist proposition.

"WRONG" REASONS TO HAVE A BABY

1. *To save (or strengthen) the relationship you have with the man in your life.*

This is still a very common and very wrong reason to have a baby. As psychotherapist Nancy Good warns, "Having a baby out of any kind of fear—especially fear of losing the man in your life—is terribly misguided and may end up backfiring on you." Both Planned Parenthood and the National Organization for Non-Parents have issued warnings in the past about using this line of reasoning. Good says, "Getting a man to support you, to love you or to share his life more with you by having his baby shouldn't be the primary motivating factor in your wanting a child. Sometimes we have basic emotional needs that did not get satisfied when we were children, and we hope that through a child and man we'll make up for this lack. But what's likely to happen is that you'll feel more drained and emptier taking care of a child and a husband. And, though you're unhappy with the results, you can't send the baby back to try another tactic."

2. *To please your parents, your friends, the people who tell you that you'd make a great mother.*

Other people—no matter how close you may feel to them—are outsiders in your life. They won't be there for the four A.M. feedings. They may even prove not to be so loving when you don't meet their fantasized expectations of doting earth-mother.

"There are at least two ways of dealing with this subtle bullying that those who elect to remain childless have to put up with," Shirley Radl says in her book *Mother's Day Is Over*. "The first is a very loud 'MIND YOUR OWN BUSINESS!' If, however, you feel obligated to answer in some way, you might try asking a question of your own," like, Radl suggests, "Where did you ever get that interesting wart?"

3. *Because everyone you know has recently become a mother.*

"To consciously choose *not* to have a child is probably the hardest conditioning a woman may have to overcome in her life," insists Dr. Formica. "When you couple what may be a very real biological drive to reproduce with your need to find your 'place' as a woman, you come up a pretty powerful force to be reckoned with. But what makes us human is our capacity to experience these drives and not be dominated by them."

Nancy Good, who is currently working on a book about couples, also warns of listening to a friend who may be quite miserable as a mother but quite adamant about why you should join her ranks. "I call them baby pushers, twisting your arm until you are uncomfortable in their presence. They keep busy so they won't think about their own secret ambivalence—which is high."

4. *To escape from the outside working world.*

Let's admit it. Having a baby is still considered a viable and important alternative to a career—especially one that is going nowhere fast.

As Angela Barron McBride, a professor of psychiatric nursing and author of *The Growth and Development of Mothers*, writes, "I wanted to have a baby because I was tired of working. My job was difficult, and I needed some time out to figure where I wanted to go in my profession." McBride adds, "Only gradually did I realize that real self-fulfillment depends on coming to terms with these preposterous fictions that all of us devise, especially when we grow up encouraged to think that having a husband and children equals automatic happiness or fulfillment."

So don't even consider baby tending as your way out of work. It's a big step in, not out of, the *work* world.

5. *To squelch a complete host of fears—once and for all.*

If you have a child out of fear of being alone in your old age, fear of what you may be missing out on, fear of never winning your mother's approval or your husband's esteem, fear of God's wrath for not answering to what your religion may deem your highest calling, you'll probably wind up sorry you took the plunge into parenthood.

6. *To be loved and treasured as a baby again yourself.*

If you haven't put your own childhood behind you, or sorted out the mistakes your mother made from the love she had for you, "then you're not ready to become a mother," insists Dr. Sanford Matthews, an Atlanta pediatrician. In fact, having a baby forces you to grow up. And, writes Angela Barron McBride: "If you conceived a child because you wanted to hold on to your own youth, you may resent the fact that picking up toys and keeping her/him away from the steps consumes so much of your energy that you feel as if you have aged 20 years in a few months."

7. *You already have a son and you want a daughter, or vice versa.*

My friend Audrey, at age 43, is still trying to prove to her parents that she is as good, as successful and as worthy of being treasured as the son she might have been. And remember all those families with no girls and six boys— or vice versa.

8. *You've been mothering your mate and you think a real baby would appreciate your efforts more.*

Babies, like some husbands, don't give as much as they take. In fact, as Dr. Matthews says, "If you are looking for the dividends your kids will someday hand you in repayment for your mothering efforts, you're in for a disappointment and at the same time turning yourself into a martyr." Investing your time in diaper changing will never assure you of being able to cash in on dividends down the road. What's more, a husband who has grown pampered and accustomed to uninterrupted doting may have an especially difficult time adjusting to the position of second place in your life, Good warns.

9. *Your own mother was not great at the task. You know you can do it better—and make up for what you missed as a child, too.*

"You can't ever make up or remedy the deficits in your own life through your children's," Formica says. "Wanting your children to live for you or do the things you never did is very dangerous." You are robbing your child of her right to a childhood of her own, one that is different from yours and different from the perfect childhood you may envision for her.

10. *To prove to the world that you are a real woman.*

"I was able to announce to the world that we were no longer irresponsible, hedonistic, immature, abnormal, sterile, frigid, impotent or homosexual," says writer Shirley Radl, describing the smugness she experienced when she and her husband expected a child after eight years of marriage. Proving a point isn't a very healthy reason to have a baby.

11. *To become closer to your own mother.*

Studies have shown that sometimes motherhood can bring a mother and daughter emotionally closer together. But the basis for their togetherness is often a far cry from a state of loving soul-sisters. By having a baby to become reunited with your mother, you may put yourself right back in the dependent role of daughter instead of independent woman.

Nancy Friday writes in *My Mother/My Self* that as a married, childless daughter she was "different" in her own mother's eyes from her sister, who'd had three children in four years. "My sister spoke to [my mother] daily about the children, relied on her for advice and financial support, and suffered her constant criticism; which my mother took as her right. My sister might be a mother herself, but in my mother's eyes, she is still thirteen."

12. *To become somebody important*

You already are somebody: yourself. In fact, if you don't love yourself, you are going to find it difficult to offer love freely to your baby, according to Dr. Matthews, co-author of *Through the Motherhood Maze*.

13. *You can afford a child financially.*

"There should be other allowances, along with the financial one, ready to be made in your life if you think you are ready for a baby," Formica insists.

I can stand at my kitchen sink, consider Lydia's predicament and know on a gut level that I've made the right decision to have my babies. But what can I tell her—except that motherhood is thrilling, exhausting and well worth my efforts?

Formica, whose own daughter just turned two, offered to "share the criteria" he and his wife used after 13 years of marriage when the question of parenthood became a serious debate for them. "We never put these seven reasons down on paper," he says apologetically. But now he has.

SOME RIGHT REASONS TO HAVE A BABY

1. *Both you and your mate want and choose to have a child.*

"Having a child is the most important decision in your life," Formica says, "and you'll both be living with the consequences for years. It's much more important than a career choice, so the more explicit and conscious the decision is, the better off you both will be. And I don't believe in compromise on this question of a baby. The wanting is a must for both partners." Too many couples spend more time analyzing what kind of car to buy than deciding whether to have a baby. "Why not?" is a question; it's insufficient as an answer.

2. *Your aim is to give, rather than to get.*

The idea here, says Formica, is to want to give "creatively, not sacrificially. Implicit in all sacrificial giving is the heavenly reward or the big payoff later on and that shouldn't be one of your reasons for wanting to give to a child. If problems in your relationship as a couple, with your life as an individual, are going to prevent you from giving easily to a child, then you may not be ready for parenthood," he explains. "Give because you have something to give and you're going to enjoy the process of giving," he adds.

3. *You are going to give from your excess.*

You aren't going to have that much extra to give if you are still desperately trying to establish yourself in the outside world, if you are still separating from your own parents, if you haven't yet put your act together. But "if you are at that point when you have more than you need, when your life is full to the brim, giving to your own baby can be very rewarding," says Formica.

4. *You are going to be available, not busy.*

This reason doesn't necessarily call for either parent to stay home with the baby 24 hours a day, seven days a week. What it means, says Formica, is "you are not so preoccupied with the external tasks of your life, with developmental goals or career ambitions that you won't be able to spend some 'present' time with your child."

5. *You want the challenge of raising a healthy, whole child.*

"In the past," says Formica, "motherhood was used as a compensation prize for failure elsewhere in the larger world." But motherhood is not for the weakhearted, this doctor says, nor is it a retreat from life. So you can't be ready for parenthood until after you have "taken on the challenge of life in the big world."

6. *You're looking forward with pleasurable anticipation to the process of raising a child.*

"This is the single most important right reason for having a baby," Formica says. "Rather than looking forward to some narcissistic product that may or may not appear in twenty years, you should be happy to share your life with a child at each stage of his or her life."

7. *You want to give birth to a personal expression of yourself.*

"You should want to share what you have already made of yourself with your child and not what you hope to become through him or her," Formica explains. "I see this as a very legitimate, healthy form of narcissism. You are saying to yourself and the world, 'I really like me. I like what I am and I want to share my values with a child.' "

Did I consider any of these points before I became pregnant?

Of course not.

There was a baby on the beach a few blankets away from where my husband and I were sitting one summer afternoon about six years ago. She was probably near two—I couldn't pin ages on children then as I can now—wearing a very wet diaper that hung very close to the sand and the most joyful expression in all the world. Her dark curly hair was most seductive. I wanted to run over and pluck her up into my arms—someone who didn't really even like babies, certainly not strange ones with obviously dirty diapers.

"I want one, just like that," I said to my husband.

"She looks like you," he said calmly. "Why do you want one now?"

"I just *want* one. Isn't that enough?"

And, *wanting*, of course, turns out to be the most important reason of all.

29 All About Birth Control

STUDY QUESTIONS

1. What are some of the possible problems and warning signs of the major birth control devices?
2. How effective are the major birth control devices?

	Birth Control Pill	I.U.D. Intrauterine Device	Diaphragm (with cream or jelly)	Contraceptive Sponge
What Is It?	A series of pills which contain synthetic hormones	Small plastic or plastic and copper device placed in the uterus	Dome-shaped rubber cup which covers the cervix when inserted correctly	Disposable sponge-like device containing spermicide
How Does It Work?	Prevents the ovaries from releasing eggs	Interferes with the implantation of a fertilized egg	With contraceptive cream or jelly, it forms a barrier which kills sperm	Sponge forms barrier at cervix so sperm is killed when it reaches sponge
How Is It Used?	Woman takes a pill every day as instructed	Inserted by a clinician and left in uterus	Used with contraceptive cream or jelly and inserted into vagina prior to each act of intercourse. Must be fitted by a clinician	Inserted by the woman into vagina and stays effective for 24 hours
What Are the Major Advantages?	Easy to use, extremely effective; does not interrupt lovemaking; shorter, lighter and more regular periods	Continuous protection; does not interfere with lovemaking; effective method	No serious side effects; only use when having intercourse; effective method	No prescription; 24-hour protection; no serious side effects
What Are Some Possible Problems?	Circulatory, heart and blood clot problems; risks increase with smoking, high blood pressure, high levels of blood fat, diabetes or if overweight	Heavier periods; anemia; infection; perforation (tear) in uterine wall	Misuse or not using it every time; may restrict spontaneity; slight irritations	Possible allergic reaction; possible increase in chances of infection; may be expensive
What Are Some Warning Signs?	A-abdominal pain C-chest pain or shortness of breath H-headaches E-eye problems S-severe leg pain	C-continuous heavy bleeding R-rise in temperature A-abnormal vaginal discharge M-missed period P-pain S-strings missing	Discomfort; burning or itching; unusual discharge	Burning; itching; abnormal discharge; odor
How Effective Is It?	98–99.5%	96–98%	87–95%	87–95%
Where Can You Get It?	Private doctor; family planning clinic	Private doctor; family planning clinic	Private doctor; family planning clinic	Relatively new method; check family planning clincs and drugstores

Source: "All About Birth Control." Planned Parenthood Association of Miami Valley (Ohio). Reprinted by permission.

Condom	Contraceptive Foam	Natural Family Planning	Abstinence	Sterilization
A thin rubber sheath which fits over the penis	Foam containing ingredients which kill sperm	Way of determining fertile days and then not having intercourse during that time	Not having intercourse at all	Operation which is considered a permanent method
Catches a man's semen which contains sperm when he ejaculates (comes)	Forms a foam barrier covering the cervix which kills sperm coming in contact with it	If no sperm is present when a woman is fertile, pregnancy can't occur	Prevents penis from entering vagina	Blocks a man's or woman's tubes to prevent sperm from meeting egg
Rolled onto erect penis BEFORE intercourse. Leave reservoir tip on end to catch semen	Inserted with applicator no more than 20 minutes before each act of intercourse	Instruction given on checking changes in vaginal mucous, temperature and other body signs	Say "No"	Doctor performs operation. May be done as outpatient or inpatient surgery
Helps prevent STD's; no prescription; no serious side effects, effective method	May help prevent some STD's; no prescription; no serious side effects; effective method	Sanctioned by most religions; no side effects	No side effects; helps prevent STD's; most effective method	Extremely effective; considered permanent; once completed no other method needed
May interrupt love-making; may decrease sensitivity; possible allergic reaction	May interrupt love-making; messy; possible allergic reaction	Other stresses on body may cause inaccurate signals to woman; may restrict spontaneity	May be difficult or not feasible for some couples	Possible infection; difficult to reverse
None	Burning or itching	None	None	Severe pain and/or rise in temperature after procedure
Condom and Foam together is 97–99%				
90–98%	70–98%	78–84%	99–100%	99–100%
Family planning clinic; drugstores	Family planning clinic; drugstores	Family planning clinic; private doctor, special classes	Anywhere	Family planning clinic; private doctor, hospital; surgi-center

30 *Voluntary Childlessness*

Lisa Kay Rogers / Jeffry H. Larson

STUDY QUESTIONS

1. What are the factors that encourage remaining child-free?

2. What are the decision-making factors that influence this decision?

Although traditional attitudes toward having children are still prevalent in American society, it is anticipated that voluntary childlessness will become an increasingly attractive lifestyle for many American couples (Burgwyn, 1981; Faux, 1984). This kind of lifestyle is encouraged by effective and convenient birth-control methods, more alternatives to the motherhood role for women, the women's movement, and concern for overpopulation (Faux, 1984).

While the rates of voluntary childlessness are likely to increase in the future, factors affecting the childbearing decision have changed (Houseknecht, 1982, 1987). Many more women are in the labor force today and many are choosing lifetime careers outside the home. The need or lure for full-time employment for married women and the evidence that employed married women usually receive little help with household or childrearing tasks from their husbands are important considerations for contemporary women and may influence their decisions about childbearing (Burgwyn, 1981; Faux, 1984; Van Meter and Agronow, 1982). The choice to remain childless allows each spouse to focus on his/her career without the added responsibility and stress of raising children.

Although education and career aspirations and the lack of desire for children are important factors that affect the choice to remain childless, perhaps the most important factor is the woman's knowledge that she has a choice. People are usually more committed and willing to defend a choice that is consciously and rationally made (Potts, 1980).

Source: Lisa Kay Rogers and Jeffry H. Larson, "Voluntary Childlessness: A Review of the Literature and a Model of the Childlessness Decision." *Family Perspective* 22:1 (1988). Reprinted by permission.

Since voluntary childlessness will likely increase in the future as more women work outside the home and take advantage of options to the motherhood role (Burgwyn, 1981; Faux, 1984), it is important to understand the decision-making process of the voluntarily childless and the unique stressors these couples face. Thus, the purpose of this study was to review the empirical research literature on voluntary childlessness and to develop a model of the decision-making process. It was anticipated that the model can serve to identify factors that are involved in the decision-making process and thereby contribute to both the research and educational concerns related to the childlessness decision.

REVIEW OF THE LITERATURE

For the purpose of this study, *voluntary childlessness* refers to couples or individuals who are physiologically able to have children but prefer not to have children. This review includes studies of the lifestyle, demographic and personal characteristics of the voluntarily childless couple, social pressures that affect the decision to be voluntarily childless, and decision-making dynamics.

Lifestyle and Demographic Characteristics of the Voluntarily Childless

Place of Residence. Several studies show that the incidence of voluntary childlessness is higher in urban areas than in rural areas (Burgwyn, 1981; Gustavus and Henley, 1971; Poston, 1976; Veevers, 1973b, 1979). One might expect that the availability of better medical care and a higher standard of living in urban areas compared to rural areas would tend to minimize involuntary childlessness in urban areas. Therefore, childlessness in urban areas is more likely to be voluntary. Urban communities may be more conducive to voluntary childlessness than rural areas because the social norms in urban areas tend to be less traditional and urban areas offer women more opportunities to attend college and work full-time. There is no clear reason to expect systematic differences in fertility between urban and rural populations; hence, the relationship between voluntary childlessness and place of residence is not fully understood.

Education and Career. Voluntary childlessness appears to be related to the wife's education level. In general, the more highly educated a woman is, the more likely she is to be voluntarily childless (Barnett and MacDonald, 1976; Bram, 1984; Feldman, 1981; Gustavus and Henley, 1971; Macklin, 1980; Rao, 1974; Veevers, 1973b). Many women who pursue an advanced education delay or postpone marriage and childbearing. This delay in childbearing may continue after college if the occupation of the husband and/or wife becomes more important and satisfying than the prospects of having children (Gustavus and Henley, 1971; Hoffman and Manis, 1979; Houseknecht, 1982; Rao, 1974; Veevers, 1973b, 1979). Some wives may also consider the problems involved in juggling careers and childrearing simultaneously and decide they cannot cope with both stressors (Burgwyn, 1981; Feldman, 1981; Martin and Martin, 1984; Myers-Walls, 1984; Veevers, 1979).

A woman who is college educated is not only more likely to be working but also probably has a higher-paying job than a less-educated woman. Wives who are employed have substantially higher rates of childlessness than housewives (Barnett and MacDonald, 1976; Bram, 1984; Macklin, 1980; Pohlman, 1970; Ramu, 1985; Veevers, 1979). Voluntarily childless wives tend to have professional careers (Bram, 1984; Gustavus and Henley, 1971; Poston, 1976; Rao, 1974; Veevers, 1979). For these high-achieving women committed to a fulltime career, voluntary childlessness may be seen as a career-facilitating decision (Bottinelli, 1976; Burgwyn, 1981; Faux, 1984; Harper, 1980; Movius, 1976). Seeking an education and a career may be either a cause or an effect of voluntary childlessness, but the exposure to different lifestyles and values gained through an education and career may expose one to the voluntarily childless lifestyle and, therefore, influence a woman to choose childlessness.

Feldman (1981) found no differences between the education and occupation levels of childless husbands and fathers. This lack of a difference for husbands may be partially due to husbands' traditional belief that "she has the children." Hence, they may be more willing to let her make the decision about childbearing (Guttentag and Secord, 1983).

Age at Marriage and Length of Marriage Without Children. A factor related to higher education, career attainment, and childlessness is age at first marriage. The older a person is at first marriage, the more likely that he/she is to be highly educated, career-oriented, and voluntarily childless (Burgwyn, 1981; Macklin, 1980; Veevers, 1979). Age at marriage influences the childlessness decision in that the older a woman is when she marries, the more likely it is that she has established a childless lifestyle and the fewer the number of fertile years she has left before menopause (Burgwyn, 1981).

Length of marriage without children is also associated with childlessness (Rao, 1974). Couples who are childless after five years of marriage are likely to remain childless. A woman who has not had children by age 30 or after 10 years of marriage is most likely to remain childless for life (Gustavus and Henley, 1971; Poston, 1976; Rao, 1974; Veevers, 1979). For example, among childless wives ages 30–34, there is a 93.3% chance that they will never have a child (Poston, 1976).

While age at first marriage and length of marriage without children are associated with voluntary childlessness, whether they precede or are a result of voluntary childlessness is not known. It seems obvious that a woman who marries late has fewer fertile years of marriage; it is not obvious whether she is childless because she married late or married late because she did not want children.

Personal Characteristics of the Voluntarily Childless

Family-of-Origin Factors. Family background affects voluntary childlessness through birth order, childhood memories, and experiences (Burgwyn, 1981; Faux, 1984; Friday, 1977). Barnett and MacDonald (1976) conducted a survey of the membership of the National Organization for Nonparents to examine the personal characteristics of this group of voluntarily childless couples. They found 53% of the members were only-children or firstborn children. Ory's (1978) study of 27 voluntarily childless couples and 54 couples who were parents found 37% of the voluntarily childless individuals were only-children, and 25% were firstborn children.

Firstborn individuals are likely to have experienced the duties of child care as a child whereas only-born individuals are likely to have had little child-care experience. Ory (1978) reported 37% of the individuals with children in her sample had child-care experience in childhood, whereas 76% of the voluntarily childless couples reported childhood child-care responsibilities. Some reported resentment for having been put into a parenting role with their younger siblings. It also may be that the voluntarily childless individuals who had child-care experience as children know what to expect from children and are aware of the responsibility and work involved. This knowledge and experience may inhibit them from assuming child-care responsibilities as adults (Brougher, 1974; Faux, 1984; Harper, 1980, Ory, 1978; Veevers, 1979). In contrast, the majority of the parenting couples reported no childhood childcare experience.

Kaltreider and Margolis (1977) found that some voluntarily childless women have an early sense of identity as an "achieving daughter" rather than as a "little mother" in their family of origin. The 33 voluntarily childless women in their sample perceived child-care experiences as unpleasant and involving a loss of freedom. They also expressed a fear of becoming a bad mother. Potts' (1980) childless respondents feared they would recreate an unsatisfactory family life like their family of origin. The childless women also reported not wanting to subordinate their own needs to meet the needs of their children. This attitude was related to their perception that their mothers had given up their own needs to meet the needs of their children and then later resented the children.

Reading and Amatea (1986) suggest that some voluntarily childless women may have a relationship with their fathers characterized by powerful messages of endorsement of their performance in the world outside the family. Unlike past research, they did not find that voluntarily childless women reported a much less satisfactory relationship with their parents than childbearing women.

Negative family-of-origin experiences and memories precede an awareness of childlessness as a life choice. However, many people will have experiences similar to those of the voluntarily childless and still have children (Burgwyn, 1981). Therefore, these family background factors most likely interact with other variables to influence childlessness.

VALUES AND ATTITUDES

Voluntarily childless couples appear to have different values and attitudes than childbearing couples. Several studies show that compared to childbearing couples, voluntarily childless couples more frequently report no religious affiliation (Barnett and MacDonald, 1976; Benson, 1979; Feldman, 1981; Gustavus and Henley, 1971; Macklin, 1980; Rao, 1974; Renne, 1976). This lack of religious affiliation may help these couples avoid expectations to bear children that are inherent in most religions (Burgwyn, 1981). Compared to childbearing individuals, the voluntarily childless seem more likely to value individuality, autonomy, freedom from responsibilities, travel, personal goal attainment, intimacy, personal growth, egalitarian sex roles, a flexible, nonconforming lifestyle, career attainment, and companionship (Bram, 1984; Burgwyn, 1981; Callan, 1983; Faux, 1984; Hoffman and Manis, 1979; Houseknecht, 1977, 1982; Macklin, 1980; Movius, 1976).

Many voluntarily childless women have negative attitudes toward pregnancy, childbirth, and childrearing (Burgwyn, 1981; Faux, 1984; Gustavus and Henley, 1971; Reading and Amatea, 1986). Faux (1984) and Kaltreider and Margolis (1977) found voluntarily childless women view childrearing as unpleasant. However, choosing to be childless does not necessarily mean that one does not like children (Burgwyn, 1981). Some voluntarily childless couples are motivated not to have children because of perceived disadvantages of parenthood such as less spare time, less spare money, less time for extra activities, and interference by children in the marital relationship (Blake, 1979; Burgwyn, 1981; Goodbody, 1977; Hoffman and Manis, 1979; Pohlman, 1970).

Blake (1979) found men are more likely than women to think of the disadvantages of childlessness. Men are more likely than women to agree with these statements: "A woman is likely to feel unfulfilled unless she becomes a mother" and "Childless couples are more likely to lead empty lives than couples with children."

For the woman who values a full-time career more than having children or simply does not want children, the decision to remain childless may be perceived as a liberating and growth-promoting choice (Burgwyn, 1981; Faux, 1984; Goodbody, 1977). For non-college-educated women, the value of children is more likely to be to give life more meaning and more status (Hoffman and Manis, 1979). Bearing children is important to their self-esteem. The value of having children may also be heightened by a lack of perceived alternatives to the motherhood role (e.g., college).

Sex-role attitudes and voluntary childlessness have been extensively studied (Houseknecht, 1987; Russo, 1979). Compared to parents, the childless are more likely to be egalitarian in decision-making processes and in doing housework (Bram, 1984). They are less conventional, more androgynous, and place a higher value on masculine traits such as independence (Macklin, 1980). Compared to fathers, childless men report they do more housework than fathers (Faux, 1984; Feldman, 1981; Holahan, 1983; Houseknecht, 1982). These differences may be partially due to the tendency for parenthood to foster more traditional sex-role attitudes in husbands and wives because of the division of labor inherent in the raising of children or due to the difference in education between the groups (Faux, 1984; Feldman, 1981).

In a review of 29 studies, Houseknecht (1987) listed the following most frequently reported rationales used by voluntarily childless couples: Freedom from child-care responsibilities/greater opportunity for self-fulfillment (79%), more satisfactory marital relationship (62%), female career considerations (55%), and monetary advantages (55%). Fewer respondents listed these rationales: Concern about population growth (38%), general dislike of children (38%), doubts about ability to parent (31%), concern about childbirth and recovery (24%), and concern for children, given world conditions (21%).

Many values and attitudes are learned in the family of origin. These values and attitudes are modified through life experiences, such as obtaining an education or working. The values associated with voluntary childlessness are the result of childhood and adult experiences and can affect whether one chooses to work, seek an advanced education, or be less traditional in one's marital roles. The relationship between these values and attitudes and the decision to remain childless is still not fully understood.

MARITAL SATISFACTION

The marital satisfaction of parents and nonparents has been the focus of several studies (Houseknecht, 1987). Research shows that marriages without children tend to be more satisfactory than marriages with children (Burgwyn, 1981; Campbell, 1975; Faux, 1984; Houseknecht, 1979a; Renne, 1976; Veevers, 1973b). It is not known how many childless couples view childlessness as one way of maintaining marital satisfaction or if their marriages become more satisfactory after the decision to remain childless is made. As with many of the above-mentioned factors, voluntary childlessness may precede or be the result of marital satisfaction. Marital satisfaction may also be influenced by career satisfaction and may interact with the decision to be voluntarily childless.

SOCIAL PRESSURES AFFECTING VOLUNTARY CHILDLESSNESS

Factors that Discourage Voluntary Childlessness. There are social norms in American society that influence couples to have children and, therefore, discourage voluntary childlessness. One states that married people should have children because they have a moral responsibility to procreate. Another expectation is that normal people should want children because of biological instincts (Campbell, 1975; Goodbody, 1977; Houseknecht, 1977; Kaltreider and Margolis, 1977; Ory, 1978; Poston, 1976; Ross and Kahan, 1983; Russo, 1979; Veevers, 1973b, 1975, 1979) and, hence, those who do not want children are assumed to be either physically or psychologically impaired (Veevers, 1975). Thus, the desire to have children is assumed to be universal, especially for women, and parenthood roles are assumed to be intrinsically rewarding. The fact that the percentage of couples who are childless remains low despite the availability of better contraception and more choices for women reflects in part the strength and endurance of these norms (Bram, 1984; Cook et al., 1982; Elman and Gilbert, 1984; Hoffman and Manis, 1979; Holahan,

1983; Houseknecht, 1982; Movius, 1976; Rossi, 1968; Veevers, 1973a, 1973b, 1975, 1979).

Factors that Encourage Voluntary Childlessness. There are factors that operate counter to the pronatalist attitudes found in American society and serve to promote less traditional lifestyles. A major social factor that encourages voluntary childlessness is the women's movement (Kearney, 1979). The women's movement promotes education and occupational attainment for women, egalitarian sex roles, individualism, awareness of issues, and the right to choose among alternatives (Faux, 1984). In general, the women's movement promotes a combination of mother, wife, and professional roles (Faux, 1984). The emphasis on choice and awareness of alternatives makes the women's movement an important positive factor in a woman's choice to remain childless (Barnett and MacDonald, 1976; Houseknecht, 1977). Concurrent with the women's movement has been the improvement of birth-control methods that allow a woman more choice in childbearing without a loss of freedom to fulfill her sexual needs (Burgwyn, 1981).

DECISION DYNAMICS OF THE VOLUNTARILY CHILDLESS

In the face of social pressure to bear children, it seems likely that there would be almost no voluntarily childless couples in American society. However, voluntarily childless couples do exist in our society and manage to maintain their alternative lifestyle with satisfaction (Campbell, 1975; Feldman, 1981; Houseknecht, 1987; Renne, 1976; Veevers, 1973b). Unfortunately, the process involved in the decision to remain childless has received little attention in the literature (Veevers, 1973b, 1974, 1979).

Awareness of Choice. Perhaps most basic in the decision to remain childless is an awareness that childbearing is a choice, not an inevitability (Burgwyn, 1981; Faux, 1984; Movius, 1976; Potts, 1980; Ross and Kahan, 1983; Veevers, 1975). Today, children are no longer biologically inevitable or economically necessary, and so perceived choice may now have a greater influence on whether or not a couple has children.

Although the choice to remain childless affects both spouses, the impact on the woman is more significant. Since the birth of a child does not affect the husband's life as much as his wife's life, the decision to remain childless may be less important to him (Hoffman and Manis, 1979) or he may prefer that his wife choose whether or not to have children (Van Meter and Agronow, 1982). Thus, for most couples the wife's preference usually takes precedence over her husband's desires (Houseknecht, 1982). Fortunately, most wives do not make the decision alone. Women usually consider the impact of their childbearing decision on others as well as on themselves (Holahan, 1983; Myers-Walls, 1984; Potts, 1980). Unfortunately, there is no way to try out being a parent—it is an irrevocable decision (Feldman, 1981; Potts, 1980; Rossi, 1968; Veevers, 1974, 1979).

A couple cannot make the choice to remain childless if they are not aware that this choice exists. In our society, the awareness of choice in childbearing is limited. Urban residence, advanced education, and pursuit of a career interact to make a person more aware of alternative lifestyles, including voluntary childlessness. Of course, a couple may also seek an advanced education and a career after they have chosen to remain childless as a result of personal values and attitudes and past family-of-origin experiences. Again, all these factors seem to interact together in the decision to remain voluntarily childless.

Timing of the Decision. Once an individual recognizes that childbearing is a choice, the timing of the decision becomes important (Benson, 1979; Burgwyn, 1981; Callan, 1983; Holahan, 1983; Houseknecht, 1979b; Veevers, 1979). Those individuals who make the decision about childbearing at a young age, independent of a spouse, and prior to marriage are called "early articulators," while those couples and individuals who decide through postponements are called "postponers" (Houseknecht, 1987; Macklin, 1980; Veevers, 1979). Barnett and MacDonald (1976) found that men and women usually make the decision to remain childless between the ages of 10 and 32. The average age for the decision is 22.5 years.

Benson (1979), Macklin (1980), and Veevers (1979) found as many as one-third of childless couples make the decision not to have children prior to marriage. Hence, not having children is an integral part of these couples' mate-selection process.

Callan (1983) studied 45 never-married women who wanted to remain childless and 45 never-married women who wanted to have children. All women were under 35 years of age and expected to marry in the future. In this sample, 53% of the voluntarily childless single women decided not to have children in high school, 31% decided in childhood, and 16% decided recently. In Ory's (1978) study, 9% of the voluntarily childless couples made the decision prior to engagement, 33% decided at engagement, 50% decided through postponements, 6% made no active decision, and 2% became pregnant accidentally. Ninety-two percent of the voluntarily childless couples reported they made an active childbearing choice whereas only 62.9% of the 54 couples with children said they made an active choice.

Childless couples who do not decide early in their relationship not to have children are usually pursuing activities such as continued education or career pursuits that promote the postponement of childbearing (Burgwyn, 1981; Goodbody, 1977; Holahan, 1983; Houseknecht, 1982; Veevers, 1979). In some instances, young wives do not decide to be childless but rather postpone childbearing until it becomes permanent (Goodbody, 1977; Veevers, 1979).

Cost of Raising Children. The cost of raising children is an important factor for some couples who choose not to have children (Burgwyn, 1981; Cook et al., 1982; Kimball and McCabe, 1981; Movius, 1976; Pohlman, 1970). Cook et al. (1982) found 50% of a sample of single college women chose family economic factors as a major reason not to have children.

The above-average income of voluntarily childless couples seems to undermine their concern with the cost of raising children (Faux, 1984). Childless couples may greatly exaggerate the cost of raising children in their attempt to have a more socially acceptable reason for not having children (Anonymous, 1979; Macklin, 1980). The cost of raising children may also include emotional costs, such as interference in the marital relationship by children or the postponement or neglect of one's own needs to provide for a child's needs (Faux, 1984; Potts, 1980).

The cost factor is interrelated with social factors, value and attitude factors, and lifestyle factors. The cost of raising children may be directly causal in the decision to remain childless or may simply be a socially acceptable explanation childless couples use for not having children.

Decision-Making Strategies. The few studies on decision making postulate several strategies for making the childless decision (Houseknecht, 1987). Goodbody (1977) found the decision to remain childless seemed to follow one of two patterns. The first pattern involved simply studying parenthood and nonparenthood and then deciding nonparenthood would be more comfortable. The second pattern consisted of a process that evolved gradually as a result of a series of postponements of childbearing.

Veevers (1979) suggests four strategies of postponement in the decision to be childless beginning with putting off childbearing until some objective was achieved like finishing school. In the second stage the couple becomes increasingly vague about when they want to have a child. In the third stage the couple begins to debate the pros and cons of parenthood. The final stage is the decision to never become parents.

Potts (1980) found childless couples in the process of deciding whether or not to have children are aware that the decision can be irrevocable and express fear at making a wrong choice. These couples talked to other couples with children about the changes made in the family to accommodate children and attempted to find out if these changes were viewed as worth it. Childless couples considered their immediate and long-term life goals and how these would be affected by the addition of a child.

However, Holahan's (1983) research suggests that such an "information search" may not be valuable to some women. He studied the relationship between women's perceptions of the manner in which the decision concerning childbearing was made and present life satisfaction. Life satisfaction was hypothesized to be related to a childbearing decision process involving an exhaustive information search about the effects of children on marriage and the individual. However, this relationship was not found. Nonmothers who expressed high life satisfaction utilized an active information search the least. High-satisfaction mothers utilized the active information search more than low-satisfaction mothers. Childless women who were happiest with their decision not to have children experienced little conflict without doing an information search.

Many voluntarily childless women reach the decision not to have children through a process of successive postponements until they find they have established a child-free lifestyle (Faux, 1984). Such women may avoid the psychological conflict in making the decision by delaying consideration of the issues related to childbearing until children are no longer desired or possible to have. This avoidance of psychological conflict may explain the lack of information search by such women (Holahan, 1983).

Ory (1978) offered two explanations for the childbearing decision. The normative model states that childbearing decisions are the product of social norms and sanctions. According to this model, couples have children because of social norms and sanctions that promote childbearing. The structural model states that childbearing decisions are the result of traditional sociodemographic factors or psychosocial attitudes from one's family of origin that may operate counter to prevailing norms and may produce deviance. For instance, an individual who grows up in a family in which the children are neglected may adopt an attitude that people should not have children unless they can care for them in a healthy way. This attitude may be so conservative that it discourages the person from having children, even though such a decision goes against prevailing social norms.

Decision-making strategies are not directly related to the decision to remain childless itself but are reflections of the values, attitudes, and personalities of the couple making the childbearing decision and may affect the satisfaction a couple feels about their decision not to have children. No one pattern seems more prevalent or well studied than any other; hence, decision-making strategies do not appear to be a strong factor affecting the decision to remain childless.

Social Support for Voluntary Childlessness. It is important for childless women to have a reference group and/or support group to help them cope with negative social sanctions that are a result of choosing to be voluntarily childless (Houseknecht, 1982). For the voluntarily childless, a reference group may be difficult to find in society. Houseknecht (1977) found 60% of 27 single, undergraduate women wishing to remain childless had some degree of reference group support for their childless decision. Although the voluntarily childless may be sufficiently autonomous to remain relatively unaffected by external pressures, social support still appears to be a key factor in being able to maintain the decision to remain childless (Faux, 1984; Houseknecht, 1977).

An important source of support for a voluntarily childless woman is her husband. A childless wife's self-esteem, coping effectiveness, and resistance to social pressure are all related to having a husband who concurs with his wife's decision to remain childless (Callan, 1983; Elman and Gilbert, 1984; Faux, 1984; Veevers, 1975, 1979).

Social support for the childless lifestyle may function to make one aware of voluntary childlessness as a lifestyle choice. Or, support may be influential in helping a couple maintain their decision to be childless. Once a couple has chosen not to have children, their support group may shrink to include more people who support voluntary childlessness, thereby reducing negative input regarding childlessness. The exact relationship between social support and voluntary childlessness is not well understood.

SUMMARY

An examination of the research literature on voluntary childlessness reveals a variety of factors that influence couples to remain childless. These include lifestyle and demographic characteristics such as place of residence, education level, occupation, income, age at marriage, and length of marriage. Personal characteristics include birth order, family background, values and attitudes, and marital satisfaction. Social pressures that discourage voluntary childlessness include pronatalist norms, negative stereotypes, and social sanctions. Factors that encourage voluntary childlessness include the women's movement and the improvement in birth-control methods. Finally, there are decision-making factors that influence the decision to be voluntarily childless. These include an awareness of childbearing choice, the timing of the childbearing decision, and the presence of social support. . . .

REFERENCES

Anonymous. (1979). "The parenthood decision." The Family Planner 10 (1):1–5

Barnett, L. and MacDonald, R. (1976). "The study of the membership of the National Organization for Nonparents." Social Biology 23:297–310.

Benson, D. (1979). "The intentionally childless couple." USA Today 107, 2401:45–47.

Blake, J. (1979). "Is zero preferred? American attitudes toward childlessness in the 1970s." Journal of Marriage and the Family 41:245–259.

Bottinelli, R. (1976). "Measuring motivational factors affecting birth planning decisions: an exploratory study." Dissertation Abstracts International 37:1426B.

Bram, S. (1984). "Voluntarily childless women: traditional or nontraditional?" Sex Roles 10 (3⁄4):195–206.

Brougher, T. (1974). "Women's attitudes about motherhood." Dissertation Abstracts International 35:1037–1038B.

Burgwyn, D. (1981). Marriage Without Children. New York: Harper and Row.

Calhoun, L. and Selby, J. (1980). "Voluntary childlessness, involuntary childlessness, and having children: a study of social perceptions." Family Relations 29:181–183.

Callan, V. (1983). "Childlessness and partner selection." Journal of Marriage and the Family 45 (1):181–186.

Campbell, A. (1975). "The American way of mating: marriage si, children only maybe." Psychology Today 8 (12):37–43.

Cook, A., West, J., and Hamner, T. (1982). "Changes in attitudes toward parenting among college women: 1972 and 1979 samples." Family Relations 31:109–113.

Elman, M. and Gilbert, L. (1984). "Coping strategies for role conflict in married professional women with children." Family Relations 33:317–327.

Faux, M. (1984). Childless by Choice. New York: Anchor Press/Doubleday.

Feldman, H. (1981). "A comparison of intentional parent and intentionally childless couples." Journal of Marriage and the Family 43 (3):593–600.

Friday, N. (1977). My Mother/My Self. New York: Delacorte.

Goodbody, S. (1977). "The psychosocial implications of voluntary childlessness." Social Casework 58 (7):426–434.

Gustavus, S. and Henley, J. (1971). "Correlates of voluntary childlessness in a select population." Social Biology 18 (3):277–284.

Guttentag, M. and Secord, P. (1983). The Sex Ratio Question. Beverly Hills: Sage Publications, Inc.

Harper, K. (1980). The Childfree Alternative. Brattleboro, VT: Stephen Green Press.

Hastings, D. and Robinson, G. (1974). "Incidence of childlessness for United States women, cohorts born 1891–1945." Social Biology 21 (2):178–184.

Hoffman, L. and Manis, J. (1979). "The value of children in the United States: a new approach to the study of fertility." Journal of Marriage and the Family 41:538–596.

Holahan, C. (1983). "The relationship between information search in the childbearing decision and life satisfaction for parents and nonparents." Family Relations 32:527–535.

Houseknecht, S. (1977). "Reference group support for voluntary childlessness: evidence for conformity." Journal of Marriage and the Family 39 (2):285–294.

(1979a). "Childlessness and marital adjustment." Journal of Marriage and the Family 41 (2):259–265.

(1979b). "Timing of the decision to remain voluntarily childless: evidence for continuous socialization." Psychology of Women Quarterly 4:81–96.

(1982). "Voluntary childlessness in the 1980s: a significant increase?" Marriage and Family Review 5 (2):51–69.

(1987). "Voluntary childlessness." In M. Sussman and S. Steinmetz (eds.), Handbook of Marriage and the Family. New York: Plenum Press.

Kaltreider, N., and Margolis, A. (1977). "Childless by choice: a clinical study." American Journal of Psychiatry 134 (2):279–282.

Kearney, H. R. (1979). "Feminist challenges to the social structure and sex roles." Psychology of Women Quarterly 4:16–31.

Kimball, K., and McCabe, M. (1981). "Should we have children? A decision-making group for couples." The Personnel and Guidance Journal 60 (3):153–156.

Macklin, E. (1980). "Nontraditional family forms: a decade of research." Journal of Marriage and the Family 42 (4):905–922.

Martin, D., and Martin, M. (1984). "Selected attitudes toward marriage and family life of college students." Family Relations 33:293–300.

Movius, M. (1976). "Voluntary childlessness—the ultimate liberation." The Family Coordinator 25:57–63.

Myers-Walls, J. (1984). "Balancing multiple role responsibilities during the transition to parenthood." Family Relations 33:267–271.

Ory, M. (1978). "The decision to parent or not: normative and structural components." Journal of Marriage and the Family 40 (3):531–539.

Pohlman, E. (1970). "Childlessness, intentional and unintentional." The Journal of Nervous and Mental Disease 14 (1):2–12.

Poston, D. (1976). "Characteristics of voluntarily and involuntarily childless wives." Social Biology 23 (3):198–209.

Potts, L. (1980). "Considering parenthood: group support for a critical life decision." American Journal of Orthopsychiatry 50 (4):629–638.

Ramu, G. (1985). "Voluntarily childless and parental couples: a comparison of their lifestyle characteristics." Lifestyles: A Journal of Changing Patterns 7:130–145.

Rao, S. (1974). "A comparative study of childlessness and never-pregnant status." Journal of Marriage and the Family 36 (1):149–157.

Reading, J. and Amatea, E. S. (1986). "Role deviance on role diversification: reassessing the psychosocial factors affecting the parenthood advice of career-oriented women." Journal of Marriage and the Family 48:255–260.

Renne, K. (1976). "Childlessness, health, and marital satisfaction." Social Biology 23 (3):183–197.

Ross, J., and Kahan, J. (1983). "Children by chance: the perceived effects of parity." Sex Roles 9 (1):69–77.

Rossi, A. (1968). "Transition to parenthood." Journal of Marriage and the Family 30:26–39.

Russo, N. F. (1979). "Overview: sex roles, fertility and the motherhood mandate." Psychology of Women Quarterly 4:7–15.

Van Meter, M., and Agronow, S. (1982). "The stress of multiple roles: the case for role strain among married college women." Family Relations 31:131–138.

Veevers, J. (1973a). "The social meanings of parenthood." Psychiatry 36:291–310.

(1973b). "Voluntary childlessness: a neglected area of family study." The Family Coordinator 22:199–205.

(1974). "Voluntary childless and social policy: an alternative view." The Family Coordinator 23:397–406.

(1975). "The moral careers of voluntarily childless wives: notes on the defense of a variant world view." The Family Coordinator 24:473–487.

(1979). "Voluntary childlessness: a review of issues and evidence." Marriage and Family Review 2 (2):3–26.

8 *Living with Children*

Moving from the question of whether to have children to the actuality of living with children is the next step in the examination of family development. The transition to parenthood, according to Alice Rossi in the first article of Chapter 8, is unique from other roles in that it is abrupt—from not being to being a parent; irrevocable—it cannot be given back; total—no respite from the chores, and mostly unprepared for. It is this latter item that leads to the belief that this "crucial social unit, the family, is assembled primarily by sheer dumb luck" (Duggan 1981). That is, society expects the family to produce well-educated, healthy, law-abiding citizens and yet makes no requirements of parents to undergo training for this role (Duggan 1981). The issue of how to raise children would appear to be twofold: What are the tasks of parenthood and how can one best cope with them?

Parenting requires five major tasks:

1. providing for the child's physical well-being in regard to shelter, nutrition, and medical care;

2. promoting emotional well-being and normal personality development by helping the child to develop a sense of belonging and self-esteem by making the child feel loved, wanted and valued;

3. encouraging optimum intellectual and creative potential by understanding the relationship between such potential and the child's physical and emotional environment;

4. developing acceptable social relations by learning about opposite-sex social relations and adult roles as well as learning about such concepts as money, success, work, and future goals; and

5. teaching moral values, that is, society's "rules," which is in line with the social relations task.

(Golanty & Harris 1982)

However, parents should understand that within the biological and personal qualities related to child development, parental power is limited to only two of them, according to Jerome Kagan in the second article of this chapter. Also, as noted, parents are often ill-prepared and lack consistent guidelines for fulfilling these tasks. Michael Meyerhoff and Burton White, in the third article of Chapter 8, indicate some of the means needed for parents to deal with these important needs of development. Basically, they include:

a. being aware of the child's capabilities at various stages in its development,

b. modeling appropriate behavior,

c. managing the environment for stimulation and safety,

d. establishing effective communication, and

e. setting standards and limits as well as using discipline and reward consistently.

It is this last item that has produced much debate of late since some people see in the term "discipline" a pseudonym for abuse. Child abuse is one manifestation of the violence ingrained in all stages of family relations. Though better reporting has made abuse more visible, it is clear that underreporting is still a problem. The different forms of abuse include physical abuse, neglect, emotional abuse, and sexual abuse. Each has distinctive characteristics and produces distinct symptoms in its victims. Since a positive relationship exists between corporal punishment and other forms of family violence, there would appear to be a need to remove the sanctions and general acceptance of physical punishment for disciplining children (Steinmetz 1977). It is this theme that Joanne Guinn has chosen to deal with in the last article of this chapter. Her thesis is that there is a right way for disciplining—a needed factor in socialization of children. Other helpful factors in eliminating violence would be, as noted in Chapter 5, the recognition that conflict is normal and can be settled by negotiation and compromise, that violence is not acceptable at any time, and the understanding that the "home is the castle" concept of noninterference means responding to abuse only after the fact.

It is this last item that returns us to an earlier theme in this chapter—the fact that many parents are deficient in basic child-rearing skills. It is for this reason that the White House Conference on Families recommended that the government acknowledge that family life education can play an important role in strengthening families and providing the means necessary to teach such factors as human development, marriage and the family, parenting education and child-care skills, interpersonal relationships, communication and decision making, and human sexuality (Alexander 1981). It is only in this manner that child welfare can move away from the secondary stage of preventing further maltreatment to the primary stage of prevention.

REFERENCES

1. Alexander, S. T. 1981. "Implications of the White House Conference on Families for Family Life Education." *Family Relations* (October).
2. Golanty, E., & B. B. Harris. 1982. *Marriage and Family Life*. Boston: Houghton Mifflin.
3. Steinmetz, S. K. 1977. "The Use of Force for Resolving Family Conflict: The Training Ground for Abuse." *The Family Coordinator* (January).

31 *Transition to Parenthood*

Alice S. Rossi

STUDY QUESTIONS

1. Explain briefly the four unique features of the parenthood role.
2. What are the four factors involved in the lack of preparation for parenthood?

FROM CHILD TO PARENT: AN EXAMPLE

What is unique about this perspective on parenthood is the focus on the adult parent rather than the child. Until quite recent years, concern in the behavioral sciences with the parent-child relationship has been confined almost exclusively to the child. . . .

The very different order of questions which emerge when the parent replaces the child as the primary focus of analytic attention can best be shown with an illustration. Let us take, for our example, the point Benedek makes that the child's need for mothering is *absolute* while the need of an adult woman to mother is *relative*. From a concern for the child, this discrepancy in need leads to an analysis of the impact on the child of separation from the mother or inadequacy of mothering. Family systems that provide numerous adults to care for the young child can make up for this discrepancy in need between mother and child, which may be why ethnographic accounts give little evidence of postpartum depression following childbirth in simpler societies. Yet our family system of isolated households, increasingly distant from kinswomen to assist in mothering, requires that new mothers shoulder total responsibility for the infant precisely for that stage of the child's life when his need for mothering is far in excess of the mother's need for the child.

Source: Alice S. Rossi, "Transition to Parenthood." *Journal of Marriage and the Family*, February 1968, pp. 26–39. Copyrighted 1968 by the National Council on Family Relations, 3989 Central Ave., N.E., Suite 550, Minneapolis, MN 55421. Reprinted by permission.

From the perspective of the mother, the question has therefore become: what does maternity deprive her of? Are the intrinsic gratifications of maternity sufficient to compensate for shelving or reducing a woman's involvement in nonfamily interests and social roles? The literature on maternal deprivation cannot answer such questions, because the concept, even in the careful specification Yarrow has given it, has never meant anything but the effect on the child of various kinds of insufficient mothering. Yet what has been seen as a failure or inadequacy of individual women may in fact be a failure of the society to provide institutionalized substitutes for the extended kin to assist in the care of infants and young children. It may be that the role requirements of maternity in the American family system extract diversified interests and social expectations concerning adult life. Here, as at several points in the course of this paper, familiar problems take on a new and suggestive research dimension when the focus is on the parent rather than the child. . . .

ROLE-CYCLE STAGES

A discussion of the impact of parenthood upon the parent will be assisted by two analytic devices. One is to follow a comparative approach, by asking in what basic structural ways the parental role differs from other primary adult roles. The marital and occupational roles will be used for this comparison. A second device is to specify the phases in the development of a social role. If the total life span may be said to have a cycle, each stage with its unique tasks, then by analogy a role may be said to have a cycle and each stage in that role cycle to have its unique tasks and problems of adjustment. Four broad stages of a role cycle may be specified:

1. Anticipatory Stage

All major adult roles have a long history of anticipatory training for them, since parental and school socialization of children is dedicated precisely to this task of producing the kind of competent adult valued by the culture. For our present purposes, however, [we use] a narrower conception of the marital role, pregnancy in the case of the parental role, and the last stages of highly vocationally oriented schooling or on-the-job apprenticeship in the case of an occupational role.

2. Honeymoon Stage

This is the time period immediately following the full assumption of the adult role. The inception of this stage is more easily defined than its termination. In the case of the marital role, the honeymoon stage extends from the marriage ceremony itself through the literal honeymoon and on through an unspecified and individually varying period of time. Raush has caught this stage of the marital role in his description of the "psychic honeymoon": that extended postmarital period when, through close intimacy and joint activity, the couple can explore each other's capacities and limitations. I shall arbitrarily consider the onset of pregnancy as marking the end of the honeymoon stage of the marital role. This stage of the parental role may involve an equivalent psychic honeymoon, that post-childbirth period during which, through intimacy and prolonged contact, an attachment between parent and child is laid down. There is a crucial difference, however, from the marital role in this stage. A woman knows her husband as a unique real person when she enters the honeymoon stage of marriage. A good deal of preparatory adjustment on a firm reality base is possible during the engagement period which is not possible in the equivalent pregnancy period. Fantasy is not corrected by the reality of a specific individual child until the birth of the child. The "quickening" is psychologically of special significance to women precisely because it marks the first evidence of a real baby rather than a purely fantasized one. On this basis alone there is greater interpersonal adjustment and learning during the honeymoon stage of the parental role than of the marital role.

3. Plateau Stage

This is the protracted middle period of a role cycle during which the role is fully exercised. Depending on the specific problem under analysis, one would obviously subdivide this large plateau stage further. For my present purposes it is not necessary to do so, since my focus is on the earlier anticipatory and honeymoon stages of the parental role and the overall impact of parenthood on adults.

4. Disengagement-Termination Stage

This period immediately pecedes and includes the actual termination of the role. Marriage ends with the death of the spouse or, just as definitively, with separation and divorce. A unique characteristic of parental-role termination is the fact that it is not closely marked by any specific act but is an attenuated process of termination with little cultural prescription about when the authority and obligations of a parent end. Many parents, however, experience the marriage of the child as a psychological termination of the active parental role.

UNIQUE FEATURES OF PARENTAL ROLE

With this role-cycle suggestion as a broader framework, we can narrow our focus to what are the unique and most salient features of the parental role. In doing so, special attention will be given to two further questions: (1) the impact of social changes over the past few decades in facilitating or complicating the transition to and experience of parenthood and (2) the new interpretations or new research suggested by the focus on the parent rather than the child.

1. Cultural Pressure to Assume the Role

On the level of cultural values, men have no freedom of choice where work is concerned: They must work to secure their status as adult men.

The equivalent for women has been maternity. There is considerable pressure upon the growing girl and young woman to consider maternity necessary for a woman's fulfillment as an individual and to secure her status as an adult.[1]

This is not to say there are no fluctuations over time in the intensity of the cultural pressure to parenthood. During the depression years of the 1930s, there was more widespread awareness of the economic hardships parenthood can entail, and many demographic experts believe there was a great increase in illegal abortions during those years. Bird has discussed the dread with which a suspected pregnancy was viewed by many American women in the 1930s. Quite a different set of pressures were at work during the 1950s, when the general societal tendency was toward withdrawal from active engagement with the issues of the larger society and a turning in to the gratifications of the private sphere of home and family life. Important in the background were the general affluence of the period and the expanded room and ease of child rearing that go with suburban living. For the past five years, there has been a drop in the birth rate in general, fourth and higher-order births in particular. During this same period there has been increased concern and debate about women's participation in politics and work, with more women now returning to work rather than conceiving the third or fourth child.[2]

2. Inception of the Parental Role

The decision to marry and the choice of a mate are voluntary acts of individuals in our family system. Engagements are therefore consciously considered, freely entered, and freely terminated if increased familiarity decreases, rather than increases, intimacy and commitment to the choice. The inception of a pregnancy, unlike the engagement, is not always a voluntary decision, for it may be the unintended consequence of a sexual act that was recreative in intent rather than procreative. Secondly, and again unlike the engagement, the termination of a pregnancy is not socially sanctioned, as shown by current resistance to abortion-law reform.

---

[1] The greater the cultural pressure to assume a given adult social role, the greater will be the tendency for individual negative feelings toward that role to be expressed covertly. Men may complain about a given job, not about working per se, and hence their work dissatisfactions are often displaced to the nonwork sphere, as psychosomatic complaints or irritation and dominance at home. An equivalent displacement for women of the ambivalence many may feel toward maternity is to dissatisfactions with the homemaker role.

[2] When it is realized that a mean family size of 3.5 would double the population in 40 years, while a mean of 2.5 would yield a stable population in the same period, the social importance of withholding praise for procreative prowess is clear. At the same time, a drop in the birth rate may reduce the number of unwanted babies born, for such a drop would mean more efficient contraceptive usage and a closer correspondence between desired and attained family size.

The implication of this difference is a much higher probability of unwanted pregnancies than of unwanted marriages in our family system. Coupled with the ample clinical evidence of parental rejection and sometimes cruelty to children, it is all the more surprising that there has not been more consistent research attention to the problem of *parental satisfaction*, as there has for long been on *marital satisfaction* or *work satisfaction*. Only the extreme iceberg tip of the parental satisfaction continuum is clearly demarcated and researched, as in the growing concern with "battered babies." Cultural and psychological resistance to the image of a nonnurturant woman may afflict social scientists as well as the American public.

The timing of a first pregnancy is critical to the manner in which parental responsibilities are joined to the marital relationship. The single most important change over the past few decades is extensive and efficient contraceptive usage, since this has meant for a growing proportion of new marriages, the possibility of and increasing preference for some postponement of childbearing after marriage. When pregnancy was likely to follow shortly after marriage, the major transition point in a woman's life was marriage itself. *This transition point is increasingly the first pregnancy rather than marriage.* It is accepted and increasingly expected that women will work after marriage, while household furnishings are acquired and spouses complete their advanced training or gain a foothold in their work. This provides an early marriage period in which the fact of a wife's employment presses for a greater egalitarian relationship between husband and wife in decision-making, commonality of experience, and sharing of household responsibilities.

The balance between individual autonomy and couple mutuality that develops during the honeymoon stage of such a marriage may be important in establishing a pattern that will later affect the quality of the parent-child relationship and the extent of sex-role segregation of duties between the parents. It is only in the context of a growing egalitarian base to the marital relationship that one could find, as Gavron has, a tendency for parents to establish more barriers between themselves and their children, a marital defense against the institution of parenthood as she describes it. This may eventually replace the typical coalition in more traditional families of mother and children against husband-father. . . .

There is one further significant social change that has important implications for the changed relationship between husband and wife: the increasing departure from an old pattern of role-inception phasing in which the young person first completed his schooling, then established himself in the world of work, then married and began his family. Marriage and parenthood are increasingly taking place *before* the schooling of the husband, and often of the wife, has been completed. An important reason for this trend lies in the fact that, during the same decades in which the average age of physical-sexual maturation has dropped, the average amount of education which young people obtain has been on the increase. Particularly for the college and graduate or professional school population, family roles are often assumed before the degrees needed to enter careers have been obtained. . . .

The major implication of this change is that more men and women are

ALICE S. ROSSI

achieving full status in family roles while they are still less than fully adult in status terms in the occupational system. Graduate students are, increasingly, men and women with full family responsibilities. Within the family many more husbands and fathers are still students, often quite dependent on the earnings of their wives to see them through their advanced training. No matter what the couple's desires and preferences are, this fact alone presses for more egalitarian relations between husband and wife, just as the adult family status of graduate students presses for more egalitarian relations between students and faculty.

3. Irrevocability

If marriages do not work out, there is now widespread acceptance of divorce and remarriage as a solution. The same point applies to the work world: we are free to leave an unsatisfactory job and seek another. But once a pregnancy occurs, there is little possibility of undoing the commitment to parenthood implicit in conception except in the rare instance of placing children for adoption. We can have ex-spouses and ex-jobs but not ex-children. This being so, it is scarcely surprising to find marked differences between the relationship of a parent and one child and the relationship of the same parent with another child. If the culture does not permit pregnancy termination, the equivalent to giving up a child is psychological withdrawal on the part of the parent.

This taps an important area in which a focus on the parent rather than the child may contribute a new interpretive dimension to an old problem: the long history of interest, in the social sciences, in differences among children associated with their sex-birth-order position in their sibling set. . . .

Some birth-order research stresses the influence of sibs upon other sibs, as in Koch's finding that second-born boys with an older sister are more feminine than second-born boys with an older brother. A similar sib-influence interpretation is offered in the major common finding of birth-order correlates, that sociability is greater among last-borns and achievement among first-borns. It has been suggested that last-borns use social skills to increase acceptance by their older sibs or are more peer-oriented because they receive less adult stimulation from parents. The tendency of first-borns to greater achievement has been interpreted in a corollary way, as a reflection of early assumption of responsibility for younger sibs, greater adult stimulation during the time the oldest was the only child in the family, and the greater significance of the first-born for the larger kinship network of the family.

Sociologists have shown increasing interest in structural family variables in recent years, a primary variable being family size. . . . The question posed is: what is the effect of growing up in a small family, compared with a large family, that is attributable to this group-size variable? Unfortunately, the theoretical point of departure for sociologists' expectations of the effect of the family-size variables is the Durkheim-Simmel tradition of the differential effect of group size or population density upon members or inhabitants. In the case of the family, however, this overlooks the very important fact that family size is determined by the key figures *within* the group, i.e., the parents. To find that children in small families differ from children in large families is not simply due to the impact of group size upon individual members but to the very different involvement of the parent with the children and to relations between the parents themselves in small versus large families.

An important clue to a new interpretation can be gained by examining family size from the perspective of parental motivation toward having children. A small family is small for one of two primary reasons: either the parents wanted a small family and achieved their desired size, or they wanted a large family but were not able to attain it. In either case, there is a low probability of unwanted children. Indeed, in the latter eventuality they may take particularly great interest in the children they do have. Small families are therefore most likely to contain parents with a strong and positive orientation to each of the children they have. A large family, in contrast, is large either because the parents achieved the size they desired or because they have more children than they in fact wanted. Large families therefore have a higher probability than small families of including unwanted unloved children. Consistent with this are Nye's finding that adolescents in small families have better relations with their parents than those in large families, and Sears and Maccoby's finding that mothers of large families are more restrictive toward their children than mothers of small families.

This also means that last-born children are more likely to be unwanted than first-or middle-born children, particularly in large families. This is consistent with what is known of abortion patterns among married women, who typically resort to abortion only when they have achieved the number of children they want or feel they can afford to have. Only a small proportion of women faced with such unwanted pregnancies actually resort to abortion. *This suggests the possibility that the last-born child's reliance on social skills may be his device for securing the attention and loving involvement of a parent less positively predisposed to him than to his older siblings.*

In developing this interpretation, rather extreme cases have been stressed. Closer to the normal range of families in which even the last-born child was desired and planned for, there is still another element which may contribute to the greater sociability of the last-born child. Most parents are themselves aware of the greater ease with which they face the care of a third fragile newborn than the first; clearly parental skills and confidence are greater with last-born children than the first-born children. But this does not mean that the attitude of the parent is more positive toward the care of the third child than the first. There is no necessary correlation between skills in an area and enjoyment of that area. Searls found that older homemakers are *more* skillful in domestic tasks but experience *less* enjoyment of them than younger homemakers, pointing to a declining euphoria for a particular role with the passage of time. In the same way, older people rate their marriages as "very happy" less often than younger people do. It is perhaps culturally and psychologically more difficult to face the possibility that women may find less enjoyment of the maternal role with the passage of time, though women themselves know the difference between the romantic expectation concerning child care and the incorporation of the first baby into the household and the more realistic expectation and sharper assessment of their own abilities to do an adequate job of mothering as they face a third confinement. Last-born children may experience not only less verbal stimulation from the parents than first-born children but also less prompt and enthusiastic response to their demands— from feeding and diaper changes as infants to requests for stories read at three or a college education at eighteen—simply because the parents experience less intense gratification from the parent role with the third child than they did with the first. The child's response to this might well be to cultivate winning, pleasing manners in early childhood that blossom as charm and sociability in later life, showing both a greater need to be loved and greater pressure to seek approval.

One last point may be appropriately developed at this juncture. Mention was made earlier that for many women the personal outcome of experience in the parent role is not a higher level of maturation but the negative outcome of a depressed sense of self-worth, if not actual personality deterioration. There is considerable evidence that this is more prevalent than we recognize. On a qualitative level, a close reading of the portrait of the working-class wife in Rainwater, Newsom, Komarovsky, Gavron, or Zweig gives little suggestion that maternity has provided these women with opportunities for personal growth and development. So, too, Cohen notes with some surprise that in her sample of middle-class educated couples, as in Pavenstadt's study of lower-income women in Boston, there were more emotional difficulties and lower levels of maturation among multiparous women than primiparous women. On a more extensive sample basis, in Gurin's survey of Americans viewing their mental health, as in Bradburn's reports on happiness, single men are less happy and less active than single women, but among the married respondents the women are unhappier, have more problems, feel inadequate as parents, have a more negative and passive outlook on life, and show a more negative self-image. All of these characteristics increase with age among men. While it may be true, as Gurin argues, that women are more introspective and hence more attuned to the psychological facets of experience than men are, this point does not account for the fact that the things which the women report are all on the negative side; few are on the positive side, indicative of euphoric sensitivity and pleasure. The possibility must be faced, and at some point researched, that women lose ground in personal development and self-esteem during the early and middle years of adulthood, whereas men gain ground in these respects during the same years. The retention of a high level of self-esteem may depend upon the adequacy of earlier preparation for major adult roles in the occupational system, as it does for those women who opt to participate significantly in the work world. Training in the qualities and skills needed for family roles in contemporary society may be inadequate for both sexes, but the lowering of self-esteem occurs only among women because their primary adult roles are within the family system.

4. Preparation for Parenthood

Four factors may be given special attention on the question of what preparation American couples bring to parenthood.

(a) Paucity of preparation. Our educational system is dedicated to the cognitive development of the young, and our primary teaching approach is the pragmatic one of learning by doing. How much one knows and how well he can apply what he knows are the standards by which the child is judged in school, as the employee is judged at work. The child can learn by doing in such subjects as science, mathematics, art work, or shop, but not in the subjects more relevant to successful family life: sex, home maintenance, child care, interpersonal competence, and empathy. If the home is deficient in training in these areas, the child is left with no preparation for a major segment of his adult life. A doctor facing his first patient in private practice has treated numerous patients under close supervision during his internship, but probably a majority of American mothers approach maternity with no previous child-care experience beyond sporadic baby-sitting, perhaps a course in child psychology, or occasional care of younger siblings.

(b) Limited learning during pregnancy. A second important point makes adjustment to parenthood potentially more stressful than marital adjustment. This is the lack of any realistic training for parenthood during the anticipatory stage of pregnancy. By contrast, during the engagement period preceding marriage, an individual has opportunities to develop the skills and make the adjustments which ease the transition to marriage. Through discussions of values and life goals, through sexual experimentation, shared social experiences as an engaged couple with friends and relatives, and planning and furnishing an apartment, the engaged couple can make considerable progress in developing mutuality in advance of the marriage itself. No such headstart is possible in the case of pregnancy. What preparation exists is confined to reading, consultation with friends and parents, discussions between husband and wife, and a minor nesting phase in which a place and the equipment for a baby are prepared in the household.[3]

(c) Abruptness of transition. Thirdly, the birth of a child is not followed by any gradual taking on of responsibility, as in the case of a professional work role. It is as if the woman shifted from a graduate student to a full professor with little intervening apprenticeship experience of slowly increasing responsibility. The new mother starts out immediately on 24-hour duty, with responsibility for a fragile and mysterious infant totally dependent on her care.

If marital adjustment is more difficult for very young brides than more mature ones, adjustment to motherhood may be even more difficult. A woman can adapt a passive dependence on a husband and still have a successful

---

[3] During the period when marriage was the critical transition in the adult woman's life rather than pregnancy, a good deal of anticipatory "nesting" behavior took place from the time of conception. Now more women work through a considerable portion of the first pregnancy, and such nesting behavior as exists may be confined to a few shopping expeditions or baby showers, thus adding to the abruptness of the transition and the difficulty of adjustment following the birth of a first child.

ALICE S. ROSSI

marriage, but a young mother with strong dependency needs is in for difficulty in maternal adjustment, because the role precludes such dependency. This situation was well described in Cohen's study in a case of a young wife with a background of coed popularity and a passive dependent relationship to her admired and admiring husband, who collapsed into restricted incapacity when faced with the responsibilities of maintaining a home and caring for a child.

(d) Lack of guidelines to successful parenthood. If the central task of parenthood is the rearing of children to become the kind of competent adults valued by the society, then an important question facing any parent is what he or she specifically can do to create such a competent adult. This is where the parent is left with few or no guidelines from the expert. Parents can readily inform themselves concerning the young infant's nutritional, clothing, and medical needs and follow the general prescription that a child needs loving physical contact and emotional support. Such advice may be sufficient to produce a healthy, happy, and well-adjusted preschooler, but adult competency is quite another matter.

In fact, the adults who do "succeed" in American society show a complex of characteristics as children that current experts in child-care would evaluate as "poor" to "bad." Biographies of leading authors and artists, as well as the more rigorous research inquiries of creativity among architects or scientists, do not portray childhoods with characteristics currently endorsed by mental-health and child-care authorities. Indeed, there is often a predominance of tension in childhood family relations and traumatic loss rather than loving parental support, intense channeling of energy in one area of interest rather than an all-round profile of diverse interests, and social withdrawal and preference for loner activities rather than gregarious sociability. Thus, the stress in current childbearing advice on a high level of loving support but a low level of discipline or restriction on the behavior of the child—the "developmental" family type as Duvall calls it—is a profile consistent with the focus on mental health, sociability, and adjustment. Yet, the combination of both high support and high authority on the part of parents is most strongly related to the child's sense of responsibility, leadership quality, and achievement level, as found in Bronfenbrenner's studies and that of Mussen and Distler.

Brim points out that we are a long way from being able to say just what parent-role prescriptions have what effect on the adult characteristics of the child. We know even less about how such parental prescriptions should be changed to adapt to changed conceptions of competency in adulthood. In such an ambiguous context, the great interest parents take in school reports on their children or the pediatrician's assessment of the child's developmental progress should be seen as among the few indices parents have of how well *they* are doing as parents.

32 The Powers and Limitations of Parents

Jerome Kagan

STUDY QUESTIONS

1. What are the universals of human development?

2. What are the personal qualities of child development?

This paper is about the mystery of human development. Because human development is of such concern to all of us, whether citizens or parents, we care about the facts that are true. We want certain beliefs to be valid, and we resist giving credence to facts we do not like.

Major changes have occurred in our views of family and child since the early 18th century. In the first place, historical changes made possible a large middle class that could afford to relieve women of the task of gathering food and so give them more time for leisure. As European cities grew and a larger middle class emerged, three beliefs—which are still with us—became established. In my view these beliefs are stronger now than they were two-and-a-half centuries ago.

The first belief is that the experiences of the infant in the family set the course of the child's development, and once these original qualities are established they are difficult to change. The second belief is that the most critical ingredient for the child's psychological growth is the mother's love. And beginning in the late 19th century this love had to be physical—embraces and kisses—rather than only verbal affirmations. The third belief is that the mother is the central figure in the child's development.

Although each of these beliefs might be true, the scientific basis for their truth remains meager. If a petit jury were to decide on the truth of these statements, I suspect they would determine that they should be tried in the court of science to see how innocent or guilty they are.

Source: Jerome Kagan, *The Powers and Limitations of Parents*. Austin, TX: Hogg Foundation for Mental Health, 1986. Reprinted by permission.

We now ask why these three beliefs grew so strong. Of the many revelant factors, I suggest that three were most central. I've already mentioned one—namely, the rise of a powerful middle class that did not need female labor. However, women needed an assignment, and all citizens agreed on one that was important. Total devotion to raising the infant and child became the central mission for the married woman. As a result, the dignity of women in the West rose considerably. European and American women have more dignity in this century, and especially during the last two decades, than they ever had in any society in the past.

An important corollary of the rise in dignity was the awarding of an enhanced importance to love and affection. As I read history, it appears that whenever a society celebrates women it also celebrates the moods and acts of love and affection.

The third factor involves the set of philosophical premises we call the Protestant tradition. The assumption that the mother was a central figure and that love should be in the family, not outside the family, was an important credo in the Protestant Reformation. Luther was troubled by the high rate of adultery in his society and urged men to select wives who would be not only good mothers but also attractive and gratifying love objects, as well. A final component of the Protestant credo is the imperative to train character. The task of training character belongs to the mother.

I trust you appreciate that the belief in the power of early experience, the significance of love, and the centrality of the mother cannot be as true as contemporary magazines and books imply. With so many other factors influencing the growing child, the assumptions that stem from these beliefs must be less valid than current ideology pretends.

TWO DEVELOPMENTAL STORIES

Human development has two different stories to tell. One describes the growth of the universal characteristics that are present in all human beings because humans possess a particular set of genes. Humans have a generative language, apes do not; humans experience guilt, shame, and pride; apes do not; humans create laws and mathematics, and apes do not. As long as a child is not locked in a closet or confined to a basement, he or she will resemble other children around the world. The reasons for this universality comprise an interesting story, especially to psychologists, psychiatrists, and pediatricians. The moral of the story is that regardless of the family in which a child grows, he or she will demonstrate some of these universal qualities.

The second plot, which is of greater interest to citizens, seeks to explain the psychological differences among us. One hundred people, of any age, are different. In textbooks this idea is called personality. And therefore it is interesting to ask what factors create different personalities.

I shall deal first with the universals and then turn to what we know about the causes of personality.

BIOLOGICAL PREPAREDNESS

As the brain grows in accord with its genetic script, the infant becomes able to behave and think in new ways. A six-month-old can neither understand nor speak language no matter what parents do because the brain is not sufficiently mature. However, when the child is twelve to fifteen months old it has reached a level of maturity that enables it to use the experiences of hearing speech to begin to utter words. We say that children are biologically prepared to learn, as long as they hear some language. The key phrase is "biologically prepared." Zoologists say that birds are biologically prepared to sing the song of their species if they hear that song. So if a canary, hatched and raised in a laboratory and isolated from all birds, hears on tape the song of a canary at the right time in its development, it will later sing its proper song. All the bird needs is a brief exposure. Let us now examine four examples of biological preparedness in the psychological growth of children.

The Growth of Memory

At around eight to ten months of age the human brain reaches an important milestone when the number of synapses in most parts of the brain has reached a peak. As a result the infant can now retrieve memories of the past, as you can remember what you ate for breakfast or what you did last evening. Before infants are eight months old they cannot retrieve the past because their brains are not sufficiently mature to permit them to reach back and recall what happened a minute earlier. After eight months they can. As a result, infants become vulnerable to a special form of anxiety.

One basic occasion for anxiety is remembering the past and comparing it with the present and noting that the two memories do not correspond. Now the person has a problem and if he or she cannot solve that cognitive problem, anxiety results. If the engine on a jet sounds odd, you only become anxious if you can remember what the engine ordinarily sounds like. If you could not retrieve that sound you would not become anxious. You may have noticed that older people who begin to lose their recall memory become less anxious.

At about eight months babies begin to show fear of strangers and fear of separation from their caretakers. You may remember that at about eight to nine months your own child cried when you left the house. A four-month-old rarely cries to that event. The eight-month-old cries because, as the mother leaves, he or she is able to compare the memory of her presence moments ago with the current perception that she is absent. The infant cannot understand that inconsistency and so has a problem. The mother was present moments ago but is not present now. As a result the infant becomes anxious.

The anxieties of infancy are a nice illustration of the principle of preparedness. All infants are prepared to become anxious about unfamiliar people and separation from their mothers at a certain age because of the maturation of the brain.

Moral Sense and Empathy

A second example of preparedness that is equally important to our species concerns our moral sense. The tree of knowledge allegory in the Bible may be the wisest statement ever written about humans. You will remember that when Adam and Eve ate from the tree of knowledge God warned them that from then on humans would be different from animals because they would know the difference between right and wrong. Every moral philosopher has acknowledged, in one way or another, that deep truth about our species.

But, after the First World War, American psychology was caught up in a rampant and dogmatic environmentalism that implied that if you didn't teach a child right from wrong he might never know the difference. Psychologists taught their students in the thirties and forties that if a parent did not punish a child and inform him what was right and what was wrong, that child might grow up to be a criminal. But Genesis and Kant were closer to the truth. All children with an intact brain will, between seventeen and twenty-four months, become concerned with broken and flawed objects. This is a time when a child may point to a frayed thread on its shirt and say to the mother, "Mommy, look." The child understands there is something wrong with the shirt. This concern with right and wrong is a prepared characteristic, no different from speech or the improvement in memory at one year.

Another quality that appears at this time is empathy for the emotional state of another. Two-year-olds who live with human beings are able to infer that a person or an animal might be suffering or feeling distress. Hume, the Scottish philosopher, called that feeling sympathy and regarded it as the most fundamental human emotion. Psychologists call it empathy. Empathy for the state of another is a fundamental human emotion that does not have to be taught. It will emerge in all children in the second year. The two-year-old who is capable of empathy has also matured enough to know that if he or she caused the distress of another guilt will also appear. Like empathy, guilt does not have to be taught. Thus humans are biologically prepared to possess a minimal conscience.

Modern psychiatry made a mistake when it invented the word psychopath to apply to criminals. Applying that word to someone who murders with no emotion implies that the killer never had a conscience at any point in his development. I doubt that. As long as the killer was not brain damaged, he once knew right from wrong, and at age two had empathy. What may have happened was that life experiences during childhood and adolescence impaired his adult capacity for empathy. One may lose temporarily a basic human emotion—love is a good example. If a woman is rejected in love twelve times it will become harder for her to fall in love the next time the occasion arises. The experiences of life can reduce the adult capacity for empathy, but every child has that capacity.

Preparedness for Responsibility

Jean Piaget, one of the great psychologists of the twentieth century, said that children passed through stages of intellectual development and that one important stage occurred at about six or seven years of age, although children living in isolated, illiterate villages without schools pass through this stage two or three years later. I believe that at this time the brain has matured in new ways permitting a new set of mental abilities to be actualized.

You will remember that the Catholic church does not require confession of a child before age seven; English Common Law did not view a child as responsible for a crime prior to seven years of age. These facts mean that our ancestors, long before there was child psychology, understood that something profound happens to a child at about seven years of age. In my work in rural Guatemala I found that parents with eight or nine children who did not know their ages would assign a boy the cutting of a new field for corn or assign to a daughter the responsibility of caring for an infant at about seven or eight years of age. Thus it must be that children are giving off some sign informing their parents they are ready for responsibility.

A second characteristic that occurs at this age is the talent to compare oneself to others. Now the child understands that he or she is prettier, less brave, or a better reader than a friend. A four-year-old cannot compare him or herself with another. This competence or ability to understand how one's qualities compare with those of a larger group has a major effect on the sense of self or self-concept. One of the components of the self-concept is the result of a psychological comparison of self with others. A child cannot know how intelligent he or she is unless he evaluates the other children in his classroom or neighborhood. Without comparative information there is no way to know how attractive, strong, brave, or intelligent one is.

Recognition of Inconsistency

The last preparedness I shall discuss is more abstract but is critical for human functioning. As puberty begins another important maturational change occurs. By twelve or thirteen years of age adolescents begin to examine their beliefs on a particular theme, and if they detect inconsistency among these beliefs they become troubled. Consider the following illustration. An eight-year-old boy can hold these two beliefs and yet not feel uneasy—"My father is a wonderful man;" "My father yells at my mother." Although these ideas are inconsistent, an eight-year-old does not sense their lack of concordance. By contrast, a thirteen-year-old cannot help but sense the inconsistency and is driven to resolve it.

Adolescents experience the dissonance that is inherent in their sets of beliefs about God, sex, family, and their future. The tension and stress we attribute to adolescence has less to do with an increase in sex hormones than with a new ability to recognize that one's beliefs are discordant.

This special psychological tension is stronger in the West than in isolated village communities around the world where almost everybody in the community holds the same set of beliefs. As a result, there is little inconsistency and adolescence is a less troubling period than in Western communities where there is so much pluralism in ideology.

Each of these phenomena, the anxiety of infancy as well as the cognitive dissonance of adolescence, will appear whether ones's parents are kind or cruel, permissive or restrictive.

PERSONALITY

I now turn to the second developmental story which asks how one can account for the differences among children and adults. In order to begin this discussion we have to decide what specific differences we will consider as important. Should we concentrate on swimming ability, how long a person sleeps, or whether a person laughs with gusto at jokes? Each culture values a small number of human qualities, awarding them more seriousness than others.

I believe that four such qualities valued in contemporary American society are: the acquisition of technical abilities, especially academic ones; differences in wealth and status; differences in the ability to enter into close and satisfying social relationships with others; and, finally, differences in happiness. Americans want to know why people differ on these four psychological qualities. Depending upon which of the four you pick, the profile causative forces will be different.

Influencing Factors

I now want to suggest six conditions which I believe contribute to the differences in technical ability, status, social relationships, and happiness that we see among adults. Depending upon which criterion you pick the balance of the six conditions will vary. Although the six conditions do not exhaust the domain of causative factors, they are important. You will also note at the end of the discussion that only one of the six is completely within the power of the parent. The remaining five are harder for parents to influence, although they are not beyond their will.

1. Biological Temperament. The biological temperament of the infant is one of the most basic factors. The biological and psychological differences among infants that we call temperamental can be genetic or prenatal. Babies differ in activity level, irritability, and in how easily they establish a schedule when they return home from the hospital. The temperamental quality I wish to dwell on is one that our research group has been studying for almost eight years.

During the second year of life one sees infants who are extremely timid, fearful, cautious, and shy. They rush to their mother if a stranger comes into the house, and they cry when taken to the doctor. They don't let their mother leave them the first month or two of nursery school and cling whenever they're in an unfamiliar situation, at least until they have become more relaxed. We believe about 10 to 15 percent of children who behave this way were born with a biological predisposition to develop this style. Obviously, it is possible to make a child shy and timid through family experiences.

Another 15 percent of children are born with a predisposition to develop a more sociable, outgoing, and fearless behavioral style. It is hard to frighten such children. We have been following two groups of children who were noted in the second or third year of life to be either timid and shy or sociable and outgoing. We had to observe over 400 volunteer children in our laboratory in order to find these 100 children—50 who are consistently shy and timid and 50 who are sociable, fearless and outgoing. The children in the middle are less consistent. We have followed these children for six years and find remarkable consistency in their styles of behavior. We believe this consistency is due, in part, to differences in the biochemistry of their brains.

Deep in our brains there is an area called the limbic lobe which is the origin of the stress circuits that discharge when we are fightened. The activity of these stress circuits leads us to secrete cortisol, a hormone of the adrenal gland, increases the tension in our muscles, and makes our hearts beat faster. The timid, shy children are reactive in all three of the stress circuits—namely, the pituitary-adrenal axis, the motor system, and the sympathetic chain. The fact suggests that the limbic lobe in the shy, timid children is at a lower threshhold of excitability to events that are unfamiliar or challenging.

However, some of these children have changed. We have seen parents of timid two-year-olds gently urge their children to be less shy, and over the years these children have changed. Specifically, about half of our timid, shy children at seven-and-a-half years of age are not extremely shy or timid. However, many families are fatalistic about their children and do not make gentle efforts to alter the child's temperamental qualities. When timid children enter school, many become isolated and loners. If such children come from middle-class families who promote high academic standards they are likely to choose an academic vocation such as history, poetry, or science. I believe that T. S. Eliot was one of these children.

If, on the other hand, the parents put excessive pressure on the child to succeed in some domain and the child does not have successes, that child may become extremely anxious and may show pathology later in life.

2. Birth Order. A second condition contributing to personality differences is the child's birth order; that is, whether the child is first, second, or third born. If we compared a thousand first borns with a thousand later borns we would find that, among middle-class Americans, first borns are generally more responsible and seek to control their environment. First borns get better grades, end up going to better colleges, and, as adults, commit fewer crimes. When a stress or challenge occurs first borns are less likely to develop symptoms.

By contrast, when later borns are faced with stress they are more likely to develop problems. Later borns are more pragmatic, less idealistic, and a little more likely to be rebellious. Historical studies show that more of the rebels and terrorists of the world are later borns, and more of the idealists and abstract thinkers are first borns. For example, Trotsky the activist was a later born, Marx the scholar a first born.

Let me try to explain these differences. To a first born growing up in a traditional middle-class home, the world looks orderly. Parents are nurturant, predictable, kind people who set high standards. The child is closely attached to and identified with them and the child looks at the world as a just place

JEROME KAGAN

where, if you do what you are told, all will be well. As first borns enter the period of childhood they ask their parents, "What is it that you want me to do? I will do it."

But the world looks different to a later born. Imagine a later born lying in his crib when suddenly a first born unpredictably shows up and intrudes into the sphere of the younger child. When a later born talks to his older sibling the latter doesn't necessarily reply, but he may seize a toy or pinch the child. Additionally, the first born can stay up until 10 o'clock, while the later born has to go to bed at sunset. Imagine these experiences happening week after week, year after year.

What might you predict to be the consequences of this regimen? One reasonable prediction is that later borns should see the world as a little less fair and just, while first borns should be more concerned with the approval of authority and less prone to disagree with or rebel against authority. First borns should want to keep harmonious relationships with authority and have less hostile feelings toward authority. If, as an adult, the person picks science as a vocation, one might predict that if a new scientific theory opposed what authority believed to be correct, and, therefore, threatened the society, the first born would be more likely to question the new idea. The more defiant later born would be more likely to favor it.

We are talking here about theories for which citizens have strong opinions. Educated citizens cared when Copernicus and Darwin said that the Bible's interpretation of the heavens or of man's place in nature was wrong. By contrast, the laser, although a brilliant discovery, did not threaten the average person's beliefs about man and nature. We are concerned here not with brilliant discoveries but with brilliant, new ideas about which most people have fixed beliefs.

Frank Sulloway, a young historian, has done research on this issue. He studied a large number of revolutions in science where the themes were of concern to the society. Some of these revolutions included the ideas of Copernicus, Francis Bacon, Freud, and, of course, Darwin. He then sought to determine what the eminent scientists of the time said about each revolutionary idea in a ten-year period after its original discovery. Was the scientist for or against the new idea and was he a first or later born? In studies of a dozen different scientific revolutions and many hundreds of scientists, he found that those who agreed with a new idea were likely to be later borns, while those who opposed it were likely to be first borns.[1] Thus one's attitude about a new scientific idea is influenced by one's ordinal position and seems to have little to do with that child's specific relationship to its parents.

3. Parental Influence. Parents assume importance in our third condition, which deals with parental behavior toward the child. Parental behavior tends to assume its greatest importance during the first six or seven years of life.

There are three experiences that parents can provide that have a profound influence on their children. One of the least impeachable facts in child

[1] Sulloway, F. Family constellations, sibling rivalry and scientific revolutions. Unpublished manuscript, 1972.

development is that the child's mental development will be stimulated if a parent provides a great deal of variety for the infant. Hence, parents who play with and talk to their children and present them with tameable variety will promote their children's mental development. Obviously, this variety can be supplied by a babysitter or a daycare center.

Some of the intellectual differences between a working- and a middle-class child are apparent by two to three years of age. Although working-class mothers love their children, they generally provide less variety during the period of infancy. It is not clear why they behave this way. Perhaps they don't believe in the effectiveness of presenting variety to the child.

A second way parents influence their children is through praise and punishment. The child does learn values in accord with what is rewarded and punished. Thus if parents discipline a child for dirtying his shirt or not cleaning his hands and do so consistently, they will get a five-year-old who is a little worried about keeping his shirt and hands clean. If a parent praises schoolwork, the child will become more concerned with doing well in school, at least during the early years of school.

A final source of parental influence involves communicating to the child that the parents value him or her. This experience is more important in our society in this century than it was in the past. You will recall that human beings have a natural tendency to evaluate themselves as good or bad. We all want our consciences to be gentle with us. When the day is done and we ask ourselves in the quiet of the evening, "How are you doing?" we want to be able to answer, "I am a good person." We are essentially moral creatures; in our daily lives we are engaged in a moral mission. A child growing up in a Third World village has to gather wood for the family, prepare supper, or wash clothes in the river. As a result it is obvious to such children that they are good. These seven-year-olds know that they are making a contribution to the family's vitality. Hence no adult has to say to them—and they usually don't—"I love you very much, Maria." Maria has less of a need for this communication because she knows she is of value.

In a society like ours, however, where children make no economic contribution to the family they have to be reassured about their goodness. That is one reason why love, the communication of value, has become so important. Historical changes made loving children, and the communication of love to children, important.

Loving a child does not necessarily mean giving that child a great deal of physical affection. John Stuart Mill recalled that his father was a wonderful person but not an emotionally close one. I have been reading an autobiography by a colleague, George Homans, who is now an emeritus professor. He writes of his father, "I could not have been blessed with a better father. I always enjoyed being with him. I respected him. Yet, I must say, I never felt emotionally close to him." A child can feel loved and can love a parent, even though there is not a great deal of physical affection between them. Some young Americans have a hard time understanding that idea because our culture has come to equate parental love with kissing and embracing.

4. Identification with Role Models. The fourth set of conditions is, in my opinion, the most important, and almost every philospher has made this point, but we continue to forget it. In modern dynamic pyschology the phenomenon I am referring to is called identification. Let me explain this idea. The child believes that some of the qualities of his or her parents also belong to the child. The child, as well as the adult, go beyond the objective facts and conclude, "I have the same last name as my family, I have the same color hair as my father, and my aunt noticed that my father and I both have dimples in our chins." The child goes beyond those facts and concludes that "because my father is popular I must be popular too; because my father is talented, I must be talented." Or the child can conclude, "No one respects my father, therefore no one will respect me." An identification with the parent can be positive or negative.

I believe that a parent's most important influence on a child originates in his or her status as a role model with whom that child can identify. One problem is that most parents find it difficult to hide their deep qualities, especially if these are undesirable. If a child perceives that the mother is competent, kind, nuturing, and attractive, then, fair or unfair, that seven-year-old girl will feel better about herself than she would otherwise. But if the mother is incompetent, not liked, and perceived to be unjust, then the child, even though she possesses none of those qualities, will feel bad, perhaps guilty. Many schizophrenics have identified with a rejecting mother they labeled as bad. As a result, they have these anxious feelings about themselves. A typical statement from a young schizophrenic woman to her psychiatrist is, "I'll tell you my problem, deep inside of me there is a great deal of evil." That feeling is a result of identification with a parent whom one perceives as bad.

Even though parents have limited control over how they present themselves to their children, it is their strongest power for it will influence the child's conception of self for many years. The child can also identify with his or her class or ethnic group. A child who is a member of a disadvantaged minority group is likely to perceive his or her group to be rejected by the larger society. As a result, the child will feel anxiety. In contemporary American society, disadvantaged Hispanic and Black children live with this burden if they identified with their ethnic group when they were young. Even though some grow up to be sucessful, they can carry the vulnerability for many years. A book that will bring a tear to your cheek, written by John Henry Wideman, is about a pair of Black brothers growing up in a ghetto in Pittsburgh. The older brother, a professor of English at the University of Wyoming, has written three novels and is respected in his community. His younger brother is serving a life sentence in a Pennsylvania prison for murder. The older brother, in an attempt to understand his younger brother, wrote a book called *Brothers and Keepers*.[2] In this book he confesses that although he is a professor of English who has written many books, every morning when he wakes up he is afraid he will be discovered. That feeling of vulnerability is a product of an earlier identification. Mr. Wideman may go to his grave anxious and suspecting that one day the larger society will discover this mysterious lack of goodness.

[2] Wideman, John Edgar. *Brothers and Keepers*. New York: Holt, Reinhart, and Winston, 1984.

5. Success and Failure. A fifth condition that influences the child resides in actual environmental successes and failures. Success in school depends in part on the size of the school. Many studies show that if the talent of a child is held constant, the probability of that child being successful is higher if he or she goes to a small school than to a very large one. Similarly, whether the peer group accepts or rejects the child is important. My colleague George Homans was not very popular with his peers and he writes that his classmates bullied and teased him. As a result he decided that he would become talented in schoolwork. The rejection by his peers and the subsequent decision set his life career.[3] It had less to do with his parents that with his experiences in school.

6. Chance and History. Finally we consider chance as a factor. Unlike the Chinese and the Malaysians, we in the West are less willing to acknowledge the role of chance in our lives. The Greeks acknowledged the power of the god's moods. You will remember that in *The Odyssey*, Athena decides what will happen to Odysseus; maybe she will cause a storm or arrange conditions to beach his boat on the rocks. But Americans want to believe that each is a master of his or her fate. If an adult is successful, he wants to believe that he did it through talent and motivation. If one fails, he or she did something wrong. And in our theories of human development we give chance events very little power.

Let me cite a few factors that are outside the control of children or families and, therefore, from that perspective are chance events. What was the size of the town in which the child grew up? If one leafs through *Who's Who in America* and notes the places where each person grew up, you will find that over 60 percent came from towns under 50,000 although the vast majority of Americans grow up in urban areas. How can we explain that anomaly?

Consider a nine-year-old girl with an I.Q. of 120 who is skilled and has kind parents. On the one hand, let us have her grow up in Salado, Texas; on the other in Chicago. In Salado there will be very few girls as talented as she, and if she stays there through high school she will graduate as a seventeen-year-old who feels very good about herself because she has compared herself with the other girls in the town and realized that she was in the top 5 percent. In Chicago she will know over two-hundred girls who are more talented and pretty than she and, as a result, she will learn humility.

That's why those listed in *Who's Who* spent their childhoods in small towns. Among the first group of astronaut candidates, three-quarters grew up in small towns—towns without great museums, large aquariums, or six-story libraries.

If one is going to succeed in an extraordinary way it is necessary to have an illusion about the self. The adolescent must believe that he or she is much better than others are. Illusion is harder to establish if there are several hundred children one's own age who are more talented, attractive, or courageous.

Historical events that influence the entire society comprise another chance factor. The Depression of the 1930s is one example. Sociologists have found that if a child was between seven and fifteen years of age during the Depression,

---

[3] Homans, G. C. *Coming to My Senses* New Brunswick, N.J.: Transaction Books, 1984.

his adult behavior was influenced profoundly. Many who were adolescents in Europe after World War I, the spiritual war that was to solve all of the world's problems, became skeptics for the rest of their lives.

An American youth in high school or college during the Vietnam War was also influenced in a serious way. I would like to find two hundred 35-year-olds who were ages fifteen to eighteen during the Vietnam protests in cities like San Francisco, Chicago, New York, and Boston and compare them with similar groups who are five years younger or five years older. I believe that I would find profound differences among these groups because of the experiences that occurred to them during the Vietnam era. These experiences had little to do with the kindness or meanness of their parents but were the result of events that were totally outside familial control.

With computers gaining ascendance, a child between seven and fifteen years old today will be influenced by the introduction of computers into the schools and society.

CONCLUSION

I have listed six factors that can have important effects on the growth of children. Two involve parents. They pertain to what parents do and what they are—their actual practices with their children and how they are viewed as role models for identification. But parents have far less control over the other four factors. That is why I said earlier that parents have power but that power is constrained. The limitation does not mean that parents should not invest effort and care in rearing children. They should be loving and conscientious as parents and should reflect on their actions. Indeed, they cannot do otherwise, for humans are prepared to believe that they can have an effect on the world. But they also must realize that the growing child is a product of the coming together of many, many coherent events, including the child's temperament, historical era, and birth order. An individual life is a complex story with many collaborators.

33 *Making the Grade as Parents*

Michael K. Meyerhoff / Burton L. White

STUDY QUESTIONS

1. What are several important things to do in dealing with the needs of child development?

2. What are several important items to avoid in this regard?

Danny and Emily Richardson and their 1-year-old daughter Rebecca live in a large, neatly kept home in the suburbs. The Richardsons, college graduates, have decided to give Rebecca the best possible start in life. She has a nursery that is stocked with all the latest educational toys. During the day, she spends much of her time in her well-equipped playpen, which Danny and Emily routinely place in front of the television set so she can be exposed to *Sesame Street*. Both parents set aside 30 minutes every day for "learning sessions," during which they teach Rebecca to recognize numbers, the alphabet and objects in pictures, and they have enrolled her in a professionally run playgroup two mornings a week.

David and Laura Taylor, high school graduates with two older children and a 1-year-old named Andrew, live in a crowded apartment that is clean but usually quite cluttered. They can't afford special toys or equipment, and their busy schedule does not allow them to set aside special blocks of time for Andrew. He spends much of his time roaming around the house playing with pots, pans, empty boxes and whatever else he can find. Sometimes he follows his parents around as they perform their household chores, interrupting them every now and then to ask for help or to share his excitement over something he has discovered. David and Laura always respond warmly and enthusiastically,

Source: Michael K. Meyerhoff and Burton L. White, "Making the Grade as Parents." *Psychology Today,* September 1986, pp. 38, 42–45. Reprinted with permission from *Psychology Today* magazine. Copyright © 1986 (PT Partners, L.P.).

but they rarely can give Andrew more than a couple of minutes of their undivided attention.

On the surface, it would appear that the Richardsons have the advantage in the child-rearing game. But our 20 years of child-development research indicate that Andrew is more likely than Rebecca to develop into a well-adjusted, competent preschool child. Some of our findings often defy popular notions and even "common sense," but they are supported by our recently completed "New Parents as Teachers" project in Missouri.

The new parents project was based on the idea that a great deal of important learning takes place during the first three years of life, that home is the first schoolhouse and parents are the first teachers. If parents are adequately prepared for and supported in their role as teachers, they will have a better chance of doing that job well.

The roots of the project go back to the early 1960s when an increasing number of parents and educators began to realize that many children were already "educationally disadvantaged" by the time they entered kindergarten. Our research with the Harvard Preschool Project, which began in 1965, identified a large sample of preschool children who, by anyone's definition and in everyone's opinion, were "most likely to succeed." They came from a wide range of socioeconomic and cultural backgrounds but shared a variety of intellectual, linguistic and social skills that clearly set them apart from their average and below-average peers. It soon became clear to us that they were exhibiting this impressive pattern of abilities by the time they were 3 years old.

We then went to the families of these children and found out which ones were expecting another child. When the new infants were between 1 and 3 years old, we began visiting their homes every other week and recording everything we could about their experiences and the child-rearing practices of their parents.

Later, we took what we had learned, combined it with the research of other developmental psychologists and translated it into information and support programs for new parents. Although much research remained to be done, we were convinced that effective programs could be developed to provide new parents with a great deal of reliable, useful information that was not then routinely available to them.

With this in mind, we established in 1978 the Center for Parent Education in Newton, Massachusetts. The primary goals were to increase public awareness of these issues and to provide resource, consulting and training services to professionals concerned with the education of children during the first three years of life. We were especially interested in those who wanted to work with parents in their role as a child's first and most important teachers.

In 1981, the Missouri State Department of Education, with funding from the Danforth Foundation, hired us to design a model parent-education program and help set it up in four school districts across the state: one urban, one suburban, one small town and one rural. Together, the families they served represented the total population of Missouri, covering a wide range of social and economic backgrounds. One full-time and two part-time parent educators were hired to serve between 60 and 100 families in each district. We provided them with specialized training, helped equip resource centers and supplied ongoing guidance and supervision for the entire effort. By January of 1982, everything was ready, and services to families began. They continued for three years at a cost of approximately $800 per family per year.

The services included group get-togethers, at which 10 to 20 parents would meet with a parent educator at the resource center, and individual home visits by a parent educator. Services began during the final three months of pregnancy and continued until the child's third birthday, with increasing emphasis on private visits after the child was 5 or 6 months old. The average amount of contact with families was once a month for an hour to an hour and a half.

Comprehensive screening procedures were used to monitor each child's intellectual, linguistic and social progress, and an extensive referral system ensured that parents could obtain prompt assistance if there were any signs of educational difficulty. Parents who had monetary, medical or other noneducational problems were referred to appropriate agencies.

Parents also used the resource centers to examine books, magazines, toys and other materials related to early development and parenting and to get guidance from the staff in selecting the most useful items.

During group and private sessions, parents were given basic information about what kinds of parenting practices are likely to either help or hinder their children's progress (see "A Primer for Parents"). They watched videotapes that demonstrated typical behavior of infants and toddlers and were given pamphlets and other materials that outlined the interests and abilities of children at each stage of development, suggested appropriate activities and told them what new developments to expect.

The information and advice provided were remarkably simple. Since we were interested in promoting well-balanced, all-round development, we did not advocate high-pressure procedures designed to produce child prodigies. Unlike the many "infant stimulation" or "superbaby" programs that have sprung up in recent years, the Missouri program focused on a comfortable, constructive style of parenting designed to make the early educational process enjoyable as well as effective rather than intensive and highly structured. In our opinion, such high-pressure programs tend to dampen the children's intrinsic interest in learning and take much of the fun out of the typical daily interactions between parents and children.

All too often, for example, parents overemphasize the importance of their child's spoken vocabulary. Our research shows that although many well-developing children do not say much until they are almost 2 years old, their capacity to understand simple words and instructions begins well before their first birthday, usually when they are between 6 and 8 months old. Unfortunately, since most people tend not to talk to things that don't talk back—such as chairs, fire hydrants, and little babies—many parents miss out on many months worth of opportunities for teaching language.

In homes where children were developing impressive linguistic abilities, we noticed that the parents talked to them frequently almost from birth. Moreover, once the children showed an awareness of language, the parents did not push them into vocabulary exercises using flashcards, labeling books or other such devices. Instead, they simply waited for the many times every day their children approached them for comfort, assistance or to share their excitement over some discovery. When this happened, the parents would use simple language to talk about and expand upon whatever topic the child introduced.

Intellectual development is an area in which "doing what comes naturally" also can be counterproductive at times. For instance, when children reach the second half of the first year, they start crawling and climbing, making accidental falls, poisonings and other serious mishaps likely. Many well-meaning parents react by restricting their children to a small but safe area, such as a playpen. They then provide an abundance of "educational" toys to keep the children occupied and occasionally let them loose for supervised "learning" sessions.

We noticed, however, that in homes where children were developing impressive intellectual abilities, parents often took a much different tack. Rather than restricting their children, they simply redesigned their homes, making most of the living area safe for (and from) newly mobile babies. This gave the children access to a very large, interesting learning environment in which they could experiment with, explore and investigate a whole world of exciting and enriching objects virtually at will.

The parents of these exceptional children were also ready and willing to provide new learning opportunities, not through expensive toys or specific games, but by letting the children help bake cookies, accompany them on a trip to the supermarket and so on. In other words, instead of setting aside specific and structured "teaching" time, they set up interesting environments, allowed the children to indulge their natural curiosity and then followed the children's leads.

Social skills are also beginning to develop during the first three years, but many parents, especially first-timers, make the mistake of assuming that children come civilized, or at least acquire common courtesies on their own. Even when presented with increasing evidence to the contrary, a lot of parents have trouble cracking down on unacceptable behavior, fearing they might lose the child's love. The "terrible twos" and the unpleasant temper tantrums of the third year of life are an all too common result.

But they are not inevitable. Our earlier studies had shown that in homes where children were both bright and a pleasure to live with, the parents were not afraid to set realistic but firm boundaries on behavior before their children's first birthday. During the first months of life, these parents lavished love and attention on their children and responded almost unconditionally to every demand. However, starting at about 8 months, and especially during the normal period of "negativism" between 15 and 24 months of age, when many children's demands were simply tests of what they could get away with, these parents reacted by letting the children know in no uncertain terms that other people had rights, too.

We had also learned that persistency in setting such limits was most important. Sooner or later, all parents would admonish their children for certain undesirable activities. But the effective parents always made sure to follow through. If the admonishments were ignored, then or later, they acted swiftly, using disciplinary strategies appropriate to their children's level of understanding. For instance, with an 18-month-old, rather than saying something like, "If you don't stop pulling on the drapes, we won't take you to Nana's house next Christmas," they quickly removed the child from the scene and physically prevented a return.

These few examples represent the sorts of things we stressed and the style of child rearing we encouraged the parents to adopt. Since participation in the Missouri program was voluntary, we could not require them to follow our advice, but we've always found that first-time parents are eager for guidance that will help them cope.

As the children of the participating families approached their third birthdays, we had an independent organization, Research and Training Associates of Overland Park, Kansas, evaluate the effectiveness of the program. A group of 75 randomly selected children from our project was compared with a carefully matched sample of children who had not been in the project. The evaluators found that the social development of the project children was outstanding, but since it is difficult to measure social skills in such young children, there was no reliable way to make comparisons.

Sophisticated measures of linguistic and intellectual development, however, left little doubt that the program had enhanced the educational prospects of the children involved in the project. The Kaufman Assessment Battery for Children and the Zimmerman Preschool Language Scale were used to measure intellectual and linguistic development, and the Missouri project children scored significantly higher in both areas.

Not all families in the four school districts were included in the evaluation. In some cases children had severe problems, such as cleft palate or Down's syndrome. In others, the parents had overwhelming problems that overshadowed educational issues, such as alcoholism or abject poverty. We included these families in the project, but we made it clear that our program could not deal with their extraordinary circumstances. To that extent, we cannot say that this type of program will be successful for every family with young children.

On the other hand, the results of the evaluation seem applicable to the approximately 85 percent of the population without such special problems. We had success with families in which both parents had doctoral degrees and with families in which both parents had failed to finish high school. In some families, the annual income was more than $40,000, and in others it was below the poverty line. There were black families and white families. Some parents were in their late 30s, others were still teenagers and a number of them were single parents.

We feel that we have clearly demonstrated some basic principles that could revolutionize the traditional approach to education in this country and around the world. First, you are likely to make the greatest difference in the academic prospects of young children if you reach them during the first three years, when the foundations for later development are laid.

Furthermore, the most inexpensive and efficient method is to work through the people who have the greatest influence on children's lives during this period—their parents. Finally, most parents, regardless of social status, educational level or cultural background, are eager to receive and can benefit from the information and support they need to be effective in their role as their children's first and most important teachers.

A PRIMER FOR PARENTS

The following recommendations are based on the lessons we learned from the parents of linguistically, intellectually and socially competent preschool children.

Things to Do

Provide your children with maximum opportunity for exploration and investigation by making your home as safe and accessible as possible.

Remove fragile and dangerous items from low shelves and cabinets, and replace them with old magazines, pots and pans, plastic measuring cups and other suitable playthings.

Be available to act as your children's personal consultant during the majority of their waking hours. You don't have to hover, just be nearby to provide attention and support as needed.

Respond to your children promptly and favorably as often as you can, providing appropriate enthusiasm and encouragement.

Set limits—do not give in to unreasonable requests or permit unacceptable behavior to continue.

Talk to your children often. Make an effort to understand what they are trying to do and concentrate on what they see as important.

Use words they understand but also add new words and related ideas. For example, if your child gives you a red ball, say, "This ball is red, just like my shirt. Your shirt is blue and it matches your pants."

Provide new learning opportunities. Having children accompany you to the supermarket or allowing them to help you bake cookies will be more enriching than sitting them down and conducting a flash-card session.

Give your children a chance to direct some of your shared activities from time to time.

Try to help your children be as spontaneous emotionally as your own behavior patterns will allow.

Encourage your children's pretend activities, especially those in which they act out adult roles.

Things to Avoid

Don't confine your children regularly for long periods.

Don't allow them to concentrate their energies on you so much that independent exploration and investigation are excluded.

Don't ignore attention-getting devices to the point where children have to throw a tantrum to gain your interest.

Don't worry that your children won't love you if you say "no" on occasion.

Don't try to win all the arguments, particularly during the second half of the second year when most children are passing through a normal period of negativism.

Don't try to prevent your children from cluttering the house—it's a sure sign of a healthy and curious baby.

Don't be overprotective.

Don't bore your child if you can avoid it.

Don't worry about when children learn to count or say the alphabet. Don't worry if they are slow to talk, as long as they seem to understand more and more language as time goes by.

Don't try to force toilet training. It will be easier by the time they are 2.

Don't spoil your children, giving them the notion that the world was made just for them.

---

34 *Daring to Discipline*

Joanne Guinn

STUDY QUESTIONS

1. In what ways is discipline different from punishment?

2. What are several factors to keep in mind while disciplining?

In the normal course of childhood, no doubt your child will misbehave, which means you will be called upon to discipline. As a parent, the way you handle these situations can make the difference between getting cooperation or getting resentment.

Punishment and discipline are different things. Punishment has no application to the upbringing of children; it is a method of controlling the deliberate, destructive acts of people who threaten the well-being of society. Discipline, on the other hand, is the opportunity to constructively correct behavior that is unacceptable to you. Discipline should be instructive, that is, your child should know WHY he is being corrected so he can learn from his mistakes.

Showing love is probably the most important interaction between parent and child, and the certainty of being loved is absolutely essential to a child. If he has that assurance, he can accept discipline as constructive, not as a threat. The old adage of "show, don't tell" is particularly applicable to love. Expressions of love involving physical contact are much more readily recognized by a child than just telling him (although verbal reassurances are important, too). Expressions of affection and appreciation should be genuine and spontaneous, not mechanical. "The quality of love expressed has a greater effect in instilling feelings of security and self-confidence than does the frequency with which it is demonstrated," according to Psyche Cattel, author of *Raising Your Child with Love and Limits.*

Source: N. Joanne Guinn, R.N., B.S., "Daring to Discipline." *The Single Parent*, March 1984, pp. 25–96. Reprinted by permission.

The guarantee of his parent's unqualified love is the foundation on which a child's self-confidence and sense of self are built. Never, never withdraw, or threaten to withdraw, your love. When a child has misbehaved, you must be sure he understands that it is his actions, not him, that bring your disapproval. Your love should be a constant.

Along with love comes praise. Praise should be sincere, and for specific behavior or visible achievements, rather than for some vague character or personality trait. We all desire recognition for good deeds—for our initiative and thoughtfulness. Such recognition fosters an adult who is considerate of others, who is giving and forgiving. How you treat your child today will be reflected in how he interacts with siblings, peers, adults, and ultimately, how he treats his own children. Genuine praise, like love, cannot be overdone.

Be consistent with your discipline. Set limits or guidelines. Be sure your child understands the boundaries of what is acceptable, and then *stick to the limits*. Don't allow him to get away with something when you're feeling permissive, then crack down on him for the same infringement the next time. Inconsistency is confusing, children need to know where they stand.

Patience is a virtue—one that every parent should expect to lose sometimes. Don't feel guilty when you do lose your temper; it happens to everyone. The wonderful thing about children is that they are forgiving. They'll give you another chance, and they won't stop loving you. But when you *are* wrong, don't be afraid to admit it or to apologize. They should know that no one is always right.

"How-to" books for parents can be misleading. They might be interpreted as expecting us to be perfect parents. There is no such thing. The manuals can't teach us how to love, or how to be patient or discipline. These are all functions of our own upbringing and social mores. What they might teach us is that each family is unique, and each child is an individual. The suggestions in such books are helpful to the extent that we weigh the information and adapt it to our own families.

MAKE IT EASY ON YOURSELF

I doubt if anyone enjoys having to discipline, so make it easy on yourself:

1. Create an atmosphere that encourages acceptable behavior. It is easier to distract and guide a child into another constructive activity than to allow him to persist at a behavior, the continuance of which requires discipline.

2. Show alternatives: "Why don't you *ask* to use his crayons instead of taking them?"

3. I like to use rewards for good behavior or a job well done, rather than bribery: "I'll give you a sucker if you do this." When a reward comes *afterward*, your child develops his own incentive and sense of control. He learns to have a goal and initiates behavior to accomplish it.

When you DO discipline:

4. Do it privately. In the corporate world, a good supervisor does not need an audience to reinforce his sense of authority. Allow your child to retain his sense of dignity by not embarrassing him in front of others. Don't be tempted to discipline him in front of siblings to set an example. Members of the same family usually are aware of disciplinary measures and privileges withheld. You needn't broadcast the fact.

5. Be sure the discipline fits the crime. Discipline at the *time* of the misbehavior or it will be ineffective. Don't build up discipline in little steps. Stop the behavior promptly. Don't say something unless you intend to go through with it.

6. Often suspended privileges are a powerful discipline, but it is not fair to withdraw a privilege already agreed upon. Just because he has disappointed you with some spontaneous misbehavior does not justify failure to keep a promise already made. You might say, "I'll let you go to the birthday party because I know you've been counting on it, and because I already said you could go, but you aren't allowed to ride your bike for two days."

7. Enlist his cooperation. Talk to him calmly, using eye and touch control. Be firm but gentle. Don't make him feel guilty. Help him to understand his behavior: "Why do you think this happened? What do you think we can do to correct it?" Let him express himself instead of telling him what *you* think. Ask him what discipline he thinks is appropriate or fair.

8. For aggressive behavior, encourage a physical activity so he can vent his energy in a harmless way (punching bag etc.).

9. For persistent misbehavior, ask yourself why. Does your child need more attention? Negative attention is better than none at all, even at the risk of discipline. If he is doing something that harms himself, another person, or property, he must be stopped immediately. But as a general rule, if you ignore bad behavior (name calling, etc.), it will disappear. Before you ignore a bad behavior, make every effort to understand its reason, and try to eliminate the *cause*. Pay attention to behavior you want to encourage—it will be repeated.

"Most of the time, the paths that lead to maturity can be kept smooth by a parent who combines intelligence and common sense with an understanding of how to set limits with love," Cattel writes in *Raising Your Child*.

Children *want* limits; they prove you care what happens to them. Adolescents often say, "My parents wouldn't like me doing that," because it takes the pressure of peer conformity off of *them*.

Enjoy your relationship with your child. You can be a friend without being a buddy. A child is not a contemporary. You are the parent and should maintain your authority and his respect for you (and yours for him) and your respective positions in the family. Discuss the situations or decisions that affect the family, but don't use him as a sounding board. This could result in burdening him with pressures and worries he is powerless to affect.

When discipline is necessary, common sense, fairness, a large measure of love and respect for your child as an individual are the best criteria. Your common goal of a harmonious family relationship can be achieved with mutual respect, cooperation, positive expectations, and love—the more you give, the greater the return.

9 *Family Variations: Social Differences*

The difficulties of parenting are compounded in the single-parent and stepparent families since they lack institutional guidelines and support. Although they are speaking about single-parent families, Edward Thompson and Patricia Gongla, in the first article of Chapter 9, could just as easily be speaking of stepfamilies when they say that their rapid growth as an alternative family form means that single-parent families have become part of the mainstream. That is, the single-parent family has become a viable, legitimate family form in contemporary society. Nonetheless, the lack of institutional support leads many to picture single parenthood as pathological. However, these authors' research has shown that this is an inaccurate belief, "that single-parent family systems are not inherently disorganized nor detrimental to individual members." An example is seen with children from single-parent families. Although they often perform less well academically and physically and engage in more deviant behavior than two-parent children, they are usually as "normal" as other children and may have closer relationships with their custodial parents (Amato & Ochiltree 1987).

The demands on the single parent include their being a stabilizing influence for their children while shouldering the added responsibility of making major decisions and coping with financial needs alone. In addition, they must deal with conflicting home and job responsibilities, inadequate child-care facilities, the lack of time and privacy for separate social life, and loneliness.

These demands on the custodial single parent lead to responsibility, task, and emotional overloads, often complicated by economic strain. This latter item is seen in the growing "feminization of poverty." Low pay and lack of child support and alimony are major factors in bringing about the inclusion of the vast majority of female-headed, single-parent households under this heading.

In the second article of Chapter 9, Blaine Porter summarizes the demands of being a single parent under the two broad headings of personal adjustments and parenting responsibilities. He concludes that the important question to ask is not why we are here or how we got in this situation but where do we go from here. He makes some adjustment suggestions.

Like the single-parent family, the stepparent family is a rapidly growing alternative family form. Also like the single-parent family, the stepparent family lacks institutional support. The result is inconsistent cultural expectations of the roles of a stepparent, and this gives rise to ambiguity and role conflict, as well as to negative connotations regarding the stepmother or stepfather. In addition, the stepparent faces adjustment problems in dealing with finances, division of labor, ex-spouses, in-laws, and food preferences, as well as with personal expectations regarding sexual intimacy and personal space (Anderson 1981).

Despite its unusual developmental history, the stepfamily does transform into a new, reliable, established unit. Patricia Papernow, in the third article of Chapter 9, describes the seven stages of this transition with the different and sometimes conflicting needs of each person at each step.

As a means of dealing with the personal problems of this transition, Sharon and James Turnbull, in the final article of Chapter 9, indicate ten commandments that stepfamilies can follow to ease their difficulties. There is also a need, however, for more understanding of the problems faced by stepparents and a need to integrate and institutionalize stepfamilies into the mainstream of society.

REFERENCE

1. Amato, P. R., & G. Ochiltree. 1987. "Child and Adolescent Competence in Intact, One-Parent, and Step-parent Families: An Australian Study." *Journal of Divorce.* 10:3–4 (Summer).

35 Single-Parent Families: In the Mainstream of American Society

Edward H. Thompson, Jr. / Patricia A. Gongla

STUDY QUESTIONS

1. Describe several types of single-parent families.

2. Describe several of the problems faced by single-parent families.

The single-parent family has recently become a renewed topic of national concern. Much of the attention has resulted from the dramatic increase in the proportion of American families maintained by a single mother or single father. By the end of the 1970s, however, a conflict between lifestyle choice and cultural scripts also called attention to these families. Some of this attention is due to the emergence of single parenting as a more deliberately intentional and less transitional lifestyle for many than has previously been the case. Some is due to the recent shift in cultural scripts and family policy from tacit concern for the welfare of all families to intentional support of the conventional two-parent family, a shift that may presage the increased vulnerability of single-parent families in the 1980s. The combined effect of these changes has been to arouse some concern with regard to how mainstreamed single-parent families have and will become. The question is raised: Are single-parent families a viable, legitimate, albeit still alternative, family form in contemporary American society? . . .

SOCIETAL REACTION

The most significant commonality across single-parent families is the structural characteristic that only one parent lives with the children. Because the other parent is "absent," and perhaps because nearly 90 percent of the single-parent

Source: Edward H. Thompson, Jr., and Patricia A. Gongla, "Single-Parent Families: In the Mainstream of American Society." In *Contemporary Families and Alternative Life Styles*, E. D. Macklin and R. H. Rubin (eds.). Copyright 1983 by Sage Publications, Inc. Reprinted by permission of Sage Publications, Inc.

families have been "headed" by women for over a century (Seward, 1978), single-parent families have long been thought to be in trouble. Whether trouble is defined as mothers managing a family unit alone and unattached, or as "father absence" depriving children of the necessary experiences and role models for satisfactory adult moral behavior, public interest in single-parent families has manifested itself as concern. The common belief is that these families are "broken" and "disorganized" (Burgess, 1970), and that the presence of both a mother and a father are prerequisites for a child's normal development (Blechman, 1982; Levitin, 1979). Benson's 1909 article, entitled "Alarming Changes in American Homes," called attention to the turn-of-the-century "social problem" (cited in Blechman and Manning, 1976: 62), and Malinowski's (1930/ 1974) proposed sociological law that "no child should be brought into the world without a man—and one man at that—assuming the role of sociological father" underscored the professional community's concern with father absence.

Early public and professional interest in single-parent families focused on the children growing up in these "partial" families. Although the single parent was usually widowed, at worst deserted, and also a "victim," public sympathies and worries focused almost exclusively on the children.

By 1980, however, death of a parent has become the least frequent factor in the establishment of a single-parent family. Separation and divorce are now the most common causes of single-parent families, although since the 1970s, there has been a major increase in the number of families created by single women having babies. In effect, Americans are increasingly choosing single parenthood over unhappy marriages, to remain single parents rather than quickly remarrying (Brown et al., 1976; Staples, 1980; Weiss. 1979), to create a single-parent family rather than aborting an unplanned pregnancy or releasing the baby for adoption (Grow, 1979; Haring, 1975), and to create single-parent families through adoption or planned premarital conception (Doughtery, 1978; Kadushin, 1970; Shireman and Johnson, 1976).

These lifestyles choices can probably be attributed to a variety of factors, among them the diminished moral stigma associated with divorce, parenting alone, and premarital conceptions. However, despite the diminished stigma attached to individuals, public concern with the single-parent family has not diminished. Indeed, as the number of single-parent families increased through-out the 1970s, so did public alarm (e.g., The Consortium for the Study of School Needs, 1980; Goldstein et al., and Solnit, 1979; Hatch, 1981; Lynn, 1974). There is still concern that single-parent families are "partial" and "broken" and thus are harming children (Anthony, 1974). In addition, there is now widespread alarm about the future of the traditional nuclear family. Social critics suggest that the choice to single parent is threatening the legitimacy of the traditional two-parent family and thus the stability of society. Rather than viewing the single-parent family as one type of family in American society, these families are defined as deviant family systems (Bernard, 1979; Levitan and Belous, 1981; Schorr and Moen, 1979). Social policymakers are often encouraged to reform existing family policy on the *assumption* that single-parent family systems are detrimental to the welfare of both the children and the economy (e.g., Senate bills 1070 and 1378, 97th Congress).

In hindsight, Ross and Sawhill's (1975) proposal for a neutral family policy, which would neither encourage nor discourage various kinds of family organization, clearly forecasted these trends and presently would seem too liberal. The 1980s have begun with a rise in a family protectionism ideology that does not speak well for family pluralism or for the welfare of all families (see Fox, 1981; Wiseman, 1981). Rather, this new wave of familism appears to support only the "neoclassical" family of Western nostalgia, where the married individuals are in their first marriage, living together, and natural parents to their children. Whether intended or not, governmental bureaucracies are thus likely to become increasingly involved in the lives of single-parent families (Hawkins, 1979; Schorr and Moen, 1979; Zimmerman, 1976, 1979).

CHARACTERISTICS OF SINGLE-PARENT FAMILIES

The paths along which single-parent families evolve are varied. Some begin as two-parent families, and as a result of separation, divorce, desertion, or death, the family becomes single parent. Others begin as one-parent families, as when a single person chooses to adopt a child or when a single woman delivers and keeps her own child. Despite the different routes to the single-parent situation, single-parent families are frequently viewed as alike and collectively referred to as *the* single-parent family. The assumption is made that single-parent families are more similar to one another than to other family types, and that they share a common lifestyle and common problems (Billingsley and Giovannoni, 1971). In some aspects of everyday life these families *may* share certain experiences. For example, they commonly experience a major reduction in family income (Bane and Weiss, 1980), a sense of isolation and loneliness (Greenberg, 1979; Katz, 1979; Nock, 1981; Smith, 1980), role overload (Glasser and Navarre, 1965; Weiss, 1979), and unequal access to the material and social resources more easily available to two-parent families (Cherlin, 1981; Schorr and Moen, 1979).

Nonetheless, it is impossible to discuss "the single-parent family" since the concept covers a wide variety of types of families. One must distinguish between single-father and single-mother families (which differ in composition) the paths along which the family system evolved, the extent to which an outside parent is involved in child care and consultation, manner and level of functioning, patterns of interaction, and subjective well-being. Furthermore, they differ in economic lifestyles, opportunities and resources, social class, racial and ethnic background, and age of parent. The conclusion to be drawn is deceptively simple: Single-parent families are not a homogeneous group. Failure to see the diversity among families, however, has been a frequent conceptual error and, until recently, has hindered our understanding of these families. To paraphrase Billingsley and Giovannoni (1971) and Sprey (1967), understanding the diversity across single-parent families may be more important theoretically, clinically, and politically than the search for the common denominators of single-parent family life. . . .

EDWARD H. THOMPSON, JR. / PATRICIA A. GONGLA

Family Systems

The everyday reality of single-parent families suggests a wide variety of interaction patterns and family boundaries, ranging from the noncustodial parent being minimally present as in the "sole executive" family system (Mendes, 1979) to being maximally involved as in the "binuclear" family system (Ahrons, 1979). The extent to which the nonresidential parent is *psychologically* and *interactively* present in the family system depends to a large extent on the person's availability and freedom of access (Abarbanel, 1979; Boss, 1977, 1980a; Fulton, 1979; Hetherington et al., 1978; Wallerstein and Kelly, 1980; Weiss, 1979), and on the extent to which the noncustodial parent was "inside the family system" prior to the onset of single parenthood (Kantor and Lehr, 1975; Kelly and Wallerstein, 1977; Minuchin, 1974; Rosenthal and Keshet, 1980).

A number of studies suggest that parents living apart from their children may still be *interactively* inside the single-parent family boundary for some time (Clapp and Raab, 1978; Earls and Siegel, 1980; Fischer and Cardea, 1981; Furstenberg and Talvitia, 1980; Hetherington et al., 1976). This parent may frequently visit the child(ren), babysit for the custodial parent, and share responsibility in decision making. Mendes (1979) identified this type of parent as an "auxiliary parent," and several authors have previously addressed this phenomenon within their discussion of the part-time father (Atkin and Rubin, 1976) or visiting parent (Wallerstein and Kelly, 1980). In cases in which both parents desire to continue their parenting roles, two interrelated households can form one family system, the binuclear family system (Ahrons, 1979). This pattern can occur whether joint custody has been awarded or not, as long as a coparenting relationship is maintained. Ahrons (1980a) and other observers of custody arrangements (Abarbanel, 1979; Galper, 1978; Greif, 1979; Newsome, 1977; Roman and Haddad, 1978) estimate that this coparenting pattern may soon be the rule rather than the exception.

However, with few institutional supports for the noncustodial parent's role, the nonresidential parent/child subsystems that emerge vary considerably, usually falling between the extremes of an "empty shell" relationship involving erratic and infrequent interaction and a "vital" relationship involving recurring interaction and cohesiveness. Tentative findings suggest that the quality of the noncustodial parent/child(ren) relationship initially improves, at least for a while (Earl and Lohmann, 1978; Earls and Siegel, 1980; Greif, 1979; Hetherington et al., 1976). Over time, though, this relationship often decomposes as the frequency of interaction decreases. The absent parent's interactive presence is often diminished when custody is not shared (Abarbanel, 1979; Ahrons, 1980a), when loss of everyday contact with family rituals and routines is either blocked by visitation restrictions or a strained relationship with the custodial parent (Benedek and Benedek, 1979; Cline and Westman, 1971; Fulton, 1979; Weiss, 1979), or when the noncustodial parent was only marginally involved inside the family in the first place (Keshet, 1980; Minuchin, 1974).

Even when strained interaction characterizes the ex-marital subsystem, "most single-parents do what they can to foster their children's relationships with their noncustodial parents. They do so despite their own feelings, because they believe it important for the children" (Weiss, 1979: 159). Goldsmith (1979) and Wallerstein and Kelly (1980) corroborate this finding, reporting that the majority of parents (both fathers and mothers) felt it important for the noncustodial parent to stay involved with the child. Thus the absent parent may be *psychologically* inside the single-parent family boundary for some time, even in families where the parent is *physically* absent (Boss, 1980a; Lopata, 1979). It would also be misguided to assume that the "absent parent" diminishes in saliency in the eyes of the child even if the interaction is reduced. Children frequently continue to think of themselves as children of two parents, despite the degree of interaction with the "absent parent." Based on their study of children of divorce, Wallerstein and Kelly (1980: 307) comment: "Although the mother's caretaking and psychological role became increasingly central in these families, the father's psychological significance did not correspondingly decline."

Evidently there is good reason to question the stereotype of "parent absence." Yet a perspective commonly found in the literature appears to be: When a marriage dissolves, the family dissolves; and if a marriage was never present, as is the case for many single mothers, a family never existed. But as Sprey (1979: 155) says: "Divorce [or any other form of marital dissolution] ends a marriage but not a family. It removes one parent from the household." It changes the relationship between the parents, it does not end the relationship; psychological and interactive ties continue to connect all family members, but under widely different circumstances.

There are apparent risks, however, with the noncustodial parent's active involvement in the family's life. Inability to manage the conflict within the ex-spouse subsystem can add subjective stresses to the lives of all family members, and an interactively absent but psychologically present parent can increase boundary ambiguity and jeopardize the family's ability to reorganize. As Boss (1980b: 449) has suggested, "Stress continues in any family until membership can be clarified and the system reorganized regarding (a) who performs what roles and tasks, and (b) how family members perceive the absent parent."

Internal Family Boundaries

Until recently, there was no systematic research on the single-parent family as a system with its own authority structure, norms, processes of conflict management and boundary maintenance, patterns of exchange and reciprocity, and decision-making rules. The second, albeit corollary, sphere of family life that remains virtually uncharted thus has to do with the concept of "boundary redefinition" and life inside single-parent families over the course of the family career.

When one parent leaves the family household, two dramatic changes follow. First, as Weiss (1979) noted, the loss of a parent tends to decrease the social distance, and open the normal boundary between the custodial parent and the child(ren). More specifically, the authority structure in a two-parent family is grounded on the implicit coalition of two adults aligned against the child(ren). In single-parent families, this superordinate/subordinate "echelon

EDWARD H. THOMPSON, JR. / PATRICIA A. GONGLA

structure" collapses. Weiss suggests that the children are promoted: The custodial parent relinquishes some decision-making control and then begins to engage the children "as if" they were junior partners. "The parent wants to be able to rely on the children as fully participant in the functioning of the family," and "once children accept the increased responsibility, it becomes natural for the single-parent to consult the children regarding household decisions"

Second, decomposition of the authority structure and group size, to paraphrase Simmel (Wolff, 1950), increases communication and disclosure. Given this and the fact that single-parent families are often more isolated from friends and community groups, a type of parent/child(ren) "dyad" forms, which is markedly different from the traditional parent/child bond. Characterized by greater equity, more frequent interaction, more discussion, and heightened cohesiveness (i.e., greater intimacy and companionship), the relationship fosters a wholly different affective structure. "The condition of intimacy consists in the fact that the participants in a given relationship see only one another, and do not *see*, at the same time, an objective, super-individual structure which they feel exists and operates on its own" (Simmel, cited in Wolff, 1950: 127–128). . . . Results suggest that it is the psychosocial characteristics of the family unit, independent of the number of parents, that affect the individuals. Living in a single-parent family need be no more harmful than living in a two-parent family.

However, there is as yet little evidence indicating the *comparative effects* of living in a single-parent family. Single-parent life is probably less detrimental for children than living in an unhappy, conflict-ridden two-parent system (Nye, 1957; Staples, 1980), and less permanently troubling than previously anticipated (Kulka and Weingarten, 1979; Loge, 1977; Luepnitz, 1979). But at present there is little information grounded in methodologically sophisticated work. For the time being, conclusions must remain tentative. . . .

SINGLE-PARENT FAMILIES IN SOCIETY

The interface between single-parent families and their larger social environment has largely gone undiagnosed. Reviewing titles listed in the *Inventory of Marriage and Family Literature*, it is as if single-parent families exist in a vacuum, unattached to major social institutions, service organizations, or personal support systems.

Economics and Employment

One obvious exception to the above is the research on the interface between single-parent families and the economy. Evidence has accumulated to conclusively document the low economic status of single-parent families—their low incomes, high rates of poverty, and fewer employment opportunities than two-parent families (Bane and Weiss, 1980; Bianchi and Farley, 1979; Bradbury et al., 1979; Brandwein et al., 1974; Dinerman, 1977; Espenshade, 1979; Hoffman, 1977; Ross and Sawhill, 1975; Sawhill, 1976; Wattenberg and Reinhardt, 1979). As Cherlin (1981) and Colletta (1979a) have summarized, the major problem faced by single-parent families is not the lack of a male's presence, but the lack of a male income.

Nowhere is the linkage between major social institutions and single-parent families as pointed as it is in the areas of economics and employment. Throughout most of the 1970s, the income of single-mother families remained less than one-third the income of two-parent families, and the income differential appears to be increasing. By the end of the decade, single mothers commanded half the income of single fathers, and half again the average income of the two-parent family. The most recent figures for family incomes show that in 1979, single mothers raising two children had a median income of $8,314, whereas a married couple with two children had $23,000 (U.S. Bureau of the Census, 1981c).

With such an income differential, it is no surprise that families maintained by a single mother are over three times more likely than those headed by single fathers, and six times more likely than two-parent families, to have incomes below the poverty threshold (U.S. Bureau of the Census, 1980: Table 19). A major reason of the single parent's poor economic status, especially the single mother's status, is the sizable reduction in family income most families experience following marital disruption. In recent years the magnitude of this reduction has become even more severe; it is the single most important factor explaining the economic gap between single-parent and two-parent families (Bane and Weiss, 1980; Bianchi and Farley, 1979; Espenshade, 1979; Hoffman, 1977). Reexamining the data on single-parent families within the Institute of Social Research's study of 5000 U.S. families, Bane and Weiss (1980: 13) found the average income of widowed mothers falls 31 percent after the death of a spouse, while divorced mothers and separated mothers experience 43 and 51 percent drops in family income, respectively. One would expect that the economic plight of the never married would be worse, given the generally younger age, lower education, and higher percentage of minority families that this group comprises (Wattenberg and Reinhardt, 1979). These data strongly suggest that reduced economic circumstances are an inevitable condition of single parenthood, especially in the case of families maintained by single mothers.

A number of other factors contribute to the poor economic conditions of the single-parent family: the father's inability or unwillingness to contribute to the family's income (U.S. Bureau of the Census, 1981d; Wattenberg and Reinhardt, 1979); the costs of child care (Sawhill, 1976; Schorr and Moen, 1979); the "Catch-22" governing policies of public assistance and "workfare" (Dinerman, 1977); the labor market "squeeze," which results in younger single mothers receiving the lowest income, experiencing the highest rate of unemployment, and obtaining the fewest benefits (Schorr and Moen, 1979; Wattenberg and Reinhart, 1979); and the recurring problem of discrimination against women in the workplace (Sawhill, 1976; Schorr and Moen, 1979).

Links to Other Institutions

Policymakers who would consult family specialists for more comprehensive information regarding single-parent families vis-à-vis other institutions discover little systematic research. One finds only scattered references, indicating that the flow of influence and control between single-parent families and major social institutions is unidirectional, from institutions to families, but little systematic data exist to support this contention. It is therefore difficult to describe with any certainty the present societal status of single-parent families. With this in mind, what can be said about the linkages between single-parent families and their environment? Are these families viewed as within the mainstream by the major social institutions, such as education, government, religion, and medicine?

Burgess (1970) and Schorr and Moen (1979) contend that many organizations and their programs view single parenthood as a temporary condition and transitional phase in a family career. The conventional wisdom is that the single-parent family will "go away" when the single-parent (re)marries. With marriage, never-married mothers will form a complete family, and with remarriage, broken families will be reconstituted or blended. In this sense, then, single-parent families are not recognized as "real" families. The conventional standard that a marriage is necessary before a social group will be defined as a legitimate family system (Sprey, 1979) may inhibit major social institutions from seeing a family nucleus when just a father/child or mother/child bond exists.

This assumption, like most common-sense assumptions, is in part justified. The reality is that the median interval between divorce and the second marriage is three years for those 35 to 54 years old (Glick, 1980). In recent years, the interval has been increasing, and the remarriage rates for both widowed and divorced single parents have been dropping (U.S. National Center for Health Statistics, 1980a, 1980b). When the unit of analysis is shifted from each to all single-parent families, however, the common-sense assumption is not justified. The reality is that by the time (re)marriage ends the single-parenting experience for one family, another has taken its place. Single-parent families are one family type in American society. The view that single parenthood is temporary can thus become a powerful though tacit policy where a lack of accommodation to and recognition of these families is acceptable (Blechman and Manning, 1976; Hawkins, 1979; Hulme, 1976; Moroney, 1980; Parks, 1981; Schorr and Moen, 1979; Wilk, 1979). Paraphrasing Simmel, when the plurality of organizations in a society tacitly defines a group as being outside the mainstream, members of that group will fare badly. With the plurality of institutions believing that "two parents are better than one," single-parent families face not only discrimination but attendant feelings of humiliation as well (Wolff, 1950: 224–265).

Cogswell and Sussman (1972: 513) noted a decade earlier that the interface between single-parent families and institutional systems was as Simmel would predict: dictated by institutions failing to support or acknowledge single-parent family systems as legitimate or viable families. Instead, institutional systems.

> make certain assumptions about the family. They gear their services toward an ideal of what the family ought to be, namely, a nuclear traditional one. . . . Because agencies idealize the traditional family, their programs are aimed at restoring this form and, thus, are ill-equipped to provide relevant supportive services to variant family forms.

Lindahl's (1979) analysis of the interface between local churches and single-parent families, for instance, concludes with such a restorative approach: "The church . . . must provide a message and an experience of reconciliation and redemption to its members who suffer the anguish of broken human relationships." Horowitz and Perdue (1977: 508) found that when health professionals come into contact with single-parent families, the institutional approach often ignores their unique group composition and indiscriminately offers solutions designed for two-parent families, or it recognizes the one-parent structure as "abnormal" and provides treatment aimed at helping the family members accept a regrettable situation (see Blechman and Manning, 1976; Wilk, 1979). Discussing single mothers who may have problems with external social service agencies and schools, Moroney (1980: 49) points out: "She may have a problem, but, if so, it often is with the system which tends to be rigid."

Although individual family members may benefit from their contact with specific organizations and their programs, organizations continue to provide a rather inimical climate for single-parent families as *families* (Blechman and Manning, 1976; Hawkins, 1979). Given the slow rate of change in large-scale organizations, it is not surprising that there have been few accommodations to single-parent families since Cogswell and Sussman wrote the above quote. For example, they noted that health care services for children are organized for the convenience of the medical care professionals and not around the availability of adults to accompany children to the agency. A decade later, clients are still supposed to adjust to the schedules of the health care agencies (Hulme, 1976; Moroney, 1980; Wilk, 1979). Yet the single parent may lose income and even jeopardize a job by having to accommodate the health organization's schedule (Brandwein et al., 1974).

Thus, institutions actually discriminate against one-parent families in two ways: by indiscriminately treating them as similar to two-parent families (Hawkins, 1979; Horowitz and Perdue, 1977) and by viewing the one-parent structure as "abnormal" (Blechman and Manning, 1976). Both approaches are dysfunctional for single-parent families. In the first case, they are obliged to fulfill the same functions and conditions as two-parent families, yet the limitations on their ability to do so are ignored (Brandwein et al., 1974; Horowitz and Perdue, 1977; Schorr and Moen, 1979). In the second case, the institutionalized view of the single-parent family as both temporary and deviant generates a daily barrage of subtle discrimination, for example, banks demanding cosigners for loans, landlords unwilling to rent housing (Brandwein et al., 1974), lack of easily available and affordable child care options (Rossi, 1977; Sawhill, 1976; Woolsey, 1977), and reduction in employment opportunities (Bane and Weiss, 1980; Bradbury, et al., 1979).

There is a social psychological analogue to the subtle, albeit formal, discrimination that single-parent families encounter. Because many families are treated as "nonfamilies" or are stigmatized as deviant, and a social distance is erected between "normal" and "abnormal" families, a self-fulfilling prophecy is put into operation. Schorr and Moen (1979: 18) state that all single-parent family members suffer from public images of the ideal and the single-parent family: "The most moving effect of misrepresentation is that many single parents believe what is said of them and add belief to the problems they face. The stereotypes involved are about as legitimate as most that are involved in discriminatory behavior—and as destructive."

Links to Other Support Networks

The relationships single-parent families maintain with friends and kin can only be obtained by piecing together studies that have focused on the parent's social ties or the child's kin relationships. Because we must borrow bits and pieces from the available information, the linkage between single-parent families and their social networks cannot be clearly defined.

Some literature suggests that single parents maintain or increase their exchange and affectional ties with their own relatives (consanguine kin) after the single-parent family evolves (Anspach, 1976; Clapp and Raab, 1978; Gongla, 1977; Spicer and Hampe, 1975). Relatives basically feel a commitment to help, and that commitment provides the family a sense of continuity and security whether help is actually given or not (Weiss, 1979). This is particularly true in the case of the never-married mother (Clapp and Raab, 1978; Grow, 1979). Nonetheless, turning to the child(ren)'s grandparents for help can create a "Catch-22." Returning home for services and support often results in tension and dependant feelings (Clapp and Raab, 1979; Colletta, 1979b; Dell and Applebaum, 1977; Weiss, 1975, 1979). Particularly acute are the problems of boundary ambiguity when grandparents offer unsolicited advice about child rearing or when children fail to turn to the custodial parent for emotional support.

Interaction with in-laws usually diminishes with divorce, unless the non-custodial parent continues to maintain contact with the family and thus provides a pathway to the in-laws (Anspach, 1976; Gongla, 1977). In effect, relationships with in-laws remain contingent upon the interactive presence of the noncustodial parent and generally worsen as the noncustodial parent withdraws from the single-parent family.

Ties to friends seem to follow a different pattern. As the single-parent family emerges, defines, and reorganizes itself, so too does the family's community of friends. For both the previously married and never married, the first reaction is a sense of being marginal to the family's former community and a sense of social, if not emotional, isolation (Clapp and Raab, 1979; Hetherington et al., 1979; Kitson et al., 1980; Rosenthal and Keshet, 1980;

Smith, 1980; Weiss, 1979). Unlike single fathers, many single mothers are nonetheless able to maintain or increase their intimacy pattern with their old friends (Clapp and Raab, 1979; Gongla, 1977). As time goes on and the family is able to more clearly define itself, a new community of friends is often formed (Clapp and Raab, 1979; McLanahan, Wedemeyer and Adelberg, 1981; Rosenthal and Keshet, 1980; Weiss, 1979). Loge (1977) contends such friends may be more effective than kin, providing more support for the single parent and respecting the family's external boundaries (see Greenberg, 1979). However, this finding may only be valid for those custodial parents who strongly identify with the role of single parent and who are attempting to reorganize their lives in a way that increases their independence (McLanahan et al., 1981).

The importance of different kinds of networks cannot be understated: Serving as a buffer to external stresses and providing emotional and instrumental assistance as needed, social supports do seem to have an effect on the *fact* and the *feeling* of going it alone (Bloom et al., 1978; Chiriboga et al., 1979; Kurdek and Siesky, 1980; McLanahan et al., 1981; Wilcox, 1981).

IMPLICATIONS AND GENERAL DISCUSSION

The intent of this chapter has been to examine public views and research traditions regarding single-parent families in American society. Demographically, it is clear that single-parent families are now within the mainstream of American society. Moreover, after at least four decades of work that emphasized their deviation from the two-parent family and the pathological effect on individual members (Shaw and McKay, 1932), single-parent families are now gradually coming to be recognized and studied as whole, often healthy, families.

Some manage to adapt and reorganize easily, even to thrive, coping effectively with stresses from both within and outside the family unit. Others do not. Research findings suggest that the factors directly associated with successful families are the age of the single parent and child(ren) (Clapp and Raab, 1978; Wallerstein and Kelly, 1980), family income (Colletta, 1979a; Ross and Sawhill, 1975; Wattenberg and Reinhardt, 1979), residential stability (Bane and Weiss, 1980), development of an adaptive informal support system (McLanahan et al., 1981), systematic separation of marital and parenting roles (Keshet, 1980; Weiss, 1979), the interactive *and* psychological presence of the nonresidental parent (Boss, 1977), ability to manage conflict (Goldsmith, 1979; Raschke and Raschke, 1979; Weiss, 1979), abandoning old rules and rituals and establishing new family norms (Ahrons, 1980b; Weiss, 1979), and access to child care alternatives (Sawhill, 1976; Schorr and Moen, 1979).

Before proceeding, a caveat is in order. This summary of factors associated with single-parent families' success must be interpreted cautiously. Few studies have been designed to compare families, and our knowledge is too limited to suggest what resources have an ameliorative effect on the life in a single-parent family in a two-parent society. Most, if not all, of the factors mentioned above also probably apply to the maintenance of well-functioning two-parent families. Data suggest that there are more variations within single-parent and two-parent families than between them. Hence continued concern with the structural variable of number of parents within the household may be less helpful than a search for those characteristics all well-functioning families share.

Single-parent families desperately need to be studied as family systems that involve internal and external boundaries and some degree of embeddedness in a social environment. There must be a continued focus on single-parent *families*, with attention to the diversity of their internal organization and boundary reorganization over time, the degree of involvement with kin and friends outside the household, and their interaction with the large social environment. Recent research strongly suggests that new investigations of single-parent families recognize the possible existence of a second parent who continues to be present within the family system. While findings are at present tentative, the second parent continues to play an important role in the family after separation, divorce, or death, and when unmarried mothers keep their babies. The interactive and/or psychological presence of the second parent must certainly have its attendant benefits and costs, but it is difficult to specify when benefits will outweigh costs.

Although most single-parent families will continue to experience the effect of their low economic status, and although the full impact of the change in economic lifestyle is far from fully explored, families appear to differ in their degree of vulnerability and with regard to the stage in their family career at which they are most vulnerable. There is increasing evidence that individuals and family systems are often at greater risk immediately following a transition than they are after a period of reorganization. Thus while most single-parent families will experience some degree of burden, it may not necessarily accompany them throughout their careers. More work is needed on the developmental career of the single-parent family. Research suggests that the single-parent family career is a several-stage process, that single-parent families often functionally exist *before* the crisis event (Bohannon, 1970), that the "absent" parent continues to be present at least for a while (Clapp and Raab, 1979; Earls and Siegel, 1980; Hetherington et al., 1976; Mendes, 1979), and that the family system continually renegotiates its boundaries to include or exclude the absent parent (Ahrons, 1979; Rosenthal and Keshet, 1980; Wallerstein and Kelly, 1980; Weiss, 1979), as well as kin and friends (Colletta, 1979b; McLanahan et al., 1981). These findings are consistent with the notion that the postdivorce adjustment process for individuals involves several stages, but much remains to be understood.

In the emergence of a more conservative era, when the 1980s "hands-off families" mandate seems instead to be an appeal for a "hands-on" policy to support and restore the traditional, two-parent family system, single-parent families seem increasingly vulnerable to challenges from outside forces. For family specialists, the 1980s offer the challenge of coming to understand the particular needs and dynamics of single-parent families, and how best to facilitate their effectiveness. It is time that researchers and policymakers alike acknowledge the prevalence of the single-parent family, and welcome it within the mainstream of American society.

REFERENCES

Abarbanel, A. (1979) "Shared parenting after separation and divorce: a study of joint custody." American Journal of Orthopsychiatry 49 (April): 320–329.

Ahrons, C. (1980a) "Joint custody arrangements in the postdivorce family." Journal of Divorce 3 (Winter): 189–205.

——— (1980b) "Divorce: a crisis of family transition and change." Family Relations 29 (October): 533–540.

——— (1979) "The binuclear family: two households, one family." Alternative Lifestyles 4 (November): 499–515.

Atkin, E. and E. Rubin (1976) Part-Time Father. New York: Signet.

Bane, M. and R. Weiss (1980) "Alone together: the world of single-parent families." American Demographics 2, 5: 11–15.

Benedek, R. and E. Benedek (1979) "Children of divorce: can we meet their needs?" Journal of Social Issues 35, 4: 155–169.

Bernard, J. (1979) "Forward," in G. Levinger and O.S. Moles (eds.) Divorce and Separation: Context, Causes, and Consequences. New York: Basic Books.

Bianchi, S. and R. Farley (1979) "Racial differences in family living arrangements and economic well-being: an analysis of recent trends." Journal of Marriage and the Family 41 (August): 537–551.

Billingsley, A. and J. Giovannoni (1971) "Family: one parent," in R. Morris (ed.) Encyclopedia of Social Work, Vol. 1. New York: National Association of Social Workers.

Blechman, E. (1982) "Are children with one parent at psychological risk? A methodological review." Journal of Marriage and the Family 44 (February): 179–195.

——— and M. Manning (1976) "A reward-cost analysis of the single-parent family," in E. Mash (eds.) Behavior Modification and Families. New York: Brunner/Mazel

Bloom, B., S. Asher, and S. White (1978) "Marital disruption as a stressor: a review and analysis." Psychological Bulletin 85 (July): 867–894.

Bohannon, P. (1970) Divorce and After. Garden City, NY: Doubleday.

Boss, P. (1980a) "The relationship of psychological father presence, wife's personal qualities and wife/family dysfunction in families of missing fathers." Journal of Marriage and the Family 42 (August): 541–549.

——— (1980b) "Normative family stress: family boundary changes across the life-span." Family Relations 29 (October): 445–450.

——— (1977) "A clarification of the concept of psychological father presence in families experiencing ambiguity at boundary." Journal of Marriage and the Family 39 (February): 141–151.

Bradbury, K., S. Danziger, E. Smolensky, and P. Smolensky (1979) "Public assistance, female headship and economic well-being." Journal of Marriage and the Family 41 (August): 519–535.

Brandwein, R., C. Brown, and E. Fox (1974) "Women and children last: the social situation of divorced mothers and their families." Journal of Marriage and the Family 36 (August): 498–514.

Brown, C., R. Feldberg, E. Fox, and J. Kohen (1976) "Divorce: chance of a new lifetime." Journal of Social Issues 32, 1: 119–134.

Burgess, J. K. (1970) "The single-parent family: a social and sociological problem." Family Coordinator 19 (April) 137–144.

Cherlin, A. (1981) Marriage, Divorce, Remarriage. Cambridge, MA: Harvard University Press.

Chiriboga, D., A. Coho, J. Stein, and J. Roberts (1979) "Divorce, stress and social supports: a study in help-seeking behavior." Journal of Divorce 3 (Winter): 121–135.

Clapp, D. and R. Raab (1978) "Follow-up of unmarried adolescent mothers." Social Work 23 (March): 149–153.

Cline, D. and J. Westman (1971) "The impact of divorce on the family." Child Psychiatry and Human Development 2: 78–83.

Cogswell, B. and M. Sussman (1972) "Changing family and marriage forms: complications for human service systems." Family Coordinator 21 (October): 505–515.

Colletta, N. (1979a) "The impact of divorce: father absence or poverty?" Journal of Divorce 3 (Fall): 27–35.

——— (1979b) "Support systems after divorce: incidence and impact." Journal of Marriage and the Family 44 (November): 837–846.

Consortium for the Study of School Needs of Children from One-Parent Families (1980) The Most Significant Minority: One-Parent Children in the Schools. Arlington, VA: National Association of Elementary School Principles and the Institute for Development of Educational Activities.

Dell, P. and A. Applebaum (1977) "Trigenerational enmeshment: unresolved ties of single parents to family of origin." American Journal of Orthopsychiatry 47 (January): 52–59.

Dinerman, M. (1977) "Catch 23: Women, work and welfare." Social Work 22 (November): 472–477.

Doughtery, S. (1978) "Single-adoptive mothers and their children." Social Work 23 (September): 311–314.

Earl, L. and N. Lohmann (1978) "Absent fathers and Black male children." Social Work 28 (November): 413–415.

Earls, F. and B. Siegel (1980) "Precocious fathers." American Journal of Orthopsychiatry 50 (July): 469–480.

Espenshade, T. (1979) "The economic consequences of divorce." Journal of Marriage and the Family 41 (August): 615–625.

Fischer, J. and J. Cardea (1981) "Mothers living apart from their children: a study in stress and coping." Alternative Lifestyles 4. (May): 218–227.

Fox, G. (1981) "Family research, theory and politics: challenges of the eighties." Journal of Marriage and the Family 43 (May): 259–261.

Fulton, J. (1979) "Parental reports of children's post-divorce adjustment." Journal of Social Issues 35 (4): 126–139.

Furstenberg, F., Jr. and K. Talvitie (1980) "Children's names and paternal claims: bonds between unmarried fathers and their children." Journal of Family Issues 1 (March): 31–57.

Galper, M. (1978) Co-parenting. Philadelphia: Running Press.

Glasser, P. and E. Navarre (1965) "Structural problems of the one-parent family." Journal of Social Issues 21, 1: 98–109.

Goldsmith, J. (1979) "Relationships between former spouses: descriptive findings." Presented at the Annual Meeting of the National Council on Family Relations, Boston.

Goldstein, J., A. Freud, and A. Solnit (1979) Before the Best Interests of the Child. New York: Macmillan.

Gongla, P. (1977) "Social relationships after marital separation: a study of women and children." Ph.D. dissertation, Case Western Reserve University.

Greenberg, J. (1979) "Single-parenting and intimacy: a comparison of mothers and fathers." Alternative Lifestyles 2 (August): 308–330.

Greif, J. (1979) "Fathers, children and joint custody." American Journal of Orthopsychiatry 49 (April): 311–319.

Grow, L. (1979) "Today's unmarried mothers: the choices have changed." Child Welfare 58 (July): 363–371.

Haring, B. (1975) "Adoption trends, 1971–1974." Child Welfare 54 (July): 524–525.

Hatch, O. (1981) "Family issues and public policy." COFO Memo 3 (Winter/Spring): 4–5.

Hawkins, L. (1979) "The impact of policy decisions on families." Family Coordinator 28 (April): 264–272.

Hetherington, E. (1978) "The aftermath of divorce," in J. Stevens and M. Mathews (eds.) Mother-child, Father-child Relations. Washington, DC: National Association for the Education of Young Children.

———— (1976) "Divorced fathers." Family Coordinator 25 (October): 417–428.

Hoffman, S. (1977) "Marital instability and the economic status of women." Demography 14 (February): 67–76.

Horowitz, J. and B. Perdue (1977) "Single-parent families." Nursing Clinics of North America 12 (September): 503–511.

Hulme, T. (1976) "Health concerns of the single-parent family," in S. Burden, P. Houston, E. Kriple, R. Simpson, and W. Stultz (eds.) Proceedings of the Changing Family Conference V: The Single-Parent Family. Iowa City: University of Iowa.

Kadushin, A. (1970) "Single-parent adoptions: an overview and some relevant research." Social Service Review 44, 3: 263–274

Kantor, D. and W. Lehr (1975) Inside the Family: Toward a Theory of Family Process. New York: Harper & Row.

Katz, A. (1979) "Lone fathers: perspectives and implications for family policy." Family Coordinator 28 (October): 521–528.

Kelly, J. and J. Wallerstein (1977) "Part-time parent, part-time child: visiting after divorce." Journal of Clinical Child Psychology 6, 2: 51–54.

Keshet, H. and K. Rosenthal (1978) "Fathering after marital separation." Social Work 23 (January): 11–18.

Keshet, J. (1980) "From separation to stepfamily: a subsystem analysis." Journal of Family Issues 1 (December): 517–532.

Kitson, G., H. Lopata, W. Holmes, and S. Meyering (1980) "Divorcees and widows: similarities and differences." American Journal of Orthopsychiatry 50 (April): 291–301.

Kulka, R. and H. Weingarten (1979) "The long-term effects of parental divorce in childhood on adult adjustment." Journal of Social Issues 35, 4: 50–78.

Kurdek, L. and A. Siesky, Jr. (1980) "Sex role self-concepts of single divorced parents and their children." Journal of Divorce 3 (Fall): 249–261.

Lamb, M. (1977) "The effects of divorce on children's personality development." Journal of Divorce 1 (Winter): 163–174.

Levitan, S. and R. Belous (1981) What's Happening to the American Family. Baltimore: Johns Hopkins University Press.

Levitin, T. (1979) "Children of divorce: an introduction." Journal of Social Issues 35, 4: 1–25.

Lindahl, A. (1979) "An evaluation of divorced single parents' views of local church ministries." Dissertation Abstracts 40(A): 1708.

Loge, B. (1977) "Role adjustments to single parenthood: a study of divorced and widowed men and women." Dissertation Abstracts 38(A): 4647.

Longhaugh, R. (1973) "Mother behavior as a variable moderating the effects of father absence." Ethos 1: 456–465.

Lopata, H. (1979) Women as Widows: Support Systems. New York: Elsevier-North Holland.

Luepnitz, D. (1979) "Which aspects of divorce affect children?" Family Coordinator 28 (January): 79–85.

Lynn, D. (1974) The Father: His Role in Child Development. Monterey, CA: Brooks/ Cole.

Malinowski, B. (1930/1974) "Parenthood, the basis of social structure," in R. Coser (ed.) The Family: Its Structure and Functions. New York: St. Martins.

McLanahan, S., N. Wedemeyer, and T. Adelberg (1981) "Network structure, social support, and psychological well-being in the single-parent family." Journal of Marriage and the Family 43 (August): 601–612.

Mendes, H. (1979) "Single-parent families: a typology of lifestyles." Social Work 24 (May): 193–200.

——— (1976) "Single-fathers." Family Coordinator 25 (October): 439–444.

Minuchin, S. (1974) Families and Family Therapy. Cambridge, MA: Harvard University Press.

Moroney, R. (1980) Families, Social Services, and Social Policy: The Issue of Shared Responsibility. Washington, DC: U.S. Department of Health and Human Services, DHHS Publication No. (ADM) 80–846.

Newsome, O. (1977) "Postdivorce interaction: an explanation using exchange theory." Dissertation Abstracts 37(A): 8001.

Nock, S. (1981) "Family life-cycle transitions: longitudinal effects on family members." Journal of Marriage and the Family 43 (August): 703–714.

Parks, A. (1981) "Single-parent families: meeting the challenge of the 1980s." Presented at The Groves Conference on Marriage and the Family, Mt. Pocono.

Raschke, H. and V. Raschke (1979) "Family conflict and children's self-concepts: a comparison of intact and single-parent families." Journal of Marriage and the Family 41 (May): 367–374.

Roman, M. and W. Haddad (1978) The Disposable Parent: The Case for Joint Custody. New York: Holt, Rinehart & Winston.

Rosenthal, K. and H. Keshet (1980) Fathers Without Partners: A Study of Divorced Fathers and Their Families. Totowa, NJ: Rowman & Littlefield.

Ross, H. and I. Sawhill (1975) Time of Transition: The Growth of Families Headed by Women. Washington, DC: Urban Institute.

Rossi, A. (1977) "A biosocial perspective on parenting." Daedalus 106 (Spring): 1–32.

Sawhill, I. (1976) "Discrimination and poverty among women who head families." Signs 1 (1–3): 201–211.

Schorr, A. and P. Moen (1979) "The single-parent and social policy." Social Policy 9 (March/April): 15–21.

Sennett, R. (1974) Families Against the City. New York: Vintage.

Seward, R. (1978) The American Family: A Demographic History. Beverly Hills, CA: Sage.

Shaw, C. and H. McKay (1932) "Are broken homes a causative factor in juvenile delinquency?" Social Forces 19: 514–525.

Shireman, J. and P. Johnson (1976) "Single-persons as adoptive parents." Social Service Review 50 (March): 103–116.

Smith, M. (1980) "The social consequences of single-parenthood: a longitudinal perspective." Family Relations 29 (January): 75–81.

Spicer, J. and G. Hampe (1975) "Kinship interaction after divorce." Journal of Marriage and the Family 37 (February): 113–119.

Sprey, J. (1979) "Conflict theory and the study of marriage and the family," in W. Burr, R. Hill, F.I. Nye, and I. Reiss (eds.) Contemporary Theories About the Family, Vol. 2. New York: Macmillan.

——— (1967) "The study of single-parenthood: some methodological considerations." Family Coordinator 16 (January): 29–34.

Staples, R. (1980) "Intimacy patterns among black, middle-class single parents." Alternative Lifestyles 3 (November): 445–462.

U.S. Bureau of the Census (1981c) Money Income and Poverty Status of Families and Persons. Current Populations Reports, Series P-60, No. 127. Washington, DC: Government Printing Office.

——— (1981d) Child Support and Alimony. Current Population Reports, Series P-23, No. 112. Washington, DC: Government Printing Office.

——— (1980a) Marital Status and Living Arrangements: March 1979. Current Population Reports, Series P-20, No. 349. Washington, DC: Government Printing Office.

Wallerstein, J. and J. Kelly (1980) Surviving the Breakup: How Children and Parents Cope with Divorce. New York: Basic Books.

——— (1979) "Children and divorce: a review." Social Work 24 (November): 468–475.

Wattenberg, E. and H. Reinhardt (1979) "Female-headed families: trends and implications." Social Work 24 (November): 460–467.

Weiss, R. (1979) Going It Alone: The Family Life and Social Situation of the Single-Parent. New York: Basic Books.

——— (1975) Marital Separation. New York: Basic Books.

Wilcox, B. (1981) "Social support in adjusting to marital disruption: a network analysis," in B. Gottlieb (ed.) Social Networks and Social Support. Beverly Hills, CA: Sage.

Wilk, J. (1979) "Assessing single-parent needs." Journal of Psychiatric Nursing 17, 6: 21–22.

Wiseman, J. (1981) "The family and its researchers in the eighties: retrenching, renewing, and revitalizing." Journal of Marriage and the Family 43 (May): 263–266.

Wolff, K. (1950) The Sociology of Georg Simmel. New York: Macmillan.

Woolsey, S. (1977) "Pied piper and the child care debate." Daedalus 106 (Spring): 127–145.

Zimmerman, S. (1979) "Policy, social policy, and family policy: concepts, concerns, and analytical tools." Journal of Marriage and the Family 41 (May): 487–495.

——— (1976) "The family and its relevance for social policy." Social Casework 57 (November): 547–554.

36   *Single-Parent Families*

Blaine R. Porter

STUDY QUESTIONS

1. Explain several of the challenges of being a single parent.
2. Describe four of the unique characteristics facing single-parent families.

INTRODUCTION

Incidence of Single-Parent Families

The fastest growing family form in America today is the single-parent family. More than 11.7 million U.S. children under the age of 18 now live with only one parent. Another 2.5 million are not living with either parent. Approximately 95% of these children living in one-parent family situations are in female-headed families. Heads of households who were female and single (widowed, divorced, unwed mothers) increased 33.8% in the six-year period between 1970 and 1976. The rapidity of this growth and the number of children involved are both demonstrated in the following statistics:

1. In 1974, one child in eight under age 18 was living in a one-parent family.
2. In 1975, one child in seven under age 18 was living in a one-parent family.
3. In 1976, one child in six under age 18 was living in a one-parent family.

These data reveal only the incidence of this phenomenon. They do not reveal the trauma and hardships that many single parents and their children face daily. . . .

Source: Blaine R. Porter, "Single-Parent Families." Reprinted from *Building Family Strengths: Blueprints for Action,* edited by Nick Stinnett, by permission of University of Nebraska Press. Copyright© 1979 by the University of Nebraska Press.

CHALLENGES OF THE SINGLE PARENT

Personal Adjustments

One is confronted with many adjustments upon returning to the single state after having been married. Although there are many differences between graduating from high school or college, or taking a new job, and that of being widowed, divorced or separated under other circumstances, there are some similarities. Both situations involve leaving behind certain familiarities and securities. Both are shaded with fears of the new and the unknown. Both provide opportunities for exploring, growing, becoming something new and even better.

Most formerly married persons whom I have interviewed responded that they feel like second-class citizens. This is especially true of those who have been divorced or who are unwed parents. They claim that society has put them in a classification which denies them the status and sense of belonging they would like to enjoy.

If children are involved in a family that has been broken, then the remaining spouse (in the case of bereavement) and the spouse granted custody of children (in the case of divorce) have greater responsibility. At the same time, for those who are divorced, approximately one-half of single parents (those who don't have custody) are usually deprived of a close association with their children. The task of parenting in any one of these situations will be dealt with later in this paper, but the point here is that these are required of the individual, personal adjustments that are usually new and frequently difficult.

Not only is one deprived of the more acceptable status in our society, but the companionship that was once there is missing. Regardless of the unpleasant times that may have been involved where couples have separated by choice, there are still memories of times spent together that were good and that are missed. It is sometimes difficult to maintain a healthy level of self-esteem as one reflects upon being abandoned or having failed or having been faced with a situation which did not seem to provide any attractive alternatives. In such a situation, one often faces a future of uncertainty and asks, "What is ahead for me now?" Unfortunately, the social supports that exist for intact families are frequently missing for the single parent.

Another of the personal adjustments required of the individual returning to the single state is dealing with the hurt of death or divorce. Others may try to sympathize and to offer assistance, but in most cases one has to cope with this challenge in his/her own unique way.

As one proceeds to try to carry on a meaningful and full and reasonably normal life after having returned to the single state, he/she often is faced with the reality that there are new restrictions placed on relationships with other adults. For example, a divorced woman, or even a widow, often discovers that her former female married friends view her as a threat now and are very jealous about her relationship with their husbands. Married men, in turn, are often afraid or uncomfortable in relationships with a divorced or widowed woman because of how their wives may react. The relationship becomes strained on both sides. Some men are on the make believing that single or divorced women are an easy mark, and the newly divorced or widowed woman may discover that she is faced with overtures and approaches that she has not had to deal with for quite some time—if ever. Probably one of the greatest personal adjustments in this regard is learning how to put up with being misunderstood, for both actions and words are frequently misinterpreted. A net result is that often, if not usually, the single parent must establish ties with new social groups and establish new personal relationships. Previous relationships usually change, even though one may not wish it so.

There is a danger of focusing too much on one's miseries and problems and, therefore, not engaging in activities that help one seek and find healthy solutions. We often share our feelings with others and occasionally derive strength from meeting with others who have common situations. However, it is important to avoid reinforcing self-defeating behaviors. Such persons often talk too much—especially about their problems. It is like talking about physical illness in a hospital—it is common and natural, but not healthy or productive.

Single parents often feel that others are watching more closely and that they are quick to criticize, often in a condescending way. For example, one may be confronted with a statement such as: "It is hard for you isn't it, Jane, when your son behaves that way, since you don't have a husband to help you out?" Her son's behavior may not be materially different from that of his age mates coming from intact families, but single parents are seldom given the benefit of the doubt.

One of the challenges facing new single parents is having feelings of discouragement and being overwhelmed with responsibilities and not having one with whom to share them. Sometimes the single parent may feel that he/she is making headway and then have an event, statement, picture, song or some other stimuli bring back memories and feelings that one thought had been processed and handled.

Coping effectively or ineffectively with personal adjustments will determine the single parent's potential success in dealing effectively with the parenting responsibilities which he/she will face. It is important to make reasonable progress in resolving personal problems, otherwise it is difficult if not impossible to be an effective parent. The task of parenting is a challenging one, even under the *best* of circumstances.

Parenting Responsibilities

The basic principles of effective parenting are the same whether or not the marriage dyad is complete or broken. I will not spend time discussing those here, but it is important to remember that a father and a mother may decide they will no longer remain together as husband and wife, but they must realize that they will be parents forever.

There are certain features or characteristics that seem to be unique to one-parent families. Let me now share with you some observations and experiences that are referred to most frequently by single parents. These are not inclusive but merely illustrative.

1. Many single parents identify a feeling of being incomplete. A vital feature seems to be missing. They are faced with the dilemma of whether to try to fulfill two roles or one. Of course, it is not realistic for one person to fill the roles of father *and* mother. Professionals need to help single parents not feel guilt about not being able to be all things to their children. Singleness may necessitate modification of tasks (cooking, shopping, breadwinning, etc.) but the role should be kept clear in the eyes of the parent and children.

2. Children in single-parent families are most often deprived of a consistent, present sex-role model for the absent parent. It is difficult to provide this role model on a substitute basis with regularity and consistency. Since 95% of children in single-parent families are living with a female head of household, it means that several million children are primarily receiving their male model as it is interpreted through the eyes of their mother. In some cases this, no doubt, has serious consequences.

3. Single parents are faced with the challenge of explaining death/divorce to children. This may be especially difficult for some, especially if the parent's feelings are still unclear or if he/she is not sure how much information to give.

4. There is often a temptation to place too much responsibility too early on children. A mother, for example, may say to a 10- or 12-year-old boy: "You have to be the man of the family now." That is too heavy a burden for a 10- or 12-year-old boy.

5. Parents also face the challenge of helping children cope with the stigma of being different—especially the divorced. Children, like their parents, sometimes feel like second-class citizens at school, church, or in the community. I recall the pathetic situation of one youngster who was invited to attend a party. As he cautiously rounded the corner into a room where considerable activity was taking place, he shyly inquired, "Is this the party for divorced kids?" But we need to remember that some children are better off being with one parent who is relatively happy and well adjusted than being in a situation where parents are constantly bickering, arguing and fighting. Some children seem to be rather indifferent and cope effectively, and others experience serious emotional trauma and sometimes require psychiatric treatment.

6. Unfortunately, battles often continue after a divorce. Some divorced couples fall into the trap of confronting each other in marriage and end up in a win/lose or lose/lose battle long after the divorce. They do not realize that the idea of "winning" a conflict is an illusion and that one person's victory inevitably turns into a loss for both of them, and even more seriously, if children are involved, it turns into a loss for the children also. In such a situation, everybody loses. . . .

SUMMARY

A parent without a partner is faced with:

1. The usual challenge of life and its responsibilities.

2. The task of adjusting to a usually hurting and/or traumatic experience of death or divorce or separation.

3. The responsibilities of parenthood—alone—which are often complicated by:

   a. Financial problems

   b. Children suffering from low self-esteem

   c. Children suffering from guilt, thinking that they are the cause of the divorce

   d. An uncooperative and difficult ex-spouse

   e. The temptation to use children as "sympathetic ears"

   f. The temptation to use children as "spies"

   g. The struggle of two parents trying to "win" children's approval, applying tactics that are known in legal circles as "the lollipop game"

   h. Children playing one parent against the other

4. Living in a society that provides very few social supports for his/her particular situation.

5. The overcoming of added burdens often imposed by "friends," relatives and social institutions

6. The difficulty of trying to finance two households instead of one (sometimes)

7. Uncertainty about the future

8. The dilemma of remarriage (sometimes)

9. The challenge of learning to know oneself, gaining control over one's life and future. This future is more bright with greater opportunities for women than ever before.

10. Not settling for less than one can achieve. We all have choices to make in given situations. I firmly believe that some individuals do not perform at as high a level as they are capable because they are unwilling to try the experience of pain, to take risks. We have discovered that many individuals have survived experiences they thought they could not endure: illness; accident; being lost in the mountains, desert, or wilderness; plane crashes; humiliating and torturing experiences in concentration camps. Usually these experiences were endured and individuals survived because they had no other choice or easy escape. Many times when we do have a choice we take what appears to be the easiest, least painful way rather than carefully analyzing the course of action that would be best in terms of long-range consequences.

We desperately need more research. The picture, circumstance, attitude and opportunities for single parents are changing rapidly. Very little empirical research is available about that and most of what we have deals with the affective dimensions of single-parent families. In the absence of the research we need I have shared with you my observations and experiences.

It is possible that the single parent feels as thousands of others have felt, namely, that he/she has been picked on, that fate has dealt him/her an unfair blow, that he/she does not deserve to be in the situation in which he/she finds himself/herself. Most of us have had things come our way that we did not deserve—both good and bad. The important considerations are not why we are here or how we got in this situation, but where we go from here.

May I share with you an account of a friend of mine as he recuperated in a New York room following surgery for cancer in his throat. He entered with fear; faced pain, risk, and an uncertain future. Loss was experienced; suffering occurred. He relived much of his past. He survived. He conquered. He achieved peace. He closed with the following:

> Some days have passed. Last night I had a full night of sleep without any medication. How glorious! The pigeons are cooing more pleasantly this morning. The Central Park birds are singing more lustily. Pain, the ugly, sadistic companion of the past three weeks, has moved out to give place first to the mild-mannered gentleman Distress, which in turn has now given way to the friendly person Comfort. And with Comfort comes Peace, and with Peace a return of memory of a certain Time, the Time with which I was formerly acquainted. The Time which has now rubbed its eyes, taken a deep breath, saluted, clicked its heels, and comes marching its way back into the normal sixty-second minutes and sixty-minute hours and twenty-four-hour days.
>
> TIME has been resurrected, peace restored, and life is good again![1]

I believe that a parent without a partner, through self-evaluation, goal-setting, determination, and discovering and building upon the strengths which he/she possesses, can have Peace restored and reach greater heights of achievement than have yet been experienced. Unfortunately, hundreds of thousands of single parents do not have the personal skills and resources to accomplish these alone. It is the task of professional persons to play a major role in providing help, leadership and influencing public policy so that more single-parent families can be effective, fully functioning ones.

Hasten the day!

---

[1] Spencer W. Kimball, *One silent, sleepless night.* Salt Lake City, Utah: Deseret Book Company.

37 *The Stepfamily Cycle*

Patricia L. Papernow

STUDY QUESTIONS

1. Briefly describe the seven stages of stepparent development.
2. What are the therapeutic tasks involved in moving from assimilation to awareness?

A REVIEW OF STEPFAMILY STRUCTURE

We know that stepfamilies begin their lives together with a very different history and structure from biological families. Briefly, biological families usually have some time together to develop a couple subsystem, and what Zinker (1981) called a "middle ground"—a solid area of shared interests, values, and rhythms of functioning. Children are added to the system one by one, allowing the couple to slowly resolve differences, create shared values, and evolve a cooperative parenting style.

When a couple divorces, a "double single parent stage" (Sager et al., 1983) begins in which children become part of two single parent families. A natural part of this process is the dissolution of intergenerational boundaries, as the single parent turns to his or her children for nourishment and support previously provided by the spouse. These relationships have been variously described in the literature as "overcathexis" (Neubauer, 1960), "pathologically intensified" (Fast & Cain, 1966), "intense overdependence" (Messinger, 1976), and more simply, "exceptionally close" (Visher & Visher, 1979). By whatever

Source: Patricia L. Papernow, "The Stepfamily Cycle: An Experiental Model of Stepfamily Development." *Family Relations,* July 1984, pp. 355–363. Copyrighted 1984 by the National Council on Family Relations, 3989 Central Ave., N.E., Suite 550, Minneapolis, MN 55421. Reprinted by permission.

name, enmeshment seems to be a normal part of single parent/child relationships!

The stepfamily begins with the stepparent as an outsider to a biological subsystem with much shared history and many unfamiliar rhythms, rules, and ways of operating which have been built over years of connection and often intensified in the single parent stage. This biological subsystem includes an ex-spouse, dead or alive, with intimate ties to the children.

This structure—a weak couple subsystem, a tightly bounded parent-child alliance, and potential "interference" in family functioning from an "outsider"— would signal pathology in a biological family (Minuchin, 1974). It is simply the starting point for normal stepfamily development.

THE STEPFAMILY CYCLE

In analyzing the data from in-depth interviews with stepparents (Papernow, 1980), the Gestalt Experience Cycle proved a useful framework for characterizing qualitative changes in stepparents' experience over time. Seven stages of stepparent development emerged: (1) Fantasy; (2) Assimilation; (3) Awareness; (4) Mobilization; (5) Action; (6) Contact; and, (7) Resolution (see Figure 1, inner circle).

Over the past few years, data describing the experience of biological parents and of children in stepfamilies have been integrated into the model. In addition, development of the stepfamily system has been more explicitly described. The resulting model, the Stepfamily Cycle, describes the above seven stages of individual development of stepfamily members, interacting with three stages of family development. In the three Early Stages (1. Fantasy, 2. Assimilation and 3. Awareness), the family remains primarily divided along biological lines, with most nourishment, agreement on rules and rituals and cycle completion happening within the biological subsystem(s).

In the two Middle Stages (4. Mobilization and 5. Action), the stepfamily begins the tasks of loosening old boundaries and restructuring itself to strengthen step subunits, with the couple first beginning to complete cycles together in the Action phase. In the two Later Stages (6. Contact and 7. Resolution) contact finally becomes regular and reliable within step subsystems, ushering in a period of structural solidification during which a clear stepparent role emerges for the first time.

In the initial interview study (Papernow, 1980), the two "fast" families completed the entire Stepfamily Cycle in about 4 years, four "average families" took about 7 years. Three "slower" families remained stuck in the Early Stages after 5, 8, and 12 years. (Two of these latter three later divorced. The third moved on to Mobilization in the 9th year and at this writing, several years later, appears to have reached Resolution.)

Early Stages: Getting Started

Stage 1. Fantasy. The fantasies of people beginning a stepfamily and the danger of these myths to stepfamily development have been well articulated in the literature (Goldstein, 1974; Schulman, 1972; Visher & Visher, 1978,

1979), making it enticing for family practitioners to wade in with combat boots to challenge them. While fantasy must give way to reality for stepfamilies to progress, this phase seems to be a universal and normal part of stepfamily development. It is crucial that stepfamily members be approached with gentleness and empathy about their myths and fantasies. Not only are these myths and fantasies powerful, but their owners almost universally look back upon this phase with a sense of chagrin and self-deprecation bordering on deep shame.

Adult members of stepfamilies ruefully describe shared fantasies: rescuing children from the excesses or inadequacies of the exspouse, healing a broken family, stepparents adoring their stepchildren and being welcomed by them; for stepparents, marrying a nurturing parent, and for biological parents, having someone with whom to share the load. For mental health professionals the shared fantasy is: "We understand this so it won't be so hard for us."

Meanwhile the child's fantasies are markedly different: "I thought that maybe if I just didn't pay attention to him, this new guy would go away." Most powerful and most enduring is, "I really hoped for a long time that my parents would get back together."

Stage 2. Assimilation: We're Glad You're Here But Don't Come In. The term "Assimilation" captures the intention, not the accomplishment of this phase, as adult stepfamily members join in attempting to carry out the fantasy of the new family. Looking back, one stepmother put it, "I was trying so hard to make these two broken pieces of plate go together. But they were from different plates and they just didn't fit!"

Stepparents, straining to join the intimate biological parent-child unit, find themselves assaulted by unexpectedly powerful and negative feelings: jealousy, resentment, confusion and inadequacy, as they are unable to join the powerful rhythm of cycle completion firmly established in the parent-child relationship. The fantasy of marrying a nurturing parent becomes a bad dream as stepparents find themselves watching their spouses relate more intimately and protectively toward their children than toward their mates.

Acting on their normal eagerness to be liked, most stepparents reach out to their stepchildren, only to find them rejecting or indifferent. "For two whole years Julie would march in the front door for weekend visits, walk right past me and throw her arms around her father." It is now known that for most children every move toward a stepparent places a child in a loyalty conflict (Visher & Visher, 1979) ("If I love my stepfather, have I betrayed my father?"). Furthermore while divorced or widowed adults may be eager to move on, children often struggle for many years with their grief over the breakup of their original family. This original family has been replaced by a single parent family with its intimate parent-child relationship. The stepparent now threatens to dislodge the child once more in order to create a new couple relationship. Unfortunately, all too few stepparents have information about these threats and conflicts, leaving many stepparents straining to make contact, withdrawing in defeat, or alternating between the two.

While the stepparent struggles with rejection and loneliness, the biological parent has a source of nourishment and support in his or her children. In this phase, the biological parent may interpret the stepparent's very different experience of the children, difficulty in joining, and need for withdrawal as a lack of desire to be part of the family—a frightening thought—as it means another failure or loss. Fear, and a very different experience of family functioning, combine so that biological parents may find themselves greeting even the stepparent's tentative expression of negative feelings with disbelief, protectiveness toward children, and even criticism.

For adult stepfamily members, the experience of the Assimilation Stage is much like the sensation phase of the Gestalt Experience Cycle—a strong sense that something's not right, and great difficulty figuring out just what it is. In addition, both members of the stepcouple face powerful forces against moving to awareness. The stepparent's feelings of jealousy, resentment, and rejection and the biological parent's feelings of grief, guilt, and fear of another loss, are nobody's favorite and are more easily denied than acknowledged. Lack of validation from intimate others adds to the confusion for stepparents. For stepparents this confusion is often intensified by the fact that the biological parent's perceptions and sense of "what's normal" are often shared by an extended family of in-laws, aunts, uncles, and friends of the previous marriage.

It is important to note the confusion of the Early Stages reverberates throughout the extended stepfamily system. For instance, how do grandparents conduct their long established relationship with their now ex-daughter-in-law? Moves to continue the relationship may create acute discomfort in the new stepfamily. To abandon such a long-term relationship is equally impossible.

Stage 3. Awareness: Getting Clear. At first falteringly and then with more confidence, stepfamily members can begin to make more sense out of what is happening to them. For stepparents this means beginning to put names on painful feelings as well as experiencing them more fully, without the self-deprecation of the Assimilation Stage. The increasing clarity includes another qualitative shift for stepparents, as they begin to see patterns to their experience: "I'm jealous and resentful because I'm left out over and over again, not because I'm childish." While the pain doesn't go away, the picture of where it comes from and why it hurts so much gets clearer. As self-acceptance grows, stepparents who continue through the cycle begin to form more definitive statements about their needs from their spouses and stepchildren. Compare these two statements made a year apart by a stepmother named Barbara struggling with an ex-wife's desire to be included in holiday dinners:

I feel so guilty. It's so hard to put words on the feelings. When she asks to have dinner with us I get so confused. I want two separate families, and when we get together, it feels like one family. And I'm the outsider. (Papernow, 1980, p. 139)

And a year later:

I finally got clear that I don't want her at our family events. It's just too hard for me. I want her to have a separate birthday and a separate

Thanksgiving with her kids. I don't think there's any way my husband can understand—it seems natural to him to have her here. But it's just not OK with me any more.

As is implicit in this quote, it is often the stepparent who first becomes aware of a need for change in the stepfamily. This is not surprising, as the old family rules and boundaries continue to be much more supportive and syntonic to the biological parent than they are to the stepparent.

Meanwhile, biological parents report that they begin to gain clarity about the pressure inherent in their central position in the stepfamily structure as the person closest to children, stepparent, and ex-spouse. Biological parents naturally want to protect their children from further hurt and from too much additional change. On the other hand, intimacy with a new partner requires excluding children and imposing new rules. The task of resolving the relationship with the previous spouse may not yet be complete, yet the new couple relationship creates pressure to sever old ties. Many single parents fear that even desirable changes in the ex-spouse relationship could jeopardize their access to their children. While this central position may have created a vague sense of discomfort in the Assimilation Stage, it becomes a clearer source of conflict in the Awareness Stage. As one biological father put it:

I realized I had this precarious position in the middle. I realized I was always watching: Is this going to work out or isn't it? Will I be able to have a woman I care about and keep my relationship with my kids? Will I have to choose one?

While much internal change is taking place within the adults in the Early Stages, the awareness process remains fairly private. The lay literature exhorts stepcouples to speed stepfamily integration by talking to each other from the beginning. Observational research at the Gestalt Institute of Cleveland (Zinker & Nevis, 1981) has demonstrated that completed cycles of communication about differences require that each individual be able to articulate his or her own awareness and be heard by the other. In the Early Stages of stepfamily development, most biological parents and stepparents cannot hear (much less elicit) each other's very different experience of the family. The stepparent remains tentative in the face of what one person called the "biological force field" of established rules and norms. The biological parent is frightened of another failure and protective of his or her children. The combination makes communication about step issues almost impossible at this time. Thus stepfamily structure remains much the same throughout the Early Stages. Most communication nourishment and completed interaction cycles continue to take place within the biological parent-child subsystem.

It is not surprising that many stepfamilies get stuck in the Early Stages. A supportive spouse seems to provide the best insurance of speed and ease of movement through the Early Stages of the Cycle. Spouses in the two fast families reported in Papernow (1980) were able to articulate their experience as well as empathize with each other very early in their stepfamily's development.

However, stepfamily structure militates against such mutual support in the couple relationship until the Action Stage. Both the initial interview study and subsequent data indicate that average families take 2 to 3 years to complete the Early Stages. Slower families can remain stuck there for many years. Like 2 year old temper tantrums, the problem is not how to avoid the Early Stages, but how to get through them and on to the next phase of development within 2 or 3 years. It is interesting to note that timing of stepparent movement from Assimilation to Awareness and from Awareness to more active Mobilization, is often related to an infusion of support from someone or something outside the couple relationship: contact with another stepparent who really understood, a book which clarified stepfamily struggles, a therapist who happened to be knowledgeable about stepfamilies, a move from the biological unit's home to a house or community new to the entire family.

Middle Stages: Restructuring

Stage 4. Mobilization: Airing Differences. Many stepparents can mark a specific time when they finally began speaking up with more energy and strength about their perceptions, needs, and feelings. The particular issue around which stepparents mobilize themselves varies: some ask their spouses to restrict phone calls from and to the ex-spouse to particular hours; others finally insist on a door to the parental bedroom. Some more vigorously lobby for support on a particular disciplinary issue. Some overwhelmed stepmothers make their first moves to divest themselves of lopsided parenting responsibilities they had absorbed from an apparently "ineffective" ex-spouse.

While in some families the stepparent's request is met with relieved support by the biological parent ("Finally I know what he needs in order to be part of this family!"), in many families this ushers in a period of conflict and chaos as highly charged differences become aired for the first time. Even couples able to handle differences in other areas of their relationship find conflict over these stepfamily issues deeply polarizing.

It is important for both family practitioners and stepfamily members to know that many fights in this phase appear to be trivial, but are actually major struggles over whether the biological subsystem will continue to function as it has, or the family will change its structure. A stepfamily arguing wildly about the appropriate bedtime for a teenager may actually be struggling over whether the girl and her father will continue to have a special time together in the evening, as they had throughout her childhood (especially in the single parent stage), or the stepmother will have time alone with her husband. At this point in the Stepfamily Cycle the biological parent may begin to feel much more acutely distressed, as the stepparent's demands intensify the biological parent's conflict between meeting the child's needs (or keeping peace with the ex-spouse) and supporting the new couple relationship.

Stepparents often initiate these fights, as they are the excluded and dissatisfied members. In this sense stepparents may often act as change agents to begin the crucial process of loosening the boundaries around the biological subsystem.

Stage 5. Action: Going Into Business Together. The energy and expressiveness of the Mobilization Stage begins what organizational consultants call the "unfreezing" of the old system (Hersey & Blanchard, 1979). The Action Stage marks the beginning of building a new one, as couples begin to work together to resolve their differences.

In Gestalt terms, the couple must now travel together back to the Awareness Stage. In a stepfamily this means articulating the very different perceptions, needs, and feelings experienced by stepparents and biological parents. It also means staying engaged long enough and with enough mutual empathy to create enough shared awareness so that the family can now mobilize and act as a unit to meet their diverse needs. Most workable solutions which result from this mutual effort will leave some of the "old" ways of doing things intact while creating brand new rituals, rules and boundaries. Thus, father and daughter may establish a "special time" together, but during the daytime on the weekend, leaving evenings after 11:00 P.M. for couple time.

The moves in this phase have in common a quality of firmness, clarity, the shared investment of both spouses, and the fact that they actually change the family structure. Most crucial for stepfamily integration are moves which establish stepcouple boundaries: carving out time alone together, closing the bedroom door, consulting each other on child rearing and visitation issues. Boundaries around the stepparent stepchild relationship also begin to be built. The process may include the biological parent remaining in the background when stepparent and stepchild interact, especially when they are fighting, and the stepparent beginning to ally with stepchildren against their biological parent at times.

Moves toward establishing firmer family boundaries include creating new stepfamily rituals, and more clearly defining differences between stepfamily and ex-spouse's family. It is crucial to the adjustment of all family members, but particularly that of the children who have loyalties to *two* families, that the differences between their two families be described without connotations of right or wrong: "In this family it's OK to swear, but only 3 hours of television per day. In your Mom's house you can't swear and you can watch as much television as you like."

Just as the disequilibrium of the Early Stages reverberated throughout the stepfamily suprasystem, new rules and boundaries established in the Middle Stages affect the entire extended stepfamily. For instance, a stepfamily decision to initiate a new Christmas ritual may conflict with established extended family rituals, requiring renegotiation not only with the ex-spouse, but with four sets of grandparents, uncles, and aunts. (The numbers involved in stepfamily politics can be overwhelming at times.)

As in all stages, the changes of the Middle Stages take place little by little over time, with some overlap with other stages. Nonetheless these moves seem to be concentrated in a period of about 1 to 3 years.

Movement through the first half of the Stepfamily Cycle is clearly experienced as uphill, until the Action stage when the couple first begins to function as a unit. While this material provides no hard numbers, data from both the initial study (Papernow, 1980) and subsequent input indicate that most

PATRICIA L. PAPERNOW

families who make it to the Action stage seem to do so in a total of about 4 years. This is consistent with findings in the clinical literature that the first 3 to 4 years of stepfamily living seem to be a "critical period" in which the family either makes it or breaks up (Mills, 1980; Visher & Visher, 1978, 1979).

Later Stages: Solidifying the Stepfamily

Developmental schema in the literature thus far take us solidly into the Middle Stages with some elements of the Contact Stage appearing (McGoldrick & Carter, 1980). However, there is very little describing the Resolution Stage—the experience of stepfamily living after patterns of nourishment have been established in steprelationships and after the stepparent role has been solidly established.

Stage 6. Contact: Intimacy in Step Relationships. As the changes of the Action Stage ease children out of the couple relationship and the biological parent out of the stepparent-child relationship, a new phase emerges, the Contact Stage, marked by increasing intimacy and authenticity in steprelationships. In the indepth interviews reported in Papernow (1980), quotes describing stepparent-child interaction began to run several pages of richly detailed exchanges over what names to call each other, what it was like in the beginning, how the stepparent and child experienced each other and what they wanted and didn't want from each other.

In this phase, the couple relationship, previously polarized by step issues, is now more often felt as an intimate sanctuary in which to share these issues, including painful or difficult feelings. While couples in the Contact Stage still describe intense struggles over some step issues, these exchanges are now characterized by a quality of freshness and completeness. In Gestalt language, members of step relationships are now able to move through the entire experience cycle together, so that real contact is made, resolution is reached, and exchanges feel satisfying and finished leaving a sense of well-being. In family systems language, steprelationships are no longer triadic, ushering in the possibility of real one-to-one exchanges within step subsystems. An appropriate subtitle for this phase might be, "Now that we're alone together, who are you anyway?"

It is not until the Contact Stage, after the major restructuring moves of the Middle Stages, that stepparents can confidently describe a solid stepparent role. These data support that of others who maintain that the development of a stepparent role is inextricably intertwined with stepfamily restructuring (Waldron & Whittington, 1979).

Many attempts to define the stepparent role appear in the literature (Draughon, 1975; Fast & Cain, 1966; Waldron & Whittington, 1979). Despite many differences in details of the workable stepparent roles described by stepfamily members in this phase, they seem to have in common the following major qualities: (a) The role does not usurp or compete with the biological parent of the same sex; (b) The role includes an intergenerational boundary between stepparent and child; (c) The role is sanctioned by the rest of the stepfamily, particularly the spouse; (d) The role incorporates the special qualities this stepparent brings to this family.

It is interesting to note that differences which had created great discomfort in the Early Stages and intense conflict in the Mobilization Stage, often form the foundation for the stepparent role in this phase. A woman who enters a very hang-loose family becomes "the one who teaches the girls how to take care of their clothes, and how to buy nice things." A very expressive man who enters a fairly polite family becomes "the one who teaches them about feelings."

Stage 7. Resolution: Holding on and Letting Go. As the following quote from a stepfather so eloquently describes, in the Resolution Stage, steprelationships now not only provide occasional satisfaction, they begin to feel solid and reliable:

> Deep down I really know now that my stepdaughter and I have a very special connection. That can't be threatened by anything. And I know it is a lifetime connection. And there is a real bottom line of security there where I know I have already made a really big difference to her, and I know she's made a big difference to me. (Papernow, 1980, p. 208)

In Gestalt language, steprelationships can now, finally, go to the background, and no longer require constant attention and maintenance. In this stage, norms have been established, a history has begun to build, and the family now has a particular and reliable rhythm of cycle completion in which all members can join. Although issues of inclusion and exclusion reappear occasionally as biological ties remain more intense than steprelationships, these have primarily been resolved. In some families this has meant a decision to have a much more distant relationship with one or more stepchildren.

The Resolution Stage is also a time of grieving. It is a cruel paradox of stepparenting that the holding on which becomes possible between stepparents and their children in the Contact Stage now sharpens the sense of loss at sharing this child with another biologically more entitled parent. This is especially acute at visitation times.

For the biological parent, grief centers around the reality of interrupted parenting. This is particularly painful for noncustodial parents of teenagers (often fathers) whose children begin visiting less as peer relationships based in the custodial community become primary. "I feel as if the father part of me has been castrated," said one father. It is as if, in the Resolution Stage, stepfamily members bring to awareness and relinquish the last fantasies of living like a biological family.

Letting go of children, a major life crisis in many biological families, is a regular occurrence in most stepfamilies, and will continue to be as joint custody becomes the norm. Despite the more acute pain involved in facing this reality once more, by the Resolution Stage, stepfamilies have invented ways to make this regularly, and prematurely, occurring crisis of "holding on and letting go" a normative event in their lives: "We always go to MacDonald's on the way to and from the airport." "We always try to have time alone as a couple before and after visit. When we do that it goes fine. When we don't, it's chaos." "We have no visitors in our house before 2:00 P.M. on the Sunday the kids arrive to spend their week with us." "I finally learned that my stepson needs time alone before he leaves to visit his father, and again after he comes back."

One of the most satisfying aspects of the mature stepparent role experienced during the Resolution Stage, is that the stepparent is now solidly established as an "intimate outsider"—intimate enough for children to confide in, and outside enough to share in areas which might prove too threatening to bring up with biological parents. Stepparents may now find themselves a special confidante to stepchildren in areas as sex, peer relationships, drugs, distress that a biological parent is holding on too tightly during visitations, and unresolved grief about the divorce.

New step issues continue to arise throughout stepfamily life—decisions about childbearing, shift in visitation arrangements, disagreements between families about money, joint decision making about schools, etc. On particularly stressful issues, families may find themselves reexperiencing the entire Stepfamily Cycle, with some period of confusion and lack of articulation, occasional periods of panicked conflict and polarization along biological lines. However, generally, issues which would have remained as "lumps under the rug" in the Assimilation Stage, or created great disequilibrium in the Mobilization Stage, now occur within the context of a solid couple and stepfamily structure whose members regularly come to resolution together. Tom again captures the feeling of solidarity and reliability of the Resolution Stage:

> I can feel that we've moved. Not easily because it's been a pain in the ass. But I feel very clear that our family works. That is resolved. It's been proven over the years that we could do it and we're doing it. We're happy for the most part. There's a lot of love. You can feel that the family is working. (Papernow, 1980, p. 201)

IMPLICATIONS FOR PRACTITIONERS

Recently, practitioners have advocated family therapy for stepfamily problems (Kaplan, 1977; Ransom et al., 1979; Sager et al., 1983; Schulman, 1972; Waldron & Whittington, 1979). In the Early Stages it is the stepparent who is most likely to appear for help, complaining of depression, anxiety and a sense of worthlessness. While development from the Mobilization Stage of the Stepfamily Cycle onwards is a family task, the primary tasks of the Early Stages are individual ones. For the stepparent, the goal is to move from the self-doubt and confusion of the Assimilation Stage to solid enough awareness to engage fruitfully in the stepfamily system. Individual therapy can be very helpful in this differentiation task (see also Visher & Visher, 1979).

The therapeutic tasks of moving from Assimilation to Awareness include: helping stepparents to identify and separate shoulds ("I should love these children") from real experience; education about the stepchild's dilemma; tying powerful and seemingly mysterious feelings like jealousy and resentment to real events; education about the roots of those events in stepfamily structure; support to pursue interests and friendships outside the stepfamily which can provide some of the mastery and nourishment missing for the stepparent in early stepfamily structure; and, finally, identification of a few specific needs from spouse and stepchildren, followed by help generating spousal support. In some families this is enough to launch the restructuring process.

Often intrapsychic issues, for instance chronic difficulty identifying needs or mobilizing to meet them, are intertwined with stepfamily issues. The informed practitioner must treat these without discounting the power of early stepfamily structure to create apparent pathology in the healthiest of us. Furthermore, all individual work with stepparents must be done with an awareness of the entire system's needs. While it is rarely supportive of clients' intimate relationships to side with them against their partners, it is especially enticing and particularly destructive for individual therapists of stepparents to do so. The challenge is to empathize with the stepparent, providing lots of support, while also understanding and empathizing with the struggles of other stepfamily members. Placing these struggles within a developmental framework makes this task easier for both therapist and client.

While individual therapy may be supportive to stepfamily development in the Early Stages, the difficulties of the Mobilization Stage are systems problems for which individual therapy may be quite destructive and much less effective. Family therapy is suggested as the treatment of choice. Sager et al. (1983) in their seminal work in this field suggest that when possible the entire "suprasystem" (i.e., members of both families) should be involved for best results.

Once the uphill half of the Stepfamily Cycle has been completed, the need for therapeutic intervention will be less intense. The form of assistance in the Resolution Stage may now depend on the locus of the problem. For example, unresolved grief may be adequately handled in individual therapy unless the couple is having trouble supporting each other. Differences in childbearing generations which often become more intense in the Resolution Stage (when the biological parent is "finished" with childbearing and the childless stepparent wants a child) is a couples issue, while a school problem will be most successfully resolved by involving the entire suprasystem.

It is worth stating explicitly that education of stepfamily members about normal stepfamily development is a powerful therapeutic tool in itself. Such education will usually play an important role in successful therapeutic work with stepfamilies and their members.

While support appears crucial for the uphill effort, it is sobering and important for mental health professionals to remember that very few stepfamily members will seek assistance through psychotherapy. Family practitioners will do their best service to stepfamilies by making information about normal stepfamily development available to the general public, offering educational groups (Jacobson, 1979; Messinger, 1976; Messinger, Walker & Freeman, 1978; Visher & Visher, 1983) through churches, PTAs, day care centers, and schools. We also need to encourage colleagues, pediatricians, ministers, lawyers, and others to make lay publications about stepfamily living (Burt & Burt, 1983; Einstein, 1982; Lewis, 1980; Visher & Visher, 1979) available in their waiting rooms; to make photocopied articles from the professional literature available to clients and to post copies of the *Stepfamily Bulletin* visibly on their bulletin boards.

A more detailed and realistic picture of the impact of stepfamily structure on members' experience, as well as an understanding of the awareness tasks of the Early Stages may help stepfamily members to move more steadily through Assimilation to Awareness. Understanding the normal panic over differences and subsequent hard work and specific Action steps which begin the restructuring process in the Middle Stages, as well as more vivid and detailed pictures of the fruits this work bears in the Later Stages, may enable stepfamily members to hang in with more hope and productive effort through the crucial uphill half of the Stepfamily Cycle and coast with more awareness of what has been accomplished over the bumps in the later stages.

CONCLUSION

The Stepfamily Cycle facilitates organization of themes and strains of stepfamily living as stepfamily members experience them over time. This phenomenological approach has created a framework which enables stepfamily members to easily recognize their stage in the cycle.

As an educational tool, the qualitative descriptions upon which the Stepfamily Cycle is built also seem to help stepfamily members empathize across their diverse experience of stepfamily living, as well as enabling family practitioners to use language and examples which join empathetically with all stepfamily members while moving for structural change.

In both therapeutic and educational work with stepfamilies, the Stepfamily Cycle has proven to be very helpful in placing difficult and confusing experiences within a normal chronological developmental framework. It gives clues to areas of difficulty and provides a guide to what kinds of moves might lead onward.

REFERENCES

Burt, M. S., & Burt, R. B. (1983). *What's special about our stepfamily?* Garden City, NY: Doubleday & Co.

Draughon, M. (1975). Stepmother's model of identification in relation to mourning in the child. *Psychological Reports*, **36**(1), 183–189.

Einstein, S. (1982). Stepfamilies: Living, loving, and learning. New York: Macmillan.

Fast, I., & Cain, A. C. (1966). The stepparent role: Potential for disturbances in family functioning. *American Journal of Orthopsychiatry*, **36**(3), 485–491.

Goldstein, H. S. (1974). Reconstituted families: The second marriage and its children. *Psychiatric Quarterly*, **48**(3), 433–440.

Hersey, P. & Blanchard, K. H. (1979). *Management of organizational behavior*. New Jersey: Prentice-Hall.

Jacobson, D. S. (1979). Stepfamilies: Myths and realities. *Social Work*, **24**(3), 202–207.

Kaplan, S. L. (1977). Structural family therapy for children of divorce: Case reports. *Family Process*, **16**(1), 75–83.

Keshet, J. K. (1980). From separation to stepfamily: A subsystem analysis. *Journal of Family Issues*, **1**(4), 517–532.

Lewis, H. C. (1980). *All about families—The second time around*. Atlanta: Peachtree Publishers.

Messinger, L. (1976). Remarriage between divorced people with children from previous marriages: A proposal for preparation for re-marriage. *Journal of Marriage and Family Counseling*, **2**(2), 193–200.

Messinger, L., Walker, K. N. & Freeman, S. J. (1978). Preparation for remarriage following divorce: The use of group techniques. *American Journal of Orthopsychiatry*, **48**(2), 263–272.

Mills, D. (1980). *Issues in remarriage: A clinical perspective*. Paper presented at the annual meeting of the National Council on Family Relations, Portland, Oregon.

Minuchin, S. (1974). *Families and family therapy*. Cambridge, MA: Harvard University Press.

Neubauer, P. D. (1960). The one-parent child and his oedipal development. *Psychoanalytic Study of the Child*, **15**, 286–309.

Papernow, P. (1980). A phenomenological study of the developmental stages of becoming a stepparent: A Gestalt and family systems approach (Doctoral dissertation, Boston University, 1980). *Dissertation Abstracts International*, **41**, 8B, 3192–3193.

Ransom, J. W., Schiesinger, S., & Derdeyn, A. P. (1979). A stepfamily in formation. *American Journal of Orthopsychiatry*, **49**(1), 36–43.

Sager, C. J., Brown, H. S., Crohn, H., Engel, T., Rodstein, E., & Walker, L. (1983). *Treating the remarried family*. New York: Brunner/Mazel.

Schulman, G (1972). Myths that intrude on the adaptation of the stepfamily. *Social Casework*, **53**, 131–139.

Visher, E. B., & Visher, J. S. (1979). *Stepfamilies: A guide to working with stepparents and stepchildren*. New York: Brunner/Mazel.

Visher, E. B., & Visher, J. S. (1983). *Stepfamily workshop manual*. Palo Alto: Stepfamily Association of America.

Waldron, J. A., & Whittington, R. (1979). The stepparent/stepfamily *Journal of Operational Psychology*, **10**(1), 47–50.

PATRICIA L. PAPERNOW

38 To Dream the Impossible Dream: An Agenda for Discussion with Stepparents

Sharon K. Turnbull / James M. Turnbull

STUDY QUESTIONS

1. Explain five of the do's and don'ts of stepparenting.

2. Why does the author say there is a need for more understanding of the problems faced by stepparents?

Only recently have those who counsel families become aware of their need to become more sensitive to the emotional complexities faced by the stepparent. By and large, stepparents are an invisible group who are often reluctant to seek help or even to discuss the unique adjustment problems they face. There has been a recent increase in interest in the problems of stepfamilies, and a number of popular books such as the one by Noble and Noble (1977), are now available to assist the stepparent.

In a perceptive paper published in 1972, Shulman identified two important characteristics which distinguish stepfamilies from "ordinary" families: (1) fantasies and hopes play a much larger role in the family member's interactions; and (2) the stepparent expects more gratitude and acknowledgement from the stepchild. Research on stepparenting remains scanty. Following a survey of over 2,000 stepfamilies, Bowerman and Irish (1962) concluded that stepchildren experienced "greater levels of uncertainty of feelings and insecurity of position" and noted a "tendency of the parent to see the child as the source of all tension." Messinger (1976) reported the frequent presence of "guilt feelings about the lack of positive emotions or, frequently, negative feelings toward their partner's children. Similarly, the children who were required to respond

Source: Sharon K. Turnbull and James M. Turnbull, "To Dream the Impossible Dream: An Agenda for Discussion with Stepparents." *Family Relations* 32(1983):227–230. Copyrighted 1983 by the National Council on Family Relations, 3989 Central Ave., N.E., Suite 550, Minneapolis, MN 55421. Reprinted by permission.

to the parent's new mate as though they were the child's 'real' parents often reacted with feelings of guilt, hostility, rebellion, or withdrawal" (p. 196).

According to Visher and Visher (1979):

> Stepparents' expectations of themselves are usually unrealistically high; since they may not be able to live up to these expectations, they often consider that there is something wrong with their feelings and with themselves. . . . So there is anger, guilt, and low self-esteem—and a need to conceal these feelings. (pp. 11–12)

Counselors and therapists, however, often express dismay at the seemingly trivial complaints of the stepparent who is painfully striving to achieve a "real" family. On the surface, their problems sound identical to those that arise, without undue trauma, in the daily lives of all parents. But the issues, however mundane, are imbued with extra meanings for the stepparent who is striving for perfection.

There is a need for more understanding of the problems faced by these families, and perhaps more importantly, for the provision of support and encouragement for the stepparent as he or she faces the difficult task of developing a role for which few realistic guidelines exist. Regardless of the therapeutic approach which is used, the most critical element for success in counseling the stepparent is the development of a relationship of warmth and understanding. The "Ten Commandments of Stepparenting" which follow were developed to facilitate a familiarity with, and appreciation for, some of the conflicts and stresses commonly faced by the stepparent. They have been used by the authors as a stimulus for discussion with stepparents in individual, family, and group therapy situations. While they obviously do not represent a comprehensive catalogue of the problems faced by the stepparenting family, they provide a useful starting point for discussion.

THE TEN COMMANDMENTS OF STEPPARENTING

The natural family presents hazards enough to peaceful coexistence. Add one or two stepparents, and perhaps a set of ready-made brothers and sisters, and a return to the law of the jungle is virtually ensured. Some guidelines for survival include the following advice for stepparents:

1. *Provide neutral territory.* Just as the Romans had gods that lived in the house and protected it, stepchildren have a strong sense of ownership. The questions: "Whose house is it? Whose spirit presides here?" are central issues. Even the very young child recognizes that the prior occupation of a territory confers a certain power. When two sets of children are brought together one regards itself as the "main family" and the other as a subfamily . . . and the determining factor is whose house gets to be the family home. One school of thought suggests that when a couple remarries they should

SHARON K. TURNBULL / JAMES M. TURNBULL

move to a new house, even if it means selling the family heirlooms. If it is impossible to finance a move to neutral territory, it is important to provide a special, inviolate place which belongs to each child individually.

2. *Don't try to fit a preconceived role.* When dealing with children the best course is to be straight right from the start. Each parent is an individual with all his or her faults, peculiarities and emotions, and the children are just going to have to get used to this parent. Certainly a stepparent should make every effort to be kind, intelligent and a good sport, but that does not mean being saccharine sweet. Children have excellent radar for detecting phoniness, and are quick to lose respect for any adult who will let them walk all over him or her.

3. *Set limits and enforce them.* One of the most difficult areas for a natural parent and stepparent living together is to decide on disciplinary measures. The natural parent has a tendency to feel that the stepparent is being unreasonable in demands that the children behave in a certain way. If the parents fight between themselves about discipline, the children will quickly force a wedge between them. It is important that the parents themselves work out the rules in advance and support one another when the rules need to be enforced. The rules need to be relatively minimal in the beginning but should attend to issues such as meal time, bed time, what to do about fighting, and getting ready for school in the morning.

4. *Allow an outlet for feelings by the children for natural parent.* It is often difficult for the stepparent to accept that his or her stepchildren will maintain a natural affection for their natural parent who is no longer living in the household. The stepparent may take this as a personal rejection. Children need to be allowed to express feelings about the natural parent who is absent. This needs to be supported in a neutral way so that the children do not feel disloyal.

5. *Expect ambivalence.* Stepparents are often alarmed when children appear on successive days or successive hours to show both emotions of strong love and strong hate toward them. Ambivalence is normal in all human relationships, but nowhere is it more accentuated than in the feelings of the stepchild towards their stepparent.

6. *Avoid mealtime misery.* For many stepfamilies meals are an excruciating experience. This, after all, is the time when the dreams of blissful family life confront reality. Most individuals cling to a belief in the power of food to make people happy. There is enormous satisfaction in having one's food enjoyed, and it is not coincidence that in fairy tales the food that the wicked stepmother offered was often poisoned. Since it is the stepmother who is most often charged with serving the emotionally laden daily bread, she often leaves the table feeling thoroughly rejected. If the status quo becomes totally unbearable, it is forgivable to decide that peace is more important and turn a blind eye, at least temporarily, to nutrition. Some suggested strategies include: daily vitamins, ridding the house of all "junk"

foods, let the children fix their own meals, eat out a lot, and/or let father do some of the cooking so he can share in the rejection. Stepfathers tend to be less concerned about food refusal but more concerned about table manners. Obviously, constant fighting at the dinner table is not conducive to good digestion; but children can master the prerequisite etiquette with reasonable speed when both parents reinforce the message that table manners are expected.

7. *Don't expect instant love.* One of the problems facing a new stepparent is the expectation of feeling love for the child and for that love to be returned. It takes time for emotional bonds to be forged, and sometimes this never occurs. All stepparents must acknowledge that eventuality.

Alternately, nonacceptance by the children is often a major problem. Some children make it very clear that "You are not *my* mother or father!" This can be very painful or anger provoking, especially if it is the stepparent who is doing the cooking and laundry, and giving allowances. Most children under three have little problem adapting with relative ease. Children over five have more difficulty. Some children are initially devoted in their excitement at having a "new" mother or father, but later find that the words "I hate you" are potent weapons. This discovery frequently coincides with puberty. A thick skin certainly helps!

8. *Don't take all the responsibility. The child has some too.* Ultimately, how well the stepparent gets along with the stepchild depends in part upon the kind of child he or she is. Children, like adults, come in all types and sizes. Some are simply more lovable than others. If the new stepmother has envisioned herself as the mother of a cuddly little tot and finds herself with a sullen, vindictive twelve year old who regards her with considerable suspicion, she is likely to experience considerable disappointment. Like it or not, the stepparent has to take what he or she gets. But that doesn't mean taking all the guilt for a less than perfect relationship.

9. *Be patient.* The words to remember here are "things take time." The first few months and often years have many difficult periods. The support and encouragement of other parents who have had other similar experiences can be an invaluable aid.

10. *Maintain the primacy of the marital relationship.* It has been our experience that most stepparenting relationships have resulted from divorce by one or both members of the couple. There is a certain amount of guilt left over about the breakup of the previous relationship which may spill over into the present relationship and create difficulties when there are arguments. The couple needs to remember that their relationship is primary in the family. The children need to be shown that the parents get along together, can settle disputes, and most of all will not be divided by the children. While parenting may be a central element in the couple's relationship, both partners need to commit time and energy to the development of a strong couple relationship; this bond includes, but is greater than, their parental responsibilities.

SHARON K. TURNBULL / JAMES M. TURNBULL

REFERENCES

Bowerman, C., and D. Irish. 1962. Some relationships of stepchildren to their parents. *Marriage and Family Living* 24:113–31.

Messinger, L. 1976. Remarriage between divorced people with children from previous marriages: A proposal for preparation for remarriage. *Journal of Marriage and Family Counseling* 2:193–200.

Noble, J., and W. Noble. 1977. *How to live with other peoples' children.* New York: Hawthorne Books.

Schulman, G. 1972. Myths that intrude on the adaptation of the stepfamily. *Social Casework* 49:131–39.

Visher, E., and J. Visher. 1979. *Stepfamilies: A guide to working with stepparents and stepchildren.* New York: Brunner/Mazel.

10 *Family Variations: Subcultural Differences*

A point made in Chapter 9 was the growing feminization of poverty. It was noted that unequal pay and professional opportunity mean that women earn about a third less than men earn. In addition, women's household responsibilities limit their outside opportunities while facilitating men's ability to pursue career and leisure activities. What is being seen here is the use of biological differences between the sexes to assign and rationalize unequal gender roles benefiting men at the expense of women.

Gender stratification is, however, not the only type of stratification which leads to variations in family structure in America. Although the "democratization" of the possession of amenities, the blurring of distinctions between blue- and white-collar jobs, and the economic integration of neighborhoods leads to the impression that America is a classless society, almost all Americans identify with a particular socioeconomic class and recognize class-based differences in beliefs and lifestyles. The chief distinguishing factor among the classes is the availability of money.

Members of the poverty-stricken lower class work erratically at unskilled jobs or sometimes illegal activities, draw welfare benefits, pool basic resources, and have a constantly changing family structure as they seek the maximum available financial and emotional support. A lack of economic resources also limits the "opportunity structure" for the poor leading to:

a. greater medical problems,

b. shorter life expectancy,

c. greater chance of criminal involvement,

d. lower educational attainment, and

e. greater likelihood of abuse, desertion, and homelessness. (Zinn & Eitzen 1987)

Since working-class people usually hold blue-collar and clerical white-collar jobs that are vulnerable to economic fluctuations, they often suffer the same low-income side effects as the poverty stricken.

A wide range of lifestyles, economic security, and occupations make the middle class a heterogenous group. However, only those at the upper end of the middle-class spectrum achieve fairly high levels in the areas of home and car ownership, recreation, nutrition, and savings. Members of this class—the upper-middle—have strong career identification and orientation, since their occupations provide power and prestige as well as money.

The upper class derives its income from ownership and control of major segments of the economy. It centers family life on the maintenance of its elite, exclusive position and inherited wealth.

Another basic variation in American families is seen in the main emphasis of this chapter—the many subcultures of American society. What should be remembered in this examination is that these subcultures are part of the American system and so it should not be surprising that they are marked by the gender and class stratification distinctions noted above.

Bill Burgess, in the first article of Chapter 10, looks at parenting in the native-American community and the penalties they pay for their nonassimilation. Although assimilated, black American families suffer from racial discrimination. Their disproportionately low pay and high unemployment mean, according to Robert Staples in the second article of this chapter, that about half of all blacks are in the lower class and that they suffer from high rates of marital instability. Based on the socioeconomic level of the family there are several variations of Chicano families; however their culture is characterized by a distinct set of values centering on the family. As Rosina Becerra notes in the third article of Chapter 10, they include:

a. a strong familistic orientation,

b. highly integrated extended kin network, and

c. reliance on the extended family for support.

The final culture to be examined—Asian-American families—offers a different picture economically from the prior cultures examined. However as Bob Suzuki notes in the final article of this chapter, they too suffer from restrictions and stereotypes.

Explanations for a group's place in the socioeconomic system tend to "blame the victim" and call for the group to abandon its cultural values as a way out of poverty. What this examination has shown, however, is that it is the larger social structures of gender, class, and racial/ethnic inequality that are the culprits since they create and perpetuate an environment of unequal opportunity.

REFERENCE

1. Zinn, M. B., & D. S. Eitzen. 1987. *Diversity in American Families*. New York: Harper & Row.

39 *Parenting in the Native-American Community*

Bill J. Burgess

STUDY QUESTIONS

1. What are the penalties afflicting native Americans for not assimilating?
2. What are several values that occur more frequently in native-American families than in non-native-American families?

This chapter will concentrate on the nature of parent-child relationships within the native-American community. Generalizations about native Americans tend to distort the truth due to the difference in life styles between tribes, and the differences between rural-reservation residents and urban residents. The reader is cautioned to keep in mind that this overview of native-American life is based on the typical and traditional rural-reservation situation. No attempt is made to consider the urban native American or to deal with the middle class or professional groups.

First, this chapter will illustrate briefly the distinct position of the native-American community in contrast to the dominant North American society. Next, it will present an overview of the patterns of parent-child relations that are unique to the native-American community. Third, it will describe the differences in the behavior of native- and non-native-American children. Finally, it will review the problems that plague the native-American community and illustrate how these problems endanger good parenting relationships.

Whenever we use the term "native American," we must remind ourselves that this term cannot adequately describe a "people." For the most part, "tribalism," with pronounced differences in life-style and language, is paramount. Although these differences vary immeasurably among the tribes, from

Source: Bill J. Burgess, "Parenting in the Native-American Community." From *Parenting in Multicultural Society* by Mario D. Fantini and Rene Cardenas. Copyright © 1980 by Longman, Inc. Reprinted by permission of Longman, Inc., New York.

patterns conditioned during years of living as nomads to those of a sedentary domestic semiurban style, there are some common values or characteristics which consistently appear. A distinct pattern of parent-child and family relationships is one of those areas that appears with regularity within, as well as among, tribes.

The destructive forces to which native Americans were exposed for over two hundred years took a terrible toll. Among the effects were a variety of disruptions in family structure. Prior to the arrival of the "Anglo" ("Anglo" is the term used by many native Americans when speaking of the dominant society in the United States), tribal societies, customs, and traditional ways of life had developed. Family, and then tribal education, stressed and encompassed the principal social values of cooperation and collective organization, making possible both individual variation and tribal solidarity. In the collective, cooperative, and noncompetitive native-American society, the family, and through it the tribe, became the primary social and educational organization. . . .

Parenting in the traditional native-American community must be examined in the context of the extended family. And for many tribes, matriarchal influence is a tradition. Dennis (1940) writes about social organization among the Hopi:

> The closest ties of a Hopi are with the members of his immediate family— his parents, his brothers and sisters . . . he has a host of relatives, all of whom usually live in his own village and whom he sees almost daily. The sisters of his mother are called 'mothers,' although the young child knows which is his 'true' mother. The brothers of his father are likewise called 'fathers,' and all children of his mothers and fathers are called brothers and sisters, so that he is surrounded by a large number of relatives who, nominally at least, are very close to him. The mother's mother is, of course, his grandmother, as is his father's mother, but in addition all sisters of these grandmothers are also called grandmother. . . . Between the individual and any relative exist a number of mutual obligations which tend to bind them together. . . .

Beyond the Hopi family is a wider group, the clan. The child's clan is the clan of his mother; that is, clan membership is inherited in the female line. All clan members consider themselves to be related, and they have a number of obligations to each other. There are numerous occasions when one would call upon a clan member for aid or services before asking the cooperation of others. The child owes obedience to his mother and father, to his mother's brothers, and to some extent to his father's brothers who are called "fathers." Grandparents are to be respected, but they are not disciplinarians and do not enforce obedience. The younger child usually obeys the older child, but in cases in which this does not occur, the older sibling must appeal to the parents: "Other people . . . may not command the child, not threaten, nor punish the child, but they are free to reprove him for wrongdoing and to report his misbehavior to his parents" (Dennis, 1940).

Dr. Robert Bergman (Byler, 1977), a psychiatrist, noted for his work on

BILL J. BURGESS

the Navajo Reservation, describing the extended-family relationships of the Navajo, stated:

> One of the most significant differences between Navajo family structure and that of ordinary middle-class Americans is the relationship of the child to a number of caring people. In general, the relationship to aunts and uncles is much more important in the Navajo family than it is to the middle-class American family. A great deal more responsibility is given to other members of the extended family, and there is considerable attachment of the child to the entire group. . . . They (grandparents) would serve as models that the children would follow in their behavior—teacher, probably the final authority to which the children could appeal. In the ordinary good family they would be the leaders of the group, and the most respected people.

Generally, the extended-family concept is still practiced by native-American families, both on and off the reservation. During tenure as Dean of Bacone Indian College, Muskogee, Oklahoma, and Haskell Indian Junior College, Lawrence, Kansas, this writer can recall many incidents that illustrate the continuation of this practice.

- Very often in communication with grandparents, aunts, and uncles, an individual would refer to his "son" or "daughter" as if the relationship were an absolute, direct one.
- Students often arrived at college with expensive articles (baskets, rugs, jewelry, and so forth) that had been given to them by extended-family members, to be sold in the event they needed money while they were away.
- Young married students, upon the birth of a child, would bring the grandmother to live with them so the child could learn tribal language and culture from the most respected teacher. This activity was endorsed and expected by all of the members of the extended family.

The role of grandparents in the parent-child relations of the native-American family is unique. Native-American children are taught to respect elders. Many Anglo and other non-native-American children are taught to love and respect their elders, but, this writer feels, not with the same intensity and depth as young native-American children. In addition, the advent of nursing homes and extended-care facilities has seriously diminished the effective role Anglo grandparents might have, or once had, in child-rearing. It appears that, at best Anglo grandparents are utilized as babysitters, or as someone to visit on "special" holiday occasions.

The native-American child is taught that age is a gift, a "badge of honor," if you please. To have grown old is to have done the right things, to have pleased your creator, to have been in "tune" with nature and your fellowman. In the native-American community, respect increases with age. Older people are expected to give advice and counsel. It is expected that grandfathers will take sons (grandsons or nephews) for long walks to talk about life, nature, and self, and that grandmothers will very carefully arrange time and events during the winter to tell and retell stories of creation, culture, and relationships of nature and people. These teaching-learning activities are not happenstance or informal. They are structured and command adherence, participation, and support by everyone concerned. Parents would not dare plan an activity or event that would break this traditional relationship.

In addition to those items mentioned above, one would need exposure to native American "values" to fully comprehend their effect on parent-child relationships. The traditional native-American community places particular emphasis on the values of brotherhood, personal integrity, generosity (sharing), and spirituality. Oftentimes, values of the native-American community are in direct contrast to those observed and reflected in the Anglo community. In addition, some values not in direct conflict with Anglo practices are taught and promoted with such an intensity that the net result is almost as if they were opposites. For instance, a native-American child is taught that wealth is measured by the amount that one shares with (gives to) others rather than the amount one obtains and keeps for his or her own personal welfare.

Native-American parents worry about these differences and are forced to give serious consideration to how to deal with them while rearing children through their early and formative years. Parents ask themselves: Are we holding to strict traditional culture? Should we give up our traditional ways so that our children can "make it" in the Anglo world? Should we compromise, and hope that our children make it in both worlds? A dilemma is created by the conflicting values which exist between the traditional native-American society desiring to retain what it believes in, and a dominant society that has been unresponsive to these differences and reluctant to acknowledge the positive contributions of "cultural pluralism."

Observation and study through the years have led this writer to conclude that, in spite of the many problems which exist, positive parent-child relationships in the native-American community are equal to, and often better than, those of most other North American ethnic communities. The illustrations of some of the practices listed below are valued in most societies, but it is believed that they occur more frequently in the native-American community than in the non-native-American community. Some of the more significant characteristic elements that are visible in the native-American community follow.

- Children—from birth—are regarded as important units of the family and heirs to its concerns and belongings. Children are considered . . . by Native Americans . . . as more important than material possessions.
- Songs and lullabies sung to children by the parent and grandparents carry messages of hope and aspiration, the appreciation of beauty, sharing, and physical strength (so as to be of service to each other).
- Families engage only in those social activities which include their children; if the children cannot go, no one goes.
- Native American children are seldom, if ever, struck by an adult: not parents,

uncles, aunts . . . no adults. This custom has enormous implications which may indicate the superiority of Native American parenting to Anglo-American customs.

- Considerable parental time and effort is devoted to making items for children to play with, or operate, or use when participating in popular activities and ceremonies. (Ex.: costumes for special dances, looms for weaving, tools for gardening, hunting, and fishing.)

- Respectfulness is taught by example as well as by precept. Respect is paid to a large number of worthy objects . . . parents, grandparents, members of the extended family, elderly people, various totem animals and objects, and various abstractions such as natural beauty and nature, dignity, and modesty.

- Talking loudly, especially while correcting children, is highly disapproved of.

- Spiritual qualities are taught and emphasized in special rituals and ceremonies.

- Artifacts (baskets, rugs, pottery, etc.) are made with *purposeful imperfections,* as a lesson to children that no one is perfect; we all make mistakes, and hence, censure and punishment are very minimal.

- Competition is considered acceptable as long as the object is not to get the best of (hurt) someone.

- Children are taught that the land . . . and all that grows . . . are only lent to us for our care and sharing, not for exploitation. [Menninger, to be published]

These features of the native-American family philosophy and parenting practice seem eminently healthy, wise, and useful for fostering parent-child guidance and development. They are conducive to self-confidence, serenity, and nonaggressive personality development. No doubt, the above list could be extended, but the major point is that children are extremely important extensions of the family and community; there is also a tendency to include the natural needs and activities of children in the whole of family and community life.

A classic example of conflicting values between the Anglo and native-American communities appeared as an advertisement in a major periodical that dedicated a particular issue to effective parenting (*Psychology Today*, 1976). The journal carrying the advertisement is generally accepted as respectable and knowledgeable. Some of the key phrases from the advertisement follow:

- Keep your kid ahead of the Jones kid.

- Get him the advantage of Montessori learning.

- Turn average kids into gifted ones.

- Your kid needs every advantage he can get to make it in this world.

- The difference between winning and losing is education.

- Make sure he doesn't bring home a discouraging report card and announce that "school is a drag."
- Don't wait another day. Time goes fast in a child's life.

It is difficult for this writer to relate in a positive manner the message of the advertisement to the goals and values of effective parent-child relations of any society or group. The goals mentioned, as well as those implied, are contradictory to the goals and methods supported by the native-American community in child-rearing. Native-American parents want their children to be successful, just as other parents do, but in a manner that is consistent with the cooperative and noncompetitive tribal, community, and family values and aspirations. . . .

In terms of intellectual potential, there seems to be considerable research to indicate that the achievements of native-American youth, up to a given level, are equal to those of non-native-American children. Most studies show that the two groups are equal at school-entry level, and some studies reported native-American children to be at a higher level than non-native-American children. After that, a common pattern emerges. Native-American children fall behind non-native-American children in terms of traditional scores on achievement tests. This is especially true after the eighth grade.

In some instances, native-American children at an early age have shown higher achievement or intelligence potential than the non-native-American children in their community. One particularly important study is illustrated by Erikson. In reviewing a previous study that had been conducted by McGregor on the Dakota Sioux personality, Erickson (1963) stated: "To settle one question, which I am sure many a reader has wanted to ask: The intelligence of the Dakota children is slightly above that of White children. Their health, however, corresponds to that of underprivileged rural Whites."

There are a number of other studies to indicate that native-American children enter kindergarten or the first grade at an intellectual and social-readiness level that is equal to or superior to that of non-native-American children. If this is true, one might credit the family and community environment of the Indian children prior to school age with this achievement.

Native-American children, then, appear to have equal or superior intellectual potential, at least at an early age. Marked differences between native-American children and Anglo children can be found in affective measures—such as emotions and values. In fact, Erikson (1963) illustrates the Dakota Sioux child by stating: "My conclusion would be as before, that early childhood among the Dakota . . . is a relatively rich and spontaneous existence which permits the school child to emerge from the family with a relative integration, i.e. with much trust, a little autonomy, and some initiative."

An important comparative study of native-American children and others, *American Indian and White Children: A Sociopsychological Investigation*, was undertaken by Havighurst and Neugarten (1955). Their work studied the moral, emotional, and intellectual development of native-American children in six native-American tribes. The study included 1,000 children, age six to eighteen. A similar control group of white children was also studied.

The primary instrument utilized was the *Emotional Response Test* developed by Stewart (Havighurst and Neugarten, 1955). The test asks for open-ended responses to questions concerning children's feelings about happiness, sadness, fear, anger, shame, and the best and worst things that could happen to them. In this particular study, the Anglo children were asked to write responses in a group-test setting. The native-American children were interviewed, and translation from English to a native-American language was often necessary.

This study revealed differences in the emotional character of native-American and Anglo children, differences with roots in the culture of the two societies. Anglo children were more concerned about their personal achievement, were more self-centered in describing happiness and pleasure, and were more troubled about getting their own way. They were less concerned about property and possessions, possibly an indication of the relative wealth. The possession of food and clothing was an important factor in the daily lives of the native-American children, while Anglos probably took these essentials for granted.

An interesting difference was reported as a result of a measure of children's feelings about "shame." Answers for both groups tended to center around two basic interpretations of the word "shame": "embarrassment" and "guilt." More native American than Anglos reported shameful incidences in which they were simply embarrassed, such as falling down in public or doing something awkward in front of others. Anglo children, on the other hand, tended to associate shame with their own guilt—bad judgment, moral wrongs, transgressions for which they were caught. This behavior is consistent with the methods of control of children as practiced by native Americans versus Anglos. For native Americans, warnings about the consequences of bad behavior are couched in community terms like, "What will people say—they will laugh at you." Rarely is a threat of physical punishment made. Shame, otherwise known as embarrassment, is a common disciplinary tool with native Americans.

Of significant importance were the differences in attitudes about family, as revealed by the Emotional Response Test. The study revealed that community members play a greater part in producing both pleasant and unpleasant emotions in native-American children. Both nuclear and extended families played a greater part in the statements about happiness, sadness, and the best and worst things in their lives. Anglo children did associate family members with their feelings, but were much more likely to associate them with punishment of negative emotions. Apparently the native-American community outside of the family has considerable influence on children, and native-American parents are less likely to be thought of in terms of punishment or unpleasantness.

In a study of the Hopi child, Dennis (1940) reflected,

> It seemed to us that the absence of a culturally determined goal of power and prestige has its effects upon the younger members of the community as well as the adults. We thought we saw less rivalry among Indian children, and less desire to be important, superior, and distinguished. This does not mean, however, that Hopi children make no invidious comparisons. . . . but the ridicule which they deal out is as likely to be

turned against the individual who tries to excel as against one who is aberrant in some other way.... Another guess which we hazard with respect to the Hopi child is that he has a world which he knows intimately and which accepts him completely ... while the child may early learn the unfriendliness of the climate and the danger of starvation which faces the entire village, he lives in a social world in which he has an indubitable place.

Another important work is that of Beuf, *Red Children in White America* (1977). Beuf, in her work, studied native-American youngsters and their development of racial attitudes in the light of four concepts: institutional racism, nonconscience ideology, the principle of constancy, and associatedness. Beuf's research was conducted during the summer and fall of 1971 with preschool children from the southwestern and midwestern United States: A total of 229 children took part in the study, 134 native Americans, and 95 Anglo children from the Midwest and Southwest.

In summarizing her findings, Beuf reported that the midwestern and southwestern young non-native-American children tend to portray a rather placid and comfortable attitude in all four concept areas, while native-American children tend to tell stories and enact dramas which reflect the realities of their lives. The social hierarchies, which are both cause and consequence of the physical circumstances of their life, did not escape the attention and comprehension of the native-American youngsters.

Beuf also reported that native-American children, at the five- to six-year-old level, for the most part, were similar to non-native-American children of the same age in identifying racial preferences. She found that native-American children would select a "white'" doll as often as they might a "red" or "brown" doll to play with. A dramatic difference was observed in testing native-American and non-native-American youngsters in the early adolescent years. While being tested, the adolescent native-American children, with few exceptions, indicated a pronounced tendency to select native-American objects. The same adolescent children were permitted to observe during the testing of the younger children. The adolescent children reacted quite visibly and emotionally when the younger children failed to indicate a preference for native-American objects. Although non-native-American children showed a decided tendency to select objects reflective of their own race as they grow older, the tendency for native-American children to do likewise appeared to be considerably more consistent.

From these examples, it would appear that native-American children are different from their Anglo counterparts. In positive instances, it might be concluded that this could be due to the pleasant and wholesome environment directly associated with good parent-child relations which exists in the native-American community. Other differences, particularly negative, are due in part to the social and political burdens borne by the ethnic minorities of this country.

The final area to be considered in this chapter relates to the problems that endanger good parenting relationships within the native-American community. As in any society, the family is recognized as the central unit of all activities. If the family, as an institution, is disturbed or altered, then the entire group is affected. In a recent speech, Dr. Karl Menninger (1977), Dean of American Psychiatry, and renowned friend of native Americans, made the following statements:

> The family is the most wonderful educational and character shaping institution of human life. . . . It is similar everywhere in the world because it is biologically the same. It is the unit of *human* social life.
>
> In most cultures, the family structure . . . is not interfered with or impaired by design; accidentally sometimes, by death or disaster or war . . . but not by human intention.
>
> In the case of the American Indians, however, it *has been* interfered with, purposely—with good intention, no doubt, but we psychiatrists think wrongly and harmfully, however well intentioned.

The problems are many and varied; for example, the dynamics of native-American extended families are in danger. They are little understood by outsiders. A native American may have scores or perhaps more than a hundred relatives who are counted as close, responsible members of the family. Many outsiders, untutored in the ways of native-American life, assume only the parents to be responsible, and interpret the acceptance of responsibility for a child by persons outside of the nuclear family as neglect or abuse.

The extended family, by its example of sharing responsibilities for child-rearing, tends to strengthen the native-American community's commitment to its children. At the same time, it diminishes the capability of the nuclear family in mobilizing itself quickly if an outside agency acts to assume custody for a child.

Non-native Americans often show concern about the relative freedom a native-American child is given and what seems to be a lack of parental concern about his or her behavior. Although this may appear as excessive permissiveness or indulgence, in fact, it is often a different and perhaps more effective way of allowing youngsters to develop in a healthy way. Discipline may be administered in other ways and in other forms not noticeable to outsiders. Native-American children are not punished often, nor are they in continual fear of punishment. On the other hand, native-American children do not expect praise for doing what is required of them. Parents occasionally praise children for doing well, indicating approval through a smile or pleasant tone of voice, or a friendly pat. There is strong affection between parents and children; knowledge of approval and disapproval is undoubtedly, in itself, a powerful means of social control.

Current programs that take native-American children away from families and place them in boarding schools or in foster homes have created havoc in the parent-child relationships in native-American communities. There are two trends: (1) Native-American children are being placed outside their natural homes at an alarming rate, and (2) they are being given to non-native Americans for foster care. Children involved are subject to ethnic confusion and a sense of abandonment, which tends to adversely affect their own potential parenting capacities. There is a growing concern among native-American tribes and communities over the loss of children as well as the absence of appropriate child welfare services.

A number of research studies indicate overwhelming problems of institutional racism in the United States. These problems have a most disruptive impact on the native-American community and family. In a country that equates "brown" and "poor" as synonymous terms, it is a difficult task to ensure that young native-American children develop a positive self-image.

The continuing lack of recognition of native Americans as a people by the institutions and agencies empowered to direct native-American land, education, health, and social service activities, perpetuates disintegration of the tribal and family structure. Until those agencies and institutions, and the dominant society in general, are willing to recognize and respect the unique differences in social values of a collective, cooperative, noncompetitive society, the tribe and the family will continue to be threatened and disrupted. These conditions will continue to contribute to the overall conditions of powerlessness, hopelessness, and poverty which exist in the native-American community. . . .

BIBLIOGRAPHY

Beuf, Ann H. *Red Children in White America.* Philadelphia: University of Pennsylvania Press, Inc., 1977.

Byler, William. *The Destruction of American Indian Families.* Steven Unger, Editor. New York: Association of American Indian Affairs, 1977.

Dennis, Wayne. *The Hopi Child.* The University of Virginia Institute for Research in the Social Sciences. New York: D. Appleton-Century Company, Inc., 1940.

Erikson, Erik H. *Childhood and Society.* New York: W. W. Norton and Company, Inc., 1963.

Fuchs, Estelle, and Havighurst, Robert. *To Live on the Earth.* Garden City, New York: Doubleday, 1972.

Havighurst, Robert J., and Neugarten, Bernice L. *American Indian and White Children: A Sociopsychological Investigation.* Chicago: University of Chicago Press, 1955.

McGregor, Gordon. *Warriors Without Weapons.* Chicago: University of Chicago Press, 1946.

Mead, Margaret. *Changing Culture of an Indian Tribe.* New York: Columbia University, 1932.

Menninger, Karl A., M.D. Speech, Navajo Nation Health Symposium, Navajo Community College, Tsaile, Arizona, August 22, 1977 (to be published).

Psychology Today, Vol. 10, No. 6, November, 1976.

40 *The Black American Family*

Robert Staples

STUDY QUESTIONS

1. Staples claims that significant changes have occurred among black family patterns. What are they?
2. Describe the husband-wife relationship among blacks.

INTRODUCTION

As the United States' largest visible minority, the black population has been the subject of extensive study by behavioral scientists. Its family life has been of particular concern because of the unique character of this group, as a result of a history that is uncharacteristic of other ethnic groups. There are four cultural traits of the black group that distinguish it from other immigrants to the United States: (1) blacks came from a country with norms and values that were dissimilar to the American way of life; (2) they were from many different tribes, each with its own language, culture, and traditions; (3) in the beginning, they came without women; and, most importantly, (4) they came in bondage (Billingsley, 1968).

The study of black family life has, historically, been problem-oriented. Whereas the study of white families has been biased toward the middle-class family, the reverse has been true in the investigation of black family patterns. Until relatively recently, almost all studies of black family life have concentrated on the lower-income strata of the group, ignoring middle-class families and even stable, poor black families. Moreover, the deviation of black families from middle-class norms has resulted in them being defined as pathological. Such labels ignore the possibility that although a group's family forms may not fit

Source: Robert Staples, "The Black American Family." Reprinted by permission of the publisher from *Ethnic Families in America* 3rd ed., C.A. Mindel, R.W. Haberstein, and R. Wright (eds.). Copyright 1988 by Elsevier Science Publishing Co., Inc.

into the normative model, it may instead have its own functional organization that meets the needs of the group (Billingsley, 1970). . . .

Changing Patterns of Black Family Life

Recent years have brought about significant changes in the marital and family patterns of many Americans. Americans have witnessed an era of greater sexual permissiveness, alternate family life-styles, increased divorce rates, and reductions in the fertility rate. Some of these changes have also occurred among black families and have implications for any public policy developed to strengthen black family life.

The sexual revolution has arrived, and blacks are very much a part of it (Staples, 1981). By the age of 19, black women were twice as likely as white women to have engaged in intercourse. Although the percentage for white females was lower, they were engaging in premarital coitus more often and with a larger number of sexual partners. However, a larger number of sexually active black females were not using reliable contraceptives, and 41 percent had been, or were, pregnant (Zelnik and Kantner, 1977).

One result of this increased premarital sexual activity among blacks is the large number of black children born out of wedlock. More than one-half of every 1,000 black births were illegitimate in the year 1980. Moreover, the rate was higher in this period for blacks than in the most recent earlier periods. The racial differences in illegitimacy rates also narrowed in the last 20 years (U.S. Bureau of the Census, 1983). One reason for the continued racial differential is the greater use by white women of low-cost abortions. In one study, 26 percent of pregnant black women received an abortion, compared with 41 percent of white women (Cummings, 1983). In all probability, the black out-of-wedlock birth rate will continue to increase as a higher percentage of black children are born to teenage mothers.

When blacks choose to get married, the same economic and cultural forces that are undermining marital stability in the general population are operative. In the last decade, the annual divorce rate has risen 120 percent. For white women under the age of 30, the chances are nearly two out of four that their marriage will end in divorce. Among black women, their chances are two out of three. In 1981, 30 percent of married black women were separated or divorced, compared with 14 percent for white women. The divorce rate of middle-class blacks is lower, because the more money that a family makes and the higher their educational achievements, the greater are their chances for a stable marriage (U.S. Bureau of the Census, 1983).

A combination of the aforementioned factors has increased the percentage of black households headed by women. The percentage of female-headed families among blacks increased 130 percent in the last decade, from 21 percent to 47 percent. One-third of these female household heads worked and had a median annual income of only $7,510 in 1981. The percentage of black children living with both parents declined in the last decade, and currently, only 42 percent of children in black families are residing with both parents. It is apparently the increasing pressures of discrimination, urban living, and poverty that cause black fathers to leave their homes or never marry. At the income level of $20,000 and over, the percentage of black families headed by a man is similar to that for white families (U.S. Bureau of the Census, 1983).

The fertility rate of black women is hardly a factor in the increase of female-headed households among blacks. Between 1970 and 1980, the total birth rate for black women decreased sharply. The fertility rate of black women (2.3 children per black woman) is still higher than the 1.7 birth rate for white women. However, the average number of total births expected by young black wives (2.6) and young white wives (2.4) are very similar. As more black women acquire middle-class status or access to birth control and abortion, one can expect racial differentials in fertility to narrow (U.S. Bureau of the Census, 1983). The birth rate of college-educated black women is actually lower than their white counterparts.

This statistical picture of marital and family patterns among blacks indicates a continued trend toward attenuated nuclear families caused by the general changes in the society and the effects of the disadvantaged economic position of large numbers of black people. An enlightened public policy would address itself to the needs of those families rather than attempt to mold black families into idealized middle-class models, which no longer mean much, even for the white middle class. What is needed is a government policy that is devoid of middle-class puritanism, the protestant ethic, and male-chauvinist concepts about family leadership.

Sex Roles

In recent years the issue of sex roles and their definition has received much attention. Although the debate has centered on the issue of female subordination and male dominance and privilege, blacks have considerably different problems in terms of their sex-role identities. They must first overcome certain disabilities based on racial membership—not gender affiliation. However, that does not mean that sex-role identities within the black community do not carry with them advantages and disadvantages. In many ways they do, but instead of fighting over the question of who is the poorest of the poor, blacks must contend with the plaguing problem of an unemployment rate that is as high as 45 percent among black men. Factors correlating to that central problem are the declining life-expectancy rate of black men and rises in drug abuse, suicide, crime, and educational failures. These facts do not warrant much support for a movement to equalize the condition of men and women in the black community (Staples, 1982).

Along with the economic conditions that impinge on their role performance, black men are saddled with a number of stereotypes that label them as irresponsible, criminalistic, hypersexual, and lacking in masculine traits. Some of these stereotypes become self-fulfilling prophecies because the dominant society is structured in a way that prevents many black men from achieving the goals of manhood. At the same time, the notion of the castrated black male is largely a myth. Although mainstream culture has deprived many black men of the economic wherewithal for normal, masculine functions, most function in a way that gains the respect of their mates, children, and community.

Along with all the dynamic changes occurring in American society are slow but perceptible alterations in the role of black women. The implications of these changes are profound in light of the fact that they are central figures in the family life of black people. Historically, the black woman has been a bulwark of strength in the black community. From the time of slavery onward, she has resisted the destructive forces that she has encountered in American society. During the period of slavery, she fought and survived the attacks on her dignity by the slave system, relinquished the passive role ascribed to members of her gender to ensure the survival of her people, and tolerated the culturally induced irresponsibility of her man in recognition of this country's relentless attempts to castrate him.

Too often, the only result of her sacrifices and sufferings have been the invidious and inaccurate labeling of her as a matriarch, a figure deserving respect but not love. The objective reality of the black woman in America is that she occupies the lowest rung of the socioeconomic ladder of all sex-race groups and has the least prestige. The double burden of gender and race has put her in the category of a super-oppressed entity. Considering the opprobrium to which she is subjected, one would expect her to be well-represented in the women's liberation movement. Yet, that movement remains primarily white and middle class. This is in part the result of the class-bound character of the women's movement—it being middle class whereas most black women are poor or working class. Their low profile in that movement also stems from the fact that many of the objectives of white feminists relate to psychological and cultural factors such as language and sexist behavior whereas the black woman's concerns are economic.

There is a common ground on which blacks and women can and do meet—on such issues as equal pay for equal work, child care facilities, and female parity in the work force. Instead of joining the predominantly white, middle-class women's movement, many black women have formed their own organizations such as the Welfare Rights Organization, Black Women Organized for Action, and the Black Feminist Alliance. There is little question that there is a heightened awareness among black women of the problems they face based on their sex-role membership alone. Whether the struggle of black women for equal rights will come into conflict with the movement for black liberation remains to be seen. It is fairly clear that black women must be freed from both the disabilities of race and sex. . . .

Husbands and Wives. Marriages are very fragile today. Fewer people are getting married, and the divorce rate in the United States is at an all-time high. There are many forces responsible for this changing pattern including changing attitudes and laws on divorce, changing and conflicting definitions of sex roles and their functions in the family, economic problems, and personality conflicts. Although divorce is on the rise and its increase cuts across racial and class lines, it is still more pronounced among blacks. Only one out of every three black couples will remain married longer than 10 years.

ROBERT STAPLES

It is not easy to pinpoint unique causes of black marital dissolution because they are very similar to those of their white counterparts. In some cases, it is the severity of the problems they face. Economic problems are a major factor in marital conflict and there are three times as many blacks as whites with incomes below the poverty level. The tensions blacks experience in coping with the pervasive incidents of racism often have their ramifications in the marital arena. One peculiar problem blacks face is the imbalanced sex ratio, which places many women in competition for the available males. Too often, the males they compete for are not available, and this places serious pressure on the marriages of many blacks.

At the same time, many blacks are involved in a functional marriage at any given point in time. Many adult blacks are married and have positive and loving relationships with their spouses. Unfortunately, practically no research exists on marital adjustment and satisfaction among blacks. What little research does exist indicates that black wives are generally less satisfied with their marriages than white wives. However, the source of their dissatisfaction is often associated with the problems of poverty and racism.

The last decade witnessed a significant increase in interracial dating and marriage. Among the reasons for this change in black-white dating and marriage was the desegregation of the public school system, the work force, and other social settings. In those integrated settings, blacks and whites met as equals, which facilitated homogenous mating. There were, of course, other factors such as the liberation of many white youth from parental control and the racist values they conveyed to them.

Not only has the incidence of interracial relations increased but their character has changed as well. Over 25 years ago, the most typical interracial pairing was a black male and a white female with the male partner generally being of a higher status. This pattern was so common that social theorists even developed a theory of racial hypergamy. In essence, it was assumed that the higher-status black male was exchanging his socioeconomic status for the privilege of marrying a woman who belonged to a racial group that was considered superior to all members of the black race. Contemporary interracial relations are much more likely to involve people with similar educational background and occupational status.

Although no research studies have yet yielded any data on the subject, there appears to be a change in interracial unions toward a decline in black male/white female couples and an increase in black female/white male pairings. Several factors seem to account for this modification of the typical pattern. Many black women are gravitating toward white men because of the shortage of black men and disenchantment with those they do have access to. In a similar vein, some white men are dissatisfied with white women and their increasing vociferous demands for sex-role parity. At the same time, there is a slight but noticeable decrease in black male/white female unions. One possible reason is that it is no longer as fashionable as it was a few years ago. Also, much of their attraction to each other was based on the historical lack of access to each other and the stereotype of black men as superstuds and white women as forbidden fruit. Once they had had extensive interaction, the myths exploded and the attraction consequently diminished (Poussaint, 1983).

We should be fairly clear that there are relatively normal reasons for interracial attractions and matings. At the same time, it would be naive to assume that special factors are not behind them in a society that is stratified by race. Given the persistence of racism as a very pervasive force, many interracial marriages face rough sledding. In addition to the normal problems of working out a satisfactory marital relationship, interracial couples must cope with social ostracism and isolation. One recent phenomenon is the increasing hostility toward such unions by the black community, which has forced some interracial couples into a marginal existence. Such pressures cause the interracial-marriage rate to remain at a very low level. Less than 5 percent of all marriages involving a black person are interracial (Poussaint, 1983).

Childhood and Childrearing

One of the most popular images of black women is that of "Mammy," the devoted, affectionate nursemaids of white children who belonged to their slavemaster or employer. This motherly image of black women probably has some basis in fact. Motherhood has historically been an important role for black women, even more meaningful than their role as wives (Bell, 1971). In the colonial period of Africa, missionaries often observed and reported the unusual devotion of the African mother to her child. The slave mother also developed a deep love for, and impenetrable bond to, her children (Ladner, 1971). It would appear that the bond between the black mother and her child is deeply rooted in the African heritage and philosophy that places a special value on children because they represent the continuity of life (Brown and Forde, 1967).

Many studies have conveyed a negative image of the black mother because she does not conform to middle-class modes of childrearing. Yet, black mothers have fulfilled the function of socializing their children into the multiple roles they must perform in this society. They prepare them to take on not only the appropriate sex and age roles but also a racial role. Children must be socialized to deal with the prosaic realities of white racism that they will encounter daily. Black females are encouraged to be independent rather than passive individuals because many of them will carry family and economic responsibilities alone (Iscoe et al., 1964). Taking on adult responsibilities is something many black children learn early. They may be given the care of a younger sibling, and some will have to find work while still in the adolescent stage. The strong character structure of black children was noted by child psychiatrist Robert Coles (1964) who observed their comportment under the pressure of school integration in the South during a very volatile era.

The black mother's childrearing techniques are geared to prepare her children for a kind of existence that is alien to middle-class white youngsters. Moreover, many white middle-class socialization patterns may not be that desirable for the psychological growth of the black child. The casual upbringing of black children may produce a much healthier personality than the status anxieties associated with some rigid middle-class childrearing practices (Green, 1946). Using threats of the withdrawal of love if the child fails to measure up to the parent's standards is much more common among white parents than black parents of any class stratum. One result of the black child's anxiety-free upbringing is a strong closeness to his parents (Nolle, 1972; Scanzoni, 1971).

Although black parents are more likely to use physical rather than verbal punishment to enforce discipline than white parents, this technique is often buttressed by the love they express for their children. Moreover, as Billingsley (1969:567) has noted, "even among the lowest social classes in the Black community, families give the children better care than is generally recognized, and often the care is better than that given by white families in similar social circumstances." One indication of the decline in this attitude is found in the statistics, which show that child abuse has become more common in black families than in white families (Gil, 1971). Some of the racial differences can be attributed to reporting bias, but much of it reflects the effect of poverty and racism on black parent-child relationships.

The most undesirable aspect of the black child's life is reputed to be the absence of a positive male figure (Moynihan, 1965; Rainwater, 1966). A plethora of studies have found that the black child has low self-esteem because of his "blackness" and the fact that many children grow up in homes without a male role model. A number of studies have emerged that are in opposition to the theories of low self-esteem among blacks. In reviewing the literature on black self-esteem, some have concluded that much of it is invalid, and others have concluded that blacks are less likely to suffer from low self-esteem because of such countervailing influences as religion, reference groups, group identification, and positive experiences in the extended family (Staples, 1976:82–84).

Problems in child development are alleged to be a function of the father's absence or ineffectiveness. There has yet to be found a direct relationship between the father's absence and child maladaption (Hare, 1975; Rubin, 1974). In part, the black child continues to have male role models among the male kinsmen in his extended family network, and the mother generally regards her children's father as a friend of the family who she can recruit for help rather than as a father failing his parental duties. However, one must be careful not to overromanticize the single-parent family as a totally functional model. They are the poorest families in the United States and are overrepresented among the society's failures in education, crime, and mental health.

The ineffective black father has been assumed to be pervasive among black families. Much of the more recent literature suggests that black fathers have warm, nurturing relationships with their children and play a vital role in their children's psychology and social development (Lewis, 1975; Scanzoni, 1971). How well they carry out the paternal role may be contingent on the economic resources available to them. Hence, we find better patterns of parenting among middle-class black fathers who have the economic and educational resources, and, consequently, participate more in child care, are more child-oriented, and view their role as different from the mother's (Cazanave, 1979; Daneal, 1975). As far as the male child's sexual identity is concerned, Benjamin (1971) discovered that black male youth had a better conception of the male role when their father had one or more years of college education, indicating a strong relationship between the opportunity to play a role and the actual playing of that role.

The Aged

As a result of the declining fertility rate among blacks, the elderly represent a larger percentage of the total black population than in previous times. By 1979, blacks over the age of 65 years constituted 8 percent of the black population, in contrast to half the corresponding percentage in 1910. Increasingly, the black elderly population is disproportionately female. As a result of the growing gap in mortality rates between black men and women, widowhood occurs at an earlier age for black than white women. For example, during the years 1939–1941, there was only a difference of two years in the life-expectancy rate of black men and women. As of 1979, that gap had widened to 12 years (U.S. Bureau of the Census, 1983). Based on his calculations from 1975 fertility and mortality data, Sutton (1977) estimated that the chances of becoming a widow among married black women prior to age 65 are nearly one out of two. Those who become widows could expect to have a tenure of nine years in that status before their 65th birthday. Their chances of remarriage are undermined by the extremely low sex ratio among blacks 65 years of age and over. For every 100 black females in that age category, there were only 72 males in 1976 (U.S. Bureau of the Census, 1983).

Compounding the problems of early widowhood among the black elderly is the lingering problem of poverty. Approximately 36 percent of the black elderly were poor in 1977, compared with only 12 percent of elderly whites. Moreover, while the percentage of poor elderly decreased from 13 percent to 12 percent between 1975–1977, the number of poor black persons 65 years of age and over increased by 110,000 during the same period, maintaining the same percentage in poverty in 1975. One result of this overwhelming poverty is that a much larger percentage of elderly black wives continue to work after reaching the age of 65 years than their white counterparts (U.S. Bureau of the Census, 1983).

Despite their poverty, the extended-kin network manages to buttress the problems attendant to aging among its elderly members. When Hutchinson (1974) compared black and white low-income elderly, his results indicated that blacks and whites were identical in their expectations for the future, feelings of loneliness, amount of worrying, perception of others, and general life satisfaction. Moreover, the black elderly were more likely to describe themselves as being happier. One of the reasons the black elderly do not experience previous adjustment problems with growing old is that they continue to play a vital role in the extended family. Very few, for instance, are taken into the households of younger relatives. Only 4 percent of black families have relatives 65 years of age and over living with them. Instead, young black children often are taken into the households of elderly relatives, usually a grandmother. This process of informal adoption is so common that half of all black families headed by elderly women have dependent children, not their own, living with them (Hill, 1977).

CHANGE AND ADAPTATION

The last 30 years have culminated in the gradual disintegration of the black nuclear family. Changes in the black family structure are in tune with the changes in American families. A number of social forces account for the increase in the number of single adults, out-of-wedlock births, divorces, and single-parent households. As women have become economically and psychologically independent of men, they have chosen to remain single or leave marriages they regarded as not satisfying their needs. Simultaneously, the growing independence of women and the sexual revolution of the 1960s and 1970s have allowed many men to flee from the responsibility attendant to the husband and father roles (Ehrenreich, 1983).

Although these sociocultural forces have an impact on the marriage and family patterns of many Americans, they are more pronounced among blacks because of one critical etiological agent: the institutional decimation of black males. As an Urban League report concluded, "the attrition of Black males . . . from conception through adulthood finally results in an insufficient number of men who are willing and able to provide support for women and children in a family setting" (Williams, 1984). Thus, many black women are denied a real choice between monogamous marriage or single life. Most do choose to bear and raise children because that is deemed better than being single, childless, and locked into dead-end, low-paying jobs. Although many would prefer a monogamous marriage, that is no longer possible for the majority of black women. The same forces that drive many black men out of social institutions also propel them out of the family.

Those forces have their genesis in the educational system. Black women are more educated than black men at all levels except the doctoral level. This, again, is in the overall direction of change in American society. White men have also been losing ground to white women in educational achievements. The reasons for the ascendency of women in the school system are unclear. Some speculate that because teachers are disproportionately female, the behaviors tolerated and most encouraged are those that are more natural for girls (Hale, 1983). The higher educational level of black women endows them with educational credentials and skills that make them more competitive in the job market. The changing nature of the economy has placed women at an advantage. While the industrial sector has been declining, the service and high-technology sectors of the economy have been expanding. Black women are more highly concentrated in the expanding sector of the economy whereas black men are overrepresented in the shrinking industrial jobs.

One consequence of the aforementioned factors is the attrition of black men in the labor force. According to a study by Joe and Yu (1984) almost 46 percent of the black men of working age were not in the labor force. As a rule, unemployed males are not good marriage prospects. The percentage of black women heading families alone in 1982 (42 percent) corresponds closely to the percentage of black males not in the labor force. Along with the number of black males not gainfully employed is the imbalance in the sex ratio, especially in the marriageable age ranges (18–35 years). Guttentag and Secord (1983) have shown that imbalanced sex ratios have certain predictable consequences for relationships between men and women. They give rise to higher rates of single adults, divorce, out-of-wedlock births, and female-headed households in different historical epochs and across different societies. Another analysis by Jackson (1971) revealed that among blacks, the percentage of female-headed households increases as the supply of males decreases. On the other hand, the percentage of female-headed households decreases when the supply of black males increases.

The crisis of the black family is, in reality, the crisis of the black male and his inability to carry out the normative responsibilities of husband and father in the nuclear family. The family's disintegration is only a symptom of the larger problem, that problem being the institutional decimation of black males. One should be clear that the institutional decimation of black males represents the legacy of institutional racism. The implications of this problem extend beyond the family. A majority of black children live in one-parent households today, and the median income available to those families is less than $7,500 per year. Although many children rise out of poor families to become successful adults, the odds are against them. Large numbers of them, especially the males, will follow their biological fathers to an early grave, prison, and the ranks of the unemployed. Only by resolving the problems of the black male can we restore the black family to its rightful place in our lives. The future of the race may be at stake.

REFERENCES

Abzug, Robert H. 1971. "The Black Family During Reconstruction," in Nathan Huggins, et al. (eds.), *Key Issue in the Afro-American Experience*. New York: Harcourt, Brace and Jovanovich, 26–39.

Adams, Bert N. 1970. "Isolation, Function and Beyond: American Kinship in the 1960s," *Journal of Marriage and the Family*, 32(November):575–598.

Bell, Robert. 1971. "The Relative Importance of Mother and Wife Roles Among Negro Lower-Class Women," in *The Black Family: Essays and Studies*. Belmont, CA: Wadsworth, 248–256.

Benjamin, R. 1971. *Factors Related to Conceptions of the Black Male Familial Role by Black Male Youth*. Mississippi State University Sociological-Anthropological Press Series.

Billingsley, Andrew. 1968. *Black Families in White America*. Englewood Cliffs, NJ: Prentice-Hall.

———. 1969. "Family Functioning in the Low-Income Black Community," *Social Casework*, 50(December):563–572.

———. 1970. "Black Families and White Social Science," *Journal of Social Issues*, 26(November):127–142.

Brown, A. R. Radcliffe, and Darryle Forde. 1967. *African Systems of Kinship and Marriage*. New York: Oxford University Press.

Cazanave, Noel. 1979a. "Middle-Income Black Fathers: An Analysis of the Provider Role," *The Family Coordinator*, 28(November).

————. 1979b. "Social Structure and Personal Choice in Intimacy, Marriage and Family Alternative Lifestyle Research," *Alternative Life Styles*, 2(August):331–358.

Coles, Robert. 1964. "Children and Racial Demonstrations," *The American Scholar*, 34(Winter):78–92.

Cummings, Judith. 1983. "Breakup of Black Family Imperils Gains of Decades," *New York Times* (November 20):1–2.

Daneal, Jealean Evelyn. 1975. "A Definition of Fatherhood as Expressed by Black Fathers." Ph.D. diss., University of Pittsburgh.

Ehrenreich, Barbara. 1983. *The Hearts of Men: American Dreams and the Flight from Commitment.* Garden City, NY: Doubleday.

Gil, David. 1971. Violence Against Children. *Journal of Marriage and the Family*, 33(November):637–648.

Green, Arnold. 1946. "The Middle-Class Male Child and Neurosis," *American Sociological Review*, 11(February):31–41.

Hale, Janice. 1983. *Black Children.* Provo, UT: Brigham Young University Press.

Hare, Bruce R. 1975. "Relationship of Social Background to the Dimensions of Self-Concept." Ph.D. diss., University of Chicago.

Hill, Robert. 1977. *Informal Adoption Among Black Families.* Washington, DC: National Urban League Research Department.

Iscoe, Ira, Martha Williams, and Jerry Harvey. 1964. "Age, Intelligence and Sex as Variables in the Conformity Behavior of Negro and White Children," *Child Development*, 35:451–460.

Jackson, Jacqueline. 1971. "But Where Are the Men?" *The Black Scholar*, 4(December):34–41.

Joe, Tom, and Peter Yu. 1984. *The "Flip-Side" of Black Families Headed by Women: The Economic Status of Black Men.* Washington, DC: The Center for the Study of Social Policy.

Ladner, Joyce. 1971. *Tomorrow: The Black Woman.* Garden City, NY: Doubleday.

Lewis, Diane R. 1975. "The Black Family: Socialization and Sex Roles," *Phylon*, 36(Fall):221–237.

Moynihan, Daniel Patrick, 1965. "Employment, Income, and the Ordeal of the Negro Family," *Daedalus*, 94(Fall):745–770.

Nolle, David. 1972. "Changes in Black Sons and Daughters: A Panel Analysis of Black Adolescents' Orientation Toward Their Parents," *Journal of Marriage and the Family*, 34(August):443–447.

Poussaint, Alvin. 1983. "Black Men—White Women: An Update," *Ebony*, 38(August):124–131.

Rubin, Roger H. 1974. "Adult Male Absence and the Self-Attitudes of Black Children," *Child Study Journal*, 4:33–44.

Scanzoni, John. 1971. *The Black Family in Modern Society*. Boston: Allyn and Bacon.

Staples, Robert. 1976. *Introduction to Black Sociology*. New York: McGraw-Hill.

——. 1981. *The World of Black Singles: Changing Patterns of Male/Female Relations*. Westport, CT: Greenwood Press.

——. 1982. *Black Masculinity: The Black Male's Role in American Society*. San Francisco: Black Scholar Press.

Sutton, Gordon F. 1977. "Measuring the Effects of Race Differentials in Mortality upon Surviving Family Members," *Demography*, 14(November):419–429.

U. S. Bureau of the Census. 1983. *America's Black Population, 1970 to 1982: A Statistical View, July 1983*. Series P10/POP83. Washington, DC: U.S. Government Printing Office.

Williams, Juan. 1984. "Black Male's Problems Linked to Family Crises," *The Washington Post*, August 1, p. A-6.

Zelnick, Melvin, and John Kantner. 1977. "Sexual and Contraceptive Experience of Young Unmarried Women in the United States, 1976 and 1971," *Family Planning Perspectives*, 9(May/June):55–59.

41 *The Mexican American Family in Historical Perspective*

Rosina M. Becerra

STUDY QUESTIONS

1. According to Becerra, the Mexican-American family is marked by heterogeneity and homogeneity. Explain.

2. Compare the traditional and contemporary Mexican-American family structure.

Mexican American families consist largely of individuals who are descended from or who are themselves unskilled immigrants who come to the United

Source: Rosina M. Becerra, "The Mexican American Family." Reprinted by permission of the publisher from *Ethnic Families in America* 3rd ed., C.H. Mindel, R.W. Haberstein, and R. Wright (eds.). Copyright 1988 by Elsevier Science Publishing Co., Inc.

States to work in low-wage sectors of the southwestern economy (McWilliams, 1968; Grebler, Moore, and Guzman, 1970). Unlike the members of some other Hispanic groups, very few Mexicans entered the United States as professional people.

Because of the Southwest's geographic proximity to Mexico and its demand for low-wage labor, the Mexican population is highly concentrated in the southwestern states. In fact, in 1979, 76 percent of Mexican Americans lived in one of two states: California or Texas (Pachon and Moore, 1981). From 1870 through 1980, these two states have always been home to between 70 percent and 80 percent of the Mexicans in the United States (Jaffe, Cullen, and Boswell, 1980). During most of their time in the Southwest, Mexicans have been the victims of prejudice and discrimination, varying in intensity from time to time and place to place but always present (Grebler, Guzman, and Moore, 1970; Hoffman, 1974; Estrada et al., 1981).

Because of their long history of settlement in the United States and continuous emigration from Mexico, the Mexican American population is far more generationally diverse than other Hispanic groups. In 1970, 16 percent were first-generation immigrants (i.e., foreign born), 34 percent were second generation, and 50 percent were third or later generations (Jaffe, Cullen, and Boswell, 1980). The generational diversity of the Mexican American people implies a corresponding diversity of social and economic statuses within the population.

What makes the situation of the Mexican American any different than that of other immigrating groups, who with the passage of time have been acculturated into mainstream America? Although change and, presumably, acculturation are taking place, Mexican Americans have more continuous interaction with first-generation immigrants and proximity to their original homeland. First-generation community members constantly reinforce traditional values. The rate and direction of acculturative change are thus greatly influenced and cause some cultural values to remain unchanged. The proximity of Mexico to the United States, regardless of the amount of flow back and forth, reinforces the familial ties—and the family values—that span the two countries (Becerra, 1983).

Heterogeneity and Homogeneity

Because family socialization takes root in the economic and political forces of society, the history of the Mexican American family must be anchored in the context of the American economy (Saragoza, 1983). Mexican Americans are a highly heterogeneous population. An important factor accounting for this variability is history. Mexican groups in the United States have different histories of immigration and settlement. Some trace their roots to the Spanish and Mexican settlers who first settled the Southwest before the arrival of the pilgrims, whereas others are immigrants or children of immigrants who began to arrive in large numbers by the beginning of the twentieth century (Martinez, 1985). Saragoza (1983) points out that this history supports the fundamental cultural variation and social differentiation among Mexican American families.

Crucial factors are variability across region (including Mexico) and changes over time. Mexican American families in different historical periods have adapted differently to economic and political forces, and family socialization patterns have responded differently to societal pressures (Baca-Zinn, 1983).

The traditional structure of the Mexican family grew out of the socioeconomic needs dictated by the agrarian and craft economies of Mexico. For the traditional Mexican, the word *familia* ("family") meant an extended, multigenerational group of persons, among whom specific social roles were ascribed. By dividing functions and responsibilities among different generations of family members, the family was able to perform all the economic and social support chores necessary for survival in the relatively spartan life circumstances of the rural Mexican environment. Mutual support, sustenance, and interaction among family members during both work and leisure hours dominated the lives of persons in these traditional Mexican families (Becerra, 1983).

After the conquest of the Southwest, Mexican families who remained or moved to the United States out of necessity tended to work and live in ethnically homogeneous settings. Minimally influenced by Anglo American culture, these communities supported the maintenance of Mexican familial structures as they might have been practiced in rural Mexico. The male took the role of authority figure and head of the household, and the female took the role of childbearer and nurturer (Sanchez, 1974). This family form was a response to particular economic and political forces, as are all family forms, that resulted in the Mexican American family carrying both these ideals and values and the need for modification under the new economic and political circumstances in the United States.

Traditional Family Structure

Much has been written about the traditional structure of Mexican American families. Depending on the author, these structures appear rigid, cold, and unstable on one end of the continuum or warm, nurturing, and cohesive on the other end. The three main characteristics of the Mexican American family that are addressed by these polar views are the following: (1) male dominance, (2) rigid sex and age grading so that "the older order the younger, and the men the women", and, (3) a strong familial orientation (Mirande, 1985:152).

Male Dominance. Of all the popular stereotypes surrounding the Mexican American family, none has become so much a part of American usage as the concept of *machismo*. Machismo is often equated with male dominance. Male dominance is the designation of the father as the head of the household, the major decision maker, and the absolute power holder in the Mexican American family. In his absence, this power position reverts to the oldest son. All members of the household are expected to carry out the orders of the male head.

The concept of machismo has various interpretations. For many, machismo is equated with excessive aggression, little regard for women, and sexual prowess. The macho demands complete allegiance, respect, and obedience from his wife and children. Madsen (1973:20) states that "ideally the Latin male acknowledges only the authority of his father and God. In case of conflict between these two sources, he should side with his father."

In contrast, genuine machismo is characterized by true bravery, or valor, courage, generosity, and a respect for others. The machismo role encourages protection of and provision for the family members, the use of fair and just authority, and respect for the role of wife and children (Mirande, 1985).

Although male dominance is a Mexican American cultural entity, as well as a structural component, its counterpart, the self-sacrificing, virtuous, and passive female, is no more true than the selfish, sexually irresponsible, and aggressive male. In fact, since 1848, many men have, for economic reasons, had to leave the family home to search for work, leaving the woman behind to head the household. Mexican American history is full of examples of women who have deviated from the submissive role. The ideals encompassed in the patriarchal tradition were often contradicted by the circumstances of day-to-day life. The types of jobs available to Mexican American men kept them away from their families for long periods of time working as teamsters, wagon drivers, miners, and farm workers. Over time, more and more women who were heads of households (even temporarily) were forced into the job market, further changing the expected roles of women (Griswold del Castillo, 1984).

Partriarchal values did not disappear under the impact of economic and political changes. Mexican American men continued to expect women to be submissive, but in this respect, they were no different from other men. Family life became a mixture of the old and new values regarding paternal authority and the proper role of women. Increasing poverty and economic insecurity intensified the pressures on Mexican American nuclear families and led to increased matriarchy and more working, single mothers. As a result, the ideology of patriarchy found less confirmation in everyday life. As a system of values and beliefs, however, the ideology of patriarchy continues to exist (Griswold del Castillo, 1985:39).

Sex and Age Grading. Complementing the concept of male dominance is the concept of sex and age subordination, which holds that females are subordinate to males and the young to the old. In this schema, females are viewed as submissive, naive, and somewhat childlike. Elders are viewed as wise, knowledgeable, and deserving of respect.

To some degree, these designations were derived from division of labor. Women as childbearers and childrearers did not perform the so-called more physically difficult jobs and therefore needed to be more protected by the man. If the women needed protection, the man took the role of overseeing the family. Nonetheless, the power of the male was more apparent than real. Respect for the breadwinner and protector rather than dominance was more key to the family. Roles within the familial network were stressed so that the constellation of the minisystem operated to the betterment of the individual and the familial system (Mirande, 1985).

In the isolated rural areas where many of the Mexican American families lived, the coordination of role expectations facilitated survival on the frontier. Each person behaviorally and institutionally carried out those roles that would ensure family survival.

The female child learned the roles and skills of wife and mother early, because she would carry them out both in the absence of the mother and as a future wife and mother. The eldest female child was expected to oversee the younger children so that the mother could carry out her tasks in the upkeep of the family. The eldest male, after puberty, had authority over the younger children as well as his elder sisters, because he would take on the responsibility for the family in his father's absence and for his own family as a future father.

The older family members, after they physically could no longer work, assumed the role of assuring family continuity. They were the religious teachers, family historians, nurturers of small children, and transmitters and guardians of accumulated wisdom. Their accumulated wisdom and numerous years of labor for the family was repaid by the respect given to them for their years (Becerra, 1983).

Thus, although particular role expectations are based on gender and age, and these dictate relationships and interactions, these roles were originally developed in response to a means for family maintainance and survival.

Familistic Orientation. The Mexican American family form was a result of a style that was brought from Mexico, modified in the United States, and adapted to fit a pattern of survival in the isolated, rural areas of the Southwest. Because of this history, there is an assumption that the Mexican family and the Mexican American family are isomorphic, allowing one to evaluate the Mexican American family from knowledge of the Mexican family, which is, in fact, fallacious (Montiel, 1970). However, the importance of the familial unit continues as a major characteristic among Mexican Americans to this day.

The familistic orientation continues because the family is viewed as a warm and nurturing institution for most Mexican Americans. It is a stable structure, in which the individual's place is clearly established and secure (Mirande, 1985). The family, as Murrillo (1971:99) indicates, offers "emotional security and sense of belonging to its members," and offers support throughout the individual's lifetime. The family is a major support system, a unit to which the individual may turn for help when in stress or in other types of need. Key to the family system is the value of sharing and cooperation.

Extended kinship ties assume a prominent place within the Mexican American culture. The extended family may include godparents and/or very close friends. Studies show that Mexican families tend to live near relatives and close friends, have frequent interaction with family members, and exchange a wide range of goods and services that include babysitting, temporary housing, personal advice, nursing during times of illness, and emotional support (Muller et al., 1985:67).

In sum, numerous studies (Ramirez 1980; Ramirez and Arce, 1981) demonstrate that familial solidarity among Mexican Americans is not just a stereotypical ideal, but a real phenomenon. Although expressed differently today because of changing cultural values and socioeconomic pressures, the pattern of a strong familistic orientation continues. It appears that Mexican Americans continue to have more cohesive family support systems than other groups (Griswold del Castillo, 1984).

THE CONTEMPORARY MEXICAN AMERICAN FAMILY

Marriage and Divorce

Marriage patterns among Mexican Americans are similar to those of other groups. Among those individuals ages 15 and over, 59.6 percent of Mexican Americans are married, compared with 59.2 percent for the total United States population. Interestingly, the percentage of never-married Mexican Americans is larger than that for persons of non-Hispanic origin (31 percent compared with 25.8 percent). This could be accounted for by the large proportion of younger persons in the Mexican American population (U.S. Bureau of Census, 1983).

Mexican Americans have a divorce rate of 5.4 percent, the lowest rate of all groups, compared with the United States population average of 7.2 percent (U. S. Bureau of Census, 1983).

With respect to family stability among Mexican American families, 75.7 percent are headed by married couples, compared with 52 percent for Puerto Rican families, 80.9 percent for non-Hispanic families, and 80.3 percent for the total population. Furthermore, 18.6 percent of Mexican American families are female-headed households, compared with a high of 44 percent for Puerto Rican families and a low of 16 percent for Cuban families. Interestingly, of male-headed (no wife present) families, Mexican males are more likely (5.8 percent) to take on the single parent role than any other group (compared with 3.6 percent for the entire population of the United States). Thus, Mexican families generally appear to be stable, two-parent families with a relatively lower rate of divorce than other ethnic families. The men seem to take over the household more often when there is no mother present.

Assimilation and Intermarriage

Assimilation is a multidimensional process in which ethnic groups begin to blend into a total community. One major dimension in this process is structural integration (Yinger, 1985). Considering the structural dimension, Yinger (1985:32) defines integration as the "degree to which members of a group are distributed across the full range of associations, and regions of a society in a pattern similar to that of the population as a whole." According to this definition, Mexican Americans are only moderately assimilated. As previously noted, they are beginning to be a political strength, a voting bloc sought after, and a strong enough constituency to promote and elect their own politicians (e.g., nine of the 13 Hispanics in the House of Representatives are Mexican Americans). In this arena, it appears that this political force will continue to increase.

In other areas, however, considerable inequities prevail. Economically, Mexican American family income is still only 73 percent of the median income for all United States families, Mexican American unemployment rates are 60 percent higher than for non-Hispanic whites, and Mexican Americans continue to be concentrated in blue-collar jobs and underrepresented in white-collar jobs. Educationally, only approximately two out of five Mexican Americans complete high school. Although there has been some progress in these areas, as indicated by the higher proportion represented in colleges and universities, greater numbers in white-collar jobs, and increased incomes, the gains are only moderate.

Intermarriage is often considered one major measure of integration, reflective of the degree of other assimilative processes (Yinger, 1985). Intermarriage in this context usually means marriage between a Mexican American and an Anglo American. Murguia (1982) has compiled one of the most extensive studies on Mexican American intermarriage. His findings suggest that among the three most populous southwestern states (which have high concentrations of Mexican Americans), the intermarriage rates range from 9–27 percent in Texas, from 27–39 percent in New Mexico, and from 51–55 percent in California. Intermarriage rates are greatly influenced by the forces that influence integration. As educational levels increase, residential segregation decreases, and social-class mobility increases with decreases in discrimination, intermarriage should probably increase accordingly. Furthermore, as the Mexican American socioeconomic profile moves closer to the socioeconomic profile of the population as a whole, the assimilation process should move accordingly.

CHANGE AND ADAPTATION

Today's Mexican American family is a unique culture in American society in that it is fully characterized by neither the Mexican culture nor the American culture—it maintains elements of both. The Mexican family has been modified by the social and economic pressures of American life, yet the proximity of the Mexican border provides a continual influex of Mexican nationals that serve to maintain the familial and emotional ties to Mexico and to enhance the Mexican culture values.

One key element encouraging change has been the increased movement of families from rural to urban life. Today, 85 percent of all Mexican American families reside in the urban centers of the southwestern and midwestern United States. This factor has had a profound impact on the familial structure. Although a familial orientation remains, Mexican American families today are less likely to be composed of extended kin residing in the same household than to be residing nearby, which still facilitates more frequent interaction. The supportive family system is much more characterized by voluntary interaction than by the necessity for economic survival that characterized the rural environment of their forefathers.

Because of the various patterns of immigration, there exists much heterogeneity among the Mexican American population. Mexican American families span the continuum of acculturation and assimilation, depending on the conditions of their immigration, length of time in the United States, and their sense of relatedness to Mexico.

Since the advent of the Chicano movement, Mexican American families have increasingly become more involved in the political process. For example,

Los Angeles, the home of the largest concentration of persons of Mexican origin outside of Mexico City, have shown their political strength by electing the first Mexican American state senator to the California legislature, the first Mexican American female assemblywoman, the first Mexican American city councilman in many years (California's Ed Roybal was the first), several other state assemblymen, and another member of the House of Representatives. This show of political strength is becoming more apparent throughout the nation.

Although there continues to be a disproportionate number of Mexican American families in the lower socioeconomic levels, there has been increasing social and economic mobility, as characterized by a growing number of Mexican American students in colleges and universities, an increase in Mexican Americans in professional and managerial positions, and a stronger Mexican voice in all aspects of society.

As has been true of all women in society, more Mexican American women are entering the labor force. There are greater numbers entering professions and participating more fully in various walks of life.

These factors come together to continually modify the Mexican American family by changing roles and expectations of all family members. As more opportunities emerge, social forces affect family life, and responses to an economic and political structure occur, the Mexican American family will continue to change and adapt to the forces around them. However, although the traditional Mexican American family has changed and will continue to change, there will continue to be a family form among Mexican Americans that fuses the culture of its roots and that of its American homeland.

REFERENCES

Acuna, R. 1981. *Occupied America: A History of Chicanos* (2nd ed.). New York: Harper and Row.

Baca-Zinn, M. 1983. "Ongoing Questions in the Study of Chicano Families," in A. Valdez, A. Camarillo, and T. Almaguer (eds.), *The State of Chicano Research on Family, Labor, and Migration*. Stanford, CA: Stanford Center for Chicano Research.

Bean, F. D., R. M. Cullen, E. H. Stephen, and C. G. Swicegood. 1984. "Generational Differences in Fertility among Mexican Americans: Implications for Assessing the Effects of Immigration," *Social Science Quarterly*, 65(June):573–582.

Becerra, R. M. 1983. "The Mexican American: Aging in a Changing Culture," in R. L. McNeeley and J. L. Colen (eds.), *Aging in Minority Groups*. Beverly Hills: Sage Publications, pp. 108–118.

Estrada, L.F., F. C. Garcia, R. F. Macias, and L. Maldonado. 1981. "Chicanos in the United States: A History of Exploitation and Resistance," *Daedalus*, 110:103–131.

Grebler, L., J. W. Moore, and R. C. Guzman. 1970. *The Mexican American People*. New York: Free Press.

Griswold del Castillo, R. 1984. *La Familia: Chicano Families in the Urban Southwest, 1848 to the Present*. Notre Dame: University of Notre Dame Press.

Hoffman, A. 1974. *Unwanted Mexican Americans in the Great Depression*. Tucson: University of Arizona Press.

Jaffe, A. J., R. M. Cullen, and T. D. Boswell. 1980. *The Changing Demography of Spanish Americans*. New York: Academic Press.

Madsen, W. 1973. *The Mexican-Americans of South Texas* (2nd ed.). New York: Holt, Rinehart, and Winston.

Martinez, M. A. 1985. "Towards a Model of Socialization for Hispanic Identity: The Case of Mexican Americans," in P. San Juan Cafferty and W. C. McCready (eds.), *Hispanics in the United States: A New Social Agenda*. New Brunswick, NJ: Transaction Books, pp. 63–85.

McWilliams, C. 1968. *North From Mexico*. New York: Greenwood Press.

Mirande, A. 1985. *The Chicano Experience: An Alternative Perspective*. Notre Dame: University of Notre Dame Press.

Montiel, M. 1970. "The Social Science Myth of the Mexican-American Family," *El Grito: A Journal of Contemporary Mexican-American Thought*, 3(Summer):56–63.

Muller, T., et al. 1985. *The Fourth Wave: California's Newest Immigrants*. Washington, DC: Urban Institute Press.

Murguia, E. 1982. *Chicano Intermarriage: A Theoretical and Empirical Study*. San Antonio, TX: Trinity University Press.

Murrillo, N. 1971. "The Mexican-American Family," in N. N. Wagner and M. J. Haug (eds.), *Chicanos: Social and Psychological Perspectives*. St. Louis: C. V. Mosby, pp. 97–108.

Pachon, H. P., and J. W. Moore. 1981. "Mexican Americans," *Annals, American Academy of Political and Social Science*, 454:111–124.

Ramirez, O. 1980. "Extended Family Support and Mental Health Status among Mexicans in Detroit," *La Red*, 28 (May).

Ramirez, O., and C. Arce. 1981. "The Contemporary Chicano Family: An Empirically Based Review," in A. Barton, Jr. (ed:), New York: Praeger.

Sanchez, P. 1974. "The Spanish Heritage Elderly," in E. P. Stanford (ed.), San Diego: Campanile Press.

Saragoza, A. M. 1983. "The Conceptualization of the History of the Chicano Family," in A. Valdez, A. Camarillo, and T. Almaguer (eds.), *The State of Chicano Research on Family, Labor, and Migration*. Stanford, CA: Stanford Center for Chicano Research.

U. S. Bureau of the Census. 1983. *General Social and Economic Characteristics: United States Summary*. Washington, DC: U. S. Government Printing Office, 1985.

Yinger, J. M. 1985. "Assimilation in the United States: The Mexican Americans," in W. Conner (ed.), *Mexican Americans in Comparative Perspective*. Washington, DC: Urban Institute Press, pp. 30–55.

42 *The Asian-American Family*

Bob H. Suzuki

STUDY QUESTIONS

1. What are some sociohistorical changes affecting Asian-Americans?
2. Indicate the structure in both Chinese and Japanese families.

. . . Since it will not be possible to present a comprehensive picture of all Asian-American families within the scope of this article, only the families of the two largest Asian-American ethnic groups, the Chinese and Japanese, will be treated. The term, Asian-American, will be used to refer to only those two groups, and not to other groups, such as the Koreans, Philipinos, Pacific Islanders, East Indians, and Indochinese that are often included in the generic use of the term. . . .

IMMIGRATION

The first of the Asian immigrants, the Chinese, began arriving in the 1850's, lured initially by the discovery of gold in California and later by recruiters seeking cheap labor for the sugar plantations in Hawaii and for railroad construction, mining, and agriculture in the western states. The vast majority were poor peasants, nearly all men, from the Canton area of southeastern China. Most of them came to earn money, hoping to return home reasonably prosperous after a few years. Those who were married left their wives at home, while single men hoped to marry when they returned. Only a few realized their hopes. The rest ultimately resigned themselves to remaining in the United States (Coolidge, 1909; Sung, 1967; Chinn, 1969).

Source: Bob H. Suzuki, "Asian-American Families." From *Parenting in Multicultural Society* by Mario D. Fantini and Rene Cardenas. Copyright © 1980 by Longman, Inc. Reprinted by permission of Longman, Inc., New York.

By 1880, some 105,000 Chinese were living in the western states and another 12,000 in Hawaii. Men outnumbered women by more than twenty to one. In 1882, as a result of a virulent anti-Chinese movement, Chinese immigration was brought to a halt by an exclusion act passed by the United States Congress (Lyman, 1970).

The major proportion of the Japanese immigrants arrived in Hawaii and on the United States mainland between 1890 and 1920. They were brought in to work as cheap laborers in many of the same areas in which the earlier Chinese immigrants had worked. Most of them were peasants or destitute small farmers in their twenties who came from the more economically distressed prefectures of southwestern Japan (Conroy, 1953; Daniels, 1962).

As in the case of the Chinese, males, predominantly unmarried, far outnumbered females. While most of them hoped to marry upon returning to Japan, they later realized, like the Chinese before them, that such a goal would be nearly impossible to achieve. Their hopes further faded in 1908 when, under pressure from the United States, Japan began restricting emigration.

It was at this time that the practice of "picture-bride" marriages, arranged through photographs, became popular. These marriages redressed the male-female imbalance considerably among the Japanese immigrants. Nevertheless, thousands of Japanese men were still unmarried in 1924 when Japanese immigration was halted by the United States Congress, this time as a result of intense anti-Japanese agitation. At the time, there were about 110,000 Japanese living on the United States mainland, mainly in the three Pacific Coast states, and an equal number in Hawaii (Ichihashi, 1932; Hosokawa, 1969)....

FAMILY STRUCTURE AND RELATIONSHIPS

Both the Chinese and Japanese kinship systems, though fundamentally different, generally led to extended families consisting usually of three generations living under one roof. In addition to the parents and their children, the residential family would often include the paternal grandparents. Contrary to popular image, however, the Confucian ideal of the large extended family of several generations and dozens of members was a rarity to be found only among the upper classes (Lang, 1946; Embree, 1939).

Perhaps the best known characteristic of the traditional Asian family has been its patriarchal structure. True to Confucian precepts, the father was the dominant authority figure in the family, while other members were in clearly prescribed, subordinate roles. However, the authoritarian role of the father has frequently been overdrawn (Wagatsuma, 1977; Wolf, 1970). In fact, in rural families in which the wife often worked alongside her husband, the mother also exerted considerable authority (Hsu, 1949; Fukutake, 1967).

The eldest son was accorded the next highest position in the family hierarchy, followed by his younger brothers. Females were considered inferior to males, and accordingly, daughters were relegated to lower-status roles. As

BOB H. SUZUKI

Wong (1974) has noted, however, the position of females in Asian societies was probably not too different from that of women in traditional western societies.

The grandparents occupied a special position of honor in the family. As its most elderly members, their wisdom was respected and their advice often sought on important family matters.

While the children were expected to show filial piety to both the father and mother, their relationships with each were distinctly different. In order to command their respect and obedience, the father tended to establish a rather distant and formal relationship with his children, especially the older sons who often viewed him with trepidation. In contrast, the relationship of the children to the mother was generally one of greater intimacy, affection, and informality. Especially close, affective ties tended to develop between the mother and her sons, particularly the eldest son.

Due to the custom of arranged marriages and the hierarchical structure of the family, the husband-wife relationship was neither the strongest nor the most intense one within the family, and was usually overshadowed by father-son and mother-son relationships (Hsu, 1975).

Finally, the relationship between the mother and daughter-in-law has received much attention in Asian folklore. Stories about the suffering of new brides under the domination of a despotic mother-in-law are well known not only in Asia but also in the West. However, due to the strong tradition of extended families and the dictates of filial piety, the burden of the role in Asian societies was much less avoidable and probably more onerous (Lang, 1946; Benedict, 1946).

CHILD-REARING

In both China and Japan, the early years of childhood were characterized by the permissiveness of parents toward their children. By American standards, young children were indulged, receiving close attention, much soothing care, and little discipline. Close intimate contacts with the mother were continual during this stage of early childhood. The child was seldom left alone or to cry, and was almost always being fed, carried, soothed, or played with. Children usually slept with their mothers until weaning, which usually occurred at one or two years of age, but sometimes continued for years. Mothers seldom left their children alone. Thus, the infant was quiet and content most of the time, and came to relate the physical presence of the mother with emotional security (Hsu, 1949; Benedict, 1946).

At the age of five or six, children were assumed to have reached the age of reason and to be ready to begin their entry into the world of adulthood. Discipline was rather suddenly imposed at this age by both the father and mother as they began to more strictly control the conduct and behavior of the child. Minor infractions, such as boastful or selfish behavior, were controlled by ridicule or teasing. More serious misbehavior, such as emotional tantrums or fighting, was more sternly handled, usually by scolding or through the inculcation of shame and, in rare instances, by corporeal punishment.

In more direct ways, parents taught their children the ethics of good conduct, their obligations to the family, and the virtues of filial piety and self-control. They also soon learned that acts of serious social deviance such as stealing would greatly stigmatize the entire family; whereas, outstanding achievements such as success in school would be a source of much collective pride. Through this process, the child was gradually socialized from an egocentric to a family-centered orientation (Lang, 1946; Wolf, 1970; Embree, 1939).

Sex-role differentiation also commenced at about five or six years of age. Boys began to spend more time with their fathers, helping them in their work and following their example. Girls followed suit, only with their mothers. Although girls sometimes worked in the fields with boys in rural areas, they were trained primarily for household chores and subjected to many restrictions not imposed on boys. By the age of adolescence, sex roles were clearly differentiated. . . .

SOCIOHISTORICAL CHANGES

Since the Chinese and Japanese faced different circumstances at different times in history, the sociohistorical changes undergone by their families will be described separately for each group.

Chinese-American Families

Due to the exclusion act of 1882 and the resulting shortage of women, families were practically nonexistent among the early Chinese immigrants. The few Chinese wives present were married to the wealthier merchants. Although many of the immigrants had left families behind in China, most of them, together with their unmarried compatriots, were destined to live out their lives as homeless bachelors (Lyman, 1974).

It was not until the 1920's that the bachelor-society character of the Chinatowns began to change as families became increasingly visible (Nee and Nee, 1972). Many of these families were started by former laborers who achieved merchant status and were finally eligible to bring wives over from China. Others were started by marriages between immigrants and the few American-born Chinese women. Because wives were prized, they had more status than their counterparts in China, and indeed, sometimes assumed more authority than their husbands. Since grandparents were usually absent they also did not have to contend with the dictates of mothers-in-law. Moreover, the traditional extended patrifocal family was generally replaced by the nuclear family (Sung, 1967).

Many of the children in these early families grew up in the familiar surroundings of their parents' small shop, laundry, or restaurant, where they lived and helped in the family business. While most of them were subjected to strict, traditional upbringing, their early childhoods were generally secure and family-centered. However, when they began school and were exposed to Western ideas and values, cultural conflicts with parents frequently broke out

BOB H. SUZUKI

and led to strained relations (Lowe, 1943; Wong, 1950). Parents were inevitably forced to make some concessions to this Americanization process, but still managed to inculcate their children with many traditional values and norms. . . .

Japanese-American Families

The early Japanese immigrants were more fortunate than their Chinese predecessors in that most of them were able to bring wives from Japan before the cutoff of immigration. Consequently, they were able to begin family life in the United States within a decade or two after their arrival. Since the majority were engaged in farming, they tended to continue many of the traditional ways of rural family life in Japan.

There were, however, a few significant departures from these traditional ways. As in the case of the early Chinese immigrant families, wives generally had more say in family matters than their counterparts in Japan, and the extended family was replaced by the nuclear type due to the absence of grandparents. Parental authority tended to diminish as the Nisei became Americanized through the schools and occasionally rebelled against traditional mores, such as filial piety (Masuoka, 1944; Iga, 1957).

The childhood of most Nisei was spent under the close, protective care and supervision of their parents either on the family's farm or in its place of business. In farming families, mothers often took their infant children out into the fields and cared for them as they worked. As the Nisei grew older, they were expected to help their parents on the farm or in the family business. Thus, except while they were in school, they were almost always in close contact with their parents. Even out in the Japanese community they could not escape scrutiny by relatives and family acquaintances.

Perhaps no event had a greater impact on Japanese-American families than the internment experience of World War II (Broom and Kitsuse, 1956; Thomas and Nishimoto, 1946). The sudden uprooting of families and the oppressive conditions in the concentration camps had traumatic, long-lasting effects on the family which even today have not been fully assessed (Morishima, 1973).

Many Japanese-Americans, especially the Nisei, felt deeply stigmatized by their internment experience. After their release from the camps many of them undoubtedly decided, consciously or unconsciously, to reject all vestiges of Japanese culture and to acculturate as quickly as possible into the American mainstream (Okimoto, 1971). This attitude appears to have had a strong influence on the subsequent development of familial patterns among the Nisei and Sansei on the mainland (Kiefer, 1974). . . .

FAMILY STRUCTURE AND RELATIONSHIPS

It has become almost axiomatic to describe the Asian-American family as patriarchal; that is, as vertically structured with the father as undisputed head and all others in subordinate roles (Kitano, 1969a; Sung, 1967). While this traditional structure may have prevailed in many first-generation families, it has almost certainly been modified in second- and third-generation families. In fact, as mentioned earlier, even in first-generation families the mother frequently assumed much more authority than her counterpart in Asia.

In second- and third-generation Asian-American families, husbands and wives appear to play complementary roles. One study (Johnson, 1972) of Nisei and Sansei families found that most husbands and wives made major decisions jointly and that their relationships were more often cooperative than disjunctive. Moreover, the investigator found that in such family matters as finances, social activities, and child-rearing, the wives were usually the decision-makers. Although more research is needed, these findings seem consistent with the impressions of many Asian-Americans themselves and are probably generalizeable to a large proportion of contemporary Asian-American families.

Paradoxically, despite such findings, the Asian-American male is generally seen as more chauvinistic than his Anglo counterpart (Fujitomi and Wong, 1973). Even in the study described above, most of the wives saw their husbands in the dominant position. The persistence of such views may be partly attributed to the strong mutual dependency that develops between Asian-American husbands and wives as a result of early socialization patterns (Caudill, 1952). One aspect of this relationship is the tendency for the husband to depend heavily on his wife to provide moral and ego support through responses that may appear indulgent and subservient by middle-class Anglo standards, even though their relationship may be more egalitarian in terms of actual power distribution.

Relationships between Asian-American parents and their children have also become more egalitarian. While they are still differentially socialized, boys enjoy little, if any, preferential treatment or status over girls with regard to the allocation of family resources. Furthermore, the duties and obligations expected of children are less demanding and restrictive than in the past. However, they are still generally subjected to stricter limits and constraints than their Anglo peers (Kriger and Kroes, 1972).

Verbal communication within Asian-American families is relatively restrained compared to that in Anglo families. This verbal reticence is not only rooted in traditional cultural norms but may also have been strongly reinforced by racial discrimination (Watanabe, 1973). On the other hand, there appears to be much greater utilization of nonverbal and indirect modes of communication. Family members generally become quite sensitive to using nonverbal cues and to reading between the lines of indirect statements.

Unlike traditional Asian families, contemporary Asian-American families are not dominated by parent-son relationships. The strongest relationships appear to be those between husband and wife and between the mother and her children. Husbands and wives appear to enjoy much closer companionship today than in previous years. Since mothers continue to assume most of the responsibility for child-rearing they develop the closest relationships with their children. Fathers still tend to maintain some distance from their children in order to engender respect and obedience. While fathers play with their children, they do not try to become close companions in the way that Anglo fathers do.

BOB H. SUZUKI

Parents are more likely to show affection for their children in indirect ways (for instance, by sacrificing their own needs for their children's), rather than with words or overt displays of affection, such as hugging or kissing.

These relationships have served to make the Asian-American family a close-knit social unit. This cohesiveness is reflected in the social activities of Asian-American families, which tend to be more family-centered than those of Anglo families. Children are more likely to be included in Asian-American social gatherings since parents appear less comfortable about leaving them at home with babysitters (Hsu, 1971; Kitano, 1969).

CHILD-REARING

While acculturation toward Anglo middle-class patterns has taken place, many aspects of traditional Asian child-rearing practices appear to be continued among contemporary Asian-American families (Young, 1972; Sollenberger, 1968; Johnson, 1972; Kitano, 1969a). The early years of childhood are still characterized by close, nurturant care by the mother, who tends to be more permissive with the young infant than her Anglo counterpart. Infants are seldom allowed to cry for prolonged periods before they are picked up by their mothers. Mothers tend to feed their infants on demand rather than by scheduling. On the average, weaning takes place at a later age than for Anglo infants. Toilet training is also more gradual. Parents often allow the young child to sleep with them, occasionally tolerating such behavior even after the child begins school.

Such indulgences would very likely be viewed by middle-class Anglo parents as a sure way of spoiling the child and retarding his/her development into a mature, independent, and autonomous adult. However, such an approach to child-rearing develops close, affective ties within the family and the child's sense of belonging to the family. It also results in the child's becoming strongly dependent on the mother to satisfy his/her needs and, in turn, enables the mother to use various deprivation techniques to control the child's behavior. Moreover, even as the Asian-American mother caters to the needs of her child, she inculcates the child with a sense of obligation, which she continues to reinforce as the child grows older. Consequently, she is able to use shame and guilt to control behavior by appealing to this sense of obligation whenever the child deviates from her expectations.

Despite their seemingly permissive child-rearing methods, Asian-American mothers are able to use nonphysical disciplinary techniques described above together with limited amounts of physical punishment very effectively to control their children's behavior. Although much childish behavior is tolerated, aggression, especially fighting, is strongly disapproved of and quickly admonished. Mothers maintain close supervision over all of their children's activities, carefully selecting their playmates and rarely leaving them alone or on their own. This protective care is reflected in the low childhood accident rates suffered by Asian-American children (Kurokawa, 1966).

Although their role appears to be increasing, most Asian-American fathers still play a relatively minor role in the rearing of children during their years of infancy. Since the time the father spends with his children usually is quite limited, he tends to take a rather tolerant attitude toward them, leaving most of the disciplining to the mother. However, when the children reach school age they are no longer indulged and begin to assume duties and responsibilities in the household. They also are subjected to stricter discipline and taught in various ways that their actions will reflect not only on themselves but on the entire family. In cases of serious misbehavior by older children, the disciplining often is done by the father since his authority evokes greater fear and respect. He also spends more time with the older children, particularly if they are boys, joining them in recreational activities and having them assist with household chores.

As Asian-American children reach adolescence, many of them join peer groups and begin showing interest in the opposite sex. Their friends are now even more carefully screened by the parents. Dating among Asian-American teenagers is often on a group basis, whereby girls and boys go out as a group without necessarily pairing off. Dating on an individual basis generally does not start until later; in fact, group dating patterns sometimes persist even into college.

Parental attitudes toward pre-marital sexual exploration are still relatively strict but are becoming more tolerant. In fact, it is not uncommon to find unmarried couples living together among Asian-American college students. However, while marriages among Asian-Americans today are based on romantic love and free choice, parents still exert considerable influence on their children in this matter.

KINSHIP AND COMMUNITY

The nuclear family consisting of the parents and their children is the norm today among Asian-American families. However, close ties are still maintained with many relatives outside the immediate residential family through frequent visits and telephone calls, mutual assistance, reciprocal gift-giving, and various social get-togethers. The bonds appear particularly strong between married sisters and between a mother and her married daughters. While grandparents generally do not live with their married children, they often live nearby and become quite involved with their children's families.

Due to the extent and closeness of these ties, the Asian-American family has been referred to as a modified extended family (Johnson, 1972). Although it is residentially nuclear, it is in many respects functionally extended. Such patterns appear to be particularly prevalent among Japanese families in Hawaii. To a lesser extent they are also found among second- and third-generation Asian-American families on the West coast (Kiefer, 1974; Nee and Nee, 1972) and in other areas, such as New York City, where there are relatively high concentrations of Asian-Americans.

Strongly complementing these family ties are the extensive networks of affiliations and communications that exist in the Asian-American communities.

These include both informal networks, such as family friends and social groups, and formal networks, such as ethnic newspapers, churches, family and business associations, recreational clubs, and various other community organizations (Hsu, 1971; Kiefer, 1974). Many of these formal networks are outgrowths of those originally established by the early Asian immigrants through their adaptations of the Chinese clan and Japanese *dozoku* systems of kinship. In recent years, as numerous national Asian-American organizations have come into being, similar networks are developing even at the national level.

It is these networks that made the Asian-American communities very close-knit social entities. They strongly reinforce the sanctioning techniques of the family for controlling behavior by serving as very effective channels for gossip and news about both misdeeds and achievements of individuals in the community. Through such communications, the "good families" and "bad families" are readily identified. Thus, community members are quite aware that their actions will become widely known and ultimately reflect on their families' reputations. . . .

Recent Immigrant Families

Since 1965 when discriminatory immigration quotas were finally elimi-nated, well over 200,000 Chinese immigrants have entered the United States, principally from Hong Kong and Taiwan. Most of them have crowded into the Chinatowns of San Francisco, New York City, Boston, and other major cities. These Chinatowns are stricken with some of the worst conditions to be found in any of the inner-city ghettoes, including increasing crime and delinquency, grossly inadequate health care, overcrowded and substandard housing, chronic underemployment, and a multitude of other pressing social problems (Chin, 1971; Wong, 1971; Lyman, 1974).

The families of these immigrants must contend with circumstances quite different from those faced by earlier Asian immigrant families. Parents no longer work and live with their children in small business establishments, but are now generally wage workers in restaurants, garment factories, and other large enterprises. Both parents usually must work, often ten hours a day, seven days a week, for subsistence-level wages. Consequently, they have little time to spend with their children and must live under poverty conditions (Chao, 1977).

Parents also no longer can rely on traditional techniques for controlling the behavior of their children. Unlike earlier Asian immigrants, most of the recent immigrants have come from urban areas, which have experienced major changes under the impact of modernization and Western influences. Values and lifestyles have undergone corresponding changes. Furthermore, the youth are far more sophisticated in their perceptions about the society in which they live.

All of these factors have subjected recent Chinese immigrant families to severe strains. Due to the absence of their parents and traditional constraints, the teenage youth of these families have been especially prone to acts of rebellion and social deviance. Since many of them cannot speak English and experience traumatic family/school discontinuities, they frequently become alienated from school, drop out and join their peers in street gangs (Sung, 1977). A large number of such gangs have formed over the past few years in all of the major Chinatowns and have been increasingly involved in crime and acts of violence, including an estimated forty-five killings attributed to intergang warfare (Wu, 1977). . . .

Deculturalization

A number of serious problems faced second-, third-, and fourth-generation Asian-Americans as a result of their deculturalization, which is defined here as the combined process of both acculturation and discrimination. Although a wide range of these problems could be discussed, we shall touch just briefly on some of the major problems in the areas of education, employment, and mental health.

. . . Despite their high achievement levels, Asian-American students face many subtle forms of discrimination in education due to the Anglo-centric orientation of most schools. The curriculum usually omits or badly distorts the experience and contributions of Asian-Americans. Teachers often stereotype Asian-American students as quiet, hard-working, and docile, and tend to reinforce conformity and stifle creativity. Therefore, Asian-American students frequently do not develop the ability to assert and express themselves verbally, and are channeled mainly into technical/scientific fields (Watanabe, 1973). As a consequence of these influences, many Asian-American students suffer from low self-esteem, are overly conforming, and have their academic and social development narrowly circumscribed.

Subtle forms of discrimination against Asian-Americans also appear widespread in employment. Although they have gained access to many professional occupations because of their high educational attainment levels, most Asian-Americans appear to be relegated to lower-echelon, white-collar jobs having little or no decision-making authority and low mobility. They are consistently passed over by Anglos for most supervisory and administrative positions, apparently because they are viewed as not having the requisite personality traits, such as aggressiveness, verbal fluency, and self-confidence, for such positions (Suzuki, 1977a). . . .

. . . Fortunately, there do appear to be countervailing forces at work. Perhaps the most important has been the emergence of the Asian-American movement, which has played a major role in raising the ethnic consciousness and social awareness of Asian-Americans. As a consequence, Asian-Americans are having second thoughts about the merits of acculturating further into the mainstream of American society, and are becoming concerned about preserving important traditional aspects of their own cultures. Many of them are also currently seeking to redefine their identity and role in American society on their own terms and can be expected to take a far less accommodating approach in this quest than in the past. . . .

THE CONTEMPORARY ASIAN-AMERICAN FAMILY: A SUMMARY

Several broad generalizations may be drawn from our description of the contemporary Asian-American family:

1. While they have acculturated toward middle-class Anglo norms, Asian-Americans still subscribe to many traditional Asian cultural values, such as group orientation and obligation to parents and family.

2. The educational level and median family income of Asian-Americans are among the highest of any ethnic group; and their rates of social deviance have been among the lowest.

3. Although the Asian-American family is often characterized as patriarchal, husbands and wives appear to enjoy a more egalitarian relationship than do their Anglo counterparts. However, except during early childhood, Asian-American parents tend to impose stricter discipline on their children. While verbal interaction between family members is relatively restrained, there is greater utilization of nonverbal and indirect modes of communication.

4. By middle-class Anglo norms, Asian-American mothers tend to indulge, if not spoil, their infant children. However, due to the close, affective ties that result from such an upbringing, mothers are able to very effectively employ nonphysical sanctions such as shame and deprivation to control their children's behavior.

5. By instilling their children with a strong sense of obligation to the family and with the idea that their actions will reflect not only on themselves but on the entire family, Asian-American parents are able to maintain a high degree of social control over their children. This control is strongly reinforced by the tightly knit Asian-American communities in which extensive networks of affiliations provide very effective channels for communicating both the misdeeds and achievements of individual community members.

6. The Asian-American family continues to be a close-knit, cohesive social entity. Although residentially nuclear, many Asian-American families are functionally extended due to the close ties that are maintained with many relatives outside the immediate residential family. Social activities tend to take place within the extended family and the ethnic community.

7. The families of recent immigrants constitute a significant proportion of all Chinese-American families. Most of them are crowded into Chinatown ghettoes and must contend with chronic underemployment, grossly inadequate health care, and overcrowded and substandard housing. Growing rates of social deviance, especially crime and delinquency, indicate that these families are experiencing serious dislocations. Language and cultural barriers prevent access to social services and job programs that could otherwise help ameliorate some of these problems.

8. The effects of deculturalization are creating serious problems for Asian-

Americans in many areas, including education, employment, and mental health. The resulting psychological strains could have long-term, detrimental effects on the Asian-American family. Perhaps the major countervailing force to deculturalization is the Asian-American movement, which has raised the ethnic consciousness and social awareness of Asian-Americans.

It must be reiterated that these generalizations should not be misused to stereotype all Asian-American families. Given the wide range of variations which exist among these families, one can be certain that many of them will not fit our modal description. . . .

BIBLIOGRAPHY

Benedict, Ruth. 1946. *The Chrysanthemum and the Sword*. Boston: Houghton Mifflin.

Broom, Leonard, and Kitsuse, John I. 1956. *The Managed Casuality: The Japanese-American Family in World War II*. Berkeley: University of California Press Reprint, 1973.

Caudill, William, 1952. "Japanese-American Personality and Acculturation." *Genetic Psychology Monographs*, 45 (February):3–102.

Chao, Rose. 1977. *Chinese Immigrant Children*. Preliminary Report, Betty L. Sung (Ed.). New York: Department of Asian Studies, City University of New York.

Chin, Rocky. 1971. "New York Chinatown Today." *Amerasia Journal*, 1 (March):1–24.

Chinn, Thomas, (Ed.). 1969. *A History of the Chinese in California: A Syllabus*. San Francisco: Chinese Historical Society of America.

Conroy, Hilary. 1953. *The Japanese Frontier in Hawaii, 1868–1898*. Berkeley: University of California Press.

Coolidge, Mary R. 1909. *Chinese Immigration*. New York: Arno Press Reprint, 1969.

Daniels, Roger. 1962. *The Politics of Prejudice: The Anti-Japanese Movement in California and the Struggle for Japanese Exclusion*. Berkeley: University of California Press.

Embree, John F. 1939. *Suye Mura: A Japanese Village*. Chicago: University of Chicago Press.

Fujitomi, Irene, and Wong, Diane. 1973. "The New Asian-American Woman." In *Asian-Americans: Psychological Perspectives*, Stanley Sue and Nathaniel N. Wagner (Eds.). Palo Alto, CA: Science and Behavior Books.

Fukutake, Tadashi. 1967. *Japanese Rural Society*. Ithaca: Cornell University Press Reprint, 1972.

Hosokawa, Bill. 1969. *Nisei: The Quiet Americans*. New York: William Morrow.

Hsu, Francis L. K. 1949. *Under the Ancestor's Shadow*. London: Routledge and Kegan Paul.

———. 1971. *The Challenge of the American Dream: The Chinese in the United States*. Belmont, CA: Wadsworth.

————. 1975. *Iemoto: The Heart of Japan*. Cambridge, MA: Schenkman.

Ichihashi, Yamato. 1932. *Japanese in the United States*. New York: Arno Press Reprint, 1969.

Iga, Mamoru, 1957. "The Japanese Social Structure and the Source of Mental Strains of Japanese Immigrants in the United States." *Social Forces*, 35:271–278.

Johnson, Colleen L. 1972. *The Japanese-American Family and Community in Honolulu: Generational Continuities in Ethnic Affiliation*. Ph.D. Dissertation in Anthropology. Syracuse: Syracuse University.

Kiefer, Christie W. 1974. *Changing Cultures, Changing Lives: An Ethnographic Study of Three Generations of Japanese Americans*. San Francisco: Jossey-Bass.

Kitano, Harry H. L. 1969a. *Japanese Americans: The Evolution of a Subculture*. Englewood Cliffs, N. J.: Prentice-Hall.

Kriger, Sara F., and Kroes, William H. 1972. "Child-rearing Attitudes of Chinese, Jewish, and Protestant Mothers." *Journal of Social Psychology*, 86:205–210.

Kurokawa, Minako. 1966. "Family Solidarity, Social Change and Childhood Accidents." *Journal of Marriage and the Family*, 28 (November):498–506.

Lang, Olga. 1946. *Chinese Family and Society*. New Haven, CT: Yale University Press.

Lowe, Pardee. 1943. *Father and Glorious Descendant*. Boston: Little Brown and Company.

Lyman, Stanford. 1970. *The Asian in the West*. Social Science and Humanities Publication No. 4. Reno: Western Studies Center, Desert Research Institute, University of Nevada System.

————. 1974. *Chinese Americans*. New York: Random House.

Masuoka, Jitsuichi. 1944. "The Life Cycle of an Immigrant Institution in Hawaii: The Family." *Social Forces*, 23 (October):60–64.

Morishima, James K. 1973. "The Evacuation: Impact on the Family." In *Asian-Americans: Psychological Perspectives*, Stanley Sue and Nathaniel N. Wagner (Eds.). Palo Alto, CA: Science and Behavior Books.

Nee, Victor, and Nee, Brett D. 1972. *Longtime Californ': A Documentary History of an American Chinatown*. New York: Pantheon Books.

Okimoto, Daniel I. 1971. *American in Disguise*. New York: Walker/Weatherhill.

Sollenberger, Richard T. 1968. "Chinese-American Child-rearing Practices and Juvenile Delinquency." *Journal of Social Psychology*, 74:13–23.

Sung, Betty L. 1967. *The Story of the Chinese in America*. New York: Collier Books.

————. 1977. *Gangs in New York's Chinatown*. New York: Department of Asian Studies, City University of New York.

Suzuki, Bob H. 1977a. "The Education and Socialization of Asian Americans: A Revisionist Analysis of the 'Model-Minority' Thesis." *Amerasia Journal*, 4:2:23–51.

Thomas, D. S., and Nishimoto, R. 1946. *The Spoilage: Japanese-American Evacuation and Resettlement During World War II*. Berkeley: University of California Press.

Wagatsuma, Hiroshi. 1977. "Some Aspects of the Contemporary Japanese Family: Once Confucian, Now Fatherless?" *Daedalus*, 106 (Spring):181–210.

Watanabe, Colin. 1973. "Self-Expression and the Asian American Experience." *Personnel and Guidance Journal*, 51 (Feb.):390–396.

Wolf, Margery. 1970. "Child Training and the Chinese Family." In *Family and Kinship in Chinese Society*, Maurice Freedman (Ed.). Stanford, CA.: Stanford University Press.

Wong, Aline K. 1974. "Women in China: Past and Present." In *Many Sisters: Women in Cross-Cultural Perspective*, Carolyn J. Matthiasson (Ed.). New York: Free Press.

Wong, Buck. 1971. "Need for Awareness: An Essay on Chinatown San Francisco." In *Roots: An Asian American Reader*, Amy Tachiki, Eddie Wong and Franklin Odo (Eds.). Los Angeles: Continental Graphics.

Wong, Paul. 1972. "The Emergence of the Asian American Movement." *Bridge*, 2:32–39.

Wu, Robin. 1977. "Front Page Chinatown: What the *** is Going on?" *Bridge*, 5 (Fall):4–7.

Yamamoto, Joe. 1968. "Japanese American Identity Crisis." In *Minority Adolescents in the United States*, Eugene Brody (Ed.). Baltimore: Williams and Wilkins.

Young, Nancy F. 1972 "Socialization Patterns among the Chinese in Hawaii," *Amerasia*, 1(Feb.):31–51.

11 *The Post-Parental Period*

The final two stages of the family life cycle involve a middle period consisting of a prelaunch period before the child leaves home plus the post-parental middle years and the later years between retirement and death. Smaller families and longer life expectancies have made the post-parental period the longest in the family life cycle. Like all stages, these too have developmental tasks which need to be accomplished.

The developmental tasks of the middle years center on:

a. reallocating resources to first deal with prelaunch expenses and then to enjoy the period of greatest financial security,
b. adjusting to the changing social roles of the post-parental period, and
c. reestablishing the marital relationship at home (Duvall & Miller 1985).

As was indicated in Chapter 7, part of the pronatalist belief is that children add to a marriage. One of the outcomes of such a belief is the idea that marital happiness must decline after the departure of the last child from the home. Also noted was the often-confirmed fact that couples are happier without children at home. This does not mean, however, that there will not be a short period of readjustment, known as the "empty nest syndrome," after the last child leaves home. The syndrome reflects the fact that there has been a change in routine and a seeming abrupt cessation of emotional transaction. However, greater involvement of women in careers and a trend toward more androgynous role behavior may decrease this trauma in the future since couples will be less dependent for their identity on their roles as nurturer and breadwinner.

Earlier- or later-than-expected launchings of children cause more problems than on-schedule ones (Blieszner 1986). However, these are becoming more prevalent as adult children either delay leaving home or return after a time to "clutter the nest" with their own offspring as a result of economic factors and a change of attitudes regarding children leaving home after reaching adulthood. The question, then, may be not how to adjust to an "empty nest" but how to empty the nest.

Since 1965, the retirement stage population of those 65 and older has grown twice as fast as the rest of the population. The growth will be even more rapid beginning around 2010 as the baby boomers reach retirement age.

Despite the specter of aging, Jack Horn and Jeff Meer, in the first article of Chapter 11, refer to this period as the vintage years since most are not, as believed, lonely, isolated, or abandoned by their families. However, there are developmental tasks to be accomplished. They include:

a. adjusting to a lower income,

b. maintaining intimacy, interdependence, and couple identification,

c. keeping active in order to avoid "secondary aging," and

d. maintaining relationships with children and other family and friends.

Greater longevity, with the concomitant likelihood of chronic illness, can lead, as Lynn Osterkamp notes in the second article of this chapter, to the family stresses of caregiving, particularly for unmarried daughters. Intergenerational "war," warns Carter Henderson in the final article of this chapter, is another problem that may result from this increased longevity as both the elderly and the young conflict over their economic needs. Thus, the major issues concerning the aged are the myths surrounding retirement, the misconceptions about the elderly, and the possibility that the growing ratio of retired to working people may lead to an intergenerational "war" over economic matters.

REFERENCES

1. Blieszner, R. 1986. "Trends in Family Gerontology Research." *Family Relations* (Vol. 35, October).

2. Duvall, E. M. & B. E. Miller. 1985. *Marriage and Family Development.* New York: Harper & Row

43 *The Vintage Years*

Jack C. Horn / Jeff Meer

STUDY QUESTIONS

1. Indicate several stereotypes and the truth about aging.

2. Why do Horn and Meer claim that the best is yet to come?

Our society is getting older, but the old are getting younger. As Sylvia Herz told an American Psychological Association (APA) symposium on aging last year, the activities and attitudes of a 70-year-old today "are equivalent to those of a 50-year-old's a decade or two ago."

Our notions of what it means to be old are beginning to catch up with this reality. During the past several decades, three major changes have altered the way we view the years after 65:

- The financial, physical and mental health of older people has improved, making the prospect of a long life something to treasure, not fear.

- The population of older people has grown dramatically, rising from 18 million in 1965 to 28 million today. People older than 65 compose 12 percent of the population, a percentage that is expected to rise to more than 20 percent by the year 2030.

- Researchers have gained a much better understanding of aging and the lives of older people, helping to sort out the inevitable results of biological aging from the effects of illness or social and environmental problems. No one has yet found the fountain of youth, or of immortality. But research has revealed that aging itself is not the thief we once thought it was; healthy older people

Source: Jack C. Horn and Jeff Meer, "The Vintage Years." *Psychology Today*, May 1987, pp. 76–77, 80–84, 89–90. Reprinted with permission from *Psychology Today* magazine. Copyright © 1987 (PT Partners, L.P.).

can maintain and enjoy most of their physical and mental abilities, and even improve in some areas.

Because of better medical care, improved diet and increasing interest in physical fitness, more people are reaching the ages of 65, 75 and older in excellent health. Their functional age—a combination of physical, psychological and social factors that affect their attitudes toward life and the roles they play in the world—is much younger than their chronological age.

Their economic health is better, too, by almost every measure. Over the last three decades, for example, the number of men and women 65 and older who live below the poverty line has dropped steadily from 35 percent in 1959 to 12 percent in 1984, the last year for which figures are available.

On the upper end of the economic scale, many of our biggest companies are headed by what once would have been called senior citizens, and many more of them serve as directors of leading companies. Even on a more modest economic level, a good portion of the United States' retired older people form a new leisure class, one with money to spend and the time to enjoy it. Obviously not all of America's older people share this prosperity. Economic hardship is particularly prevalent among minorities. But as a group, our older people are doing better than ever.

In two other areas of power, politics and the law, people in their 60s and 70s have always played important roles. A higher percentage of people from 65 to 74 register and vote than in any other group. With today's increasing vigor and numbers, their power is likely to increase still further. It is perhaps no coincidence that our current President is the oldest ever.

Changing attitudes, personal and social, are a major reason for the increasing importance of older people in our society. As psychologist Bernice Neugarten points out, there is no longer a particular age at which someone starts to work or attends school, marries and has children, retires or starts a business. Increasing numbers of older men and women are enrolled in colleges, universities and other institutions of learning. According to the Center for Education Statistics, for example, the number of people 65 and older enrolled in adult education of all kinds increased from 765,000 to 866,000 from 1981 to 1984. Gerontologist Barbara Ober says that this growing interest in education is much more than a way to pass the time. "Older people make excellent students, maybe even better students than the majority of 19- and 20-year-olds. One advantage is that they have settled a lot of the social and sexual issues that preoccupy their younger classmates."

Older people today are not only healthier and more active; they are also increasingly more numerous. "Squaring the pyramid" is how some demographers describe this change in our population structure. It has always been thought of as a pyramid, a broad base of newborns supporting successively smaller tiers of older people as they died from disease, accidents, poor nutrition, war and other causes.

Today, the population structure is becoming more rectangular, as fewer people die during the earlier stages of life. The Census Bureau predicts that by 2030 the structure will be an almost perfect rectangle up to the age of 70.

The aging of America has been going on at least since 1800, when half the people in the country were younger than 16 years old, but two factors have accelerated the trend tremendously. First, the number of old people has increased rapidly. Since 1950 the number of Americans 65 and older has more than doubled to some 28 million—more than the entire current population of Canada. Within the same period, the number of individuals older than 85 has quadrupled to about 2.6 million (see "The Oldest Old," this article).

Second, the boom in old people has been paired with a bust in the proportion of youngsters due to a declining birth rate. Today, fewer than one American in four is younger than 16. This drop-off has been steady, with the single exception of the post-World War II baby boom, which added 76 million children to the country between 1945 and 1964. As these baby boomers reach the age of 65, starting in 2010, they are expected to increase the proportion of the population 65 and older from its current 12 percent to 21 percent by 2030.

The growing presence of healthy, vigorous older people has helped overcome some of the stereotypes about aging and the elderly. Research has also played a major part by replacing myths with facts. While there were some studies of aging before World War II, scientific interest increased dramatically during the 1950s and kept growing.

Important early studies of aging included three started in the mid or late 1950s: the Human Aging Study, conducted by the National Institute of Mental Health (NIMH); the Duke Longitudinal Studies, done by the Center for the Study of Aging and Human Development at Duke University; and the Baltimore Longitudinal Study of Aging, conducted by the Gerontological Institute in Baltimore, now part of the National Institute on Aging (NIA). All three took a multidisciplinary approach to the study of normal aging: what changes take place, how people adapt to them, how biological, genetic, social, psychological and environmental characteristics relate to longevity and what can be done to promote successful aging.

These pioneering studies and hundreds of later ones have benefited from growing federal support. White House Conferences on Aging in 1961 and 1971 helped focus attention on the subject. By 1965 Congress had enacted Medicare and the Older Americans Act. During the 1970s Congress authorized the establishment of the NIA as part of the National Institutes of Health and NIMH created a special center to support research on the mental health of older people.

All these efforts have produced a tremendous growth in our knowledge of aging. In the first (1971) edition of the *Handbook of the Psychology of Aging*, it was estimated that as much had been published on the subject in the previous 15 years as in all the years before then. In the second edition, published in 1985, psychologists James Birren and Walter Cunningham wrote that the "period for this rate of doubling has now decreased to 10 years . . . the volume of published research has increased to the almost unmanageable total of over a thousand articles a year."

Psychologist Clifford Swenson of Purdue University explained some of the powerful incentives for this tremendous increase: "I study the topic partly to discover more effective ways of helping old people cope with their problems, but also to load my own armamentarium against that inevitable day. For that is one aspect of aging and its problems that makes it different from the other problems psychologists study: We may not all be schizophrenic or neurotic or overweight, but there is only one alternative to old age and most of us try to avoid that alternative."

One popular misconception disputed by recent research is the idea that aging means inevitable physical and sexual failure. Some changes occur, of course. Reflexes slow, hearing and eyesight dim, stamina decreases. This *primary aging* is a gradual process that begins early in life and affects all body systems.

But many of the problems we associate with old age are *secondary aging*—the results not of age but of disease, abuse and disuse—factors often under our own control. More and more older people are healthy, vigorous men and women who lead enjoyable, active lives. National surveys by the Institute for Social Research and others show that life generally seems less troublesome and freer to older people than it does to younger adults.

In a review of what researchers have learned about subjective well-being—happiness, life satisfaction, positive emotions—University of Illinois psychologist Ed Diener reported that "Most results show a slow rise in satisfaction with age . . . young persons appear to experience higher levels of joy but older persons tend to judge their lives in more positive ways."

Money is often mentioned as the key to a happy retirement, but psychologist Daniel Ogilvie of Rutgers University has found another, much more important, factor. Once we have a certain minimum amount of money, his research shows, life satisfaction depends mainly on how much time we spend doing things we find meaningful. Ogilvie believes retirement-planning workshops and seminars should spend more time helping people decide how to use their skills and interests after they retire.

A thought that comes through clearly when researchers talk about physical and mental fitness is "use it or lose it." People rust out faster from disuse than they wear out from overuse. This advice applies equally to sexual activity. While every study from the time of Kinsey to the present shows that sexual interest and activity diminish with age, the drop varies greatly among individuals. Psychologist Marion Perlmutter and writer Elizabeth Hall have reported that one of the best predictors of continued sexual intercourse "is early sexual activity and past sexual enjoyment and frequency. People who have never had much pleasure from sexuality may regard their age as a good excuse for giving up sex."

They also point out that changing times affect sexual activity. As today's younger adults bring their more liberal sexual attitudes with them into old age, the level of sexual activity among older men and women may rise.

The idea that mental abilities decline steadily with age has also been challenged by many recent and not-so-recent findings (see "The Reason of Age," *Psychology Today*, June 1986). In brief, age doesn't damage abilities as much as was once believed, and in some areas we actually gain; we learn to compensate through experience for much of what we do lose; and we can restore some losses through training.

For years, older people didn't do as well as younger people on most tests used to measure mental ability. But psychologist Leonard Poon of the University of Georgia believes that researchers are now taking a new, more appropriate approach to measurement. "Instead of looking at older people's ability to do abstract tasks that have little or no relationship to what they do every day, today's researchers are examining real-life issues."

Psychologist Gisela Labouvie-Vief of Wayne State University has been measuring how people approach everyday problems in logic. She notes that older adults have usually done poorly on such tests, mostly because they fail to think logically all the time. But Labouvie-Vief argues that this is not because they have forgotten how to think logically but because they use a more complex approach unknown to younger thinkers. "The [older] thinker operates within a kind of double reality which is both formal and informal, both logical and psychological," she says.

In other studies, Labouvie-Vief has found that when older people were asked to give concise summaries of fables they read, they did so. But when they were simply asked to recall as much of the fable as possible, they concentrated on the metaphorical, moral or social meaning of the text. They didn't try to duplicate the fable's exact words, the way younger people did. As psychologists Nancy Datan, Dean Rodeheaver and Fergus Hughes of the University of Wisconsin have described their findings, "while [some people assume] that old and young are equally competent, we might better assume that they are differently competent."

John Horn, director of the Adult Development and Aging program at the University of Southern California, suggests that studies of Alzheimer's disease, a devastating progressive mental deterioration experienced by an estimated 5 percent to 15 percent of those older than 65, may eventually help explain some of the differences in thinking abilities of older people. "Alzheimer's, in some ways, may represent the normal process of aging, only speeded up," he says.

Generalities are always suspect, but one generalization about old age seems solid: It is a different experience for men and women. Longevity is one important reason. Women in the United States live seven to eight years longer, on the average, than do men. This simple fact has many ramifications, as sociologist Gunhild Hagestad explained in *Our Aging Society*.

For one thing, since the world of the very old is disproportionately a world of women, men and women spend their later years differently. "Most older women are widows living alone; most older men live with their wives . . . among individuals over the age of 75, two-thirds of the men are living with a spouse, while less than one-fifth of the women are."

The difference in longevity also means that among older people, remarriage is a male prerogative. After 65, for example, men remarry at a rate eight times that of women. This is partly a matter of the scarcity of men and partly a matter of culture—even late in life, men tend to marry younger women. It is also a matter of education and finances, which, Hagestad explains, "operate quite differently in shaping remarriage probabilities among men and women. The more resources the woman has available (measured in education and income), the less likely she is to remarry. For men, the trend is reversed."

The economic situations of elderly men and women also differ considerably. Lou Glasse, president of the Older Women's League in Washington, D.C., points out that most of these women were housewives who worked at paid jobs sporadically, if at all. "That means their Social Security benefits are lower than men's, they are not likely to have pensions and they are less likely to have been able to save the kind of money that would protect them from poverty during their older years."

Although we often think of elderly men and women as living in nursing homes or retirement communities, the facts are quite different. Only about 5 percent are in nursing homes and perhaps an equal number live in some kind of age-segregated housing. Most people older than 65 live in their own houses or apartments.

We also think of older people as living alone. According to the Census Bureau, this is true of 15 percent of the men and 41 percent of the women. Earlier this year, a survey done by Louis Harris & Associates revealed that 28 percent of elderly people living alone have annual incomes below $5,100, the federal poverty line. Despite this, they were four times as likely to give financial help to their children as to receive it from them.

In addition, fewer than 1 percent of the old people said they would prefer living with their children. Psychiatrist Robert N. Butler, chairman of the Commonwealth Fund's Commission on Elderly People Living Alone, which sponsored the report, noted that these findings dispute the "popular portrait of an elderly, dependent parent financially draining their middle-aged children."

There is often another kind of drain, however, one of time and effort. The Travelers Insurance Company recently surveyed more than 700 of its employees on this issue. Of those at least 30 years old, 28 percent said they directly care for an older relative in some way—taking that person to the doctor, making telephone calls, handling finances or running errands—for an average of 10 hours a week. Women, who are more often caregivers, spent an average of 16 hours, and men five hours, per week. One group, 8 percent of the sample, spent a heroic 35 hours per week, the equivalent of a second job, providing such care. "That adds up to an awful lot of time away from other things," psychologist Beal Lowe says, "and the stresses these people face are enormous."

Lowe, working with Sherman-Lank Communications in Kensington, Maryland, has formed "Caring for Caregivers," a group of professionals devoted to providing services, information and support to those who care for older relatives. "It can be a great shock to some people who have planned the perfect retirement," he says, "only to realize that your chronically ill mother suddenly needs daily attention."

Researchers who have studied the housing needs of older people predictably disagree on many things, but most agree on two points: We need a variety of individual and group living arrangements to meet the varying interests, income and abilities of people older than 65; and the arrangements should be flexible enough that the elderly can stay in the same locale as their needs and abilities change. Many studies have documented the fact that moving itself can be stressful and even fatal to old people, particularly if they have little or no influence over when and where they move.

This matter of control is important, but more complicated than it seemed at first. Psychologist Judith Rodin and others have demonstrated that people in nursing homes are happier, more alert and live longer if they are allowed to take responsibility for their lives in some way, even in something as simple as choosing a plant for their room, taking care of a bird feeder, selecting the night to attend a movie.

Rodin warns that while control is generally beneficial, the effect depends on the individuals involved. For some, personal control brings with it demands in the form of time, effort and the risk of failure. They may blame themselves if they get sick or something else goes wrong. The challenge, Rodin wrote, is to "provide but not impose opportunities. . . . The need for self-determination, it must be remembered, also calls for the opportunity to choose not to exercise control. . . ."

An ancient Greek myth tells how the Goddess of Dawn fell in love with a mortal and convinced Jupiter to grant him immortality. Unfortunately, she forgot to have youth included in the deal, so he gradually grew older and older. "At length," the story concludes, "he lost the power of using his limbs, and then she shut him up in his chamber, whence his feeble voice might at times be heard. Finally she turned him into a grasshopper."

The fears and misunderstandings of age expressed in this 3,000-year-old myth persist today, despite all the positive things we have learned in recent years about life after 65. We don't turn older people into grasshoppers or shut them out of sight, but too often we move them firmly out of the mainstream of life.

In a speech at the celebration of Harvard University's 350th anniversary last September, political scientist Robert Binstock decried what he called The Spectre of the Aging Society: "the economic burdens of population aging; moral dilemmas posed by the allocation of health resources on the basis of age; labor market competition between older and younger workers within the contexts of age discrimination laws; seniority practices, rapid technological change; and a politics of conflict between age groups."

Binstock, a professor at Case Western Reserve School of Medicine, pointed out that these inaccurate perceptions express an underlying ageism, "the attribution of these same characteristics and status to an artificially homogenized group labeled 'the aged.' "

Ironically, much ageism is based on compassion rather than ill will. To protect older workers from layoffs, for example, unions fought hard for job security based on seniority. To win it, they accepted mandatory retirement, a limitation that now penalizes older workers and deprives our society of their experience.

A few companies have taken special steps to utilize this valuable pool of older workers. The Travelers companies, for example, set up a job bank that is open to its own retired employees as well as those of other companies. According to Howard E. Johnson, a senior vice president, the company employs about 175 formerly retired men and women a week. He estimates that the program is saving Travelers $1 million a year in temporary-hire fees alone.

While mandatory retirement is only one example of ageism, it is particularly important because we usually think of contributions to society in economic terms. Malcolm H. Morrison, an authority on retirement and age discrimination in employment for the Social Security Administration, points out that once the idea of retirement at a certain fixed age was accepted, "the old became defined as a dependent group in society, a group whose members could not and should not work, and who needed economic and social assistance that the younger working population was obligated to provide."

We need to replace this stereotype with the more realistic understanding that older people are and should be productive members of society, capable of assuming greater responsibility for themselves and others. What researchers have learned about the strengths and abilities of older people should help us turn this ideal of an active, useful life after 65 into a working reality.

GREAT EXPECTATIONS

If you were born in 1920 and are a . . .

	. . . white man	*. . . white woman*
your life expectancy was . . .		
at birth	*54.4 years*	*55.6 years*
at age 40	*71.7*	*77.1*
at age 62	*78.5*	*83.2*

If you were born in 1940 and are a . . .

	. . . white man	*. . . white woman*
your life expectancy was . . .		
at birth	*62.1 years*	*66.6 years*
at age 20	*70.3*	*76.3*
at age 42	*74.7*	*80.7*

If you were born in 1960 and are a . . .

	. . . white man	*. . . white woman*
your life expectancy was . . .		
at birth	*67.4 years*	*74.1 years*
at age 22	*73.2*	*80.0*

---

44   *Family Caregivers*

Lynn Osterkamp

STUDY QUESTIONS

1. Who are the caregivers and what care do they provide?

2. What are the needs of the caregivers?

"Aging is a family affair." "Caregivers need care too!" Such familiar slogans reflect the recent emphasis on the needs of American families caring for frail elderly relatives. Professional organizations, advocacy groups, and the popular media remind us that informal caregivers, primarily families, are providing most of the help needed by frail elderly persons, and that these caregivers themselves need help.

We know that in the past 20 years, the U.S.A.'s elderly population (age 65 and above) has grown twice as fast as the general population, and that the most rapidly growing age group is the "old-old" (over age 85). This oldest group numbers approximately 2 million and will increase to about 16 million by the mid-21st Century. While only about 5 percent of those aged 65 to 74 require help, by age 85, about 33 percent need personal assistance.

Families are our nation's primary resource for providing this help. Approximately 80 percent of the frail elderly in the community report that informal caregivers are their major source of assistance. In 1982 the National Long Term Care Survey found that approximately 2.2 million caregivers aged 14 or older were providing unpaid assistance to 1.6 million noninstitutionalized disabled elderly persons who had one or more limitations in activities of daily living. An estimated 6 million elderly Americans need some assistance from family or friends with activities ranging from personal care to household maintenance, shopping and transportation.

Even though providing care imposes extensive demands on families, home

Source: Lynn Osterkamp, "Family Caregivers: America's Primary Long-term Care Resource." *Aging* 358(1988):2–5. Reprinted by permission.

care is likely to continue to increase in the future for several reasons: families prefer it over institutional care, family caregiving costs less than hospital or nursing home care, and the number of patients now requiring extensive home care is increasing.

To help caregivers effectively, we need a picture of who they are, how they manage, what problems they face, and what types of assistance they need. Although there is considerable research describing caregivers, we find from the data that caregivers are not a homogeneous group who can be easily represented by some typical caregiver. As we consider caregivers' problems, it is important to keep in mind that this diverse population requires a broad range of assistance to meet its varying needs.

WHO ARE THE CAREGIVERS? WHAT CARE DO THEY PROVIDE?

Surveys consistently find that the majority of caregivers (about 75 percent) are women and that their average age is between 55 and 60, with approximately one-third over age 65. The frail person's spouse is the most likely to become the caregiver; next likely are adult daughters, then daughters-in-law, sons and other relatives. Wives of severely impaired men provide the most informal care.

Caregivers described by research tend to be those who are caring for seriously impaired elderly persons, as, for example, the 6,400 elderly studied in the National Long Term Care Survey. That survey estimates that these 6,400 represent an actual 1.6 million frail elderly receiving care at home. Thus, when we use this research data to describe caregivers, we must realize that we are depicting primarily the estimated 2.2 million unpaid caregivers who care for these frail elderly. We cannot necessarily assume that we are also describing the larger population of family and friends who assist elderly people needing limited amounts of help with activities such as transportation, finances or home maintenance.

The frail elderly described in research are impaired on an average of two to three activities of daily living (such as bathing, feeding and toileting) and on an average of five instrumental activities of daily living (such as housework, meal preparation and shopping). The majority of their caregivers assist them with such tasks seven days a week, averaging between four and five hours a day. About half of their caregivers have been providing care for less than four years, but about a fifth have been caregivers for five years or longer. Approximately three-fourths of the caregivers live with the care recipient.

Family caregivers increase the level of services they provide to match the older person's needs, and some, especially adult daughters, serve as a link between the elderly person and community services. In general, women give more overall help and more help with personal and household tasks, while men help more with home repairs, transportation, and financial management.

LYNN OSTERKAMP

HOW MUCH HELP DO CAREGIVERS GET?

Most frail elderly people have one primary caregiver who assumes overall responsibility for their care. When the primary caregiver is an adult child, that child is most often a daughter who is geographically close to the parent. There is no evidence that oldest versus youngest or middle children are most likely to become caregivers or that the "most loved" child is chosen for the job.

Primary caregivers tend to take on most of the caregiving tasks themselves, often with little help from other family members or from community services. In general caregivers who do get help and support from family feel less burdened by the demands of caregiving. This does not necessarily imply, however, that family members can easily step in and relieve the primary caregiver's burden. In fact, professionals have repeatedly observed that the family dynamics surrounding caregiving are complex, and that not all primary caregivers are willing to ask for or even accept help.

Caregivers also use relatively few community services. Surveys show that only 10 to 20% of caregivers use paid helpers and that the frail elderly receive an average of five times as many hours per week of help from informal caregivers as they do from formal services. In general, families begin using formal services only when the older person's needs become too much for them to handle.

WHAT IS THE IMPACT OF CAREGIVING ON CAREGIVERS?

Although the most frequently mentioned effects of caregiving on the caregiver are negative, some benefits are reported. Three quarters of caregivers say providing care makes them feel useful, and many anecdotal reports attest to caregivers' satisfaction in knowing that their older relative is receiving adequate care while remaining in the community. About one-fourth of caregivers report that the older person helps financially or with household chores.

The impact of caregiving on physical health has been investigated with confusing results. Reports of poor health are higher for women who are caregivers than for women of the same age who don't have this responsibility, but whether or not this difference is due to caregiving is unclear. Caregivers in some studies have reported rather large declines in their physical health over several years of caregiving; other studies have not found much decline.

Emotional strain and feelings of being burdened are the most often cited negative effects of caregiving, but again effects are by no means universal. Some caregivers report much more stress than do others, but interpretations are difficult because of the many different methods used to study caregiver stress. Caregivers don't necessarily agree on what constitutes "a great deal of strain," and may weigh such factors as obligation and family tradition when responding.

In general, it seems that the types of tasks caregivers must perform, the amount of assistance they get, and specific characteristics of caregivers, such as problem-solving style, are most related to the amount of strain the caregiver reports. Apparently, providing personal care is more burdensome than performing less intimate tasks. Several studies have found that women find care giving more stressful than men do, but the reason for such differences is not clear.

Caregivers who take a passive approach to problem-solving, using such strategies as avoidance, report more feelings of burden, as do those who feel little control over their situation or do not have confidence in their problem-solving abilities. Also, caregivers caring for elders who engage in disruptive behavior such as yelling and swearing report more stress. However, the burden does not necessarily increase as the severity of an older person's cognitive impairment increases.

While caregivers' feelings of stress and burden are subjective states that are difficult to investigate, other negative effects of caregiving are more obvious. Between a quarter and a third of caregivers report that limitations on their social life and on relationships with family and friends pose a serious problem; about half report some problems in these areas.

Ten to twenty percent of caregivers report leaving their jobs to be full-time caregivers. Among employed caregivers, one-fifth to one-third say they have rearranged or restricted their working hours because of caregiving demands. Blue collar workers, who have the least flexibility, are most likely to take time off without pay to handle caregiving tasks, thus adding lost income to their problems.

Some caregivers have conflicting demands. About a quarter of adult child caregivers have dependent children competing for their time and attention. Forty to fifty percent of spousal caregivers have problems with their own health, assessing it as fair to poor.

WHAT IS THE CONTRIBUTION OF FAMILY CAREGIVING?

Decades of research have shown that feelings of family responsibility to the elderly are firmly rooted in our society. The idea that families today are abandoning their elderly has been repeatedly demonstrated to be false. In fact, family care is the most critical factor in preventing or delaying nursing home placement of the frail elderly.

Among elderly who do enter nursing homes, those who have family support enter at a higher level of impairment than do those without such support. Families tend to exhaust their own resources before turning to institutionalization. One study found that the majority of families in a sample who had placed relatives in nursing homes reported that their patient required 24-hour care or supervision before placement. On admission these patients had an average of four health problems per person, two other precipitating problems (such as frequent falls, confusion, incontinence), and more than 80 percent had been recently hospitalized. Nevertheless, families had been providing

LYNN OSTERKAMP

nearly total care before nursing home admission; only 19 percent of the elderly patients had been receiving any formal community-based services.

Several studies have shown that the level of family care does not decrease even when formal community-based servides are used. Increased use of formal services seems to serve primarily to improve the quality of life for caregivers and patients.

Obviously American families who care for frail elderly relatives are contributing immensely to society, both in terms of the quality of life for these elderly and in terms of the financial responsibility society would otherwise have to assume for such care. If families are to continue to carry this responsibility, however, they need more help.

WHAT DO CAREGIVERS NEED?

This is a complex question since caregivers are a diverse group whose needs and resources vary, and since the effects of interventions designed to help them are difficult to evaluate.

Caregivers Need Education and Training. Surveys consistently show that caregivers want to know more about the disease and conditions that afflict their elderly relatives. They want to know what to expect and how best to respond. They want to understand and know how to administer the drugs and treatments their relatives need. They want specific training in performing the increasingly complex medical procedures needed to care for their relatives when they are discharged from the hospital. They want to know what services are available to help their older relative and how to go about getting them. They want to learn how to cope with complex health care reimbursement forms and regulations.

Caregivers Need Assistance. The types of assistance needed obviously vary with the caregiving situation and caregiver resources. We do not know why some caregivers use services while others do not or whether some services are more helpful than others. Research on the effects of providing such services as respite, adult day care, or case management is difficult to interpret since programs differ and varying measures of the impact of the services on caregivers have been used.

Although caregivers' anecdotal reports of the effects of new programs and services tend to be positive, specific consistent benefits generally have not shown up on measuring instruments. We need more carefully controlled research investigating the effects of specific interventions so that we can tailor programs to meet caregivers' needs most effectively. We also need to find ways of assuring families that accepting help does not mean that they are giving up or failing in their caregiving role.

Caregivers Need Emotional Support. Caregivers who participate in support groups find comfort in being able to express their feelings in a supportive setting and in realizing that they are not alone in their emotional reactions. Again, the benefits of such groups are difficult to quantify, and research to date has yielded confusing results. Nevertheless, professionals and caregivers alike overwhelmimgly report that caregivers need support in setting limits for themselves, in considering the effects of taking on or continuing caregiving responsibilities, and in making difficult decisions. Whether they can best find this support from friends and family, through a support group or in individual counseling may vary from case to case.

Caregivers Need Relief from Financial Strain. Fewer caregivers than we might expect actually report financial strain due to caregiving. Nevertheless, the costs of giving up or reducing employment, or straining one's physical and mental health to provide care for a long period may not be immediately apparent. We must carefully investigate what partnership between government and family will be most cost-effective in the long run.

Caregivers Need to Know We Care. Most of all caregivers need to know that they are not alone, that society supports them and is willing to share the burden. Families want to provide for their elderly, ideally as part of a coordinated societal approach to long term care.

45 *Old Glory: America Comes of Age*

Carter Henderson

STUDY QUESTIONS

1. Why does Henderson refer to the elderly age period as the "golden oldies"?

2. Give several factors that could lead to an intergenerational war.

Older people in the United States have never had it so good. They're richer, healthier, happier, more respected, more involved, living longer and—as their numbers increase—inexorably changing America's character from youth to maturity.

Basketball superstar Wilt Chamberlain has announced plans to make the 1988 U.S. Olympic team as a discus thrower at age 51. Actress Joan Collins of *Dynasty* is a sex symbol at 55. Movie tough guy Charles Bronson is invincible at

Source: Carter Henderson, "Old Glory: America Comes of Age." *The Futurist*, March/April 1988, pp. 36–40. Reprinted by permission.

65. Ronald Reagan is president of the United States at 77. And comedian George Burns is still packing 'em in at 92.

Even the medical profession, traditionally more concerned with the young than the old, is seeing the elderly in a new light. At a recent University of Pennsylvania forum on medical ethics, a panel of physicians, lawyers, and academicians was asked who should receive a kidney transplant—a 60-year-old man who has an outstanding record of professional excellence in his field, or a 25-year-old man who had dropped out of school, served time in prison, and been negligent in keeping to the prescribed regimen of dialysis and dietary restrictions. The panel opted, by a fairly wide margin, to give the kidney transplant to the older man.

But as life-spans lengthen and age comes into its own, the weakening U.S. economy may prove unable to pay for older Americans' hard-won retirement programs, from Social Security and Medicare to impending protection against catastrophic illness and the ruinous cost of long-term nursing-home care.

This could trigger a battle royal between politically powerful retired Americans financially dependent on such government transfer payments and young workers just starting out in life from whose paychecks these payments are being extracted.

"In the first half of the next century," says *The Economist,* "age could become a more divisive influence on the world than race, sex, and class have been."

THE METHUSELAH PROGRESSION

The number of elderly Americans is expected to double within the next 30 years. This is not surprising since life expectancy is being lengthened by better diet, greater emphasis on physical fitness, and stunning advances in medical science—with more to come. Two examples of the sort of medical advances we can expect:

• New discoveries in biotechnology and genetic engineering will lead to the replacement of nerve cells, arteries, hormone-producing cells, and even brain cells. Medical science is also on the verge of generating or regenerating body parts such as skin, bones, and vital organs and inducing injured nerve cells in the brain and spinal cord to repair themselves.

• New psychotherapeutic drugs will benefit victims of senility by moderating behavioral abnormalities such as anxiety, depression, schizophrenia, and memory loss. This will help elderly people take better care of themselves, live fuller and happier lives, and be less of a burden on their families.

Longevity is also being extended by research into the aging process itself. This research has shown that old age is a distinct and separate stage of life that's been little studied and about which we are still profoundly ignorant.

Chronological age is no longer a valid indicator of where a person stands in the continuum from birth to death. Saying someone is 65 or 75 is no longer meaningful; more important are individuals' physical and mental condition and circumstances such as whether they are working, married, etc.

Older people think of themselves as being much younger than they actually are. One researcher asked a group of elderly people to describe themselves, and a woman in her 80s brought out a picture of herself taken 40 years earlier. When asked if she had a more recent photo, she reluctantly handed over one taken the year before, protesting, "It's terrible. It's not me at all."

AMERICA THE ELDERLY

Five thousand Americans reach age 65 every day, says the U.S. Census Bureau, and by 1990 more than 31 million Americans will be 65 or older, up from 25.5 million in 1980. By 2030, more than 20% of all Americans will be 65 or olders. Americans over 85, whose numbers could approach 7 million by 2012, are the fastest-growing segment of the population.

This demographic shift toward the elderly means, among other things, that:

- U.S. productivity should improve, since older workers have more job stability and work experience than younger workers.
- The United States should become a less crime-ridden society since the peak age for burglary and auto theft is 16, for violent crime 18, and for murder 20.
- U.S. highways should become safer, as older drivers have fewer accidents and are arrested less often for speeding or driving while intoxicated.

But the demographic shift toward the elderly also means:

- New household formation will decline as the baby-boom generation matures and the number of young people setting up homes declines. This will significantly reduce the demand for new houses, furniture, appliances, etc.
- Today's executives are living longer and hanging on to their jobs, making it difficult for younger professionals to get ahead.
- Caring for the elderly will continue as one of America's fastest-growing new industries—and may be one of its major problems.

GOLDEN OLDIES

Older Americans are better off financially than they've ever been before. Households headed by people 50–55 are the wealthiest, according to recent studies, followed by those headed by people 55–60. Houses headed by people 65 and older have a higher after-tax income than all age groups under 50.

CARTER HENDERSON

The big reason for this is the fairly recent appearance of generous pension and inflation-linked entitlement programs. Today's retirees have their money stretched even further by income tax breaks for those 65 and over, not to mention widespread senior-citizen discounts for goods and services ranging from medical care to special hotel and restaurant rates.

The number of America's elderly living in poverty has declined by two-thirds over the last 25 years. While 12% of the country's elderly, or some 3.5 million people, remain below the poverty line, the poverty rate for the elderly is now less than that of the general population.

One obvious upshot of all this is the increasing financial independence of the elderly. In 1946, for example, 30%–40% of elderly parents received most of their financial support from their children. Today, thanks largely to Social Security, the figure is less than 1%. In fact, older parents are now twice as likely to give their children money as to receive it from them.

Americans over 50 make up about 25% of the population but account for 77% of the nation's wealth and nearly 50% of its discretionary spending. Yet these big spenders—who are almost as numerous as the baby boomers—have only recently been studied, let alone courted, by Madison Avenue, even though they spend more than $800 billion on goods and services annually.

Advertisers who once feared offending the old by publicly calling attention to wrinkles, receding hairlines, and other manifestations of the aging process are now pushing products to cope with everything from varicose veins and liver spots to bladder-control problems.

The finance industry is pushing new products to market such as the "upside-down conventional mortgage" that pays homeowning senior citizens so much money every month until they die or sell their home. At that point, the mortgage company's monthly payments are repaid with interest plus a percentage of any appreciation in the value of the house from the time the reverse mortgage was taken out.

And the medical profession is cashing in by making youth-restoring plastic surgery commonplace, along with more exotic treatments to increase the elders' energy and sex drive.

AMERICA'S OVER-THE-HILL ECONOMY

But all is not rosy for today's—and tomorrow's—senior citizens. The U.S. economic outlook has turned gloomy as a result of the nation's soaring debt, falling competitiveness, deteriorating infra-structure, and declining working-age population. This threatens to arrest years of inflation-adjusted economic advantages enjoyed by older Americans—at the very time that elders' longevity is increasing at a record pace.

The nation's lackluster competitiveness has already forced a number of companies such as steelmaker LTV Corp. to declare bankruptcy and slash pensions. This has caused some retired workers to picket the company with signs reading, "LTV Motto: Stick It to the Old Folks," and has led other retired workers to contemplate suicide.

Such bankruptices and pension cutbacks are putting an impossible burden on the federal government's Pension Benefit Guaranty Corporation, which was set up in 1974 to safeguard retirement incomes. The Corporation is already $4 billion in the red and continues to pay out more than it takes in.

Even more seriously jeopardized are retirees' health-insurance benefits, which, unlike pensions, do not have to be funded with money employers put aside for that purpose. Unfunded retiree health costs played a large part in LTV's bankruptcy proceedings, just as they did in the more recent bankruptcy filing of Allis-Chalmers Corporation.

The Employee Benefit Research Institute in Washington, D.C., estimates that employers now have $85 billion in unfunded liabilities for their current retirees' health benefits and that the unfunded liabilities for workers who have not yet retired range from $98 billion to more than $2 trillion.

One bright note is that the Social Security system is expected to run up huge surpluses well into the next century—before being swamped by deficits. But even this optimistic outlook, assumes that:

- The United States will have no more recessions.
- Inflation will never exceed 4% annually.
- Economic growth will average 2%–3% a year.
- Unemployment will remain below 6% after 1993.
- The U.S. birthrate will rise nearly 10% by 2010.
- The increase in life expectancy will hold fairly steady between now and the year 2060.
- Wages, adjusted for inflation, will rise by 16% before the turn of the century and will double by 2037.

This seems, to many, a highly unlikely scenario. If it is not an accurate reading of future events, the United States will have to either greatly increase the already burdensome Social Security tax or greatly reduce the benefits.

THE AGING BABY BOOMERS

Social Security payments to 30 million older Americans are being largely underwritten by working-age baby boomers, born between 1946 and 1964, who are being forced to shoulder this financial millstone at the very time most of them are struggling to get a start in life and raise a family.

To make matters worse, the boomers themselves are growing older. Millions of them began hitting 40 in the last two years, and millions more will hit 40 in the late 1980s and 1990s.

It's the boomers—and their children, often called the "baby-boom echo" generation—whose incomes are being squeezed by climbing living costs, relentlessly rising Social Security taxes, and heavy income taxes that can only get worse as the nation pays for years of living beyond its means. The boomers may be the first generation in U.S. history that won't live materially richer lives than their parents.

The very idea that a battle may be looming between the increasingly hard-pressed young and the affluent old was pooh-poohed as "The Phony War" in a survey financed by the American Association of Retired Persons' *Modern Maturity* magazine.

But as the young see the good life evaporate, their attitude toward the old is bound to change. "The only reason the AARP survey found so much support from young workers," wrote one *Modern Maturity* reader following the magazine's article, "is that they haven't yet realized what we're doing to them."

This thinking is widely shared. For example, a group of more than 50 business and government leaders in Florida recently released a report that, among other things, looks at the kind of problems they see ahead for Floridians, whose average age is the highest in the United States. Toward the top of the list is the prediction that by the year 2000 "age warfare will pit workers against retirees on issues such as Society Security taxes, educational goals, and community projects."

Phillip Longman, research director of Americans for Generational Equity, a Washington, D.C.–based lobby, and author of *Born to Pay: The New Politics of Aging in America,* noted in a letter to *The New York Times,* "Since 1939, the maximum Society Security tax has increased by more than 10,000%, from $60 to $6,006. The government projects that Medicare's hospital insurance trust will be exhausted by the year 2003. And, according to projections by the Social Security Administration, the system's pension trust will collapse well before the youngest baby boomers reach retirement age unless the United States meanwhile experiences unprecedented rates of economic and population growth."

The number of Social Security recipients 65 and older will double by the year 2020 and triple by 2050, when some 70 million Americans will be receiving monthly retirement checks from the U.S. Treasury.

Today there are three workers for every retiree, but by 2020 there will be only two. This compares with 46 workers for each retiree when the plan was introduced in 1936. No wonder two-thirds of America's young workers doubt that the Social Security system will pay off when it comes time for them to collect.

This is one reason the U.S. Congress is looking into private-sector options to help provide older Americans with financial security. These include legislation to establish health-care savings accounts, medical IRAs combined with insurance, Medicare vouchers for the purchase of private long-term-care insurance, and risk pools to provide protection for uninsurable older Americans.

As young people search for alternative ways to insure their own retirement security, both they and politicians sensitive to their predicament will have to contend with both rising deficit-induced taxes and individual Social Security taxes already scheduled to increase. "Politicians have expressed deep concern about the economic and ethical implications of passing tax burdens to the future through the budget deficits we are running now," says Stanford economics professor Michael J. Boskin. "Yet the burden we are passing on through Social Security could dwarf the budget deficits."

The idea that old people are burdensome seems to be gaining credence throughout the world. East Germany, for example, has long permitted retired people to visit friends and relatives in West Germany in the hope they'll stay there, thus relieving the state of paying them social-security benefits. And in Japan, the Ministry of International Trade and Industry has suggested that older people be invited to spend the final years of their lives enjoying a "comfortable, soul-enriching" life in "Silver Towns" to be built in countries thousands of miles away such as Australia, Spain, or possibly the United States.

THE AGE OF THE ELDERLY

America must come of age. It must replace the strength and competitive vigor of its fading adolescence with the wisdom of its on-rushing maturity.

The United States must urge its older citizens to continue using the knowledge, skills, and experience they've built up over a lifetime, instead of letting them rot in early retirement.

"America has the largest population of educated old people in the world, yet we have somehow failed to realize the miracle we have produced—a whole new manpower resource of healthy, largely self-financed people," says Merrel Clark, founder of Elderworks Inc. of Scarsdale, New York, a firm that helps find second careers for people after retirement.

A flurry of recent federal legislation is also making it easier for older Americans to continue pulling their load past age 65. Older people are being allowed to stay on in their present jobs longer, and they can no longer be discriminated against in vying for new job openings.

Older workers are even being given the chance to continue working after retirement in collegial surroundings. This can be seen in the nonprofit Inter-American Institute of Science in Titusville, Florida, where retired agronomists, physicists, chemists, and others are provided with research facilities and staff support. Here, they can continue their work in disciplines such as plant research, marine biology, environmental studies, biomedical research, and human nutrition.

If elders are to enjoy the glorious old age awaiting so many of them, they must be encouraged to continue contributing to the nation's economic vitality—and to temper the financial demands made on America's young taxpayers.

CARTER HENDERSON

MARITAL ALTERNATIVES AND FAMILY TRANSITIONS

12 *Variations on a Theme*

Despite the loss of various functions in regard to education, recreation, economics, and security, the family is still seen in America as providing the important functions of psychic well-being by providing love, stability, and loyalty as well as being the matrix for the development of personality. It is little wonder, then, that the institution of marriage is thought of as the natural order of things. As a result, Americans are socialized early to expect that they will eventually marry and there is little social support for those who would prefer to remain single.

Such values have led to the development of beliefs in which marriage is seen as something good, whereas singleness is seen as an unfortunate circumstance, a bad state. Thus, it is perceived that people remain single because they are immature and unwilling to assume responsibility; because they are unattractive ("real losers") or unhealthy either physically or mentally (latent homosexuals), because they are socially inadequate (oddballs) and so failed in the dating game, because they were overly concerned with economics (self-centered), or because they were unlucky (Kuhn 1955).

In the first article of Chapter 12, Leonard Cargan and Matthew Melko examine these stereotypes and the retorts of the singles. Their study indicates that the "reality" of being single depends on one's marital status. For example, singles could be considered deviant since they do not do as the majority does—get married. In the second article of the chapter, Peter Stein carries this examination a step further by noting who the singles are, what their needs are, and how they cope with these needs. He indicates that their greatest need would appear to be a substitute network of social relationships to meet the needs of intimacy, companionship, and an enduring bond of social support. Fortunately for singles, numerous factors have emerged to make singlehood a more viable lifestyle, and these have led to a recent growth spurt in the never-married population. Some of these factors are:

a. value changes toward sexual permissiveness, women's career goals, and societal acceptance of singlehood;

b. technological changes such as contraception and convenience foods and services;

c. the institutionalization of singlehood;

d. lowered expectations for marriage as a source of happiness; and

e. demographics and other problems in finding a mate.

However, being never-married is still a temporary state for most. The increase in their numbers reflects the postponement of marriage until a later age rather than its ultimate rejection.

A variation of traditional marriage noted in Chapter 4 was that of cohabitation. The strong acceptance of this variation is seen in its dynamic fivefold growth since 1970. However, it is not a substitute for marriage since most cohabitants expect to eventually marry. Being similar to marriage, however, means cohabitation has many of its same problems, including those of family violence and a need for social agency support.

As noted in the introduction, there is a growing concern with self-growth. One of the outgrowths of this idea is the belief that conventional marriage "imposes severe limitations on the personal growth of marital partners." The result is a dilemma between "the desire for personal growth and the restriction imposed by conventional marriage" (Myers 1977, p. 35). Various factors such as the growing egalitarianism of male/female relationships, the greater acceptability of premarital sex, the advent of contraceptive technology, and the isolation of the nuclear family are all leading to increases in nonexclusive behavior. They may involve extramarital sexual relationships, "swinging," sexually open marriage, intimate friendship networks, multilateral marriage relationships, and extramarital nonsexual relationships. For example, the misunderstood term, "swingers" applies to married people who engage in extramarital sexual behavior as a form of recreation. The people involved are in most ways typical middle-class whites and although their sexual behavior may raise issues of jealousy, guilt, disease, and community censure, it does not appear to have major negative effects on their marriages or lives (Gilmartin 1977). Similarly, open marriages do not lessen the likelihood of breakup but they also do not bring about the benefits claimed for this lifestyle. It is believed by those involved that by providing for companionship, sexual equality, and role flexibility, the marriage can be honest and open and change as the partners grow and change.

James Ramey, in the third article of Chapter 12, carries these ideas a step further by noting the impact of various other changes on family forms. He indicates that such experimental family forms as group marriage and communes are coming to fruition due to our obsessions with personal freedom, the effects of revolutions in demography, biology, economics and communication, and the transformation of our sexual attitudes.

The final article in Chapter 12, by Joseph Harry, deals with the emerging recognition of homosexual couples as an alternative to traditional marriage. With this emergence, he notes, it is important to deal with the beliefs held about this segment of the population. His findings reveal that many of the beliefs about homosexual people and their relationships are false. As he indicates, most homosexuals are normal people with a nonconforming sexual orientation.

REFERENCES

1. Gilmartin, B. G. 1977. "Swinging: Who Gets Involved and How?" In *Marriage and Family Alternatives: Exploring Intimate Relationships*, R. W. Libby & R. N. Whitehurst (eds.). Glenview, IL: Scott, Foresman.

2. Kuhn, M. 1955. "How Mates Are Sorted." In *Family, Marriage, and Parenthood*, H. Becker & R. Hill (eds.). Lexington, MA: Heath.

3. Myers, L. 1977. A Couple Can Also Be Two People. In *Marriage and Family Alternatives: Exploring Intimate Relationships*, R. W. Libby & R. N. Whitehurst (eds.). Glenview, IL: Scott, Foresman.

46 *Being Single on Noah's Ark*

Leonard Cargan / Matthew Melko

STUDY QUESTIONS

1. Describe three of the myths uncovered by this study.

2. Describe three of the realities claimed by this study.

The world throughout history goes marching two by two. From Noah's Ark to the socialization process of today's society, two is the proper number, and in a world that counts by twos, the pressure to marry has been overwhelming.

THE GROWING SINGLES POPULATION

Whatever the social pressures, it is clear that singles have been growing as a percentage of the population in America. Since 1960, there has been a marked increase in the number of single households with a resultant decline in the number of nuclear families. Between 1960 and 1975, the number of adults between the ages of 20 and 34 who have never been married increased by 50 percent, while in the same period, the divorce rate doubled. The large increase in divorce is emphasized when it is noted that 39 percent of first marriages now end in divorce within 10 years, and 40 percent of second marriages end so within five years. In addition, the time interval between divorce and remarriage has increased, and so the number of those divorced but not remarried has doubled in the decade from 1963 to 1973. Thus, there has been a slowdown of marriage and remarriage versus a speed-up in the rate of divorce; the annual rate of first marriages has not been keeping pace with the growth of the prime age group for first marriages, and the divorce rate is now

Source: "Being Single on Noah's Ark." In *Singles: Myths and Realities* by Leonard Cargan and Matthew Melko. Beverly Hills, CA: Sage, 1982. Reprinted by permission.

at the highest point in our history. The result is that there are now over 58 million single adults aged 18 and over (Stein, 1983, p. 27).

Why is the percentage of singles increasing? Consider first why we marry. Reasons given by marriage authorities include the bond of love or sex, mutual aid in the struggle for existence, and the desire for children (Ackerman, 1972, p. 12).

The changes that have occurred in the industrial age have undermined much of the logic behind these marriage imperatives of providing children, mutual aid, and love. The processes of urbanization and industrialization have reduced the percentage of people involved in farming occupations from more than 90 percent to fewer than 10 percent; more recent developments in organizational structure have meant a decline in the percentage of people engaged in family businesses; developments in medicine have reduced infant mortality. All of these factors have greatly reduced the importance of the child-bearing functions of the family. Then came the development of effective means of preventing conception: oral contraceptives and outpatient sterilization.

There have also been changes in the need for mutual aid in the struggle for existence. National highway systems and air transportation have greatly increased mobility, which in turn has contributed to the undermining of the extended family and therefore, for many people—married and single alike—a greater dependence on an extended community of friendships. Add to this a complicated change in attitudes that is partly independent of the change in family structure and partly reinforced by it: continued secularization of religion, a changing perception of the individual, and a widening perception of the rights of minorities, including women, blacks, the handicapped, and homosexuals.

For example, greater attention has been given to equal opportunity hiring practices, and this has provided women with greater opportunities for financial independence. It may also have reduced the perception of the single man as irresponsible and thus reduced pressure on him to marry or remain married.

Other factors that have emerged fortuitously have added to the independence of individuals from the need for marriage: the emergence of fast food restaurants, for instance, and, even more important, frozen foods, along with the development of laundromats, clothes that do not require ironing, and various convenience services. The increase in singles and a perception of them as a market have resulted in the development of bars and clubs for singles, packaged vacations for singles, small cars, new insurance policies, and various other benefits that, in turn, provide further incentive to people to remain single (Stein, 1976, p. 38). Also affecting the traditional appeal of marriage and family life for young people is the rising divorce rate and increasing criticism of this life-style by scholarly and mass media sources (Stein, 1978, p. 5).

In sum, there are many pressures which militate toward marriage, such as economic security, cultural pressures that idealize marriage, peer and parental socialization, and a desire for a family. However, there are also factors that make singlehood attractive in comparison to marriage, such as freedom from the restrictions of a binding relationship, self-sufficiency, increased opportunities for geographical mobility, and the existence of supportive groups (Kain, 1981, p. 3).

STEREOTYPES ABOUT SINGLES

Because there is a natural lag between the various steps of the scientific process, from awareness of an issue to the formation of hypotheses, it is not surprising that social scientists did not really begin to focus on the growth of singles until the 1970s. In the 1960s, family sociologists "either ignored singles or relegated them to boring out-of-date discussions of dating" (Libby, 1978, p. 164). Even in the seventies "they seem to deny that change was possible in family structure, the relations between the sexes, and parenthood" (Skolnick and Skolnick, 1977, p. 3). With the values of society strongly in favor of marriage and family (Ackerman, 1972; O'Brien, 1973) and little scientific knowledge of singles, singles were not perceived as a distinct social entity "that had its own characteristics, dynamics and unique features" (Adams, 1976, p. 10). Instead, singles were described with stereotypical images, usually negative, that implied they were carefree but incomplete, lonely, and undesirable. In addition, there was a change in the terminology being applied to the unmarried. The terms "bachelor" and "spinster" were replaced by the term "single" (Readers Guide). Although the concept was supposed to be specific to the never-married, it has been applied to all of the unmarried, thus blurring the distinctions between never-marrieds, divorced, redivorced, and widows. This has led to all unmarrieds being tainted with the same stereotypes and to ignoring their particular needs.

The stereotypes must be investigated because they may lead to serious and often unperceived discrimination. In order to deal with these stereotypes, a survey was made from a probability proportionate to size sample of 400 households from the Dayton metropolitan area—an area considered by George Gallup to be one of the ten typical areas of the nation (*Dayton Journal-Herald*, 1976, p. 1). Because it was not believed that all singles (or, for that matter, all marrieds) were alike, the sample data was subdivided into the categories of never-married, divorced, married, and remarried. Widows constituted too small a percentage of the respondents and were replaced via the sampling technique.

MYTHS AND REALITIES

It was believed at the beginning of the study that most of the stereotypes would prove to be myths and that singles would turn out to be similar to marrieds. However, as will be seen, stereotypes are indeed myths but others are or have become realities.

Myths

Singles Are Tied to Their Mother's Apron Strings. This stereotype is the belief that an attractive man or woman has not married due to an unresolved relationship with a parent. The data indicates that there is little difference between the never-married and married in their perceptions of relations with their parents. The divorced are not usually part of this image since they did, after all, get married.

Singles Are Selfish. The stereotype is that singles do not get married because they are too centered on themselves. But the selfish single does not emerge from the data. Singles were indeed more likely than marrieds to go nightclubbing (38 percent versus 16 percent) than to visit grandparents (19 percent versus 10 percent). So, even though likely to value success (36 percent versus 30 percent) and personal growth (56 percent versus 47 percent) whereas marrieds are more likely than singles to value love (63 percent versus 45 percent) and community service (28 percent versus 24 percent). Singles, however, are more likely than marrieds to value friends (56 percent versus 35 percent) and proved to be greater contributors to community service of two or more hours per week (19 percent versus 10 percent). So, even though marrieds are likely to value community service more, the singles deliver.

Singles Are Rich. Singles ought to be richer than marrieds—they have no spouses and children to support, they live in fancy condominiums or bachelor pads, and they are always out a'roaming. This "Joe Namath" image does not seem to be realized by most singles. Many are young, at the bottom of the economic ladder. Others are divorced, trying to support children and two households. On the whole, marrieds are better off economically than singles.

Singles Are Happier. Generally most people say they are happy most of the time. But on a number of specific questions about areas that would seem to contribute to happiness, the responses indicate there is more unhappiness than would be expected from the answer to the general question. On most of these responses, the indications are that singles are less happy than marrieds. For instance, on the loneliness questions singles were more likely than marrieds to be depressed when alone (24 percent versus 15 percent), much more often feel they have no one with whom they can really share (71 percent versus 44 percent) or discuss (66 percent versus 49 percent). Regarding health, singles are more likely to feel anxious (25 percent versus 17 percent), guilty (21 percent versus 11 percent), despondent (18 percent versus 10 percent), and worthless (19 percent versus 10 percent). Two possible signs of trying to compensate for unhappiness might be using pep pills and getting drunk often. Sure enough, singles are more likely than marrieds to use pep pills (11 percent versus 49 percent) and more likely to get drunk once a week or more (21 percent versus 7 percent). Finally, in total contemplated or attempted suicides, singles were again higher (55 percent versus 35 percent). All in all, there is very little here to support the idea that singles are happier than marrieds and much to suggest that they are, by several measurements, considerably less happy.

Singles Are Increasing in Numbers. This is true in America if we are considering numbers. But the percentage of singles in the population is lower today than it was at any time before World War II, and today's percentage appears to have peaked and to be approaching decline. It could be that even in numbers singles will be declining by the late eighties or early nineties. In sum, a demographic survey indicates that the growth of singles in the sixties and seventies was largely a function of the baby boom of the forties and fifties, and that even if the percentage of divorced population continues to increase, it is not likely to compensate for the decrease in the percentage of young adults.

Being Single Is Acceptable. This is a myth advocated but not accepted by singles. A review of titles in the *Readers Guide* throughout the century indicates that there has been little change in the preoccupation of singles with marriage. Titles about mate finding were as prevalent as ever in the seventies, and so were articles about making the best of it—implying that one must endure it if one cannot change it.

There Is Something Wrong with Singles. By measures of happiness or loneliness, singles may not be as well off as marrieds. However, there is nothing wrong with being lonely or sad some of the time. By measures of freedom singles may be better off than marrieds, but that does not make it wrong to marry. A married person may sometimes or often wish for freedom from the responsibilities of marriage, but on the balance she may consider it better to remain married. So may a single consider it on the balance to remain single, even if loneliness is a price to be paid. No, there is nothing wrong with being single.

Realities

Singles Are Deviant. It may seem incongruous to state that the image of something wrong with singles is a myth, but that singles are nonetheless deviant. But normality and deviance are defined by perceptions and the stereotype perceives marriage as normal. The label is usually applied to the singles who are in the 30–50 age bracket. Singles in this age bracket have been labeled deviant because they are not following the norm, not because their behavior can be demonstrated to be abnormal.

Singles Have More Time. This image has been posed in a different way. The marital image is that singles are free—they come and go as they please without worrying about baby sitters, they sleep nights without waking for children, and they go on vacation where they like. Focusing on time, it does appear that singles have more time than marrieds. More of them are likely to be spending more time visiting friends (66 percent versus 39 percent), and more are likely to be spending more time on hobbies (71 percent versus 56 percent). Singles are more likely than marrieds to go out socially twice a week (22 percent versus 16 percent) and much more likely to be out three or more times (30 percent versus 8 percent).

Singles Have More Fun. It may seem something of a contradiction to assert that although singles are less happy, they have more fun than marrieds, especially since they do not think so themselves (75 percent versus 83 percent). Then why say singles have more fun? Because in most specifics in which fun is imagined to be involved, singles are more involved. As just indicated, singles have more social outings. When they do go out, they are more likely than marrieds to go to movies, nightclubs, and theaters while the marrieds are going to social clubs, restaurants, or visiting relatives. When singles visit friends, they are three times as likely as marrieds to sit around smoking marijuana—a sharing, pleasurable experience—or getting drunk—which may be fun while you are doing it. In sum, it is possible that a person can go to dances and nightclubs, go out bicycling and camping more, and, in general, have high experiences but still on a day-to-day basis feel less happy.

Singles Are Swingers. From the standpoint of variety, singles have had more sex partners than marrieds at every level of involvement, 24 percent to 19 percent at 2–3 partners, 23 percent to 16 percent at 4–10 partners, and a decisive 19 percent to 6 percent at 11 or more partners.

Singles Are Lonely. It was expected that singles are neither happier nor lonelier than marrieds. The evidence from this study indicates that neither of these expectations were met. Thus, singles are more likely than marrieds to feel that they have no one to share with or discuss matters with. They are also more likely to feel that most people are alone. They are more likely to feel depressed just being alone and join social organizations because of loneliness. The answers on these specific kinds of activities reinforced the impression that singles are more lonely than marrieds.

Life for Singles Is Changing for the Better. Despite such continuities as a continued anticipation of marriage in the future, life and perceptions were qualitatively different for singles in the seventies and eighties from what they had been in previous decades of this century. The universal norm of marriage was being challenged for the first time in the seventies. There was an increase of articles in the sixties and seventies about single life, articles that took the lifestyle for granted and gave practical advice on the special problems of singleness. Another example seems to be the reduction of sexual frustration in the seventies. Though singles may not be as satisfied sexually as marrieds, the channels to satisfaction seem to be opening. There is also the changes involved with technology such as wash-and-wear clothing, laundromats, frozen foods, and fast-food restaurants. Finally, there is a perception of singles as a market and the accompanying development of items specifically for them such as apartments, vacation spots, and tours.

This examination of the myths and realities of being single allows for the dealing with the specific needs of singles. That is, by recognizing rather than ignoring such realities, singles can make a reality of that which earlier was referred to as a myth—being single is acceptable.

REFERENCES

Ackerman, Nathan W., in Harold Hart (ed). *Marriage for and Against*. New York: Hart, 1972.

Adams, Margaret. *Single Blessedness: Observations on the Single Status in Married Society*. New York: Basie, 1976.

Gallup, George. *Polster Visits Nation's Barometer. Dayton Journal-Herald*, June 22, 1976.

Kain, Edward L. Social determinants of the decision to remain never married. *American Sociological Association*, 1981.

Libby, Roger W. Creative singlehood as a sexual lifestyle: Beyond marriage as a rite of passage. In Bernard I. Murstein (ed). *Exploring Intimate Lifestyles*. New York: Springer, 1978.

O'Brien, Patricia. *The Woman Alone*. New York: Quadrangle, 1973.

Skolnick, Arlene and Jerome Skolnick (Eds). *Family in Transition*. Boston: Little, Brown, 1977.

Stein, Peter. The lifestyles and life changes of the never married. *Marriage and Family Review*, July/August 1978, 1–11.

Stein, Peter. Singlehood. In Eleanor Macklin and Roger H. Rubin (Eds). *Contemporary Families and Alternative Lifestyles*. Beverly Hills, California: Sage, 1983.

Stein, Peter. *Singles*. Englewood Cliffs, New Jersey: Prentice-Hall, 1976.

47 *Major Tasks Faced by Single Adults*

Peter J. Stein

STUDY QUESTIONS

1. What are the major tasks faced by singles?

2. Indicate the coping styles of never-married adults.

Included among the major tasks faced by single adults are: achieving and maintaining friendships, intimacy, and fulfilling sexuality; maintaining emotional and physical well-being; making satisfactory living arrangements; seeking and finding productive work; becoming successful parents; and adjusting to aging. These issues are faced by all adults and they require decision making, the expenditure of physical and emotional energy, value and goal clarification, and resource allocation. The accomplishment of these tasks yields varying degrees of satisfaction, pleasure, discord, stress, and happiness. The discussion that follows is not meant to be exhaustive, but rather to highlight the major tasks and issues for single persons.

Source: Peter J. Stein, "Major Tasks Faced by Single Adults." In *Contemporary Families and Alternative Lifestyles*, E.D. Macklin and R.H. Rubin, (eds.). Copyright© 1983 by Sage Publications, Inc. Reprinted by permission of Sage Publications, Inc.

FRIENDSHIP, INTIMACY, AND SEXUALITY

All humans need intimacy, yet the experiences of intimacy differ for single and married people, and among singles. Society today is undergoing a well-publicized revolution with regard to sexual attitudes and behaviors, and gender roles. One product of this is the growing acceptance of sexual relationships outside marriage, thus increasing the options available to single men and women (Libby, 1977).

Increased social and sexual availability presents both opportunities and problems. Personal enrichment, access to a variety of ideas and encounters, and the opportunity to select associates and activities consistent with one's own needs and goals are obvious advantages. Problems include limited access to the world of the married, the stress of juggling ever-shifting emotional commitments, the uncertainty of the commitment of others, and the lack of role clarity and social endorsement.

An important sexual outlet for singles, as well as for married people, is masturbation. Though there are no data regarding whether singles masturbate more or less than the general population, it can be assumed that its incidence is at least as high as the adult average, that is, 95 percent of men and 63 percent of women (Hunt, 1974).

Some single men and women choose celibacy (Brown, 1980), either as a long-term voluntary state, or as a temporary, perhaps difficult, state between relationships. Celibacy may be a religious requirement, may arise out of moral conviction, may be a means of conserving energy for creative endeavors, or may represent a flight from intimacy. The celibate person's degree of satisfaction with this lifestyle depends on the degree of motivation and on the freedom of choice.

Some singles have elected to be part of a new movement called the "New Celibacy." Its proponents argue that they are celibate by choice, not through default, often because of the disappointments, displeasures, and stresses of one-night stands. Some, such as Gabrielle Brown in *The New Celibacy* (1980), discuss the value of taking a vacation from sex. Critics argue that if celibate singles had a choice, they "would prefer a loving, sexual relationship with a partner" (Shostak, forthcoming). This debate will undoubtedly continue.

For many singles, sexual experimentation is a part of their single identity, enjoyed for itself or used as a stage leading to marriage or choice of a single sexual partner. Those who try a variety of relationships can learn much about the world and about themselves. They may avoid commitment in order to work on a career or on personal growth, or to recover from a painful past relationship. Some set up a hierarchy of relationships involving special obligations to a primary partner and lesser responsibilities to others. Personal enrichment is a possible benefit of this style of relationship, but the stress of managing conflicting commitments and a lack of clarity about one's role are potential problems (Clayton and Bokemeier, 1980).

There are two other sexual lifestyles that bear mention. Casual sexuality—whether heterosexual or homosexual—is more frequently practiced by single men than by single women. Many women find it difficult to be assertive enough to find a variety of partners, and women's commonly held ideas of love are more likely to be violated by this seeming promiscuity. "Relationship" sexuality is a more popular choice with women, whether as part of a monogamous or a sexual experimental lifestyle. A relationship is considered to be "leading somewhere" and sexual intercourse symbolizes a degree of caring between the partners (Laws and Schwartz, 1977).

Many singles believe that an individual cannot love more than one person at a time. Those who adhere to the Judeo-Christian ethic often prefer a monogomous relationship—a single sexual partner—even if it is without the obligations and daily responsibilities of marriage. As needs and desires change, these persons may move on to new partners, in a kind of serial monogamy.

Nonmarital cohabitation is a major source of intimacy for growing numbers of singles. Most cohabitors consider their relationship important, affectionate, supportive, and exclusive of other sexual involvements. Those who live together often claim to gain deeper self-understanding and emotional growth. Many homosexual as well as heterosexual couples choose cohabitation as a shorter-or longer-term alternative to marriage (Macklin, 1980).

Persons who elect a homosexual lifestyle often remain single because of legal constraints on gay marriage. Same-sex relationships may be just as diverse as heterosexual relationships. Some gay people prefer a permanent partner in a marriagelike arrangement, while others prefer living a single lifestyle. Public acceptance of homosexuality is an increasingly important issue for gays, as is active participation in the gay subculture. Political consciousness of the gay community is growing as are various gay and lesbian support systems (Vida, 1978; Levine, 1979).

EMOTIONAL AND PHYSICAL HEALTH

Historically, studies have shown that married people live longer than unmarrieds and that they use health care facilities less often. The complex cause-and-effect relationship between marital status and better health has been acknowledged, but more recent studies suggest that this relationship may no longer be as strong.

In a comprehensive review based on data from two national health surveys, Verbrugge (1979) writes that limiting chronic and work-disabling conditions are rather low for "noninstitutionalized single people." Among singles, the divorced and separated have the worst health status, followed by the widowed and the never married. Noninstitutionalized never marrieds "are the healthiest of all marital groups. . . . They take the least time off for health problems and have lowest utilization of physician and hospital services" (Verbrugge, 1979: 270). However, institutionalization rates for the never married are relatively high, and the total singles population is, in fact, less healthy than the total married population.

What happens to singles when they become ill? The lucky ones have a support group to which they can turn: family, neighbors, fellow communards, or roommates. Indeed, the crucial factor may not be marriage versus singlehood, but the strength of the support network. As the single state comes to be seen as less deviant, and more friends and groups become available to single adults, their general health and well-being should improve. Today, however, as single people grow older and their health deteriorates, they enter institutions more readily than do the married, having fewer opportunities for home care and fewer social responsibilities (Verbrugge, 1979).

A recent study of 400 single adults (Cargan and Melko, 1982) found no differences between marrieds and singles in terms of reported nightmares or crying spells, but did find that more singles worry and/or feel guilty, despondent, worthless, or lonely. However, it is the divorced that report feelings of despondency, worthlessness, sexual apathy, and loneliness more often than the never married. They note that if frequent contemplation of suicide is used as a measure, the figures are highest for the divorced (20 percent), followed by the never married (10 percent), and the married (7 percent).

In an important article examining the relationship between social class, marital status, life strains, and depression, Pearlin and Johnson (1981) reject the traditional interpretation that the poorer physical and mental health of singles reflects the unmet inner needs and emotional frustrations of never-married and formerly married people. Rather, this study examines the consequences of economic hardship, social isolation, and obligations of parents. These are three basic conditions of life to which unmarried people are both more exposed and more vulnerable. However, Pearlin and Johnson find that the greater life hardships of the unmarried only partly explain their greater incidence of depression. Even when hardships of married and unmarried persons are equally severe, the effects of these hardships are more devastating among the unmarried. "The combination most productive of psychological distress is to be simultaneously single, isolated, exposed to burdensome parental obligations, and most serious of all, poor." To what extent does marriage help fend off the psychological assaults of economic and social problems? Is its protective function the reason for the continued survival of marriage as an institution?

LIVING ARRANGEMENTS

Among the important decisions single men and women face is where to live. This involves not only such fundamental matters as one's financial resources and the availability of housing, but also such questions as with whom to live, for what period of time, and what these decisions say to the world about oneself. Living arrangements are a central issue of single life, since each alternative involves many possibilities and limitations.

Shostak (forthcoming: 25) cites a recent MIT-Harvard Joint Center for Urban Studies report indicating that in the 1980s "only 50 percent of households will be headed by married couples compared with 80 percent in 1950. People will spend more years living alone or with roommates or partners. They will increasingly delay marriage, divorce more, remarry more slowly."

A single person may live alone, with friends or family, as head of a household, or as part of an unmarried couple. He or she may choose a commune, a single-family home, an apartment, or a dormitory. The most common trends in living arrangements for singles are the following.

Living Alone. In 1980 there were 17.8 million people living alone, an increase of 61 percent from the 10.9 million of 1970. Over those years the number of single residences maintained by persons under the age of 35 more than tripled, from 1.4 million to 4.8 million. A majority of these men and women are living in urban areas. New York City, Chicago, Los Angeles, Houston, and San Francisco are the most prominent. In each of these cities, and in others, there are areas that are occupied primarily by single adults living alone. But the greatest number of people living alone are not younger singles. Persons over the age of 45 constitute 65 percent of all those living alone, the largest group of which is elderly widows. Of all women living alone, more than half are widows over the age of 65.

While ideally single adults might choose living arrangements that reflect their needs and values, it is more likely that their household situations will reflect their economic status. For example, census data show that in 1977 the median income of women living alone was $3412, which means that half of these women actually received less than that figure. Since "housing choices will be somewhat limited, even for those with incomes up to $8000 . . . the wonder is not that so few aged parents share a home with an adult child, but that so many do not" (Hess and Markson, 1980).

Heading Households. About six out of ten single adult households are headed by single women. The number of single-parent households headed by women is now about 8.2 million, or 10.6 percent of the population, while only 1.6 million, or 2.1 percent of the population, are headed by men in the absence of a woman.

Cohabiting. Cohabitation is defined as a "more or less permanent relationship in which two unmarried persons of the opposite sex share a living facility without legal contract" (Cole, 1977:67). Cohabitation has been around for a long time, but has become increasingly popular in the last ten years (Macklin, 1978, 1980). In 1980, some 3.2 percent of all "couple households" were unmarried men and women living together. In 1980 there were 1.56 million unmarried couples living together—three times as many as in 1970, when there were 523,000. Unmarried couples with no children represent about three-fourths of all unmarried couples. Some 63 percent of all unmarried couples were composed of two adults under the ages of 35. In 20 percent of all households, both partners were under age 25.

Why are so many singles choosing to live together as unmarried couples? The following factors are influential:

1. financial considerations such as the higher cost of living alone;

2. housing shortages in urban areas;

3. greater social tolerance of alternative living arrangements;

PETER J. STEIN

4. greater tolerance and support for cohabitation among undergraduates and graduate students and among postcollege adults;

5. greater acceptance of premarital sex;

6. changing gender role definitions; and

7. the sheer force of greater numbers of singles.

Paul Glick and Graham Spanier (1981) used data from the U.S. Bureau of the Census to estimate the prevalence of cohabitation in the United States. "Rarely does social change occur with such rapidity," they write. "Indeed, there have been few developments relating to marriage and family life which have been as dramatic as the rapid increase in unmarried cohabitation" (1981: 65). They mention the trend toward smaller families and the increase in age at which women begin childbearing as contributing to this phenomenon. They report that unmarried cohabitation is more common in large cities, more common among Blacks than among Whites, and most likely to end for any given couple within two years.

WORK, CAREERS, AND OCCUPATIONS

Income and wealth derived from paid work is, for most of us, a central resource. Society places a high value on what we do for a living; so do the people we meet; so do we ourselves. Work provides the means for obtaining the goods and pursuing the activities that are the essence of the single lifestyle. Marketing experts recognize the impact of singles' consumption patterns in the marketplace and they create product lines and selling strategies to lure singles' dollars. From townhouses to sports cars, from tape decks to vacations in Mexico, goods are created and singles work to obtain the money to enjoy them.

Beyond the marketplace, work provides a crucial source of identity. Power, prestige, and privilege all flow from occupational involvement, as does a sense of self-worth. Single people are far more likely to place their career goals above interest in family. Some devote longer hours to work than their married colleagues, and many feel that they receive significant emotional support from their co-workers (Stein, 1976).

Though single women and men can make superior employees, some continue to receive lower wages than married colleagues and are sometimes passed over for promotion on the basis of their single status. A survey of fifty major corporations found that in 80 percent of the responding companies, the official corporate position was that marriage was not essential to upward mobility within the corporation. However, in a majority of these same companies, only 2 percent of their executives, including junior management levels, were single. Over 60 percent of the replies stated that single executives tend to make snap judgments, and 25 percent said that singles are "less stable" than married people (Jacoby, 1974). Discrimination may range from overt cases to more subtle ones involving the complex networks that exist in every institution: business-related friendships, luncheon conversations, and other informal contacts that affect job retention and promotion. Since race, sex, ethnic origin, and religion are also bases for discrimination, discrimination based on singleness is often difficult to isolate. Whatever its cause, such discrimination victimizes many men and women who hope to get ahead in their work, or hope just to get by.

The marital status and the socioeconomic status of women and their families are particularly influential in determining choices of occupation. Natalie Sokoloff's 1981 study of women college graduates showed that single and married women differed in their early career activities and in their occupational choices. The differences in career activities were due less to marital status than to socioeconomic status. Some of Sokoloff's findings were:

1. Almost all single women from all socioeconomic classes were employed, and 25 percent were involved in postbachelor's studies.
2. Married women were less likely to be employed or in school three years after graduation from college.
3. A larger percentage of women from lower socioeconomic status families remained single three years after graduation. This was true even when the women had children.
4. The largest percentage of single and married women were employed in professions traditionally considered "female."

For many women, obtaining a good education and entering a profession take priority over marrying and establishing a family, at least for a period of time. This is true of Black and White women from lower-middle-class families. Higginbotham's studies (1981, 1982) of middle- and lower-middle-class Black, college-educated women compared the relevant emphasis placed on marriage by the two groups. The upwardly mobile women from lower-middle-class backgrounds had parents who did not see future marriage prospects as assuring the desired mobility for their daughters. They therefore focused on educational success to the exclusion of other goals, including marriage. On the other hand, women from Black middle-class homes were expected to integrate careers with family life.

The problem of successfully integrating personal and professional life is compounded for many gay men. Keeping one's job often means hiding one's homosexuality. How this is accomplished, what happens when one is found out, and the extent of discrimination against gays throughout the working world are the focus of Martin Levine's "Employment Discrimination Against Gay Men" (1981). Public opinion polls report strong support for barring gays from high-status occupations; application forms are constructed to weed out gays; there is discrimination even in government licensing and security clearances. The struggle to conceal their sexual orientation from co-workers often leaves gay people feeling alienated and anxious, and if they fail to conceal it, the situation can be worse. Many companies enforce a policy of firing gays upon discovery. Others keep employees at a low level or transfer them to a "more suitable" job.

PARENTING

Single parents may be separated, divorced, or widowed, or may never have been married at all. They tend to be older than most singles and their social lives are shaped by the daily responsibilities of child care. They may be independent and self-sufficient, but most are overburdened and financially strained (Benjamin, 1981).

There were 5.7 million one-parent families in 1978, an increase of 9 percent over 1977. More than 90 percent of these families are maintained by women. In 1980, 11.1 million children were living with their mothers alone, while about 1 million were living with their fathers alone. Overall, 19.7 percent of all children under 18 were living in one-parent families (U.S. Bureau of the Census, 1981).

Single parents experience three major worries: loneliness, children, and money. Their problems evolve over time. The first months after the breakup of a marriage are the most traumatic. The newly divorced person must deal with disputes over child support and custody as well as personal problems of depression, self-doubt, desire for revenge, and the need for new emotional involvements. Then come financial worries (Weiss, 1979). The median income in two-parent families is two to three times that of one-parent families. The economic hardships faced by single parents reflect the lower wages paid all women, particularly minority women, who make up 35 percent of all single mothers. Less than 30 percent of families headed by women report incomes as high as $10,000, compared with 70 percent of two-parent families. These single parents need skilled child care, part-time jobs with benefits, and easily available health care facilities (Stein, 1981).

The difficulties of providing for their own and their children's physical, social, and emotional needs often result in role overload and fatigue. It is difficult to develop and maintain a satisfying social/sexual life. Nonparents often consider single parents, with their attached responsibilities, less than "marriageable." Many single parents are reluctant to expose their children to dates who spend the night, and getting away for weekends or vacations requires child care arrangements. Not surprisingly, single mothers are somewhat less likely to remarry than other single women (Duberman, 1975).

How do women heading families feel about their situations? "Rarely is the concept put forward that the female-headed family is an acceptable family form or that, once divorced, it is all right for a mother to stay divorced," report Kohen, Brown and Feldberg (1981: 288). But presumptions in favor of the male-headed family have begun to be questioned as the advantages of single-hood emerge. When a couple divorces, the woman not only loses most of her right to the man's resources, but she also loses her personal dependence and obligations of service. For some women, the experience of heading a family may be more rewarding than were their marriages.

Rosenthal and Keshet (1981) found that young single fathers experience role conflicts between work and child care similar to conflicts experienced by single mothers. Moreover, full-time and half-time fathers averaged considerably less income than did men in intact marriages. Yet at home, men who learned to meet children's practical daily needs began to feel better about themselves and their relationship with their children. Bringing the criteria of work performance to the parenting role made them more at ease with their new obligations.

AGING

Only 12 percent of the 11 million single persons over the age of 65 have never married; 3 percent are separated, 77 percent widowed, and 7 percent divorced. There are dramatic differences in the statistics for men and women. Most notably 75 percent of men over the age of 65 are married and 14 percent are widowed, while only 37 percent of the women in this age group are married and 52 percent are widowed. The number of older never-married people is significant and their characteristics are varied.

What do we know about singles and aging? One of the few analyses done on the elderly never married tells us that they are not especially lonely in old age. They are similar to the married elderly in that both groups are more positive in outlook than the divorced or widowed elderly. Moreover, having never been married means that one avoids the desolation of bereavement following the death of one's spouse (Gubrium, 1975). A study of older women points out that the never marrieds had the best physical and psychological health and were the best able to cope in terms of facing up to problems and taking action. Experience with living alone appears to increase independence and autonomy and to have some beneficial effects for coping effectively (Wood, 1979). . . .

COPING STYLES OF NEVER-MARRIED ADULTS

Margaret Adams (1976), in a pioneering study of single women who had made successful life adjustments, cited three major factors responsible for making singleness a viable lifestyle for them: economic independence, social and psychological autonomy, and a clear intent to remain single by choice.

In his summary of the literature, Shostak (forthcoming) identifies six major coping mechanisms employed by singles. Three are traditional coping mechanisms for singles: permissive social attitudes, same-sex friendships, and marriage-deriding attitudes. The three more recent coping mechanisms are: assertive social attitudes, dating support systems, and prosinglehood options.

Citing a 1976–1977 Harris poll for *Playboy* of 684 never-married men, Shostak reports that "about twice as large a proportion of the never-married as the married males were designated 'innovators,' the most liberal of the four possibilities,[1] and less than half as many singles as married men were labeled conservative 'traditionalists'" (forthcoming: 19).

Single women have similar liberal attitudinal profiles, according to the 1980 Virginia Slims Poll. Though cautious about the incomplete data, Shostak indicates that single women and men "stand out . . . in their comparative permissiveness, liberality and acceptance of change" (forthcoming: 19).

Singles stress the importance of close, caring friendships, based on free choice and developing into a sense of mutuality. Stein (1976) interviewed sixty single men and women between the ages of 25 and 45, mostly college graduates employed and living in New York and Boston. In their departure from traditional family structures, they expressed a strong need for substitute networks of human relationships that provide the basic satisfactions of intimacy, sharing, and continuity.

Intimacy for these women and men came from both opposite or same-sex friendships. Groups of friends, formal or informal, are especially well suited to meeting the needs of single people, helping them to deal with life choices and to pursue personal growth. For many of the single people interviewed, friendships meant survival.

Marriage-deriding attitudes may be used to justify the unwed state. Some take a very critical stance with reference to marriage, feeling that "it is better to be single than caught in an unfulfilling marriage." There is a need among singles to develop a consistent and supportive world view.

Assertive social attitudes are apparent in the emergent ideology of positive singlehood, which is now documented in a number of magazines, journals, seminars, and the like. The positive aspects of singlehood are stressed in such titles as "Living Alone and Liking It," "Single Can Be Fun," and so on. The traditional appeal of marriage as a conveyor of respectability has been considerably weakened by the recent liberalizing of our social norms, and having children is no longer considered necessary for either full adulthood or for a full and happy marriage relationship (Burnley and Kurth, 1981; Cheung, 1982; Greenwood, 1978).

Dating support runs the gamut from singles' magazines and clubs catering to singles, to computer dating services, singles' bars, and vacation resorts. More formal structures are also emerging to provide intimacy and continuity among adults. They frequently take the form of group living arrangements, one type of "experimental family" (Cogswell and Sussman, 1972). While communal homes might include the socialization of children, they also focus on the needs for identity, intimacy, and interaction of adult members. Other structures include women's and men's groups, therapy and encounter groups, and organizations formed around specialized interests. Although not restricted to singles, they are particularly well adapted to meeting the needs of single people and were cited by the singles interviewed as examples of positive experiences in their lives (Stein, 1976). Such group interactions foster friendships and spur personal growth by providing a supportive context.

Shostak indicates the need to alter certain public policies that affect singles. "Nonmarried Americans need a fair hearing and positive changes in their roles as learners, as citizens, as renters, as cohabitors, as parents, as purchasers of 'singles only' services, and especially as the subjects of social science research" (forthcoming: 38). Shostak echoes the need for further research (see also Stein, 1978). For example:

1. What are the similarities and differences between voluntary and involun-

tary, temporary and stable singles (Shostak's ambivalents, wistfuls, resolveds, and regretfuls)?

2. How do women and men make decisions regarding preferred marital status and how committed are they to these choices?

3. To what extent are people "embedded" in their present married or single state?

4. How do singles opt for transitory versus long-term single life?

5. How does the experience of singlehood differ for men and women?

6. How do gender differences coupled with age intersect with work experiences, life arrangement, and social supports?

7. How much variation is there in the singlehood experiences of different ethnic, religious, and racial groups?

8. To what extent do existing social support systems provide help for singles, and what new forms of support are still needed?

9. What kinds of adults cope well and enjoy the single experience and who are those who are discontent? What social and psychological factors seem to account for these similarities and differences?

10. Have the stereotypes of single life changed to reflect its heterogeneity?

11. What are the work and career experiences of today's singles?

A crucial need also exists for a systemic comparison of cohorts of nonmarried and married men and women based on both aggregate and individual data that would lead to the development of concepts, typologies, and theories. Testable hypotheses must be generated and existing statistics need to be replicated. Interested social scientists will find many research opportunities; social practitioners and those concerned with social policy will find much to consider.

CONCLUSION

Singles are an important segment of the adult population. Their interests, their activities, and their lifestyles are often in the forefront of social trends. Singles take risks; they experiment; they consume; they set trends. Any one of us may some day belong to the singles population, if we are not now single. Statistics show that about one-third of young adults currently marrying will divorce; three out of four married women will become widows; many people will live together without marriage. There are many styles of adulthood in our society. Different people may choose different styles, or one person may adopt various styles in the course of a lifetime.

Although personal statements provide us with insight into single experiences, little has been done to provide a systematic examination of singlehood. Singles have often been regarded as a somewhat deviant group, different from "normal" married adults, and until very recently they have been avoided as a

PETER J. STEIN

subject of serious research. Recognition of the variations that exist within the singles population, and of the goals and concerns they hold in common with other people, such as meaningful work, friendship, financial security, health care, a comfortable and secure home, and self-esteem, is a result of recent research on this lifestyle. The interested researcher and practitioner will find many opportunities to do creative and constructive work.

NOTE

[1] The other three categories were traditionalist, conventional, and contemporary.

REFERENCES

Adams, M. 1976. *Single blessedness* New York: Basic Books.

Benjamin, E. 1981. It's not easy being single after years of marriage: the social world of separated and divorced parents. Paper presented at the Annual Meetings of the SSSP.

Bloom, B., W. Hodges, R. Caldwell, L. Systra, and A. Cedrone. 1977. Marital separation: a community survey. *Journal of Divorce* 1 (Fall): 7–19.

Brown, G. 1980. *The new celibacy.* New York: McGraw-Hill.

Burnley, C. and S. Kurth. 1981. Never married women's perceptions of adult life transitions. Paper presented at the Annual Meetings of the SSSP.

Cargan, L. and M. Melko. 1982. Singles. Beverly Hills, Calif: Sage.

Cheung, L. M. 1982. Single Chinese-American women. Paper presented at the Annual Meetings of the Eastern Sociological Society.

Clayton, R. R. and J. L. Bokemeier. 1980. Premarital sex in the seventies. *Journal of Marriage and the Family* 42 (November): 759–75.

Cogswell, B. and M. Sussman. 1972. Changing family and marriage forms. *The Family Coordinator* 21 (September): 505–16.

Cole, C. L. 1977. Cohabitation in social context. In R. Libby and R. Whitehurst (eds.), *Marriage and alternatives*, pp. 62–79. Glenview, Ill: Scott, Foresman.

Duberman, L. 1975. *The reconstituted family.* Chicago: Nelson-Hall.

Glick, P. C. 1979. Future Americans. Washington COFO Memo 2 (Summer/Fall): 2–5.

———— and G. Spanier. 1981. Cohabitation in the U.S. In P. J. Stein (ed.), *Single life: Unmarried adults in social context*, pp. 194–209. New York: St. Martin's.

Greenwood, N. A. 1978. Safely single or wisely wed? A sociological analysis of singleness as a positive lifestyle. Master's thesis, California State University, Sacramento.

Gubrium, J. F. 1975. Being single in old age. *International Journal of Aging and Human Development* 6 (Fall): 29–41.

Hess, B. and E. Markson. 1980. *Aging and old age*. New York: Macmillan.

Higginbothan, E. 1982. Educated single Black women: marital options and limits. (unpublished).

———. 1981. Is marriage a priority? Class differences in marital options of educated black women. In P. J. Stein (ed.), *Singles life: Unmarried adults in social context*, pp. 259–67. New York: St. Martin's.

Hunt, M. 1974. *Sexual behavior in the 1970s*. Chicago: Playboy.

Jacoby, S. 1974. 49 million singles can't all be right. *New York Times Magazine* (February 17): 41–49.

Kohen, J., C. Brown, and R. Feldberg. 1981. Divorced mothers. In P. J. Stein (ed.), *Single life: Unmarried adults in social context*, pp. 288–305. New York: St. Martin's.

Laws, J. L. and P. Schwartz. 1977. *Sexual scripts: The social construction of female sexuality*. Hinsdale, Ill: Dryden.

Levine, M. 1981. Employment discrimination against gay men. In P. J. Stein (ed.) *Single life: Unmarried adults in social context*, pp. 268–73. New York: St. Martin's.

———, ed. 1979. *Gay men: The sociology of male homosexuality*. New York: Harper & Row.

Libby, R. 1977. Creative singlehood as a sexual lifestyle: beyond marriage as a rite of passage. In R. W. Libby and R. N. Whitehurst (eds.), *Marriage and alternatives*, pp. 37–61. Glenview, Ill.: Scott, Foresman.

Macklin, E. D. 1980. Nontraditional family forms: a decade of research. *Journal of Marriage and the Family* 42 (November): 905–22.

———. 1978. Nonmarital heterosexual cohabitation. *Marriage and Family Review* 1 (March/April): 1–12.

Pearlin, L. I. and J. S. Johnson. 1981. Marital status, life strains, and depression. In P. J. Stein (ed.), *Single life: Unmarried adults in social context*, pp. 165–78. New York: St. Martin's.

Rosenthal, K. and H. Keshet. 1981. Childcare responsibilities of part-time and single fathers. In P. J. Stein (ed.), *Single life: Unmarried adults in social context*, pp. 306–24. New York: St. Martin's.

Shostak, A. (Forthcoming.) Singlehood: the lives of never-married employed Americans. In M. Sussman and S. Steinmetz (eds.), *Handbook on marriage and the family*. New York: Plenum.

Sokoloff, N. 1981. Early work patterns of single and married women. In P. J. Stein (ed.), *Single life: Unmarried adults in social context*, pp. 238–59. New York: St. Martin's.

Stein, P. J., ed. 1981. *Single life: Unmarried adults in social context*. New York: St. Martin's.

———. 1976. *Single*. Englewood Cliffs, N. J.: Prentice-Hall.

U.S. Bureau of the Census. 1981. *Marital status and living arrangements: March 1980*. Current Population Reports, Series P-20, No. 365. Washington, D. C.: Government Printing Office.

Verbrugge, L. 1979. Marital status and health. *Journal of Marriage and the Family* 41 (May): 267–85.

Vida, V., ed. 1978. *Our right to love: A lesbian resource book.* Englewood Cliffs, N.J.: Prentice-Hall.

Weiss, R. 1979. *Going it alone.* New York: Basic Books.

———. 1975. *Marital separation.* New York: Basic Books.

Wood, V. 1979. Singles and aging. Paper presented to the Annual Meetings of the National Council on Family Relations.

48 Experimental Family Forms—The Family of the Future

James Ramey

STUDY QUESTIONS

1. Indicate three areas of change and how they affected experimental family forms.
2. Name several benefits of group marriages and communes.

WHAT IS AN EXPERIMENTAL FAMILY FORM?

Americans have trouble defining experimental family forms, perhaps because they are unaware of the family pluralism in our society. The latest Bureau of Labor (March 1977, Note 1) figures indicate that in 1975, adults were distributed in United States households as follows:

Heading single-parent families	16%
Other single, widowed, separated, or divorced persons	21
Living in childfree or postchildrearing marriages	23
Living in dual-breadwinner nuclear families	16
Living in single-breadwinner nuclear families	13
Living in no-breadwinner nuclear families	1
Living in extended families	6
Living in experimental families or cohabiting	4
	100%

Source: James Ramey, "Experimental Family Forms—The Family of the Future, *Marriage and Family Review*, January/February 1978, pp. 1–9. Reprinted by permission.

With the exception of the final category, these are variant family forms, not experimental family forms, although within them there may be some experimental forms, such as the single person who deliberately chooses to conceive and raise a child out of wedlock. Neither lay persons nor professionals avoid confusing the issue by lumping together those who actually change family structure with those who merely modify or redefine sex roles within the existing family structure—a process that occurs in almost every generation. Cogswell and Sussman explored this area in some depth in an article in 1972.

Bookshelves are crowded with titles on alternative marriage and family forms, including contract marriage, childfree marriage, trial marriage (cohabitation), homosexual marriage, sexually open marriage, family clusters, intimate groups and networks, multiadult households, consensual and nonconsensual adultery, single-parenting, swinging, communes, group marriage, and singlehood. We are now beginning to see a rash of information about yet another family form, one heretofore so taboo that it was mentioned only in whispers—the incestuous family. During the single month of April 1977, four major television programs were devoted to this subject.

How does one relate these seemingly disconnected and sometimes overlapping variations on interpersonal relating? How many people are they likely to attract? In a 1972 article, expanded in *Intimate Friendships* (1976), this author suggested a paradigm for establishing a complexity continuum on which they could be located. This continuum is anchored at one end in the absence of relationships—the celibate hermit—and then ranges through ever more complex nonprimary relationships, such as uncommitted dating, intimate groups and networks, or having a lover, to variations of primary relationships, such as cohabitation, contract marriage, traditional monogamous marriage, voluntary childfree marriage, or homosexual marriage. Even more complex are primary relationships plus nonprimary relationships, as in the case of consensual or nonconsensual adultery in marriage, sexually open marriage, or multiadult households. Multiple primary relationships are found in group marriages. Finally, the most complex form is a combination of multiple primary relationships and nonprimary relationships. One example is a partner in a group marriage who is also a member of an intimate network with an outside lover.

There appears to be high association between the number of adherents to a particular lifestyle and its complexity; the more complex the lifestyle, the fewer practitioners. Constantine and Constantine (1973) estimate 1,000 group marriages or fewer in the United States. Zablocki (1977) estimates fewer than 50,000 individuals live in communes in the United States. The overwhelming majority of adults live in the least complex lifestyles, alone or with a single partner.

Despite these small numbers, communes and group marriages capture the imagination of behavioral scientists and popular writers. The vast outpouring of both serious and popular writing about experimental family forms has concentrated on such multiadult households or on such nonmonogamous relationships as swinging (couple-front consensual adultery) and sexually open marriage.

One clue to this preoccupation with complex lifestyles is revealed by the second part of the title of this review article—the future of the traditional nuclear family. What is considered to be the traditional nuclear family, a breadwinner-father, a housewife-mother, and two children under eighteen accounted for only 7 percent of the population in 1975 (Bureau of Labor Statistics, Note 1)! Etzioni, while not reporting the source of the data, declared, "the proportion of married households out of total households declined from 72.5% in 1965 to 64.9% in 1976. . . . While the average annual rate of decline was 33% for the first three years of this period, it tripled to 97% for the last three years" (1977, p. 487). He suggested that a generation from now, should this trend continue, there would not be a married household left. While this was not a prediction, he nevertheless said it sufficed to show that the family is an endangered species.

Those who predict the demise of the family fail to take into account that we have always had a plurality of family forms. It is unrealistic to use the monogamous nuclear family as the common starting point for all explorations of current experimental family forms, much less for an assessment of future family forms. Plural family forms have been the ideal in most cultures and times and are still preferred in some societies today, although even in these societies most people can only afford a dyadic marriage. Murdock (1949) stated that only 43 of the 238 societies he surveyed could be classified as monogamous, when preferential marriage form was used as the criterion. It is not the mere complexity of multiadult households that mitigates against them in our society.

In the United States, especially since the Civil War, we have idealized the nuclear family form even though we have not all lived in this type of family. Most individuals actually experience several family forms during their lives. Perhaps the reason we assume that we all live in a nuclear family is because we overwhelmingly tend to adopt dyadic primary relationships or none at all, despite the family form in which we live.

Much of the change in family form in the future can be expected to involve shifts in the number of individuals living in existing family forms. As the population ages there is an expansion in postchildrearing marriages. In the past five years, single-parent families have grown 11.5 times the rate of dual-parent families. Cohabitation now accounts for nearly 1 percent of all adults (Bureau of the Census, Note 2). Deliberately childfree couples account for almost 5 percent of all adults, yet the percentage of never-married individuals is not as high today as it was before World War I. The percentage of single parents is about the same as it was in 1910, and the percentage of childfree couples is less than one-fourth the percentage in the 1920s (Glick, 1977).

HISTORICAL CONTEXT

Three areas of change in our society are critically important to the current development of experimental family forms. The first of these is the American obsession with *personal freedom*. In the early days of the Republic this urge was expressed by striking out for the western frontier and carving oneself a place from the wilderness. As the physical frontier began to disappear, the Horatio

Alger tradition began to emerge whereby one carved one's place out of the economic or technological frontier through the exercise of "Yankee ingenuity." That individualistic tradition has not abated in our society, but it has been reshaped in recent decades. While part of the population has remained steeped in the rugged individualist tradition of marriage, kids, a house, a boat, two cars, and a place in the country, others have responded to a new emphasis on individual growth and freedom that may include, but clearly transcends, the economic emphasis of rugged individualism. Maslow's vision of self-actualism has been stripped of its emphasis on responsibility and reduced to "do your own thing." More about this later.

The second area of change that must be considered in any realistic appraisal of experimental family forms is the impact of *four revolutions* that have occurred in this country over the past hundred years. The demographic revolution has wrought vast changes. In 1900, the average woman lived 47 years, 18 of them being childbearing years. By 1974, the average woman lived 74 years and only 8 involved childbearing (Francoeur, 1972). Today, the couple that remains married has better than one out of three chances to celebrate their 50th wedding anniversary. In fact they can expect to have over 30 years together after their children are grown and gone. 'Til death do us part takes on a very different meaning today than it did in 1900.

The biological revolution is of more recent vintage and is still occurring. Already the pill, which became generally available as recently as 1962, has been superseded by contraceptive sterilization as the most popular means of birth control among married couples. By 1973, contraceptive sterilization had tripled within three years even among the 15–24 age group (Westoff, 1976). In 1975, a survey of a sample of 3,403 married white men and women was conducted, the fourth in a series of National Fertility Studies. It was reported in 1975 that about 6.8 million couples chose surgical sterilization compared to 7.1 million wives using the pill to prevent an unwanted birth. Medical reasons accounted for 1.1 million additional sterilizations (*Sentinel*, 1977). Today in the United States, as in the rest of the world, sterilization is the preferred means of contraception. Women can at last control their own biology.

The economic revolution is also extremely relevant to our examination of change, for it has brought us to a point in history when for the first time the family is no longer the basic unit in society. Today the individual, male or female, can perform all the functions once reserved to the family—economic self-sufficiency, maintaining a household, meeting sexual needs, and raising children. The individual can now be the basic unit and in growing numbers is exercising this ability. Over a third of our adult population is single and living alone or with children. The individualistic tradition brought us first to the isolated nuclear family unit, with its instability and atomizing influence on the community, and now, because it is no longer possible to keep women "barefoot and pregnant," it is giving rise to a shift from family to individual units.

Finally there is the fourth revolution in communication. My father, grandfather, and great-grandfather grew up in essentially the same world. New ideas took decades and sometimes a generation to become part of general knowledge in their day—long enough to be processed, modified, accepted or rejected, and integrated into one's store of information. I have little more than a foothold in my father's world, and my children even less in mine, for the pace of change has been immeasurably speeded up, not alone by the acceleration of technological development but perhaps even more by instantaneous communication. We were armchair participants in the war in Vietnam. We all walked on the moon, and hundreds of millions of people all over the world simultaneously cheered a 14-year-old girl as she exhibited perfect form in the Olympic games in Montreal. Today we are innundated with information—more than we can process, much less integrate.

The change that is being wrought by these four revolutions is vast and cumulative, and most of it is yet to come. Already we have seen the flowering of the women's rights movement, a flowering that could not come about until women controlled their own economic and biologic futures. And this issue is very germaine to our examination of experimental family forms.

THE SEXUAL TRANSFORMATION

There is still one area of change that we must examine in order to understand the intellectual history underlying our current concern with experimental family forms—the transformation of our sexual attitudes. Sexual modernists (Robinson, 1976) contend that sexual experience neither threatens moral character nor drains vital energies, as the Victorians were wont to say. They practically denied women any sexual life, while the modernists contend that she is at least the sexual equal of the male. In addition, the modernists raise serious doubts about whether marriage and the family can or should be the only context for the expression of sexuality. Although European Romantic sexual doctrine also affirmed the essential worth of erotic experience, they also split with the modernists over the concept of sex for sex's sake, arguing that sex is of value only within the context of an intense psychological relationship, even if that relationship should occur outside marriage.

Havelock Ellis was a romantic, according to Robinson, who argued for broadening the spectrum of acceptable sexual behavior based on animal behavior and cultural relativism. He was an early spokesman for looking at homosexuality as variant rather than deviant and he defused the explosive issue of masturbation in young boys by pointing out that it was especially common in females. As an investigator of normal, rather than pathological sex, Ellis switched the traditional concern about the control of sexual activity in courtship to concern about sexual arousal as a potential problem. Ellis coined the term "trial marriage" for the preparenting stage of marriage many years before Margaret Mead advocated two-step marriage. He was in favor of divorce as an automatic right to either party so long as the children are taken care of. He believed in licensing parents rather than nonparents (Robinson, 1976, pp. 4–30).

According to Robinson, Ellis believed that men and women sought not just variety in sex but variety in romance and he hoped that the bonds of marriage could be loosened enough to accommodate this need. He felt that a number of simultaneous relationships were possible and that in an atmosphere of trust and truth about outside relationships there would be no jealousy. In other words, his stress was on psychological fidelity rather than sexual exclusivity (pp. 32–33).

Alfred Kinsey sought to undermine established categories of sexual wisdom rather than to create new ones. He concentrated on showing that sexual differences could be plotted on a curve or spectrum and avoided concern about the emotional aspects of sexuality by evaluating sexual experience in terms of counting orgasms without regard to how they occurred. He debunked the importance of marriage by showing that more than half of all orgasms were derived from sources outside intercourse between marriage partners, i.e., they were derived from socially disapproved and in large part illegal sources (Robinson, 1976, pp. 54–76).

Kinsey argued that while premarital sexual experience contributed to sexual success in marriage, once the knot was tied the problem of sexual outlet was largely resolved. Thus it was not until 1948 that he began asking his subjects about extramarital petting. However, in contrast to Ellis, he seemed to feel that extramarital sex should not be emotionally involved, lest it adversely affect the marriage. The idea that sex was permissible only when people loved each other was no less absurd to Kinsey than the belief that masturbation caused insanity. Only when repressed did sexual urges threaten emotional stability so that a rational society, in his view, would promote not only a positive but essentially a casual attitude toward sex, especially among the young.

Robinson feels that Masters and Johnson primarily differ from Kinsey in their antithetical sexual values and in their explicitly therapeutic intent. He is particularly concerned about their bias toward female masturbators, exhibitionists, older individuals, upper-class subjects, and sexual inclinations.

> Their emphasis on the similarity of female and male response, their belittling of the penis and the lore associated with it, their campaign against the vaginal orgasm, and their inclination to judge sexual experience from an essentially marital, even monogamous, perspective all exemplify tendencies that are subtly supported by the bias of their sample. Their conservatism manifests itself in three broad areas of sexual inquiry. . . . They conceive of sexual life in terms of enduring, heterosexual relationships of substantial affection. They seem at times as much concerned with procreation as with pleasure. They betray an antibehavioral bias and a weakness for upbeat psychologizing in the manner of the neo-Freudians. On the other hand, they take genuinely progressive or even radical positions on women, on the elderly, and on masturbation. (pp. 140–41)

For Masters and Johnson an extramarital affair is a confession of marital failure and is itself a significant contributor to sexual inadequacy. A marriage should be saved no matter how emotionally bankrupt it may be.

Robinson concludes that the distinctive feature of contemporary culture is the casual and often brief extramarital alliances that are both known to and approved by the marriage partner and that this is the crux of the unresolved tensions of modern sexual tradition. We want to rid ourselves of the repressions of a romantic past but we fear emotional emptiness in a deromanticized future, even while we anticipate its greater freedom.

In review, there are three intertwined threads that establish the historical perspective for experimental family form evaluation; the press toward individual freedom and growth; the impact of the demographic, biologic, economic, and communications revolutions; and the unresolved conflict between sex as a physical need and sex as part of an elaborate emotional relationship.

CURRENT UNDERSTANDING OF EXPERIMENTAL FAMILY FORMS

Alice Rossi (1977) defends the monogamous nuclear family and takes issue with those who argue for sexual equality: "Sexual liberation seems to mean that increasing numbers of women are now following male initiatives in a more elaborate, multipartner sexual script [in which] to be faithful, possessive, exclusively heterosexual, and able to postpone gratification are signs of immaturity and oppression. . . . In the post-nuclear-family era, the adult can turn parenthood on and off and exchange children as well as sexual partners. It is not at all clear what the gains will be for either women or children in this version of human liberation. . . . recreational sex has contemporary ascendence over procreational sex (pp. 14–16)."

I have argued elsewhere that equity rather than equality should be the goal of human liberation (Ramey, 1976). Already we are seeing some women who have taken on male roles succumbing to typical male stress diseases, such as ulcers, heart disease, and loss of hair due to increased production of androgens. Much of Professor Rossi's critique is directed at the pop writers and propagandists for alternative lifestyles who have generated so much heat and so little light on the contemporary scene, rather than at those who are making a serious attempt to understand what is happening. The latter group, almost without exception, is convinced that most people will continue to live in familiar family forms.

What is required are hard facts about current behavior in experimental family forms and theory frameworks within which to assess these family forms, relate them to more conventional family forms, and predict the likelihood that they will persist, grow, or decline. We need to know what happens to practitioners of experimental family forms and to their relationships. Actual research data on experimental family forms is sparse and most of what exists is exploratory, descriptive, and based on opportunity samples.

Group Marriages

Larry and Joan Constantine have published the only study on group marriage or, as they call it, "multilateral marriage" (1973). (These are nonlegal marriages where three or more adults of both sexes live together as a family.) They found over a hundred groups, corresponded and met with more than

30, and intensively studied the 11 groups that form the basis for their book. Their in-depth study was considerably more thorough than most studies of the family ever attempted, involving multiple visits, separate interviews with each adult and child in the group as well as with the group as a whole, the use of both group and individual interview forms and questionnaires, and feedback sessions with both individuals and groups. In addition they secured psychological profiles, marital adjustment and satisfaction scores, and personality inventory scores on their 40 participants. They investigated their subjects' beliefs and values, their individual expectations and motives for forming a group marriage, and the disadvantages and problems they found. They examined the way the group related to significant others, to job, and to the community, and how they shared responsibilities, finances, and chores. They looked at the impact of the group on its children, if any, at the type of planning and structure they used in setting up the group, and at how they dissolved it.

Their results can best be summed up in their own words:

> Multilateral marriage is, of course, an ideological extreme in which the traditional family boundary is completely eliminated, while a new, similar boundary is erected around the multilateral unit. But our research does not show this to be happening; internal boundaries are present, though highly diffuse; primary dyadic relationships are recognizable. . . . We do not expect that more than a small minority of families will be based on multilateral marriage. In many ways, it is the most difficult and extreme departure from previous models. Surprisingly, in its purest form its moral base is not at all distant from conventional morality. Sex and intimacy remain tied to marriage, and the boundaries of several of the intact groups in our knowledge are traditionally tight. Some couples have felt comfortable about cross-marital sex only after they regarded themselves as "engaged to be group married." (pp. 233, 235)

Communes

The most comprehensive study of communes so far undertaken in the United States is the Urban Communes Project, a three-year study, headed by Ben Zablocki. This project involves a sample of almost 700 men and women in 60 urban communes in Los Angeles, Houston, Atlanta, Minneapolis, Boston, and New York. In each city the study focused on religious, political, craft, music, art, and therapeutic groups. Some were intensely ideologic, while others were merely places where people chose to share economically. Some were highly structured, some were not. Some included children, but most did not. The overwhelming majority of the participants were single, and all groups included both sexes. These groups were found to constitute an important form of social support for some single individuals. Participants listed the following reasons for joining a commune, in rank order:

1. Economic
2. Order and regularity

3. Friendship and support from caring people in a noncaring world
4. As a way to leave home
5. To break with the past
6. In search of a viable alternative to things they had tried but did not like
7. Exploratory—a way of trying out a new lifestyle just for the sake of new experience
8. A way to live with a lover
9. A way to live in a single state in the company of others
10. A search for like-minded people
11. Companionship, or community

Participants indicated a number of activities made easier by communal living:

To be single	70%
To find out what you want in life	70
To be the kind of person you want to be	72
To meet financial emergencies	72
To find out who you are	74
To meet new people	77
To relate to people openly and spontaneously	80
To solve emotional problems	81
To be cared for when physically ill	82

Despite the wide variation in the types of communes studied, there was considerable uniformity regarding reported advantages. For some respondents joining was a hard decision, while others joined friends who were already there. Communes located in Houston, Boston, and Los Angeles found it easier to find suitable housing. The average participant stays for two years. Some move on to another commune in the same town. Some attempt to change the structure of the commune and, if unsuccessful, move on to one more to their liking. Some leave to marry, often to persons they met while living communally, while others just drop out to return to their previous lifestyle. A significant proportion of the sample was steadily employed and led normal, rather than freaky lives, while pursuing undergraduate and graduate education or careers.

In contrast to the urban communes studied by Zablocki, most rural communes have involved a drop-out philosophy and few have survived for more than a season, with a few notable exceptions, such as Twin Oaks, The Farm, or the Hutterite communities. What these survivors have in common is discipline, structure, goals, rather than a "do your own thing" philosophy. The religious communes, such as the Hutterites, are the most highly structured and have the strongest, most centralized leadership. Such highly structured groups have much lower turnover than other types of communes, but this is achieved at the cost of isolation from the rest of the world.

For many people who have not yet experienced such a commitment or who do not wish to make such a choice, multiadult households, such as communes, represent a way of finding community and economic sharing without making a marriage or cohabitation commitment. For those who have already tried marriage or cohabitation and found such an arrangement too constricting—not providing sufficient freedom to grow and develop—multiadult households also promise a way to remain single, but within the structure of a strong support group. This is particularly relevant to divorced women with small children. There are also happily married or cohabitating couples who want to open up their relationships even more than would be the case if they were simply to practice sexually open relating, by actually sharing living quarters with other married and/or unmarried adults. Other studies of communes have found similar results (Kanter, Jaffe, & Weisberg, 1975; Alam, Note 3).

Swinging

Several descriptive studies of swinging have been published (Symonds, 1971; Bartell, 1971; Palson & Palson, 1972), but the most rigorous study to date had been Gilmartin's 1975 study in which 100 swinging couples were matched with 100 control couples on age, income, neighborhood, marital status, education, and children. Contrary to the stereotype of the swinger as portrayed by Bartell and others, this carefully conducted study found that swingers became romantically interested and involved earlier in life, began dating and courtship earlier, and appeared to have a greater need for social-heterosexual interaction than did the controls. In general they were more involved in the community than nonswingers, but were less religious. They reported much more frequent intercourse with their own spouses and were less bored with life than the controls. No divorces were reported to have occurred after the couple began swinging. Gilmartin concluded that "As far as any outsider can tell, swinging has not had any apparent negative effect on their marriages or lives" (p. 58).

In their forthcoming book on the Sexual Freedom Movement, James and Lynn Smith (Note 4), who followed a sample of 700 swingers over several years, report a progressive expansion of boundaries on the part of many married couples in their study. These couples first tested the feasibility of comarital sex, or couple-front swinging, in which the couple always participated together, either in the same room or at least at the same party in different rooms. If this proved comfortable, they then expanded their relationship boundary further, to allow individual rather than couple-front extramarital sex. If this was also found to be compatible, the boundary was further extended to allow for intimate friendships, i.e., friendships that include social, emotional, intellectual, family, and career intimacy as well as sexual intimacy. Such relationships tend to be long-term, rather than short-term ones. Their book, tentatively titled *Consenting Adults*, should add considerably to our understanding of swinging, which appears to involve about 4 percent of the adult population.

Sexually Open Marriage

To date, only three studies have been reported on sexually open marriage (Ramey, 1975, 1977; Knapp, 1976; Knapp & Whitehurst, 1977). The (1975) Ramey study of 380 participants in intimate groups and networks concentrated on those who had practiced sexual openness for at least ten years (15 + years was the average reported), since the focus was on the effect of sexual openness on the primary relationship. One-third of the respondents were single but 80 percent of the total sample were in primary relationships. Knapp concentrated on those who were married and had only recently opened their relationship since her interest was in the transition to sexually open relating and its effect on the couple. The Whitehurst study included some of both types.

Respondents in all three studies were remarkably similar except in age. They were uniformly upper-middle class, with above-average education, income, and interest in community affairs. The women as well as the men tended to be in full-time careers in academic, professional, managerial, or creative arts areas, and the women tended to be "liberated," i.e., willing to initiate relationships with men. Respondents were strikingly secure in their primary relationships, and exhibited a strong sense of self. Most had established definite ground rules for relating to others, although these were sometimes more implicit than explicit.

Perhaps the most striking factor about these respondents was the very high percentage of first-borns. Knapp found 53 percent and Ramey 57 percent first-borns (Ramey, 1977). Kagan (1977) found that "The combination of a firm commitment to the standards of adults and an affinity for coherence, consistency, and order among standards leads first-borns to adopt more idealistic philosophical positions and to prefer single, unifying principles in both morality and science, in preference to ones that are pluralistic or expedient." This is consistent with the findings of these three studies that their subjects' personal philosophies were holistic and humanistic and unaccepting of a view of marriage that excluded meaningful intimacy with anyone else.

Knapp (Knapp & Whitehurst, 1977) reported that on the Myers-Briggs Type Indicator (MBTI), which measures personality differences that result from the way people perceive and the way they judge, "72% of the sample fell into one of three categories: the extravert-intuitive (39%), the introvert-intuitive (18%), and the introvert-feeling type (15%). While estimations place the number of intuitives in the general population at about 25%, they made up 80% of the sample, most closely resembling standardization groups of highly creative artists" (p. 155). The Ramey respondents appeared to fall largely into these same categories.

The composite characteristics of people who practice sexually open marriage or are otherwise involved in intimate groups or networks—many are single or cohabitating—as indicated by these samples suggest that a particular type of person is more likely to try sexually open relating. Such a person would be imaginative, a risk-taker, self-assured, unconcerned about convention, an opinion leader, an idealist, one who thinks for him or herself, a "mover and shaker" as they say in Philadelphia. Knapp concludes that "if current trends persist, such persons would be females more often than males" (p. 156). Knapp further suggests that sexually open marriages are the most viable experimental family form because "they have very low visibility, do not require special living arrangements, and are based upon intactness of the marital unit. . . . When it works well, participants combine the security and specialness of the marital commitment with the freedom and individuality required for self-actualization" (p. 159).

LOOKING TO THE FUTURE

In addition to the Ramey complexity continuum paradigm discussed above, there are two others which provide a framework for understanding more about experimental family forms. Libby (1977) describes a paradigm for understanding how people move from one type of relationship to another. He uses role, exchange, and symbolic interaction theory. The suggestion is that we should explore with research subjects the nature of their past as well as present relationships and work through the process of rewards and costs they associated with the transition decisions they made and are making as they consider and anticipate future relationships. He suggests that we use role models in reevaluating our relationships with significant others as crucial events occur in those relationships and that bonding or unbonding occurs as a result of these evaluations, thus leading the individual to move from one type of relationship to another, possibly, but not necessarily of the same type (pp. 50–57). Unfortunately Libby's paradigm is descriptive and tells us nothing about the likelihood that the individual will pick one or another lifestyle, and would involve extremely difficult and expensive research.

Whitehurst (1977) presents a "Fallout Model" as "a means of examining how alternative lifestyle choices occur in the process of leakage from the social controls that keep most people tracked into conventional marriage" (p. 319). Assuming the same independent variables for all people, Whitehurst suggests that those who search for alternatives will exhibit such intervening variables as

> High sense of personal security, high personal autonomy need, similarity of lifestyle, opportunity, and support system availability. Those who remain in conventional marriages will exhibit opposite intervening variables: Low sense of personal security, low need for personal autonomy, lack of perceived opportunity or support systems (or presence of conventional supports). (p. 321)

He assumes that only a few individuals will fit his model because the masses are scripted by their early socialization toward conventional marriage. He hypothesizes distribution of fallout from conventional to alternative systems somewhat analogous to Ramey's continuum of growing complexity. Whitehurst sees a future in which conventional marriages that include nonconsensual adultery will predominate, followed by modified open marriages (not sexually open), traditional monogamous marriages, postmarried singles, and variations on sexually open marriage, with multiadult households and triads or group marriages at the low end of the scale of probability (p. 324).

It is interesting to note that the Libby, Whitehurst, and Ramey paradigms are not competing but rather explain different aspects of the phenomenon of involvement in experimental family forms. The Ramey paradigm predicts the likelihood that a particular lifestyle will become popular by suggesting that there is an inverse relationship between the complexity of the lifestyle and the number of adherents it will have. The Libby paradigm suggests the actual mechanism by which individuals are likely to shift from one lifestyle to another, and the Whitehurst paradigm suggests the intervening variables that differentiate which individuals are most likely to shift to an alternative lifestyle.

ANALYSIS

What has not occurred in this field up until now, although many have ventured predictions about the future, is the use of available sophisticated techniques for prediction. The Delphi Method, for example, has been well researched and applied in many settings, as documented by Linstone and Turoff (1975) in a highly readable and comprehensive book. The Delphi Method involves getting individual opinions from a group of experts about when a particular event or innovation will occur, then feeding back the resultant information to the group, giving each a chance to refine and/or defend his contribution. After several iterations, the findings are then presented as the group consensus. The assumption is that this method will make possible utilization of the best known input to a set of common problems. It is interesting to note that Delphi predictions usually err on the conservative side. Application of this process might be of value in clarifying our understanding of where we are and where we are going as American families.

This review paper has sought to explain where we are and how we got here, vis a vis experimental family forms. It has identified the social imperative toward ever greater individualism; the biological, economic, demographic, and communication revolutions; and the indecision of the modernists' sexual doctrine as the reasons why we are today and will be increasingly in the future concerned about experimental family forms. In spite of our concern, very few studies have been published to date that provide hard data about experimental family forms. These were reviewed, together with several paradigms that have sought to explain various aspects of the phenomenon.

Much remains to be done. There has not yet been a single national probability sample research project funded in this area. Several have been proposed, but funding from federal agencies has been parsimonious. We need to study the connection between experimental family forms and the law. We need to relate the experimental family form to social change. We need to collect census data that clearly reflects the number of citizens living in multiadult households or cohabitating. We need to extend the preliminary work relating specific experimental family forms with specific personality types. So far, this work indicates some very interesting patterns but tells us nothing about causality.

We are in need of longitudinal studies of persons who have been identified as having participated in *any* experimental family form. Just as the same people show up at many different humanistic psychology programs such as encounter, est, primal therapy, and the like, it would appear that those who are interested in experimental family forms move from group to group until they find the right group, if indeed they ever do.

We need control studies of people practicing sexually open marriage, people practicing group marriage, and people living in multiadult households. A dollars-and-cents evaluation of the benefits of the multiadult household as compared to a control group with the same income would also be revealing. It is time to stop doing descriptive research and start working on the tough problems of comparing the efficacy of experimental family forms with the more common variations detailed in the first section of this review.

NOTES

[1] Bureau of Labor Statistics, *News release*, USDL 77–191 (March 8, 1977).

[2] Bureau of the Census, *Population characteristics* Series P-20, No. 306 (January 1977).

[3] S. F. Alam, "Middle class communities" (Paper presented at the annual meeting of the National Council on Family Relations, St. Louis, October 1974).

[4] J. Smith, and J. Smith, "Consenting adults: An exploratory study of the sexual freedom movement" (Book in preparation, 1977).

REFERENCES

Bartel, G. 1971. *Group sex.* New York: Wyden.

Cogswell, B. E., and M. B. Sussman. 1972. Changing family and marriage forms: Complications for human service systems. *Family Coordinator* 21 (4): 505–16.

Constantine, L. L., and J. M. Constantine. 1973. *Group marriage.* New York: Macmillan.

Etzioni, A. 1977. Science and the future of the family. *Science* 196 (4289): 487.

Francoeur, R. T. 1972. *Eve's new rib.* New York: Dell.

Gilmartin, B. G. 1975. That swinging couple down the block. *Psychology Today* 8 (9): 54–58.

Glick, P. C. 1977. Updating the life cycle of the family. *Journal of Marriage and the Family* 39 (1): 5–13.

Kagan, J. 1977. The child in the family. *Daedalus* 106 (2): 33–56.

Kanter, R., D. Jaffe, and K. Weisberg. 1975. Coupling, parenting, and the presence of others: Intimate relationships in communal households. *Family Coordinator* 24 (4): 433–52.

Knapp, J. 1976. An exploratory study of seventeen sexually open marriages. *Journal of Sex Research* 12 (3): 206–19.

Knapp, J., and R. Whitehurst. 1977. Sexually open marriage and relationships: Issues an prospects. In R. Libby and R. Whitehurst (eds.), *Marriage and alternatives*, pp. 147–60. Glenview, Ill.: Scott, Foresman.

Libby, R. 1977. Creative singlehood as a sexual lifestyle: Beyond marriage as a rite of passage. In R. Libby and R. Whitehurst (eds.), *Marriage and alternatives*. Glenview, Ill.: Scott, Foresman.

Linstone, H., and M. Turoff. 1975. *The Delphi method*. Reading, Mass.: Addison-Wesley.

Murdock, G. 1949. *Social structure*. New York: Macmillan.

Palson, C., and R. Palson. 1972. Swinging in wedlock. *Society* 9 (4): 28–37.

Ramey, J. 1972. Emerging patterns of innovative behavior in marriage. *Family Coordinator* 21 (4): 435–56.

Ramey, J. 1975. Intimate groups and networks: Frequent consequence of sexually open marriage. *Family Coordinator* 24 (4): 515–30.

Ramey, J. 1976. *Intimate friendships*. Englewood Cliffs, N.J.: Prentice-Hall.

Ramey, J. 1977. Sexual behavior and alternative lifestyles. *Society* 14 (3).

Robinson, P. 1976. *The modernization of sex*. New York: Harper and Row.

Rossi, A. 1977. A biosocial perspective on parenting. *Daedalus* 106 (2): 1–32.

Symonds, C. 1971. Sexual mate swapping and the swingers. *Marriage Counseling Quarterly* 6: 1–12.

The Sentinel. (Winston-Salem, N. C.). 1977. July 22, p. 31.

Westoff, C. F. 1976. Trends in contraceptive practice: 1965–1973. *Family Planning Perspectives* 8 (2): 54–57.

Whitehurst, R. 1977. Changing ground rules and emerging life-styles. In R. Libby & R. Whitehurst (eds.), *Marriage and alternatives*. Glenview, Ill.: Scott, Foresman.

Zablocki, B. 1977. *Alienation and investment in the urban commune*. New York: Center for Policy Research.

49 *Gay Male and Lesbian Relationships*

Joseph Harry

STUDY QUESTIONS

1. What is the butch/femme hypothesis and its reality?

2. What is the truth concerning gay and lesbian parents?

A decade review of the literature on lesbian and gay couples and family relationships is particularly appropriate since it is only within the last 10 years that there has been reported research on the topic.

GAY COUPLES

The Butch/Femme Hypothesis

Tripp (1975: 152) has observed that persons unfamiliar with gay male relationships often tend to heterosexualize them by viewing one partner as masculine (i.e., doing the masculine household chores, being dominant in sexual activities and decision making, and financially supporting the partner) and the other as engaging in complementary feminine activities. However, the one thing that the literature most clearly shows about intimate gay relationships is that they infrequently approximate this version of husband and wife roles. Bell and Weinberg (1978: 323–325) found specialization in sex-typed tasks to occur in fewer than 10 percent of their 686 interviews of gay male respondents in San Francisco. Westwood (1960: 119), in a study of 127 English homosexuals, reported little evidence that masculine and feminine gay men were mutually attracted to each other and found that the large majority preferred masculine

Source: Joseph Harry, "Gay Male and Lesbian Relationships." In *Contemporary Families and Alternative Life Styles*, E.D. Macklin and R.H. Rubin (eds.). Copyright 1983 by Sage Publications, Inc. Reprinted by permission of Sage Publications, Inc.

partners. Similarly, Saghir and Robins (1973: 74–75), in a study of 89 homosexual males, found that few gay couples pattern their relationships according to a traditional husband/wife model. Although a few gays may organize their relationships in a "butch/femme" manner, the literature strongly indicates that gay relationships are more likely to be patterned after a "best friends/roommates" model than after a heterosexual sex role model. . . .

Harry and DeVall (1978b: 104–108) analyzed preferences among 241 Detroit gay men for erotic techniques, using questions that did not oblige respondents to make forced choices. Exploring preferences for the activities of oral insertee, oral insertor, and anal insertee, and anal insertor, they found that the most popular combination was a liking for all of these activities, again indicating greater flexibility than a simple insertee/insertor dichotomy would suggest. When respondents were asked, "If I lived with a lover (or do live with), I would probably make most of the decisions" (Harry and DeVall, 1978b: 112), responses to this item showed no significant association with the four sexual techniques. However, among those who preferred inegalitarian forms of decision making, the associations among the four sexual techniques were consistent with the butch/femme hypothesis. It thus seems that the butch/femme hypothesis, while not completely lacking in empirical support, may hold only for those gay men who bring expectations or values of inegalitarianism to a relationship. Further evidence that the butch/femme hypothesis may hold only for a small minority of gay relationships is reflected in findings from Harry's (1982a: 213) study of 1556 gay men in Chicago who responded by mailback questionnaire. Gay men who rated their hypothetical preferred erotic partners as "very masculine" were about 40 percent more likely to agree that "it is very important for me to look masculine." Thus masculinity when valued in the self appears to be also valued in erotic partners. Since masculinity of appearance is positively evaluated by many gay men, it is suggested that a butch/butch pattern may be the more dominant pattern.

Equality in Relationships

Peplau and her associates (Peplau, 1981; Peplau and Cochran, 1981) have compared the values and relationship expectations of 128 gay men, 127 lesbians, and 130 unmarried heterosexual men and women. Of their gay male respondents 92 percent said that both partners to a relationship should "have exactly equal say," although only 37 percent of the currently coupled reported that their relationship was exactly equal. Peplau (1981) found that, regardless of sexual orientation, women were somewhat more likely than men to value equality, emotional expressiveness, and similarity of attitudes between partners. Peplau concluded that gender of respondent rather than sexual orientation was the major predictor of differences in relationship values, with the exception that heterosexuals were somewhat more likely than homosexuals to value sexual exclusivity than gays. Only 13 percent of the coupled lesbians versus 54 percent of the coupled gays had been sexually nonexclusive in the preceding six months.

Peplau and Cochran (1981) also indicate that a large majority of persons value equality in relationships regardless of sex or sexual orientation, although in practice there often may be departures from equality. A common reason for departure from equality in relationships is differential access to resources outside of the relationship (Blood and Wolfe, 1960: 29–30). This also seems to hold in gay relationships, since it has been found that income differences between gay partners are associated with self-reported differences in decision making (Harry and DeVall, 1978b: 99). However, in gay and lesbian relationships such incomes differences seem to be considerably less than in the case of heterosexual couples. Housepersons in gay relationships are quite rare, and most couples are dual-worker, dual-career units. Harry (1979; 1982b) found that only 1 percent of his Detroit gay respondents and none of his Chicago respondents were economically supported by another man. Since the analogue of a housewife is unusual among gay couples, and typically both parties work, the economic basis for inequality in relationships is virtually absent. Income differentials in gay or lesbian relationships are also reduced due to the fact that both parties are of the same sex and hence likely to be subject to the same degree of sex discrimination in jobs and income. In contrast, working wives in heterosexual couples are likely to earn considerably less than their husbands and hence are more likely to be somewhat economically dependent on them. These two factors—the general absence of housepersons and the approximate similarity of incomes—suggest that gay relationships often may be more egalitarian than heterosexual ones.

A major source of potential inequality in relationships is age difference between partners. Blood (1972: 526) has reported that older partners in heterosexual relationships tend to be dominant in decision making, although the age difference must be fairly large, e.g., 10 or more years, to have an effect. Harry (1982a: 209) also reports that older partners in both past and present gay relationships say they were more likely to make the decisions in the relationship. He summarizes, (1982a: 209): "If a gay relationship is inegalitarian in decision making, it is likely to be one between age-different persons, although age difference predict less well to decision making."

Age-Related Characteristics

The extant data indicate that there is more variability in the age difference between gay partners than among heterosexual couples. While the age difference between heterosexual partners is approximately two years, Harry (1982b) reported the median age difference between gay male partners to be 4.9 years. (This corrects his earlier, erroneously reported figure of zero years; Harry, 1979.) Cotton (1972) also reported age differences between gay partners in a majority of his 36 gay men, but did not indicate the extent of the age difference. Bell and Weinberg (1978: 319) found an age difference of six or more years in 49 percent of their coupled gay male respondents. While Blood (1972: 523) found that 58 percent of his married heterosexual respondents were within three years of their spouses' age, the comparable statistic from Harry's Chicago data is 36 percent among gay partners.

The greater variability of age differences among gay partners may arise for two reasons. First, there are fairly widely agreed upon norms concerning preferred age differences for heterosexual couples while there are no corresponding norms for gay couples. Second, age segregation in institutions containing large percentages of young heterosexuals in their marrying years (e.g., universities and leisure organizations) may be greater than in the gay world. While the gay world is often young and youth oriented and does display tendencies toward age segregation of settings (Gagnon and Simon, 1973: 149–150; Harry and DeVall, 1978a; Harry, 1974), it does not seem to be as greatly divided into settings for the young and unmarried versus those for the older and married as among heterosexuals. For these reasons, there may be greater leisure-time interaction between age-different partners, and hence greater age differences in subsequent couplings, in the gay world than in the heterosexual world.

Being in a coupled state—whether the couple lives together or not—seems curvilinearly related to age among gay men. Based on their Detroit data, Harry and DeVall (1978b: 85) reported that 35 percent of gay men 18 to 29 years of age had been currently coupled for at least a year; 46 percent of those 30 to 39 and 39 percent of those 40 and older had been coupled for a year. Similar findings were reported from his Chicago data (1982a: 221), with 47 percent of those under 24 years of age being currently coupled, approximately 55 percent of those aged 25 to 40, 44 percent of those aged 41 to 54, and 32 percent of those 55 and older. The higher percentages of currently coupled found in the Chicago data are likely due to the fact that the question for the Detroit data required that the respondent had been going with a partner for at least a year. Saghir and Robins (1973: 56–57) reported a similar curvilinear association between age and current involvement with another man. Bell and Weinberg (1978: 282) found no significant association between age and current involvement, although their measure of association would not have detected a curvilinear association. When respondents are asked whether they were *currently involved with another man*, the percentages were as follows: 51 percent (Harry, 1982a: 221), 59 percent in West Germany (Schafer, 1977), 41 percent (Peplau and Cochran, 1981); *currently involved for at least one year*: 32 percent (Westwood, 1960: 114–115), 40 percent (Harry and DeVall, 1978b: 85); *currently living with a lover:* 31 percent (Robinson et al., 1982); *currently living with a lover among those over* 40: 43 percent (Berger, 1980). The studies that at any given time 40 to 50 percent of gay men are currently involved with someone else, and that being involved is curvilinearly related to age with a peak at about 40 years of age.

While the literature is in substantial agreement on the extent to which gay men may be currently coupled and on the relationship between being coupled and age, one must raise the question of the extent to which these findings may be artifacts of sampling. The principal places from which gay men have been sampled are gay bars, gay organizations, and gay friendship networks (Weinberg and Williams, 1974; Bell and Weinberg, 1978; Harry and DeVall, 1978b; Harry 1982a). Since older gay men are less likely to attend gay bars and clubs (Weinberg and Williams, 1974; 314), they are less likely to be included in the studies of gay men. Also, if one assumes that the age distribution of gay men should approximate that of heterosexual men, it is clear that all of the studies have systematically underrepresented the older age groups. If, as the data suggest, those over 50 are less likely to be coupled, the extent of coupledness may be overestimated in the published data while, if the coupled avoid the typical settings where gay men are sampled, the published data may have underestimated the extent of coupledness.

To explore these contradictory possibilities, the relationship between being currently coupled and going to gay bars, being a member of a gay organization, and having mostly gay friends was explored by Harry in a sample of 1556 gay men located in a variety of settings in the Chicago area (see Harry, 1982a, for a description of sampling procedures). Findings from mailback questionnaires indicated that men currently involved with another man were somewhat less likely to attend gay bars once or more a week (46 percent versus 56 percent) and somewhat more likely to have all or mostly gay friends (54 percent versus 44 percent); they did not differ from the uncoupled on membership in gay organizations. Among the currently coupled, those in relationships of greater duration were less likely to go to gay bars. Of those in relationships of less than a year duration, 57 percent went to gay bars once or more a week; 43 percent of those in relationships of one year to less than five years duration and 35 percent of those in relationships of five or more years duration went to gay bars once or more a week. The Chicago data also show that the curvilinear relationship between age and being coupled is largely confined to those who go to gay bars less than once a week.

The implications of these data appear to be that: (1) The studies of gay men may have underrepresented the frequency of long-term relationships because men in such relationships are less likely to go to bars, older men are less likely to go to bars, and, among the coupled, it is the older who are more likely to be in long-term relationships. (Among the coupled, the percentage who are in relationships of five or more years duration rises from 4 percent of those under 25 years of age to 60 percent of those 45 and over.) (2) The strength of the curvilinear relationship between being coupled and age has been somewhat underestimated in the literature because that relationship is largely confined to the less frequent bar goers, and such men are less likely to be included in surveys. (3) The extent of coupledness among gay men remains uncertain because, although the coupled and especially the long-term coupled are less likely to go to gay bars, the older are both less likely to go to bars and are less likely to be coupled. It is hoped that someday these questions may be answered through the inclusion of a question on sexual orientation in general probability surveys.

Sexual Exclusivity

The literature clearly shows that gay male relationships are considerably less sexually exclusive then heterosexual ones or lesbian relationships. Peplau (1981) found that 46 percent of her coupled gay males had been sexually exclusive during the last six months compared to 87 percent of the lesbian counterparts. Schafer (1977) reported similar findings when comparing West

German gay and lesbian couples. Harry and DeVall (1978b: 88) found that a quarter of their coupled gay males had been exclusive during the last year, a finding that supports figures reported by Saghir and Robins (1973: 57). Sexual exclusivity has been found to be negatively related to the duration of a relationship. Harry and DeVall (1978b: 92) found that 46 percent of their coupled gay men in relationships of less than three years duration had been exclusive during the last year versus 16 percent of those in longer-term relationships. The Chicago data replicate this finding and show complete exclusivity to have been the case for 39 percent of persons in relationships of one to less than five year's duration, and 9 percent of those in relationships of five or more years duration. Apparently, exclusivity is more common during the honeymoon stage of gay relationships.

Hoffman (1968: 154–177) has interpreted the common nonexclusivity of gay relationships as a major problem, often leading to jealousy and termination of relationships. However, Warren (1974: 72–76) has suggested that exclusivity may be nonnormative and problematic principally in the heterosexual community. She has suggested that, although it may be characteristic of the honeymoon stage of gay relationships, nonexclusivity often becomes accepted as the most common expectation for "mature" relationships and represents an adjustment to reality. Harry and DeVall (1978b: 91–92) found support for Warren's hypothesis in that in longer-term relationships there was greater agreement between partners on *either* fidelity or infidelity, while disagreement decreased with length of relationships. Couples in relationships of three or more years duration were divided into three roughly equal groups; those who were agreed on exclusiveness, those who agreed on nonexclusiveness, and those who disagreed. It would seem that since gay couple relationships lack the conventional cultural guidelines that govern heterosexual relationships, they develop in more diverse directions and exclusivity may be either approved or disapproved. Since Peplau (1981) found that sexually exclusive coupled gay men did not differ from nonexclusives on measures of relationship intimacy or satisfaction, both of these adaptations seem workable.

Perhaps the major problem encountered by gay couples is reaching an agreement regarding exclusivity. Silverstein (1981:140) has suggested that "at some point in the life of every gay couple, the monogamy battle will be fought." Dividing gay men into "excitement seekers" and "home builders" (1981: 113–138), he suggests that gay relationships are more workable when both parties to a relationship are of the same type, since their eventual choice of lifestyle is more likely to flow from their personal predispositions than from the imposition of the heterosexual cultural norm of monogamy. An emphasis on exclusivity by one partner when paired with a partner seeking excitement may be perceived to be too constraining to the latter, who would prefer an open relationship. Some suggestive data consistent with Silverstein's hypothesis have been reported by Harry and Lovely (1979), who found that those who formerly had been coupled for at least a year—"the divorced"—were more likely to favor sexual exclusivity than the currently coupled or the single, thus suggesting that their emphasis on exclusivity may have been a barrier in their own couple-forming attempts. This group was also the only group for which there was a significant association between intimacy scores and the item "gay lovers should be completely faithful to each other." Thus it may be that an emphasis on exclusivity, possibly borrowed from the heterosexual marriage model, may interfere with the relationships of gay men.

GAY FATHERS

Because a percentage of gays have been heterosexually married, many gay men are also fathers. The percentages of gays who have ever married, as reported in the literature, are: 25 percent (Dank, 1972); 18 percent (Saghir and Robins, 1973:11); 17 percent (Weinberg and Williams, 1974: 128); 20 percent (Harry and DeVall's Detroit data); 19 percent (Bell and Weinberg, 1978: 374); 16 percent (Harry, 1982a: 42); 14 percent (Robinson et al., 1982). Thus it is safe to say that about 20 percent of gay men have been heterosexually married. Of these marriages, about half (52 percent) resulted in children (Bell and Weinberg, 1978: 391); a similar percentage (56 percent) was found for lesbians who have been married (Bell and Weinberg, 1978: 391). In a few cases children have been adopted by gay or lesbian couples through marginally legitimate channels (Miller, 1979).

The reasons that gay men have married include a lack of awareness of their own homosexuality, a belief that their homosexuality was a peripheral part of their lives, or an assumption that marriage would help them overcome their homosexuality (Dank, 1972). In a third of the cases it appears that the spouse was aware of the gay man's homosexuality before the marriage but believed that the marriage would eliminate the husband's homosexuality (Bell and Weinberg, 1978: 386). The marriages, which lasted three or four years (Bell and Weinberg, 1978: 388), were typically full of problems, especially sexual problems. In over half of the cases the men fantasized about other men during sexual relations with the wife (Bell and Weinberg, 1978: 384). The majority of gay men who either have been or currently are married tend to give negative descriptions of these marriages (Ross, 1971). Reporting on thirteen currently married gay men, Ross (1971) found many of these marriages filled with resentment and bitterness over the infrequency of sexual relations, the nonexclusivity of the husband due to his search for male sexual partners, and the feeling that the husband had deceived the wife at time of marriage.

During the course of the marriage, as the husband's need for sexual fulfillment through sex with other men became more conscious and pressing, most resorted for a period to furtive sexual encounters in a variety of places. Many such encounters are described in Humphrey's classic study, *Tearoom Trade* (1970). Of the men who had had sex in restrooms, 54 percent were heterosexually married (1970: 112). This period of their lives was one in which the husbands engaged in quick sex at the sleazy periphery of the gay world, hated themselves for doing it, and lied to their wives about where they had been and what they had been doing. Men in occupations permitting greater freedom in their movements and control over their time commitments appear to have managed this phase with less worry and more grace. Movement from this lifestyle to an acceptance of one's own homosexuality, becoming socially active in the gay world, and, usually, getting a divorce, was motivated principally by coming to see gay men and homosexuality in a more positive light and falling in love with another man (Miller, 1978).

All of the forty gay fathers interviewed by Miller (1979) feared disclosure of their homosexuality to their children and most feared disclosure to their wives. When they did disclose to their wives, the wives, after a period of initial shock, sometimes agreed to arrangements that permitted the marriage to continue while allowing the husband to pursue homosexual activities outside of the marriage (Bozett, 1981). These included allowing a "night out with the boys," understanding that the husband would only have sex with other men when in other cities, and an occasional *menage à trois* (Bozett, 1981; Ross, 1971). While Bozett (1981), reporting on eighteen gay fathers, has described these arrangements as mutually consensual "permission giving," they also appear to have been last-minute attempts to keep a marriage that was near collapse together. Virtually all of the gay fathers studied stated that the principal reason they remained in their marriages as long as they did was because they loved their children (Miller, 1979; Bozett, 1980).

Those gay fathers who disclosed to their children, either before or after a divorce, reported that, after the initial surprise, the children generally responded quite acceptingly. Although the numbers involved in the various studies are small, there is the suggestion that acceptance by female children is more forthcoming than by male children. Both Miller (1978) and Bozett (1980) report that relationships with children tended to improve after disclosure. "Children who showed the greatest acceptance were those who, prior to full disclosure, were gradually introduced by their parents to homosexuality through meeting gay family friends, reading about it, and discussing the topic informally with parents" (Miller, 1979).

While a number of gay men are fathers, the large majority of these fathers do not retain custody of the children at the time of divorce. This arises because the couple often decides that the children are to live with the mother, the courts have traditionally preferred to give custody to the mother, and, when custody is contested and the father's sexual orientation is an issue in the case, gay fathers rarely win custody (Maddox, 1982). In contested custody cases where a parent's sexual orientation is an issue, lesbian mothers win in about 15 percent of the cases with gay fathers winning less frequently. Indeed, the courts are so averse to giving custody to gay fathers that the contested issue is usually visiting rights while for lesbian mothers the issue is usually custody (Hitchens, 1980).

Another way in which gay men sometimes become fathers is through becoming foster fathers. During the 1970s, there arose a number of gay foster homes in some large cities (New York Times, May 7, 1974: 47). Gay adolescents who had either run away from home or been thrown out by parents after learning of the child's homosexuality have been occasionally placed with gay male couples. Of course, the foster parents have been carefully screened to eliminate the inappropriately motivated. Such placements, typically done by private agencies, often encounter a number of legal problems since the natural parents usually retain legal custody. Such placements seem a promising development since gay adolescents often do not fare well in institutions for juveniles or in heterosexual foster homes. For some young gays the relationship with the gay foster father may be the first positive relationship with an adult male in their life.

LESBIAN COUPLES

Lesbian partners are somewhat more likely to live together than are gay male partners (Bell and Weinberg, 1978: 319; Schafer, 1977; Cotton, 1975) and to value the importance of living together (Bell and Weinberg, 1978: 322). Approximately three-quarters of lesbian couples live together compared with somewhat more than half of all gay male couples. Lesbian couples are also more likely to be sexually exclusive than are gay couples (Peplau et al., 1978; Peplau, 1981; Cotton, 1975). Exclusivity seems to be characteristic of 75 to 85 percent of the cases. The differences in degree of exclusivity between lesbians and gay men have been attributed by Simon and Gagnon to their respective gender role socialization and are said to parallel the differences in exclusivity among heterosexual males and females (Kinsey et al., 1948: 585; Hunt, 1974: 257–258; Kinsey et al., 1953: 435–438). Males are socialized to engage in sexual behaviors both with and without affection while women are more expected to combine the two. As a result, when two men enter a partnership, nonexclusiveness can be expected, while when two women enter a relationship, exclusiveness could be expected. Aside from exclusivity, men and women do not seem to differ in the values, e.g., romanticism, that they bring to a relationship (Peplau, 1981). Laner (1977) reported great similarity among student samples of gay men, lesbians, heterosexual men, and heterosexual women in what they expect in a partner. The great majority (89 to 92 percent) of all four groups wanted a permanent partner with little difference among groups. It thus seems that the principal sex difference is not in relationship values but in how sexuality is combined with those values.

The butch/femme hypothesis has also been applied to lesbian couples (Jensen, 1974). While a small minority of lesbian couples do play gender roles, role playing is relatively rare (Tanner, 1978: 99–101; Ponse, 1978: 114–116; Wolf, 1979: 49–43). The division of household tasks is typically done by turns or by talent and both parties to the relationship are usually employed. Both Ponse and Wolf report that role playing seems to have been more common in the 1950s and 1960s and is somewhat more common among older lesbian couples. This seems supported by the one study that found gender-typed division of household tasks in the large majority of the 17 couples studied (Jensen, 1974). It should be noted that these seventeen couples were interviewed in the mid-1960s and the majority were Mormons living in Salt Lake City and Denver, highly gender-conservative environments.

Role playing as a relationship style has become quite unpopular in lesbian circles, probably due to the fact that a large percentage of lesbian women became affiliated with the women's movement of the late 1960s and the 1970s

(Wolf, 1979: 85). One goal of the lesbian/feminist movement has been to create identities as women rather than in relationship to men. Toward this end, one fairly large segment of the lesbian world advocates and practices separatism from men. Such separatism sometimes extends to advocating that lesbian mothers should give up their male children to the father, although the voluntary practice of this is rare (Wolf, 1979: 156–158). The rise of the women's movement and of feminist theory has had the effect of creating a quite varied spectrum of lesbian circles, ranging from traditional and often closeted role players on the "right" to lesbian/feminists in the "center" to lesbian/feminist/separatists on the "left." At the left may be found communal households containing one to three pairs of lovers plus a few single women (Wolf, 1979: 98–101). Household boundaries tend to coincide with political boundaries and having the proper political credentials may be a condition for admission to a household.

While gay couples tend to interact within such gay institutions as the gay bar, the gay church, and gay organizations, lesbian couples tend to live within social networks of lesbians, although there is some overlap between the gay world and that of lesbians (Ponse, 1978: 89–90; Tanner, 1978: 66–70). The lesbian bar plays a much smaller role in the world of lesbians than does the gay bar in the gay world (Tanner, 1978: 67–68). The principal forms of socializing in the lesbian world include inviting other lesbian couples to one's home, attendance at lesbian coffee houses and theater, and participation in women's organizations. The lesbian bar seems somewhat more significant in the lives of unattached women (Tanner, 1978: 67; Cotton, 1975), although some lesbians disparage lesbian bars as places for socializing because of the "role-playing, fighting, or drug use" that may occur there (Chafetz et al., 1974). Since roughly three quarters of lesbians are currently coupled compared to 40 to 50 percent of gay men (Bell and Weinberg, 1978: 318; Schafer, 1977; Harry and DeVall, 1978b: 85; Peplau and Amaro, 1982), the social world of lesbians tends to be a world of couples whereas the world of gay men is one of singles *and* couples.

Lesbians tend to meet their partners through lesbian friendship networks (Tanner, 1978: 66–71). There subsequently follows a period of courtship lasting from one to nine months. In contrast, the courtship period for gay men is considerably truncated and may be preceded by sexual relations. Thus among lesbians a sexual relationship usually arises out of a developing affectional relationship while among gay men affection may develop out of a sexual relationship.

The literature is inconsistent regarding whether lesbian or gay relationships last longer. While (Schafer (1977) found that lesbian relationships last longer than gay ones, Bell and Weinberg (1978: 320) reported that 38 percent of their currently coupled gay men were in relationships of four or more years duration compared with 30 percent of the comparable lesbian respondents. Saghir and Robins (1973: 225) found no difference in the length of gay and lesbian relationships. For both groups, the average length of a relationship appears to be approximately two to three years (Peplau and Amaro, 1982). It appears that the gender difference in relationship longevity has been exaggerated and that a principal difference between the two groups is in the amount of one's life that is spent in relationships (i.e., the between-partner time spent outside of relationships seems to be shorter for women). This interpretation is supported by Bell and Weinberg's (1978: 315) finding that among lesbians romantic involvement with another woman was the most commonly mentioned reason for the breakup of their first affair, while this reason was fourth among gay men (29 percent versus 14 percent). Hence it seems that more lesbians go directly from one relationship to another. It should be noted that the studies of lesbian couples, even more so than for gay couples, have been largely based on samples of persons in their twenties and thirties and that the duration of lesbian relationships in general may be greater than is estimated from these studies.

Satisfaction in lesbian relationships has been found to be positively associated with equality in decision making (Peplau et al., 1982). This also seems to hold for gay relationships. Of the currently involved gay men studied by Harry (1982a), 72 percent of those who said that decisions were made equally reported that they and their partner got along "very well," compared to 50 percent of those who said that they made the decisions and 43 percent of those who said that the partner made the decisions. Being low in decision-making power in lesbian relationships is, in turn, associated with having less education and less income than one's partner (Caldwell and Peplau, 1982). Relationship satisfaction has also been found to correlate strongly ($r = +.63$) with the expectation that the current lesbian relationship would continue for another five years and with equality of emotional involvement (Peplau et al., 1982). Factors negatively associated with relationship satisfaction include differences in interests, conflicting attitudes about sex, conflicting attitudes about exclusivity, and desire for independence (Peplau et al., 1982). No significant associations were found between satisfaction and scores on a Sex-Role Traditionalism Scale, age, number of previous relationships, education, and the extent of closetedness. While satisfaction was not found to be related to closetedness, it would be useful to explore whether differences in closetedness between partners may create problems for a couple. Since few lesbians or gay men are totally uncloseted toward all the heterosexuals with whom they may interact, differing degrees of closetedness could be expected to create tensions in a relationship.

In recent years there appear to have been some changes in lesbian relationships induced by the women's movement. As an expression of identification with women, a number of bisexual or heterosexual women have come to have affairs with lesbian women (Ponse, 1978: 122–124). Sometimes referred to as "political lesbians," these women are often distrusted in lesbian circles because there is always the chance that the political lesbian may end a relationship and return to men or to their husbands. "Political gay men" seem unheard of, although a few might exist. Another effect of the women's movement has been some decline in sexual exclusivity and an increase in "cruising," i.e., the search for brief sexual encounters at lesbian bars and by younger lesbians (Lewis, 1979: 178–180). Since much feminist writing is directed toward the elimination of gender roles and the traditionally structured inegalitarian heterosexual family, this sometimes is extended in lesbian writing to include the elimination of romanticism and monogamy (Lewis, 1979: 168–171), customs that are seen to hold women in emotional dependency. Among lesbians, acceptance of nonexclusivity in relationships tends to be associated with less traditional attitudes toward women (Peplau et al., 1978). It thus appears that the nonexclusivity and the cruising found among gay men have made an appearance on the lesbian scene.

LESBIAN MOTHERS

Lesbian households are considerably more likely to contain children than are gay households. This is largely due to the fact that a higher percentage of lesbians have been heterosexually married: approximately one-fifth of gay men have been married versus one-third of lesbians (Bell and Weinberg, 1978: 374; Saghir and Robins, 1973: 255; Cotton, 1975; Schafer, 1977). Also contributing to the greater presence of children in lesbian households is the tradition of the courts awarding custody to the mother *as long as the mother's homosexuality is not an issue in the divorce* (Maddox, 1982). A further reason for the greater presence of children is that lesbians tend to "come out" a few years later than gay men. While gay men usually come out during late adolescence at approximately 18 or 19 years of age (Dank, 1971; Harry and DeVall, 1978b: 65; Saghir and Robins, 1973: 67), lesbians do so during their early 20s (Schafer, 1977; Saghir and Robins, 1973: 232). One effect of this is that lesbians are at risk of marriage for a longer time than are gay men, particularly at the age when a large percentage of their heterosexual peers are getting married.

Courts give two primary reasons for their reluctance to grant custody or even visiting rights to lesbian mothers and gay fathers. First is the possibility that the children might become homosexual if raised in a lesbian or gay household. The extant data show that there is little ground for this concern. Green (1978) examined the erotic fantasies of 37 children raised in lesbian, gay male, and transsexual households and found all of the children, with one possible exception, to be heterosexual. Hoffer (1981) examined the toy preferences of 20 children of lesbian mothers and 20 children of heterosexual mothers and found no differences between the two groups of children. (Toy preferences seem to be the best childhood indicator of future adult gender atypicality (Green, 1976; Bell et al., 1981: 75–76, 147; Whitam, 1980). From the reports of 40 gay fathers on their 21 sons and 27 daughters who were old enough for their sexual orientations to be assessed, it was found that one of the sons and three of the daughters were homosexual (Miller, 1979). Hotvedt and Mandel (1982) compared the 56 children of 50 lesbian mothers with the 48 children of 40 heterosexual single mothers while controlling on ages of mother and children, race, income, time since separation, education, and religion. For boys, there was no difference in toy preferences, with boys of both groups consistently choosing masculine toys. The daughters of lesbian mothers chose somewhat less feminine toys than did the daughters of heterosexual mothers, but they did not choose masculine ones. These data suggest no disproportionate amount of homosexuality among the children of homosexual parents, although more research clearly needs to be done.

The second concern of the courts is that the children of homosexual parents will be harrassed by others because of their parents. Children in three of the thirteen families studied by Green (1978) had been teased by other children, e.g., "Your mother is a lezzie," "Your mother is a queer," "homoson." However, Bruce Voeller, former president of the National Gay Task Force and a person whose homosexuality has been quite visible through appearances on numerous television shows, reported that his children who live with him have never been teased about their father (Voeller and Walters, 1978). Of the eighteen gay fathers studied by Bozett (1980), one reported that his child had been teased. Hotvedt and Mandel (1982) reported from interviews with the children of lesbian and heterosexual single mothers that the two groups of children did not differ in their popularity with other children of either sex. Interviews with the mothers on the children's popularity also showed no differences.

Like gay fathers, lesbian mothers often advise their children to be guarded in providing information about the home life to neighbors and school teachers (Wolf, 1979: 153). It appears that in those cases in which a gay father has disclosed his gayness to a child a common tactic has been for the father to suggest that the child practice discretion (Bozett, 1980). For example, the father's live-in lover is referred to as an "uncle" in the presence of other children. The evidence suggests that, while the lives of the children of gay and lesbian parents are not problem free, harrassment is not common and seems typically manageable.

Because of the court's strong propensity not to accord custody of children, and especially male children, to lesbian mothers, these mothers are often fearful of losing their children and attempt to conceal their homosexuality from ex-husbands, grandparents, welfare workers, landlords, neighbors, and school personnel (Pagelow, 1980). In a study of 20 lesbian and 23 nonlesbian single mothers, Pagelow (1980) reported that lesbian mothers may be somewhat more likely to live in houses rather than apartments since the former housing permits greater privacy. They were also more likely to be self-employed, thus permitting a greater measure of both privacy and freedom.

There has been some question about whether male children are out of place or unwelcome in lesbian circles. Hall (1978) described a situation in which persons planning a mother's day celebration for lesbians and their children questioned the appropriateness of allowing male children to participate and yet hesitated to exclude them. However, it seems that lesbian mothers are usually aware of the needs of their male children and are more likely than single heterosexual mothers to be concerned about providing adult male figures for their boys (Kirkpatrick et al., 1981). Nungesser (1980) reported that 80 percent of the male children of lesbian mothers had adult male figures involved in their lives, including a number of gay men. Some have suggested that lesbian mothers may, because of their relatively unique situations, bend over backwards to assure that male children have exposure to adults of both sexes. It does seem fairly clear that lesbian mothers in general attempt to raise their children in nonsexist ways and to bring them up without the constraints of traditional gender roles (Kirkpatrick et al., 1981: Wolf, 1979: 152).

Kirkpatrick et al., (1981) compared ten boys and ten girls living with lesbian mothers to a similar sample of boys and girls living with single heterosexual mothers and found no differences with regard to emotional disturbance, toy preferences, or gender identifications. While they did find a high level of problems in both groups of children, they attributed this to the fact that both groups had experienced parental divorces in recent years. As in the case of stepfamilies, children of lesbian mothers may require a period of adjusting to the mother's lover (Hall, 1978; Lewis, 1979: 120). The scanty literature suggests that most such children come to accept and love the mother's lover, although Lewis (1977) found in a study of 21 children of lesbian mothers that older adolescent boys reacted negatively to their mother's homosexuality.

FUTURE RESEARCH AND POLICY QUESTIONS

Although much remains to be explored, the studies do permit a few policy suggestions. Sometimes judges have imposed on a lesbian mother the condition that she can have custody only if she does not live with, or sometimes even associate with, her lover (Hall, 1978). This condition may do serious damage to the household functioning, since two-income and two-adult households typically have superior financial resources and more personpower for child care arrangements. Judges thereby condemn the household to poverty. Similarly, gay fathers have usually been denied custody and often visiting rights. Yet since the extant evidence negates the hypothesis that the father's sexual orientation will rub off on the children, and suggests that parent/child relations may improve once the father discloses to the child, such court actions seem both to deprive the child of a father and to tell the child that his or her father is bad.

Although there have been a number of attempts by gay and lesbian couples to obtain legal marriages, no court to date has recognized such unions (Rivera, 1979). The acquisition of legal marriages by gays and lesbians would bring with it the advantages of symbolic equality, spouse social security benefits, spouse health insurance benefits, lower car insurance, family membership in various organizations, and inheritance rights. In the case in which there are children in the lesbian or gay household, the lack of these benefits also accrues to these children. However, there are also disadvantages to the acquisition of legal marital status. The termination of the relationship would obligate the parties to undergo the bother and expense of legal and financial disentanglements. A legal marital status would also grant to the state a right to regulate relationships that are essentially private, and a major thrust of the gay/lesbian movement has been to get the state out of the bedroom.

Because of the limited research to date, many questions remain to be answered. If, as Peplau and Amaro (1982) suggest, lesbian relationships typically last approximately three years, they can be characterized by a pattern of serial monogamy. Since most children in lesbian households have already experienced a heterosexual divorce, what is the effect on the child of a subsequent series of homosexual divorces? Do male children in lesbian households feel comfortable living in social circles so heavily populated with women? Does the heterosexual model of monogamy and sexual exclusivity create problems when gay men attempt to pattern their relationships after it? Has the advent of gay/lesbian liberation had the effect of lowering the age at which homosexual persons come out and thus reduced the frequency with which homosexual persons attempt heterosexual marriages? It is hoped that as these questions and others are answered, counselors to lesbians and gays of the future will be able to give more accurate and useful information to their counselees and parents, and relatives of gays and lesbians will be able to relate to the latter in a more positive manner.

REFERENCES

Bell, A. and M. Weinberg (1978) Homosexualities. New York: Simon & Schuster.

——— and S. Hammersmith (1981) Sexual Preference. Bloomington: Indiana University Press.

Blood, R. (1972) The Family. New York: Macmillan.

——— and D. Wolfe (1960) Husbands and Wives. New York: Macmillan.

Bozett, F. (1981) "Gay fathers: evolution of the gay-father identity." American Journal of Orthopsychiatry 51: 552–559.

——— (1980) "Gay fathers: how and why they disclose their homosexuality to their children." Family Relations 29: 173–179.

Caldwell, M. and L. Peplau (1982) "The balance of power in lesbian relationships." Sex Roles.

Chafetz, J., P. Sampson, P. Beck, and J. West (1974) "A study of homosexual women." Social Work 19: 714–723.

Cotton, W. (1975) "Social and sexual relationships of lesbians." Journal of Sex Research 11: 139–148.

——— (1972) "Role playing substitutions among male homosexuals." Journal of Sex Research 8: 310–323.

Dank, B. (1972) "Why homosexuals marry women." Medical Aspects of Human Sexuality 6: 14–23.

——— (1971) "Coming out in the gay world." Psychiatry 34: 180–197.

Gagnon, J. and W. Simon (1973) Sexual Conduct. Chicago: Aldine.

Green, R. (1978) "Sexual identity of 37 children raised by homosexual or transsexual parents." American Journal of Psychiatry 135: 692–697.

——— (1976) "One hundred ten feminine and masculine boys." Archives of Sexual Behavior 5: 425–426.

Hall, M. (1978) "Lesbian families: cultural and clinical issues." Social Work 23: 380–385.

Harry, J. (1982a) Gay Children Grown Up: Gender Culture and Gender Deviance. New York: Praeger.

—— (1982b) "Decision making and age differences among gay couples." Journal of Homosexuality.

—— (1979) "The marital liaisons of gay men." Family Coordinator 28: 622–629.

—— (1974) "Urbanization and the gay life." Journal of Sex Research 10: 238–247.

—— and W. DeVall (1978a) "Age and sexual culture among homosexuality oriented males." Archives of Sexual Behavior 3: 199–209.

—— (1978b) The Social Organization of Gay Males. New York: Praeger.

Harry, J. and R. Lovely (1979) "Gay marriages and communities of sexual orientation." Alternative Lifestyles 2: 177–200.

Hitchens, D. (1980) "Social attitudes, legal standards, and personal trauma in child custody cases." Journal of Homosexuality 5: 89–95.

Hoffer, B. (1981) "Children's acquisition of sex-role behavior in lesbian-mother families." American Journal of Orthopsychiatry 51: 536–544.

Hoffman, M. (1968) The Gay World. New York: Bantam.

Hotvedt, M. and J. Mandel (1982) "Children of lesbian mothers," in J. Weinrich and B. Paul (eds.) Homosexuality: Social, Psychological, and Biological Issues. Beverly Hills, CA: Sage.

Humphreys, L. (1970) Tearoom Trade. Chicago: Aldine.

Hunt, M. (1974) Sexual Behavior in the 1970s. New York: Dell.

Jensen, M. (1974) "Sexual differentiation in female quasi-marital unions." Journal of Marriage and the Family 36: 360–367.

Kinsey, A., W., Pomeroy, and C. Martin (1948) Sexual Behavior in the Human Male. Philadelphia: W.B. Saunders.

—— and P. Gebhard (1953) Sexual Behavior in the Human Female. Philadelphia: W. B. Saunders.

Kirkpatrick, M., C. Smith, and R. Roy (1981) "Lesbian mothers and their children." American Journal of Orthopsychiatry 51: 545–551.

Laner, M. (1977) "Permanent partner priorities: gay and straight." Journal of Homosexuality 3: 21–39.

Lewis, K. (1977) "Lesbian mother survey results." Boston: Gay Community News (September 6): 7.

Lewis S. (1979) Sunday's Women. Boston: Beacon.

Maddox, B. (1982) "Homosexual parents." Psychology Today 16: 62–69.

Miller, B. (1979) "Unpromised paternity: the life-styles of gay fathers," pp. 240–252 in M. Levine (ed.) Gay Men. New York: Harper & Row.

—— (1978) "Adult sexual resocialization." Alternative Lifestyles 1: 207–232.

Nungesser, L. (1980) "Theoretical bases for research on the acquisition of social sex-roles by children of lesbian mothers." Journal of Homosexuality 5: 177–187.

Pagelow, M. (1980) "Heterosexual and lesbian single mothers." Journal of Homosexuality 5: 189–204.

Peplau, L.A. (1981) "What homosexuals want in relationships." Psychology Today 15: 28–38.

—— and H. Amaro (1982) "Understanding lesbian relationships," in J. Weinrich and W. Paul (eds.) Homosexuality: Social, Psychological, and Biological Issues. Beverly Hills, CA: Sage.

Peplau, L. A. and S. Cochran (1981) "Value orientations in the intimate relationships of gay men." Journal of Homosexuality 6: 1–19.

—— K. Rook, and C. Padesky (1978) "Loving women: attachment and autonomy in lesbian relationships." Journal of Social Issues 34: 7–27.

Peplau, L. A., M. Hamilton, and C. Padesky (1982) "Satisfaction in lesbian relationships." Journal of Homosexuality.

Ponse, B. (1978) Identities in the Lesbian World. Westport, CT: Greenwood.

Rivera, R. (1979) "Our straight-laced judges: the legal position of homosexual persons in the United States." Hastings Law Journal 30: 799–955.

Robinson, B., P. Skeen, C. Hobson, and M. Herrman (1982) "Gay men's and women's perceptions of early family life and their relationships with parents." Family Relations 31: 79–83.

Ross, L. (1971) "Mode of adjustment of married homosexuals." Social Problems 18: 385–393.

Saghir, M. and E. Robins (1973) Male and Female Homosexuality. Baltimore: Williams & Wilkins.

Schafer, S. (1977) "Sociosexual behavior in male and female homosexuals." Archives of Sexual Behavior 6: 355–364.

Silverstein, C. (1981) Man to Man. New York: William Morrow.

Simon, W., and J. Gagnon (1967) "Femininity in the heterosexual community." Social Problems 15: 212–221.

Tanner, D. (1978) The Lesbian Couple. Lexington, MA: D. C. Heath.

Tripp, C. A. (1975) The Homosexual Matrix. New York: Signet.

Voeller, B. and J. Walters (1978) "Gay Fathers." Family Coordinator 27: 149–157.

Warren, C. (1974) Identity and Community in the Gay World. New York: John Wiley.

Weinberg, M. and C. Williams (1974) Male Homosexuals. New York: Viking.

Westwood, G. (1960) A Minority. London: Longmans.

Whitam, F. (1980) "The prehomosexual male child in three societies: the United States, Guatamala, Brazil." Archives of Sexual Behavior 9: 87–99.

Wolf, D. (1979) The Lesbian Community. Berkeley: University of California Press.

13 *Transitions*

The subtitle of this anthology is *Coping with Change* and so, in reality, the topic of transitions has been a consistent theme throughout this anthology. Thus, the title of this chapter is a misnomer if it implies a theme not previously discussed. Its use here as a chapter title is to emphasize the major alterations from the dominant marital lifestyle to be discussed in this chapter: divorce, widowhood, and remarriage.

The way in which the large increase in the divorce rate is perceived depends on what role the marriage and family institution is expected to play. For those who see the nuclear family as the norm of society, the increased divorce rate is seen as an indicator of the breakdown of the social structure. For those who believe in the marriage vow of "until death do us part," the increased divorce rate is a sign of moral decay. However, those who see marriage as a personal choice for personal fulfillment regard the higher divorce rate as a sign that this goal is being accomplished (Schultz 1982). It is people's expectations, then, that define what is acceptable and desirable in marriage and these expectations, as noted in Chapter 1, are being changed toward an emphasis on self-fulfillment, personal happiness, personal growth, and personal sexual satisfaction. Add to this our immense, romantic expectations of marriage and our lack of preparation for it, and few are prepared for the conflicts which occur or how to resolve them. Perhaps, then, the divorce rate is high, not because marriage is so little regarded, but rather because we expect so much of it—affection, companionship, empathy, and self-actualization.

Factors influencing the rise in the divorce rate include:

a. the greater freedom promoted by industrialized, urban society;

b. more effective contraception;

c. value changes involving subjective choice of mate, acceptance of divorce, easier legal facilitation, greater social and economic independence for women, greater sexual equality, and greater religious tolerance for divorce; and

d. demographic factors such as smaller families and longer life span.

Some or all of these factors make divorce a viable option in the case of marriage deterioration. Whether it actually leads to such depends upon the costs of the relationship as measured against its rewards. However, there still may be barriers to going the divorce route to obtain ease from the existing situation. Barriers such as personal religious beliefs; the presence of children; lack of financial abilities; negative counsel from family, friends, or religious leaders; fear of the unknown; and/or the difficulty of a state's divorce laws. As can be seen, it is almost never easy for the individuals involved in a marriage to make the decision to terminate that marriage. Yet, the rise in divorce rates has seemingly led to divorce being held in a romantic view. Complementing the myth of romantic love and marriage, the myth of romantic divorce leads to the expectation that divorce will mean less stress and conflict, joys of greater freedom, and delights of self-discovery. The result may mean a lack of preparedness for the traumas and stresses that follow. The divorce, then, may resolve a number of dissatisfactions with a marriage but the process produces stress and requires a number of adjustments. Paul Bohannan, in the first article of Chapter 13, refers to the process as the need to adjust to a new style of life and it involves really six divorces: an emotional divorce for dealing with the bitterness of the divorce; the legal divorce involving causes and complaints; the financial divorce dealing with property settlement, child support and, perhaps, alimony; the coparental divorce involving decisions regarding the children, such as custody and visitation; the community divorce, which is the recognition of new friends and community activities; the psychic divorce, which involves the transition to being an autonomous social individual.

Leonard Cargan and Robert Whitehurst, in the second article of this chapter, note a number of factors aiding adjustment to divorce and that such adjustment may be even more difficult the second time around. These include personal and financial resources, social activities, disengagement from the former spouse, and feelings of having been treated unfairly.

Although most divorces do not involve children, 40 percent to 50 percent of children spend some time in single-parent families. Effects of divorce on children differ at different ages but often include, to varying degrees, feelings of fear, rejection, sadness, worry, anger, shame, and conflicting loyalties. However, it should be realized that supportive single-parent households are less stressful to children than unhappy interactions. Ellen Levy and her associates discuss what helps children of divorce, in the third article of Chapter 13. It appears that a major factor is the parents' own ability to cope with the situation.

Divorce is, of course, not the only means of losing a mate. In fact, up to the 1960s more marriages were ended by death than by divorce. But since that time, marriages ended by death have remained fairly steady and actually declined, whereas the divorce rate has doubled. Death is also a more acceptable means of ending marriage than divorce, since it is considered a tragedy rather than a failure. It is this viewpoint that leads to help in the early stages of grief. Nonetheless, problems exist for both the widow and widower. Widows frequently encounter a loss of social status and identity as well as financial uncertainty, while widowers suffer from their lack of preparation in social and housekeeping skills. In the fourth article of this chapter, Lyn Lofland describes this change in the mortality picture and the experience of loss. Sidney Wolfe, in the fifth article of this chapter, adds to this examination of the experience of death by indicating the means of dealing with its various phases.

The increased divorce rate and large number of widows does not mean, however, that marriage has been rejected. In fact, one of the most telling reminders of the importance of marriage in our society is seen in the remarriage rates—most of the divorced will remarry. The figures tell us that it is not marriage that is being rejected, it is a particular mate. The figures are somewhat lower for the widowed due to wide differences in the number of available potential mates and such personal factors as age and income.

Remarriage does not mean that the problems of being divorced or widowed are ended; rather, they are only changed. As the final two articles in Chapter 13 indicate, there are complications and numerous adjustments to be made in the new state. In the sixth article, Monica McGoldrick and Elizabeth Carter note the complications that make the development tasks of remarriage difficult. In the final article, Ann Goetting likens these adjustments to those being made in a divorce; that is, there are also six developmental tasks to the adjustment of being remarried. She summarizes these as the need to reestablish trust and commitment, a reinstating of one's identity as a couple, establishment of the couple relationship with friends and community endeavors, making decisions regarding the role with children, dealing with the financial needs and obligations of a dual household, and adjusting to the legal and social factors concerned with ex-spouses and in-laws. It would appear that remarriage, like marriage, could use a premarital contract or at least discussions involving the above areas. Specifically, this would mean discussions revolving around the division of labor, responsibilities, views of child rearing, financial arrangements, relations with the ex-spouse and kin, and partner's children.

REFERENCE

Schultz, D. A. 1982. *The Changing Family.* Englewood Cliffs, N.J.: Prentice-Hall.

50 *The Six Stations of Divorce*

Paul Bohannan

STUDY QUESTIONS

1. Explain the six stations of divorce.

2. Which of the six stations would seem to be the most difficult? Why?

Divorce is a complex social phenomenon as well as a complex personal experience. Because most of us are ignorant of what it requires of us, divorce is likely to be traumatic; emotional stimulation is so great that accustomed ways of acting are inadequate. The usual way for the healthy mind to deal with trauma is to block it out, then let it reappear slowly, so it is easier to manage. The blocking may appear as memory lapses or as general apathy.

On a social level we do something analogous, not allowing ourselves to think fully about divorce as a social problem. Our personal distrust of the emotions that surround it leads us to consider it only with traditional cultural defenses. Our ignorance masquerades as approval or disapproval, as enlightenment or moral conviction.

The complexity of divorce arises because at least six things are happening at once. They may come in a different order and with varying intensities but there are at least these six different experiences of separation. They are the more painful and puzzling as personal experiences because society is not yet equipped to handle any of them well, and some of them we do not handle at all.

I have called these six overlapping experiences (1) the emotional divorce, which centers around the problem of the deteriorating marriage; (2) the legal divorce, based on grounds; (3) the economic divorce, which deals with money and property; (4) the coparental divorce, which deals with custody, single-parent homes, and visitation; (5) the community divorce, surrounding the

Source: "The Six Stations of Divorce," from *Divorce and After* by Paul Bohannan. Copyright © 1968, 1970 by Paul Bohannan. Reprinted by permission of Doubleday & Company, Inc.

changes of friends and community that every divorcee experiences; and (6) the psychic divorce, with the problem of regaining individual autonomy.

The first visible stage of a deteriorating marriage is likely to be what psychiatrists call emotional divorce. This occurs when the spouses withhold emotion from their relationship because they dislike the intensity or ambivalence of their feelings. They may continue to work together as a social team, but their attraction and trust for one another have disappeared. The self-regard of each is no longer reinforced by love for the other. The emotional divorce is experienced as an unsavory choice between giving in and hating oneself and domineering and hating oneself. The natural and healthy "growing apart" of a married couple is very different. As marriages mature, the partners grow in new directions, but also establish bonds of ever greater interdependence. With emotional divorce, people do not grow together as they grow apart—they become, instead, mutually antagonistic and imprisoned, hating the vestiges of their dependence. Two people in emotional divorce grate on each other because each is disappointed.

In American society, we have turned over to the courts the responsibility for formalizing the dissolution of such a marriage. The legislature (which in early English law usurped the responsibility from the church, and then in the American colonies turned it over to the courts) makes the statutes and defines the categories into which every marital dispute must be thrust if legal divorce is possible. Divorce is not "legalized" in many societies but may be done by a church or even by contract. Even in our own society, there is only one thing that a divorce court can do that cannot be done more effectively some other way—establish the right to remarry.

The economic divorce must occur because in Western countries husband and wife are an economic unit. Their unity is recognized by the law. They can—and in some states must—own property as a single "legal person." While technically the couple is not a corporation, they certainly have many of the characteristics of a legal corporation. At the time the household is broken up by divorce, an economic settlement must be made, separating the assets of the "corporation" into two sets of assets, each belonging to one person. This is the property settlement.

All divorced persons suffer more or less because their community is altered. Friends necessarily take a different view of a person during and after divorce—he ceases to be a part of a couple. Their own inadequacies, therefore, will be projected in a new way. Their fantasies are likely to change as they focus on the changing situation. In many cases, the change in community attitude—and perhaps people too—is experienced by a divorcee as ostracism and disapproval. For many divorcing people, the divorce from community may make it seem that nothing in the world is stable.

Finally comes the psychic divorce. It is almost always last, and always the most difficult. Indeed, I have not found a word strong or precise enough to describe the difficulty or the process. Each partner to the ex-marriage, either before or after the legal divorce—usually after, and sometimes years after— must turn himself or herself again into an autonomous social individual. People who have been long married tend to have become socially part of a couple or a family; they lose the habit of seeing themselves as individuals. This is worse for people who married in order to avoid becoming autonomous individuals in the first place.

To become an individual again, at the center of a new community, requires developing new facets of character. Some people have forgotten how to do it— some never learned. The most potent argument against teen-age marriages is that they are likely to occur between people who are searching for independence but avoiding autonomy. The most potent argument against hurried remarriage is the same: avoidance of the responsibilities of autonomy.

Divorce is an institution that nobody enters without great trepidation. In the emotional divorce, people are likely to feel hurt and angry. In the legal divorce, people often feel bewildered—they have lost control, and events sweep them along. In the economic divorce, the reassignment of property and the division of money (there is *never* enough) may make them feel cheated. In the parental divorce they worry about what is going to happen to the children; they feel guilty for what they have done. With the community divorce, they may get angry with their friends and perhaps suffer despair because there seems to be no fidelity in friendship. In the psychic divorce, in which they have to become autonomous again, they are probably afraid and are certainly lonely. However, the resolution of any or all of these various six divorces may provide an elation of victory that comes from having accomplished something that had to be done and having done it well. There may be ultimate satisfactions in it. . . .

51 *Adjustment Differences in the Divorced and Redivorced*

Leonard Cargan / Robert N. Whitehurst

STUDY QUESTIONS

1. What are the four factors that would aid divorce adjustment?

2. Who is most likely to have the easier/harder adjustment and why?

Source: Leonard Cargan and Robert N. Whitehurst, "Adjustment Differences in the Divorced and Redivorced." Society for the Study of Social Problems, 1988 Annual Meeting. Used by permission.

INTRODUCTION

Over the past century the overall rate of marital dissolutions due to death, desertion and divorce has remained the same. The change during this period has been the increased share of the total attributed to divorce (Nadelson and Poledsky, 1984). The result has been greater attention to divorce and postdivorce relationships in current social studies. Although many of the problems associated with divorce are being clarified, it is still considered a "noninstitution" (Price-Bonham and Balswick, 1980), and, as a result, the transition for those involved is never easy (Weiss, 1976).

Even though the literature identified a number of variables that may aid divorce adjustment, there has been little attention paid to the effects of the combination of these variables and whether their impact is different after a redivorce. Due to the increasing rate of redivorce since the late 70's, the literature must be expanded beyond the usual female-male analysis. This paper covers both the adjustment variables and the divorce cycle.

THEORETICAL REVIEW AND HYPOTHESIS

Four general areas have been hypothesized as aiding adjustment to divorce: resources, activity, attachment, and a sense of fairness.

Concepts

The initial concept to be used in the theoretical model is *resources*. The link between resources and divorce is the subject's self-defined perception of having "enough resources" to meet one's current situation. Such resources can be concrete or symbolic (Foa and Foa, 1980), such as money/goods, information/services, status/love. Thus, Menaghan and Lieberman (1985) reiterated the findings of others in a study showing that the increase in depression following divorce was reflected by greater economic problems and reduced availability of personal support. In this study "resources" refers to the variables of financial well-being, support of family, friends and others, help from counseling, and the happiness one derives from social life.

Borrowing from a study by Raschke (1977), the second concept uses an activity theory as a framework for post-divorce adjustment. . . . In sum, socially active people are happier and better off than inactive people (Spanier and Lachman, 1980). Combining this idea of frequency with the idea of valued activity allows as a test for this concept the frequency of one's social activities and the length of time needed to obtain replacements for the missing social/sexual partner.

The third concept to be developed is attachment. Generally, it is important in intimate relationships and of great importance in the adjustment to separation and divorce. Weiss notes that whether the marriage is happy or not, whether the dissolution is sought or not, a sense of bonding to the spouse remains. The disruption of this attachment is a major cause of emotional problems (1976:

204–7). . . . In this study, the attachment between the respondent and the ex-spouse, as well as friends, will be examined.

The concept of distributive justice has been related to cognitive dissonance by Geschwender (1971). This implies that persons who feel unrewarded or punished by their circumstances will likely have fewer positive resources to share and thus attain a lower level of overall adjustment. We suggest that, insofar as divorced persons accept as fair the new status accorded them, their adjustment will be facilitated. Fairness then revolves around the desire for the divorce; that is, who initiated and/or favored the divorce. . . .

Hypothesis

For purposes of this study, the guiding hypothesis involves the test of the adjustment potential for both the divorced and the redivorced of the above concepts: their resources, the degree and kind of activities, feelings of attachment, and sense of justice. The hypothesis can be stated as:

Insofar as divorced persons have resources at their disposal they feel meet their needs, experience accustomed and valued activity levels, have a satisfactory sense of attachment, and experience fairness in their arrangements, they will make positive adjustments to divorce.

The data from which inferences are drawn about the above hypothesis involve suggestive, rather than full tests of conclusiveness about the linkages. Thus, the aim of this exploratory study is to create more fruitful hypotheses rather than to test significance of relationships from the present sample. . . .

FINDINGS

Resources

The first factor hypothesized as leading to a better divorce adjustment is supportive resources. It is assessed by current economic situation, emotional support received, counseling received, and social life satisfaction.

The divorced males were far more likely than their female counterparts to note being better off financially after the divorce (45% vs. 30%). This is especially true for the redivorced male. Over half of the redivorced males were better off financially whereas 60% of the redivorced women were worse off financially.

Gender role descriptions imply that females have closer, more supportive relationships than males. The findings in this study support this belief, except in regard to children. In every category examined, the divorced female was more likely than her male counterpart to receive support from the family (76% vs. 72%), friends (85% vs. 76%), other relatives (51% vs. 47%), acquaintances (62% vs. 57%), and the children (60% vs. 33%). The findings were similar for the redivorced female as compared to her male counterpart, except in regard to other relatives (36% vs. 45%). The breakdown among the categories implies that divorce the second time around lessens this supportive network. The redivorced males received more critical reactions or non-support than their divorced-once counterparts from their family (16% vs. 5%), from their friends (15% vs. 0%) and their acquaintances (16% vs. 4%). The critical or non-support response from the children (32%) for the redivorced females stands out from those received by the other respondant categories since it is almost double any of them.

Another resource could be the support received from counseling. The findings reveal that there is little difference between the various categories in this regard. About three fifths of each category received counseling. The redivorced were slightly more likely to seek counseling than the divorced (60% vs. 55%).

Satisfaction from one's social life can also be a support resource in divorce adjustment. A majority (68%) were satisfied with their social life. Despite this large satisfied majority, there were differences among the categories in degree of satisfaction, with the redivorced females (80% vs. 65%) and the divorced-once males somewhat more likely than their counterparts to be satisfied with their social life.

Except for financial well-being the females of both categories appear generally more supported by the variables in the resource concept.

Activity

The second factor is social activity. Three elements were considered: the current level of social activity, dating, and heterosexual activity. A majority of the respondents (57%) go out at least twice per week. However, it is the divorced male—once or redivorced—who is more likely to be going out this frequently (70% vs. 50%). Actually, the difference between the sexes occurs at the "going out three or more times per week" level. At this level, 42% of the males go out versus 23% of the females.

The assessment of dating repeats the above findings. Although most of the sample (68%) had started dating within six months of the separation, it was the males who were more likely to have begun this soon (76% vs. 63%). Similarly, the largest difference in this activity is between the divorced female and the redivorced male (62% vs. 85%).

Considering the above findings, it is perhaps not surprising to find that males were more likely than their counterparts to have resumed a heterosexual relationship (97% vs. 86%) and to have done so sooner (72% vs. 55%). The breakdown between the divorce categories reveals that it is the divorced female who had the most difficulty in starting a heterosexual relationship.

The three variables all indicate that the males, regardless of divorce cycle, were more likely than the females to have made this adjustment.

Attachment

The third factor of the hypothesis is the need for a replacement of the primary relationship to provide a feeling of closeness. An indicator could be the beginning of a heterosexual relationship, but such activity reveals nothing about closeness. A better measurement would be the relationship existing between the respondent and the ex-spouse or friends. The study reveals that the large difference in "relationship to the ex-spouse" is within the divorce categories. Thus, both the female and male divorced categories were more likely than redivorced counterparts to have friendly (41% vs. 26%) or supportive (24% vs. 13%) relationships with their ex-spouses. The redivorced, especially the redivorced females, were more likely to have non-supportive (24% vs. 21%) or argumentative relations (36% vs. 16%) with their former spouses.

There was little difference between the categories in attachment to friends. The males were somewhat more likely than the females to no longer be close with former friends (52% vs. 47%). The largest contrast is among the redivorced (F = 39% vs M = 47%).

It would appear from the data that the redivorced are less likely to have supportive attachments.

Fairness

The question of fairness revolves around the divorce itself and whether or not it was desired. Females were more likely to have perceived the divorce in a favorable light, since they were more likely to have both initiated the divorce (61% vs. 39%) and to have favored it (71% vs. 48%). These results indicate that both categories of females would be more likely to have a positive feeling of fairness.

Adjustment

Up to now, we have been investigating factors that aid adjustment to divorce. It is now necessary to explore signs of adjustment, both positive and negative.

The data imply that less adjusted respondents would be more likely to feel lonely, to get drunk, and to contemplate or attempt suicide. The redivorced were more likely than the divorced to reveal such loneliness feelings as having no one to share happy/sad moments (31% vs. 20%), having no one with whom to discuss problems (22% vs. 17%), feeling that no one cares about them (15% vs. 99%), feeling isolated (19% vs. 18%), and needing others around (38% vs. 33%). The redivorced male stands out. In his need for having others around (63% vs. 31% average).

Considering the findings on loneliness, it is not surprising that the redivorced male is far more likely to get drunk once per week or more (35% vs. 6% average). In contrast to his male and female counterparts, the redivorced male is four times more likely than the divorced male to get drunk this often, whereas no redivorced female indicated that she got drunk this often.

The redivorced male again shows up as less positively adjusted when we turn to plans for and attempts at suicide. Although twice as likely as his divorced counterpart to attempt suicide (20% vs. 9%), he is not as likely to attempt this negative act as his female counterpart (20% vs. 40%).

On a more positive note most of the sample indicated that they were "pretty happy" (63%) or "very happy" (15%). Among those more likely to note that they were not too happy was the redivorced male. This was true in comparison to both his divorced counterpart (35% vs. 25%) and his female counterpart (35% vs. 20%).

An indication of adjustment might be the respondent's attitude toward a future relationship, that is, willingness to risk marriage again. In this regard, most of the respondents think they will be either remarried (73%) or cohabiting (15%) within five years. However, there are some significant differences in this desired picture. Significantly more of the divorced females than their redivorced counterparts see themselves as remarried in the future (70% vs. 55%). Somewhat similar is the picture with males. Significantly more of the divorced males than the redivorced males see themselves married (70% vs. 57%). Seemingly, after at least two marriages, a cohabiting relationship is more appealing to the redivorced (24% vs. 13%), especially the male (43%). On the other hand, it is the females who are the least likely to want to risk again (14% vs. 5%) and this is more so for the redivorced female (20%).

In an outright question on adjustment, most of the sample (75%) have the positive belief that they are adjusting very well to their new lifestyle. The females are somewhat more likely than the males to have this outlook (78% vs. 68%). Again, the redivorced male was the most likely to have a negative feeling; 20 percent as compared to an average of 6 percent of the others noted that they were not adjusting well.

Summation

Overall, the variables regarding the concept of resources revealed mixed results. Although both categories of males were better off financially, both categories of females were more likely to be receiving emotional support from their possible relationships. The other two variables of this concept, support from counseling and social life, revealed little difference between the categories.

The second concept of activity is the male's strong area of adjustment. Both male categories were far more likely than the females to be active in going out socially in dating, and in starting a heterosexual relationship early after divorce. Although these activities are important in adjustment, support from the other variables may be overriding since the redivorced males' negative adjustment was not in line with their seemingly positive activity responses.

On a sexual basis, the smallest differences occur on measures of attachment. Apparently, the deciding item in this concept is that of divorce cycle—a redivorce seemingly makes it more difficult to maintain an attachment to an ex-spouse since both categories of the divorced had lesser contact with their ex-spouse. The concept of attachment has also been shown to be an important factor in divorce adjustment, but, again, our findings indicate that this variable must have support from other variables in order to aid adjustment. Thus, the redivorced females' lack of attachment here is not shown in the negative adjustments—loneliness or drunkenness—but in suicide attempts.

The variable utilized for fairness may have been self-determining since national statistics reveal that females are more apt to file for divorce. However, the study revealed that this is not just a question of legality since both categories of females were also more likely than the males to have favored the divorce. Also, the strong difference between the sexes indicates that this area is easier for females than males. However, the mixed results from prior studies (Spanier and Thompson, 1983; Buehler, 1986) and here would imply that initiator status, although clinically useful, is only part of the adjustment-needs picture.

DISCUSSION

The four concepts were measured by 15 variables. The breakdown of these variables revealed that aids to adjustment vary according to both the sex and divorce cycle. The redivorced male apparently benefits least from these aids. Compared to the other categories, he is the least likely to be getting support from his family, friends and acquaintances, to be maintaining attachment to the former spouse or have favored the divorce. On the other hand, he was likelier to be better off financially, be going out more often, and to be dating relatively early in the proceedings.

The redivorced female revealed a somewhat more positive balance than her male counterpart. Compared to the other categories, she is more likely to have financial difficulties, to lack support from other relatives and children, and to lose attachment with her ex-spouses. But she is likely to receive support from the family, friends and acquaintances. She is also likely to be satisfied with her social life, to have started a heterosexual relationship fairly early in the proceedings, to be close with her friends, to have initiated and favored the divorce.

The divorced reveal a picture of involvement similar to their redivorced, sexual counterparts, but not to the same degree. Thus, the divorced-once male is less likely than the other categories in receiving support from the children, retaining closeness with friends, and initiating the divorce whereas, more likely to have begun a heterosexual relationship early in the proceedings and in having attachment with his ex-spouse. The divorced female had more difficulties in getting out socially frequently and in getting started in a heterosexual relationship early. On the other hand, she is likelier to be receiving support from other relatives, and the children, and in favoring the divorce.

What stands out in this overall picture, is the lack of adjustment by the redivorced male. If this is so then it should be reflected in negative responses to various life situations and such is the case. Of the ten life situations, the redivorced male is the likeliest of the categories to have a negative response to six:—having someone to share happy and sad moments, having feelings that no one cares for him, needing others, getting drunk frequently, being unhappy most of the time, and about his adjustment to the new lifestyle. He is also likely to contemplate or attempt suicide and to have less positive feelings about a future marriage.

The somewhat more balanced picture of the redivorced female is also seen in the life situations. She was the most likely to attempt suicide and to believe that she would remain divorced. She also has some difficulties in finding someone to share happy/sad moments and believes that no one cares about her.

The two divorced categories also have a better adjustment picture. The divorced male is not found as the likeliest in any of the negative life adjustments but does seem to have some problems with feelings of isolation, getting drunk frequently, with claims of unhappiness, and in adjusting to his new lifestyle.

The divorced female reveals the best adjustment picture of the categories. She is the least likely to note the combined loneliness items, to plan or attempt suicide, to feel unhappy, and to believe that she is not adjusting well to her new lifestyle.

CONCLUSION

Although the data do not lead to definitive conclusions, some useful trends may be noted. The hypothetical model implies that those people who have supportive resources, activities, attachments, and a sense of fairness are more likely to make a positive adjustment to their divorce. The data supported the hypothesis. It was also shown that both sex and the divorce cycle had an impact on the adjustment variables. That is, the redivorced male had the least positive adjustment and the divorced-once female had the most positive adjustment. The other two categories showed no clear-cut association between the adjustment elements and the negative behaviors.

In sum, the four hypothetical elements are important for aiding divorce adjustment, but other factors, such as divorce experience and gender roles, are also important. Thus, despite their prior experience, divorce adjustment appears to be more difficult for the redivorced, especially the redivorced male. This may be a result of the implications of a second divorce: it may imply the belief of a permanent end to a desired status, the greater stigma and guilt over being a "two-time loser," and/or it may also mean a lesser support from the "usual" resources.

Further research to clarify these findings is needed and should be expanded to include in comparative focus the above categories: the married once, remarried, the never-married and the widowed.

REFERENCES

Buehler, Cheryl. 1986 "Initiator Status and the Divorce Transition," *Family Relations*, 1986.

Foa, E. B. and U. G. Foa. 1980 "Resource Theory: Interpersonal Behavior as Exchange," in K. L. Gergen, M. S. Greenberg and R. H. Willis, (eds), *Social Exchange: Advances in Theory and Research*, New York: Plenum Press, 77–94.

Geschwender, James A. 1971 "Continuities in Theories of Status Consistency and Cognitive Dissonance," in: *Contemporary Sociological Theory*, ed by Fred E. Katz, New York: Random House 392–342.

Menaghan, Elizabeth and Morton A Lieberman. 1985 "Changes in Depression following Divorce: A Panel Study," *American Sociological Association*, Meeting.

Price-Bonham, Sharon and Jack O Balswick. 1980 "The Non-Institutions: Divorce, Desertion and Remarriage," *Journal of Marriage and the Family*, vol 42, Nov., 959–972.

Raschke, Helen J. 1977 "The Role of Social Participation in Postseparation and Postdivorce Adjustment," *Journal of Divorce*, vol 1(2), Winter, 129–140.

Spanier, Graham B. and Margie E. Lachman. 1980 "Factors Associated with Adjustment to Marital Separation," *Sociological Focus*, vol 13, no. 4, Oct. 369–381.

Spanier, Graham B. and Linda Thompson. 1984 *Parting: The Aftermath of Separation and Divorce*. Beverly Hills: Sage.

Weiss, R. S. 1976 "The Emotional Impact of Marital Separation," *Journal of Social Issues*, vol. 32(1), 135–145.

52 *What Helps Children Of Divorce*

Ellen Levy / Virginia Nuta / Ann Parks

STUDY QUESTIONS

1. What do the authors imply when they say that the parents' own coping helps the child?

2. What are several factors that would aid children of divorce to adjust?

Does divorce harm children? Researchers still don't entirely agree, even after years of study and more research reports than anyone wants to read. The reason for this is that—as single parents know—the effects of divorce on all parties involved vary with the circumstances of each family. Much has to do with the economic facts, the educational level of parents, the community in which the family lives, the coping ability of the parents, the age and sex of the children, the stability of family life after divorce, and the degree of conflict in the family before divorce. Furthermore, increasing community acceptance may have the effect of decreasing stress for children and parents.

    To complicate matters further, researchers have also discovered something else single parents knew all along. Divorce is a process, and much has to do with all of the above factors at each of the several stages a divorcing family

Source: Ellen Levy, Virginia Nuta, and Ann Parks, "What Helps Children of Divorce." *The Single Parent*, May 1985, pp. 11–15. Reprinted by permission.

goes through. The quality of family life before divorce, the way the separation occurs, the resolution of the separation into a divorce, the first years of reconstituting the family after divorce, the later years of stabilization, remarriage—all have an effect on how well the kids will do eventually, and the children will also show different strengths and problems at any given time during the divorce process.

Nearly all recent research agrees that divorce probably harms children much less than was previously believed, because of the above factors. In fact, most research says that the vast majority of children whose parents have separated or divorced seem to do rather well. One study, by Martin Levin at Emory University in Georgia, of about 8000 children in a national sample, found that sometimes children of divorce raised by their mothers do *better* than children in intact homes. Most other researchers don't agree, but still find that differences between divorced children and other children are not so sizeable. Nearly everyone agrees, as well, that the children in most trouble are those whose married parents fight for years and display physical violence.

What is becoming apparent is that the real questions must be "What conditions help or harm children of divorce?" and "What can parents do to help their children?" The new research is beginning to explore some of these areas, and while some situations may be out of your control, others will not be. And what is quite clear is that there are many, many ways for children to come out of the painful experience of a divorce as healthy, happy adults.

Following are some of the key factors researchers have identified.

Research indicates a high correlation between your ability to cope and your child's sense of well-being. This may seem obvious, but it is worth discussing because it is easier said than done. If you accept the premise, then you will want to get to the next step of figuring out what you can do to learn to cope.

Researcher Frank Furstenberg, in a University of Pennsylvania project that measured the well-being of children over time, found that "parent's coping ability affects their adolescent children's well being. Children whose parents were frequently depressed and generally discontented and those whose parents exhibited a lack of confidence and control were more likely to have behavioral and psychological symptoms of maladjustment."

After a divorce, there is a period like the quiet after the storm. Accompanying this, however, you are likely to feel a sense of grief, loneliness and loss at a time when your children need your reassurance more than ever.

Some people turn to self-destructive behaviors or relationships when they are feeling lonely, needy and unloved. As a responsible parent, this must be avoided. You cannot be as self-indulgent as separated and divorced couples who are childless and can take time to enjoy their freedom, and then go on, when they are ready, to healing and starting anew. And sometimes with especially understanding children, there is role reversal and the parents lean on their children for a while. Be careful not to do this with your school age or adolescent children.

Work on constructive behaviors. Remember that with children, there are ongoing responsibilities and decisions during the transition period. At this time, precedents are set about new routines and life style that will continue throughout the rest of your childrearing days: custody arrangements, communicating about children, planning for the future about housing and employment.

For help in dealing with practical matters, check out job training programs, local social services, counseling centers for displaced homemakers and the like. Try parent education classes. If you do not feel overwhelmed in coping with your children and family matters, you will find that you have the energy to pursue job, school or other opportunities that may come your way.

Whatever you do, you will call upon strength from within that you may not have known you had. Acknowledge your feelings. Avoid isolating yourself from others. Join a single parent support group. Look for community services that may help you. And remember that you do have qualities that will help you cope. According to researcher Frank Furstenberg, those qualities within you are flexibility, sensitivity and honesty mixed with good common sense and a positive outlook.

Research indicates that the age of children at the time of divorce affects their ability to cope with the divorce and may have long term effects on their future adjustment. Children whose parents divorced early in their lives were more likely to be held back a grade in school, have disciplinary problems and were more likely to be recommended for or have received counseling. The most vulnerable ages are from 3–9, especially boys.

Researcher Frank Furstenberg postulates that young children "may be more susceptible to the effects of divorce because they are cognitively and emotionally less equipped to interpret the experience."

It is important to take this into consideration if you divorce when your children are under the age of nine: they may need more support and understanding at that age to make up for the early disruption and loss. It is best not to assume that they completely recovered from the divorce which took place before they were able to reason. Reassure them of what a comfort they were to you during your time of crisis; tell them stories about your joy at their birth and milestones shared by both parents such as when they first talked and walked, just as you would had the family not undergone a divorce.

If your child is younger than age seven and you are divorced or divorcing, take time to explain to him/her as best you can what is going to be the same and what is going to be different in your family life. Emphasize that the child is loved and will be protected; *he/she is not the cause of divorce nor is being divorced.* Encourage questions. Repeat things that your child likes to hear often: young children learn through repetition. Have available as many friends and relatives as possible to help you help your child to feel secure and well taken care of.

Be consistent and adhere as closely as possible to normal routines of the child's life. Avoid making the mistake of saying things in front of your children that you think will go over their heads. Your young child may not be able to interpret what you say but he/she hears every word and may come to conclusions that are frightening and damaging to his/her self image.

During the separation and ensuing divorce keep in touch with your child's other parent and kin. If one parent has left the home, arrange for time to be spent on a regular basis with that parent, during the initial separation and thereafter. Have your children talk on the telephone with their other parent every day. The younger the child the more important the continuity of contact because young children live in the here and now and need constant positive reinforcement.

Young children are resilient and this can be the key to helping them to cope with divorce. Researcher Nicholas Zill writes "transitory conflict is something with which most children can cope." Persistent conflict, however, within marriage, during a custody battle or carried over into post divorce anger between ex-spouses is unbearable for children. Adults have an obligation to their children to protect them from relentless tension resulting from unresolved parental conflict. Your child will cope with divorce if you and your ex-spouse let go of marital ties and begin a new relationship as co-parents, so your child, who needs both of you, will heal from your divorce and thrive.

If you want to remarry, you probably eventually will. If remarriage is on your mind, it is important to consider the effects on your children. Research indicates that the immediate effect of remarriage can be detrimental to the child's well-being, if the child is still struggling with the loss of a parent, and because it is a stressful transition. But if the remarriage is stable and endures over time, it is very good for your child to become part of a stepfamily. "Remarriage seems to restore some of the balance achieved by the initial marriage . . . step-grandparents quickly assume the familiar grandparent role even for children in their middle years," writes researcher Frank Furstenberg.

However, if the second marriage should end in divorce, the effect is devastating on children. Unfortunately, one child in ten will undergo two or more family disruptions before reaching the age of 16. Children in these circumstances are in the highest risk category for maladjustment.

Should you risk remarriage or settle for the safety of single parenthood, which, all things being equal, your child can accept in time? Of course, there is no right or wrong answer here. But there are some guideposts from the research. When considering a second marriage, it would be a good idea to consider how well the potential spouse and your child are getting along. The relationship between your child and the stepparent can be very important to how well your child copes with a divorce. If you do not see kindness and attachment toward your child and if your child does not seem to accept the person; this marriage could be harmful to your child.

As far as the effect of remarriage on your relationship with your ex-spouse, the researchers agree it remains status quo. Mainly, this is because there is very little communication between ex-spouses; in fact, in many instances, not enough to establish a co-parenting relationship which experts recommend is in the best interest of your child. Before you remarry, try to evaluate whether you and your ex-spouse would describe yourselves as co-parenting or parallel parenting your children. Chances are your new mate will support you in your parenting and parenting style. The less unfinished business from a previous marriage, the easier it will be for your new mate to define his/her role.

If your first marriage was difficult and/or your life has been filled with pain, you may be in danger of settling for a marriage that seems to fill a need in you, but does not hold much promise for your child. A word of caution: your child may not recover from the second (or third) breakup. As you know, there is no formula for success. But you can try to ensure that your future marriage will last by consciously looking for a mate who will be concerned about your children. Then it will be much more likely that life will come together for you.

Above all, it is important for you to know that children are sensitive to the feelings of the parent who is not remarrying, sympathizing with him/her for the hurt or sadness that may not be verbalized. If your child sees that you, too, are sensitive to the other parent, it will bring everyone closer and help establish, perhaps, the co-parenting relationship that may not have existed or reinforce one that already exists.

Witnessing arguments and physical violence between parents is bad for children, and researchers agree that children whose parents fight a lot during marriage tend to have more problems than children for whom there is less parental conflict.

But separation and divorce that ends long-term, major hostilities may soften this effect, even if some conflict still exists after divorce.

In a major study done by Frank Furstenberg of the University of Pennsylvania and Nicholas Zill of Child Trends in Washington, D.C., 1,423 children were tested and interviewed in 1976 and then in 1981. Children in high conflict married families had more problems and needed the most psychological help.

Children whose parents fought a lot and then divorced needed more help than children whose parents fought a little and then divorced. But the need did not increase much after the divorce. Children whose custodial parent was divorced at both interview times showed a decline in need for help between the two interviews.

Many parents in the study said that conflict between parents dwindled drastically after the marital disruption. This may be, say researchers, because most of the noncustodial parents ceased to have contact with the custodial parent. But even those children whose parents still fought, and those whose parents got along well, were less affected by the parents' post-divorce relationship than by other things.

The "other things" may be the passage of time and the parents' ability to cope. Other studies of smaller groups of families who were *in* the process of divorcing show that children are affected by the conflict *during* divorce and by the departure of one parent. One study by Nancy Warren at the University of North Carolina found that children of divorce are quite resilient and most were not "at risk." But those who *were* having problems were children whose parents continued to disagree about custody and childrearing, or where the absent parent was truly absent.

What to do? Furstenburg cautions parents when it comes to working out post-divorce parental access to children, "If you can work it out, fine." If not, don't "look for a blueprint to slavishly follow that guarantees success."

But some parents think they must choose between continued conflict with the absent parent, or cutting off access to the children. This research indicates that even if you and your ex still don't get along, it is not necessarily bad for the kids. And kids who can maintain positive relationships with parents do have fewer problems. Some children may do all right without seeing the departing parent; but others may need that parent desperately.

How to work it out? Try "co-parenting," a term that describes a new relationship that can emerge between divorced parents who learn to cooperate on major decisions about their children. In research conducted by Constance Ahrons, University of Wisconsin, two thirds of 54 divorced couples said their relationship was supportive. Women usually believed the relationships were more conflictual than men. Successful co-parents talked frequently about the children, and also talked about family and mutual friends. They avoided discussing the past marriage, new romances, differences in childrearing, and financial problems.

Ahrons believes that the most important task for divorcing parents is to find out where the spousal relationship ends, and the parenting relationship begins. Parents get along best when they are able to maintain a child-centered relationship after divorce. Rules defining when and how each parent will relate to the child "are critical to the child's understanding and stabilization of his or her relationship with each parent," says Ahrons.

You say you can't get along that well? Try "parallel parenting," a term coined by Frank Furstenburg that describes what happens when former spouses stop contact. The child, however, can see the absent parent, experience different rules and values, and still come out just fine.

It's pretty much accepted that stress has a direct bearing on people's mental and physical health. Life events—such as death of a spouse or divorce at the high end of the scale to taking a vacation and Christmas at the low end of the scale—influence how we feel.

There's a lot of talk about stress. Workshops about how to reduce it are given everywhere. We now know that stress can increase your blood pressure, give you ulcers and heart attacks, cause headaches, insomnia and even predispose you to certain kinds of cancer. Your style of life, even the food you eat, influences your health and well being.

We've learned that activity such as running creates chemicals in your blood that give you a natural high. We've learned that thinking depressing thoughts can cause other blood chemistry changes. Our minds and bodies act together; there's an entire medical discipline arising around holism and wellness.

What causes stress for single parents? Emotions and feelings do. Many who divorce experience grief, feelings of loss, guilt, anger for being left alone, fear about being able to control the future, depression or self pity. Your lifestyle may change, too. Schedules become irregular, you may eat, drink or smoke more to calm yourself. You may feel anxious and cry or yell at your children more.

There may be acute stress due to the struggle to make ends meet, perhaps having to move to a less expensive place or a worse neighborhood, or maybe needing to move in with relatives. You are tense because you must go to work or get a better job. Perhaps your employer is not sympathetic to working parents. And the children—how can you manage with no back up child care; who will care for them while you work? What if they get sick? And to top it off, your old friends are fading away and you have no one to confide in.

Nancy Coletta from the University of Maryland, also found that distress in mothers and children were related to low income following divorce, *not* to the father's absence. Child rearing practices were influenced by not enough money. Mothers, thinking of the cost to replace items, constantly nagged their youngsters about touching family possessions.

You may not feel stressed. How severe a situation seems depends on your perceptions. A crisis for someone else may be to you just an obstacle to overcome. Your children, far from being stressed, may be relieved at the sudden lack of tension in the home when a parent departs and do just fine. But if the children felt close to the departing parent or perceived the family was going just great, they will not adjust as well. In this case, the separation will be more a disaster to them; you may notice a young child being anxious, withdrawn and generally regressing.

It's not surprising that children and parents who feel stressed by divorce tend to have more health problems than married couples and children from two-parent families. There's little doubt that divorce's major changes affect everyone.

Research reveals some unsettling facts. In an analysis of health—physician visits, death rate, treatment for acute and chronic conditions, and institutionalization, Lois Verbrugge from the University of Michigan, found that the healthiest people were married and the least healthy single, especially the formerly married. Overlooking the possibility that healthier people may tend to get married, one explanation could be found in the lifestyle. Married people have a miniature support group; spouses encourage each other to take action when they first feel ill, they exchange child care, freeing the other to visit the doctor, and they can usually better afford medical care.

Formerly marrieds, Verbrugge theorized, have riskier life styles, more injuries, acute and chronic health problems, and are less able to afford preventive health care. Many divorced mothers know that regular meal and bed times, being able to afford nutritionally-balanced food, and even having time to fix real meals is a luxury!

Children's health-related reactions to stress now have been documented by a nation wide study of grade school children by Dr. John Guidubaldi from Kent State University. School children from divorced homes seemed to have more problems than children from two-parent families. Yet research that uncovers negatives also points the way to preventive measures. You can maintain your child's health during your separation and divorce.

First, before you separate, you must prepare yourself with the information you need about the divorce process so you can choose the most positive way to go about it. Find out how to minimize negatives for your children. Learn skills to solve your problems. Honestly prepare your children for the changes in their lives and bend over backwards to keep them out of adult fights.

Cultivate your friends and family, since having a caring group of people around you acts as a buffer against stress. Plan your life so that changes are gradual, schedules like meal and bedtimes are regular and nutritious meals are routine. Get regular health and dental checkups.

Insist on the active involvement of the absent parent. Research consistently verifies that children do better when they visit the other parent as often as they wish.

Work on your own personal capacities—believe in your own abilities, beef up your job qualifications, and get the education you need. You will fare better as a divorced parent if you view your new role as a challenge. If you managed well and had good relationships before divorce, you'll return to your former competence.

Researchers, like Guidubaldi and Frank Furstenberg from the University of Pennsylvania go further to challenge the institutions of society to support divorcing families. They say that affordable medical and dental care can prevent health problems. They say that schools can cooperate to reduce stress—by scheduling school activities at times convenient for working single parents, offering rap sessions to kids (a problem shared is less devastating) and by sending school records and announcements to the absent parent. They also say that affordable child care must be a high priority.

Support measures like these in your community. Endorse programs to reach separating couples with information about minimizing the stress of the divorce on their children. With your awareness and knowledge, and with medical and mental health professionals, schools and your entire community working together, you can have healthy, well-adjusted children.

Time may not heal *all* wounds, but it accounts for a great deal of the eventual adjustment of children and parents to divorce. Research used to look at children of divorce without examining the length of time since the divorce. But now, social scientists are understanding that divorce is a process and that the initial trauma is softened by time.

Judith Wallerstein and Joan Kelly in California found that the significance of divorce for children changed with time, that the initial upset was usually smoothed out by two years. Sometimes, however, a seemingly well-adjusted child at the time of divorce can show problems later.

But most children do have the capacity to cope, given parental love and attention. And it may help to keep a child's life as stable as possible, even if you cannot control all change.

Resolve your situation. Long separations may be detrimental to children.

Some research shows children living in homes where separations have dragged on for years need more psychological help. Constance Ahrons of the University of Wisconsin has set forth five transitions a family must work through in divorce, and believes that the more people are clear about their roles in these transitions, the less stress.

The first stage is individual cognition, when a spouse feels distress, but may deny that the marriage is to blame. A spouse also may blame the other, escalating conflict. Eventually, one or both spouses withdraws, and seeks solutions.

The second stage is family metacognition, where the family takes stock, discusses the realization that the marriage is the problem, and prepares for separation. The amount of stress may depend on whether the crisis is voluntary or inflicted. This may be the time of greatest disequilibrium; children often seek out friends whose parents are divorced.

The third stage is actual physical separation. If the family has come to terms with the first two stages, the crisis may not be so stressful. If not, disequilibrium continues. At this stage, "on again, off again" situations often arise. The lack of clear boundaries and roles causes more stress, especially for children.

The fourth stage, systemic reorganization, is when the family does reorganize the boundaries of the new parental roles. This is also a stressful period, often resulting in "freezing out" one parent from the family system.

Finally, the fifth stage is family redefinition, where the divorced family defines itself, both to family members and the community. This stage, Ahrons believes, is "critical to the family's struggles with identity, boundaries, and individuation."

Most families eventually do work through these stages, becoming a new family with clear roles and boundaries. Moving from disequilibrium to redefinition usually takes about two years.

In research conducted by Nancy Warren of the University of North Carolina, divorcing families contacted from court records were given three different education programs. One group of families received a parenting education class, and said they appreciated the contact with other parents and information on children's needs. Another group with the children received one-to-one counseling, and were grateful to get help in dealing with the absent parent.

The third group received a book about divorce. The first two groups of parents were coping better after the programs were finished. The group who received the book didn't do better immediately, but eventually caught up after a year!

This may indicate that time heals many wounds, but also that education about divorce can help you deal with the disequilibrium you may immediately be experiencing.

It will also help your children to keep your home as stable as possible. Research indicates that stressful changes cause children to do more poorly. Try to keep as much of your child's life the same as you can. You may not be able to avoid a move to a new neighborhood, but try to organize your home life so that you have regular routines. You may not be able to avoid going to work, if you didn't work before, but try to see that your children have regular time with you every day. You don't need to be both mother and father to your child, but be there. Be consistent. Your child will feel more secure if discipline and care for his needs are quietly present.

53 When Others Die

Lyn H. Lofland

STUDY QUESTIONS

1. What are the four features of the situation of loss?
2. The author uses the term "fresh attachments" to describe the difference between elderly loss of spouse and other types of losses. What does she mean?

Everywhere and always humans form attachments—they build relationships. And everywhere and always they suffer when these attachments are broken—when these relationships are destroyed. This article is concerned with human loss engendered by death. (For a more inclusive discussion of human loss, see Marris, 1974.) The situation of a human facing the irreversible loss of a fellow human whom the person defines as significant in his or her life provides the model for understanding losses of all other sorts—pets, possessions, physical abilities and assets, and so forth.

Though humans everywhere form attachments, the patterning of those attachments is not always the same. Similarly, while loss and its accompanying pain appear to be universal, the *situation of loss* is not. Four features described below constitute the loss situation characteristic of the relatively affluent in modern developed societies. Also explored are some implications of this historically and culturally rather peculiar state of affairs.

A *first feature* of what we might think of as the modern "loss complex" is the pronounced tendency for losses to be concentrated in the middle and late years of life rather than being spread throughout the entire span, as has historically been more usual. This concentration is a product of what demographers refer to as the "mortality revolution"—a relatively recent and unprecedented radical reduction in mortality levels (Goldscheider, 1971). One aspect

Source: Lyn H. Lofland, "When Others Die." Reprinted with permission from *Generations*, 833 Market Street, Suite 512, San Francisco, CA 94103. Copyright 1986 ASA.

of this massive change in mortality is the low level of death among infants and young children. In the United States, the infant mortality rate currently hovers around 1 percent (it is even lower in much of Europe), and the death rates for children up to the age of ten are minuscule (Preston, et al., 1972). Such figures contrast markedly with those estimated to have been historically typical: an infant mortality rate of about 35 percent, with the death of one-half of all children before the age of ten. These incredible reductions in infant and child deaths are reflected in increasing average life expectancies (mid 70s and rising), but life expectancy figures also reflect an overall decline in mortality throughout youth and adulthood. The pre-modern world experienced annual mortality rates of about 50 per 1,000, but, during the recurrent periods of plague, crop failure, or other natural disasters, these rates could and frequently did surge to 300 or 400 per 1,000. For modern humans in the developed countries, a mortality rate of less than 9 per 1,000 is typical. Thus, unlike most of our ancestors to whom death (of parents, siblings, friends, spouses, children) was a constant companion, we have good reason to anticipate that our parents will not die until we reach middle age, that our siblings will all survive, that our children will outlive us, and that any serial marriages we contract will be due to divorce rather than death. From mid-life on, however, the demographics that have been working "for" us begin to work against us, and we must also anticipate, until our own deaths, a gradually increasing volume of loss.

A *second feature* of modern loss-through-death is the considerable likelihood that the relational severing will be quite drawn out. That is, in greater and greater numbers we modern humans are dying not as our ancestors did of such diseases as bubonic plague, smallpox, or diphtheria, which kill with considerable speed, but of pathologies, like cancer, that move along—even without interference—at a rather leisurely pace. That pace, of course, is slowed even further by the technological tinkerings of contemporary medicine (Lofland, 1978). Thus, not only must we anticipate an escalation in the volume of loss as we age, we must also expect that at least some of these losses will play themselves out not in hours or days but in months or even years.

A *third feature* of the modern loss complex involves the patterning of relationships. The historical and anthropological literature seems to indicate quite clearly that across time and space these patterns are highly variable. In thinking about such variation, it might be helpful to conceive of human attachment as being formed by multiple "threads of connectedness." We are connected to others by the roles we play, by the help we receive, by the wider network of others made available to us, by the selves others create and sustain, by the comforting myths they allow us, by the reality they validate for us, and by the future they make possible (Lofland, 1982). With this conception, it becomes possible to inquire into the cultural and historical differences in the way these individual threads get put together, as well as in preferences for their construction. Among many possibilities, one can imagine, for example, a human group in which the threads or linkages are quite widely distributed among different people, so that any single relationship is relatively low in significance. The Ifaluk, a people studied by the anthropologist M.E. Spiro, appear to have had a relational pattern close to this one. Commenting on

Spiro's puzzlement over the brevity of bereavement among the Ifaluk, Edmund Volkart, a sociologist, suggested that "... *in self-other relations among the Ifaluk, the other is not valued by the self as a unique and necessary personality. .... Multiple and interchangeable personnel performing the same functions for the individual provide the individual with many psychological anchors in his social environment; the death of any one person leaves the others and thus diminishes the loss.*" (Volkart, 1976)

Conversely, one can also imagine a human group in which each person is typically connected to another by multiple threads, with the total number of relationships maintained by each individual being quite small. In this situation, any single relationship would be relatively high in significance. The work of a number of social scientists indicates that this may be the dominant contemporary pattern of connectedness in the West—a pattern of relatively recent vintage (Lofland, 1985). If so, it means that while we can expect to suffer only a small number of death caused meaningful losses, each such loss will be of very high intensity.

A fourth feature of the contemporary loss situation is the voluntary character of most attachments. Many modern social orders—the United States among them—are characterized by a historically unusual degree of relational voluntarism. Marriages are a matter of mutual choice rather than familial selection, and the continuation of the coupling depends almost entirely upon the will of the partners. Even among near kin, sustained contact and mutual responsibility are more matters of preference than mandate. And, if a relationship ends, whether through death or other causes, it is the task solely of the bereft—not of family or other interested parties—to see to its replacement. In sum, the loss situation of the relatively affluent in modern developed societies is characterized by a concentration in the later years of a small but highly significant number of relational dissolutions, some of which are quite drawn out, and by the absence of any socially guaranteed replacements for the missing attachments.

The implications of this state of affairs are rather somber. There is little here to feed into the American penchant for optimism or to support our fervent belief that human tragedy is merely a set of technical, and ultimately solvable, problems. Thus, for example, this portrait of loss among modern humans leads to the conclusion that, to the degree that it involves an appraisal of what lies ahead, midlife depression is an emotional reaction fully grounded in reality. Those individuals whose lives have matched the probabilities and who have thus far been unscathed by serious illness or death face in middle age, in the foreseeable future, the *inevitable* intrusion of these melancholy companions. Those few unlucky enough to have already experienced loss have an even clearer understanding of what is in store for them.

The foregoing portrait also highlights the fact that most of us will confront death and loss unprepared by prior experience or tutoring. And this confrontation will reach its peak (both in numbers of losses and in prolonged suffering) at the same time that physical and, perhaps, mental vigor are beginning to decline or have already done so. Despite the valiant attempts of our poets and philosophers and theologians to point up the brighter side of human mortality, as a species we have never shown any great enthusiasm for this particular fact of life. We find it inconvenient, at least; more frequently, it engenders terror and despair. The confrontation with mortality is, in short, humanity's special monster. And it is ironic that among us moderns, the main forces who do battle with it are equipped with neither the armor of prior experience nor the strength of youth.

However, devastating they may seem to those who witness them, the deaths of children and young and middle-aged adults provide for most of their survivors the genuine possibility of relational replacement. Even among people for whom the only meaningful relationships are intimate ones, parents may produce or adopt another child; widows and widowers may remarry; lovers may find new loves; new friendships may be formed. In the characteristic modern loss situation, however, many survivors are older and will spend what is left of their lives uncomforted by fresh attachments. In a social order where relationships represent individual *achievements*, those with a limited supply of time or energy or opportunity are in a poor position to recreate their personal networks.

When we use the term "tragedy" in connection with death and loss, it is usual for us to be referring to what we conceive of as "untimely" death. We tend to dismiss the death that comes to the old as merely normal and timely— hardly the ingredients for emotionally stirring drama. Yet, surely, a life in which all the worst suffering is saved until the end is not a great deal less lamentable than a life in which such experiences come early and remain as constant companions.

However much we like to congratulate (and comfort) ourselves on our "medical progress and prowess," we have not escaped from the tragedy of the human condition. We have only substituted a new version. Recognition of that harsh reality is at least as conductive to the dignity of the aged as all the bromides about the pleasures of the "sunset years."

REFERENCES

Goldscheider, C., 1971. *Population, Modernization and Social Structure*. Boston: Little, Brown & Co.

Lofland, L. H., 1978. *The Craft of Dying: The Modern Face of Death*. Beverly Hills, Calif.: Sage.

Lofland, L. H., 1982. "Loss and Human Connection: An Exploration into the Nature of the Social Bond." In William Ickes and Eric S. Knowles, eds., *Personality, Roles and Social Behavior*. New York: Springer-Verlag.

Lofland, L. H., 1985. "The Social Shaping of Emotion: The Case of Grief." *Symbolic Interaction* 8(2):171–90.

Marris, P., 1974. *Loss and Change*. New York: Pantheon Books.

Preston, S. H., Keyfitz, N. and Schoen, R., 1972. *Causes of Death: Life Tables for National Populations*. New York and London: Seminar Press.

Volkart, E. H., 1976. "Bereavement and Mental Health." In Robert Fulton, ed., *Death and Identity*. Bowie, Md.: Charles Press.

54 *Bereavement*

Sidney M. Wolfe

STUDY QUESTIONS

1. What are the phases of grief?

2. What are some recommendations that the author makes to ease bereavement?

At least 8 million Americans lose a relative to death each year, and the result, for the survivors, is called bereavement. Medical writer Peggy Eastman has turned her personal tragedy, and her own response to it, into articles which have comforted many others.

"Nothing is more devastating than losing someone close to you, especially a spouse," says Ms. Eastman. Her husband, James Eastman, was a passenger on a small commuter plane, which crashed in Maine, killing him, young activist Samantha Smith and her father, as well as five others. Her first reaction was "violent tears of protest," and she later had nightmares, bouts of depression, and spiritual struggles.

One month after her husband's death, she says, "I set out to research my condition, in a desperate attempt to understand what was happening to me . . . I felt it might be the only thing that would help."

Bereavement is defined as "loss through death." The inevitability of death makes bereavement, like pregnancy, a common and natural occurrence which results in changes in both function and behavior. As each person is different, so each death is different, and every bereaved person has some unique reactions, which may depend on the deceased person's age, suddenness of death, and type of death. Each year, death of a spouse results in 800,000 new widows and widowers.

Source: Sidney M. Wolfe, "Bereavement." *Health Letter* 3:12 (December 1987), pp. 1–3. Public Citizen Health Research Group, 2000 P Street, N.W., Washington, DC 20036. Reprinted by permission.

Despite the advances of modern medicine, which have reduced childhood mortality, nearly 400,000 persons under age 25 die each year, leaving millions of siblings, parents, and friends in a state of grief. There are at least 27,000 suicides each year in the U.S. Experts feel that the loss of a spouse or the loss of a child are the two most difficult losses to adjust to.

Grief, defined as the behaviors and processes associated with bereavement, usually follows a common course. Grief, sometimes equated with mourning, is normal, and adaptive, allowing the affected person eventually to get on with their own life. Grief may have complications, however, which may require medical attention. Features of grief may be common to other losses, such as loss of a limb, or sometimes divorce.

THE PHASES OF GRIEF

Grief is frequently described as occurring in "phases," in which one follows another, but where some people move back and forth between them. The boundaries between the phases may be blurred.

Phase I

The first phase begins immediately after the loss, and may last up to a few weeks. The survivor experiences shock, numbness, and disbelief. Other common symptoms include crying, sighing, throat tightness, and a sense of unreality. The shock may be more pronounced if the death is sudden and unexpected.

Phase II

The second phase of grief is characterized by preoccupation with the deceased and a yearning to recover the lost person. The survivor frequently re-examines the past relationship, including disagreements, conflicts, and unresolved anger. Emotions can fluctuate wildly, from intense sadness, to anger, to guilt. Dreams of the deceased may be intense and vivid. Weakness and fatigue are also common. If this phase extends beyond several months and does not progress to further stages, it may signal the need for treatment, as this constitutes "pathological grief."

"Pathological grief" may refer to several abnormal patterns of grief. Absent grief, delayed grief and distorted grief are three forms of pathological grief. Distorted grief usually involves persistence of the second stage of grief. This may show itself through compulsive overactivity without a sense of loss, acquisition of the symptoms associated with the deceased, loss of health, social isolation or alienation, or severe depression. Any of these symptoms may require medical attention, or increased social support. However, cultural norms may differ, and in some cultures a single symptom may not represent a true problem.

Phase III

Disorganization and despair characterize the third phase, although the end result is that the survivor accepts the permanence and the fact of loss. The survivor ceases attempts to recover the lost person. Sadness persists in this phase, along with feelings of emptiness, and loss of interest in usual activities.

Phase IV

The fourth phase involves resolution and reorganization of behavior. Normal activities resume, and the bereaved person regains interest in usual activities. Some new social contacts are made. Occasional feelings of sadness, emptiness, and crying spells may occur, but less frequently than before, or with less intensity. The result may not be a complete return to previous activities, but a loss of the preoccupation with the deceased. Past events with the deceased person can be recalled with some pleasure.

The distress of grief and mourning was formerly thought to be short-lived, but recent studies have shown that such feelings can persist for many years. In fact, some think that it can normally last a lifetime. This has prompted some to conclude, "You really don't get over it, you get used to it." As noted before, there is a tremendous amount of individual variation.

THE CONSEQUENCES OF BEREAVEMENT

It has been a common observation, over many years, that the recently widowed are at increased risk for death. Medical studies of this phenomenon have more recent origins. Many studies have looked at the death of a spouse, and according to a 1984 National Academy of Sciences review, "some bereaved persons are at increased risk for illness and even death." Risk factors for death include male gender (widowers) and living alone. Remarriage seems to protect against this effect, but it is not clear if remarriage itself is truly protective, or if those with better support systems tend to remarry and that this protects.

Recent work has shown that the immune system becomes slightly depressed during the grieving process. This may be due to general stress, depression, bereavement itself, or for some other reason. Infections may result from this suppressed immune system, ranging from colds to pneumonia, although this is by no means universal.

Other bereaved persons at increased risk of serious consequences include those who feel a lack of a support system, those in poor prior health (physical or mental), alcoholics, those with severe financial difficulties, and those under 65. Preventive efforts may avoid some of the serious results of bereavement. Someone with many of these risk factors is more likely to need support, counselling, or some other intervention. The suicide of someone especially close also increases risk.

SIDNEY M. WOLFE

INTERVENTIONS

As noted, grief is normal and adaptive, and in most cases does not need to be "medicalized" into an illness. However, if help is needed, there are people to turn to.

1. *Support groups*, where people who have had similar experiences meet and discuss topics of concern. Peggy Eastman joined such a group about three months after the death of her husband. "My church started a new weekly support group for people who had experienced a loss of a loved one. It was made clear that this was to be a support group rooted in the healing power of love, not a psychotherapy group." Topics can include social adjustment, research discussions, the grieving process, and how to avoid stumbling blocks. She concludes, "Nonjudgemental, confidential, peer-directed support groups are one of the best ways to resolve loss because they reassure the griever that he or she is not alone."

As noted in a National Institute of Mental Health publication, "Mutual-help groups do not intend to replace physicians, therapists, and other skilled professionals. Rather, the groups function in the belief that many of our physical and mental health needs go beyond the bounds of formal care measures."

2. *Counselling* is another intervention which may help deal with grief. At its simplest, counselling may be support from friends and family, however, health care personnel can provide this service. The basic goal is to facilitate passing through the phases of mourning, by accepting the reality of the loss, dealing with feelings and emotions, and readjusting to the new environment.

3. *Medications* are a controversial part of the bereavement process, particularly because of the risk of delayed or distorted grief. Some people feel that the reason for the widespread use of medications is that physicians find it easier to write a prescription than to deal with feelings. Some bereaved persons, however, do legitimately need a *short* (7–10 day) course of sleeping pills or tranquilizers. Courses of treatment may lead to addiction, or other complications. Research into this area, as recommended by the National Academy of Sciences, is sorely needed.

4. *The hospice movement* has initiated preventive efforts for those with loved ones who have a chronic and fatal disease. They can help prepare for the eventual loss. Their effectiveness is under investigation, because they are so new.

RECOMMENDATIONS

The Institute of Medicine/National Academy of Sciences released a report in 1984 entitled, *Bereavement: Reactions, Consequences, and Care*. They had several conclusions and recommendations for future work in this area, although only some of the actions have been taken so far. Two international conferences on bereavement have been organized in response to the report, and some additional research money has become available, according to Fred Silver of the Institute of Medicine.

The report recommends:

"Health professionals and institutions have a continuing responsibility to the bereaved."

Schools should train nurses and physicians to look for warning signs, and should refer people at high risk for pathological grief for counselling.

The integration of social workers and chaplains into hospital settings, particularly those involving terminal illness, has improved the care at some medical institutions.

Increased public education may offer support indirectly to bereaved persons. The report notes that institutional care for the dying, and geographic mobility have left many people unprepared to deal with death. Many people are surprised by the intensity of their emotional reaction to the death of a loved one.

Further research is needed in several areas, notably the process and outcome of bereavement. The risk factors for death or disease following the death of someone close need to be studied to effectively plan ways to prevent such problems. Health consequences of bereavement in children, in minority groups, and in other cultures, as well as expanded research into the biology and physiology of grieving, were all highlighted as major areas in need of research.

Research into the intervention strategies described above is needed to evaluate their effectiveness and whether they may be broadly applied to the general population. In particular, the panel noted the opportunities available to evaluate the rapidly evolving hospice movement. Finally, they recommended the establishment of a research review committee by the federal National Institute of Mental Health (NIMH) to coordinate bereavement studies of all kinds.

SIDNEY M. WOLFE

55 *Remarriage and the Family Life Cycle*

Monica McGoldrick / Elizabeth A. Carter

STUDY QUESTIONS

1. Indicate at what points emotional tensions peak.

2. Describe the phases of the divorcing and post-divorce family.

While the statistical majority of the American middle and upper classes still go through the traditional family life cycle stages as outlined [in Chapter 5] the largest variation from that norm consists of families in which divorce has occurred. With the divorce rate currently at 38% and the rate of redivorce at 44% (Glick & Norton, 1976), divorce in the American family is close to the point at which it will occur in the majority of families and will thus be thought of more and more as a normative event.

In our experience as clinicians and teachers, we have found it useful to conceptualize divorce as an interruption or dislocation of the traditional family life cycle, which produces the kind of profound disequilibrium that is associated throughout the entire family life cycle with shifts, gains, and losses in family membership. As in other life cycle phases, there are crucial shifts in relationship status and important emotional tasks that must be completed by the members of divorcing families in order for them to proceed developmentally. As in other phases, emotional issues not resolved at this phase will be carried along as hindrances in future relationships.

Therefore, in this view, we conceptualize the need for families in which divorce occurs to go through one or two additional phases of the family life cycle in order to restabilize and go forward developmentally again at a more complex level. Of women who divorce, 25% do not remarry. These families go

Source: "Remarriage and the Family Life Cycle." In *The Changing Family Life Cycle*, 2nd ed., edited by Elizabeth A. Carter and Monica McGoldrick. Boston: Allyn & Bacon, 1989. Copyright © 1989, Allyn & Bacon. Reprinted by permission.

through one additional phase and can restabilize permanently as divorced families. The other 75% of women who divorce remarry, and these families can be said to require negotiation of two additional phases of the family life cycle before permanent restabilization.

Our concept of divorce and postdivorce family emotional process can be visualized as a roller-coaster graph, with peaks of emotional tension at all of the transition points.

In divorcing families, emotional tension peaks predictably at these points:

1. at the time of the *decision* to separate or divorce;
2. when this decision is announced to family and friends;
3. when money and custody—visitation arrangements are discussed;
4. when the physical separation takes place;
5. when the actual legal divorce takes place;
6. when separated spouses or ex-spouses have contact about money or children and at life cycle transition points of all family members;
7. as each spouse is making the initial adjustments to rebuilding a new life.

These emotional pressure peaks occur in all divorcing families—not necessarily in the above order—and many of them occur over and over again, for months or years. A more detailed depiction of the process appears in [Table 1].

The emotions released during the process of divorce relate primarily to the work of *emotional* divorce—that is, the retrieval of self from the marriage. Each partner must retrieve the hopes, dreams, plans, and expectations that were invested in *this* spouse and in *this* marriage. This requires mourning what is lost and dealing with hurt, anger, blame, guilt, shame, and loss in oneself, in the spouse, in the children, and in the extended family.

In our clinical work with divorcing families, we subscribe to the basic systems view that cutoffs are emotionally harmful, and we work to help divorcing spouses continue to relate as cooperative parents and to permit maximum feasible contact between children and natural parents and grandparents. Our experience supports that of others (Hetherington, Cox, & Cox, 1977), who have found that it takes a minimum of 2 years and a great deal of effort after divorce for a family to readjust to its new structure and proceed to the next developmental stage. Families in which the emotional issues of divorce are not adequately resolved can remain stuck emotionally for years if not for generations.

At the transition into remarriage, the predictable peaks of emotional tension occur at the time of serious commitment to the new relationship; at the time the plan to remarry is announced to families and friends; at the time of the actual remarriage and formation of the stepfamily; and as the logistics of stepfamily life are put into practice.

The family emotional process at the transition to remarriage consists of struggling with *fears* about investment in a new marriage and a new family:

MONICA McGOLDRICK / ELIZABETH A. CARTER

TABLE 1. Dislocations of the Family Life Cycle Requiring Additional Steps to Restabilize and Proceed Developmentally

Phase	Emotional Process of Transition: Prerequisite Attitude	Developmental Issues
	Divorce	
1. The decision to divorce	Acceptance of inability to resolve marital tensions sufficiently to continue relationship	Acceptance of one's own part in the failure of the marriage
2. Planning the breakup of the system	Supporting viable arrangements for all parts of the system	a. Working cooperatively on problems of custody, visitation, finances b. Dealing with extended family about the divorce
3. Separation	a. Willingness to continue cooperative coparental relationship b. Work on resolution of attachment to spouse	a. Mourning loss of intact family b. Restructuring marital and parent-child relationships; adaption to living apart c. Realignment of relationships with extended family; staying connected with spouse's extended family
4. The divorce	More work on emotional divorce: overcoming hurt, anger, guilt, etc.	a. Mourning loss of intact family: giving up fantasies of reunion b. Retrieval of hopes, dreams, expectations from the marriage c. Staying connected with extended families
	Postdivorce Family	
A. Single-parent family	Willingness to maintain parental contact with ex-spouse and support contact of children with ex-spouse and his or her family	a. Making flexible visitation arrangement with ex-spouse and his or her family b. Rebuilding own social network
B. Single-parent (noncustodial)	Willingness to maintain parental contact with ex-spouse and support custodial parent's relationship with children	a. Finding ways to continue effective parenting relationship with children b. Rebuilding own social network

one's own fears, the new spouse's fears, and the children's fears (of either or both spouses); dealing with hostile or upset reactions of the children, the extended families, and the ex-spouse; struggling with the ambiguity of the new model of family structure roles and relationships; rearousal of intense parental guilt and concerns about the welfare of children; and rearousal of the old attachment to ex-spouse (negative or positive). [Table 2] depicts the process in somewhat greater detail. . . .

TABLE 2 Remarried Family Formation: A Developmental Outline

Steps	Prerequisite Attitude	Developmental Issues
1. Entering the new relationship	Recovery from loss of first marriage (adequate "emotional divorce")	Recommitment to marriage and to forming a family with readiness to deal with the complexity and ambiguity
2. Conceptualizing and planning new marriage and family	Accepting one's own fears and those of new spouse and children about remarriage and forming a step-family Accepting need for time and patience for adjustment to complexity and ambiguity of the following: 1. Multiple new roles 2. Boundaries: space, time, membership, and authority 3. Affective issues: guilt, loyalty conflicts, desire for mutuality, unresolvable past hurts	a. Work on openness in the new relationships to avoid pseudomutuality b. Plan for maintenance of cooperative coparental relationships with ex-spouses c. Plan to help children deal with fears, loyalty conflicts, and membership in two systems d. Realignment of relationships with extended family to include new spouse and children e. Plan maintenance of connections for children with extended family of ex-spouse(s)
3. Remarriage and reconstitution of family	Final resolution of attachment to previous spouse and ideal of "intact" family; acceptance of a different model of family with permeable boundaries	a. Restructuring family boundaries to allow for inclusion of new spouse-stepparent b. Realignment of relationships throughout subsystems to permit interweaving of several systems c. Making room for relationships of all children with biological (noncustodial) parents, grandparents, and other extended family d. Sharing memories and histories to enhance stepfamily integration

NOTE: Variation on a developmental schema presented by Ransom, Schlesinger, and Derdeyn (1979).

In our experience, the residue of an angry and vengeful divorce can block stepfamily integration for years or forever. The rearousal of the old emotional attachment to an ex-spouse, which characteristically surfaces at the time of remarriage and at subsequent life cycle transitions of children, is usually not understood as a predictable process and therefore leads to denial, misinterpretation, cutoff, and assorted difficulties. As in the case of adjustment to a new family structure after divorce, stepfamily integration seems also to require a

MONICA McGOLDRICK / ELIZABETH A. CARTER

minimum of 2 years before a workable new structure permits family members to move on emotionally.

REFERENCES

Glick, P., and A. J. Norton. Number, timing, and duration of marriages and divorces in the U.S.: June 1975. In *Current Population Reports*. Washington, D.C.: U.S. Government Printing Office, October 1976.

Hetherington, E. M., M. Cox, and R. Cox. The aftermath of divorce. In J. J. Stevens, Jr., and M. Matthews (Eds.), *Mother-Child, Father-Child Relations*. Washington, D.C.: National Association for the Education of Young Children, 1977.

Ransom, W., S. Schlesinger, and A. P. Derdeyn. A stepfamily in formation. *American Journal of Orthopsychiatry*, 1979, 49, 36–43.

56 *The Six Stations of Remarriage: Developmental Tasks of Remarriage After Divorce*

Ann Goetting

STUDY QUESTIONS

1. Note several reasons for the large remarriage rate.

2. Describe the six stations of remarriage.

Remarriage is emerging as a common form of marriage. Currently, remarriages represent 32% of all marriages in the United States (Price-Bonham & Balswick, 1980). As the divorce rate continues to rise and the rate of remarriage remains high—it recently has been estimated that 80% of Americans who are currently obtaining divorces will eventually remarry (Glick, 1975a)—an increasing number of people are finding themselves immersed in a marital structure quite different from the one with which they are familiar. As Schlesinger (1970) pointed out, a remarriage "possesses its own constructs, characteristics, and possibilities" (p.

Source: Ann Goetting, "The Six Stations of Remarriage: Developmental Tasks of Remarriage After Divorce." *Family Relations*, April 1982. Copyrighted 1982 by the National Council on Family Relations, 3989 Central Ave., N.E., Suite 550, Minneapolis, MN 55421. Reprinted by permission.

101). Some of the most important differences between a first marriage and a remarriage are based on the ties each partner has to the previous marriage through children, through financial and custodial settlement, through the family and friends of the former spouse, and through continued commitment and/or attachment to the former spouse. It is probably true that the single visible factor which most differentiates a remarriage from a first marriage is the presence of children from a former marriage. Cherlin (1978) indicated that when neither spouse had a child from a previous marriage, the family of remarriage closely resembled families of first marriage and most of the norms for first marriages applied.

Though it has been suggested that remarriages are happier and more successful than first marriages (Rollin, 1971), the best available evidence has consistently indicated over the last two decades that while most remarriages do remain intact until death, the risk of marital dissatisfaction and divorce is somewhat greater than that associated with first marriages (Cherlin, 1978; McCarthy, 1978). It is estimated that one third of first marriages will end in divorce while close to one half of remarriages will do so (U.S. Bureau of the Census, 1976).

Furstenberg (1979) pointed out that the rate of conjugal stability in remarriage is only slightly lower than that in first marriage and might well be accounted for, not by greater difficulties inherent in the structure of remarriage, but by the fact that remarriages include a disproportionately greater number of individuals who accept divorce as a solution to an unsatisfactory marital situation. While this may be true, while remarriage may not require a *more difficult* lifestyle or adjustment process than first marriage, it can be assumed to require one that is *different* and therefore worthy of consideration because of the unique nature of remarriage.

The main purpose of this paper is to examine remarriage as a process. More specifically, the concern is to explore the various developmental tasks associated with the status passage from divorced to remarried. The question addressed here is: what are the situations which a person may expect to encounter upon entering and participating in remarried life? Furstenberg introduced the concept "normative schedule" to describe demographic processes that become relatively constant over time. As marriage, divorce and subsequent remarriage become routinized, they become part of a normative schedule, part of the life course. While the processes of marriage and divorce have been charted (Berger & Kellner, 1964; Bohannan, 1970; Vaughan, 1978), the final component of this marital normative schedule, that is remarriage, virtually has been overlooked in the family literature. A descriptive model of this status passage from divorced to remarried could aid the practitioner in guiding clients through the developmental tasks associated with their transition into remarriage after divorce.

Before addressing the developmental tasks of remarriage, attention is turned to the divorce and remarriage trends which are the sources of this emerging marital form. The concern here is with why divorce and subsequent remarriage have become increasingly common. Why are more and more people accepting divorce as a solution to an unsatisfactory marriage? And why do so many, though the proportion is declining (Norton & Glick, 1976), find their way back into the marriage market and eventually recommitted to matrimony?

EXPLANATIONS FOR DIVORCE AND REMARRIAGE

Divorce

The divorce rate in the United States has been rising almost continuously since data were first collected by the United States Census Bureau. It is estimated that about 37% of first marriages currently being contracted will end in divorce if the present conditions affecting divorce continue (Glick, 1973). In the past when divorce was relatively rare it was blamed on individual deficiencies. With the dramatic increase during the middle 1960's when divorce was chosen as a solution to marital problems by a broader spectrum of the population, however, emphasis has turned away from the deviance perspective and toward societal-level explanations. One recent analysis blamed the long term divorce increase on five components of our social structure: (1) the doctrine of individualism; (2) the trend toward equality of sexes; (3) the trend toward a general acceptance of divorce; (4) growing systemness; and, (5) affluence (Goetting, 1979). While this analysis is quite comprehensive, other components could be added to constitute a long list of factors fostering divorce. For example, Glick (1975b, p. 8) suggested that the following factors contribute to marital disruption: (1) social disruption such as the Vietnam war and inflation; (2) the secularization of life which dilutes the influence of organized religion in discouraging divorce; (3) education for marriage and family life in churches, schools and colleges which fosters more objective evaluation of marriage and divorce; and, (4) marriage and divorce counseling which assist incompatible couples in dissolving intolerable marriages. Also, divorce has been blamed on the socialization process which teaches men and women to have different and even opposing interests and social orientations. The result is that they have difficulty as adults becoming the companions required by the modern marriage ethic (Goetting, 1981).

Remarriage

Unlike divorce, little attention has been devoted to the high rate of remarriage after divorce. While single isolated explanations are scattered throughout the family literature, no attempt has been made to integrate these ideas into a comprehensive set of societallevel explanations. An attempt here to do so yields four: (1) the value of romantic love; (2) social exchange—satiation and alternatives; (3) social norms; and, (4) norm ambiguity and role instability.

Romantic Love. Romantic love was conceptualized by Goode (1959) to mean a strong emotional attachment between adolescents or adults, consisting of at least the components of sex desire and tenderness. In American society it has been taught that being romantically in love and having this love reciprocated is a major goal in life. The individual who "has no one" is pitied or at least considered to be in this way unfulfilled. Furthermore it has been taught that appropriate fulfillment of the need for romantic love is found within the institution of marriage. Biegel (1951) and Goode (1959) suggested that while romantic love serves important functions for social stability, it is based on temporary personal need satisfaction, and therefore is unstable. A marriage based on such fragile ground is conducive to divorce. Biegel stated that the "burning craving" of romantic love cannot last. Goode agreed that the passion of romantic love dies in the marital relationship. He stated that the "antithesis of romantic love is 'conjugal' love, the love between a settled couple" (Goode, 1959, p. 39). Synthesizing this series of ideas on romantic love, it is suggested here that romantic love leads to marriage, which in turn leads to conjugal love, a non-romantic form of love. If this simple process is extended, some implications for remarriage can be suggested. The individual is taught to strive for romantic love and seek satisfaction within marriage. But then marriage destroys the romantic elements of the relationship and replaces them with a relationship based on responsibility. Therefore, married individuals who are no longer romantically involved with each other would be left unfulfilled and once again in pursuit of romantic love. Extramarital romantic love relationships or at least desires or fantasies of such would then stimulate divorce and ultimately result in remarriage.

Benson (Note 1) suggested that most married individuals avoid this cycle of remarriage probably because of a lack of ambition in the continuing search for love. Because they are influenced by various social controls (for example, norms disapproving extramarital romantic involvements), they in fact remain unfulfilled romantically.

Social Exchange—Satiation and Alternatives. Exchange theory offers another cyclical scheme explaining serial monogamy. Theories of social exchange view humans as reward-seeking, punishment-avoiding creatures. The theories perceive human interaction to be analogous to economic markets, though humans can exchange things which are not measured by money. People are motivated toward profit—that is, an excess of reward (something valuable) over cost (something punishing or loss of reward). From the perspectives of Homans (1961) and Thibaut and Kelley (1959) divorce and subsequent remarriage can be viewed as the exchange between marital partners, and explained in the following way: A and B choose to interact with one another (marry) because each obtains the highest profit (such as companionship, romantic love or whatever is valuable) relative to interacting with alternative persons in that kind of relationship. But eventually satiation will weaken that relationship. This is based on the assumption that the more of a rewarding activity a person receives from another, the less valuable the further units of that activity ("diminishing returns"). At the same time that the relationship is becoming weakened due to satiation, it is becoming further weakened because of the increase in alternative marriage partners resulting from social changes including industrialization, urbanization, the doctrine of individualism, and the increased proportion of women in the labor force. The many alternative spouses raise what Thibaut and Kelley refer to as the "comparison level for alternatives." Therefore, because of the satiation of marital rewards and the increase in alternative spouses, A and B will divorce and both find new partners who will again offer them the best profit (remarriage) until once again satiation sets in and a better alternative presents itself.

While under the principle of satiation it is assumed that the individual seeks rewards from interacting with a variety of people, a person *may* get such variety of interaction while being married. The need for variety may be satisfied by interacting with family, friends, colleagues or an extramarital lover. This is how exchange theorists would explain the marriages that last. If the spouses do not limit themselves to interacting with each other, that is, if they spend time together as well as time with others, satiation does not occur and so alternatives are less attractive. Thibaut and Kelley (1959) devoted a chapter to nonvoluntary relationships. They suggested that some below-comparison-level relationships (relationships that are below the person's standards of satisfaction) are maintained because alternatives are unacceptable. In other words, the marriage may provide too little reward, but the costs of divorce (one alternative) outweigh its rewards.

Social Norms. Another explanation for remarriage after divorce is that it represents an adaptation to social norms. One such norm is Farber's (1964) "permanent availability." Like romantic love, permanent availability is useful in explaining divorce and remarriage. According to Farber the norm of permanent marriage is being replaced by the norm of permanent availability. This notion implies that divorce can be explained by greater attractions to new spouses. It implies an expectation to better one's lot in society by progressing on to more attractive marital partners in somewhat the same way that one would move to a new position that offered a higher salary or better working conditions.

Another norm which has implications for remarriage is that of success in marriage. To the extent that divorce represents some kind of failure, marriage represents success. While there is social pressure on both sexes for success in marriage, such pressure is greater for women because the marriage and family have traditionally been her primary domain of responsibility. Whether a marriage is a "success" or "failure" is commonly largely attributed to the wife's "expressive" skills in maintaining the marriage. After an individual becomes divorced, the sense of failure can often be relieved by success within subsequent remarriage. In this sense, divorce carries within it the seeds of remarriage. Remarriage is an attempt to alleviate feelings of failure.

The third and final norm to be considered here which is conducive to remarriage after divorce is that of marriage itself. Marriage is the "normal" life-style, and society tends to organize social life on the basis of couples and families. Duberman (1974) stated: "Ours is a two-by-two world, and there is little room in it for the unaccompanied individual. . . . To justify their own state, married people think of marriage as 'natural' and anyone who does not conform to this point of view is challenging the social values" (p. 115). Being without a spouse places one in an awkward position often resulting in a truncated social life. Single persons may be excluded from social affairs because of their proverbial "fifth wheel" status. Adult singleness, not necessarily the divorced status, represents deviance from the norm, and in that way exerts social pressure toward marriage.

The pressure to become "normal" in terms of becoming a partner in marriage may be greater for parents than for other categories of singles because there are more individuals involved in the striving for a normal family life. Single parents may feel added pressure in terms of accomplishing normal lives not for only themselves but for their children.

Norm Ambiguity and Role Instability. In contrast to the view that remarriage after divorce is an adaptation to social norms is Goode's argument that such remarriage represents adaptation to norm ambiguity associated with the status of divorce. In his classic volume *Women in Divorce*, Goode (1956) suggested that the lack of norms associated with the status of being divorced created pressures toward remarriage, and in this way minimized social disruption caused by divorce. It was his contention that such norm ambiguity provided institutional pressures conducive to remarriage which allowed a high divorce rate to exist while kinship institutions were maintained and major societal disruption was avoided. Goode (1956) described the following four areas of norm ambiguity associated with the divorced status:

1. There are no ethical imperatives for relatives or friends to furnish needed material or emotional support during and after the crisis to divorcees *as* divorcees.

2. Issues are unclear concerning the readmission of divorcees into their former kinship structure or into a new one. We are not at all clear as to where members of the divorcing family ought to go. Families of orientation are under no obligation to take them back, nor are former in-laws, even though in the case of the woman, they all have surnames in common.

3. There are no clear avenues for the formation of new families. It is unclear as to what constitutes appropriate behavior in terms of finding a second husband or wife. Such norm ambiguity permeates the relationships of the divorcees with parents, friends and children.

4. There is no clear definition concerning the general proper behavior and emotional attitudes of the divorced. They don't know whether they should be grieved or relieved. Lacking specification of behavior expectations, divorcees are subject to criticism by some regardless what they do.

It was Goode's assumption that the norm ambiguity associated with divorce places sufficient stress on most divorcees to pressure them back into the comfortably norm-regulated state of marriage. He believed that the lack of institutionalization of postdivorce adjustment functions to create pressures toward new marriages, which in turn maintain the kinship structures necessary for the survival of society. It should be noted that while such norm ambiguity could create pressure toward remarriage, it could instead lead to the development of clear norms for the divorced.

Bernard (1956) argued along the same general lines as Goode in her explanation of the high rate of remarriage after divorce. She referred to the inherent instability in the status of "divorced" and the resulting drive toward remarriage. She contended that even if divorced persons have no children, they cannot resume the status of being single because marriage has fundamentally altered their self-images, daily habits and leisure activities, relations with friends and family and even their identities.

> Dissolution of marriage disrupts a complex integration of role, which requires a corresponding role to be played by someone in the outside world . . . his need for a partner who will play a complementary role and thus render functional a longstanding role of one's own is undoubtedly a strong motivational drive toward remarriage. (p. 125)

THE STATIONS OF REMARRIAGE

While there are clear factors favoring remarriage after divorce such as experience and maturity, it remains a trying experience for most who pursue it. As suggested earlier, a great portion of the problems associated with remarriage are related to the complexities introduced by children from former marriages. The complexity of an institution in itself need not present problems, but if society fails to provide guidelines for the relationships involved, the outcome may be one of chaos and conflict. For lack of such guidelines in Western culture, the remarried pair is often expected to function in the same way as does a first married pair, despite the fact that in addition to the new husband and wife there may be two former spouses, two sets of children, four sets of grandparents, and numerous other relatives and friends associated with a former marriage. In addition, there may be many unresolved feelings carried over into the new marriage.

Undoubtedly, remarriage after divorce is a complex process with several interrelated components. That process is described here through use of Bohannan's (1970) model outlining developmental tasks of divorce. His six "stations" of divorce consist of those tasks which must be mastered in order to exit successfully from an existing marriage. They include the emotional, legal, economic, coparental, community and psychic divorces. Those stations are revisited here in the course of moving from divorce to remarriage. As Furstenberg (1979) pointed out, a successful remarriage must involve undoing or refashioning many of the adaptations made to a successful divorce. As is true of the divorce stations, all six stations of remarriage need not necessarily occur to all remarrying people with the same intensity and in the same order. In fact, some individuals may avoid some stations altogether. The six stations of remarriage are ordered here in such a way that the first three can occur independent of the existence of children from a former marriage, while the last three assume the involvement of such children.

Emotional Remarriage

Typically the remarriage process begins with the emotional remarriage. This is the often slow process by which a divorced person reestablishes a bond of attraction, commitment and trust with a member of the opposite sex. After having experienced severe disappointment in a previous relationship, the divorcee learns to release emotions in an effort to once again secure comfort and love. Often this process is wrought with the fear that this emotional investment will lead to loss and rejection. Such fears may justifiably be intense because an additional failure at relationships threatens not only to leave the individual once again disappointed and alone, but also to damage identity and self-concept. Another divorce could strongly suggest to others as well as self a deficiency in those skills, whatever they may be, which are necessary to sustain a marriage. While there is always ambiguity in terms of cause and fault with one divorce—possibly it was at least partially the fault of the other spouse, or maybe the divorce could be blamed on a situation which surrounded that particular marriage—additional failures begin to single out an individual as a "loser." Due to the loss, rejection and failure that are typically associated with divorce, the emotional remarriage is a unique and often arduous and volatile process which is not satisfactorily completed by all who attempt it.

Psychic Remarriage

Psychic remarriage is the process of changing one's conjugal identity from individual to couple. It involves relinquishing the personal freedom and autonomy established by the psychic divorce, and resuming a lifestyle in which a person is expected to be viewed as one component of a partnership.

The psychic remarriage affects different individuals in different ways. For example, men and women are likely to differ in the amount of stress experienced in their respective transitions in conjugal identity. In general the psychic remarriage may represent less change for men than for women, and therefore mean less potential for difficulties in adjustment. Since the role of adult male in our society dictates a primary identity with occupational status thereby deemphasizing conjugal identity, men are likely to experience a relatively mild identity shift as they pass from the status of single person to that of mate. In other words, since the social status and therefore personal identity of a man is relatively independent of his marital status, a shift in his marital status would not represent an extreme alteration in personal identity. But the situation may be very different for women, who in accordance with traditional gender roles, identify strongly with their marital status. While the occupational sphere tends to be the domain of the man, the conjugal sphere is seen as the domain of the woman. It is the woman, then, who is faced with the more extreme identity shift when there is an alteration in marital status.

But the shift is not of equal intensity among all women. Changes in marital status would seemingly have a greater affect on women who hold traditional gender role attitudes than on those who hold non-traditional attitudes. The traditional women would suffer a great loss with psychic divorce, a true identity

ANN GOETTING

crisis. But upon remarriage these women would adjust easily in the psychic realm. For them psychic remarriage represents the recovery of their valued identity as wife. Non-traditional women, on the other hand, are likely to view the psychic divorce in positive terms as a period of growth into autonomous identity, an opportunity to do away with the restraints of couple identity. It is these women who are likely to have adjustment problems associated with psychic remarriage. To them the wife role is less important, and psychic remarriage represents loss of the more highly valued independence and freedom. It is interesting to note that the suggestion presented here that non-traditional women, when compared with traditional women, are likely to discover satisfaction in psychic divorce and severe stress in psychic remarriage has some empirical support in 1970 census statistics. Those data indicate that women with five or more years of college education (an index of non-traditional attitude) are divorcing more often than other divorced men and women (Glick, 1975b).

It becomes clear that psychic remarriage represents a different kind of process for different categories of people, but it safely can be assumed that in most, if not all, cases it represents some disruption and the consequent need for adjustment.

Community Remarriage

The community remarriage like the community divorce represents an alteration which a person often must make in relationships with a community of friends. Where the community divorce involves breaking away from the world of couples, entering what Hunt (1966) called "the world of the formerly married," the community remarriage involves re-entrance into the couple's world. Like the community divorce, the community remarriage may be a turbulent process. Unmarried friends are typically lost for lack of a common lifestyle, especially friends of the opposite sex. These friends are replaced by married couples, often remarried couples with whom remarrieds share important aspects of biography.

In some ways the process of community remarriage has potential for being more strenuous than does the process of community divorce because it can result in the loss of closer friends. With the community divorce one must give up couples, that is *pairs* of friends who were shared with a spouse. Often the friendships had not been intimate. Instead, they were secondary to, convenient to, and dependent upon, the marital relationship. They were not one's own friends, selected as a reflection of one's interests and needs. They were relationships based on the combined interests and needs of the spouses. But with the community remarriage, one may be put in a position of severing the close personally-tailored ties established while divorced, and replacing them with less intimate, couple-oriented relationships. Furthermore, those bonds of friendship established during that period of time when one was divorced may be particularly valuable because they lent support at a time of personal crisis. These were the friends who were there to help the individual through the typically devastating experiences associated with the divorce process.

So the community remarriage, while representing re-entrance into the "normality" of the couples' world, also may mean the eventual loss of valuable friendship bonds. Married life is often intolerant of relationships with unmarried friends. Its structure discourages those connections with the past, those ties with the world of the formerly married.

Parental Remarriage

The parental remarriage is necessary if there are children. It is the union of an individual with the children of this new spouse. Parental remarriage may be the most difficult developmental task of remarriage as suggested by one recent study (Messinger, 1976). It is certainly the one that has received the most attention in the literature as is indicated by the fact that a series of bibliographies on steprelationships, the product of parental remarriage, is periodically compiled and distributed for the use of social scientists (Sell, 1977). Unprecedented numbers of people find themselves living with other peoples' children, and many view the process of combining with them to form a family unit as challenging at best.

Fast and Cain (1966) suggested that the problems of stepparenthood are based on the fact that the role definition of stepparent in this society is poorly articulated, and implies contradictory expectations as "parent," "stepparent" and "nonparent." The stepparent cannot fully assume any of these roles, and therefore must individually work out behavior patterns for interacting with one's spouse's children. Folk tradition describes the stepmother as wicked and cruel—in a word, unparentlike—so to enact that role would be socially unacceptable. Instead, the stepparent is encouraged to assume the role of parent, for which there is legal support in the explication of the rights and duties entailed by the "in loco parentis" relationship. But the stepparent cannot totally assume the role of father or mother. The natural parent is typically still active in the parental role, which requires that the stepparent gracefully accede to the parental rights of another and behave as nonparent. The stepparent and the natural parent are placed in a position of sharing the residential, educational, financial, health, and moral decisions incumbent on the parental role. Society provides no guidelines for this sharing of rights and responsibilities which can easily lead to confusion, frustration, and resentment.

Another explanation for the difficulties associated with parental remarriage and the associated steprelationships is that marital role expectations between husband and wife are not worked out prior to the assumption of parental roles. Spouses are not allowed the opportunity to develop workable and comfortable marital relationships and to establish a primary husband-wife bond prior to the birth of children. Marital and parental adjustment must be confronted simultaneously which could encourage the inappropriate involvement of children in marital dissention. Marital and parental problems could easily confound one another. The natural parent's prior relationship to his child can serve as a threat to the establishment of a primary husband-wife bond. In that way it may detract from the integration of the new family unit.

One problem relating to stepparenthood that appears often in the literature is discipline. The stepparent is often reluctant to provide discipline because the clear authority vested in a natural parent is lacking. If the stepparent does actually attempt to discipline, such action may not be well-received by the child or may not be interpreted as acceptable by the spouse. This problem of discipline would seemingly be more common for stepfathers than stepmothers, since children typically stay with their mothers after divorce. It is the stepfather who most often enters a formerly single-parent family unit and who, therefore, actually experiences daily interaction with his stepchildren. The stepmother, on the other hand, usually spends limited time with her visiting stepchildren.

Another specific problem associated with parental remarriage concerns children as a link to the former marriage, and was expressed by Messinger's (1976) subjects. Some felt that continued ties through the children with previous family members made it more difficult for the new spouse to integrate into the new family unit. In this way they saw the children as a source of marital disruption. New mates frequently felt that such continued ties made them feel as though they were outsiders.

Economic Remarriage

The economic remarriage is the reestablishment after divorce of a marital household as a unit of economic productivity and consumption. Like the parental remarriage, it is a particularly difficult developmental task of remarriage, as evidenced by the Messinger study, which suggested that the problem of finances in remarriage was surpassed in severity only by problems associated with children. The economic remarriage as a developmental task can be considered as being an extension of the parental remarriage in that its main difficulties stem from the existence of children from a former marriage. When there are such children involved, the economic remarriage becomes complex in that it emerges as an open system, dependent on or at least interrelated with the economic behavior of individuals other than the two spouses.

Typically the standard of living increases at remarriage due to the simple fact that financial resources which had formerly maintained two residences are combined to support only one. So the problem is not so much one of insufficient funds as it is one of financial instability and resource distribution. One source of instability stems from the sporadic nature of incoming child support payments, especially after the mother has remarried. Many reconstituted families are simply unable to predict how much money will be available from month to month because of the uncertainty associated with the arrival of child support payment. Information (Note 2) collected in 1978 from a sample of United States women indicates that continuity of support payments declined somewhat with the remarriage of the mother; only 43% of the remarried wives reported having received their payments always, as opposed to 51% of the divorced but not remarried. Not knowing whether that next payment will arrive can introduce significant inconvenience into the remarriage household. A second source of economic instability lies in the unpredictable nature of the needs of the husband's children, who typically reside with their mother. While outgoing child support payments may be constant, the possibility of unexpected needs requiring extra financial cost (medical, educational, etc.) can loom as a dark cloud over the remarriage. It can bring the same kind of uncertainty and consequent inconvenience into the remarriage household as lack of continuity associated with incoming child support payments.

The problem of resource distribution refers to the issue of how the money should be spent; who should get how much of what is available? For example, if *his* daughter is given ballet lessons, should not *her* son be allowed tennis lessons, even though the sources of support for the two children are quite different? If the resources available to her son from her ex-spouse preclude such tennis lessons, should the stepfather finance such lessons for the sake of equity? Messinger (1976) reported frequent statements of discomfort and embarrassment on the part of mothers over the financial cost incurred for her new husband on behalf of her children. Society fails to provide guidelines for these kinds of situations, which can lead to stress in the remarital relationship.

The economic remarriage unites individuals from two different family systems and two different generations who have learned different and possibly opposing earning and spending habits. The problems involved in integrating such persons into a smooth functioning economic unit may provide a true challenge for all involved.

Legal Remarriage

Remarriage as a form of marriage is a creature of the law. Since it is such a relatively newly recognized way of life, its legal ramifications are only beginning to be explored. By the time a remarriage takes place, alimony, child support, and the division of property have already been set regarding the former marriage. The new marriage may cause additional legal considerations concerning responsibility toward relationships from the former marriage. The complexity of what Bohannan (1970) referred to as the pseudokinship system created by remarriage after divorce requires decisions regarding his and her financial resources, his and her former spouses, and his, her, and their children. In consideration of all of these, people need to evaluate their legal responsibilities and to decide how they want their resources distributed. Remarriage after divorce does not mean that a person exchanges one family for another; instead it means that the individual takes on an additional family. Since legal responsibilities associated with this action have not been clearly charted, individuals are left to base legal decisions on their own moral guidelines. For some this can be a difficult process because it involves assigning weights of importance to members of their complicated pseudokinship networks. Such questions arise as to which wife deserves the life and accident insurance, medical coverage, retirement benefits, pension rights and property rights. Is it the former wife who played a major role in building the estate or is it the current wife who has contributed less but is currently in his "good graces"? Also, to which children should he lend support for college education—his children, her children or their children? Since state inheritance laws typically favor a person's current spouse and natural children, inheritance rights need to be clearly defined at the point of legal remarriage if the person wishes to will benefits to a former spouse or to stepchildren.

Until the time that state legal codes respond to the needs of the remarried, individuals will continue to be left to work out the legal problems and decisions of remarriage after divorce. The imposition of structure by the state in this area not only would make the legal remarriage logistically simpler, but might contribute to increased affability for the relationships involved. The implementation of a standard procedure for the distribution of resources, for example, would eliminate the sense of competition and jealousy which is now encouraged by the lack of guidelines. If, for example, it was predetermined by the state that the resources of remarried persons would be divided among all of their surviving spouses in proportions corresponding to the length of each marriage, bitterness on the part of any of those spouses toward one another before or after death regarding equity in inheritance rights might be reduced. The burden of responsibility for distribution of resources would have been lifted from the individual by the state. Such legal structure could relieve tension among spouses, former spouses, parent-child relationships and steprelationships, and therefore contribute to the maintenance of the complex pseudo-kinship structure created by remarriage after divorce.

CONCLUDING STATEMENT

As divorce and subsequent remarriage become increasingly common, adjustment to their developmental tasks becomes a greater concern for family practitioners. While individuals face different tasks in varying orders, it has been suggested here that the six developmental tasks of divorce outlined by Bohannan are also important developmental tasks of remarriage. Remarriage can be a complex process, and its adjustment accordingly difficult. The problems associated with remarital adjustment are often heightened by the fact that partners in remarriage may still be adjusting to their divorces. At remarriage, a person may be compelled to commence the stations of remarriage while having not yet completed the stations of divorce. For example, as an individual struggles with establishing bonds of affection, commitment and trust with a new partner, he or she may still be contending with the severance of emotional ties with the former spouse. In order to be able to provide guidance and support to individuals in the throes of remarital adjustment, the practitioner needs to be familiar, first, with the general complexity of remarriage after divorce and, second, with the specific developmental tasks which can be anticipated as part of the adjustment process.

NOTES

[1] Benson, L. Personal communication. 1969.

[2] These data were obtained from a combination of the March and April 1979 Current Population Surveys conducted by the United States Bureau of the Census. Although the information has not been published by the Bureau, it has been made available on computer tapes.

REFERENCES

Berger, P. L. and H. Kellner, 1964. Marriage and the construction of reality. *Diogenes* 46:1–23.

Bernard, J. 1956. *Remarriage: A study of marriage.* New York: Dryden Press.

Biegel, H. 1951. Romantic love. *American Sociological Review* 16:326–34.

Bohannan, P. 1970. The six stations of divorce. In P. Bohannan (ed.), *Divorce and after.* New York: Doubleday.

Cherlin, A. 1978. Remarriage as an incomplete institution. *American Journal of Sociology* 84:634–50.

Duberman, L. 1974. *Remarriage and its alternatives.* New York: Praeger.

Farber, B. 1964. *Family: Organization and interaction.* San Francisco: Chandler.

Fast, I., and A. C. Cain. 1966. The stepparent role: Potential for disturbances in family functioning. *American Journal of Orthopsychiatry* 36:485–91.

Furstenberg, F. F. 1979. Recycling the family. *Marriage and Family Review* 2 (3), 1:12–22.

Glick, P. C. 1973. Dissolution of marriage by divorce and its demographic consequences. *International Population Conference* 2:65–69. Liege, Belgium: International Union for the Scientific Study of Population.

———. 1975a. A demographer looks at American families. *Journal of Marriage and the Family* 31:15–26.

———. 1975b. Some recent changes in American families. *Current Population Reports: Special Studies*, Series P-23, No. 52. Washington, D.C.: Government Printing Office.

Goetting, A. 1979. Some societal-level explanations for the rising divorce rate. *Family Therapy* VI (2):71–87.

———. 1981. Divorce outcome research: Issues and perspectives. *Journal of Family Issues* 2:350–78.

Goode, W. J. 1956. *Women in divorce.* New York: Free Press.

———. 1959. The theoretical importance of love. *American Sociological Review* 24:38–47.

Homans, G. C. 1961. *Social behavior: Its elementary forms.* New York: Harcourt, Brace and World.

Hunt, M. M. 1966. *The world of the formerly married.* New York: McGraw-Hill.

McCarthy, J. 1978. A comparison of the probability of the dissolution of first and second marriages. *Demography* 15 (3):345–59.

Messinger, L. 1976. Remarriage between divorced people with children from previous marriages: A proposal for preparation for remarriage. *Journal of Marriage and Family Counseling* 38:193–200.

Norton, A. J., and P. C. Glick. 1976. Marital instability: Past, present and future. *Journal of Social Issues* 32:5–20.

Price-Bonham, S. and J. O. Balswick. 1980. The noninstitutions: Divorce, desertion and remarriage. *Journal of Marriage and the Family* 42:959–72.

Rollin, B. 1971. The American way of marriage: Remarriage. *Look*, September 21, pp. 62–67.

Schlesinger, B. 1970. Remarriage as family reorganization for divorced persons: A Canadian study. *Journal of Comparative Family Studies*, 1 (1):101–18.

Sell, K. D. 1977. *Divorce in the 1970's*. Salisbury, N.C.: Department of Sociology, Catawba College.

Thibaut, J. W. and H. H. Kelley. 1959. *The social psychology of groups*. New York: Wiley.

U.S. Bureau of the Census. 1976. Number, timing and duration of marriages and divorces in the United States: June, 1975. *Current Population Reports*, Series P-20, No. 297. Washington, D.C.: Government Printing Office.

Vaughan, D. 1978. Uncoupling: The social construction of divorce. In H. Robboy, S. L. Greenblatt, and C. Clark (eds.), *Social Interaction: Introductory readings in sociology*. New York: St. Martins.

14 *Continuing the Change*

Since changes in other aspects of the social system have a strong impact on the family, it is necessary to know about present and future changes in society as a whole in order to understand and prepare for new family situations.

Such factors as the family's loss of functions and moral influence, the decline in family size, the recognition and thus a seeming rise in family violence, and the higher divorce rate have raised the question regarding the death of the family and a yearning for the "good old days." As Alvin Toffler notes in the first article of Chapter 14, a return to the idealized 1950s requires a return to yesterday's world—a fact few would accept since it would mean the loss of many items now accepted and cherished. Besides, a closer historical analysis reveals that the current situation may reflect more a change in values and interpretation than in the basic "goodness" or deterioration of family life. Thus, current problems may be a result of economic, social, and medical advances which improved upon earlier conditions.

Arthur Norton, in the second article of this chapter, believes that there will be little change from the current picture in families in the year 2000. The trends, then, indicate that:

a. the longer period of premarital singlehood will continue as will the issues they raise regarding greater sexual permissiveness and the need for sex education;

b. the continuing trend toward increasing marital equality will mean a continuing increase in dual-career families, role flexibility, and improvements in child care arrangements;

c. the trends toward smaller families, child-free and single-parent families, and stepfamilies will continue, as will the questions they raise as to family quality;

d. the longer post-parental married life will continue as will the possible clash between the needs of a large retired population and a relatively smaller working group.

In the final article of Chapter 14, Gordon Clanton carries these trends a bit further into the future and comes up with a few surprising results. The message from these findings is simple—we must learn to cope with new and changing conditions.

57   *Families of the Future*

Alvin Toffler

STUDY QUESTIONS

1. Indicate several items that would have to be accomplished if we are to return to the idealized family of the fifties.
2. What are several features of the family of the Third Wave?

During the Great Depression of the 1930's millions of men were thrown out of work. As factory doors clanged shut against them, many plunged into extremes of despair and guilt, their egos shattered by the pink layoff slip.

Eventually unemployment came to be seen in a more sensible light—not as the result of individual laziness or moral failure but of giant forces outside the individual's control. The maldistribution of wealth, myopic investment, runaway speculation, stupid trade policies, inept government—these, not the personal weakness of laid-off workers, caused unemployment. Feelings of guilt were, in most cases, naïvely inappropriate.

Today, once more, egos are breaking like eggshells against the wall. Now, however, the guilt is associated with the fracture of the family rather than the economy. As millions of men and women clamber out of the strewn wreckage of their marriages they, too, suffer agonies of self-blame. And once more, much of the guilt is misplaced.

When a tiny minority is involved, the crack-up of their families may reflect individual failures. But when divorce, separation, and other forms of familial disaster overtake millions at once in many countries, it is absurd to think the causes are purely personal.

The fracture of the family today is, in fact, part of the general crisis of industrialism—the crack-up of all the institutions spawned by the Second Wave. It is part of the ground-clearing for a new Third Wave socio-sphere. And it is this traumatic process, reflected in our individual lives, that is altering the family system beyond recognition.

Today we are told repeatedly that "the family" is falling apart or that "the family" is our Number One Problem. President Jimmy Carter declares, "It is clear that the national government should have a pro-family policy.... There can be no more urgent priority." Substitute preachers, prime ministers, or the press, and the pious rhetoric comes out very much the same. When they speak of "the family," however, they typically do *not* mean the family in all its luxuriant variety of possible forms, but one particular type of family: the Second Wave family.

What they usually have in mind is a husband-breadwinner, a wife-housekeeper, and a number of small children. While many other family types exist, it was this particular family form—the nuclear family—that Second Wave civilization idealized, made dominant, and spread around the world.

This type of family became the standard, socially approved model because its structure perfectly fitted the needs of a mass-production society with widely shared values and life-styles, hierarchical, bureaucratic power, and a clear separation of home life from work life in the marketplace.

Today, when the authorities urge us to "restore" the family it is this Second Wave nuclear family they usually have in mind. By thinking so narrowly they not only misdiagnose the entire problem, they reveal a childish naïveté about what steps would actually be required to restore the nuclear family to its former importance.

Thus the authorities frantically blame the family crisis on everything from "smut peddlers" to rock music. Some tell us that opposing abortion or wiping out sex education or resisting feminism will glue the family back together again. Or they urge courses in "family education." The chief United States government statistician on family matters wants "more effective training" to teach people how to marry more wisely, or else a "scientifically tested and appealing system for selecting a marriage partner." What we need, say others, are more marriage counselors or even more public relations to give the family a better image! Blind to the ways in which historical waves of change influence us, they come up with well-intentioned, often inane proposals that utterly miss the target.

THE PRO-NUCLEAR CAMPAIGN

If we really want to restore the nuclear family to its former dominance, there *are* things we could do. Here are a few:

1) Freeze all technology in its Second Wave stage to maintain a factory-based, mass-production society. Begin by smashing the computer. The computer is a greater threat to the Second Wave family than all the abortion laws and gay rights movements and pornography in the world, for the nuclear family *needs* the mass-production system to retain its dominance, and the computer is moving us beyond mass production.

ALVIN TOFFLER

2) Subsidize manufacture and block the rise of the service sector in the economy. White-collar, professional, and technical workers are less traditional, less family-oriented, more intellectually and psychologically mobile than blue-collar workers. Divorce rates have risen along with the rise in service occupations.

3) "Solve" the energy crisis by applying nuclear and other highly centralized energy processes. The nuclear family fits better in a centralized than a decentralized society, and energy systems heavily affect the degree of social and political centralization.

4) Ban the increasingly de-massified media, beginning with cable television and cassette, but not overlooking local and regional magazines. Nuclear families work best where there is a national consensus on information and values, not in a society based on high diversity. While some critics naïvely attack the media for allegedly undermining the family, it was the mass media that idealized the nuclear family form in the first place.

5) Forcibly drive women back into the kitchen. Reduce the wages of women to the absolute minimum. Strengthen, rather than relax, all union seniority provisions to assure that women are further disadvantaged in the labor force. The nuclear family has no nucleus when there are no adults left at home. (One could, of course, achieve the same effect by reversing matters, permitting women to work while compelling men to stay home and rear the children.)

6) Simultaneously slash the wages of young workers to make them more dependent, for a longer time, on their families—and thus less psychologically independent. The nuclear family is further denuclearized when the young leave parental control to go to work.

7) Ban contraception and research into reproductive biology. These make for the independence of women and for extramarital sex, a notorious loosener of nuclear ties.

8) Cut the standard of living of the entire society to pre-1955 levels, since affluence makes it possible for single people, divorced people, working women, and other unattached individuals to "make it" economically on their own. The nuclear family needs a touch of poverty (not too much, not too little) to sustain it.

9) Finally, re-massify our rapidly de-massifying society, by resisting all changes—in politics, the arts, education, business, or other fields—that lead toward diversity, freedom of movement and ideas, or individuality. The nuclear family remains dominant only in a mass society.

In short, this is what a pro-family policy would have to be if we insist on defining family as nuclear. If we truly wish to restore the Second Wave family, we had better be prepared to restore Second Wave civilization as a whole—to freeze not only technology but history itself.

For what we are witnessing is not the death of the family as such, but the final fracture of the Second Wave family system in which all families were supposed to emulate the idealized nuclear model, and the emergence in its place of a diversity of family forms. Just as we are de-massifying our media and our production, we are de-massifying the family system in the transition to a Third Wave civilization.

NON-NUCLEAR LIFE-STYLES

The coming of the Third Wave, of course, does not mean the end of the nuclear family any more than the coming of the Second Wave meant the end of the extended family. It means, rather, that the nuclear family can no longer serve as the ideal model for society.

The little-appreciated fact is that, at least in the United States where the Third Wave is most advanced, most people *already* live outside the classical nuclear family form.

If we define the nuclear family as a working husband, a housekeeping wife, and two children, and ask how many Americans actually still live in this type of family, the answer is astonishing: 7 percent of the total United States population. Ninety-three percent of the population do not fit this ideal Second Wave model any longer.

Even if we broaden our definition to include families in which both spouses work or in which there are fewer or more than two children, we find the vast majority—as many as two thirds to three quarters of the population—living *outside* the nuclear situation. Moreover, all the evidence suggests that nuclear households (however we choose to define them) are still shrinking in number as other family forms rapidly multiply.

To begin with, we are witnessing a population explosion of "solos"—people who live alone, outside a family altogether. Between 1970 and 1978 the number of persons aged fourteen to thirty-four who lived alone nearly tripled in the United States—rising from 1.5 million to 4.3 million. Today, a fifth of all households in the United States consists of a person living solo. Nor are all these people losers or loners, forced into the solo life. Many deliberately choose it, at least for a time. Says a legislative aide to a Seattle councilwoman, "I would consider marriage if the right person came along, but I would not give up my career for it." In the meantime she lives alone. She is part of a large class of young adults who are leaving home earlier but marrying later, thus creating what census specialist Arthur Norton says is a "transitional living phase" that is "becoming an acceptable part of one's life cycle."

Looking at an older slice of the population, we find a large number of formerly married people, often "between marriages," living on their own and, in many cases, decidedly liking it. The growth of such groups has created a flourishing "singles" culture and a much publicized proliferation of bars, ski lodges, travel tours, and other services or products designed for the independent individual. Simultaneously, the real estate industry has come up with "singles only" condominia, and has begun to respond to a need for smaller apartments and suburban homes with fewer bedrooms. Almost a fifth of all home buyers in the United States today are single.

ALVIN TOFFLER

We are also experiencing a headlong growth in the number of people living together without bothering about legal formalities. This group has more than doubled in the past decade, according to United States authorities. The practice has become so common that the United States Department of Housing and Urban Development has overthrown tradition and changed its rules to permit such couples to occupy public housing. The courts, meanwhile, from Connecticut to California, are wrestling with the legal and property complications that spring up when such couples "divorce." Etiquette columnists write about which names to use in addressing partners, and "couple counseling" has sprouted as a new professional service alongside marriage counseling.

THE CHILD-FREE CULTURE

Another significant change has been the growth in the number of those consciously choosing what is coming to be known as a "child-free" life-style. According to James Ramey, senior research associate at the Center for Policy Research, we are seeing a massive shift from "child-centered" to "adult-centered" homes. At the turn of the century there were few singles in society, and relatively few parents lived very long after their youngest child left the home. Thus most households were, in fact, child-centered. By contrast, as early as 1970 in the United States only one in three adults lived in a home with children under eighteen.

Today organizations are springing up to promote the child-free life, and a reluctance to have children is spreading in many industrial nations. In 1960 only 20 percent of "ever-married" American women under age thirty were child-free. By 1975 this had shot up to 32 percent—a 60 percent jump in fifteen years. A vocal organization, the National Alliance for Optional Parenthood, has arisen to protect the rights of the childless and to combat pronatalist propaganda.

A similar organization, the National Association for the Childless, has sprouted in Britain, and many couples across Europe are also deliberately choosing to remain childless. In Bonn, West Germany, for example, Theo and Agnes Rohl, both in their mid-thirties, he a city official, she a secretary, say "We don't think we'll have children . . ." The Rohls are modestly affluent. They own a small home. They manage a vacation trip to California or Southern France now and then. Children would drastically alter their way of life. "We're used to our life-style the way it is," they say, "and we like being independent." Nor is this reluctance to bear children a sign of capitalist decadence. It is present in the Soviet Union, too, where many young Russian couples echo the sentiments of the Rohls and explicitly reject parenthood—a fact that worries Soviet officialdom in view of the still-high birth rates among several non-Russian national minorities.

Turning now to those *with* children, the breakdown of the nuclear family is even more sharply evidenced in the spectacular increase in single-parent families. So many divorces, breakups, and separations have occurred in recent years—mainly in nuclear families—that today a staggering one-in-seven American children is raised by a single parent, and the number is even higher—one in four—in urban areas.*

The huge growth in such households has brought a growing recognition that despite severe problems, a one-parent household can, under certain circumstances, be better for the child than a nuclear household continually torn by bitter strife. Newspapers and organizations now serve single parents and are heightening their group consciousness and political clout.

Nor, once again, is the phenomenon purely American. In Britain today nearly one family in ten is headed by a single parent—nearly a sixth of them headed by men—and one-parent households form what *New Society* magazine calls "the fastest growing group in poverty." A London-based organization, the National Council for One-Parent Families, has sprung up to champion their cause.

In Germany, a housing association in Cologne has constructed a special block of apartments for such families and provided them with day-time child care so the parents can work. And in Scandinavia a network of special welfare rights has grown up to support these families. The Swedes, for example, give one-parent households first crack at nursery and day-care facilities. In both Norway and Sweden, in fact, it is sometimes possible for a single-parent family to enjoy a higher standard of living than that of the typical nuclear family.

A challenging new form of family has arisen in the meantime that reflects the high rate of remarriage after divorce. In *Future Shock* I identified this as the "aggregate family," in which two divorced couples with children remarry, bringing the children of both marriages (and the adults as well) into a new, expanded family form. It is now estimated that 25 percent of American children are, or will soon be, members of such family units. According to Davidyne Mayleas, such units, with their "poly-parents" may be the mainstream family form of tomorrow. "We're into economic polygamy," says Mayleas—meaning that the two merged family units typically transfer money back and forth in the form of child support or other payments. The spread of this family form, she reports, has been accompanied by a rising incidence of sexual relations between parents and nonblood-related children.

The technologically advanced nations today are honeycombed with a bewildering array of family forms: Homosexual marriages, communes, groups of elderly people banding together to share expenses (and sometimes sex), tribal groupings among certain ethnic minorities, and many other forms coexist as never before. There are contract marriages, serial marriages, family clusters, and a variety of intimate networks with or without shared sex, as well as families in which mother and father live and work in two different cities.

Even these family forms barely hint at the even richer variety bubbling under the surface. When three psychiatrists—Kellam, Ensminger, and Turner—attempted to map the "variations of families" found in a single poor black neighborhood in Chicago, they identified "no less than 86 different combinations of adults," including numerous forms of "mother-grandmother"

---

*The total is also fed by out-of-wedlock births and by adoptions by single women and (increasingly) single men.

ALVIN TOFFLER

families, "mother-aunt" families, "mother-stepfather families," and "mother-other" families.

Faced with this veritable maze of kinship arrangements, even fairly orthodox scholars have come around to the once radical view that we are moving out of the age of the nuclear family and into a new society marked by diversity in family life. In the words of sociologist Jessie Bernard, "The most characteristic aspect of marriage in the future will be precisely the array of options available to different people who want different things from their relationships with one another."

The frequently asked question, "What is the future of the family?" usually implies that as the Second Wave nuclear family loses its dominance some other form will replace it. A more likely outcome is that during Third Wave civilization no single form will dominate the family mix for any long period. Instead we will see a high variety of family structures. Rather than masses of people living in uniform family arrangements, we shall see people moving through this system, tracing personalized or "customized" trajectories during the course of their lives.

Again, this does not mean the total elimination or "death" of the nuclear family. It merely means that from now on the nuclear family will be only one of the many socially accepted and approved forms. As the Third Wave sweeps in, the family system is becoming de-massified right along with the production system and the information system in society.

"HOT" RELATIONSHIPS

Given this flowering of a multiplicity of family forms, it is too early to tell which will emerge as significant styles in a Third Wave civilization.

Will our children live alone for many years, perhaps decades? Will they go childless? Will we retire into old-age communes? What about more exotic possibilities? Families with several husbands and one wife? (That could happen if genetic tinkering lets us preselect the sex of our children, and too many parents choose boys.) What about homosexual families raising children? The courts are already debating this issue. What about the potential impact of cloning?

If each of us moves through a trajectory of family experiences in our lives, what will the phases be? A trial marriage, followed by a dual-career marriage with no children, then a homosexual marriage *with* children? The possible permutations are endless. Nor, despite the cries of outrage, should any of these be regarded as unthinkable. As Jessie Bernard has put it, "There is literally nothing about marriage that anyone can imagine that has not in fact taken place. . . . All these variations seemed quite natural to those who lived with them."

Which specific family forms vanish and which ones proliferate will depend less on pulpit-pounding about the "sanctity of the family" than on the decisions we make with respect to technology and work. While many forces influence family structure—communication patterns, values, demographic changes, religious movements, even ecological shifts—the linkage between family form and work arrangements is particularly strong. Thus, just as the nuclear family was promoted by the rise of the factory and office work, any shift *away* from the factory and office would also exert a heavy influence on the family.

It is impossible, in the space of a single chapter, to spell out all the ways in which the coming changes in the labor force and in the nature of work will alter family life. But one change is so potentially revolutionary, and so alien to our experience, it needs far more attention than it has received so far. This is, of course, the shift of work out of the office and factory and back into the home.

Assume for a moment that twenty-five years from now 15 percent of the work force is employed part- or full-time in the home. How would working at home change the quality of our personal relationships or the meaning of love? What would life be like in the electronic cottage?

Whether the work-at-home task is programming a computer, writing a pamphlet, monitoring distant manufacturing processes, designing a building, or typing electronic correspondence, one immediate change is clear. Relocating work into the home means that many spouses who now see each other only a limited number of hours each day would be thrown together more intimately. Some, no doubt, would find this prolonged proximity hateful. Many others, however, would find their marriages saved and their relationships much enriched through shared experience.

Let us visit several electronic cottages to see how people might adapt to so fundamental a change in society. Such a tour would no doubt reveal a wide diversity of living and working arrangements.

In some houses, perhaps the majority, we might well find couples dividing things up more or less conventionally, with one person doing the "job-work" while the other keeps house—he, perhaps, writing programs while she looks after the kids. The very presence of work in the home, however, would probably encourage a sharing of both job-work and housekeeping. We could find many homes, therefore, in which man and wife split a single full-time job. For example, we might find both husband and wife taking turns at monitoring a complex manufacturing process on the console screen in the den, four hours on, four hours off.

Down the street, by contrast, we would likely discover a couple holding not one, but two quite different jobs, with each spouse working separately. A cellular physiologist and a CPA might each work at his or her craft. Even here, however, with the jobs differing sharply in character, there is still likely to be some sharing of problems, some learning of each other's work vocabulary, some common concerns and conversation relating to work. It is almost impossible under such conditions for the work life of an individual to be strictly segregated from personal life. By the same token, it is next to impossible to freeze one's mate out of a whole dimension of one's existence.

Right next door (continuing our survey) we could well come upon a couple holding two different jobs but sharing *both*, the husband working as a part-time insurance planner and part-time as an architect's assistant, with the wife doing the same work on alternating shifts. This arrangement would provide more varied, and therefore more interesting, work for both.

ALVIN TOFFLER

In such homes, whether one or several jobs are shared, each partner necessarily learns from the other, participates in the problem-solving, engages in complex give-and-take, all of which cannot help but deepen intimacy. Forced proximity, it goes without saying, does not guarantee happiness. The extended family units of the First Wave era, which were also economic production units, were hardly models of interpersonal sensitivity and mutual psychological support. Such families had their own problems and stresses. But there were few uncommitted or "cooled out" relationships. Working together assured, if nothing else, tight, complete "hot" personal relationships—a committedness many people enjoy today.

In short, the spread of work-at-home on a large scale could not only affect family structure but transform relationships within the family. It could, to put it simply, provide a common set of experiences and get marriage partners talking to one another again. It could shift their relationships along the spectrum from "cool" to "hot." It could also redefine love itself and bring with it the concept of Love Plus.

LOVE PLUS

We saw how, as the Second Wave progressed, the family unit transferred many of its functions to other institutions—education to the school, care of the ill to hospitals, and so on. This progressive stripping away of the functions of the family unit was accompanied by the rise of romantic love.

A First Wave person looking for a mate might properly have asked "Is my proposed spouse a good worker? A good healer? A good teacher for the children to come? Can we work together compatibly? Will she (or he) carry a full load or prove to be a shirker? Peasant families actually asked "Is she strong, good at bending and lifting, or is she sickly and weak?"

As the functions of the family were hived off during the Second Wave era, those questions changed. The family was no longer a combination of production team, school, field hospital, and nursing home. Instead, its psychological functions became more important. Marriage was supposed to supply companionship, sex warmth, and support. Soon this shift in the functions of the family was reflected in new criteria for choosing a mate. They were summed up in the single word *love*. It was love, the popular culture assured us, that makes the world go round.

Of course, real life seldom lived up to romantic fiction. Class, social status, and income continued to play a role in the choice of a mate. But all such considerations were supposed to be secondary to Love with a capital L.

Tomorrow's rise of the electronic cottage may very well overthrow this single-minded logic. Those who look ahead to working at home with a spouse, instead of spending the main part of their waking lives away, are likely to take more into consideration than simple sexual and psychological gratification—or social status, for that matter. They may begin to insist on Love Plus—sexual and psychological gratification *plus* brains (as their grandfathers once favored brawn), love *plus* conscientiousness, responsibility, self-discipline, or other work-related virtues. We may—who knows?—hear some John Denver of the future croon lyrics like:

I love your eyes, your cherry lips,

the love that always lingers,

your way with words and random blips,

your skilled computer fingers.

More seriously, one can imagine at least some families of the future taking on additional functions rather than shedding them, and serving as a multipurpose, rather than a narrowly specialized, social unit. With such a change the criteria for marriage, the very definition of love, would be transformed.

THE CAMPAIGN FOR CHILD LABOR

Children, meanwhile, would also be likely to grow up differently in the electronic cottage, if for no other reason than that they would actually see work taking place. First Wave children, from their first blink of consciousness, saw their parents at work. Second Wave children, by contrast—at least in recent generations—were segregated in schools and divorced from real work life. Most today have only the foggiest notion of what their parents do or how they live while at work. One possibly apocryphal story makes the point: An executive decides to bring his son to his office one day and to take him out to lunch. The boy sees the plushly carpeted office, the indirect lightning, the elegant reception room. He sees the fancy expense-account restaurant with its obsequious waiters and exorbitant prices. Finally, picturing their home and unable to restrain himself, the boy blurts out: "Daddy, how come you're so rich and we're so poor?"

The fact is that children today—especially affluent children—are totally divorced from one of the most important dimensions of their parents' lives. In an electronic cottage kids not only observe work, they may, after a certain age, engage in it themselves. Second Wave restrictions on child labor—originally well-intentioned and necessary, but now largely an anachronistic device to keep young people out of the crowded job market—become more difficult to enforce in the home setting. Certain forms of work, indeed, might be specifically designed for youngsters and even integrated with their education. (Anyone who underestimates the capacity of even very young people to understand and cope with sophisticated work has not run into the fourteen- or fifteen-year-old boys who served probably illegally, as "salesmen" in California computer stores, I have had kids with braces still on their teeth explain the intricacies of home computing to me.)

The alienation of youth today flows in large measure from being forced to accept a nonproductive role in society during an endlessly prolonged adolescence. The electronic cottage would counteract this situation.

In fact, integrating young people into work in the electronic cottage may offer the only real solution to the problems of high youth unemployment. This problem will grow increasingly explosive in many countries in the years ahead, with all the attendant evils of juvenile crime, violence, and psychological immiseration and cannot be solved within the framework of a Second Wave economy except by totalitarian means—drafting young people, for example, for war or forced service. The electronic cottage opens an alternative way to bring youth back into socially and economically productive roles, and we may see, before long, political campaigns *for*, rather than against, child labor, along with struggles over the necessary measures to protect them against gross economic exploitation.

THE ELECTRONIC EXPANDED FAMILY

Beyond this, one can easily imagine the work-at-home household becoming something radically different: an "electronic expanded family."

Perhaps the most common family form in First Wave societies was the so-called extended family, which brought several generations together under the same roof. There were also "expanded families" which, in addition to the core members, included an unrelated orphan or two, an apprentice or additional farm hand, or others. One can likewise picture the work-at-home family of tomorrow inviting an outsider or two to join it—for example, a colleague from the husband's or wife's firm, or perhaps a customer or supplier engaged in related work, or, for that matter, a neighbor's child who wants to learn the trade. One can foresee the legal incorporation of such a family as a small business under special laws designed to foster the commune-cum-corporation or the cooperative. For many the household would become an electronic expanded family.

It is true that most of the communes formed in the 1960's and 1970's fell rapidly apart, seeming to suggest that communes, as such, are inherently unstable in high-technology societies. A closer look reveals, however, that the ones that disintegrated most rapidly were those organized primarily for psychological purposes—to promote interpersonal sensitivity, to combat loneliness, to provide intimacy, or the like. Most had no economic base and saw themselves as utopian experiments. The communes that have succeeded over time—and some have—are, by contrast, those that have had a clear external mission, an economic base, and a practical, rather than purely utopian, outlook.

An external mission welds a group together. It may, indeed, provide the necessary economic base. If this external mission is to design a new product, to handle the "electronic paper work" for a hospital, to do the data processing for an insurance company department, to set up the scheduling for a commuter airline, to prepare catalogs, or to operate a technical information service, the electronic commune of tomorrow may, in fact, turn out to be a quite workable and stable family form.

Moreover, since such electronic expanded families would not be designed as a rebuke to everyone else's life-style or for demonstration purposes but rather as an integral part of the main wiring of the economic system, the chances for their survival would be sharply improved. Indeed, we may find expanded households linking up to form networks. Such networks of expanded families could supply some needed business or social service, cooperating to market their work or setting up their own version of a trade association to represent them. Internally, they might or might not share sex across marriage lines. They might or might not be heterosexual. They might be childless or child-ful.

In brief, what we see is the possible resurrection of the expanded family. Today some 6 percent of American adults live in ordinary extended families. One might easily imagine a doubling or tripling of this number in the next generation, with some units expanding to include outsiders. This would be no trivial event but a movement involving millions in the United States alone. For community life, for patterns of love and marriage, for the reconstitution of friendship networks, for the economy and the consumer marketplace, as well as for our psyches and personality structure, the rise of the electronic expanded family would be momentous.

This new version of the extended family is not presented here as inevitable, not as better or worse than some other type of family, but simply as one example of the many new family forms likely to find viable niches in the complex social ecology of tomorrow.

PARENTAL MALPRACTICE

This rich diversity of family forms won't come into being without pain and anguish. For any change in family structure also forces change in the roles we live. Every society, through its institutions, creates its own architecture of roles or social expectations. The corporation and trade union between them more or less defined what was expected of workers and bosses. Schools fixed the respective roles of teachers and pupils. And the Second Wave family allocated the roles of breadwinner, housekeeper, and child. As the nuclear family goes critical, so to speak, the roles associated with it begin to shiver and crack—with excruciating personal impact.

From the day that Betty Friedan's bombshell book, *The Feminine Mystique*, launched the modern feminist movement in many nations, we have seen a painful struggle to redefine the roles of men and women in terms appropriate to a postnuclear-family future. The expectations and the behavior of both sexes have shifted with respect to jobs, legal and financial rights, household responsibilities, and even sexual performance. "Now," writes Peter Knobler, editor of *Crawdaddy*, a rock music magazine, "a guy's got to contend with women breaking all the rules. . . . Many regulations need breaking," he adds, "but that doesn't make it much easier."

Roles are shaken by the battle over abortion, for instance, as women insist that they—not politicians, not priests, not doctors or even husbands—have a right to control their bodies. Sexual roles are further blurred as homosexuals demand and partially win "gay rights." Even the role of the child in society is changing. Suddenly advocates spring up to lobby for a Children's Bill of Rights.

Courts are swamped by cases involving role redefinition, as alternatives to the nuclear family multiply and gain acceptability. Do unmarried spouses have to share their property after they break up? Can a couple legally pay a woman to bear a child for them by artificial insemination? (A British court said no—but for how long?) Can a lesbian be a "good mother" and retain custody of her child after a divorce? (An American court says yes.) What is meant by being a good parent? Nothing underlines the changing role structure more than the lawsuit filed in Boulder, Colorado, by an angry twenty-four-year-old named Tom Hansen. Parents can make mistakes, Hansen's lawyer argued, but they must be held legally—and financially—responsible for the results. Thus Hansen's court action claimed $350,000 in damages on an unprecedented legal ground: parental malpractice.

EASING INTO TOMORROW

Behind all this confusion and turmoil, a new Third Wave family system is coalescing, based on a diversity of family forms and more varied individual roles. This de-massification of the family opens many new personal options. Third Wave civilization will not try to stuff everyone willy-nilly into a single family form. For this reason the emergent family system could free each of us to find his or her own niche, to select or create a family style or trajectory attuned to individualized needs.

But before anyone can perform a celebratory dance, the agonies of transition must be dealt with. Caught in the crack-up of the old, with the new system not yet in place, millions find the higher level of diversity bewildering rather than helpful. Instead of being liberated, they suffer from overchoice and are wounded, embittered, plunged into a sorrow and loneliness intensified by the very multiplicity of their options.

To make the new diversity work for us instead of against us, we will need changes on many levels at once, from morality and taxes to employment practices.

In the field of values we need to begin removing the unwarranted guilt that accompanies the breakup and restructuring of families. Instead of exacerbating unjustified guilt, the media, the church, the courts, and the political system should be working to lower the guilt level.

The decision to live outside a nuclear family framework should be made easier, not harder. Values change more slowly, as a rule, than social reality. Thus we have not yet developed the ethic of tolerance for diversity that a de-massified society will both require and engender. Raised under Second Wave conditions, firmly taught that one kind of family is "normal" and others somehow suspect, if not "deviant," vast numbers remain intolerant of the new variety in family styles. Until that changes, the pain of transition will remain unnecessarily high.

In economic and social life, individuals cannot enjoy the benefits of widened family options so long as laws, tax codes, welfare practices, school arrangements, housing codes, and even architectural forms all remain implicitly biased toward the Second Wave family. They take little account of the special needs of women who work, of men who stay home to take care of their children, of bachelors and "spinsters" (hateful term!), or of between-marrieds, or "aggregate families," or widows living alone or together. All such groupings have been subtly or openly discriminated against in Second Wave societies.

Even while it piously praised housekeeping, Second Wave civilization denied dignity to the person performing that task. Housekeeping is productive, indeed crucial, work, and needs to be recognized as part of the economy. To assure the enhanced status of housekeeping, whether done by women or by men, by individuals or by groups working together, we will have to pay wages or impute economic value to it.

In the out-of-the-home economy, employment practices in many places are still based on the obsolete assumption that the man is the primary breadwinner and the wife a supplemental, expendable earner, instead of a fully independent participant in the labor market. By easing seniority requirements, by spreading flextime, by opening part-time opportunities, we not only humanize production, we adapt it to the needs of a multistyle family system. Today there are many indications that the work system is beginning to accommodate itself to the new diversity of family arrangements. Shortly after Citibank, one of the largest banks in the United States, began to promote women to managerial jobs, it found that its male executives were marrying their new colleagues. The bank had a long-standing rule barring the employment of couples. It had to change that rule. According to *Business Week*, the "company couple" is now flourishing with benefits both for company and for family life.

It is likely that before long we will go far beyond such minor adaptations. We may see demands not merely for the hiring of "company couples" but of whole families to work together as a production team. Because this was inefficient in the Second Wave factory doesn't mean it is necessarily inappropriate today. No one knows how such policies would work out but, as in other family matters, we ought to encourage, perhaps even publicly fund, small-scale experiments.

Such measures could help us ease our way into tomorrow, minimizing for millions the pain of transition. But whether painful or not, a new family system is emerging to supplant the one that characterized the Second Wave past. This new family system will be a core institution in the novel socio-sphere taking shape alongside the new techno-sphere and info-sphere. It is part of the act of social creation by which our generation is adapting to and constructing a new civilization.

58 Families and Children in the Year 2000

Arthur J. Norton

STUDY QUESTIONS

1. Why does Norton claim that major trends involving the family have leveled off?

2. What are the features of the family in the year 2000?

Changes over the past two decades affecting the lives of children provide the backdrop for describing the social, economic and demographic circumstances of childhood between now and the end of this century. Children as a group are nearly totally dependent upon the individual and collective actions of a number of social and economic institutions. The ability of these institutions to meet the needs of children have important immediate and long-range or developmental consequences for the structure and quality of life for children. One of those institutions is the family. Family, in the broadest definition, encompasses a variety of living arrangements. This article focuses on this broad concept of family to give an overview of several important recent trends influencing families in general and children in particular.

Most major trends involving family life appear to have levelled off or established a predictable (for the meantime) pattern, and it seems likely that conditions which generally characterize childhood in 1987 will prevail in the year 2000. Patterns of childbearing, marriage, divorce, remarriage, and employment in the paid labor force of mothers have changed dramatically during the past 20 years.

Source: Arthur J. Norton, "Families and Children in the Year 2000." *Children Today*, July/August 1987, pp. 6–9. Department of Health & Human Services, Office of Human Development Services.

AGE AT MARRIAGE

The ages at which young brides and grooms have been marrying for the first time have been increasing rather steadily since the 1960s. In fact, in the last decade alone, the estimated median age at first marriage for men and women has risen by about two full years reaching 25.7 for men and 23.1 for women in 1986. About one-third of all women and one-half of all men who were 25 years old in 1986 had never been married, in each case more than doubling the percent never married for 25-year-olds in 1970. Some people have suggested that these age-at-marriage trends indicate a movement toward a much greater proportion of the adult population never marrying at all. There is not much doubt that proportionally fewer young adults today will ever marry than has historically been true in the United States. Nevertheless, the vast majority of men and women will eventually marry. Probably about nine of every 10 young adults today will marry during their adult years as compared with a standard of about 95 percent ever marrying for previous generations.

A later age at first marriage has important implications for children and their families. If the long-standing inverse relationship between age at marriage and likelihood of divorce continues, then marital stability will increase. Recent studies have reaffirmed the association between age at marriage and "marital success," and this and other factors may contribute to a decrease in divorce in the next several years. However, the expected decline in divorce is not forecast to be precipitous and the U.S. will likely continue to be among the countries with the highest divorce rates in the world.

Another consequence of later marriage is that more young adults have the time for pursuing educational and career goals without the limitations of family responsibilities. The investments made by young adults in education and work are likely to be looked upon for lifelong returns. This is especially important for determining the structure of family life after these people have married. The percent of married couple families with both spouses in the paid work force is likely to continue to increase regardless of whether childbearing has begun or not. However, once children are born, the dimension of child care becomes a major concern because parents are more likely than ever before to continue in the paid work force after childbirth. The Bureau of Labor Statistics reports that in the last decade the labor force participation rate for women with very young children (under three years old) has increased from one-third to one-half. Labor force participation rates for all mothers have increased markedly and, in general, the older the children the more likely the mother is to be in the paid work force.

The most notable increase in working among mothers has been for women in married couple families. Currently, more than six in 10 married women with a husband and children under 18 present in the home are in the paid labor force. However, among all mothers with children present, women maintaining single-parent families are still the most likely to be in the labor force. Clearly, what was once the exception regarding working wives and mothers is now the rule, and one result of this shift is an emerging demand by working parents for an accommodation of their child care needs.

ARTHUR J. NORTON

Recent studies show that there has been no measurable increase in what is popularly termed "latchkey" situations but that for all children there has been an increased use of "alternative" types of child care. Parents are moving away from using care in the child's home and care in another private home to group care arrangements like those provided by day care centers and nursery schools. Data show that in the short span of years between 1982 and 1985, the percent of mothers employed full time who used organized child care for their youngest child under five rose from 20 percent to 30 percent. Also, a surprising proportion of children whose mothers are in the labor force are reported as cared for by a parent. This may suggest some accommodation in the work place for the child care needs of workers. It may also reflect what one social scientist has termed a trend toward the "destandardization of American work life," meaning more flexitime, shiftwork, etc. It seems reasonable to expect that high labor force participation rates for both parents in 2-parent families and for persons maintaining single-parent families are here to stay, as are the attending concerns about child care.

There are other, more subtle changes occurring in family life that are associated with the increased labor force participation of mothers and fathers who have young children at home. These changes involve the roles husbands and wives and children play vis-a-vis each other in a changing home environment. New research on interaction among family members is needed to assess the nature and consequences of these changes.

Another development associated with later age at marriage is a drop in family size. Postponement of marriage usually means postponement of childbearing. As the age at childbearing has increased and as effective measures of fertility control have become widely available *and used* (allowing more parents to achieve a balance between family, job and other aspirations), fertility has declined. Women are currently bearing children at a rate of slightly under two per woman. The fertility rate in this country has not changed appreciably over the last decade, nor is it expected to change in the near future. Birth expectations of young women indicate little change is likely to occur in desired family size in the next several years. Young women today expect to have, on average, about two children per woman when they have completed their childbearing. Small families, for several reasons, will remain the norm in our society for the foreseeable future.

Later age at marriage also results in a larger at-risk period for women to bear children before marriage. Increasingly more single-parent situations involve a never-married mother and her child(ren). Today, one of every five of the seven million single-parent families is maintained by a never-married woman.

In summary, a major change in age at first marriage for men and women has been associated with several important changes in family life for parents and children. There are more working parents and presumably less time is available for parent-child interaction; families are smaller and children therefore have fewer siblings; married couples may be less likely to divorce; on average parents are older and perhaps more established than in the past; and more single-parent families are created by never-married women having babies.

DIVORCE

Nearly everyone is familiar with the litany of divorce statistics covering trends in the U.S. over the past 20 years. Between 1965 (when the incidence of divorce began to turn upward) and 1980, the divorce rate doubled, reaching a point where one of every two marriages could be expected to end in divorce.

Since 1980, there has been little change in the divorce rate and there is some reason to expect the rate to drop somewhat in the near future. Factors such as an increasing age at first marriage, recognition of the heavy societal costs of divorce, the ending of a period of dramatic institutional change in this country and the beginning of a period of adaptation to new circumstances surrounding marriage are associated with the predictions of a drop in divorce. Irrespective of causation, it does not appear that the drop in the divorce rate will alter the position of the U.S. as the country with the highest reported divorce rate in the world. Thus, the serious consequences of a large portion of the population, especially children, experiencing the trauma of a marriage breaking up will remain a major concern for society.

A direct result of a high divorce rate is a growth in the number and percent of people who live in single-parent situations. In recent years, divorce has been the largest contributor to the growth in the number of one-parent families. About 43 percent of all one-parent families in 1986 were maintained by a divorced parent. Nine of every 10 single-parent families in the U.S. are mother-child(ren) families—a statistic that has remained virtually unchanged over the past 30 years. These families suffer more deprivation than other families. For example, about 60 percent of the children under 18 years old in mother-child families live in poverty, compared to approximately 25 percent of the under-18 child population as a whole. Single-parent families are characterized by high minority representation, low education and high residential mobility. In short, they are a group with little equity or stature in U.S. society and yet a group with usually pressing social and economic needs involving housing, social and psychological services, work place considerations and child care, to name a few. Currently, close to one-fourth of the nation's 60 million children under 18 live with only one parent.

Furthermore, because being in a one-parent family is a temporary status for many, the chances of a child under 18 ever experiencing living with only one parent for at least one year are greater than one in two. The lifetime likelihood for a child to live in a one-parent family probably will not change significantly in the near future and, consequently, it is important to remind those whose responsibility is to provide in some way for the well-being of children of the prevalence of this experience.

A natural consequence of the high divorce rate in the U.S. has been an increasing pool of people eligible for remarriage. The primary reason that living in a one-parent family is a transitional status for many is that about 80 percent of people who divorce eventually remarry, not necessarily to each other. (A secondary reason for the transitional nature of the one-parent family is that the vast majority of women who bear children before marriage eventually do marry.) Remarriage is leading to an increase in the number and percent of

　　　　　　　　　　　　　　　　　　　　　　　　　　　　ARTHUR J. NORTON

families involving "step" relationships and other previously "atypical" family relationships (the presence of one or more combinations of step-siblings or half-siblings, for example).

Sixteen percent of all married-couple families today involve step situations, and there is little question that this proportion will continue to grow. The introduction of a substantial number of stepfamilies, blended families and/or reconstituted families into U.S. society has happened so fast that there is little well-documented information about the impact of this phenomenon on the lives of children. The small but rapidly growing body of knowledge about these families indicates that stepfamilies are more complex and, in some respects, more fragile than other families. A major challenge for researchers during the next several years will be to learn more about how parents and children in these relationships cope with the circumstances of everyday life and how family members interact in the relatively new family structures that have been identified.

Past fluctuations in fertility trends, immigration and internal migration and improvements in longevity have—and will continue to have—a profound influence on the lives of children in the United States. Even with the fertility rate below replacement level (2.1 births per woman), the absolute annual number of births in the U.S. has been rising since the mid 1970s. This is because of the entry into childbearing ages of women who are members of the disproportionately large baby boom generation. The so-called "echo effect" of the baby boom has resulted in about 3.7 million births per year during the 1980s, a figure that is projected to rise to about 3.9 million for 1990 before falling to about 3.5 million births for each year during the 1990s. These numbers are only exceeded by the figures during the baby boom years, and they indicate that for the rest of this century relatively numerous students will be attending school at the primary and secondary levels.

There is also growing social and ethnic diversity among children in the United States. In 1985, 70 percent of all births were white non-Hispanic. By the year 2000, the projected percent of white non-Hispanic births among all births will be 64 percent.

Greater longevity for the adult population and generally low fertility in recent years have resulted in an "aging" of the U.S. population. While this may create additional competition for resources between the youngest and oldest segments of the population, it also provides a circumstance whereby the youngest members of society can benefit from the experiences of the oldest members. More than ever before, grandparents and even great-grandparents will be present in a child's life.

Population redistribution in the U.S. has resulted in very high growth rates in the South and West regions as compared with growth in the Midwest and Northeast regions. This pattern of difference in growth rates is likely to continue over the next several years. The South and West have gained population both by receiving migrants from the Midwest and Northeast and by high rates of natural increase (births minus deaths). Each component has contributed about equally to the regional growth in the South and West. For the Midwest and Northeast, however, there has been net out-migration for the past 15 years, compensated for by a modest amount of natural increase. So, children, like the population in general, will be influenced by and share in the changing regional distribution of the U.S. population. The importance of this extends from realigning representation in the U.S. House of Representatives to problems associated with the physical infrastructures of regions experiencing different rates of population growth.

In a general sense and from an adult perspective, today's children and children of the near future live and will live in a world of increasing complexity. Changes are happening so quickly that experientially there is substantial diversity within the various age groups constituting the "youth" population (that is, persons under 18 years old). Technological development causes continual alterations in the educational curricula of students as our schools try to make students "literate" in a setting where aspects of the definition of "literacy" are constantly changing. Children are confronted with a new openness regarding drug use, sexual activity, AIDS, and the possibility of child abuse.

These considerations, when added to the range of possible changes regarding family structure, point to a period between now and the year 2000 of challenge for children, parents and others upon whom children rely for assistance. The challenge for researchers in this field is to more fully investigate causes and consequences and assist in developing programs of action that will meet the growing list of family and child needs.

59 *Social Forces and the Changing Family*

Gordon Clanton

STUDY QUESTIONS

1. Compare the traditional values versus the contemporary values of the future.

2. Describe the child-rearing policies of the future.

FAMILY LIFE IN THE TWENTY-FIRST CENTURY

As Americans lowered their expectations with regard to material prosperity, there was also a tendency to develop more realistic expectations concerning

Source: Gordon Clanton, "Social Forces and the Changing Family." From *Marriage and Family in the Year 2020*, edited by Lester A. Kirkendall and Arthur E. Gravatt. (Buffalo, NY: Prometheus Books, 1984), © Lester A. Kirkendall and Arthur E. Gravatt. Reprinted by permission of the publisher.

love relationships, marriage, and family life. Men and women today are still seeking intimacy. Most choose to commit themselves to others in love relationships, to marry, to have children, to love their children, and to want the best for them. But, in contrast with marriage in the late twentieth century, contemporary marriage is a less central fact of a person's life and, therefore, it is not so crucial that it be completely satisfying on every level. This sentiment would have seemed scandalous in the period from 1950 to 1970. (Even today, it is upsetting to older people with long, intact marriages which are central to their lives.) As people lowered their unrealistic expectations, many became cautiously optimistic that they could have relationships that were rewarding and worthwhile, even if they were not perfect.

Family life today is diverse, and most people are relatively tolerant of those whose values and behavior are different from their own. There is very little conflict about these matters because sex, love, marriage, and family are viewed as private matters. On this nearly all Americans now agree. After failing to ban abortion by constitutional amendment, many persons with traditional values have agreed that sexual and family issues should be viewed as private matters. Feminists softened their attack on marriage and the family and agreed that privacy is the best policy in such matters, once their first effort to win ratification of the Equal Rights Amendment ended in defeat. Leaders of the gay and lesbian community agreed that privacy in sexual matters is the best policy when they were unable to get laws passed that would guarantee homosexual rights. The majority of Americans simply grew tired of hearing about these issues. Media coverage declined. Previously controversial topics such as abortion, sexual preference, and orgasm count largely dropped out of casual conversation. Today most people discuss these matters primarily with family and close friends. Rather than demand that sex be denied, hidden, or persecuted (as did some late Victorians) or that sexual style be publicly celebrated (as did some gays and swingers in the 1960s and 1970s), most Americans today treat sexuality as a private matter. As a result, public controversy about abortion and homosexuality has diminished in the last thirty years.

The polarized debates of the 1980s between the self-appointed "Moral Majority" and their opponents gradually turned into a more constructive search for some kind of broad national moral consensus to which all Americans could subscribe. This dialogue was often guided by the slogan: "In essential matters, unity. In unessential matters, diversity. In all matters, toleration, patience, and good humor."

Most people came to feel that some of the old sexual prohibitions could be relaxed without great personal damage and without social collapse. Today most Americans, regardless of their religious or sexual preferences (or lack thereof) agree that sexual interaction should occur only when there is mutual informed consent (no force, no fraud, no manipulative seduction) and only when both partners are likely to feel good about the experience (and about each other) later. Such positive feelings after the fact, most people agree, are most likely when two persons have similar values, similar expectations for the future, and a similar understanding of their shared sexual encounter. While many Protestant fundamentalists and Roman Catholics have insisted that these broad ethical principles would "encourage people to sin," the liberal Protestant denominations (Episcopalians, Presbyterians, Methodists, the United Church of Christ, etc.) have endorsed them, with varying degrees of further qualification. Meanwhile, following Vatican III and the election of the Dutch Pope, some orders of the Roman Catholic clergy are now permitted to marry.

Two fairly distinctive understandings of sex, love, marriage, and family now coexist (more or less) peaceably. Of course, there is great diversity of attitude and behavior within these two patterns and some individuals reflect aspects of both. Nevertheless, it is helpful to contrast the traditional and contemporary viewpoints.

Traditional Values. About one-fifth of the adult population adheres to traditional (late Victorian) values. Most of these people are religious conservatives. For most Americans with traditional family values, sexual pleasure is suspect, perhaps sinful; nudity is strongly disapproved. Masturbation is discouraged and many view it as shameful. Premarital sex is disapproved and associated with guilt. Cohabitation is frowned upon. Marriage is all but required and traditional sex roles are viewed as natural and necessary. It is expected that almost every couple will have at least one child and some in this group still have large families. Child-rearing is relatively authoritarian. Extra-marital sex is condemned. Some people cheat a little. Some cheat a lot. But many are sexually exclusive (or celibate) for life. (When adultery is discovered, women are expected to be more forgiving of straying husbands than are men of straying wives, part of what critics call the "double standard.") Therapy and marriage counseling are suspect; some stigma is attached to persons who need such services. Divorce, while sometimes necessary, is considered a personal tragedy and a public scandal. Most traditional Americans are opposed to abortion under all (or nearly all) circumstances. Many disapprove of homosexuality and a few are hostile toward gay people.

Contemporary Values. In contrast, a more liberal set of attitudes and behavior is now characteristic of about four-fifths of the adult population. There is, of course, considerable diversity *within* this group but it is possible (and useful) to summarize their orientation in general terms as follows. Sexual pleasure is viewed positively. Masturbation is not stigmatized; rather, it is encouraged as a source of pleasure and self-knowledge for people of all ages. Some books about sex for young people encourage them to masturbate without guilt and, later, to share masturbation with their boyfriends and girlfriends until they are ready for the adult responsibilities assumed with intercourse, i.e., the use of contraception, controlling the spread of disease, and an acknowledged concern for the other. Most adults admit they masturbate and many share masturbation as part of their love-making. Premarital sexual intimacy is not condemned and most adults today consider it appropriate, especially for couples who are "in love" or planning to marry. About one-fifth of the population are virgins until marriage (or for life). There is no stigma attached to virginity and in some communities it is still highly prized. Nudity in adult films and magazines is taken for granted by most people and enclaves for nude swimming and sunbathing are now found in all parts of the country.

GORDON CLANTON

Most people still marry but those who do not are no longer stigmatized. Many couples, especially in the cities, live together without getting married unless and until they decide to have a child. (This had been the pattern in the Scandinavian countries since the 1960s.) In comparison with their own parents and grandparents, people today are more apt to marry later and are more likely to have several sex/love relationships before marriage or between marriages. Within marriage, gender roles are relatively flexible, although it is still easier for a woman to have a career than for a man to devote himself full-time to housekeeping and child-care. Most couples have one or more children but almost half choose to remain child-free, and there is little social disapproval of this course. Although many Americans still disapprove of abortion, about eighty percent believe that abortion is preferable to the birth of an unwanted child; therefore, abortion is permitted and (typically) paid for by National Health Insurance. Those couples who choose to have a family usually opt for one or two children. Child-rearing is relatively democratic. Although there are relatively few sexually "open marriages," occasional episodes of extra-marital sex are tolerated as preferable to divorce. Therapy and marriage counseling are viewed positively. Many people are involved in peer counseling or in groups; such efforts are directed toward relationship enrichment and the prevention of problems rather than toward the management of pathology. Divorce, although regrettable, is no longer viewed as a tragedy or a scandal. Cordial relations and shared parenting often continue beyond the end of a marriage. Most divorced people remarry.

Homosexuals and other sexual minorities are accepted (or at least tolerated) by the majority. In fact, the terms homosexual and heterosexual are rarely used today, except as a way of indicating the gender of one's living partner or of persons to whom he or she is most likely to be attracted. It is widely recognized that all human beings are inherently capable of sexual response to both males and females. Many people at least experiment with same sex relationships at some point in their lives, even if they are predominantly heterosexual most of the time. (Likewise, many adults are sexually experimental for a portion of their lives, even if they are monogamous most of their lives.) Because there is very little disapproval of or discrimination against gay people, stable homosexual couples of both genders are more common than in the twentieth century. Indeed, recent research indicates that, in general, the "family life" of gay and lesbian couples is very similar to that of childless heterosexual couples. (Lesbians are more apt to establish such stable couple relationships than are gay men.)

Children and Child-Rearing Today. It is no longer assumed that everyone ought to reproduce. Instead, parenthood is a *choice* that is made by just more than half of the adults in our society. Most people understand that having a child is a major, long-term commitment. (One popular book on parenting is entitled *The 25-Year Contract*.) While there is very little stigma attached to single parents, most parents want a partner to share the tasks of providing for and socializing a child. Most couples wait until their late twenties or early thirties to have a child. Many couples have only one child, in keeping with the slogan (borrowed from the Chinese), "One family; one child." In contrast with mid-twentieth-century attitudes, recent research shows that the only child and his or her parents are happier and healthier than children and adults in larger families.

Because there are fewer children than in the past—in the average family and therefore in the community and the society—each child is more appreciated, more "special." Each child receives more attention and support (both material and emotional) from more adults than in the late twentieth century. Adults with no small children of their own now often "borrow" the children of their relatives or friends so they can enjoy the delights of playing with children while simultaneously providing "time off" for the grateful parents and exposure to additional adult role models for the children. These "surrogate parents" make it possible for most children to have time away from their parents when they need it. When they feel like "running away from home," they can usually spend a day or two with adults other than their parents.

Because of the full-employment economy and the National Health Insurance System, very few American children today are without adequate food, shelter, and medical care. As the number of children in orphanages and reform schools declined, these formerly dismal institutions underwent a renewal. These facilities have been turned over to advocates of different approaches. Some are relatively authoritarian; others are more democratic. Some work from a behavioral orientation; others utilize depth psychologies. Some are public institutions; some have religious sponsorship; some are privately owned. Comparative longitudinal research is under way to determine which approaches are the most effective in producing relatively happy and productive adults. Preliminary data from these studies suggest that small children thrive best in small (rather than large) living groups and that they need stable relations with adult supervisors who can be with them over several years (rather than being passed through a succession of parent surrogates and adult supervisors as was common in the twentieth century).

Divorce and Beyond. The divorce rate has gone down slightly in the last decade. Of course, divorce rates are still very high; in many urban jurisdictions, there is one divorce for every two marriages. Unlike our parents and grandparents, however, most people today are not surprised, shocked, or scandalized when divorce becomes necessary. Most urban adults have come to *expect* to be divorced at least once in their lives. Those who do not divorce are pleasantly surprised and those who do divorce get what they expected. Thus, almost everyone is subjectively happier in these matters than their parents and grandparents who were quite likely to divorce but whose unrealistic expectations made the experience of ending a marriage more painful.

One hundred years ago, when children were more likely to die young, when divorce was much less common, and when child-rearing was assumed to be "woman's work," relatively little attention was given to "parenting" as a distinct activity. Over the last fifty years, parenting has grown in importance, in part because medical technology now makes it more likely that the child will live to adulthood. Equally important, millions of divorced persons discovered that *the parent-child relationship is often more lasting or more significant than the hus-band-wife relationship.* Thus, an increasing number of fathers have played larger and larger roles in the rearing of their children. Most child-care is still provided by mothers, but only a minority of adults today would say that rearing children is "woman's work." For all these reasons, divorced persons today are much more likely than in the past to share the responsibilities of child-rearing as well as child-support.

New Attitudes Toward the Elderly. As the number and proportion of older Americans increased through the late twentieth and early twenty-first centuries, they became more influential in the political and cultural life of the nation. In the 1980s mandatory retirement age was pushed up, in part because a generation of healthier older adults wanted to show that they were still useful and to some extent because of economic pressures. In the last three decades of the twentieth century, more people over the age of sixty-five made substantial contributions to the national economy through full-time, part-time, or volunteer work. A growing block of older voters called for the National Health Insurance System which Americans of all ages now take for granted. Older people assumed a greater part in helping to care for the children of relatives and friends. Those who chose to live in institutions for older people demanded and got better institutions. Many chose to live at home (rather than in an institution) for as long as possible and to die at home with loved ones nearby. Following the Swedish example, the United States built more apartments designed to allow elderly and handicapped people who do not need constant care to lead lives that are as near to normal as possible and to spare them from the depressing effects of being thrust into an institution. In all these ways, older Americans of the last few decades have escaped some of the deprivation and stigma experienced by so many older people in earlier times.

The New Pluralism. As we reflect upon the contrast between traditional and contemporary understandings of sex and the family, it is important to realize that the newer patterns did not *replace* the traditional ones. Rather, the new attitudes *joined* the old, thus making American society and culture much more pluralistic where sex, love, marriage, and family are concerned. Just as the Roman Catholic monopoly was replaced in the sixteenth century by a *choice* between Catholicism and Protestantism, so also the Victorian view of sex and the family was replaced in the twentieth century by a *choice* between late Victorian values and the more liberal ones described above. Substantial numbers of people chose some version of the more liberal orientation which predominates today. Persons with more traditional values are not stigmatized but neither are they able to impose their values on others.

Most contemporary adults, then, are not late-Victorians; they are neo-Puritans—a new, sexier version of those seventeenth-century Calvinists who believed that sexual pleasure is good and that it ought to strengthen the bond between husband and wife. As we today search for sex, love, and companionship in one relatively intense and (ideally) enduring relationship, most of us have sex with more people before, outside, and between marriages than did the Puritans who settled New England. But even today, most people are searching for that one "most important other person" with whom they can share their lives. Many still want to raise a family in partnership with another. Few willingly choose an adult life of aloneness or of large numbers of short, superficial encounters. Most of us are neo-Puritans who tolerate both the late-Victorian minority as well as the sexually-more-liberal minorities.

CONCLUSION: HISTORY AND THE FUTURE

The past is the foundation on which the future will be built. The present is stretched between memory and hope. A survey of more than two thousand years of Western history reveals that very personal experiences of sex, love, marriage, and family life are influenced by social institutions and cultural movements such as the Roman Catholic Church and the Protestant Reformation. For more than two hundred years, the development of industrial society has been a major influence on family life. Looking more carefully at the century that has passed since the end of World War I, we have traced the impact of changing economic and political conditions upon the "intimate world" of courtship, marriage, child-rearing, and personal lifestyle. Although ongoing adaptation to new techniques continues to be an important feature of social life, the major changes in personal and family life of the past fifty years have resulted from new economic, political, and social *choices* about how to use our technology and how to distribute its benefits. Such choices will continue to contribute to the shaping of our future and the futures of our children and grandchildren.

Although the forms of the family have changed over time, human beings in all times and places have mated, procreated, and provided for the socialization of each new generation into the roles required of adults. In that sense, the family has been around for thousands and thousands of years and, in that sense, the family is here to stay. As different as they were, the hedonistic, classical Greeks and the ascetic, early Christians both made provision for reproduction and primary socialization, the apparently universal functions of a relatively small social unit, the family. As Mary Jo Bane (1:141) concluded more than forty years ago,

> . . . family commitments are likely to persist in our society. Family ties, it seems clear, are not archaic remnants of a disappearing traditionalism, but persisting manifestations of human needs for stability, continuity, and nonconditional affection.

If the family as the agent of nurtured socialization survived the hedonism of classical antiquity, the fall of Rome, the rise of Christianity, the invention of courtly love, the Renaissance, the Reformation, and the early Industrial Revolution, we should not be surprised that it is still with us today. Acknowledging this continuity, I have focused on change, more particularly a century of changes in attitudes and expectations about sex, love, marriage, and the family.

We can understand ourselves better and be less surprised by the future if we have some historical perspective and some awareness of the influence of social forces in our own time and place. Individuals who can see their lives in a larger social context are more likely to have realistic expectations for their most important relationships. They are less likely to blame themselves for events beyond their control. Of course, they may also be tempted to use social forces as an alibi when they ought to accept responsibility for making a situation better. But, if we can avoid that pitfall, we can make good use in our own lives of the principle that all this history illustrates: *Private experience and family life are shaped by the social world around us and by our cultural inheritance.* Knowing this empowers and liberates us; ignorance of it weakens and limits us.